14th International Conference on Cognition and Exploratory Learning in Digital Age (CELDA 2017)

Cognition and Exploratory Learning in Digital Age

Vilamoura, Portugal
18 – 20 October 2017

Editors:

Demetrios G. Sampson
J. Michael Spector
Dirk Ifenthaler
Pedro Isaias

ISBN: 978-1-5108-5320-1

Printed from e-media with permission by:

Curran Associates, Inc.
57 Morehouse Lane
Red Hook, NY 12571

Some format issues inherent in the e-media version may also appear in this print version.

Printed by Curran Associates, Inc. (2018)

For permission requests, please contact International Association for Development of the Information Society (IADIS) at the address below.

International Association for Development of the Information Society (IADIS)
Rua Sao Sebastiao Da Pedreira
No. 100, 30, 1050-209
Lisbon, Portugal

Phone: 351 21 3151373
Fax: 351 21 3151244

secretariat@iadis.org

Additional copies of this publication are available from:

Curran Associates, Inc.
57 Morehouse Lane
Red Hook, NY 12571 USA
Phone: 845-758-0400
Fax: 845-758-2633
Email: curran@proceedings.com
Web: www.proceedings.com

PROCEEDINGS OF THE 14th INTERNATIONAL CONFERENCE on COGNITION AND EXPLORATORY LEARNING IN THE DIGITAL AGE (CELDA 2017)

VILAMOURA, ALGARVE, PORTUGAL

OCTOBER 18-20, 2017

Organised by

IADIS
International Association for Development of the Information Society

Edited by Demetrios G. Sampson, J. Michael Spector, Dirk Ifenthaler and Pedro Isaías

Associate Editor: Luís Rodrigues

TABLE OF CONTENTS

SHORT PAPERS

REFLECTION PAPERS

FOREWORD

These proceedings contain the papers of the 14th International Conference on Cognition and Exploratory Learning in the Digital Age (CELDA 2017), 18-20 October 2017, which has been organized by the International Association for Development of the Information Society (IADIS) and endorsed by the Japanese Society for Information and Systems in Education (JSISE).

The CELDA conference aims to address the main issues concerned with evolving learning processes and supporting pedagogies and applications in the digital age. There have been advances in both cognitive psychology and computing that have affected the educational arena. The convergence of these two disciplines is increasing at a fast pace and affecting academia and professional practice in many ways.

Paradigms such as just-in-time learning, constructivism, student-centered learning and collaborative approaches have emerged and are being supported by technological advancements such as simulations, virtual reality and multi-agent systems. These developments have created both opportunities and areas of serious concerns. This conference aims to cover both technological as well as pedagogical issues related to these developments. Main tracks have been identified. However innovative contributions that do not easily fit into these areas will also be considered as long as they are directly related to the overall theme of the conference – cognition and exploratory learning in the digital age.

The following areas are represented in the submissions for CELDA 2017:

- Acquisition of expertise
- Assessing progress of learning in complex domains
- Assessment of exploratory learning approaches
- Assessment of exploratory technologies
- Cognition in education
- Collaborative learning
- Educational psychology
- Exploratory technologies (simulations, VR, i-TV, etc.)
- Just-in-time and Learning-on-Demand
- Learner communities and peer-support
- Learning communities & Web service technologies Pedagogical issues related with learning objects
- Learning paradigms in academia
- Learning paradigms in the corporate sector
- Life-long learning
- Student-centered learning
- Technology and mental models
- Technology
- Learning and expertise
- Virtual university

The CELDA 2017 Conference received 72 submissions from more than 25 countries. Each submission was reviewed in a double-blind review process by at least two independent reviewers to ensure quality and maintain high standards. Out of the papers submitted, 27 were accepted as full papers for an acceptance rate of 38%; 23 were accepted as short papers and 2 were accepted as reflection papers. Authors of the best published papers in the CELDA 2017 proceedings will be invited to publish extended versions of their papers in a book from Springer and in a special issue of the Interactive Technology and Smart Education (ITSE) journal (ISSN: 1741-5659).

In addition to the presentation of full, short and reflection papers, the conference also includes one keynote presentation from an internationally distinguished researcher. We would therefore like to express our gratitude to the CELDA 2017 keynote speaker: Professor Pierre Dillenbourg, Director, EPFL Center for Digital Education, Swiss Federal Institute of Technology, Lausanne, Switzerland.

A successful conference requires the effort of many individuals. We would like to thank the members of the Program Committee for their hard work in reviewing and selecting the papers that appear in this book. We are especially grateful to the authors who submitted their papers to this conference and to the presenters who provided the substance of this meeting. We wish to thank all members of our organizing committee.

Last but not least, we hope that participants enjoy Vilamoura and their time with colleagues from all over the world.

Pedro Isaías, The University of Queensland, Australia
Conference Chair

Demetrios G. Sampson, Curtin University, Australia
J. Michael Spector, University of North Texas, USA
Dirk Ifenthaler, University of Mannheim, Germany and Deakin University, Australia
Program Co-Chairs

Vilamoura, Algarve, Portugal
October 2017

PROGRAM COMMITTEE

CONFERENCE CHAIR

Pedro Isaías, The University of Queensland, Australia

PROGRAM CO-CHAIRS

Demetrios G Sampson, Curtin University, Australia
J. Michael Spector, University of North Texas, USA
Dirk Ifenthaler, University of Mannheim, Germany and Deakin University, Australia

COMMITTEE MEMBERS

Alke Martens, University of Rostock, Germany
Carla Falsetti, University Politecnica Delle Marche, Italy
ChanMin Kim, The University of Georgia, USA
Charoula Angeli-Valanides, University of Cyprus, Cyprus
Chien Sing Lee, Sunway University, Malaysia
Chun-Wang Wei, Kaohsiung Medical University, Taiwan
Clark Quinn , Quinnovation.com, USA
Dirk Ifenthaler, Deakin University, Australia
Dominique Py, University Of Maine, France
Flavio Manganello, Institute of Educational Technology – CNR, Genova, Italy
Giuliana Dettori, National Research Council, Italy
Giuliana Guazzaroni, University Politecnica Delle Marche, Italy
Huei-tse Hou, National Taiwan University Of Science And Technolo, Taiwan
Janet Corral, University Of Colorado Anschutz, USA
Jay Loftus, Schulich School of Medicine & Dentistry, Canada
Jirarat Sitthiworachart, Walailak University, Thailand
Julie-Ann Sime, Lancaster University, United Kingdom
Katherine Sinitsa, International Research and Training Center of Information Technologies and Systems, Ukraine
Kuo-Liang Ou, National Hsin-chu University of Education, Taiwan
Lence Miloseva, Goce Delcev University, Macedonia
Michael Verhaart, New Zealand
Mike Joy, University Of Warwick, United Kingdom
Min Kyu Kim, Ohio State University, USA
Ming-Chi Liu, National Cheng Kung University, Taiwan
Minjeong Kim, Dankook University, Republic of Korea
Monica Divitini, Norwegian University of Science and Technology, Norway
Patrick Blumschein, University of Education Freiburg, Germany
Radu Vasiu, Politehnica University of Timisoara, Romania
Richard Huntrods, Athabasca University, Canada
Roger Hartley, Leeds University, United Kingdom
Tiong Goh, Victoria University of Wellington, New Zealand
Veronica Rossano, University of Bari, Italy
Vincent Barre, Le Mans University, France
Vive Kumar, Athabasca University, Canada
Yen-Ting Lin, National Pingtung University, Taiwan

KEYNOTE LECTURE

CLASSROOM ORCHESTRATION: FROM PRACTICAL TIPS TO FORMAL MODELS

Professor Pierre Dillenbourg
Director, EPFL Center for Digital Education,
Swiss Federal Institute of Technology, Lausanne, Switzerland

Abstract

When robots or tablets are introduced into a classroom, they do not only enable rich learning activities, they also significantly increase the complexity of classroom management. How can teachers integrate individual, team and class-wide activities, some with digital tools, some without? Some answers to this question refer to practical aspects of schools, which fall under the umbrella of 'classroom usability'. This concept emphasizes technology features that enable teachers to cope with practical constraints of their routine such as time, discipline, etc. Another answer is to develop formal models of classroom orchestration, so-called orchestration graphs, as well to elaborate quantitative measures of orchestration load. These measures connect recent work in learning analytics with the life of everyday classrooms.

Full Papers

ARE LEARNING LOGS RELATED TO PROCRASTINATION? FROM THE VIEWPOINT OF SELF-REGULATED LEARNING

Masanori Yamada, Misato Oi and Shin'ichi Konomi
Learning Analytics Center, Kyushu University, 744, Motooka, Nishiku, Fukuoka, 8190395, Japan

ABSTRACT

This study investigated the relationships between self-regulated learning (SRL) awareness, time-management awareness, learning behaviors (report submission), and learning performance. Psychometric data and learning logs for both in-class and out-of-class activities were collected in the lecture course, and their relationships were analyzed using Pearson's correlation analysis. The results indicated that awareness of self-efficacy, intrinsic value, and cognitive learning strategies use had significant correlations with the frequency of out-of-class activities, submission time of report, and learning performance. Regarding the relationships between SRL awareness and out-of-class activities, usual reading activities as well as additional actions, such as bookmarking, had significant correlations with SRL awareness.

KEYWORDS

Learning analytics, Self-regulated learning, Procrastination

1. INTRODUCTION

1.1 Self-regulated Learning

Self-regulated learning (SRL) is an important perspective for understanding learning behaviors. Many researchers have conducted research on SRL in experimental and practical educational settings. SRL is related to motivation, cognition, and self-control, as it is directed toward the accomplishment of learning purposes (Pintrich, 1999). SRL relates to many learning concepts such as metacognition (Schunk and Zimmerman, 1986), information processing (Winne and Hadwin, 1998), procrastination (Strunk et al., 2013; Yamada et al., 2016), and so on.

SRL seems to be useful concept for understanding learners' learning features. Schunk and Zimmerman (1998) compared the learning behaviors of novice and expert SRL learners in each SRL phase. For example, in the forethought phase, skilful learners articulate their final goal and the necessary steps for its accomplishment. Skilful learners also tend to have internal motivation and high self-efficacy. In the performance/volitional phase, skilful learners try to maximise the effects of learning by monitoring the learning process. In the self-reflection phase, they seek to evaluate their learning performance independently and tend to attribute its quality to learning strategies and practice.

Recent research has investigated the effects of learning behaviors on SRL awareness in e-learning settings. Azevedo et al. (2017) suggested a framework for visualising SRL awareness using multimodal data in e-learning settings. Yamada et al. (in press) suggested that the use of cognitive learning strategies, such as annotation, as well as appropriate reading time for learning materials play important roles in enhancing SRL awareness. Using Information and Communication Technology (ICT), learning behaviors that contribute to enhancing SRL awareness can be analyzed to support learning.

1.2 Procrastination

Time management, which is an important SRL element, plays an important role in fruitful learning outcomes in both e-learning and face-to-face learning environments. Goda et al. (2015) investigated learning patterns based on learning logs in computer-assisted language learning settings. They extracted seven learning patterns: procrastination, learning habit, random, diminished drive, early bird, chevron, and catch-up. They found that students of the learning habit type and chevron type achieved higher scores than the procrastination type. However, considering daily lifes, the accomplishment of learning tasks following learning plans that learners made themselves indicated high SRL skills. In this sense, procrastination is not always a harmful behavior for high learning performance. Chu and Choi (2005) proposed an 'active procrastination' learning behavior that regards procrastination as a positive learning strategy with meta-cognition. Chu and Choi (2005) found that active procrastination had significant effects on learners' perceptions of life satisfaction and self-reported performance but not on grade point average (GPA). Active procrastinators have several features that effectively and efficiently contribute to their accomplishment of learning goals. Procrastination seems to be a useful perspective for supporting successive learning for the enhancement of learning performance.

In information technology era, information technologies allow instructors to understand learner's learning behaviors, using learning logs stored in server. Learning analytics research contributes to clarify education and learning environment improvement using various data such as log about learners and learning environment, with information processing methods (e.g., Ifenthalar, 2015; Ogata et al, 2015). Oi et al (2017) investigated the relationship between learning logs in both preview and review and learning performance, using e-book logs. The results revealed that low learning performers tried to access to e-book in preview phase, but they easily gave up. Learning analytics research allows researchers and instructors to investigate various learning behaviors. Jayaprakash et al. (2014) suggested the analytical framework to predict students' academic risk, using various data such as logs and GPA. It seems to be possible to investigate learning behaviors that affect on awareness of procrastination. Yamada et al (2016). found that procrastination and timely engagement awareness promote the learning outcome submission time directly and indirectly, using time stamp log on Learning Management System (LMS). However, the findings of their research focused on the learning outcome phase, therefore, it did not mention about usual learning behaviors, which seem to be meaningful to understand learning habits including procrastination.

The review of previous research mentioned above focused on the relationships among learning logs in in-class and out-of-class settings, learning behaviors, and learning awareness, especially self-regulated learning and procrastination. This study aimed to investigate the relationships between learning behaviors and SRL awareness, especially procrastination. Therefore, we set two research questions, in order to investigate these relationships.

RQ1: From the viewpoint of self-regulated learning and procrastination, what are the relationships between learning behaviors and awareness in both in-class and out-of-class settings?

RQ2: What are the learning behaviors that contribute to the improvement of SRL awareness and procrastination?

2. METHODS

2.1 Subjects and Course

Ninety-one university students participated in this research. One was a fourth-year student, and the others were first-year students taking an introductory education class. The course consisted of fifteen classes. The main learning object was to understand educational theories, principles, and history. There were three criteria for the grade: submitting a one-minute paper after every class, a regular report, and a final report. Students had to submit the one-minute paper within a day for a normal grade, but the teacher would accept it one day late (the score would be cut by half). The one-minute paper had to contain the class abstract and discussion. Regarding the regular and last reports, the teacher explained the report themes three weeks before the submission deadlines. Students were required to submit the one-minute papers and reports on LMS.

2.2 Data Collection

Students were asked to fill out two types of questionnaires: the motivational strategies for learning questionnaire (MSLQ) (Pintrich and DeGroot, 1990) and a 2 x 2 time-related academic behavior scale (Strunk et al., 2013). The MSLQ, which consists of five factors (self-efficacy (SE), internal value (IV), cognitive strategies (CS), self-regulation (SR), and test anxiety (TA); 44 items in all, rated on a seven-point Likert scale), was used for the subjective evaluation of learners' SRL skills. The 2 x 2 model of time-related academic behavior scale consisted of 22 items: seven for procrastination approach (PAP), four for procrastination avoidance (PAV), six for timely engagement approach (TAP), and five for timely engagement avoidance (TAV). Students were asked to rate each item on a seven-point Likert scale (see Appendix). Students were asked to complete the MSLQ and 2 x 2 model of time-related academic behavior scale at the first class and again at the last class. The second method of data collection was a log that recorded learning behaviors using e-books, the submission times of the one-minute papers relative to the deadlines, and the submission times of the two reports. Submission time was converted for analysis. Submission time increased the earlier a student submitted the assignment. For example, if a student submitted the one-minute paper one hour before the deadline, submission time was 1; if a student submitted the regular report 100 hours before deadline, submission time was 100.

3. RESULTS

Seventy-three out of the ninety first-year students answered the two questionnaires in class. The fourth-year student did not answer the questionnaire. We conducted Pearson's correlation analysis to investigate the relationship between SRL, procrastination, and learning behavior. In section 3.1 below, we show the descriptive data; the results of the correlation analysis are shown in section 3.2.

3.1 Descriptive Data and *t*-test

Table 1 shows the average for each item. The score for each factor was calculated by the sum of each item in each factor. The average scores for each factor are shown in Tables 1 and 2. The average times of submission are shown in Tables 3 and 4. These results show that there were large differences between individual students in the items for self-efficacy in MSLQ, procrastination approach, and all learning behaviors due to large standard deviations.

3.2 Correlation Analysis

The *t*-test results revealed that learners were aware and not aware of SRL and time management overall. However, what kinds of learning behaviors were affected pre- and post-class in terms of SRL and time management? Is awareness of SRL and procrastination related to learning behaviors and learning performance? To investigate the relationships between psychological perspectives, learning behaviors, and learning performance, Pearson's correlation analysis was conducted. The differences between post- and pre-rating data for SRL and procrastination questionnaires were calculated. Regarding learning behaviors, we summed the learning logs for both in-class and out-of-class settings, the one-minute paper submission times within the deadline, and the submission times (hours) of both reports. Table 5 shows the results.

Table 1. Average sum scores and *t*-test results for each factor in MSLQ

Item	Average score (SD)		*t*	sig
	Pre	Post		
Self-efficacy (min: 9, max: 63)	32.438 (6.110)	33.068 (8.772)	0.654	
Internal value (min: 9, max: 63)	50.616 (5,413)	49.370 (9.001)	-1.461	$p < 0.1$
Cognitive strategy use (min: 13, max 91)	60.082 (7.176)	61.671 (9.651)	1.536	$p < 0.1$
Self-regulation (min: 9, max: 63)	39.438 (5.624)	38.288 (5.832)	-1.812	$p < 0.05$
Test anxiety (min: 4, max 20)	14.150 (4.569)	14.384 (5.358)	0.606	

Table 2. Average sum score for each factor in 2 x 2 model of time-related academic behavior scale

Item	Average score (SD)		*t*	sig
	Pre	Post		
Procrastination approach (min: 7, max: 49)	19.986 (6.657)	21.671 (7.830)	2.115	$p < 0.05$
Procrastination avoidance (min: 4, max: 28)	11.233 (4.514)	13.342 (5.463)	3.431	$p < 0.001$
Timely engagement approach (min: 6, max: 42)	24.726 (6.900)	22.726 (7.683)	-2.553	$p < 0.01$
Timely engagement avoidance (min: 5, max: 35)	22.384 (5.301)	19.178 (6.842)	-4.403	$p < 0.001$

Table 3. Average sum of learning log

Log	In class (SD)	Out of class (SD)
Add bookmark	0.110 (0.427)	0.137 (0.561)
Add marker	0.411 (1.451)	0.493 (1.376)
Add memo	3.110 (8.547)	4.931 (10.483)
Change marker	0.055 (0.369)	0.164 (0.986)
Change memo	2.726 (8.856)	7.603 (22.815)
Close	14.315 (14.273)	106.178 (83.915)
Delete bookmark	0.082 (0.340)	0.041 (0.200)
Delete marker	0.123 (0.439)	0.068 (0.254)
Delete memo	0.151 (0.462)	0.219 (0.507)
Page jump	2.151 (4.348)	8.684 (10.197)
Landscape (changing display in horizontal way)	0.274 (0.672)	1.068 (1.636)
Next	60.260 (44.812)	306.205 (180.832)
Open	14.548 (12.849)	116.274 (86.064)
Portrait (changing display in vertical way)	1.342 (1.618)	6.247 (4.684)
Prev (flipping previous page)	29.123 (28.479)	180.945 (143.949)
Search	0.027 (0.234)	0.027 (0.164)
Select bookmark	0.000 (0.000)	0.000 (0.000)
Select chapterlist	0.000 (0.000)	0.000 (0.000)
Select marker	0.014 (0.117)	0.027 (0.234)
Select memo	0.068 (0.419)	0.123 (0.551)
Select thumbnail	0.000 (0.000)	0.000 (0.000)
Zoom	6.000 (7.627)	25.589 (34.895)
Average sum of all activities	134.890 (103.732)	765.027 (481.294)

These results indicated that self-efficacy, internal value, and cognitive learning strategies had significant correlations with learning activities in out-of-class settings, one-minute paper submissions, and the final score. However, awareness of procrastination did not have a significant correlation with learning activities in either in-class or out-of-class settings. Several factors in the awareness of procrastination had significant correlations with task-management behaviors. Procrastination avoidance had negative correlations with last-report submission and the final score. It also had a weakly significant correlation with one-minute paper submission. The timely engagement approach had a significant positive relationship with submission time for the last report. Timely engagement avoidance had a significant positive relationship with the submission of the first report. However, the procrastination approach had no relationship with any SRL awareness, learning behaviors, or learning performance.

Table 4. Average submission time for one-minute paper, average submission time (hour) for reports, and average final score

Item	Average	SD
Submission time for one-minute paper in the deadline	9.918	1.579
Submission time (hour) for regular report 1	18.575	25.987
Submission time (hour) for last report	39.753	69.384
Final score	76.447	13.727

Table 5. Correlation analysis results between psychological factors, learning logs, and learning performance (upper: correlation coefficient; lower: significance)

	In-class logs	Out-of-class logs	One-minute paper submission	First report submission	Last report submission	Final score
SE	0.015	0.368 $p < 0.01$	0.322 $p < 0.01$	0.119	0.018	0.402 $p < 0.001$
IV	-0.019	0.399 $p < 0.001$	0.363 $p < 0.01$	0.172	0.032	0.372 $p < 0.01$
CS	-0.123	0.225 $p < 0.1$	0.327 $p < 0.01$	0.110	0.060	0.301 $p < 0.01$
SR	0.137	0.186	0.177	0.037	0.033	0.083
TA	-0.002	0.109	0.122	0.172	0.083	0.263 $p < 0.05$
PAP	-0.041	-0.046	0.083	-0.153	-0.077	0.097
PAV	-0.068	-0.076	-0.220 $p < 0.1$	-0.013	-0.233 $p < 0.05$	-0.272 $p < 0.05$
TAP	0.071	0.058	0.125	0.169	0.266 $p < 0.05$	0.075
TAV	-0.007	-0.019	0.191	0.301 $p < 0.01$	0.099	0.085
Final score	-0.058	0.241 $p < 0.05$	0.732 $p < 0.001$	0.184	0.121	

The correlation coefficients between learning logs for out-of-class settings, psychological data (SE, IV, CS), and final scores were calculated based on the results of the correlation analysis shown in Table 5. The learning logs 'select marker', 'select chapterlist', and 'select thumbnail' were eliminated because the learners did not take these actions at all. Table 6 shows the results.

Pearson's correlation analysis showed several significant correlations between SRL and learning behaviors in out-of-class settings: self-efficacy (add bookmark, close, next, open, prev, zoom, final score), internal value (close, next, open, portrait, prev, zoom, final score), cognitive learning strategies (zoom, final score), and final score (close, landscape, next, open). Overall, learning logs about reading activity (e.g. page flipping and zoom) had significant correlations with final score and SRL awareness. However, awareness of cognitive learning strategies was not significantly related to learning logs, except for zoom. The additional action 'add bookmark' had a significant positive correlation with self-efficacy. The learning log 'landscape' had no relationship with SRL awareness but had one with final score. All types of SRL awareness were significant with final score.

Table 6. Correlation coefficients between SE, IV, CS, learning logs in out-of-class settings, and final score (upper: correlation coefficient; lower: significance level)

	SE	IV	CS	Final score
Add bookmark	0.330 p < 0.01	0.141	0.070	0.147
Add marker	0.106	0.087	0.039	0.079
Add memo	0.193	0.116	0.077	0.153
Change marker	0.028	0.110	-0.040	0.056
Change memo	0.108	0.110	0.109	0.106
Close	0.268 p < 0.05	0.298 p < 0.05	0.189	0.242 p < 0.05
Delete bookmark	0.077	0.150	0.096	0.069
Delete marker	0.032	0.092	0.087	0.101
Delete memo	0.083	-0.004	-0.035	0.057
Jump	0.066	0.084	0.048	0.169
Landscape	0.144	0.132	0.094	0.267 p < 0.05
Next	0.357 p < 0.01	0.382 p < 0.001	0.199	0.214 p < 0.1
Open	0.313 p < 0.01	0.305 p < 0.01	0.196	0.288 p < 0.05
Portrait	0.210	0.297 p < 0.1	0.170	0.111
Prev	0.325 p < 0.01	0.385 p < 0.001	0.187	0.140
Search	-0.044	-0.215	-0.126	-0.049
Select marker	0.020	0.053	0.046	-0.012
Select memo	-0.060	0.032	-0.029	-0.002
Zoom	0.279 p < 0.05	0.281 p < 0.05	0.228 p < 0.1	0.143
Final score	0.402 p < 0.001	0.372 p < 0.01	0.301 p < 0.01	

4. CONCLUSION AND FUTURE WORK

This study aimed to investigate the relationships between SRL awareness, procrastination, and learning logs; the submission time of learning outcomes; and learning performance. There were four main findings. About RQ1, overall, several factors in the awareness of SRL (self-efficacy, internal value, and cognitive learning strategies) and all factors of time management showed significant differences between before and after classes. The awareness of SRL—in particular self-efficacy, internal value, and cognitive learning strategies—had significant relationships with learning logs in out-of-class settings and the final score. Time-management awareness was related to the submission of learning outcomes. SRL awareness was related to reading activities such as page flipping. Time management is one of the important skills in SRL (e.g. Wolters et al., 2003; Barnard et al., 2009; Yamada et al., 2016). The results about RQ2 also indicated that the awareness of SRL and time management had a positive relationship with learning logs in out-of-class settings. Procrastination avoidance had negative correlations with one-minute paper submission times, last-report submission times, and final scores. The timely engagement approach had a positive relationship with last-report submission, and timely engagement avoidance had a negative relationship with first-report submission. These results differ from those of previous research (Yamada et al., 2016). Yamada et al. (2016) demonstrated the overall causal relationships between SRL, time management, and learning behaviors. That research found that procrastination avoidance had negative effects on the submission of one-minute papers, and timely engagement avoidance had positive effects on the submission of the first report. In this research, the awareness of procrastination was regarded as a positive learning strategy through the class. However, learners were less aware of both types of timely engagement as suggested by the results of the *t*-test and the correlation analysis. A possible reason is that meta-cognition seemed to have been developed through the class. Submission deadlines were important criteria for gaining credit in the class. The change in avoidance awareness in both procrastination and timely engagement seems to indicate that learners reflected on their learning behaviors and then tried to manage their learning time. However, this consideration is only one possibility. To further examine this point, more data should be corrected, and causal data analysis should be conducted (e.g. multiple regression analysis).

Regarding the relationships between psychometric data and learning behaviors, previous research supports these results (Yamada et al., 2015). These findings provided more concrete results compared to Yamada et al. (2015). Not only usual reading activities, such as page flipping, but also additional actions, such as bookmark and zoom, had significant correlations with SRL and learning performance. Additional actions allow learners to read learning materials in detail and can therefore promote their comprehension. For example, adding a bookmark helps learners to access and read learning materials again. This feature supports a learner's intention to learn again. By learning through these actions, learners seemed to perceive their SRL skill awareness development.

Future research should clarify the relationship between SRL, learning behaviors, and learning performance with more data in order to investigate these relationships. Processes for changing SRL and time-management awareness should be investigated using learning log data. If changing points in the process can be detected in consideration of instructional design, it can help instructors improve their classes and learning materials.

ACKNOWLEDGEMENT

The research is supported by "Research and Development on Fundamental and Utilization Technologies for Social Big Data" (178A03), the Commissioned Research of the National Institute of Information and Communications Technology (NICT), Japan; Grant-in-Aid for Scientific Research (B) No. 16H03080 and the Qdai-jump Research(QR) Program of Kyushu University.

REFERENCES

Azevedo ,R., Millar, G.C., Taub, M., Mudrick, N.V., Bradbury, A.E., & Price, M.J. (2017). Using Data Visualizations to Foster Emotion Regulation during Self-Regulated Learning with Advanced Learning Technologies: A Conceptual Framework, *Proceedings of Learning Analytics and Knowledge 2017*, 444- 448.

Barnard, L., Lan, W. Y., To, Y. M., Paton, V. O. & Lai, S-L. (2009) Measuring self-regulation in online and blended learning environments. *Internet and Higher Education*, Vol.12, No.1, pp.1-6.

Chu, A.H.C. & Choi, J.N. (2005). Rethinking procrastination: Positive effects of "active" procrastination behavior on attitudes and performance. *The Journal of Social Psychology*, Vol.145, No. 3, pp.245–264.

Goda, Y., Yamada. M., Matsuda, T., Kato, H. & Miyagawa, H. (2013). Effects of Help Seeking Target Types on Completion Rate and Satisfaction in E-Learning, *Proceedings of INTED 2013*, pp. 1399-1403

Goda, Y., Yamada, M., Kato, H., Matsuda, T., Saito, Y. & Miyamaga, H. (2015). Procrastination and other learning behavioral types in e-learning and their relationship with learning outcomes, *Learning and Individual Differences*, Vol.37, pp.72-80.

Ifenthaler, D. (2015). Learning Analytics. In J. M. Spector (Ed.), *The SAGE Encyclopedia of Educational Technology* (pp. 447-451). Thousand Oaks, CA: Sage.

Jayaprakashm S.M., Moody, E.W., Lauría, E.J.M., Regan, J.R. & Baron, J.D. (2014). Early Alert of Academically At-Risk Students: An Open Source Analytics Initiative, *Journal of Learning Analytics*, Vol.1, No.1, pp. 6-47.

Ogata, H., Yin C., Oi, M., Okubo, F., Shimada, A., Kojima, K. and Yamada, M.(2015). e-Book-based Learning Analytics in University Education, Ogata, H et al (Eds.). *Proceedings of the 23th International Conference on Computers in Education*, pp.401-406.

Oi, M., Yamada, M., Okubo, F., Shimada, A. & Ogata, H. (2017). Finding traces of high and low achievers by analyzing undergraduates' e-book logs, *Workshop Proceedings of MMLA-CrossLAK 2017*, pp.15-22

Pintrich, P. R. (1999) The role of motivation in promoting and sustaining self-regulated learning. *International Journal of Educational Research*, Vol.31, No.6, pp.459-470.

Schunk, D. H., and Zimmerman, B. J. (1998) *Self-Regulated Learning: From Teaching to Self-Reflective Practice*. New York, NY: The Guilford Press.

Strunk, K.K., Cho, Y., Steele,M.R. & Bridges, S.L. (2013). Development and validation of a 2 × 2 model of time-related academic behavior: Procrastination and timely engagement. *Learning and Individual Differences*, Vol.25, pp.35–44.

Winne, P., & Hadwin, A. F. (1998). Studying as self-regulated learning. In D.J. Hacker, J.Duntosky & A.C. Graesser (Eds.) Metacognition in educational theory and practice, pp.277-304, Mahwah NJ: Erlbaum.

Wolters, C. A., Pintrich, P. R. & Karabenick, S. A. (2003) Assessing Academic Self-Regulated Learning. Paper prepared for the *Conference on Indicators of Positive Development: Definitions, Measures, and Prospective Validity*. Sponsored by ChildTrends, National Institutes of Health.

Yamada, M., Yin, C., Shimada, A., Kojima, K., Okubo, F. & Ogata, H. (2015). Preliminary Research on Self-Regulated Learning and Learning Logs in a Ubiquitous Learning Environment, *Proceedings of the 15th IEEE International Conference on Advanced Learning Technologies*, pp.93-95.

Yamada, M., Goda, Y., (2016). How does self-regulated learning relate to active procrastination and other learning behaviors?, *Journal of Computing in Higher Education*, 28(3), pp.326-343.

Yamada, M., Shimada, A., Okubo,F., Oi, M., Kojima, K., & Ogata, H. (2017). Learning analytics of the relationships among self-regulated learning, learning behaviors, and learning performance, *Research and Practice in Technology Enhanced Learning*,12, 13.doi: 10.1186/s41039-017-0053-9

Appendix: 2 x 2 measure of time-related academic behavior scale (Strunk et al., 2013)

Factor	Item
Procrastination approach	I more effectively utilise my time by postponing tasks
	I delay completing tasks to increase the quality of my work
	I put off starting tasks to increase my motivation
	I feel a stronger state of flow in my tasks when working closer to a deadline
	I intentionally wait until closer to a deadline to begin work to enhance my performance
	I delay tasks because I perform better when under more time pressure
	I rarely have difficulty completing quality work when starting a task close to the deadline
Procrastination avoidance	I put off tasks for later because they are too difficult to complete
	I avoid starting and completing tasks
	I often delay starting tasks because I am afraid of failure
	I delay starting tasks because they are overwhelming
Timely engagement approach	I work further ahead of the deadline at a slower pace because it helps me perform better
	I believe I can successfully complete most tasks because I start work immediately after being assigned a task
	I do my best work well ahead of the deadline
	I start working right away on a new task so I can perform better on the task
	I complete my tasks prior to the deadline to help me be successful
	I begin working on difficult tasks early to achieve positive results
Timely engagement avoidance	I start my work early because my performance suffers when I have to rush through a task
	I do not start things at the last minute because I find it difficult to complete them on time
	I begin working on a newly assigned task right away to avoid falling behind
	When I receive a new assignment, I try to complete it ahead of the deadline to avoid feeling overwhelmed
	For extremely difficult tasks, I begin work even earlier so I can avoid the consequences of putting them off for later

ASYMMETRY IN THE PERCEPTION OF FRIENDSHIP IN STUDENTS GROUPS

Luigi Lancieri
University of Lille, Citée scientifique, Villeneuve d'Ascq, France

ABSTRACT

Several studies point out the link between sociability and academic results. In this paper, we highlight a phenomenon of asymmetry in the perception of friendship. This occurs when a student think he has more or less friends than he really has. We present an experimental method that allows us to analyze this question in relation with the academic performances of 15 groups of students. We show that students having a symmetric view of their friendship relations tend to have the better results. Furthermore, our study shows that the link between sociability and results improvement is stronger for lower grades (i.e younger students).

KEYWORDS

Friendship perception; Social networks; Learning analytics; interactions

1. INTRODUCTION

It has been known for a long time that friendship has positive effects in our everyday life. More recently, several studies in education sciences or in economy tend to show that friendship has also a positive effect on learning and on education performances. But, the common finding of all these studies is the complexity of this question due to the large amount of influence parameters. As very basic examples, it is obvious that the "quality of friends" can leads to good or bad outcomes that also strongly impact students behavior. A lot of other parameters (socioeconomics, parental context,..) make forecasting education difficulties a hard challenge.

In this paper, we investigate a methodology aiming at having a better understanding of a class sociability context and at investigating the link that these features could have with the students' performances. In particular we analyze the phenomenon of friendship perception asymmetry that deals with the gap between the perception and the reality that an individual has of his friendship network. For example, a student can think that he has 4 close friends within his class but, finally, it may turn out that his feeling is not fully reciprocal. More globally, it appears that we can over or under estimate the strength of our social network. Depending on the point of view, this gap can also be expressed in terms of attention to others driven by social norms. This phenomenon can also be rooted in concepts such as cognitive heuristics and biases (Tversky and Kahneman, 1974) or in the theory of bounded rationality (Simon,1957).

Indeed, several studies show that asymmetries of perception are linked with cognitive biases. For example, Pronin and his colleagues studied the illusion of asymmetric insight that states that people perceive their knowledge of others as surpassing other people's knowledge of them (Pronin et al, 2001). In interpersonal interactions, this means that we think we find out more about other people than other people find out about us. As a second example, let us consider the mere ownership effect that is the observation that a seller tend to evaluate its own good more positively than a buyer. As we can imagine, this phenomenon has an important implication in trading and was widely studied in behavioral economy (Beggan, 1992). Apart from these perception biases that are supposed to be universal since they are rooted in the deep cognition, we will see in the state of the art other forms of asymmetries that are more caused by cultural factors.

Our goal is to investigate these concepts in relationships between students within small university classes. Our first results are descriptive aiming at responding to questions related to the friendship network of students. For example, how many friends have students in their class ? Is there a difference between younger and older university students ? Moreover, we may wonder what extent the friendship perception is reciprocal and what the implications (scores, achievement, ect) of this asymmetry are ?

2. BACKGROUND

Several studies on the relations between friendship and school performances point out the role of individual and collective influences (Smith et al, 2007) (Sparrowe et al, 2001) (Hinshaw, 1992). Let us note that most of these works focus on primary or middle schools. Few of them address the university population. Our results tend to show that age and autonomy of students can make the difference. This is also true for adult learning.

Sometimes, surrounding bad behaviors can lead to delinquency or at least can interrupt learning progress. Except in these extreme cases, friendship has rather a positive effect in academic achievement. For example, Son Thierry Ly and his colleagues observed over four years the transition between junior high-school and high-school for 28 000 teenagers. On average, in France, 20 % of schoolchildren find themselves in the same high-school and only 5% in the same class. The authors find that grouping low-achieving freshmen who know each other tends to decrease their current repetition rate by around 13 percent, and raise their graduation rate by the same amount (Son et al, 2014).

Another study with 629 students of 18 years old also shows a strong positive link between friendship in school and grade results. Whatever the gender or the ethnicity, the more friends a student has in class the better his results. In order to obtain the data, the authors asked the students to fill in a form and maintain a journal in which they noted their activities and the time they take to study (Witkow et al, 2010). Another study shows that peer collaboration is an effective learning strategy for primary school children. Peer collaboration, where pairs of equally skilled partners work together in problem solving, has demonstrated immediate and long-term benefits on the cognitive development of children. One still open question is whether friends should be paired together or not. Indeed, results indicated that friends outperformed acquaintances in the collaboration, but not on the individual post-test (Webber et al, 2002). But, if a link exists, the question of causality is not simple. Xinyin Chen and his colleagues found that academic achievement predicted children's social competence and peer acceptance but, children's social functioning uniquely contributed to academic achievement (Chen et al, 1997).

If friendship has a link with academic results, one question remains: what is friendship ? On a range going from intimate friends to episodic contacts, the concept of friendship may widely vary. Verkuyten shows, for example, that gender and culture have a determinant influence on the perception of friendship. The allocentrism (versus idiocentrism) is a collectivistic personality attribute whereby people center their attention and actions on other people rather than themselves (Verkuyten, 1996). Since groups are sometimes composed of mixed people, it seems logical to find nuanced levels of friendship reciprocity. Social scientists have long suspected that friendship dyads are not always reciprocal but things are not clear. When connections are reciprocal, relations are likely to be more intimate. Asian-Americans and females are the most likely to have reciprocated friendships. Interracial friendships are less likely to be reciprocal than intra-racial friendships. Further, adolescents with reciprocal friendships report higher levels of school well-being. Friendship reciprocity is an important indicator of social support above and beyond the numbers of friends reported by youth (Vaquera et al, 2008). See also the theory of Granovetter on the influence of weak ties (Grannovetter, 1973).

Outside cultural or social reasons, the difference in perception may also come from cognitive biases. We evoked in the introduction the concept of bounded rationality popularized by H.A. Simon, Nobel laureate in economics. For example, (Pronin et al, 2007) showed that people see others as more conforming than themselves. This phenomenon is "rooted in people's attention to introspective versus behavioral information when making conformity assessments. The participants displayed an introspection illusion, placing more weight on introspective evidence of conformity (relative to behavioral evidence) when judging their own susceptibility to social influence as opposed to someone else's. ".

In mediated communication, this gap can be very different than in real life (i.e. face-to-face interactions) due to the size of groups and the limited non-verbal feature of the communication. In network science, reciprocity is a measure of the likelihood of vertices in a directed network to be mutually linked (Garlaschelli et al 2004). This minimal reciprocity is not present with Twitter since you can follow someone without being followed back. In contrast in Facebook, the equal reciprocity is the rule (Golder et al, 2010). There are also several works considering the relation between centrality in social networks and performances (Joksimović et al 2016).

3. STUDY METHODOLOGY

The most difficult and longest task in our study was data collection. We got, for each student, the level of friendship with each of their mates in his group (I.e a class of students). This step took 4 years (2013-2016) for 15 groups (278 students) composed of 7 groups of 2 years of university degree (called B groups) and 8 groups of 5 years Master university degree (called M groups). Students in B groups are 20 years old on average (23 years old in M groups). The groups, mostly composed by males (90%) have from 13 to 25 students (see table 1). All students are studying for a degree in computer science. All 15 groups are completely independent one from another (different year or degree).

Our methodology takes advantage of an online platform used in class for a practical exercise dedicated to the study of social networks. This platform helped us to collect data related to students' friendship networks that we confronted with their annual scores. Each student was requested to give a value of closeness in a list where all students of the group appear. This value corresponded to the perceived frequency of contacts with their colleagues, on a scale from 1 to 3. Very frequent contacts correspond to the level 1, less frequent (level 2) or very few interactions or not at all (level 3). Interactions, here, means public contacts in university life. For example, this can correspond to students who spend time together (lunch, more often discussing between classes,...). Thereby, we make the assumption that frequent contacts involve friendship. Of course this is an approximation since, if friendship often means frequent contacts, the reciprocal is not always true. Anyway, in the free context of universities, it seems difficult to have frequent contacts without trust, which is also a key for friendship (Lusher et al, 2014).

The following figure show a partial transcript of the user interface for the data collection. Then, a process anonymizes the data and provides a matrix (student I vs student J) that can be used for the class exercise.

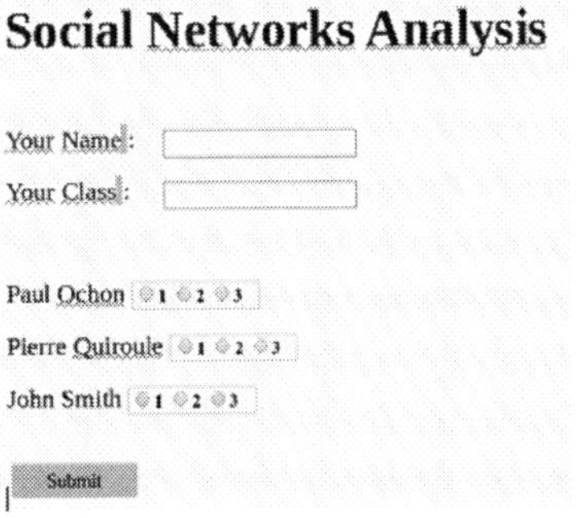

Figure 1. Look of the user interface for friendship data collection

The idea behind this exercise was to show to students how to compute and draw features of social networks (degree, centrality, ..etc). Of course, this kind of exercise could be done with artificial data but it was a good pretext to collecting real data for our study. As these data reflect public behaviors, we found no special difficulties in using them for research purposes. Anyway, in order to keep an ethical attitude, and avoid, as possible, bias effects, we clearly indicated to students that we introduced anonymity into the exercise, so that, each student name was replaced with a user identifier and it was not possible to identify individual persons behind the data. These data allow us build the social network of each group. This reveals interesting individual and collective features.

In the second step, we collected the annual score of each student. This score was computed by averaging from 12 to 14 teaching units depending on the group type (B or M). For example, B group students are evaluated with 14 teaching units. So, at the end of the year each student gets a score from 0 to 20 that is the average of its 14 scores.

4. RESULTS

In this section, we present, first, the sociability features of each category of students as well as the relation linking the sociability level and the student annual score. Then, we investigate the concept of the friendship perception asymmetry and, again, we compare this level with the annual scores.

4.1 Sociability and Academics Results

First of all, we analyze the friendship context of our 15 groups. The following table presents these data for the B and M groups. We see that on average each student has 3.3 close friends (see table 1). We also note that, in our context with a group size from 13 to 25, the number of close friends is weakly linked to the number of students in the group (R^2 =0,2).

Table 1. Sociability level of each group of students

B groups	# stud per grp	Aver friend per stud	M groups	# stud per grp	Aver friend per stud
B1	16	3.30	M1	14	2.93
B2	13	4.08	M2	16	2.13
B3	13	4.31	M3	25	4.29
B4	13	2.46	M4	19	1.95
B5	22	3.23	M5	14	2.36
B6	24	3.46	M6	17	2.71
B7	25	4.92	M7	24	3.67
			M8	23	4.22
Average		3.68			3.03
Total	126			152	

The question of the number of friends raises a recent attention with social network platforms (Facebook, ..) suspected of causing anxiety when friends are too numerous. If several studies are dedicated to the quantification of friendship in social network platforms, we found few papers that investigate this question within small class groups. S.L Field reported an average value of 2.7 close friends per college student in his study (Feld, 1991). M. Ali in another study with a population of adolescents found a value of 2,54 (Ali, 2012). There may be a kind of social constant around the value of 3 friends per individual but we have not enough data to fully support this hypothesis. Anyway, some students are less sociable than others.

The two following tables show the difference between the average score for the less sociable and the more sociable students. These two categories are simply formed by observing how many friends each student has. In each group, this value is ranked by order of increasing number of friends. The subgroup of students who have fewer friends is considered as less sociable that which has more friends. This is of course an approximation.

In table 2 (B groups) and 3 (M groups), the first column indicates the group type. The second and third columns contain the average score of the group and the standard deviation. The three last columns contain the average score respectively for the less sociable subgroup and the more sociable one, as well as the score difference in percentage between these 2 subgroups. For example, in the first row of table 2, we see that less sociable students of the B1 Group have an average score 17% lower than more sociable students.

Table 2. Score difference between high and low sociable students (B groups)

B Groups	Average	Std	Low Soc.	High Soc.	Diff (high-Low) %
B1	13.47	2.33	12.14	14.20	17.00
B2	11.79	2.14	11.56	11.99	3.72
B3	12.64	2.00	12.72	12.57	-1.16
B4	12.97	1.45	12.22	13.85	13.40
B5	12.74	1.72	12.83	12.65	-1.38
B6	13.53	1.84	12.74	14.31	12.29
B7	11.36	2.82	10.72	12.05	12.42
Averg.	12.64	2.04	12.13	13.09	8.04

Table 3. Score difference between high and low sociable students (M groups)

M Groups	Average	Std	Low Soc.	High Soc.	Diff (high-Low) %
M1	13.51	1.04	13.57	13.46	-0.78
M2	14.31	1.57	14.43	14.19	-1.66
M3	14.54	0.91	14.74	14.34	-2.72
M4	13.37	1.01	13.26	13.48	1.66
M5	14.01	0.79	13.91	14.11	1.40
M6	13.96	0.40	13.83	14.07	1.71
M7	13.59	1.24	13.68	13.51	-1.21
M8	14.06	1.05	13.65	14.44	5.78
Averg.	13.92	1.00	13.88	13.95	0.52

We see that students having the more friends have the better results. This is true for 9 groups on the 15 (5/7 on B groups and 4/8 on M groups). For all groups cumulated, the average difference represents + 4,4%. We can also see that this difference is higher for students of lower grade (8,04 % for B groups), who are also younger, than for higher grade (0,52%). As we saw in the background section, this result tends to confirm studies related to other educational contexts and also tend to show that our data are consistent. It is also important to say that even if both features are linked, we cannot say if there is any causality between friendship and academic results.

4.2 Asymmetry of Friendship Perception

Actually, the average number of friends by student we find in the previous section hides a perception asymmetry. An underestimation of this perception means that one student thinks he has fewer close friends than he really has (I.e what their friends declare). Table 4 shows that, globally, students tend, indeed, to underestimate their close social network. In this table, the first column reports the level of asymmetry as the difference between the number of friends declared by a student (out) and the number of reciprocal declarations from other students (in). For example, let us say that Paul declared John and Peter as friends (out=2), and that Peter, John and David declared Paul as a friend (in=3). This case corresponds to the sixth row (-1) of the first column. The other 3 columns represent respectively the percentage of all students, B groups and M groups, in each category of asymmetry. The last 3 rows summarize the table and show that 42.9 % of all students underestimate their friendship network, 24,1% have a realistic perception and 32,9 % overestimate it. We also see that this underestimation is more accentuated for younger students (47, 9% for B groups vs 38,6 % for M groups). The B groups also show the lowest level of symmetric perception, near twice less than for M groups (17,8 % vs 30,6).

Table 4. Under and over perception of friendship in groups

Diff. out -in	% All Stud	% B Stud	% M Stud
<= -6	0.34	0.68	0.00
-5	0.67	0.68	0.67
-4	2.01	2.05	2.00
-3	6.38	6.85	6.00
-2	11.74	13.01	10.67
-1	21.81	24.66	19.33
0	24.16	17.81	30.67
1	14.09	15.07	13.33
2	8.39	9.59	7.33
3	5.37	3.42	6.00
4	1.68	2.05	1.33
5	1.01	1.37	0.67
=> 6	2.35	2.74	2.00
% underestimation (out-in < 0)	42.95	47.95	38.67
% equal (out-in = 0)	24.16	17.81	30.67
% overestimation (out-in > 0)	32.89	34.25	30.67

We may also wonder if there is a link between this asymmetry and the students scores. In order to investigate this question, we first ranked each student in his group according to his normalized annual score. The student normalized score is computed according to the following formula in order to obtain in each group a student rank value from 0 to 1.

$$Rank_{score\ stud} = \frac{(Score_{stud} - Min_{score\ group})}{(Max_{score\ group} - Min_{score\ group})}$$

This allows us to consider all students in the same range of rank, which is not possible without normalization since the ranges of annual scores are very different from one type of group to another (average 12,6 std 2 for B groups, 13,9 std 1 for M groups, see table 2 and 3)

Then, we computed the average score rank for students that underestimate, overestimate and who have a realistic view of the number of their friends. The average rank of each category is reported in the following table as well as the corresponding typical score. This score is computed assuming a typical group with a minimal and maximal score respectively equal to 7 and 18. For comparison, the minimum and maximum scores for the B and M groups are respectively of 1,6 to 18 and 10 to 17,2)

Table 5 shows that realistic students tend to have better scores than those who overestimate (+7.6%) or underestimate (+4.9%) the number of their close friends. The realistic students have up to 1 point more in their average score. This question needs further studies but our sample also seems to say that students who underestimate have better results than those who overestimate their friendship network.

Table 5. Score difference between high and low sociable students

	Number of stud.	Average rank	Typical score
Underestimation	64	0.47	12.2
Realist perception	72	0.52	12.8
Overestimation	56	0.45	11.9

These results can be explained by the hypothesis that underestimation is a sign of a lack of self-confidence that pushes these students to work more. In the same way overestimation could be a sign of overconfidence that leads students to rest on their laurels. Social sciences show that self-confidence is linked to autonomy and motivation that are known key factors for academic achievement (Govier, 1993).

5. DISCUSSION

We presented a work aiming at investigating the implications of relational features in groups of students. Obtaining unbiased data for this kind of study is very difficult. Having enough students and enough groups in a real teaching context is a way to optimize the reliability of data collection. The consistency of the results for similar types of group (B vs M) tends to show that this data collection was of decent quality.

If the positive links between friendship and academic results have already been observed, less obvious is the influence of the asymmetry of the friendship perception. We see that young students (B groups) largely underestimate the number of their friends. Furthermore, students who have a clear view of their friendship relation also tend to have the better results.

These questions are not only useful for understanding but they could also have practical implications in terms of pedagogy or class organization. For example, we can imagine grouping together friends for class work, specially for young students. Knowing that some groups are composed with more autonomous students can allow the teacher to concentrate his attention to other groups.

In the wider context of mediated teaching, we can also evoke the design of educational tools such as friendly computer interfaces. It was shown, for example, that humorous user interfaces have positive effects on user attention or increase the motivation or the trust of students in learning situations (Morkes et al, 1998) (Nijholt, 2001). From another perspective, it is important to consider how these questions could impact large scale computer mediated education. The MOOCS or social networks platforms oriented to education can amplify the effects we observe in real classes.

ACKNOWLEDGEMENT

The research leading to these results was partially funded by a European Union Grant through the Dig-e-Lab project (Interreg France–Wallonie-Vlaanderen 2014-2020 program)

REFERENCES

Ali, M. M. (2012). Social learning theory, cigarette taxes and adolescent smoking behavior. Jahrbücher für Nationalökonomie und Statistik, 232(6), 633-651.

Beggan, James K. (1992) "On the social nature of nonsocial perception: The mere ownership effect.". Journal of Personality and Social Psychology. Vol 62(2), Feb 1992, 229-237.62 (2):. doi:10.1037/0022-3514.62.2.229.

Chen, X., Rubin, K. H., and Li, D. (1997). Relation between academic achievement and social adjustment: Evidence from Chinese children. Developmental psychology, 33(3), 518.http://www.rubin-lab.umd.edu/pubs/Downloadable%20pdfs/kenneth_rubin/cross%20cultural/DevPych97adjustment.pdf

Feld, Scott L. (1991) Why Your Friends Have More Friends Than You Do; The American Journal of Sociology, Vol. 96, No. 6, pp. 1464-1477.

Garlaschelli, Diego, Loffredo, Maria I. (2004). "Patterns of Link Reciprocity in Directed Networks". Physical Review Letters. 93 (26). American Physical Society.

Govier, T. (1993). Self Trust, Autonomy, and Self Esteem. Hypatia, 8(1), 99-120.

Golder Scott A. and Yardi Sarita. (2010) "Structural Predictors of Tie Formation in Twitter: Transitivity and Mutuality." Proceedings of the Second IEEE International Conference on Social Computing. August 20-22, 2010. Minneapolis, MN. http://www.redlog.net/papers/golder_yardi_2010.pdf

Granovetter, M. S. (1973). The strength of weak ties. American journal of sociology, 78(6), 1360-1380.

Hinshaw, S. P. (1992). Externalizing behavior problems and academic underachievement in childhood and adolescence: Causal relationships and underlying mechanisms. Psychological Bulletin, 111, 127-155.

Joksimović, S., Manataki, A., Gašević, D., Dawson, S., Kovanović, V., and De Kereki, I. F. (2016). Translating network position into performance: importance of centrality in different network configurations. In Proceedings of the Sixth International Conference on Learning Analytics & Knowledge (pp. 314-323). ACM.

Lusher, D., Kremer, P., and Robins, G. (2014). Cooperative and competitive structures of trust relations in teams. Small group research, 45(1), 3-36.

Morkes, John, Kernal, Hadyn K. and Nass, (1998) Clifford. Humor in Task-Oriented Computer-Mediated Communication and Human-Computer Interaction. In:Proceedings of CHI98, 1998.

Nijholt, Anton. (2001) Agents, Believability and Embodiment in Advanced Learning Environments. In: Proc. IEEE International Conf. on Advanced Learning Technologies: Issues, Achievements, and Challenges (ICALT 2001), T. Okamto, R. Hartley, Kinshuk & J.P. Klus (eds).

Pronin, E., Kruger, J., Savitsky, K and Ross, L (2001). "You don't know me, but I know you: the illusion of asymmetric insight". Journal of Personality and Social Psychology. 81 (4): 639–656. doi:10.1037/0022-3514.81.4.639

Pronin, E., Berger, J., and Molouki, S. (2007). Alone in a crowd of sheep: asymmetric perceptions of conformity and their roots in an introspection illusion.Journal of personality and social psychology, 92(4), 585.

Simon, H. A. (1957), Models of Man: Social and Rational. Mathematical Essays on Rational Behavior in a Social Setting, New York, Wiley, 1957

Son Thierry Ly and Riegert Arnaud. (2014) Persistent Classmates: How Familiarity with Peers Protects from Disruptive School Transitions. PSE Working Papers n2013-21. 2014. https://halshs.archives-ouvertes.fr/halshs-00842265/document

Smith, R. A., and Peterson, B. L. (2007). "Psst ... What Do You Think?" The Relationship between Advice Prestige, Type of Advice, and Academic Performance. Communication Education, 56(3), 278-291. doi:10.1080/03634520701364890

Sparrowe, R. T., Liden, R. C., Wayne, S. J., and Kraimer, M. L. (2001). Social Networks and the Performance of Individuals and Groups. The Academy of Management Journal, 44(2), 316-325. doi:10.2307/3069458

Tversky Amos and Kahneman Daniel(1974), Judgment under Uncertainty: Heuristics and Biases, Science, New Series, Vol. 185, No. 4157. , pp. 1124-1131.

Vaquera, E., and Kao, G. (2008). Do you like me as much as I like you? Friendship reciprocity and its effects on school outcomes among adolescents. Social Science Research, 37(1), 55-72. https://www.ncbi.nlm.nih.gov/pmc/articles/PMC2352147/

Verkuyten, M. (1996). Culture and gender differences in the perception of friendship by adolescents. International Journal of Psychology, 31(5), 207-217.

Webber Sean. R. and Robinson Julie (2002) The impact of friendship on primary school children's ability to effectively collaborate with peers: Learning outcomes on two scientific reasoning tasks ; Australian Association for research in Education (AARE) conference, 2002. http://www.aare.edu.au/data/publications/2002/web02411.pdf

Witkow Melissa R, and Fuligni Andrew J. (2010). In-School Versus Out-of-School Friendships and Academic Achievement Among an Ethnically Diverse Sample of Adolescents. Journal of Research on Adolescence

EXPLORING TEACHER USE OF AN ONLINE FORUM TO DEVELOP GAME-BASED LEARNING LITERACY

Amanda Barany, Mamta Shah and Aroutis Foster
Drexel University, USA

ABSTRACT

Game-based learning researchers have emphasized the importance of teachers' game literacy and knowledge of pedagogical approaches involved in successfully adopting an instructional approach (Bell and Gresalfi, 2017). In this paper, we describe findings from an online resource that teachers used to generate a repository of games for use both during their involvement in a Masters in Learning Technologies program and after the completion of the program. We argue that such a repository providing information on games in terms of their technology, pedagogy, and content may prove useful for teachers searching for games to align with their area of practice. This paper presents a descriptive analysis of a sample of 82 posts posted from September 2010 – November 2016 to demonstrate participants' emerging proficiency in assessing games for their technological, pedagogical, and content-related affordances and constraints (as supported by the Game Network Analysis (GaNA) framework) (Shah & Foster, 2015). The paper also presents a case example to illustrate a forum user's developing game literacy and the community and contextual factors that influence post content. We conclude with implications for future research.

KEYWORDS

Game-based learning, Game Network Analysis, teacher development, online forums.

1. INTRODUCTION

Serious games and games for learning have acquired greater mainstream acceptance as tools for knowledge, skill development, and behavioral change in students (Boyle et al., 2016). However, meta-analyses of game-based learning studies stress that the involvement of teachers can support meaningful learning through games, particularly through their expert intervention as content and pedagogical experts both in general and in partnership with the game being used (Clark et al., 2015; Wouters et al., 2013; Young et al., 2012).

For such integration to occur, Hanghøj (2013) stresses the need for teachers to develop both game literacy and skills in game-based learning curricular design and implementation. Teacher analysis of existing games for their pedagogical, technical, and content-related affordances and constraints (as part of GaNA) has been argued as a necessary prerequisite to game integration (Foster, 2012), particularly so that educators may determine whether a game is appropriate for their respective contexts (Foster et al., 2011). Examination of teachers' existing game selection processes also reveals that peer support, advice, and education play a key role; "what other teachers say about a game" was ranked as the biggest influence on game selection by teachers using GBL (Takeuchi and Vaala, 2014). Furthermore, teachers' limited knowledge of games has fueled their reluctance to use games in their instruction (Rice, 2007). Nonetheless, aside from small-scale in-person interactions, few structures or resources exist to support teacher development of game literacy and pedagogy (Ruggiero, 2013; Takeuchi & Vaala, 2014). Online websites or forums might serve this function, and promote wider dissemination of expertise by teachers and for teachers; however, these too are rare.

In this paper, we used the Game Network Analysis (GaNA) theoretical framework to create and examine the outcomes of the 'Learning in Game-Based Environments Web Resource' for teachers and professionals partaking in a graduate program on Learning Technologies. Game Network Analysis (GaNA) is a combination of analytical and pedagogical frameworks developed to aid teachers, researchers and designers in adopting game-based learning (GBL). The following work offers an introduction to the online resource and its purpose, followed by a description of data collection and analysis procedures to descriptively explore manifestations of teacher game literacy using GaNA as an analytical framework. First, a descriptive analysis of a sample of 82 student forum posts made on the web resource offers insight into participants' emerging proficiency in assessing games for their technological, pedagogical, and content-related affordances and constraints (as supported by GaNA) (Foster et al., 2015). The paper then presents a case example to illustrate an individual forum user's developing game literacy and the community and contextual factors that influence post content. We conclude with implications for future research on this topic, and offer preliminary suggestions for the design of future resources that develop teachers' game literacy.

2. GAME NETWORK ANALYSIS

Game Network Analysis (GaNA) is a combination of analytical and pedagogical frameworks developed to aid teachers, researchers and designers in adopting game-based learning (GBL). Analytical elements of GaNA support consideration for the ecological conditions (technological, pedagogical, and content-related) that influence the integration of game-based curricula in formal and informal learning contexts (Foster et al., 2015). The game integration frameworks in GaNA include the Play, Curricular activity, Reflection, Discussion (PCaRD) model (Foster & Shah, 2015b), and the inquiry, communication, construction, and expression (ICCE) framework (Foster & Shah, 2015a), which offer a process for employing game-based learning in classrooms in a given context (Shah & Foster, 2015).

3. THE LEARNING IN GAME-BASED ENVIRONMENTS WEB RESOURCE

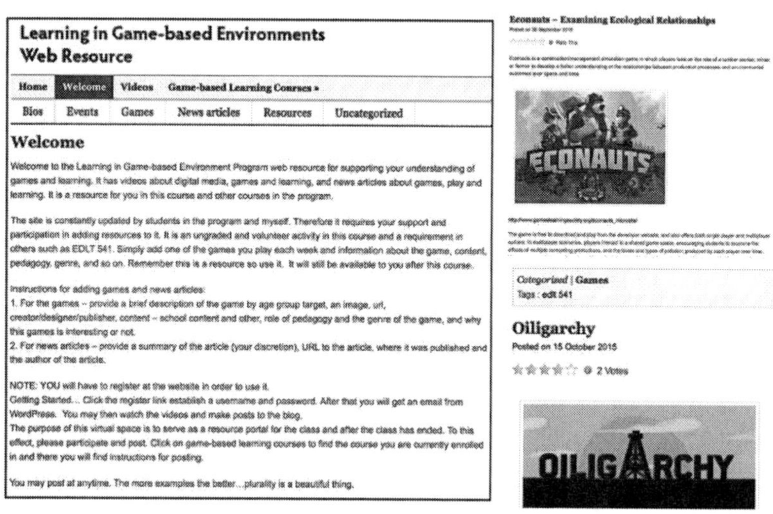

Figure 1. The homepage and sample posts from the Learning in Game-Based Environments Web Resource

The 'Learning in Game-Based Environments Web-Resource' (see Figure 1) was developed as part of an online Masters in Learning Technologies program for students taking courses in the game-based learning concentration at an urban private university in a Northeastern city in the United States. The web resource was intended to serve as a repository of videos about digital media, games for learning, and news articles about games, play and learning that would be continually updated, mostly by students and occasionally by the course instructors. The purpose of this virtual space was to serve as a resource portal for students to access both during the courses and after the courses had ended, and consists primarily of a forum where students were encouraged to contribute posts about games, links to news articles, or other game-based learning resources for peers.

The majority of these forum posts describe existing games, and their potential utility for game-based learning contexts. As part of class activities, students are encouraged to post games to the forum that had not appeared previously in the posting lists; thus, the majority of game analysis posts are unique. This tool also hosts an online discussion forum that has been active since September of 2010 (7 years), that currently contains over 250 original posts with over 280 response comments made by students with experience in education, game design, business, and other areas of career or academic expertise.

Instructors invited students to share brief descriptions of games and explain why they were or were not interesting, with posting guidelines kept intentionally open-ended to encourage students to share whatever information they found relevant. Students received instructions stating "For the games – provide a brief description of the game by age group target, an image, URL, creator/designer/publisher, content – school content and other, role of pedagogy and the genre of the game, and why this games is interesting or not. For news articles – provide a summary of the article (your discretion), URL to the article, where it was published, and the author of the article."

Resources like the Learning in Game-Based Environments have only recently been introduced. For example, Legends of Learning is a web-based platform that allows teachers/parents to create a playlist of learning games. Common Sense Media, a non-profit organization, offers a review of variety of media (e.g. games, TV shows, films) for parents and teachers to make choices for use with children and youth. The Learning in Game-Based Environments Web-Resource is unique in that it was created exclusively for educators and was tied to professional development as courses in the graduate program. Additionally, the web resource has been active for a long time, resulting in a large pool of resources for and by teachers and professionals. Thus, examination of sites that promote, develop and disseminate teacher-to-teacher game analyses is warranted, to better understand how such tools serve current and future educators.

3.1 Research Sampling and Analysis

A stratified random sample of forum posts describing games was collected across the 75 months during which the forum has been active; 33 months did not contain posts on games for education. Of the remaining 42 months, one to two posts on games was randomly sampled from each month and examined for student game analysis in terms of a game's technological, pedagogical, and content-based affordances and constraints. Months with no posts on games for learning were spread throughout the web resource, likely signifying the gaps between classes in which students contributed posts. Several posts contained multiple discrete descriptions of individual games; text from these posts was separated by game into individual data entries, to assess game literacy development for each described game. The resulting sample consisted of 82 games.

A detailed codebook was developed to analyze posts for the inclusion of specific types of information relating to elements of a game's technology (game platform), pedagogy (game genre), and elements of content (subjects or skills) (see Table 1). The objective of the analysis was to identify the extent to which participants demonstrated game literacy (i.e. were able to describe a game in terms of technological, pedagogical, and content affordances and constraints). Code lists for platform, genre, content, and skill were modeled after those used by the website Common Sense Media to categorize game reviews geared toward parents, educators, and technology advocates.

Table 1. Codes for Analyzing the Learning in Game-Based Environments Web-Resource. Codes were developed based on those hosted at https://www.commonsensemedia.org/game-reviews

Question	Label	Value	Measure
What is the genre of the game?	Genre	01 – Educational 02 – Action/adventure 03 – Roleplaying ... 26 – Other 27 – Multiple genres 00 – Information not provided	Nominal
What content (subject area) does this game focus on?	Subject	01 – Language and reading 02 – Math 03 – Science ... 07 – Other 00 – Information not provided	Nominal
What content (skills) does this game focus on?	Skill	01 – Thinking and reasoning 02 – Creativity 03 – Self-direction ... 10 – Other 00 – Information not provided	Nominal

A team of 5 researchers completed three rounds of cross-coder comparison using the codebook, at which point a moderate level of agreement was reached (k = .549), and coding of the resulting sample of 82 game posts commenced. Following descriptive statistics to characterize emerging teacher game literacy, chi square tests were calculated across each pair of codes to explore patterns of co-occurrence across descriptions of technology, pedagogy, and content.

In addition, elements of text were deductively coded for discussions of a game's technology, pedagogy, and content, providing a body of text vignettes organized by game analysis elements. These categories were then examined using open and axial coding techniques to reveal emerging qualitative themes (Glaser and Strauss, 1967) to further inform how posters discuss and analyze games. Findings present a descriptive picture of students' game analysis processes as part of GaNA – a preliminary examination that will support future in-depth qualitative and quantitative analysis.

3.2 Findings

3.2.1 Game Objectives

The majority of the game descriptions (58, 71%) reported game objectives in varying levels of detail. Some posts detailed game objectives in terms of what players might learn or experience. For instance, a post on *Diabetic Dog Game* described it as "a simulation game that teaches children how to take care of animals." Some posts instead detailed the objectives of gameplay, or objectives for game completion:

> You have to find a way to get the hamburger to the hungry cat by popping balloon like objects that are blocking the hamburger's path. You also have to keep the hamburger from falling onto an electrified grid which burns it to a crisp. (*Cat Around the World*, 04/2013)

Some posts also merged game objectives with student learning objectives, as demonstrated in the following example:

> You Make Me Sick is a game for middle school kids (ages 11-14) to teach them about the process of infection, pathogens and how infections occur. The game is made up of parts: first teaching students on the habits and weaknesses of a human, then creating an evil pathogen, and finally playing a short game in battling the pathogen against immune cells. (*You Make Me Sick*, 04/2011)

3.2.2 Technological Affordances and Constraints

In the majority of game descriptions (57, 71%), game platform information was not included in the post. Often, technological platforms were only explicitly detailed when they were particularly noteworthy in some way, such as when a game was hosted on multiple platforms:

> The game is also great because you only need an internet connection to play. You can even download the game as an application for your iphone, which makes it available at your hands even more. (*Sporcle*, 09/2010)

In 59 of the 82 game descriptions (73%), a URL was provided, or references to the hosting website or descriptions of website play were included. This suggests a potential preference among posters for games distributed online through websites, or illustrates the likely abundance of such games. When posters detailed game technological affordances or constraints, technical features were often connected to pedagogical benefits from either the teacher or learner's perspectives, as demonstrated in an example below:

> Thermometers are placed with pictures to represent high and low temperatures. Students can use them as a guide to which items get paired together. The name of the picture is also said out loud so students can learn more vocabulary and help figuring out what a picture is. (*Weather Surprise / Sid the Science Kid*, 02/2012)

3.2.3 Pedagogical Affordances and Constraints

In 57 cases (71%), posters provided some information regarding the genres of games. Post described games as educational (15, 19%), other (13, 16%), puzzle (11, 14%), multi-genre (5, 6%), roleplaying (4, 5%), strategy (4, 5%), simulation (2, 2%), action/adventure (1, 1%), and edutainment (1, 1%). Some pedagogical descriptions affirmed how the games could help educate players about specific skills or content. Some posts listed pedagogical benefits of the game for specific learning groups. Other posts described specific lesson plans or classroom activities in which other teachers could use the games:

> The game allows for spelling word lists to be created. I downloaded the game and created basic sight word lists for my 5-year-old son. I made lists like "body parts" and entered head, arm, leg, etc. and "colors" with red, blue, green, etc. I then played the game and allowed my son to play the game. We both found the game play to be very simple, requiring no real instructions to get started. Without reading, it is simple enough to understand the game play and process. The game tracks statistics of how much time is spent playing the games and percentage of correct spellings for each word list. (*Spelling Monster*, 08/2014)

3.2.4 Content-based Affordances and Constraints

In 49 cases (60%), posters provided information on the subjects covered by the games in each description. The games focused on math (10, 12%), science (9, 11%), other areas (9, 11%), social studies (7, 9%), language and reading, (6, 7%), multiple areas (6, 7%) or hobbies (2, 3%). In addition to games that were connected to a variety of subject areas including science, social studies, language and reading, hobbies, engineering, and personal finance, three posts also made explicit reference to multiple content areas, as demonstrated in an example below:

> The beautiful thing about Sporcle is that it is filled with content. It ranges from everything from Geography to Entertainment. If you want to use your math skills, you can search for math games. If you want to test your video game knowledge, you can do that as well. (*Sporcle*, 09/2010)

Thirty-three posts (40%) contained information on the types of skills embedded in or connected to each game. Specifically, posters described their games as facilitating "other" skills (11, 13%), thinking and reasoning, (8, 10%), responsibility and ethics (3, 4%), tech skills (3, 4%), multiple skills (3, 4%), self-direction (2, 2%), communication (2, 2%), and health and fitness (1, 1%). Combinations coded for games connected to multiple skills ranged from responsibility and ethics and health and fitness (*Diabetic Dog*

Game) to thinking and reasoning and tech skills (*Code Monster*). In several cases, posters explicitly highlighted the multiple skills developed through gameplay as a game asset:

> So this game not only teaches how to take care of a dog, but also money management and how to balance a diabetic's diet. These lessons could also be applied to a non-diabetic's diet. It can teach responsibility and also time management. It is also easier than a real dog and it is free. This learning experience is very interactive and it allows children to explore what it might be like to live with and take care of a diabetic. (*Diabetic Dog Game*, 03/2011)

3.2.5 Additional Themes

Additional themes that arose in game posts included poster's personal opinions and experiences with each game, as demonstrated in the following examples:

> What attracted me to this game was first the concept – it seems like a great idea for a game, to utilize biology and the bodies defense system. (*Immune System Defence Forces*, 11/2011)

> I found that not only was the game animal shelter a good game that allows children to see what it is like to take care of pets but that it can be for both girls and boys. One day I was playing this game, and my nephew wanted to give it a try. For an 8 year old, it was stimulating because it required a sense of responsibility. Although he had little experience with taking care of animals this game, gave him a look into all the things that are required to house pets. (http://www.123-games.net/games/animal-shelter, 01/2012)

Given the importance of peer reviews in teachers' game selection, it is likely such endorsements may carry particular weight for other educators. Another common theme involved the provision of information on the background, design, or other history of the game. This suggests posters may have valued background information on game development and release as useful or interesting to peers. For example:

> It has been downloaded over 25 million times and was a runner up in the IGN Game of the Year 2012 awards for 'Overall Best Strategy Game'. Overall, it was the 15th most downloaded paid iPhone game of 2012 in the U.S. and the 5th most downloaded paid iPhone game of 2013 in the U.S. In February 2014, Ndemic Creations released Plague Inc: Evolved, for PC, Mac and Linux onto Steam. The game continues to have an active community and is regularly updated. (*Plague Inc.,* 11/2014)

For 7 out of the 37 posts (19%), other site users left one or more comments on the posts. Teachers who had previous experience with the posted game, or saw particular relevance of the tool in their specific contexts, made up the majority of posted comments in 2010 through 2012. Comments made in the 2015 cohort typically contained deeper analyses of the games themselves, as the group played the games and offered affirmations and critiques.

3.2.6 Variable Associations

Chi square tests explored associations between the presence of post information on technology, pedagogy, and content; findings indicated statistically significant associations between a posts' inclusion of classroom subject and game objective (χ^2 (1, 82) = 5.068, p = 0.025), and subject and skill (χ^2 (1, 82) = 5.270, p = 0.022) (see Table 2). This informs how posters might be conceptualizing and discussing game content affordances and constraints – describing a learning objective, detailing classroom subject alignment, and then relating the game to teachable skills.

Statistically significant associations also emerged between game objectives and associated URLs (χ^2 (1, 82) = 5.319, p=0.021), which informs how posters might conceptualize and discuss technological features (if and when they do). A typical post might include a brief description of how to play and win the game, followed by a link to access it, but more often may not develop a technological assessment further to consider things like game platform.

Table 2. Chi Square tests of associations between technology, pedagogy, and content variables

Data pair	χ^2	p-value
Subject_objective	**5.068**	**0.025**
Subject_platform	3.638	0.056
Subject_genre	3.067	0.080
Subject_skill	**5.270**	**0.022**
Subject_url	5.270	0.438
Objective_platform	0.704	0.402
Objective_genre	0.224	0.636
Objective_skill	3.500	0.061
Objective_url	**5.319**	**0.021**
Platform_genre	0.550	0.458
Platform_skill	1.144	0.285
Platform_url	0.118	0.731
Genre_skill	0.775	0.379
Genre_url	0.004	0.949
Skill_url	2.778	0.096

No statistically significant associations were found between game genre and any other category, suggesting a potential disconnect between inclusion of game genre (which involves usually one word or less) and other text discussions of pedagogical, technological, and content-based affordances and constraints. This suggests the need to build teacher awareness of how genre influences pedagogy (how the game teaches), and the need for a qualitative exploration of how teachers do describe game pedagogy. The following case example illustrates how one teacher introduced technology, pedagogy, and content in her posts.

4. CASE EXAMPLE

Kai (pseudonym) posted four games on the Learning in Game-based Environments Resource – two in October of 2015 and two in November of 2015. In October, Kai posted about *The Migrant Trail* and *Rolling Fall*, while in November, she posted about the games *Superbetter* and *Yousician*. The game-based learning class asks students to make two posts to the forum resource, suggesting Kai's voluntary posting to the forum beyond the mandatory minimum. Kai was selected as an instrumental case example due to this higher number of posts, which afforded greater insight into her developing game literacy over time; though posts varied by student in terms of length and content, Kai's posts were chosen as representative of "average" game posts in terms of length and level of detail.

Kai described *The Migrant Trail as a* "text-based adventure game," *Rolling Fall as a* "puzzle game," and Yousician as an "app game," but did not share a genre for *Superbetter*. Kai described *Superbetter* as "a digital version of gamified life." As definitions of gamification often distinguish such tools from traditional games, Kai may not have known how to distinguish *Superbetter* by game genre.

In most cases, Kai did not explicitly describe the platforms needed to play these games. However, in all four cases, Kai provided a URL or mentioned a game website, which suggests that all of the games were hosted online and accessible with any platform that could access the Internet. Kai's posts also encouraged readers to explore the game sites through supportive texts (i.e. "But don't take my word for it. Go have fun killing zombies.").

Kai's post on *Yousician* offered greater detail on technological game affordances as compared to her other posts; she described it as a "web or mobile-based app game," further emphasizing that this game was hosted on multiple platforms. She also described how "the game uses the microphone of your computer and analyzes the real sounds coming from a real guitar to award...points," stressing how the technological setup of this game (as compared to *Guitar Hero*) could develop real-world musical skill.

Kai provided detailed information on the pedagogical affordances of each game in her posts. For *The Migrant Trail*, she offered in-depth descriptions of how the game promotes understanding of different perspectives and complex immigration issues by sharing the stories of key characters:

> The game can be played from the perspective of migrants as well as border control agents, which lends a level of complexity to the issue...The player is confronted with the personal story of each migrant, which humanizes them and helps the player understand why each migrant feels it is necessary to make the incredibly dangerous journey.... Playing from the perspective of the border patrol agents, is significantly less challenging and engaging, however, its main purpose is to highlight the magnitude of the crisis for migrants trying to cross the border...You also get to read the agents' bios, which explains their motivation and diversity.

Kai also provided some information on the content knowledge and skill development supported by each of these games. For instance, in her post on *Rolling Fall*, Kai listed the specific physics constructs demonstrated by the game, such as "energy conservation," "parabolic kinematics," and "rotational equilibrium," and described how the game could be integrated into a high school math unit.

Several additional posting themes emerged during analysis of Kai's posts. Kai described specific age groups, demographics, or contexts in which each game could serve an educational purpose. In her post on *Rolling Fall*, for example, Kai identified herself as a physics teacher and provided specific curriculum ideas for using the game based on student age group:

> Younger students (late elementary, early middle school) would benefit from playing this game just to gain a feel for the physical world and how it works. Older students (early high school) could play this game and tie it into real-world experiments, to learn the mathematics behind what they are playing with.

Kai also regularly integrated other elements of her personal experiences with and around these games into her posts, detailing her personal experiences playing or using the games as context for her endorsements:

> I found out about this game from a friend in a support group that I belong to, as we both have a vascular brain anomaly that can cause some issues like a traumatic brain injury. I decided to give it a go (I'm playing in 2 different challenges at the moment). I love it so much, I recommended it to my sister who deals with depression (who also loves it). I also recommended it to my colleagues to use in middle school homeroom classes to help students work on motivation and self-acceptance.

In another post that Kai made to the forum (where she shared a non-game resource), she described the forum as "a community of people who value games." This understanding of the nature purpose of the forum is perhaps reflected in the particularly active peer responses her posts engendered. Her game descriptions merged practical discussions of each game's utility for learning with relatable personal experiences as a teacher and game user. While demonstrations of Kai's game literacy varied in terms of the volume and detail of information presented on technological, pedagogical, or content-related issues, her emphases on one or more of these areas perhaps reflects an profound understanding of what information the community might find immediately relevant about a game (i.e. *Yousician* might require an initial focus on technological setup).

5. CONCLUSION

A Descriptive analysis of the Learning in Game-Based Environments Web Resource revealed gaps in representation of technological, pedagogical, and content-based affordances and constraints across the sampling of game posts, most notably in discussions of technology. Posts that provided a comprehensive analysis were rare; more often, a poster would prioritize discussion of unusual or noteworthy elements over others (i.e. a game played on a PlayStation 3 warranted more explicit discussion of technology). While game posts often shared detailed discussions of technology, pedagogy, or content, the inclusion of more specific prompts or educator supports could promote comprehensive game analysis discussions.

Kai's case example illustrates how a single student's posts might vary based on their integration of game analysis constructs due to contextual factors such as characteristics of the game itself, the poster's opinions and personal experiences, and perhaps on the poster's perceptions of what the community finds useful. A fruitful avenue of future research might explore how users decide and justify what information to include in their discussions of games to further illuminate teacher game literacy practices.

Further development of this research will also expand the sample to test for statistical differences between posters that did and did not include elements of content, pedagogy, or technology. These and future findings offer potential insights to educators working to support game literacy and pedagogy in future teachers. Just as Young et al. (2012) argued for the creation of an educational video game repository for use in research follow-up and replication, such a tool could offer manifold benefits to educators looking to develop game implementation skills and searching for games to use in their classrooms. Given the rarity of such a resource and its potential to help fill implementation gaps, an examination of this existing online repository serves as a useful example for the development of future tools and resources for teacher-driven games education and skill development.

REFERENCES

Bell, A., & Gresalfi, M. (2017). Teaching with Videogames: How Experience Impacts Classroom Integration. *Technology, Knowledge and Learning*, pp 1-14.

Boyle, E. A. et al., 2016. An Update to the Systematic Literature Review of Empirical Evidence of the Impacts and Outcomes of Computer Games and Serious Games. *Computers & Education*, Vol. 94, pp 178-192.

Clark, D. B. et al., 2015. Digital Games, Design, and Learning a Systematic Review and Meta-Analysis. *Review of educational research*, Vol. 86, No. 1, pp 79-122.

Foster, A. et al., 2011. Digital Game Analysis: Using the Technological Pedagogical Content Knowledge Framework to Determine the Affordances of a Game for Learning. *Learning to Play: Exploring the Future of Education with Video Games*. Peter Lang Publications, New York, NY, USA.

Foster, A., 2012. Assessing Learning Games for School Content: Framework and Methodology. In D. Ifenthaler, D. Eseryel, and X. Ge (eds.) *Assessment in Game-based Learning: Foundations, Innovations, and Perspectives.* Springer, New York, NY, USA.

Foster, A. and Shah, M., 2015a. The Play Curricular activity Reflection and Discussion Model for Game-Based Learning. *Journal of Research on Technology in Education*, Vol. 47, No. 2, pp 71-88.

Foster, A. and Shah, M., 2015b. The ICCE Framework: Framing Learning Experiences Afforded by Games. *Journal of Educational Research*, Vol. 51, No. 4, pp 369-395.

Foster, A. et al., 2015. Game Network Analysis: For Teaching with Games. In M. L. Niess and H. Gillow-Wiles (Eds.) *Handbook of Research on Teacher Education in the Digital Age*. Information Science Reference, Hershey, PA, USA.

Glaser, B. G. and Strauss, A. L., 1967. *The Discovery of Grounded Theory: Strategies for Qualitative Research.* Wiedenfeld and Nicholson, London, England.

Hanghøj, T., 2013. Game-Based Teaching: Practices, Roles, and Pedagogies. *New Pedagogical Approaches in Game Enhanced Learning: Curriculum Integration*, Vol. 81.

Rice, J. W., 2007. New Media Resistance: Barriers to Implementation of Computer Video Games in the Classroom. *Journal of Educational Multimedia and Hypermedia*, Vol. 16, No. 3, pp 249.

Ruggiero, D., 2013. Video Games in the Classroom: The Teacher Point of View. *Games for Learning Workshop of the Foundations of Digital Games Conference*, Chania, Greece.

Shah, M. and Foster, A., 2015. Developing and Assessing Teachers' Knowledge of Game-Based Learning. *Journal of Technology and Teacher Education.* Vol. 23, No. 2, pp 241-267. Society for Information Technology & Teacher Education, Chesapeake, VA, USA.

Takeuchi, L. M. and Vaala, S., 2014. Level Up Learning: A National Survey on Teaching with Digital Games. *The Joan Ganz Cooney Center at Sesame Workshop*, New York, USA.

Wouters, P. et al., 2013. A Meta-Analysis of the Cognitive and Motivational Effects of Serious Games. *Journal of Educational Psychology*, Vol. 105, No. 2, pp 249-265.

Young, M. F. et al., 2012. Our Princess is in Another Castle: A Review of Trends in Serious Gaming for Education. *Review of educational research*, Vol. 82, No. 1, pp 61-89.

EDUCATIONAL ASSESSMENT OF STUDENTS IN PRIMARY SCHOOL IN TUNISIA

Wiem Ben Khalifa[1,2], Dalila Souilem[3] and Mahmoud Neji[2]
[1]*University of Dammam, Dammam, Saudi Arabia*
[2] *University of Sfax, MIRACL Laborator, Sfax, Tunisia*
[3]*University of Umm Qura , Mecca, Saudi Arabia*

ABSTRACT

Regardless of the study level, the assessments applied in the different educational institutions in Tunisia raise many questions. Do these practices indicate the learners' cognitive metamorphoses? Do formative and summative evaluations intend to access knowledge acquisition at the expense of understanding? Is the content of the evaluation approaches and instruments an important part of the learners' previous knowledge? Is there any relationship between this content and the specific knowledge base of the learner? Does the evaluation instruments structure provide access to knowledge construction? Is this structure oriented towards the evaluation of low-level cognitive skills more than to the assessment of high-level cognitive skills? Does the assessment context introduce affective variables that may influence learners' results in a negative way? Do the used instruments allow consistently determining the learners' strengths and weaknesses? Do the correction criteria respect all the learner's responses worth to build up a special knowledge? Do objectivity requirements influence these criteria more than the cognitive value of responses? In fact, all of these questions risen show the seriousness and complexity of the evaluation problem in the school environment as well as the cognitive progress of the learners. They are quite related to the subject matter of the evaluation instruments and their structure as well as their objectives and the background they are taking place in than to the correction criteria. In this paper, we propose a personalized evaluation environment for mobile learning. We first introduce m-evaluation scenario. Then, we describe this personalization as well as the architecture of the evaluation environment composed of Web services and based on communication between these services carried out via Semantic web technologies. The environment presented allows assessing the learners' knowledge of a particular teaching content by first of all searching, then selecting and finally generating a test well adapted to their knowledge level. In fact, a new course will be introduced once the evaluation is accomplished. We also managed an experimentation based on concluding the student's satisfaction degree.

KEYWORDS

Assessment Technology, m-evaluation, Semantic Web, Context

1. INTRODUCTION

The evolution in the Information and communication technologies has considerably modified the organizational structures of learning and its processing through the last decade mainly because of the increase in using the Internet as well as network technologies. Consequently, there is general use of movable communication means as mobile phones and laptops that can be connected to the internet through the different wireless networks (Wi-Fi, 3G, etc.) The use of these mobile tools revolutionizes the pupils' view of space and time in the learning context. These technologies contribute the young learners with significant competences to the extent of carrying out their scholarly scheme conceivably ever. Hence, mobile technologies are valuable for pupils. Actually, they better develop their collaborative, communicative, and coordinative skills. They also promote cooperating with teachers and grant outstanding autonomy as well as improving responsiveness.

Studying many criteria in such learning approach including learner mobility, learner profile, organization of knowledge, learning time and gain and so on increases the efficiency of m-evaluation. Indeed, mobility in m-evaluation is notably detected in the context concept which indicates the learners' suitable situation. It is crucial to determine, with reference to the context, which resources to send, how to send, when to send, on which interface, etc. Therefore, the entire evaluation process must be adaptable to these developing contexts.

With the evolution of Web 3.0, the semantic web sounds to ensure technology to carry out m-evaluation system. Undoubtedly, the semantic Web is a Web intelligible to both men and machines. Thus, it represents a vast field of applying works emerging from the knowledge formality and representation reasoning (Berners-Lee et al., 2001).

In this manuscript, we suggest a flexible environment for mobile evaluation using semantic Web technologies for description and reasoning. This paper is structured as follows: First, we present related works. Then, we introduce our work based on a mobile evaluation (m-evaluation) scenario in an open learning network. Afterwards, we analyze the proposed scenario and we describe the m-evaluation process. The architecture set up for the evaluation system is depicted in section 5. In section 6, we discuss the first uses of this system and we end the paper with a conclusion and our future works.

2. RELATED WORK

Plenty of studies about using mobile technologies have been performed in mobile environments assessment. As an example, Cheniti and al. realize a Mobile and Personalized Evaluation System (MPES) using the Semantic Web and Web services. Actually, MPES connects and realizes a set of web services interacting together to provide the system needs. This approach is likewise effective to handle the semantic web technology. Web services, naturally, set up the evaluation resources corresponding to the set of the different attitudes, the learners' needs and how they collaborate with the mobile environment (Belcadhi et al., 2013). Similarly (Coulombe et al., 2011) proposed the MobileQuizz project performing a multiplatform mobile application executed with the Google Web Toolkit in Ajax. Likewise, the Context aware adaptive and personalized mobile learning systems is introduced by (Sampson et al., 2013).

The approach of Chen (Chen, C. H. 2010) is based on self-assessment research results and peer review in which he realized a Mobile Assessment Participation System (MAPS) used by PDA (Personal Digital Assistant). Moreover, Chen recommended a model of MAPS implementation simplifying and improving self-efficiency and peer assessments in classrooms. However, in (Coulby et al., 2011) and with reference to a group of students in their last year of medicine, the authors analyzed the effect of contributing a skill-based assessment via PDAs. This assessment presented the good experience of using mobile technologies to evaluate the students' level.

In the same way, Zualkernanand et al. performed an architecture that takes a QTIv2.1 evaluation test based on an XML file and systematically generates a Flash Lite to be presented and then executed on a mobile device (Zualkernan et al., 2007).

3. A MOBILE EVALUATION SCENARIO OF A LEARNER

In this section, we describe the context of our research using the following evaluation scenario: Idriss, a 7th year Basic student, would like to prepare for his exam on the Arabic grammar course. This student wants to review the nominal sentence components lesson. He also wants to evaluate his knowledge. So, he starts by selecting this lesson. The necessary prerequisites for the chosen lesson will be first researched .The corresponding questions will be, then, presented to the student. These questions form a pre-assessment on the chosen lesson. The student will, as a result, have the opportunity to revise the lesson parts that are not known and for which the corresponding questions were not answered in the correct way.

Finally, to insure that Idriss understands the essential notions of the formerly-mentioned lesson, questions will be searched and presented to form a personalized post-assessment test. The learning environment must show Idriss's process in revising the selected lesson. The tests presented to Idriss should contribute a detailed and precise assessment of his knowledge and level of understanding. Thus, all the main parts of the course must be well understood. Whenever Idriss chooses a lesson to revise, the learning environment should look for relevant assessment supports, especially the questions that should be put after the examination of the final tests, the learner's options in terms of language and learning plan parameters. Idriss wants to access the resources of this evaluation from a mobile interface. Served by a personal PDA, the student can, for instance, be in the school library for an hour. Idriss will, accordingly, access a user interface where he can choose the course to be evaluated as illustrated in figure 1. Then, he enters a set of keywords showing the theme of the evaluation. Idriss should also specify his location type. Moreover, he must specify the maximum time reserved for the self-evaluation test: 1 hour. Finally, he gives his preferences in terms of the questions types. For example, he chooses the SOAQs (Short and Open Answer Questions).

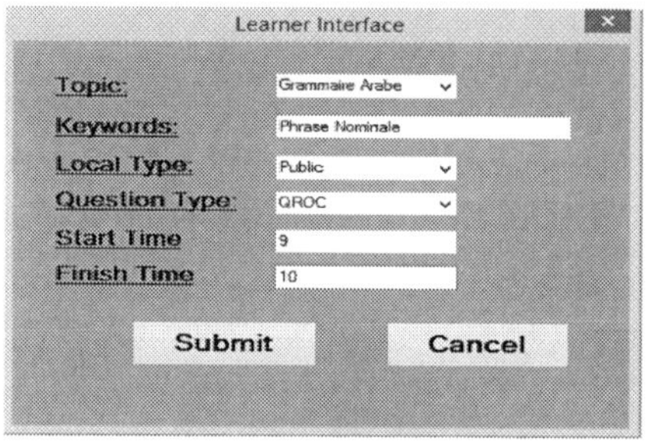

Figure 1. Learner interface

All the information indicated by Idriss must be taken into account when generating the assessment test. The evaluation environment presents itself as a context-sensitive system for the generation of personalized and mobile evaluation tests. It must also score and safeguard its progress and evaluation references in order to use them in future evaluation activities. Assessment tests, presented to the students, should be adapted to their profiles, level and prerequisites.

The environment should, thus, personalize the learning and evaluation content to the learner's level of knowledge based on two main concepts:

- Reuse and Interoperability through the design and implementation of the content in the form of learning objects: allows a dynamic generation of the content by identifying and searching teaching or evaluation resources to be regenerated. Through this design, the course will not be conceived in a monolithic way, but as a set of independent parts. These objects represent also the new approaches and reflections basis on the possibilities of electronic learning systems standardization.
- Estimation of the learner's level of knowledge at each learning stage through a personalized evaluation.

Four functionalities must then be determined in such evaluation system:

- Content presentation to the learner.
- Knowledge assessment obtained by the learner.
- A suitable content generation adapted to the assessment of the learner's knowledge.
- Consideration of the learner context and the personalization of the evaluation according to the parameters provided by the evaluation context.

4. A STUDY OF THE PROPOSED SCENARIO

Mobile learning environments are distinguished by unreliable learning situations and circumstances. In such environments, context modeling is needed to better understand the learners' activities and to personalize the learning resources. Context-sensitive environments generally refer to a class of environments that can capture environmental parameters and adapt accordingly the set of decisions and behaviors. They are essentially characterized by their heterogeneous nature involving steady change of context according to many circumstances depending mainly on the learner, location, time, place, etc. The basic goal of learning is always to yield the learner with context-relevant learning and / or evaluation resources. Thus, the learning or assessment process must be adjusted as well as adapted to the context. Contextual reasoning is an important aspect in studying the ambient intelligence. Its aiming is to figure out new knowledge based on the accessible data. It makes context-sensitive applications more intelligent and personalized according to the users 'needs. Thus, context sensitivity results from the dynamic and heterogeneous nature of the ambient environments.

In order to maintain contextual reasoning and supply the learner with a Mobile Assessment Object (MAO), First Order Logic (FOL) should be used. Indeed, FOL is a very influential and potent means of reasoning about the context in a mobile environment. The set of Framework information serves as first-order predicates. In fact, this description is very eloquent and can be used to show the various types of information.

We present personalized evaluation formalism with FOL developed from the formalism of hyper-media adaptive educational systems (Baccari et al., 2016). The choice of the predicates logic for this formal description is stimulated by the fact that this type of FOL gives a specific design of the data representations. The evaluation personalization, in a mobile environment, is influenced by a set of parameters that establish our framework. Indeed, the Mobile Assessment Framework (MAF) must be described according to a set of information combined in a group of ontological models, and the learner's interactions with the Framework must be treated in order to update the learner model and apply it in any evaluation task. The Framework must include, similarly, a personalization element allowing personalizing the assessment activity in accordance with a set of information.

5. DESIGN OF CONTEXT-SENSITIVE MOBILE EVALUATION SYSTEM

The Mobile learning environments are identified by unreliable learning conditions and circumstances. In such environments, context modeling is needed to perceive well the learners' activities and to personalize the learning resources. However, context-sensitive environments mainly indicate a class of environments that can pick up environmental parameters and accommodate the set of decisions and behaviors appropriately. They are basically characterized by their heterogeneous nature involving a steady change of context according to many circumstances mainly relying on the learner, location, time, place, etc. The fundamental objective is to ever provide the learner with context-appropriate evaluation means. The evaluation process has to be therefore diversified and of course relevant to the context.

Hence, we suggest, in this paper, the Context-Aware Mobile Assessment System based on semantic web. This architecture describes a powerful valuable approach to exploit the technology of the semantic web. Web services develop assessment resources conforming a set of ontologies, the learners' needs and how they interact to the mobile environment.

The different exchanged documents are of RDF type. As a result, in order to admit a personalized evaluation support, metadata about the field of application (courses), assessment resources (questions), learners (prerequisites and skills), context, and evaluation history are crucial. The system uses the DC standard, a group of ontologies and specifications, to promote interoperability. It is also planned to submit the IMS / QTI specification to ensure the exchange of evaluation resources. The architecture of the system is illustrated in figure 2.

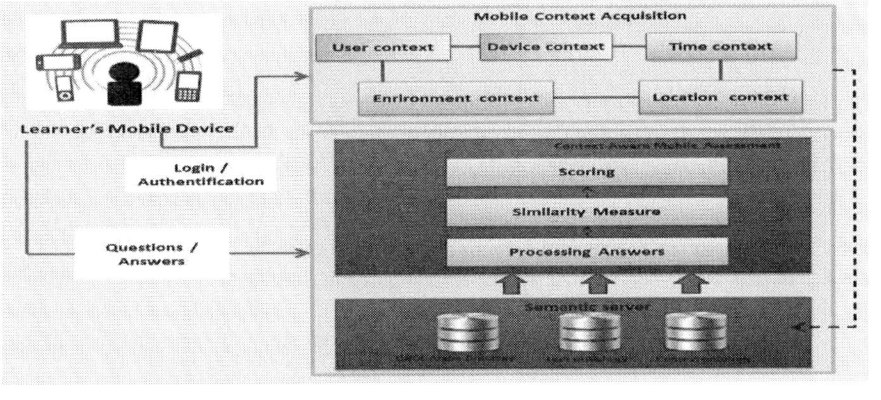

Figure 2. Aarchitecture of personalized m-evaluation system

Our system is definitely based on five modules:

1- Authentication module: consists in identifying the learner in his/her mobile environment. It is established by parameters which will be later communicated to the local database.

2- Context management module: This process is composed of three main levels:

- Acquisition: The acquisition of the environment contextual information is made by modules that directly capture information from the environment through probes, devices, means of interaction, etc.

- Aggregation and storage: The captured data are significant and coherent and interpreted for a specific use. This contextual information will be stocked for later use and accessible for processing.
- Processing: Context information processing consists in selecting resources from the user's request and applying an adaptation method to elaborate the selected resources. Contextual information and relevant resources are sent at the application level. The use of context information at this level consists in presenting this information to the user to interact, to notify him/her about the changes or to trigger the system event or action, etc.

3- Ontologies database: includes the ontologies that can be applied to model the context of the learner by indicating the user context, device context, location context and acquisition context). It also involves the ontologies of the learner response and those of the teacher (Khalifa, W. B et al., 2016).

4- Evaluation module: It rectifies the answers and then calculates the result of the learner according to his answers which will be segmented into words after performing the partial decomposition to compare them with the model answers already available for the score computing according to the similarity measure of Wu & Palmer in order to obtain the final results. Then, this module sends these results to the Interface agent which passes them to the tutor agent that displays the results to the learner. It performs this task after receiving it from the adapted test list and corrects this list by the adaptation Engine agent that prepares tests adapted to the learner's level. Finally, it saves the learner's result in his/her profile.

5- Test database and SOAQs-Arabic: It contains all the tests provided for each course and the test results for each learner. The tests are of SOAQs (Short and Open Answer Questions) type, which allows a semi-automatic correction. Indeed, each test has a defined deadline.

6. DISCUSSION

We suggested a mobile evaluation system that compels taking into consideration the context and its elements. Indeed, both of the context concepts and context sensitivity are two key terms broadly used to exploit mobile environments. In order to maintain a mobile evaluation, we need to model the context. In our work, we chose to use the ontology-based approach not only to model the context, but also to think about the described data. This approach is combined with the logic-based one allowing the deduction of a set of facts and new inferences. Besides, we introduced a mobile assessment situation as a set of evaluation context information characterized by a specific time period which can change the evaluation system behavior. As far as the evaluation objects are concerned, it is necessary to define a mobile evaluation object which considers the use of these resources in mobile environments.

To verify the system efficiency and test the aspect of personalization and adaptation, mobile evaluation system should be designed. In this work, we performed our experiments on 7th year Tunisian pupils at Bouficha High School. The aim of our study is to assess the satisfaction and the results of pupils by testing the system on different devices, such as mobile phone, touch pad, PC, employing the system at various time in order to evaluate pupils' prerequisites, and changing their locations.

The evaluation process was carried out on 30 pupils who were classified into two groups based on their Arabic grammar prerequisite: beginners and intermediate-level pupils who were given a system performance evaluation form containing 16 questions relying on 4 assumptions:

— A: Hypothesis 1: personalization aspect assessment contains 4 questions to test both the portfolio and the level of the pupils
— B: Hypothesis 2: adaptation aspect assessment contains the same number of questions as the personalization aspect assessment.
— C: Hypothesis 3: usability assessment includes also 4 questions. Students are invited to improve their opinions in terms of: navigation, generic use, etc.
— D: Hypothesis 4: system guidance and improvement evaluation

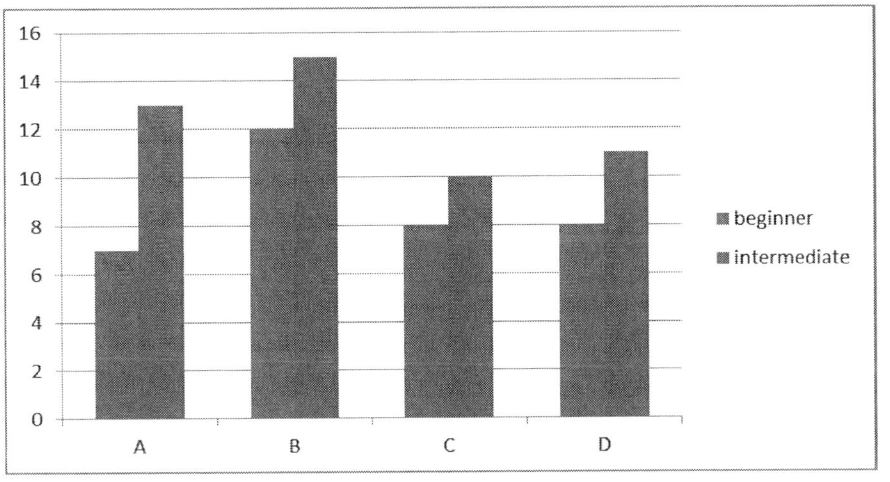

Figure 3. Histogram representing answered questions according to pupils' levels

Figure 3 represents the histogram of the answered questions based the pupils' level.

From this figure, we notice that the majority of intermediate-level pupils perceived the criteria of personalization. However, beginners did not properly recognize it. In fact, to better enhance the personalization aspect, pupils had to utilize the system several times and accurately answer some given questions. B analysis shows that the phase of adaptation was praised by the two afore-mentioned groups of pupils. Indeed, changing the device used or the location type leads to the generation of different tests.

As shown in D and C, we notice that it was confusing for beginners to use the system mainly because of the Arabic complex Grammar courses content. Furthermore, most of them liked to utilize large- screen device system because they were generally familiar with employing small-screen devices for entertainment.

Besides, pupils found that using such system is efficient in mobile learning and self-assessment. They proposed that applying this system will be expanded in other courses. The obtained findings are promising. They prove the possibility of employing this system by a wide range of pupils if the tool is introduced in various knowledge domains.

The choices of the parameters used in the discussion are marked by an open mind rather than partisan. They are guided not by a methodological blindness but by an intention to derive a rich, interesting, and original understanding of the object of study.

7. CONCLUSION AND PERSPECTIVES

We introduced, in this paper, a personalized evaluation system using the semantic web services allowing the selection and presentation of learning and evaluation resources adapted to the learner's level of knowledge. We presented also a formal description of the m-evaluation, based on FOL, and discussed its main elements to be considered when dealing with the mobile version. Moreover, we fully described the framework and recommended Logical rules based on first order logic. All these rules and other ones will be used later to personalize the assessment in a mobile learning environment and to adapt it to the assessment activity context. The architecture of the system was also well developed.

The evaluation system, in its mobile version, was tested on a group of young learners. The next step consists in developing mobile components for other types of questions and to test them on a group of learners, which will certainly boost the personalization functionalities provided to learners.

REFERENCES

Baccari, S., Mendes, F., Nicolle, C., Soualah-Alila, F., & Neji, M. (2016, June). A comparative study of the mobile learning approaches. In International Conference on Mobile, Secure and Programmable Networking (pp. 76-85). Springer International Publishing.

Belcadhi, L. C., Harchay, A., & Braham, R. (2013). Personnalisation de l'évaluation: de l'E-Evaluation vers la M-Evaluation Assessment Personalization: From E-Assessment to M-Assessment.

Berners-Lee, T., Hendler, J., & Lassila, O. (2001). The semantic web. Scientific american, 284(5), 28-37.

Boumiza, D. S., & Khalifa, W. B. (2012, July). Design of an evaluation system in e-learning Arabic language. In Education and e-Learning Innovations (ICEELI), 2012 International Conference on (pp. 1-4). IEEE.

Chen, C. H. (2010). The implementation and evaluation of a mobile self-and peer-assessment system. Computers & Education, 55(1), 229-236.

Coulby, C., Hennessey, S., Davies, N., & Fuller, R. (2011). The use of mobile technology for work- based assessment: the student experience. British Journal of Educational Technology, 42(2), 251-265.

Coulombe, C., & Ouk, N. P. Titre courant: MobileQUIZ: une application mobile multiplateforme réalisée en Ajax avec le Google Web Toolkit.2011

Harchay, A., Cheniti-Belcadhi, L., & Braham, R. (2012, June). A model driven infrastructure for context-awareness mobile assessment personalization. In Trust, Security and Privacy in Computing and Communications (TrustCom), 2012 IEEE 11th International Conference on (pp. 1676-1683). IEEE.

Khalifa, W. B., Boumiza, D. S., & Neji, M. (2016). Modeling of an evaluation system based on ontologies in a distance learning of the Arabic language. International Journal of Computer Science and Information Security, 14(11), 535

Ranganathan, A., & Campbell, R. H. (2003). An infrastructure for context-awareness based on first order logic. Personal and Ubiquitous Computing, 7(6), 353-364.

Sampson, D. G., & Zervas, P. (2013). Context-aware adaptive and personalized mobile learning systems. In Ubiquitous and mobile learning in the digital age (pp. 3-17). Springer New York.

Zualkernan, I. A., Ghanam, Y. A., Shoshaa, M. F., & Kalbasi, A. S. (2007, July). An architecture for dynamic generation of QTI 2.1 assessments for mobile devices using Flash Lite. In Advanced Learning Technologies, 2007. ICALT 2007. Seventh IEEE International Conference on (pp. 194-195). IEEE.

IMPACT OF EARLY NUMERACY TRAINING ON KINDERGARTENERS FROM MIDDLE-INCOME FAMILIES

Carla Meloni, Rachele Fanari, Andrea Bertucci and Sara Berretti
Department of Education, Psychology, Philosophy
University of Cagliari (Italy)

ABSTRACT

The aim of this work was to evaluate the effectiveness of a supplemental early numeracy skills training program for typically developing middle-income pre-school and kindergarten children (age 4-5) enrolled in a standard educational program. Three conditions were compared: cooperative learning training; individual learning training; and no training (control group). Results showed that the scores of all groups increased significantly between pre-test and post-test, but no significant differences were found between the children exposed to additional training and the control group. This finding suggests that an intervention may not be more effective than good standard schooling with such young children, and that there is a need for further investigation in this area. In a follow-up analysis, the hypothesis that the effectiveness of an early math intervention is more apparent in low-ability children was tested. For children with low early math ability, performance in terms of early numerical competence before and after the intervention was compared to a control group of equally low early math ability kindergarteners. Results showed a significant difference between pre- and post-test in both the experimental and control groups, but the training group showed higher achievement with respect to the control group. This finding suggests that it may be important to carry out interventions on children with low-ability in early math competence, even in a middle-income social context.

KEYWORDS

Early numeracy skills, training, cooperative learning, low early math ability preschoolers

1. INTRODUCTION

Recently, an increasing number of researchers have been concerned with children's early number competence and its relation to mathematics achievement. Numerical competence is a key element both in education and in everyday life, and early math skills training from the preschool level may be a preventive factor for future difficulties in learning mathematics (Geary et al., 2013). Several intervention programs have proven effective in enhancing early numeracy skills at a preschool level, with a focus on abilities such as counting, recognizing and writing numbers, one to one correspondence, comparison of numbers and dots, and understanding of numbers and quantities (e.g., Arnold et al., 2002; Ramani & Siegler, 2008). Most of the studies have been conducted in schools attended by low-income children. For instance, Ramani and Siegler (2011) compared middle-income with low-income children of different ages: the results showed that both children from low and middle-income families benefited from an early math intervention, although children from low-income backgrounds took more advantage of the intervention and learned more than less needy children.

Few studies have investigated the effects of early math skills training in children from middle-income families. In one study conducted in Italy, Passolunghi and Costa (2014) found that five year old mainstream children could benefit from domain-specific early math training.

Regarding math training, a fundamental issue is how to give effective instructions to introduce preschool and kindergarten children to numeric and quantitative concepts. One powerful method to improve learning in children is cooperative learning. Cooperative learning (CL) involves the use of small groups in which students interact with each other and work together to achieve shared goals. Although its effectiveness is well-attested in literature (Johnson et al., 2008), CL has received little consideration for children younger than six (Wiegel, 1998). Indeed, Vermette et al. (2004) underlined how the evidence about CL comes from classrooms from the third grade and "up". One of the rare studies, in which an experience of CL math training with kindergarten children is described, was conducted by Artut (2009). In this study, the effects of CL on early math ability were investigated by comparing a CL training group to a control group in which other forms of training were implemented. A significant improvement was noted in mathematical abilities in the CL group, but the work does not exactly specify the children's ages, nor does it provide details about the specific cooperative learning activities.

Our study had three main aims: to explore the effectiveness of a supplemental (i.e., in addition to the standard school curriculum) intervention in early math competence in typically developing children (aged 4-5) from middle-income families and to explore which kind of math training is the most efficient for kindergarteners, thus contributing to the discussion about the efficacy of cooperative learning in children younger than six years of age. We also wondered whether the efficacy of an early math supplemental intervention in middle-income children is more apparent in children with low early math abilities.

To achieve these aims, we assigned a sample of typically developing kindergartener (4-5 years of age) to three experimental groups: one group was exposed to structured cooperative learning early math training; a second group was assigned to individual learning early math training; and the third group was assigned to a control group involved in drawing and coloring activities. All children underwent kindergarten education in mathematics during the time of the intervention, following the standard early math curriculum established by the Italian Ministry of Instruction (Annali pubblica istruzione, 2012). Children's performances before and after math training were compared. Then, to test the hypothesis that the efficacy of an additional intervention is stronger in children with low early math abilities, in a follow-up analysis, we compared a subsample of low ability children's performance before and after the training with the performance of an equally low ability control group.

According to studies investigating the importance of early numeracy skills training in mainstream kindergarten children (Passolunghi & Costa, 2014), we expected to find an improvement in children's early math skills after a domain specific training supplemental to the standard math curriculum. Based on the literature related to children from low-income families, we expected to find the training to be especially beneficial in low-ability children (e.g. Ramani, & Siegler, 2008).

Regarding the efficacy of different kind of interventions, we decided to compare structured cooperative learning training with individual training. As discussed above, there is very little research on the effectiveness of cooperative learning for children younger than six years of age; thus, it is quite difficult to make an exact prediction regarding its effectiveness on children as young as those from our sample. According to data coming from primary and secondary schools (Johnson et al., 2008), we expected a better outcome from cooperative learning training as compared to individual training.

2. METHOD

2.1 Participants

Forty-three typically developing 4 and 5 year old Italian children (19 males and 24 females) were recruited from a public kindergarten school in the town of Cagliari (Italy). Children with significant developmental delays (as identified by local educational and health services) were excluded. Both the school and the children's parents agreed to let the students take part in the research study, signing informed consent forms. The participants involved in the study came from two different classes (sections A and B), in which the same two teachers evenly rotated. The participants' average age was 56.55 months (SD = 6.29), with a range of 47-66 months. The socioeconomic status of the sample was measured by the Family Affluence Scale (FAS) (Boyce et al., 2006) and was classified as middle-class (mean = 6.5, SD = 1.1, scale range 0-9). Children were assigned to one of the following conditions: cooperative learning (CL) training group (15 children, 6 males); individual learning (IL) training group (14 children, 7 males); and control group (14 children, 6 males). The three groups were balanced for the following variables: initial early math ability measured through a standardized early math test, the BIN 4-6 (Molin et al., 2007); gender; age; IQ score; and school class.

2.2 Procedure

The study was divided into four phases:

1. Familiarization with students and teachers: three researchers (the first author and two trained psychologists) were in the classroom during normal class activities for two weeks, interacting and playing with the children.
2. Pre-training assessment. The Italian standardization of Raven's Coloured Progressive Matrices in the Italian standardization (CPM, Belacchi et al., 2008) was used to assess children's IQ so as not to include in the study children with low levels of intelligence. The BIN 4-6 (Molin et al., 2007), an early math abilities standardized test, was used to develop a baseline of early numeracy skills.
3. The training phase. While children assigned to cooperative and individual learning were involved in the supplemental early math training with two researchers (in two different classrooms), children assigned to the control groups participated for the same amount of time in drawing activities led by the third researcher (in a third classroom). The three researchers rotated evenly between the three activities. The two experimental groups were exposed to the same learning materials (see below for details). Each math activity comprised two steps: a manipulation or movement game followed by a paper-and-pencil consolidation task. The aim of each meeting was the enhancement of different aspects of early numerical competence (Lucangeli et al., 2003). The only difference between the two groups was the way the lesson was implemented: cooperative versus individual. The training was divided into 12 weekly meetings. The individual training sessions lasted about 30-40 minutes. The CL activities, due to the longer instruction time, lasted for about an hour.
4. Post-training assessment. The children's early numerical competence was retested with the BIN 4-6 (Molin et al., 2007) to assess the effects of the training.

2.3 Training Materials

For both training activities (CL and IL), we used several structured learning materials, such as short stories, games, and practical activities about numbers, specifically developed for early math training for children from three to six years of age (Lucangeli et al., 2003) and for consolidation interventions (Judica et al., 2010). Activities were conducted that focused on the following areas: the lexical area (distinction between numerical symbols and letters, telling stories with numerical elements, association symbol/name-number, writing Arabic numerals from number 1 to number 5); the semantic area (connect the number-words to their correspondent numerical quantities; comparing Arabic numerals e.g., "Tell me which is more, 2 or 4?"); the counting area (numbers sequence, count forward, count backwards), and operations in the pre-syntactic area (comparing and ordering quantities of up to five elements).

2.4 Cooperative Learning Activities

The learning together approach (Johnson et al., 2008) was followed to complete the CL training. Students were asked to work cooperatively in pairs. Different pairs were formed for each different session, so students had the chance to work with different partners, and heterogeneous pairs in terms of skill levels were structured (Johnson et al., 2008). Children were instructed to perform the following steps to cooperate effectively: (1) listen to the different questions and formulate the answer individually; (2) share the answer by whispering to the other group member; (3) try to reach an agreement with the other group member; and (4) be ready to answer if asked.

Students whose answer was required had to share it with the class. A practical demonstration of this procedure was performed by the instructor to provide the children with a concrete behavioral model. Positive goal interdependence and positive identity interdependence were established among group members.

At the end of each activity, the scores of each pair were shared and commented by the teachers with all pairs (final evaluation) and the students were encouraged to celebrate other students for the successes obtained (Johnson et al., 2008).

2.5 Individual Learning Activities

Children in IL conditions were asked to sit on small chairs that formed a circle, while the researcher explained the instructions for the math activities. Each child then had to carry out the tasks independently without help from his/her classmates. Later, the children sat around a table, and each child received a card for a paper-and-pencil consolidation task that had to be completed independently. During all the activities, the researcher was present to offer help, support, and motivation to each child while he/she worked.

2.6 Drawing Activities

Control group children were asked to freely play with building blocks and other toys and then to make a drawing of their activity under the supervision of the third researcher.

3. RESULTS

To compare the three groups (cooperative learning training, individual learning training, and control groups), three Kruskal-Wallis tests were used to determine possible pre-training, IQ, and age effects between the three groups ($p > .05$). Three Wilcoxon tests were used to determine gender effect ($p > .05$). Non-parametric statistics were used due to the small sample size and the difficulty of checking the assumption of normality of data.

The first question of this study was related to whether additional training in early numeracy skills is effective in enhancing early numerical competence in kindergarten children from middle-income families. A Wilcoxon test for paired sample was used to compare the CL group performance in early numeracy competence (dependent variable: BIN 4-6 z-score) in the pre- and post-training evaluation. The test results showed a significant difference ($V = 0$, $p = .002$, $|r| = .88$). A second Wilcoxon test for paired sample was used to compare pre- and post-training early numeracy competence (BIN 4-6 z-score) in the IL group; the results showed a significant difference ($V = 0$, $p = .003$, $|r| = .88$). The third Wilcoxon test for paired sample was used to compare pre-and post-training early numeracy competence performance (BIN 4-6 z-score) of the control group. The results showed a significant difference between pre-test and post-test also in the control group ($V = 0$, $p = .006$, $|r| = .83$). Descriptive statistics (median, IQR, CI, V, p-value, and effect size-r) of BIN z-score are reported in Table 1.

The Wilcoxon test results showed that early math abilities grew significantly in all the groups: CL training, IL training, and control group.

Table 1. Pre-test and post-test z-scores on test BIN 4-6 in the three groups, V, p values with Bonferroni correction and effect size |r|

	pre-test			post-test					
Group	Median	IQR	95% CI	Median	IQR	95% CI	V	p	|r|
Cooperative Learning Training (n=15)	-0.48	1.28	[-1.63, 0.57]	0.50	0.44	[-0.29, 1.44]	0	.002**	0.88
Individual Training (n=14)	-0.10	0.79	[-0.84, 0.82]	0.65	0.62	[0.1, 1.2]	0	.003**	0.88
Control Group (n=14)	-0.44	0.49	[-0.96, 0.41]	0.28	0.69	[-0.29, 1.08]	3	.006**	0.83

Note. N = 43; *p < .05; **p< .01; CI = confidence interval; r = effect size

To determine if one group had improved more than the others, we created a BIN test improvement score (BIN-IS) by calculating the differences between total BIN z-scores at pre-test and total BIN z-scores at post-test, and using these as dependent variables in a Kruskal-Wallis test. The results did not reveal significant differences between the three experimental groups (χ^2 (2) = 1.79, $p = .41$). By observing median and IQR of BIN-IS in the three groups, it is evident that children involved in the CL training (median = 0.93; IQR = 0.40; 95% CI [0.18, 1.96]) seemed to achieve higher than children in the individual training group (median = 0.63; IQR = 0.53; 95% CI [0.17, 1.4]) and the control group (median = 0.71; IQR = 0.57; 95% CI [-0.06, 1.6]), although the difference was not statistically significant.

Our findings showed that all children, control group included, significantly improved their performance in early math competence from the first to the second assessment (12 weeks' time lag) without a significant difference between the three situations. The improvement demonstrated in the three groups is not dependent on age because, in statistical analysis, we used the z-scores of the standardized early math ability BIN 4-6 test to control age effects.

One of our aims was to verify if the efficacy of an early math domain specific intervention was more strongly apparent on low-ability children. To test the hypothesis that early math low-ability children may benefit from the training more than high and medium ability ones, we carried on a further analysis on a sub-group of participants. We extracted from the general sample the children who had scored at least a half standard deviation below the average normative score in the pre-test BIN 4-6. The obtained sample of 25 participants (11 males and 14 females) was divided into two groups: a training group of 14 participants (7 males and 7 females, selected from both the cooperative and individual training groups) and a control group of 11 participants (4 males and 7 female) selected from the control group. The average age participant's age was 54.4 months (SD = 6.6 months). The choice to use as a cut-off half a standard deviation below the mean was motivated by the necessity to select a sample of children with low early math ability but still with typical development: considering children with a score below one standard deviation (i.e., those included in the "request for attention" zone according to the BIN 4-6 manual), would have potentially led to an atypical development sample.

To analyze the data from the sample of 25 low-ability children, Wilcoxon tests were used. The use of non-parametric statistics was due to the small sample size and to the difficulty to check for the assumption of normality of data. Different Kruskal-Wallis and Wilcoxon tests were performed to ensure that the two groups were balanced for BIN z-scores, IQ, age and gender. No significant differences were found ($p > .05$).

A first Wilcoxon test for paired sample was used to compare the performance in early numeracy competence (BIN 4-6 z-score) in pre- and post-test in the training group and results showed significant differences ($V = 0$, $p = .002$, $|r| = .85$). A second Wilcoxon test for paired sample was used to compare the performance in early numeracy competence (BIN 4-6 z-score) in the pre- and post-test in the control group, and results showed a significant difference ($V = 1$, $p = .005$, $|r| = .76$). Descriptive statistics (median, IQR, CI, V, p-value, and effect size-r) of the BIN z-score are reported in Table 2.

The results showed that both groups enhanced their early math ability from pre-test to post-test time. To test if the training group improved more compared with the control one, the same BIN-IS score used in the previous analysis was used as dependent variable, and a Wilcoxon test was carried out to compare the two groups. The results showed a significant difference between the two groups ($W = 114$, $p = .04$; $|r| = .40$). By observing the median and IQR of BIN-IS in the two groups, it is evident that children in the training condition (median = 0.96; IQR = 0.53; 95% CI [0.65, 1.98]) achieved higher improvement when compared with the control group (median = 0.69; IQR = 0.47; 95% CI [-0.07, 1.66]).

Two Wilcoxon Tests were also performed to test for a gender difference in children's BIN-IS. Results did not show significant differences between males and females in the two experimental groups ($p > .05$).

Table 2. Low-ability children pre-test and post-test Z scores on test BIN 4-6, V, p values with Bonferroni correction and effect size (r)

	pre-test			post-test					
Group	Median	IQR	95% CI	Median	IQR	95% CI	V	P	|r|
Training group (n=14)	-0.83	0.35	[-1.65, -0.39]	0.38	0.40	[-0.30, 0.63]	0	.002**	0.85
Control group (n=11)	-0.79	0.52	[-1.23, -0.43]	0.09	0.84	[-1.21, 0.91]	1	.005**	0.76

Note. N = 25; *p < .05; **p< .01; CI = confidence interval; r = effect size

4. GENERAL DISCUSSION AND CONCLUSION

This study involved 43 middle-income, typically developing children (aged 4-5) attending kindergarten in a public school in Italy. The main aim of our study was related to whether a supplement to the standard curriculum intervention in early numeracy skills would improve early math performance by confronting children exposed to two different interventions (cooperative learning and individual learning) and a control group. We wondered also whether early math training could be useful for children starting with a low level of numerical and quantity concepts knowledge.

First, the numerical skills baseline of participants was measured. Afterwards, training in early numerical competence was implemented in a cooperative learning training group and in an individual training one, while a balanced control group was involved in drawing activities. Finally, the children's numerical skills were measured again to evaluate the effectiveness of the training.

Regarding the first aim of this study, our findings showed that all children, control group included, significantly improved their performance in early math competence from the first to the second assessment. Thus, it appears that an additional intervention was not any more effective than the standard school activity: our data showed that neither CL nor individual training was effective in terms of significantly improving children's math abilities beyond the level reached through standard teaching. The results of our study are not in line with the previous literature on the effectiveness of early math training programs (e.g., Clements, 2007), but, as already noted, most of the literature on typically developing kindergarteners has concentrated on low-income children a category generally judged to be more at risk for school math underachievement, (e.g., Ramani & Siegler, 2008). A possible explanation for our findings is that the standard school activities carried out by the teachers are enough by themselves to bring children toward a high level of numeracy competence. Moreover, it is to be noted that our children came from a middle-class environment and likely had help from their families—in addition to standard schooling—in constructing sound initial math knowledge. When we discussed the matter with the teachers involved in the study, we learned that most of the children had received a relevant numeracy input from their parents. Many had been taught the Arabic digits from 1 to 9 and other numeracy skills. This factor may be important in young children's numerical development (Gunderson & Levine, 2011). Also, it may be that, during the standard kindergarten course, a good number of children can reach a significant level of math knowledge appropriate for their age group, even in the absence of supplemental training. The literature has shown that those children who have weaknesses in a skill benefit from empowerment training (Räsänen et al., 2009; Ramani & Siegler, 2011) and taking advantage of the "zone of proximal development" (Vygotsky, 1962). If children show a high level of performance in a skill we can hardly further strengthen that skill. In our study, children were assigned to one of the three experimental groups, depending on their grade of initial ability, so that the same numbers of high, low, and medium ability children were assigned to each group. A possible explanation for our finding may lie in the presence, in our sample, of children with high scores in early math abilities: some kindergarteners' early math high abilities may have hidden the effects of the training in enhancing early numerical competence.

To explore the possibility that training effects could have been hidden by the presence of children with high initial early math knowledge, and to test the hypothesis that the efficacy of an additional intervention is more accentuated in children with low early math abilities, we ran a further analysis in a subsample of low math ability children, in which we compared children who had undergone (training group) or not undergone (control group) math training. The results confirmed our hypothesis by showing that all low-ability children improved their performance, but, as expected, the training group significantly outperformed the control one. Our findings showed that, in low ability children, the supplemental intervention caused a significant early math ability improvement compared with the normal school curriculum. This result confirms, and extends to low ability middle-income children, the previous findings on low-income children related to the possibility of improving early numeracy skills in kindergarten children using numerical games and activities (e.g., Ramani & Siegler, 2008).

For low ability children, the standard school curriculum may not be sufficient as it is for average and high-achieving children, and it may be advisable, and even necessary in many cases, to develop an added intervention to support their early competence in mathematics.

One of our aims was to explore which kind of math training is most efficient for kindergarten children: the cooperative learning approach or the individual approach. Thus, this study contributes to the discussion about the efficacy of cooperative learning in children younger than six years of age. Our findings showed that the CL training pushed the children to a better performance than the individual training, but the difference between the two intervention approaches was not significant. This result runs counter to the notion that CL is more effective than other teaching approaches as the literature involving older children suggests (e.g., Johnson et al., 2008). As already stated, there is very little research investigating the role of collaboration in kindergarteners and, in the scarce literature, studies are often described without clear details about protocols utilized (e.g. Fuchs et al., 2001; Wiegel, 1998). A possible explanation for the lack of efficacy of CL in young children may relates to the nature of CL itself. When involved in a CL situation, students are requested to accomplish both teamwork and task work (Johnson et al., 2008). Teamwork involves complex social skills, such as communication, decision making, and conflict resolution skills. Task work involves the cognitive activities students had to accomplish. All these tasks may have been excessively demanding for such young children. For the effectiveness of CL versus individual training in children under six years of age, therefore, our data do not allow to draw a definite conclusion.

A limit of this study is the limited sample size. It may be interesting to replicate the study with a larger sample that includes both medium/high and low-ability children and to verify if a structured CL intervention can be more effective than individual training.

In conclusion, even taking into account the already mentioned limitation of the small sample size, our findings suggest that, at least when in the kindergarten curriculum early math teaching is comprised, standard teaching is probably enough to bring most kindergarteners to their highest "zone of proximal development" limit. However, even in a group of children from middle-income backgrounds, it is possible to find learners at a low starting level that can benefit from supplemental math training.

In future, it would be interesting to implement pre-math trainings by means of digital technologies. Until now there are few studies investigating the effectiveness of intervention programs on kindergarteners based on digital tools, and the few studies available highlighted the inconsistency of the results due mainly to the child's difficulty to work without the constant monitoring of an adult (Stephen; Plowman, 2008). Nevertheless, the introduction of touch technology may open new possibilities in training very young children. In light of this novelty, the purpose of our next work is aimed to create new intervention protocols Information Communication Technology (ICT) based, targeting kindergarteners.

ACKNOWLEDGEMENT

This study was supported by Cagliari University (Italy). The authors thank the principal of the school in which the data were collected. Special thanks go to the children, families, and kindergarten teachers who participated in the study.

REFERENCES

Annali della Pubblica Istruzione, 2012. *Indicazioni nazionali per il curricolo della scuola dell'infanzia e del primo ciclo d'istruzione.* Le Monnier. Retrieved from http://www.annaliistruzione.it/

Arnold, D.H. et al., 2002. Accelerating math development in Head Start classrooms. *Journal of Educational Psychology*, 94(4), pp. 762–770.

Artut, P.D., 2009. Experimental evaluation of the effects of cooperative learning on kindergarten children's mathematics ability. *International Journal of Educational Research*, 48, pp. 370–380.

Belacchi, C. et al., 2008. *CPM coloured progressive matrices: standardizzazione italiana: manuale*. Giunti OS.

Boyce, W. et al., 2006. The family affluence scale as a measure of national wealth: validation of an adolescent self-report measure. *Social Indicators Research*, 78(3), pp. 473-487.

Claessens, A. et al., 2009. Kindergarten skills and fifth-grade achievement: Evidence from the ECLS-K. *Economics of Education Review*, 28(4), pp. 415-427.

Clements, D. H. and Sarama, J., 2007. Effects of a preschool mathematics curriculum: Summative research on the Building Blocks project. *Journal for Research in Mathematics Education*, pp 136-163.

Fuchs, L. et al., 2001. Enhancing kindergarteners' mathematical development: Effects of peer-assisted learning strategies. *The Elementary School Journal*, 101(5), pp. 495-510.

Geary, D. C. et al., 2013. Adolescents' functional numeracy is predicted by their school entry number system knowledge. *PloS one*, 8(1), e54651.

Gunderson, E. A. and Levine, S. C., 2011. Some types of parent number talk count more than others: Relations between parents' input and children's cardinal- number knowledge. *Developmental Science*, 14(5), pp. 1021-1032.

Johnson, D. W. and Johnson, R. T., 1999. *Learning together and alone. Cooperative, competitive and individualistic learning.* Englewood Cliffs, NJ: Prentice Hall.

Johnson, D. W. et al., 2008. *Cooperation in the classroom.* Edina, MN: Interaction Book Company.

Judica, A.et al, 2010. *Un mare di numeri. Attività di conoscenza dei numeri e del calcolo.* Erickson, Trento.

Lucangeli, D. et al., 2003. *L'intelligenza numerica. Abilità cognitiva e metacognitive nella costruzione della conoscenza numerica dai 3 ai 6 anni.* Erickson, Trento.

Molin, A. et al., 2007. *BIN 4-6, Batteria per la valutazione della Intelligenza Numerica in bambini dai 4 ai 6 anni.* Erickson, Trento.

Passolunghi, M. C. and Costa, H. M., 2014. Working memory and early numeracy training in preschool children. *Child Neuropsychology*, 22(1), pp. 81-98.

Ramani, G. B. and Siegler, R. S., 2008. Promoting broad and stable improvements in low-income children's numerical knowledge trough playing number board games. *Child Development*, 79, pp. 375-394.

Ramani, G. B. and Siegler, R. S., 2011. Reducing the gap in numerical knowledge between low-and middle-income preschoolers. *Journal of applied developmental Psychology*, 32(3), pp. 146-159.

Ramani, G. B. and Brownell, C. A., 2014. Preschoolers' cooperative problem solving: Integrating play and problem solving. *Journal of Early Childhood Research*, 12(1), pp. 92-108.

Räsänen, P. et al., 2009. Computer-assisted intervention for children with low numeracy skills. *Cognitive Development.* doi:10.1016/j.cogdev.2009.09.003

Stephen, C., and Plowman, L. (2008). Enhancing learning with information and communication technologies in pre- school. *Early Child Development and Care*, 178(6), pp. 637-654.

Vermette, P.et al., 2005. Cooperative and collaborative learning...with 4-8 year olds: How does research support teachers' practice. *Journal of Instructional Psychology*, 31(2), pp. 130-134.

Vygotsky, L. S., 1962. *Thought and language* (E. Hanfmann & G. Vakar, Eds. and Trans.). Cambridge, MA: MIT Press. (Original work published 1934)

Wiegel, H.G., 1998. Kindergarten students' organization of counting in joint counting task and the emergence of cooperation. *Journal for Research in Mathematics Education*, 29(2), pp. 202-224.

360 DEGREE VIDEOS WITHIN A CLIMBING MOOC

Michael Gänsluckner[1], Martin Ebner[1] and Isidor Kamrat[2]

[1]*Educational Technology, Graz University of Technology, Münzgrabenstraße 35, 8010 Graz, Austria*

[2]*Computer and Information Services, Graz University of Technology, Steyrergasse 16, 8010 Graz, Austria*

ABSTRACT

In this research study a course, combining both computer-supported and face-to-face teaching using the concept of blended learning, has been designed. It is a beginners climbing course called "Klettern mit 360° Videos" (climbing with 360° videos) and the online part has been implemented as a Massive Open Online Course (MOOC). This research study presents the background of the course, the course concept, the course itself and the results of the evaluation. To measure the difference between the pure online participants and the blended learning participants the MOOC has been evaluated independently from the blended learning course. It should be mentioned that all participants (whether pure online or both) evaluated the course in a positive manner. The use of technology enhanced learning realized by the concept of blended learning proved to be a well-suited method for this course setting. Furthermore, many advantages of computer based learning, blended learning and 360°-videos have been reported by the participants.

KEYWORDS

Technology Enhanced Learning, MOOC, 360 degree, Blended Learning, Climbing

1. INTRODUCTION

The opportunities of digital media in sports have already been discovered very early (Hebbel-Seeger, Kretschamen & Vohle 2013). For example, in many different sports, pictures and videos are used to visualize or track movements. In terms of computer based learning (technology enhanced learning, TEL), with a special focus to learning videos, different projects already exist. Nevertheless, surprisingly very few studies for computer based or blended learning courses in sports have been published.

In 2011 a research study took place in Germany to survey the deployment of digital media in physical education (Opitz & Fischer 2011). Sports students were asked about technical equipment in schools and their estimations for digital media usage in physical education. It turned out that most of the students reported positive experiences with digital media in physical education, but that the frequency of use was very low. About 46% stated, that they had never considered using digital media in physical education. Additionally, the majority of the interviewed students reported that the technical equipment in schools is either very bad or non-existent.

Some universities in German speaking Europe and further education institutions, like school, are currently using learning management systems when it comes to teaching sports. For example, since 2006 the platform "sports-edu" is used to support physical education in seven German institutions (Sensing & Frenger 2010). With Sports-edu, videos and additional content for different sports are provided and the platform is used to manage user profiles. The online courses are usually used in combination with practical courses following the concept of blended learning.

In the research field of Technology Enhanced Learning, Massive Open Online Courses are increasing dramatically. Since the first course created by George Siemens and Stephen Downes in 2008 (McAuley et al, 2010), followed by the famous MOOC of Sebastian Thrun, different MOOC platforms are searching for lecturers providing so called xMOOCs (Carson & Schmidt, 2012). An xMOOC can be characterized by a number of videos, additional learning objects and self-assessment presented in a structured way (mostly on a weekly basis) (Ebner et al, 2016).

After exploring existing projects in sports and bearing in mind the current trends in the field of TEL the basic idea for the study was to create a field study combining a MOOC and face-to-face-teaching. Furthermore, the use of 360 degree videos was being explored. In order to include the above-mentioned criteria, a climbing course for beginners supported by 360° videos was designed. The course has been split in two different parts. Over the course of five weeks, the stand-alone MOOC provides the basic knowledge about climbing such as rules and security with regards to climbing. Twelve different videos are used to present the main theoretical concepts of the course. Some of the videos are recorded using 360° video-technology to provide the viewers with new viewing-angles and interactive video learning. Afterwards the face-to-face part was designed and combined with the MOOC to a blended learning concept. In short, the MOOC provides theoretical background to the practical climbing lessons taught in a face-to-face manner.

We tried to answer the following research questions:

1. Is the concept of blended learning using a MOOC suitable for sports?
2. Is the use of 360 degree videos in sports appropriate for the target group?
3. What are the advantages and limitations of this learning scenario?

2. DESIGN OF THE RESEARCH STUDY

2.1 Course Design

Most traditional climbing courses take place in indoor climbing halls and cover theoretical and practical basics. During these courses a lot of time is used to teach and learn the theoretical basics that are required to ensure save climbing. Of course, in many courses the time for the practical part is limited and important practical basics are handled as briefly as possible. To use the time more efficient and to enhance the practical part, the course was designed to teach the basic knowledge beforehand by using an online course. Providing those contents online allows the participants to learn independently and more accurately. Therefore, the essentials are provided in videos and additional content is offered for a more detailed study.

The MOOC itself consists of five chapters, each building on the one before. Each chapter covers a different subject in one or more videos. Self-assessments are provided at the end of each chapter, to enable individual learning progress. The self-assessments are not mandatory, but allow the participants to check their acquired knowledge by doing some multiple-choice questions.

Following the idea of blended learning, the final face-to-face course extends the MOOC with a practical lesson for each chapter. Due to safety reasons, the blended learning course has been designed for only a small group of attendants. The practical lessons are a follow up to the weekly topics of the MOOC and rely on the theoretical part. This allows the participants to apply the learned techniques and procedures right away. To increase the improvement achieved through the course, in the first lesson a video of each participant's climbing techniques are recorded. At the end of the last lesson another video is recorded to compare and analyze the progress.

Due to the nature of a MOOC – its openness – other participants were also able to join the online course for free. We call the people who only participated in the MOOC and therefore only learned the theoretical part of the course pure-online-users. Figure 1 shows the two different learning scenarios. First the blended learning scenario represented by the changing online and face-to-face parts and second the MOOC scenario represented by just online parts.

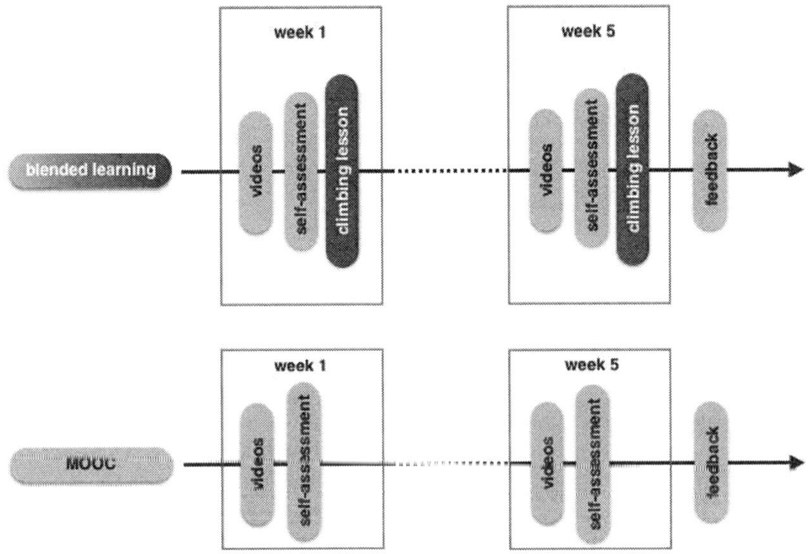

Figure 1. Course Design

2.2 Didactical Approach

The didactical approach of the course design is following three major issues:

1. The currently upcoming 360 degree video technology allows to capture engaging and immersive videos. By recording beyond the common field of view, many advantages of 360 degree videos can be used. On one hand, everything happening around a 360 degree camera is captured and on the other hand while viewing the video, the viewer is able to interactively controls his/her personal field of vision. By allowing the viewer to interact with the video, more attention is paid to the video and to the content, which enhances the learning experience. During planning and recording the videos, it was attempted to make as much use of the 360 degree camera as possible. This ensures that the viewer can continuously follow the events on the screen.
2. The self-assessment in each chapter is used to allow the learner to check their learning progress on their own. Additionally, the self-assessments aim to encourage the participants to learn the contents more precisely. These self-assessments are implemented as straightforward tests in form of multiple choice quizzes. To pass the self-assessment, participants have to engage with the material on a deeper level instead of merely watching the videos.
3. To encourage the participants of the blended learning course to learn the contents of the MOOC, participants were informed that the basics learned online were required to take part in the practical lessons. To affirm the necessary basic knowledge, the participants were asked short questions throughout the practical lessons.

2.3 MOOC Platform

The course was published on the MOOC platform imoox.at. iMoox is a redesigned learning management system operated by Graz University of Technology and the university of Graz (Ebner et al, 2015). The platform opened in 2013 and is frequently used for MOOCs about various topics as well as for university lectures (Khalil & Ebner, 2015) (Ebner et al, 2016a) (Höfler et al, 2017).

iMoox offers all capabilities that are required for the planed course. The system is well suited for managing user data and providing all course contents. Additionally, self-assessments are implemented in a very intuitive way. The platform provides a straightforward course system and also allows the participants of the MOOC to access all videos and content independent from time and place.

Figure 2 gives an overview of the final MOOC. The weekly course topics are found on the left-hand side. Above the main content, four blue buttons allow to navigate to the news, the course description, the available files and finally to the discussion forum. The main part consists of a short welcome message and an introductory 360° video. If a learner scrolls down he/she also gets additional web-based content and the weekly self-assessment.

Figure 2. Overview about the main elements of the MOOC

2.4 Course Development

All videos were recorded in an indoor climbing hall in Graz. In some videos, 360 degree video technology has been used to capture spherical videos. In order to use the full potential of the 360 degree videos, well-structured film scripts were produced beforehand. To allow viewers to have an efficient learning progress, a lot of testing of camera mountings was required.

Especially when watching 360 degree videos with virtual reality headsets, fast movements are very confusing. Even though climbing is a sport with a lot of movement, a chest mount for the 360 degree camera created steady videos. This mount also simulates a first person view.

In some videos the camera has been positioned in the middle of the room while events are happening all around the camera. In climbing one of the partners stays on the ground while the second one tries to climb to the top. In this situation, the viewer can change the point of view between the two climbing partners, depending on what is considered as important.

2.5 Research Design

Different research methods have been used in order to evaluate the MOOC and the blended learning course. When signing up for the MOOC a reason has to be given (short sign-in survey). This survey is used to analyze the intentions of the participants. In order to complete the MOOC, the participants have to give a final feedback via the iMooX system. The feedback includes multiple-choice questions about the MOOC and about the experience of the participants. Additionally, the questions cover experiences with 360 degree videos, computer based learning and blended learning. Furthermore, the course itself and the adequacy of the used concepts are evaluated. To explore the limits of 360 degree videos and blended learning in sports, the participants are asked to think about the possibilities to apply this method for other sports.

To evaluate the blended learning course scenario two different feedbacks are used. On the one hand, the participants have to take part in a survey and on the other hand interviews are carried out to get subjective impressions. The survey is quite similar to the evaluation of the MOOC but also includes questions about the practical lessons and blended learning. First they have to answer questions about their experiences, later on they are asked about their usage of the online contents and videos. The survey also covers the self-assessments and some comparisons between the blended learning climbing course and traditional climbing courses. The interview is used to analyze the recorded videos of the participants. Furthermore, every practical lesson is analyzed to determine advantages and disadvantages of the blended learning scenario.

3. FIELD STUDY

The field study took place in March 2017 with a five week MOOC and the corresponding blended learning course. To find volunteers for both course concepts, a short 360 degree promotion video has been published and promoted via social media. The MOOC took place with 103 participants and the blended learning course, for security reasons, only included eight participants. Table 1 shows details of the blended learning course participants and figure 2 shows their prior experience before attending the course.

Table 1. Participants of the blended learning scenario

Participants	Age	Sex	Experience
n = 8	mean: 24.3 min: 21 max: 33	male: 3 female: 5	none: 4 beginner: 3 intermediate: 1

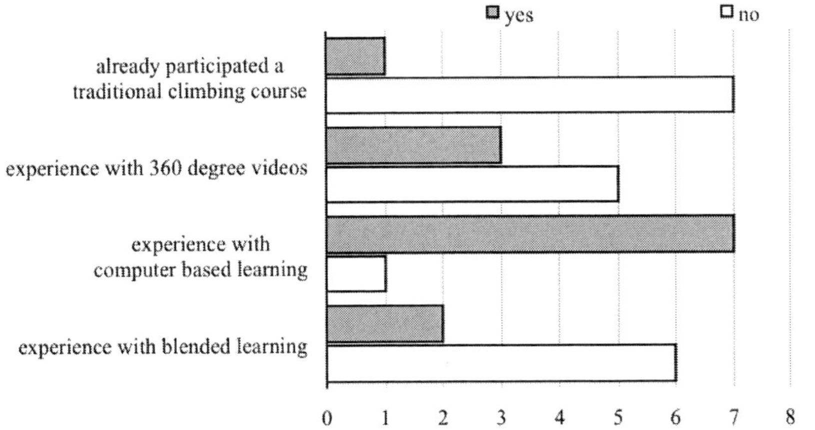

Figure 3. Experience of the blended learning course participants

4. RESULTS

4.1 MOOC

The results of the survey that took place before the start of the MOOC are presented in figure 4. It turned out that most of the participants wanted to know more about the course, but only 19% planned to pass the course from the beginning. This result already hints that only a few participants had the idea to take an active part within the course.

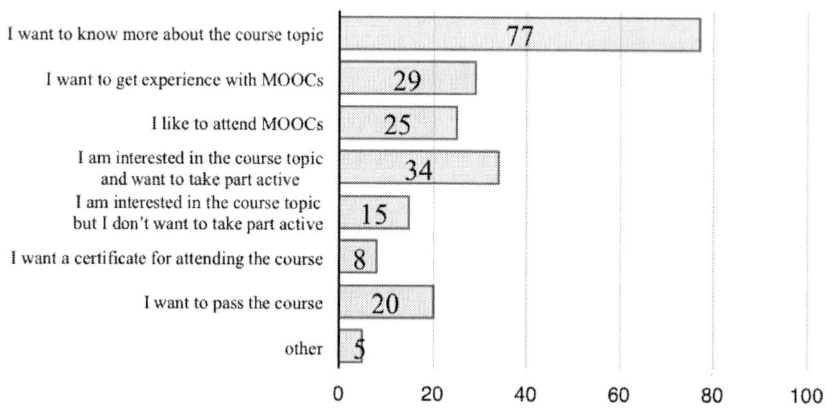

Figure 4. Experience of the blended learning course participants

This anticipation turned out to be true, since only 70 self-assessments were completed and only eight of the pure-online participants gave feedback at the end via the iMooX feedback system. Despite the small number of feedback, the results turned out to be very positive. The use of 360 degree videos has been evaluated by the majority as "much better" or "better" compared to traditional videos, while only two participants evaluated the videos equally.

One additional part of the survey was to evaluate the benefit of 360 degree videos in different subjects of the MOOC. The best-suited subject for usage of 360 degree videos turned out to be the "climbing techniques". Figure 5 shows the results of 360 degree video usage in the course. Almost all participants described the usage of 360 degree videos in the course as better, compared to traditional videos. Specially the videos about climbing techniques turned out to enable new viewing angles and learning scenarios that would not possible without 360 video-techniques. In terms of suitability of computer based learning for other sports, all participants said that 360 degree videos in combination with a blended learning scenario would be very beneficial.

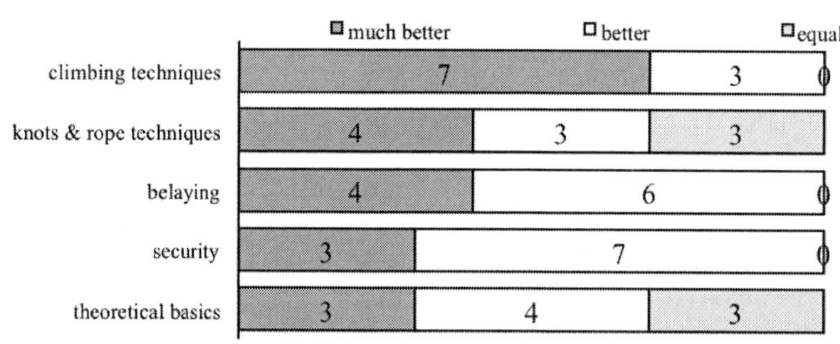

Figure 5. Results of the survey question: "Compare 360 degree videos to traditional videos"

4.2 Blended Learning Scenario

During the practical lessons, the participants, their motivation and their acquired knowledge from the MOOC have been observed. Throughout the whole course a lot of motivation and enthusiasm was observed. The participants were able to transform their prior knowledge to the practical lessons. Sometimes participants even urged to put their learned techniques into practice. During the lessons, questions regarding the videos and contents were asked. One participant described the benefits of the blended learning scenario:

"The videos and contents allowed me to acquire a basic knowledge for climbing and climbing techniques. In the practical lessons we used those techniques in fun exercises, which helped me to learn everything better and to improve my skills. "

The results of the feedback of these participants turned out be even better than the feedback of the MOOC. All of them described the online content as well prepared and well suited for blended learning. The results of the survey in figure 6, regarding the content usage show that the participants consumed the offered contents more than once.

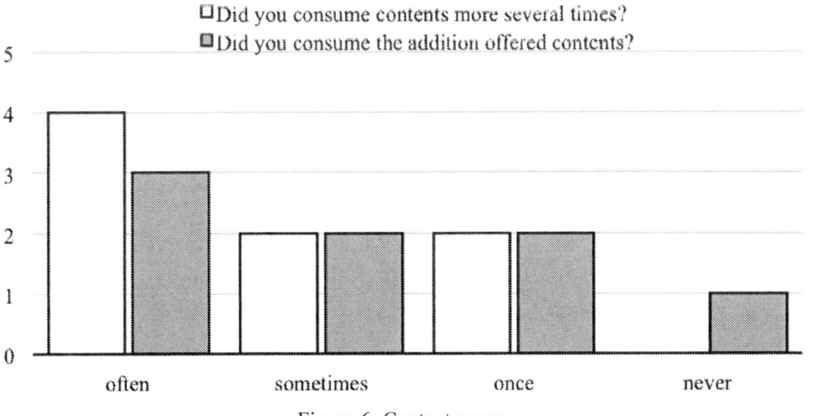

Figure 6. Content usage

The benefits of the self-assessments were also evaluated very positively . All participants rated the self-assessments as very beneficial to self-check their learning progress. Almost all participants, except one, reported that the self-assessments motivated them to learn the content of the MOOC more precisely. These statements have also been confirmed in the final interviews. All interviewed participants described the MOOC as very helpful in order to learn the basics.

One of the main aspects of the interview was the analysis of the recorded videos of the participants climbing techniques. All participants analyzed both of their videos to experience their progress through the climbing course. Later on problems and advantages encountered in the practical lessons were discussed. Besides some basic technical problems at the beginning of the course, no other problems occurred.

The last part of the feedback covered the blended learning scenario in this course and for other sports. All participants described the used concept for climbing as very reasonable. To verify that the blended learning course has been suited appropriately, all participants have been asked if they could have attended the practical lessons without learning the MOOC contents. Almost all participants agreed that it would not have been possible to follow the instructions during the practical lessons unprepared. This confirms that the blended learning scenario was used efficient. The closing question of the feedback asked about whether the blended learning climbing course motivated the participants to attend further blended learning courses. 75% replied that they are planning to attend further blended learning courses, while 25% perhaps want to attend further online courses.

5. CONCLUSION

The study clearly shows that Technology Enhanced Learning and especially blended learning are a well-suited concept for climbing. There are many benefits that can be achieved by outsourcing and reprocessing theoretical basics that are required. This on the one hand can save time in practical lessons and on the other hand allows the course participants to learn the contents individually and in their preferred learning speed. In a practical lesson this has also been mentioned by a participant. During the face-to-face lessons a traditional course took place right next to the group. In this traditional course the basic security contents were discussed very quickly. One of the blended learning course participants noted:

"I am glad that we could learn the theoretical contents regarding security and belaying more detailed at home. The course next to us covered the content in very short time, I definitely would not fell very save in that course"

This quote summarizes many of the most important aspects of a blended learning scenario and shows that the concept is very well suited for climbing. In many other sports blended learning could allow the participants to learn the basics individually and more accurate. Also 360 degree videos could bring many benefits to nearly every sport. The possibility of capturing everything that happens around an athlete or elsewhere in the room leads to new learning experiences by changing the view to a personal one.

Learning videos allow time and place independent learning and each participant can choose their own learning speed. This also supports self-responsibility by controlling the learning process. 360 degree videos bring even more benefits: Interacting with the video can raise the motivation of the viewer and draws the attention to the content.

Of course, there can also be downsides. The content has to be well prepared in order to be beneficial. But this study showed that blended learning and 360 degree videos can bring many advantages in climbing and presumable other sports as well.

REFERENCES

Carson, S., Schmidt, J. (2012) The Massive Open Online Professor Academic Matter. *Journal of higher education.* Retrieved from: http://www.academicmatters.ca/2012/05/the-massive-open-online-professor/

Ebner, M., Scerbakov, A., Kopp, M. (2015) All About MOOCs. *Digital Medien in Arbeits- und Lernumgebungen.* Jost, P, Künz, A (Ed.). S. 148-155. Pabst, Lengrich

Ebner, M., Kopp, M., Scerbakov, A., Neuböck, K. (2016) MOOCs in Engineering Education: First Practical Experiences from two MOOCs. In: *Handbook of Research on Applied E-Learning in Engineering and Architecture Education.* Fonseca, D., Redondo, E. (Eds.). pp. 224-236. doi:10.4018/978-1-4666-8803-2

Ebner, M., Schön, S., Khalil, M. (2016a) Maker-MOOC – How to Foster STEM Education with an Open Online Course on Creative Digital Development and Construction with Children. *Conference Proceeding 19th International Conference on Interactive Collaborative Learning (ICL2016)*, Belfast, pp. 1233-1244

Hebbel-Seeger A.; Kretschamen R.; Vohle F. (2013) Bildungstechnologien im Sport: Forschungsstand, Einsatzgebiete und Praxisbeispiele. In: Ebner, M.; Schön, S. (eds) *Lehrbuch für Lernen und Lehren mit Technologien.* Berlin: epubli, pp. 465–473.

Höfler, E., Zimmermann, C., Ebner, M. (2017) A case study on narrative structures in instructional MOOC designs, *Journal of Research in Innovative Teaching & Learning*, Vol. 10 Iss: 1, pp.48 - 62

Khalil, M., Ebner, M. (2015) A STEM MOOC for School Children - What Does Learning Analytics Tell us? In: *Proceedings of 2015 International Conference on Interactive Collaborative Learning* (ICL), Florence, Italy, pp. 1-7

McAuley, A, Stewart, B, Siemens, G. (2010) *Massive Open Online Courses Digital ways of knowing and learning, The MOOC model For Digital Practice.* Retrieved from: http://www.elearnspace.org/Articles/MOOC_Final.pdf

Opitz C., Fischer U. (2011) Medieneinsatz im Sportunterricht der Sekundarstufe II. *sportunterricht*, 60 (1). pp. 10-15.

Sensing C., Frenger, R. (2010) Die technologische Infrastruktur zur kooperativen Erstellung von Web-Based Trainings und deren Nutzung in innovativen Lernsettings. In: Wiemeyer J., Hansen J. (eds.), *Sport-Medien-Gesellschaft.* Sportverlag Strauß, pp. 163-168

CULTIVATING STUDENTS' READING LITERACY USING DIGITAL LEXILE-BASED READING IN A CHINESE PRIMARY SCHOOL

Patricia Norte, Joao Negreiros and Ana Correia
University of Saint Joseph, Rua de Londres, 16 NAPE Macao, China

ABSTRACT

This Macau study investigates the unwillingness of primary 5 Chinese native students to read in English on a Lexile® Framework based digital reading platform provided by their school, with visible negative consequences on their English reading literacy, and whether or not it is possible for teachers to help improve students' reading literacy by adopting specific instructional practices. The study, carried out in a school which uses Chinese (Cantonese) as medium of instruction, initially measured student's reading level and tried to identify possible reasons that deterred students from reading in a digital reading platform. The investigation was based on an action research model (to look, think, act) while a mixed method approach was deployed to collect data: numerical information from the platform which informed about students reading ability was treated with descriptive and inferential statistics and focus group interviews were conducted to allow a deeper understanding of students' attitudes towards reading. The findings revealed that students in general were not averse to reading, although they seemed to need someone to facilitate the process for them as well as to guide and encourage them to read. Extrinsic motivation strategies were found helpful and, by way of teacher's same intervention with all her students (group A), such as constant reminders to read, compulsory reading of a certain number of books per month, publicly praising students and granting them bonus points on their marks, meaningful improvement was achieved. These findings are discussed in relation to the significance of the teacher's intervention, in terms of providing constant support, facilitating the reading process and monitoring students' reading activity, by adopting varied instructional practices to appeal and motivate children to engage in reading.

KEYWORDS

Lexile®, reading literacy, children, motivation, digital reading platforms

1. INTRODUCTION

In Macau, reading in English for pleasure is not frequently seen, as most Chinese students do not read on their own initiative and they usually do not enjoy reading in a foreign language. Some of these reasons might have to do with: 1) not being their mother-tongue, hence struggling with new or difficult words which prove to be a challenge for them (Powell-Brown, 2006); 2) absence of the right motivation or boost to read; 3) lack of guidance to read – students are sometimes unaware of how to pick the right books; 4) lack of encouragement or the right stimuli/environment to engage in reading activities.

Helping Chinese students to increase their love for reading in English and instilling in them reading habits have not always been easy tasks, but are probably some of the most important responsibilities of a teacher, as gaining the habit of reading and understanding each text can help the child with comprehension, not only through their academic life, but also outside the classroom.

In terms of language acquisition, educators have recognized and accepted computer-assisted language learning in the field of English as a Second Language (ESL) and English as a Foreign Language (EFL) due to its potential and unique opportunities for developing L2 reading skills by allowing readers to access varied sources of extra information. These sources pave the way for a new concept of electronic literacy and, therefore, lead to a great deal of influence in the process of learning and teaching in the L2 (Al-Seghayer, 2016).

It is important, though, to state that according to Kahlid Al-Seghayer (2016), the ones responsible for adopting a computer-assisted reading platform are policymakers, school administrators and other stakeholders, yet educators and teachers are the ones implementing the adoption of technology and integrating computer reading programs by using instructional practices in the classroom and determining and controlling the use and implementation of these practices.

Despite the fact that Portuguese and Chinese are the two official languages in Macau, English maintains a "de facto additional working language" status in the territory, especially in the field of education. In fact, the influence of English in education can be seen mostly through secondary and higher education, with 13.4% of Macau students enrolled in schools that use English as a medium of instruction (Moody, 2008). This happens because the growing use of English has increased since the handover in 1999 with the needs of the strategic economic development, particularly in the gaming and tourism industry. English is used as a bridge in business opportunities as well as a way to publicly present itself as an 'international region' (Feng, 2011).

The concept of literacy is not only confined to reading and writing, and is evolving continuously due to technological, cultural and social changes in contemporary societies. Literacy involves listening to, reading, speaking, writing and creating oral, print, visual and digital texts, by using and changing language in a variety of contexts and with different purposes (AARE - Australian Association for Research in Education, 2017).

According to Stenner (1996), reading comprehension is one of the most tested concepts in formal education. He argues that it is an indicator of success in higher education and job performance. The ability to read well and comprehend texts has gained importance, especially as a survival skill in the "information era". Solid reading became necessary for continuing education, rapid changing technology and economical demands. Unfortunately, nearly 17% of the world's adult population is still illiterate, being two thirds of them women. The illiteracy numbers among youth are no less disappointing: 122 million youth are globally illiterate, and 67.4 million children who are out of school are likely to come across great challenges in the future, "as deficient or non-existent basic education is the root cause of illiteracy" (UNESCO, 2016).

With this in mind, this research design follows what Stenhouse (1983a) and Sturman (1999) defined as action research (AR). This concept refers to a classroom action research or school case studies undertaken by teachers who use their participant status as a basis on which they build skills of observation and analysis (Stenhouse, 1983b). As a result, the following three research questions were developed: 1) What is the role of teachers in implementing digital reading platforms at schools? 2) What are the effects of teachers' guidance and instructional practices on students' reading progress when using a digital reading platform? 3) What are the factors that impact students' motivation for reading?

The study here reported was conducted to analyze Chinese students' reading ability, their attitudes towards English reading and see whether teachers can help improve their reading literacy through a digital reading platform. Even though it would be important to follow up on these students' progress after the end of the school year, this could not be investigated as the researcher was not able to monitor students' reading activity once the school year was over. Certainly, this fact can be considered as one of the limitations of the study. Another drawback is the fact that the researcher is not Chinese-fluent. Having to communicate with Chinese native speakers in English during the focus group interviews only allowed for somehow limited dialogues between the children and moderator that could have been more descriptive if everyone was proficient in the same language.

The digital reading platform adopted by the school during the study was called Scholastic Literacy Pro Library, a browser-based eBook reader that allows students to select eBooks from its online library and read on it (Scholastic Inc., 2016). The platform had over 800 eBooks and students could access it with an individual username and password which let them see their own profile, their Lexile measure, books read and other reading information. The teacher could also monitor students' progress and carefully select books for the students. However, just like any regular school library, it won't be of any advantage if not visited frequently for reading purposes.

The key concept "Lexile" used within the digital reading platform refers to the Lexile® Framework for Reading, developed by MetaMetrics Inc. It is a scientific approach that measures reading ability and the complexity of texts by using a scale for measuring both readers' skill level and the text difficulty of materials they encounter (MetaMetrics, 2017). This scale is translated into numbers and it is known as Lexile. A student receives a Lexile reader score after taking a reading test. Currently, millions of books and other texts have a Lexile measure that allows anyone to know about their complexity level and demand. When measures are used together, it helps matching the reader with a text that has an appropriate level of difficulty.

This introduction includes the study purpose, significance, some literature review, research questions and limitations. Section two addresses the methodology for data collection and analysis. The following section presents the results, while section four delivers a deeper discussion of the findings, that are stressed in terms of pedagogical and theoretical significance. Section five presents the answers to the research questions and suggestions for further studies.

2. METHODOLOGY

For this study, an action research was used. Stringer's (2007) interacting spiral model (Figure1) presents a collaborative approach to inquiry which allows teachers to take systematic action to resolve specific problems, after observing that students were not self-motivated to read. In fact, this model provides a basic action research routine that offers a simple powerful framework, Look-Think-Act, which enables people to initiate their inquiries in a straightforward manner and build detail into procedures as the complexity of issues increase.

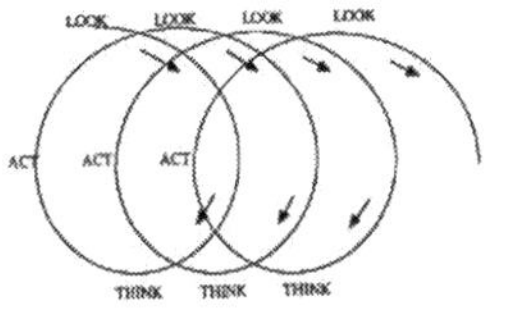

Figure 1. Stringer's action research interacting spiral

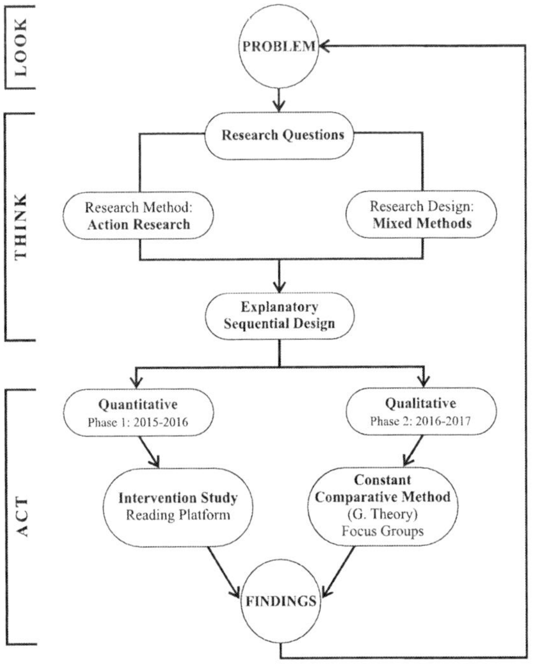

Figure 2. Adopted research framework.

A mixed methods procedure was adopted to enrich the present action research, as shown in Figure 2, allowing a combination of qualitative and quantitative data collection. According to Creswell (2012), the mixed methods use of both quantitative and qualitative methods provides a better understanding of the research problem. The explanatory sequential design (Creswell & Clark, 2011) was found to be the most appropriate method (quantitative and qualitative data are sequentially collected in two phases, with one form of data collection following/informing the other). According to them, this is perhaps the most popular form of mixing methods in educational research and consists of first collecting quantitative data to get a general picture of the research problem and then qualitative data to elaborate and explain the general picture.

In the first stage, students' numerical data was retrieved from the digital platform to track their Lexile growth, so a quantitative approach was found more suitable as the Lexile® Framework primarily uses a numerical system to measure progress. In addition, the data extracted from the platform allowed generating numerical statistics for several types of analysis.

In the second part, a qualitative approach was used; students' opinions towards reading in general and the platform were heard to assist in understanding how the platform was being used and the reasons behind the usage given by learners. By hearing students' descriptions and narrated words, data previously collected could be enriched and; therefore, attain higher credibility with the research results, by combining both methods.

3. DATA ANALYSIS

3.1 Quantitative Results

This study was conducted with 106 students who were subject to the same intervention (group A) in the school year of 2015-2016. Also from primary 5 level, 115 students were not subject to the intervention (group B). For students to be included in this study, they had to be enrolled in the school where the study was conducted in the school years of 2014-2015 for primary 4, 2015-2016 for primary 5 and 2016-2017 for primary 6.

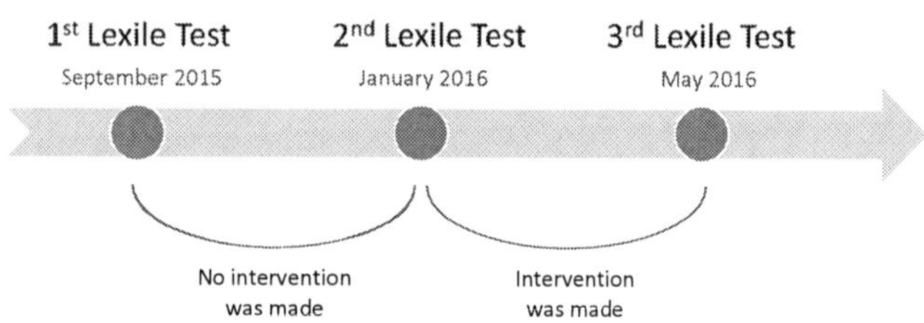

Figure 3. Intervention timeframe

Between their 1st and 2nd Lexile tests, no measures were taken. The purpose of this first cycle was to observe students' attitudes and their willingness or unwillingness to read in the digital platform. At this time, it was still possible to observe students' online reading activity which was taking place randomly. Having completed their 2nd Lexile test, students from group A were exposed to the following educational strategies: 1) Book selection: books were selected and assigned by the teacher to guarantee that the reading process would not be hindered by the uncertainty of what to read or the amount of books to choose from; 2) Monthly goals: students had to read at least five Lexile-appropriate books every month: three connected to their favourite reading topics, one connected to the current General English study unit and the remaining one was a general topic, students would have to complete an online comprehension quiz and pass to ensure that they were actually reading and comprehending the texts; 3) Bonus points: 2 to 5 p.p. bonus points on performance scores were granted to students who were reading on a regular basis. This acted as an extrinsic motivation reward for students; 4) Public praising: students who had the highest monthly reading activity were publicly praised, and reading achievements would be displayed on a notice board.

Table 1. Descriptive statistics for group A

School Year	N	Range	Minimum	Maximum	Mean	Std. Deviation
2014-2015	106	638	-240	398	105.98	128.854
2015-2016	106	549	-96	453	159.64	115.870

The relevant findings about the descriptive statistics for the Lexile growth of group A (see table 1) are: 1) By the end of the intervention, minimum negative growth (-96L) was less severe than in the previous school year (-240L); 2) By the end of the intervention, maximum positive growth (453L) was better than in the previous school year (395L); 3) By the end of the intervention, the mean Lexile growth (159.64L) was considerably higher than in the year before the intervention (105.98L).

Regarding group B, as seen in table 2, it is not possible to infer the same pattern as for group A, since findings do not reveal different outcomes in terms of minimum nor maximum growth. A result worth mentioning is that the mean Lexile growth in the school year 2015-2016 (159.42L) was not significantly high when compared to the previous year (133.77).

Table 2. Descriptive statistics for group B

School Year	N	Range	Minimum	Maximum	Mean	Std. Deviation
2014-2015	115	810	-187	623	133.77	147.464
2015-2016	115	703	-174	529	159.42	138.201

For both groups, we can statistically assert that the hypothesis of Normality distribution is accepted (Sig>0.05) for a level of confidence of 95%. Since these are respectively two random samples of 106 and 115 from the 3,000 students of this Chinese school, this means both datasets comply with the Gaussian requirements in order to apply all parametric statistics methods. For quantitative analysis purpose, a null hypothesis (H0) and an alternative hypothesis (H1) are considered, namely:

- H0: Students do not exhibit a higher rate of Lexile growth when more exposed to teachers' guidance and instructional practices in the usage of a digital reading platform.
- H1: Students exhibit a higher rate of Lexile growth when more exposed to teachers' guidance and instructional practices in the usage of a digital reading platform.

Regarding group A, it is possible to confirm in table 3 that, with a 95% level of confidence, the mean of the Lexile growth results between the academic year 2014-2015, with no intervention, and 2015-2016, with intervention, is significantly lower [Sig (2-tailed = .004] than the standardized acceptance value of Sig. (2-tailed) > 0.05, hence H0 is rejected. This test shows that the Lexile growth does not follow the same pattern between years. One can assume that the intervention had an impact in the students' Lexile growth.

Table 3. Paired samples test for group A

			95% Confidence Interval			
Paired Samples	Mean	Std. Deviatio	Lower	Upper	t	Sig. (2-tailed)
S1: 2014-2015 S2: 2015-2016	-53.66	188.25	-89.92	-17.41	-2.935	.004

The Paired Samples Correlations for Group A, (N) = 106, Correlation= -.181, Sig = .063, demonstrated a negative correlation between both years. Although it is not a perfect negative correlation (close to -.20), it reveals that there is still a slight relationship between variables for a 95% interval of confidence, as theory would dictate.

Table 4. Paired samples test for group B

			95% Confidence Interval			
Paired Samples	Mean	Std. Deviation	Lower	Upper	t	Sig. (2-tailed)
S1: 2014-2015 S2: 2015-2016	-25.65	216.19	-65.589	14.28	1.272	.206

As for group B, it is possible to scrutinize from table 4 that, with a 95% level of confidence, the mean of the Lexile growth results between the academic year 2014-2015 and 2015-2016 (both with no intervention) is significantly higher [Sig. (2-tailed) = 0.206] than the acceptance value of Sig. (2-tailed) > 0.05, hence H0 is accepted. This test shows that the Lexile growth follows a similar pattern between years, with no significant differences between years in the group of students that were subject to intervention.

3.2 Qualitative Results

In this section, the analysis of data is made according to the focused interviews carried out in the school year of 2016-2017 with students subject to intervention and other students not subject to intervention in the previous year, using the constant comparative method which revealed several patterns useful for analysis.

It was possible to observe some similarities as well as differences in students' reading habits and behaviors. Both groups hold in common the fact that all children suggest they enjoy reading in general, including English books, being quite aware of the benefits of reading for the gain of knowledge, language acquisition and further development. Both groups also mentioned reading as an activity that they use as entertainment to overcome boredom. However, the students subject to intervention conveyed the impression of having more reasons to believe that reading in English is especially important in terms of language, by mentioning about their future and career prospects, and by emphasizing the fact that English is considered an international language.

Both groups revealed that they are used to reading in the two common formats, i.e. eBooks and paper books, and that they are equally prepared to deal with both book formats with ease. Both groups also mentioned that they like selecting their own books on the platform, although they recognized that the teacher was a precious help in choosing the right texts (suitable level) for them and therefore avoid the hassle of having to browse among hundreds of books and wasting their time.

For both groups, the teacher is their biggest source of motivation. During the intervention, students from group A read more regularly and had a goal to achieve every month. They also said that the teacher frequently gave them advice about reading, explained how they could select books on the platform and, in general, gave a considerable amount of encouragement to read (even outside the platform). They mentioned that they started reading as it was given as homework. Nevertheless, the teacher facilitated the process for them. As for the children who didn't go through any reading intervention, the teacher still was a big source of motivation, although this would only happen if and when their teacher decided to choose and assign something for the children to read on the platform, which was mentioned to happen with no specific regularity. These children would do it as it would be assigned as a homework (compulsory) activity.

In terms of their opinions towards the reading platform, students from group A appeared to know the platform very well and were able to point out several positive aspects, which surpassed the negative aspects that they mentioned. They were able to tell in what ways the platform would be helpful in their daily routine and showed that they really took advantage of the positive features. The majority of students pointed out that they intended to carry on reading after the end of school year, but that they would do it outside the platform. It seemed that children relate the digital reading platform as school work, so even though they plan to engage in reading activities, they affirmed that they would use other sources to do so.

On the other hand, students from group B gave very limited opinions about the platform, and only pointed one very general advantage, being its convenience, and their given disadvantages exceeded the positive aspect. They showed that they had very little connection to this reading tool and appeared not to be taking advantage of it to its full potential. Some group B students also confessed that they would never read on the platform unless a teacher assigned them reading tasks. Others admitted only reading occasionally. This shows the importance of the teacher monitoring and following up on children's reading habits.

4. DISCUSSION

As for the quantitative analysis, several relevant findings were made. The most important one shows that there is a direct connection between the teacher's guidance and monitoring, and students' Lexile growth, which translates into reading skills improvement. Although some students subject to the intervention kept having a decrease in their Lexile level, such decrease was substantially lower than before the intervention. Also, students who historically grew their Lexile level had an even higher growth after the intervention. Statistically speaking, it is possible to assert that the intervention caused a higher than expected average Lexile growth of 51% in group A, when compared with the previous year, while the students not subject to the intervention, group B, had a significantly lower Lexile growth of 19%.

The statistical Paired Samples Test brought additional light into this analysis and the intervention effectiveness. In a nutshell, it was found that group A presented positive statistical discrepancies in the Lexile growth between the pre-intervention and post-intervention periods that were relevant to the analysis. Although the Correlation Tests were not conclusive, the Paired Samples Tests, along with other metrics used, was sufficient to reject H0.

If analyzed in terms of gender (no statistics are presented here due to the 8 pages restriction), the findings are even more interesting, since it is shown that, in the group of students subject to intervention, females, who had a significantly lower Lexile than males in the year before the intervention, grew their Lexile level by 120% while males grew 15%. These results show that the female students from this group had a slower Lexile growth when not exposed to the instructional practices included in the intervention, and when exposed to said practices had a sharp increase in the Lexile growth and even surpassed the males' results. Moreover, data showed that when the intervention stopped, females from the intervention group resumed a lower Lexile growth than males. This indicates that female students from the group subject to intervention were more sensitive to the teacher's guidance or lack thereof.

Also, it appears that the effects of guidance and instructional practices were still visible in the year following the intervention, as the 2016-2017 growth results between the first and second Lexile tests, which took place in the first and second terms, show undoubtedly that, in average, group A has improved and keeps improving much more than group B. In perspective, group A came from an initial reality where their average growth was 21% lower compared to group B. Immediately after the intervention, their average growth happened at the same pace, with a 0% mean variance between groups, and lastly, in the year following the intervention, group A had an average growth 32% higher when they took the second Lexile test of the year. This systematic growth pattern backed up by all other statistical tests positive results was the proof that the researcher was looking for the idealized study.

Concurring with Watkins & Biggs (2001) that intrinsic motivation is not applicable in Confucian Heritage Culture (CHC) because it plays a minor role in CHC classrooms and Moneta & Siu (2002) that has shown through research that students who are intrinsically motivated end up presenting lower levels of achievement than extrinsically motivated ones, during the interviews, both groups clearly admitted that the reason why they were reading or ever read at all was because the teacher assigned books and asked them to read as homework. This also restates what Lee (1996) argued that CHC societies are known not only for showing respect for education, but also for highly respecting and valuing teachers' instructions.

From the conversations with students, it was found that the teacher is their biggest source of reading motivation. Before the intervention, the lack of clear and regular educational practices from teachers, as well as lack of encouragement for reading and monitoring their reading activity, may have contributed for the low Lexile level of students. Thus, most of the students in primary 5 were Below Basic readers and had a weak reading ability before intervention.

Even though most of the children voiced out that they prefer to choose the books they read, those who were subject to intervention recognized that when the teacher chose books for them, it was indeed helpful and a trigger for them to read more online, again showing the importance of the teacher's role in the reading process of these children.

Another positive outcome from the intervention is that students who were subject to the researcher's practices and instructions were more comfortable using the platform and more aware of the advantages of such tool. Additionally, with the opportunity to read regularly in the platform, as their reading activity was being followed by the teacher researcher, improvement was achieved. The target of the intervention was to help students progress more than historically expected, rather than achieve a predetermined level or score.

On the other hand, during the interviews, students who were not subject to intervention showed they were less prone to reading in the platform. Students stated that they never read online or, if it happened, it would be occasionally or when their teacher assigned them eBooks.

Another important finding is that students who were subject to intervention expressed that they intended to continue reading even after the school year ended. Another objective of the intervention was for students to gain a reading routine. Even though most of the measures were to externally motivate students to read as they were found not internally motivated, this corroborates what Vygotsky (1978) suggested with the ZPD (Zone of Proximal Development) that, provided with scaffolding or support from a more able person, students would then be able to perform certain tasks alone after a period of time. Basically, extrinsic measures were used in a tentative way of creating reading habits in students, even after intervention.

	Complete School Year Comparison			Parcial School Year Comparison		
Timeline:	Before Intervention	End of Intervention		End of Intervention	1 Year After Intervention	
School Year:	2014-2015	2015-2016		2015-2016	2016-2017	
Grade and Term:	P4 Term 1-3	P5 Term 1-3	P4 to P5	P5 Term 1-3	P6 Term 1-2	P5 to P6
Average:	-21%	0%	▲	0%	32%	▲
Maximum:	-36%	-14%	▲	-14%	-6%	▲
Minimum:	-28%	45%	▲	45%	2%	▼
Standard Deviation:	13%	16%	▲	16%	-1%	▼

Figure 4. Lexile growth variance between group A and group B (a positive percentage indicates that group A had better results than group B. A green upward arrow represents an increase in percentage between the years, which in turn indicates that group A had better results than group B)

5. CONCLUSIONS

1. What is the role of teachers in implementing digital reading platforms at schools? This research and its results are absolutely conclusive about how important the role of teachers is in implementing digital reading platforms at schools. Teachers play a key part in this process, as many would say and one would expect. Not only the school environment and resources act as a means to motivate children into being interested in literacy, but especially teachers who directly contact and establish rapport with them every day. According to Methe & Hintze (2003), teachers are the most influential agents in students' social environment. The role of teachers in implementing a digital reading platform also encompasses the need to act as a role model, i.e., the teacher holds a vital role in modelling reading behavior. Confirmed by Bussey & Bandura (1984), children replicate the behavior of powerful models, such as teachers.

2. What are the effects of teachers' guidance and instructional practices on students' reading progress when using a digital reading platform? The effects of teachers' guidance and instructional practices on students' reading progress seem to be quite high and revealed themselves to be fairly easy to measure with the use of the Lexile-based online reading platform. Considering that the Lexile® Framework is a renowned metric system for reading, the accuracy of the results and findings of this study is undeniable. In the findings, it is clear that students react in a very positive way to guidance and instructional practices when it comes to reading progress.

3. What are the factors that impact students' motivation for reading? It is possible to conclude that children are more inclined to respond to external reading stimuli rather than internal ones that still may exist, but in a much subtle form, since Macau students are strongly influenced by CHC. This culture is more motivated by external factors, as schools don't seem to reward internally motivated students (Moneta & Siu, 2002). For this reason, children responded well to intervention strategies where teacher granted points in their performance score for books they would have completed each month. A marks-driven society consents children to think that they will be rewarded for their outcomes rather than for the learning process itself. Another extrinsic aspect is their social motivation (Biggs, 1995). Publicly awarding the top 3 students who had more reading activity, placing their names and reading achievement on a board on a monthly basis also helped boost their reading interest as they would be acknowledged in front of the whole class and showed contentment when their work was recognized in front of their peers. It is still possible to identify minor internal factors that may trigger children's interest for reading (such as students' interest topics) even though they were not found sufficiently strong to sustain reading habits for a long time without other mechanisms.

Considering that the intervention took place in a short period of time and with participants who belonged to one level only, it is suggested the same study to be carried out with different levels to find out the teacher's role in implementing digital reading platforms with children of different ages, as well as to see if the motivating aspects that encourage children to read in those platforms are the same across levels. The intervention can also be planned to take place in a full school year, thus requiring 3 complete school years to observe, intervene and evaluate results. Another suggestion would be to assess the impact of a study like this in their reading habits, for a full year after the intervention. A similar study can also be planned to include paper books alongside the digital platform which will require for the school library books to be properly Lexile-measured and labelled as well as to perform changes in the schools' reading curricula to include more activities such as book sharing, book clubs, buddy reading activities and in-class reading time for leisure. This will allow to understand if, by extending the instructional practices and strategies to paper books, the effects of an intervention are even higher.

REFERENCES

AARE - Australian Association for Research in Education. (2017). *Teaching literacy is more than teaching reading skills*. Retrieved from http://www.aare.edu.au/blog/?p=1532

Al-Seghayer, K. (2016). *ESL/EFL instructors' perceptions of the importance of computer-assisted reading in L2 reading instruction*. Theory and Practice in Language Studies, (9), 1753.

Biggs, J. (1995). *Learning in the classroom*. In Biggs & Watkins (Eds.), Classroom learning: Singapore, Prentice-Hall.

Bussey, K. & Bandura, A. (1984). *Influence of gender constancy and social power on sex-linked modelling*. Journal of Personality and Social Psychology, 47, 1292-1302.

Creswell, J. W. & Clark, V. L. (2011). *Designing and conducting mixed methods research*. SAGE Publications.

Creswell, J. W. (2012). *Educational research*. Boston: Pearson.

Feng, A. (2011). *English language education across greater China Multilingual Matters*.

Lee, W. (1996). *The cultural context for Chinese learners: Conceptions of learning in the Confucian heritage*. In D. Watkins & Biggs (Eds.), The Chinese learner: Cultural, psychological and contextual influences. Hong Kong, China and Victoria, Australia: Comparative Education Research Centre and The Australian Council for Educational Research Ltd.

MetaMetrics. (2017). *The Lexile framework for reading*. Retrieved from lexile.com/about-lexile/lexile-overview/.

Methe, S. & Hintze, J. (2003). *Evaluating teacher modelling as strategy to increase student reading behavior*. School Psychological Review, 32(4), 617-623.

Moneta, G. & Siu, C. (2002). *Trait intrinsic and extrinsic motivations, academic performance and creativity in Hong Kong college students*. Journal of College Student Development, 43(5), 664-683.

Moody, A. (2008). *Macau English: Status, functions and forms. English Today*. 24(3), 3-15. doi:10.1017/S0266078408000242.

Powell-Brown, A. (2006). *Why can't I just see the movie? Fostering motivation in children who struggle with reading*. Intervention in School and Clinic, 42(2), doi:10.1177/10534512060420020701.

Scholastic Inc. (2016). *Scholastic literacy pro library user's guide*. Scholastic Inc.

Stenhouse, L. (1983a). *Authority, education, and emancipation: A collection of papers*. Heinemann Educational Books.

Stenhouse, L. (1983b). *Case study in educational research and evaluation* (In L. Barlett, S. Lemmis and G. Gillard, Eds), Geelong, Australia: Deakon University Press.

Stenner, A. J. (1996). *Measuring reading comprehension with the lexile framework*. Durham, NC.: MetaMetrics, Inc.

Stringer, E. T. (2007). *Action research*. SAGE Publications.

Sturman, A. (1999). *Case study methods*. In J.P. Keeves and G. Lakomski (eds.), Issues in Educational Research, Oxford: Elsevier Science Ltd, 103-12.

UNESCO. (2016). *Statistics on literacy*. Retrieved from http://www.unesco.org/new/en/education/themes/education-building-blocks/literacy/resources/statistics

Vygotsky, L. S. (1978). *Mind in society: The development of high psychological processes*. Cambridge, MA: Harvard University Press.

Watkins, D. & Biggs, J. (2001). *The paradox of the Chinese learner and beyond*. In Watkins & Biggs (Eds.), Teaching the Chinese learner: Psychological and pedagogical perspectives. Hong Kong: Comparative Education Research Centre, The University of Hong Kong.

HOW TO FLIP A CLASSROOM AND IMPROVE STUDENT LEARNING AND ENGAGEMENT: THE CASE OF PSYC1030

Pedro Isaias[1], Blake McKimmie[2], Aneesha Bakharia[3], John Zornig[3] and Anna Morris[3]
[1] *Institute for Teaching and Learning Innovation (ITaLI), The University of Queensland, Brisbane, Australia*
[2] *School of Psychology, Faculty of Health and Behavioural Sciences, The University of Queensland, Brisbane, Australia*
[3] *UQx, Institute for Teaching and Learning Innovation (ITaLI), The University of Queensland, Brisbane, Australia*

ABSTRACT

The flipped classroom's pervasiveness in different educational contexts derives from the growing need to focus on student-centered and active learning approaches. The fact that the flipped classroom allocates the lecture delivery to the outside of the classroom endows teachers with the possibility of using the in-class time to develop active learning tasks. At the same time, since students gain insight of the learning material prior to attending the class, they are more prepared to actively engage with the resources and their peers inside the classroom. This paper presents a project developed by the School of Psychology from the University of Queensland in Australia that consisted in flipping a course, PSYC1030, and creating a series of four MOOCs. The students' evaluation of the experience was measured via a survey and showed that, in general, they found the outcomes to be positive, namely at the level of the assessment, collaboration, interaction and their understanding of the material.

KEYWORDS

Flipped classroom, MOOCs, active learning, higher education

1. FLIPPING THE CLASSROOM

The growing focus on student-centred approaches to learning has motivated the adoption of more flexible teaching techniques, inspired by the notion of active learning (Danker, 2015). Flipped classrooms can facilitate teaching strategies that focus on the students, namely inquiry-based and problem-based methodologies, by optimising in-class time (Sergis et al., 2017). This teaching style basically involves inverting the events that customarily take place inside and outside of the classroom, by resorting to technology and it is based on a model of blended learning (Kim et al., 2014). In general, the use of the flipped classroom method, entails the preparation of online lectures in an audio or video format that the students are asked to review prior to attending the class. Thus encouraging students to complete the information acquisition part of learning before the class (Phillips and Trainor, 2014). This then enables the development of interactive learning tasks within the time that is allocated for the lecture delivery (Aidinopoulou and Sampson, 2017).

There is a wide variation between what different studies report having used as the pre-class content delivery assignments, although the majority seems to use a combination of asynchronous online video and quizzes or closed-ended problems. This variation exists equally in the type of activities that the teachers design for the in-class engagement with the material. Most studies seem to have a preference for using interactive learning tasks based on group work (Bishop and Verleger, 2013). Teachers do not have to limit the presentation of the lecture to the use of video, they can create podcasts and use web-based whiteboards (Moffett and Mill, 2014). In terms of the support for the pre-class content attainment, the teachers can provide the students with a brief reading, a narrated presentation in PowerPoint, a brief audio or video lecture recording or ask them to use a discussion forum or chat room. With respect to the in-class activities the teachers can resort to a revision of the pre-class questions, tasks involving real life examples or case studies, simulations, group work, student presentations or field work and peer feedback (Loveys et al., 2016). During the classroom the teachers predominantly assume the role of a mentor, guiding both individual and group work and prior to the class they are required to deliver learning content by using their technology competences (Dennen and Spector, 2016).

The flipped classroom approach has the advantage of empowering students to be in control of their learning through the preparatory work that they complete and through the adoption of a more interactive stance during the class itself. Also it allows the students to learn at their own rhythm, as they can access the digital material when it's more convenient, and it assists them to develop valuable lifelong learning skills (O'Flaherty and Phillips, 2015). This approach to learning demands the students to make an investment of their time, outside of the classroom for independent self-learning (Kurtz et al., 2014). Self-regulated learning constitutes a core competence for the promotion of lifelong learning (Ifenthaler, 2012). Whereas passive learning entails receiving content by listening to a teacher and promotes only surface learning, active learning goes beyond knowledge retention, encourages a personal involvement with the content and it is connected with deep learning (Phillips and Trainor, 2014). Active learning has a positive effect on the students' learning results and on their motivations and behaviours. At the same time, active learning is responsible for encouraging the learners' engagement and promoting reflection (McLaughlin et al., 2014). Focusing on active learning is particularly important to assist students to develop communication and critical thinking competences (Ferreri and O'Connor, 2013) as well as high-order cognitive skills (Danker, 2015).

Flipped classrooms are also associated with the improvement of the learners' results, the promotion of student engagement and the enhancement of classroom participation. Since the students have time to review the lectures before going to class they can acquire a deeper knowledge of the subjects and for that reason be more proficient when engaging in high-order actions, like discussions and problem solving. Additionally, given that this part of the learning is done in the classroom, the teacher is present and it is possible for the students to receive immediate feedback (Thai et al., 2017). During the class, the teacher becomes more capable of addressing the individual needs of the students and of designing learning practices that are more suitable for particular students (McLaughlin et al., 2014). This approach is also believed to enhance the interaction among learners and between the learner and the teacher (Phillips and Trainor, 2014). With this approach the students can make sense of the content and apply in class what they've learned, by engaging in collaborative problem solving (Danker, 2015). Furthermore, the use of a flipped classroom enables teachers to reinforce the material that was covered without having to sacrifice additional content and to deliver the content in a variety of formats, thus addressing different learning preferences (Mason et al., 2013).

2. EVALUATION OF FLIPPED CLASSROOMS

Existing research about the evaluation of the flipped classroom reports an assortment of student's perceptions, nonetheless, they seem to be globally positive (Bishop and Verleger, 2013). There is a scarcity of quantitative research that supports the effectiveness of using the flipped classroom approach (Findlay-Thompson and Mombourquette, 2014) and solely a very reduced number of studies actually offers an objective assessment of the students' learning results (Bishop and Verleger, 2013). Moreover, despite the importance of evaluating the opinion of the teachers, the majority of the existing studies focuses on assessing the viewpoints of the students (O'Flaherty and Phillips, 2015). Current research on the assessment of the flipped classroom generally falls into two categories: comparison studies and case-studies (DeLozier and Rhodes, 2017).

Comparative studies establish an analogy between the conventional classroom and the flipped technique and can be more generalizable, but since sometimes they use so many different variables (teaching methods, technology, learning material) between the two types of approach it becomes difficult to conclude which of them have influence over the findings (Jensen et al., 2015). Strayer (2012) compared two classes, one had been flipped and the other had remained in the conventional format. The author used a questionnaire, field notes, interviews and focus groups to examine both classes. The students in the flipped classroom manifested a lower satisfaction level with the classroom's orientation to the learning activities, but were more welcoming of collaboration and innovation in teaching styles. Mason et al. (2013) also conducted a comparison study, where three dimensions were evaluated: content, students' performance (in quizzes and exams) and students' perceptions (via a survey). The authors concluded that the flipped classroom, allowed a wider coverage of content, the students' performance was as good or better and despite the initial difficulties, the students were satisfied and they perceived it as being effective. Findlay-Thompson and Mombourquette (2014) compared the results of students within a traditional lecture-based class and a flipped classroom and concluded that there were no differences between the two teaching styles in terms of grades. In post-term interviews, the students from the flipped classroom had mixed feelings about the experience, but appreciated the extra time to ask questions in class and they felt that they did better, even though their perceptions were not corroborated by higher grades.

Case-studies, on the other hand, usually offer a depiction of implementation practices and present mainly affective data. While they provide valuable information, they aren't usually generalizable nor do they usually offer a causal explanation (Jensen et al., 2015). Young et al. (2014) designed a quantitative questionnaire based on a Likert scale to assess the opinions of the students about the flipped classroom sessions that they had attended and used qualitative items in their inquiry of the faculty's perceptions. The students highlighted the positive side of material retention, of having a more interactive class and of actively participating. The faculty stated that the main advantages pertained to the possibility of providing feedback and of assessing the students' knowledge. Butt (2014) measured the perceptions of students that participated in a flipped classroom during a semester, using a survey at the start of the course and another survey at the end. The authors findings show that in the initial survey there was a 50/50 division between the students who believed that the flipped structure would be advantageous and those who didn't. The survey that was administered at the end of the course, after they had experienced this approach showed that 75% of the students considered the flipped classroom to be advantageous to their learning process.

3. FLIPPING A COURSE AT THE UNIVERSITY OF QUEENSLAND

In line with the goals of the Student Strategy (The University of Queensland, 2016), The University of Queensland in 2016-17 undertook a project to flip a large first year undergraduate course and evaluate its impact on students and teaching staff so as to create an exemplar for other courses to follow. The course, Introduction to Psychology: Developmental, Social & Clinical Psychology (PSYC1030) from The Faculty of Health and Behavioural Sciences at The University of Queensland has one of the largest enrolments of all courses across the institution.

The course coordinator had successfully used a UQx MOOC project in 2014 to flip a smaller second year course. In mid-2016 a collaboration with the UQx online learning unit was initiated to transform PSYC1030 in time for the Semester 1 teaching period in 2017. As in the earlier course the content for flipping PSYC1030 would be developed both for a MOOC and a SPOC (Small Private Online Course) for PSYC1030 students. Unlike many other flipped class projects, the SPOC for PSYC1030 would totally replace the content delivery, formerly the task of lectures. The MOOC course style utilised by UQx relies heavily on embedding activities for students throughout the predominantly video presentation of core concepts. These activities reinforce learning and allow students to judge how well their understanding is so that they can better direct their engagement with the content.

PSYC1030, in previous years, comprised a traditional 2-hour lecture, 1-hour tutorial format for 12 weeks of the teaching period. When flipped, it consisted of a SPOC presenting the content and a single weekly contact hour which took the form of a 120 student workshop (4 times) and a 25 student tutorial (9 times). The MOOC style of active online learning contained in the SPOC allowed students to be prepared to participate in the peer to peer and group activities orchestrated by the teaching staff during the weekly workshop or tutorial.

One of the goals of the project was to create a MOOC, called PSYC1030x, that would represent as well as could be done in a fully online and self-paced mode, the new transformed on-campus flipped PSYC1030. Experience from earlier MOOCs indicates that learners prefer shorter MOOCs with focused learning goals and narrow topics, and that this improves student engagement. This experience informed the choice to modularise PSYC1030x as a series of four MOOCs covering the primary topics. The goal of replacing the lectures entirely led to the MOOCs being very comprehensive and including content that was often skipped from lecture delivery because of time constraints and only available to students via the prescribed text book. The usual practice in MOOCs is for the content to stand alone without need for a textbook thus maintaining the goal to have the course available to a massive global audience for free. The result was that neither PSYC1030x or the transformed PSYC1030 require a textbook.

The whole process of flipping the course took eighteen months with the evaluation of the results continuing after the completion of the course delivery. The flipping process consisted of the UQx project team working with the lead course academic (course coordinator) of PSYC1030 to collaboratively create videos and activities. All previous lectures from 2015 PSYC1030 were transcribed and used as a starting point to create short video scripts of the lecture content. The lead academic created slides and some video material for insertion into the videos. The team also consisted of a UQx learning designer and faculty project officer with subject matter knowledge who worked with the course academics to refine video scripts and create interactive activities. The UQx media team filmed and edited the videos. The UQx technical team developed custom Learning Tool Interoperability (LTI) tools that the course utilised to deliver formative assessment activities. The UQx learning designer developed the created videos and formative assessment activities in the edX EDGE platform to create the SPOC. The faculty project officer built the summative quiz pools for assessment in Blackboard. A team of beta-testers from the faculty and members of the UQx team (who had not been involved in production) reviewed the four individual SPOC courses before they went live.

The tutorials were adapted from the existing tutorial sequence for PSYC1030, and focussed on supporting students to write a laboratory report on a study. This formed a major assessment item in the course and was supported by video resources created for the fourth MOOC in the PSYC1030x series. The workshop activities, one for each of the three major content areas corresponding to the first three MOOCs in the PSYC1030x series, were developed in junction with the content-area expert in that area and a lead tutor from the course.

4. EVALUATION METHODOLOGY

The evaluation methodology has been designed to include students, tutors and the course development team in the evaluation. In addition there were regular student surveys at the end of the semester to assess their satisfaction with the course and the teaching team (SECaTs).This paper focus specifically in the students' results and analysis of learner clickstream data from Blackboard.

The student experience survey included questions on Engagement, Flexibility, Assessment and Instructional Methods. The student experience survey also included two free text questions asking what the students liked about the flipped classroom model and what improvements they would suggest.

5. PSYC1030 EVALUATION RESULTS

This paper focuses on presenting results from the student experience survey, as well as an analysis of the learner clickstream data from BlackBoard. This more thorough evaluation will include student surveys of the three main course blocks, interviews with course developers and surveys and interviews of tutors. It will also include an analysis of the Blackboard clickstream data, as well as engagement with previous offerings of the course via ECHO 360 data.

This section analyses the valid responses of the 237 students who completed the student experience survey in a population of 1250 students of this course (there were 288 total responses).

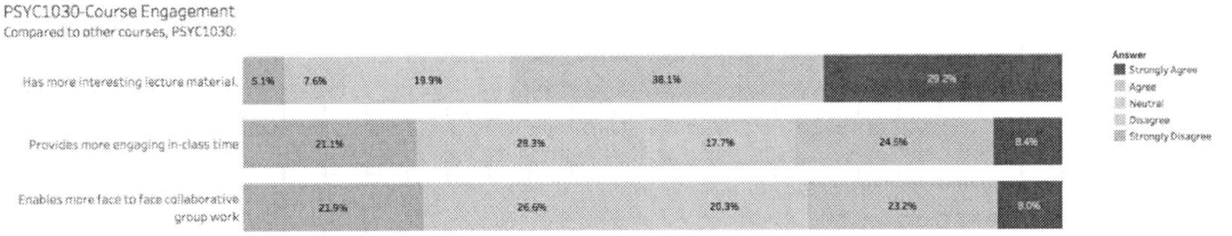

Figure 1. Course Engagement results from Student Survey

In Figure 1 we can see the results for the Course Engagement section questions of the student experience survey. This shows that compared to other courses, PSYC1030 has more interesting lecture material (29.2% strongly agree; 38.1% agree – these figures correspond to a majority of respondents). Only about 1/3 of the respondents consider that it provides more engaging in-time class and also more face to face collaborative group work, with around 18%-20% respondents in both questions being neutral about it. It must be noted that engagement goes beyond this question since it can also be assessed by how many students were watching the videos and doing the activities each week.

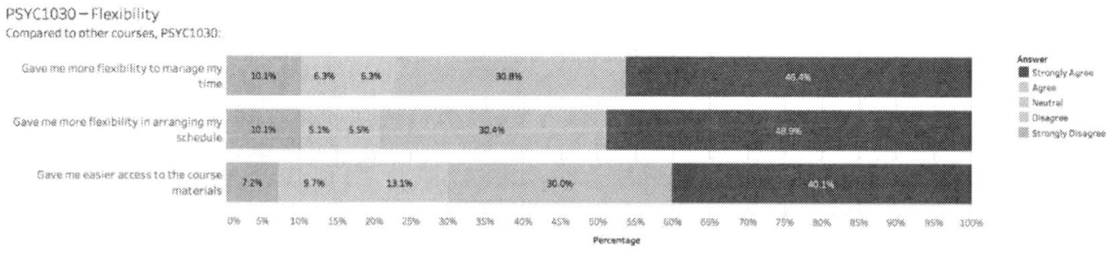

Figure 2. Flexibility results from Student Survey

In Figure 2 we can see the results for the Flexibility section questions of the student experience survey. This shows that a significant majority of students (more than 2/3) considered that it gave them more flexibility to manage their time (46.4% strongly agree and 30.8% agree) and also gave them more flexibility in arranging their schedules (48.9% strongly agree and 30.4% agree). A majority of respondents, but to a lesser extent, considered that it gave them easier access to the course materials (40.1% strongly agree and 30.0% agree).

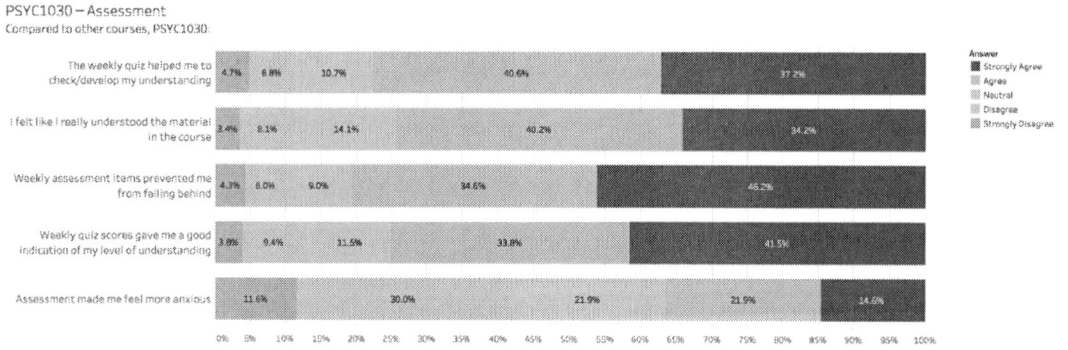

Figure 3. Assessment results from Student Survey

In Figure 3 we can see the results for the Assessment section questions of the student experience survey. This shows a very positive outcome for the first four questions. More than 2/3 of respondents strongly agree or agree that assessments were positive for them and that they also understood the material in the course. About ⅓ considered that assessments made them more anxious.

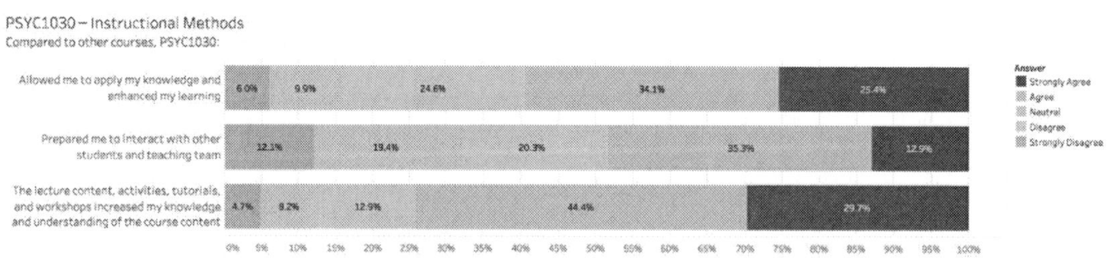

Figure 4. Instructional Methods results from Student Survey

In Figure 4 we can see the results for the Instructional Methods section questions of the student experience survey. This shows that more than 2/3 of respondents acknowledge that lecture content, activities, tutorials, and workshops increased their knowledge and understanding of the course content. Only about half of the respondents consider that it allowed them to apply their knowledge and enhanced their learning, as well as prepared them to interact with other students and teaching team.

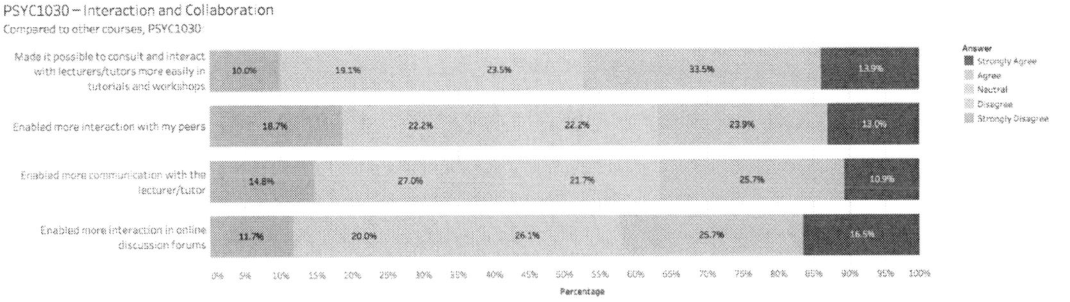

Figure 5. Interaction and Collaboration results from Student Survey

In Figure 5 we can see the results for the Interaction and Collaboration section questions of the student experience survey. This shows that only 1/3 of respondents considered that it enabled more interaction with their peers as well as more communication with the lecturer/tutor. 47.4% considered that it made it possible to consult and interact with lecturers/tutors more easily in tutorials and workshops, whilst 42.2% signalled that enabled more interaction in online discussion forums.

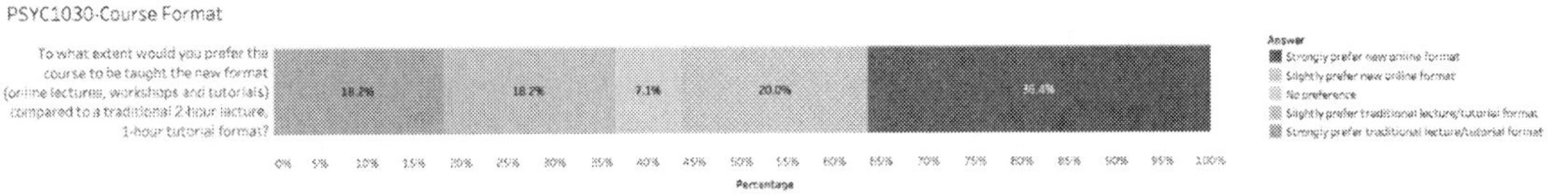

Figure 6. Preference of the course in the new format results from Student Survey

In Figure 6 we can see the results for Preference of the course in the new format question of the student experience survey. This shows that 55.4% considered that overall they preferred the course to be taught in the new flipped format, with 1/3 considering the contrary.

Qualitative content analysis was performed on the two free text questions included in the student survey. Each student response was tagged with the course element that the student was referring to (i.e., a primary category) and the feature that the student found effective (i.e., a secondary tag). Categorising student responses by both the course elements and the related aspect that the student was referring to allowed for fine grained analysis and visualisation. The main course elements included as primary categories were: Online Lectures, Weekly Quizzes, Lecture Videos, Tutorials, Workshops, Video Interactivity (i.e., the ability to pause, seek and speed up a video) and Interactive Course Elements (i.e., the inclusion of online interactive social polls and discussion forums). Only course elements (i.e. nodes) and edges mentioned by more than one student have been included in the resulting network visualisations. Edge weights represent the number of students that mentioned the primary and secondary categories together.

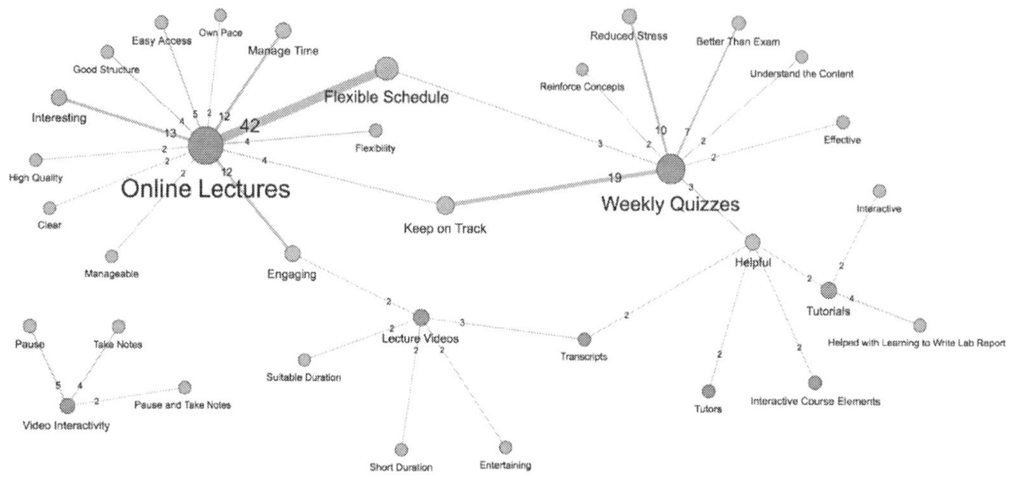

Figure 7. Network Diagram with visualization results from Student Survey –
Question: "What were the most effective parts of PSYC1030?"

Figure 7 is a network diagram visualization for the open-ended survey question: "What were the most effective parts of PSYC1030?". Results show that students thought that the online lectures provided them with a flexible schedule (n=42). Students also valued the weekly quizzes because smaller quizzes helped keep them on track (n=19), reduced stress (n=10) and were preferred over a final exam (n=10). Students felt that the duration of videos (i.e., 3 minutes on average) was also appropriate and found the Online Lectures to be engaging (n=12), interesting (n=13) and easy to access (n=5).

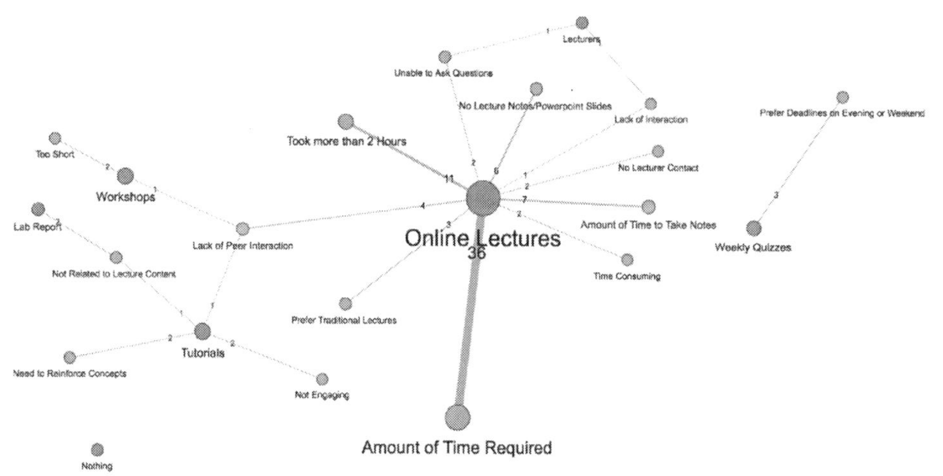

Figure 8. Network Diagram with visualization results from Student Survey –
Question: "What were the least effective parts of PSYC1030?"

Figure 8 is a network diagram visualization for the open-ended survey question: "What were the least effective parts of PSYC1030?". Results show that students thought that watching the Online Lectures and taking their own notes required a lot of time (n=36). Some students mentioned the amount of time they took to work through the online content which was between 3 to 6 hours. The University expects that students will allow 10 hours per week for each 2 unit course (PSYC1030 is a 2 unit course), however it was clear from conversations with some students and their feedback on the survey that their expectations were that they would spend two hours per week on the course content (this is the time for a traditional on campus lecture). The remainder of the time would presumably be caught up during the vacation period for courses with final exams. A small percentage of students requested Lecture Notes or Powerpoint Slides (n=5). It is not known whether the students requesting Lecture Notes were aware that a transcript was able to be downloaded. The ability to download a transcript was acknowledged as an effective course feature by students responding to the "What were the most effective parts of PSYC1030?" question. Students also referred to the lack of both peer and teaching staff interaction.

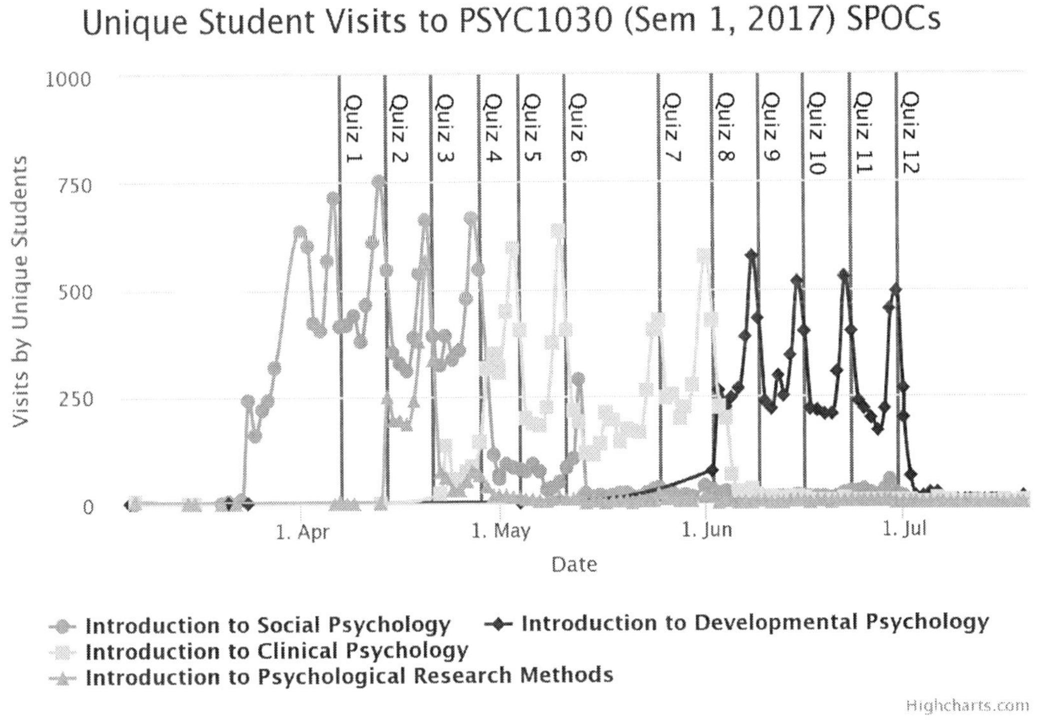

Figure 9. Unique students visiting PSYC1030 SPOCs each day in Semester 1, 2017

Figure 9 shows the unique student visits to each of the PSYC1030 SPOCs, during Semester 1 2017. The 12 quizzes deadlines are also indicated. From the figure analysis, it can be stated that the students accessed the quizzes in the days before the respective deadline, and after that, there is a clear drop rate in access. There is an interesting tendency for student access to decrease throughout the semester. This can be explained because, according to the course profile, only the 10 best scores out of the 12 quizzes' scores, are considered. Therefore, as soon as a student gets his best scores, he or she won't proceed to continue doing the quizzes. In addition to this aspect, there is a normal drop-out rate of students during the semester and thus the decrease shown.

Engagement with SPOCs seems to be very much quiz driven. Compared to previous years' face to face course attendance, these figures show higher engagement. There's more students accessing the SPOCs and engaging with them, compared to students attending face to face lectures in previous years.

6. DISCUSSION AND LESSONS LEARNT

Similarly to what previous research has concluded (Findlay-Thompson and Mombourquette, 2014, Ferreri and O'Connor, 2013, Mason et al., 2013), the project to flip PSYC1030 and create a MOOC with the same content and learning outcomes has shown that the effort involved is considerable. Hence, it should not be taken on without good resourcing and a clear vision of the end results.

The project gave an opportunity for more academics from the School of Psychology to participate in the creation of the course than would have been involved in the previous lecture style of delivery. This can be seen as both a professional development and a school collaboration outcome. Also, in agreement with Mason et al. (2013) findings on the capacity of the flipped classroom for a wider coverage of content, in this project the replacement of the entirety of the lectures caused the MOOCs to include content that was not possible to include in the lecture delivery format.

With concern to the students' evaluation of the experience, in comparison to other courses, they stated that the flipped PSYC1030 has more interesting lecture material, it endowed them with more flexibility in terms of time and arranging their schedule and provided them with an easier access to course materials. They've equally highlighted the importance of the weekly assessments as a method to prevent them from falling behind and as an indicator of their level of understanding. Also, they stated that the lecture content, its activities, tutorials and workshops did increase their knowledge and understanding of the course content, which was also reported by previous research (Young et al., 2014)

Students in the flipped course like the scheduling flexibility of fewer contact hours and the on-demand access to the content presentation in the SPOC. There was an acknowledgement from the students that the active learning format and comprehensive coverage of the content in the online materials took longer to do than simply watching two hours of recorded lectures. Current student's expectations of study hours don't appear to align with the institution's expectations, but the presentation of the content in the SPOC does seem to increase the time students spend on the course vs. the lecture format of their other courses.

7. CONCLUSIONS

Flipping courses with high quality online learning resources allows for many improvements in student experience, such as increased opportunity for staff, student and peer-to-peer interactions, greater flexibility, lower costs and more immediate feedback. Nonetheless, it is important to account for the substantial effort that this conversion means to the teaching team.

The benefits of the flipped classroom have been extensively researched, but more data of its real effectiveness is necessary. Hence, it is important to document the outcomes of the experiences with this type of teaching method. In the case of the project, the PSYC1030 course was converted into a series of four MOOCs covering the main topics and SPOCs derived from these MOOCs were used to flip the course. The results of the students' evaluation are overall positive, in particular in terms of assessment, collaboration, interaction, time management and comprehension of the material. However, the students reported that watching the lectures online and taking notes demanded a substantial amount of time.

The project's aim to be an exemplar for future course transformations has been achieved with improvements in student engagement and experience aligning with the broad goals of the The University of Queensland (UQ) Student Strategy.

Having the MOOCs and the flipped course sharing most content and learning goals will allow for a detailed assessment of the benefits to students' learning and engagement of the on-campus workshops and tutorials. The University of Queensland does not offer fully online undergraduate programs and so the value of active small group interaction in the on-campus workshops and tutorials is important to both develop and to quantify.

REFERENCES

Aidinopoulou, V. & Sampson, D. G. 2017. An Action Research Study from Implementing the Flipped Classroom Model in Primary School History Teaching and Learning. *Journal of Educational Technology & Society,* Vol. 20, No. 1 pp. 237-247.

Bishop, J. L. & Verleger, M. A. The flipped classroom: A survey of the research. ASEE National Conference Proceedings, Atlanta, GA, 2013. 1-18.

Butt, A. 2014. Student views on the use of a flipped classroom approach: Evidence from Australia. *Business Education & Accreditation,* Vol. 6, No. 1 pp. 33-43.

Danker, B. 2015. Using flipped classroom approach to explore deep learning in large classrooms. *IAFOR Journal of Education,* Vol. 3, No. 1 pp. 171-186.

DeLozier, S. J. & Rhodes, M. G. 2017. Flipped classrooms: a review of key ideas and recommendations for practice. *Educational Psychology Review,* Vol. 29, No. 1 pp. 141-151.

Dennen, V. P. & Spector, J. M. 2016. The Flipped K-12 Classroom: Implications for Teacher Preparation, Professional Development, and Educational Leadership. *In:* Avgerinou, M. D. & Gialamas, S. P. (eds.) *Revolutionizing K-12 Blended Learning through the i²Flex Classroom Model.* Hershey, PA, USA: IGI Global.

Ferreri, S. P. & O'Connor, S. K. 2013. Redesign of a large lecture course into a small-group learning course. *American journal of pharmaceutical education,* Vol. 77, No. 1 pp. 1-9.

Findlay-Thompson, S. & Mombourquette, P. 2014. Evaluation of a flipped classroom in an undergraduate business course. *Business Education & Accreditation* Vol. 6, No. 1 pp. 63-71.

Ifenthaler, D. 2012. Determining the effectiveness of prompts for self-regulated learning in problem-solving scenarios. *Educational Technology & Society,* Vol. 15, No. 1 pp. 38-52.

Ifenthaler, D., Sampson, D. G. & Spector, J. M. 2015. Interactions between cognitive psychology, educational technology, and computing in the digital age. *Technology, knowledge and learning,* Vol. 20, No. 2 pp. 129-131.

Isaías, P., Miranda, P. & Pífano, S. 2009. Designing E-Learning 2.0 courses: recommendations and guidelines. *In* A. Méndez-Vilas, A. Solano Martín, J.A. Mesa González & J. Mesa González (Eds), *Research, Reflections and Innovations in Integrating ICT in Education.* (Vol. 2, pp 1081-1085). Badajoz, Spain: FORMATEX.

Jensen, J. L., Kummer, T. A. & Godoy, P. D. d. M. 2015. Improvements from a flipped classroom may simply be the fruits of active learning. *CBE-Life Sciences Education,* Vol. 14, No. 1 pp. 1-12.

Kim, M. K., Kim, S. M., Khera, O. & Getman, J. 2014. The experience of three flipped classrooms in an urban university: an exploration of design principles. *The Internet and Higher Education,* Vol. 22, No. pp. 37-50.

Kurtz, G., Tsimerman, A. & Steiner-Lavi, O. 2014. The Flipped-Classroom Approach: The Answer to Future Learning? *European Journal of Open, Distance and E-Learning,* Vol. 17, No. 2 pp. 172-182.

Loveys, B., Riggs, K., McGrice, H., Snelling, C., Winning, T. & Kemp, A. 2016. The Rise of the Flip: Successfully engaging students in pre-class activities through the use of technology and a flipped classroom design template. In Barker, S., Dawson, S., Pardo, A., Colvin, C. (Eds*) Show Me The Learning. Proceedings ASCILITE 2016*, pp.312-317 2016.

Mason, G. S., Shuman, T. R. & Cook, K. E. 2013. Comparing the effectiveness of an inverted classroom to a traditional classroom in an upper-division engineering course. *IEEE Transactions on Education,* Vol. 56, No. 4 pp. 430-435.

McLaughlin, J. E., Roth, M. T., Glatt, D. M., Gharkholonarehe, N., Davidson, C. A., Griffin, L. M., Esserman, D. A. & Mumper, R. J. 2014. The flipped classroom: a course redesign to foster learning and engagement in a health professions school. *Academic Medicine,* Vol. 89, No. 2 pp. 236-243.

Moffett, J. & Mill, A. C. 2014. Evaluation of the flipped classroom approach in a veterinary professional skills course. *Advances in medical education and practice,* Vol. 5, No. pp. 415-425.

Natividad, G., Mayes, R. & Spector, J. M. 2015. Balancing stable educational goals with changing educational technologies: challenges and opportunities. *e-mentor,* Vol. 1, No. pp. 83-94.

O'Flaherty, J. & Phillips, C. 2015. The use of flipped classrooms in higher education: A scoping review. *The Internet and Higher Education,* Vol. 25, No. pp. 85-95.

Phillips, C. R. & Trainor, J. E. 2014. Millennial students and the flipped classroom. *Journal of Business and Educational Leadership,* Vol. 5, No. 1 pp. 102-112.

Sergis, S., Vlachopoulos, P., Sampson, D. G. & Pelliccione, L. 2017. Implementing Teaching Model Templates for Supporting Flipped Classroom-Enhanced STEM Education in Moodle. *In:* Marcus-Quinn, A. & Hourigan, T. (eds.) *Handbook on Digital Learning for K-12 Schools.* Cham: Springer International Publishing.

Strayer, J. F. 2012. How learning in an inverted classroom influences cooperation, innovation and task orientation. *Learning Environments Research,* Vol. 15, No. 2 pp. 171-193.

Thai, T. N., De Wever, B. & Valcke, M. 2017. The impact of a flipped classroom design on learning performance in higher education: Looking for the best "blend" of lectures and guiding questions with feedback. *Computers & Education,* Vol. 107, No. pp. 113-126.

The University of Queensland, 2016. The University of Queensland student strategy. Retrieved from https://www.uq.edu.au/teaching-learning/student-strategy/content/front-page

Tucker, B. 2012. The flipped classroom. *Education next,* Vol. 12, No. 1 pp. 82-83.

Young, T. P., Bailey, C. J., Guptill, M., Thorp, A. W. & Thomas, T. L. 2014. The flipped classroom: a modality for mixed asynchronous and synchronous learning in a residency program. *Western Journal of Emergency Medicine,* Vol. 15, No. 7 pp. 938-944.

EARLY NUMERICAL COMPETENCE AND NUMBER LINE TASK PERFORMANCE IN KINDERGARTENERS

Rachele Fanari, Carla Meloni and Davide Massidda
Department of Education, Psychology, Philosophy
University of Cagliari (Italy)

ABSTRACT

This work aims to evaluate the relationship between early numerical competence in kindergarteners and their numerical representations as measured by the number line task (NLT). Thirty-four 5-year-old children participated in the study. Children's early performance on symbolic and non-symbolic numerical tasks was considered to determine which was a better predictor of NLT performance. Children completed an early number competence standardized test comprising symbolic semantic tasks (Arabic digit comparison and Arabic digit linear order), lexical tasks (numbers recognition and numbers reading), and non-symbolic semantic tasks (dots comparison and picture linear order), and the NLT 0–100. The relationship between early number competence (both symbolic and non-symbolic) and performance on the NLT was analyzed using a regression model in which the predictors were identified through a forward selection based on the use of the index BIC (Bayesian Information Criterion). Results show that symbolic number knowledge tasks (Arabic linear digits order and Arabic digits comparison) are the best predictors of performance on the NLT. This suggests that knowledge of the semantics of Arabic digits is more important than non-symbolic quantity knowledge in predicting number line task accuracy among young children. This finding brings additional evidence to the debate on the relationship between non-symbolic numeral knowledge and symbolic number processing.

KEYWORDS

Early numerical competence, number line task, kindergarteners, symbolic number knowledge

1. INTRODUCTION

In numerical cognition research, it is widely believed that numeracy is founded upon an early non-symbolic system of numerical representation in which children implicitly discriminate between smaller and larger collections of objects, and represent and manipulate numerical information without using symbols (see Carey, 2001; Feigenson et al., 2004). Dehaene (1997) calls the cognitive foundation of mathematics number sense, and argues that it is represented by a mental number line, an analog magnitude representation system that serves as a core representation of quantities.

Non-symbolic numerical magnitude knowledge provides potentially useful referents for learning the magnitudes of numbers expressed symbolically. Following this approach, children acquire a symbolic system to represent numbers by repeatedly linking a quantity with its associated numeral, which is then mapped onto a pre-existing, approximate non-symbolic number system, or ANS (Barth et al., 2005; Mundy & Gilmore, 2009; see Carey, 2004 for an alternative view). This mapping idea is mainly supported by studies investigating children with number processing difficulties or developmental dyscalculia who show problems with discriminating both non-symbolic and symbolic numerosities (e.g., Landerl et al., 2009; Mazzocco et al., 2011; Mussolin et al., 2010). Additional empirical evidence supporting the mapping idea comes from studies investigating the distance effect, a phenomenon by which more distant magnitudes (e.g., 2 and 7) are easier to differentiate than neighboring numbers (e.g., 8 and 9) (for a review see Gallistel & Gelman, 2005). This effect has been observed both in symbolic and non-symbolic comparison tasks (Holloway & Ansari, 2009; Rousselle & Noël, 2007).

While the idea that early non-symbolic numerical magnitude knowledge can be the foundation for successive symbolic numerical knowledge is well established, the nature of this relationship is still unclear (see, for instance, Carey, 2001; Siegler, 2016). A number of developmental studies suggest that the link between non-symbolic and symbolic numeral knowledge is weak; some have found that non-symbolic magnitude discrimination is weakly correlated with overall math achievement (see Chen & Li, 2014 and Fazio, et al., 2014 for meta-analysis), while others have found no evidence that training children in non-symbolic numerical magnitude discrimination helps develop knowledge of symbolic magnitudes (Dewind & Brannon, 2012; Park & Brannon, 2014; Wilson, et al., 2006).

The number line task (NLT) proposed by Siegler and Opfer (2003) is commonly used to investigate children's numerical representation ability. The NLT reflects how children represent numerical magnitudes on a mental number line, asking them to translate between numerical and spatial representations without assuming knowledge of specific measurement units; in its classic version, a written or spoken number is presented to a child and he/she is asked to locate its position on a physical number line representing a certain numerical range.

The number line task has been used to measure how children represent numbers and how this representation changes over time. In Geary's words, target number placements on the external number line "that conform to the natural logarithm of the numbers, may reflect dependence on the core system that represents approximate magnitudes (Feigenson et al., 2004; Gallistel & Gelman, 1992), whereas linear placements indicate the child is learning the mathematical number line" (Geary, 2011, p. 4). Berteletti et al. (2010) observed that a transition from approximately logarithmic to approximately linear distributions in children's representations of whole number magnitudes in the NLT takes place between ages 3 and 6.

Following this line of reasoning, NLT performance at a young age should be strongly influenced by non-symbolic knowledge. It is not clear, however, how representations on the number line task relate to general non-symbolic representations.

There are few studies directly investigating the relationship between NLT and early symbolic and non-symbolic numeral knowledge, and the studies that do exist have obtained mixed results. Sasanguie et al. (2013) tested NLT and both symbolic and non-symbolic tasks in the same sample of 6- to 8-year-old children. They found a significant correlation between NLT performance and a symbolic comparison task, but no correlation with non-symbolic tasks. Bertelletti et al. (2010) investigated the NLT response pattern (logarithmic vs. linear) in 3- to 6-year-old children and found that a better knowledge of both symbolic and non-symbolic magnitudes was correlated with a more linear response pattern on the NLT.

In the present study, we examined the relationship between kindergarteners' NLT performance and their symbolic and non-symbolic numeral knowledge. Children were tested on several tasks: symbolic semantic tasks (an Arabic digit comparison task and an Arabic digits linear order task), lexical tasks (numbers recognition task and Arabic numbers reading task), and non-symbolic semantic tasks (dot comparison and a task in which different objects had to be ordered from smaller to bigger) to study which of them is predictive of NLT performance.

This work aims to clarify the nature of numerical representation systems involved in solving the number line task in young children, and to acquire additional evidence on the relationship between non-symbolic and symbolic number processing at an early stage of numerical acquisition. To our knowledge, this is the first work investigating predictors of children's NLT performance exploring both symbolic and non-symbolic abilities. If young children, to carry out the NLT task, draw on their pre-existing non-symbolic representations in addition to their symbolic number knowledge, we would find that both symbolic and non-symbolic abilities predict NLT performance. If the two kinds of knowledge are not strictly linked, as the findings of Sasanguie et al. (2013) suggest for older children, we would expect only one of them to predict good performance on the NLT.

To rule out possible interference and to explore other possible factors influencing NLT performance, we controlled for lexical symbolic numerical knowledge. We expected that semantic number processing would be more predictive of NLT performance than lexical knowledge.

2. METHOD

2.1 Participants

Thirty-four typically developing children were recruited from a public kindergarten in the town of Cagliari, Italy. The participants' average age was 69.24 months (SD = 3.32), range: 63-74 months (16 males and 18 females).

Children with clinically developmental delays (as identified by local health services) were excluded. Both the school and the children's parents agreed to let the students take part in the research study, and signed informed consent forms.

2.2 Procedure

The tests were administered in the month of March, from Monday to Friday, from 8:30 a.m. to 11:45 a.m. in one of the school's classrooms. The children were tested individually by an experienced psychologist. Each session lasted about 20 minutes.

Children's early number skills were evaluated through some of the tasks on the Battery for Numerical Intelligence from 4 to 6 years of age (BIN 4–6) (Molin et al., 2007), a standardized early math test providing norms for Italian children from 4 to 6 years of age. Two tasks assessing lexical competence with numbers (knowledge of numerical symbols) were proposed: a number recognition (NR) task (children were asked to select among three written Arabic numbers in the 1–9 range after hearing one spoken by the researcher) and an Arabic number reading (ANR) task (children were asked to read the Arabic digits in the 1–9 range). In addition, their semantic knowledge of numbers was evaluated though an Arabic digit comparison (ADC) task (children were asked to determine which of two Arabic digits was bigger, range 1–9). Children's ability to order Arabic digits was evaluated using the Arabic digits linear order (ADO) task (children were asked to order by magnitude the numbers written on five cards, range 1–5). To assess non-symbolic numerical knowledge, children were given a dots comparison (DC) task (children were shown two sets of dots with different magnitude and were asked, "Which is more?") and a task in which different objects cards (balloons of various size) had to be ordered from the smaller to the bigger (PO).

After this, the number line task NLT 0–100 was administered (Siegler & Opfer, 2003) using the software PyNLT (Massidda et al., 2015). Participants were shown on a laptop PC screen (14 inches) a 25-cm. horizontal line, marked 0 on the left end and 100 on the right end. In each trial, children were shown an Arabic digit (stimuli: 2 – 3 – 4 – 6 – 18 – 25 – 48 – 67 – 71 – 86, corresponding to Sets A and B for the interval 0–100 in Siegler & Opfer, 2003), and were asked to click with the mouse on the number line where they thought the target number should be placed. Each stimulus appeared twice.

Finally, we assessed children's IQ using the Colored Progressive Matrices test in the Italian standardization (Belacchi et al., 2008) to control for the influence of general intelligence on NLT performance. For all symbolic and non-symbolic numerical competence tasks, the number of correct answers was used as an index. The accuracy of a child's NLT estimates was assessed by calculating for each child her/his percentage of absolute error (PAE, Siegler & Booth, 2004) as follows: |[(Estimate – Estimated Quantity) / Scale of Estimate] *100|. For example, if a child was asked to locate "18" on the 0–100 number line, and placed the mark at the location that corresponded to "10," the percentage of absolute error would be 8% |[(10-18)/100]*100|.

We conducted a preliminary analysis of children's NLT estimation patterns by fitting linear and logarithmic functions to the group means and to each individual child (Siegler & Opfer, 2003). Thirty of the 34 participants were identified as having a logarithmic estimation pattern; the other four showed a linear pattern.

Descriptive statistics of the different experimental measure were calculated: means, standard deviations, and minimum and maximum scores (see Table 1).

Table 1. Descriptive statistics of children's performance in symbolic and non-symbolic tasks (n = 34)

Task type	Task name	Index	Mean	sd	Min	Max
Symbolic task	Number line task (NLT)	Percentage of Absolute Error (PAE)	21.75	9.67	21.75	9.67
	Lexical task	number recognition (NR)	8.82	0.58	7.00	9.00
		number reading (ANR)	8.88	0.41	7.00	9.00
	Semantic task	comparison of Arabic digits (ADC)	10.68	0.81	8.00	11.00
	Linear order task	Arabic digits linear order (ADO)	4.15	1.88	0.00	5.00
Non-symbolic task	Semantic task	Dots comparison (DC)	9.79	0.41	9.00	10.00
	Linear order task	Objects linear order (PO)	5.41	2.09	1.00	7.00

We examined the relations between symbolic and non-symbolic tasks and NLT performance using the correlation index Pearson's r (see Table 2). Our analysis shows a significant negative correlation between NLT performance and the comparison of Arabic digits (ADC), r (34) = -.443, p < .01, and a significant negative correlation between NLT performance and the Arabic digits linear order task (ADO), r (34) = -.601, p < .001; in other words, the better the child is at deciding which Arabic digit is larger or smaller and at ordering digits by magnitude, the more accurate were her/his estimations on the NLT. Finally, a strong correlation between the two lexical symbolic tasks (number reading and number recognition) was found, r (34) = .681, p < .001. No other significant correlations were found.

Table 2. Spearman's *rho* (top-right half) and Pearson's *r* (low-left half) correlation between symbolic and non-symbolic early numerical competence tasks. PAE: percentage of absolute error; NR: numbers recognition; ANR: numbers reading; ADC: comparison of Arabic digits; ADO: Arabic digits linear order; DC: dots comparison; PO: objects linear order

	PAE	NR	ANR	ADC	ADO	DC	PO
PAE		-0.333	-0.251	-0.331	-0.451 **	-0.019	0.101
NR	-0.131		0.645 ***	0.103	0.136	-0.158	-0.034
ANR	-0.075	0.681 ***		-0.143	0.152	-0.158	-0.161
ADC	-0.443 **	0.004	-0.119		0.207	0.112	0.002
ADO	-0.601 ***	0.137	0.260	0.213		0.157	0.205
DC	-0.150	-0.158	-0.149	-0.024	0.158		0.182
PO	-0.012	-0.139	-0.154	-0.152	0.108	0.172	

*** $p < .001$; ** $p < .01$; * $p < .05$.

Moreover, we examined the relationship between gender, age, and IQ and performance to exclude the possibility that correlations were due to differences in gender, age, or general ability. To do this, we performed a multiple regression analysis with the NLT percentage of absolute error (PAE) as dependent variable and gender, age, and IQ as predictors. These three predictors together explain only 2% of variance; thus we conclude that these variables did not influence NLT performance.

Finally, the relationship between NLT performance (with the PAE as dependent variable) and both early symbolic number competence (semantic, linear order, and lexical tasks) and early non-symbolic number competence (dot comparison and objects linear order) as predictors was examined adapting a regression model in which the predictors were identified through a forward selection based on the use of the Bayesian Information Criterion (BIC) index (Schwarz, 1978), which selected the best model from a Bayesian perspective.

Our results showed that in the best final selected model, NLT accuracy was predicted by the Arabic digits linear order (ADO) task with β = -.53, p <.001, and by the comparison of Arabic digits (ADC) task with β = -.33, p = .019 (see Figure 1), which together explained 46% of the variance in performance on the NLT, while the other investigated skills were not predictive of NLT performance.

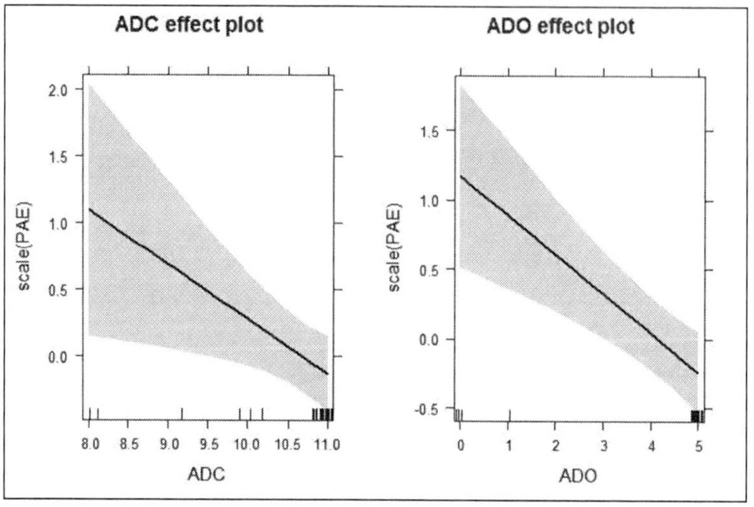

Figure 1. Effects reported in multiple regression with the dependent variable PAE in the vertical axes and the predictors Arabic Digits Comparison (ADC) and Arabic Digits Order (ADO) in the horizontal axes. The gray shadows represent the 95% confidence intervals

3. DISCUSSION AND CONCLUSIONS

The NLT is extensively used in research on numerical cognition because children's performance on this task has been identified as a predictor of future mathematics skills (e.g. Booth & Siegler, 2006; Booth & Siegler, 2008; Geary et al., 2008; Geary, 2011; Siegler, 2016). Moreover, several authors (Siegler & Opfer, 2003; Boot & Siegler, 2006; Siegler & Booth, 2004; Siegler, 2016) have considered the change over time in pattern performance on the NLT (linear vs. logarithmic) as an indicator of the shape of the mental number line, the analogical core representation of quantities hypothesized by Dehaene (1997).

In our work, we explored the ability to represent numbers on a physical number line in 5-year-old children, with the aim of determining how NLT estimation accuracy is related to both general non-symbolic representation of quantities and to symbolic number knowledge. We decided to explore the issue in kindergarteners since in children of this age, the symbolic system is starting to form but is still closely related to the early non-symbolic system.

To study the issue, the 0–100 NLT was proposed to kindergarteners. Moreover, symbolic semantic tasks (comparison of Arabic digits and linear ordering of Arabic digits) and non-symbolic tasks (dot comparison and linear object ordering) were administered to the participants. To control for the influence of numerical symbol knowledge, two lexical tasks were also administered (a number recognition task and number reading).

The results of our analysis show that kindergarten children's performance on the NLT depends exclusively on symbolic knowledge; together, performance on the comparison of Arabic digits task and the Arabic digits linear order task explained 46% of the variance in NLT performance, while non-symbolic numeral knowledge tasks did not predict NLT performance.

Although our study is the first, to our knowledge, to investigate NLT predictors among children in this age range, other studies on younger children have reported correlations between symbolic and non-symbolic tasks and NLT. For example, Berteletti et al. (2010) found that in 3- to 6-year-old children, both symbolic and non-symbolic magnitude knowledge were correlated with a linear NLT response pattern. Our results are not in line with this finding. In the Berteletti et al. study, however, the type of number line representation (logarithmic vs. linear) was considered in the correlation analysis, whereas we used PAE scores. This may explain the difference between our findings and those of Berteletti et al.

Our results are instead in line with the findings of Sasanguie et al. (2013) that in older children there is a correlation between NLT accuracy (PAE) and performance on a symbolic comparison task but not between NLT accuracy and performance on non-symbolic tasks such as magnitude comparison.

Our data, gathered from young children who have not yet begun formal schooling, show that the NLT is solved mainly based on symbolic abilities and suggest that, at least at this age, NLT performance is loosely dependent on the core system that represents approximate magnitudes, despite the fact that children were tested on an unfamiliar number range and that the vast majority of them (30 out of 34) showed a logarithmic pattern of response.

Moreover, we found that number lexical knowledge did not predict NLT performance. Thus, it seems that the ability to identify the numerical symbol corresponding to a spoken numeral or to correctly read an Arabic digit are not crucial to the NLT, whereas semantic knowledge about the meaning of a numeral is necessary.

A further interesting finding emerging from our analysis is that the two non-symbolic quantity knowledge tasks are not correlated with any of the tests exploring symbolic number knowledge. This result seems in line with studies that have considered the influence of symbolic and non- symbolic quantitative tasks on math skills in kindergarteners. For instance, in a study on 5-year-old children, Sasanguie et al. (2013) found no correlation between symbolic and non-symbolic comparison tasks. Sasanguie et al. (2012) investigated the effects of a dot comparison task and a symbolic numbers comparison task on math performance in kindergarteners, first graders, second graders, and sixth graders. Only the comparison of symbolic numbers predicted math performance in 5-year-olds. Another study by Sasanguie et al. (2014) found no association between the accuracy of the performance on a dots comparison task in 5-year-old children and the performance in a symbolic comparison task presented to the same children six months later.

The present study covered a little investigated area of numerical development yielding to new and interesting results. Its exploratory nature and relatively small sample size do not permit us to draw firm conclusions on the relationship between non-symbolic and symbolic number processing, or on the early math knowledge underlying NLT performance, but our findings suggest that symbolic knowledge about quantities and numerals may play a stronger than expected role in the stage of development in which children are not yet very familiar with culturally determined numeric symbols. Further investigation on these topics should be undertaken. In particular, a better knowledge of early magnitude estimation ability and its underlying mechanism will be critical for better understanding important stages in numerical development, such as learning to connect symbolic numbers to their non-symbolic referents or accurately representing the magnitude of rational numbers, both of which are considered crucial in recent theories on numerical development (e.g., Siegler, 2016).

ACKNOWLEDGEMENTS

This study was supported by Cagliari University (Italy). The authors want to thank the principal of the school where data collection took place. Special thanks go to the children, families, and kindergarten teachers who participated in the study.

REFERENCES

Barth, H. et al., 2005. Abstract number and arithmetic in preschool children. *Proceedings of the National Academy of Sciences of the United States of America*, 102(39), 14116-14121.

Belacchi, C. et al., 2008. *CPM coloured progressive matrices: standardizzazione italiana: manuale*. Giunti OS, Firenze, Italy.

Berteletti, I. et al., 2010. Numerical estimation in preschoolers. *Developmental Psychology*, 46(2), pp. 545-551

Booth, J. L., & Siegler, R. S., 2006. Developmental and individual differences in pure numerical estimation. *Developmental Psychology*, 42(1), pp. 189-201

Booth, J. L., & Siegler, R. S., 2008. Numerical magnitude representations influence arithmetic learning. *Child Development*, *79*(4), pp. 1016-1031.

Carey, S. 2004. Bootstrapping & the origin of concepts. *Daedalus*, 133(1), pp. 59-68.

Carey, S., 2001. Cognitive foundations of arithmetic: Evolution and ontogenisis. *Mind & Language*, 16(1), pp. 37-55.

Chen, Q., & Li, J., 2014. Association between individual differences in nonsymbolic number acuity and math performance: a meta-analysis. *Acta Psychologica*, *148*, pp. 163–172. doi:10.1016/j.actpsy.2014.01.016

Dehaene, S., 1997. *The number sense: How the mind creates mathematics*. Oxford: Oxford University Press.

Dewind, N.K., & Brannon, E.M., 2012. Malleability of the approximate number system: effects of feedback and training. *Frontiers in Human Neuroscience*, 6(68). doi:10.3389/ fnhum.2012.00068

Fazio, L.K. et al., 2014. Relations of different types of numerical magnitude representations to each other and to mathematics achievement. *Journal of Experimental Child Psychology*, pp 123, 53–72.doi:10.1016/j.jecp.2014.01.013

Feigenson, L., et al., 2004. Core systems of number. *Trends in Cognitive Sciences*, 8, pp. 307–314. doi:10.1016/j.tics.2004.05.002

Gallistel, C. R., & Gelman, R. 1992. Preverbal and verbal counting and computation. *Cognition*, 44(1), pp. 43-74.

Gallistel, C. R., & Gelman, R., 2005. *Mathematical Cognition*. Cambridge University Press.

Geary, D. C., 2011. Cognitive predictors of achievement growth in mathematics: a 5-year longitudinal study. *Developmental psychology*, 47(6), pp. 1539-1552.

Geary, D. C., et al., 2008. Development of number line representations in children with mathematical learning disability. *Developmental neuropsychology*, 33(3), pp. 277-299.

Holloway, I. D., & Ansari, D., 2009. Mapping numerical magnitudes onto symbols: The numerical distance effect and individual differences in children's mathematics achievement. *Journal of Experimental Child Psychology*, 103(1), pp. 17-29.

Landerl, K., et al.,. 2009. Dyslexia and dyscalculia: Two learning disorders with different cognitive profiles. *Journal of Experimental Child Psychology*, 103(3), pp. 309-324.

Massidda, D. et al., 2015. *An open source software application to study numerical representations in children and adults.* The 14th European Congress of Psychology -ECP- Milan, Italy 7-10 July 2015

Mazzocco, M. M. et al., 2011. Preschoolers' precision of the approximate number system predicts later school mathematics performance. *PLoS one*, 6(9), e23749.

Molin, A. et al., 2007. *BIN 4-6, Batteria per la valutazione della Intelligenza Numerica in bambini dai 4 ai 6 anni.* Erickson, Trento.

Mundy, E., & Gilmore, C. K., 2009. Children's mapping between symbolic and nonsymbolic representations of number. *Journal of Experimental Child Psychology*, 103(4), pp. 490-502.

Mussolin, C. et al., 2010. Symbolic and nonsymbolic number comparison in children with and without dyscalculia. *Cognition*, 115(1), pp. 10-25.

Noël, M. P., & Rousselle, L., 2011. Developmental changes in the profiles of dyscalculia: an explanation based on a double exact-and-approximate number representation model. *Frontiers in Human Neuroscience*, 5, 165. doi.org/10.3389/fnhum.2011.00165

Park, J., & Brannon, E. M., 2014. Improving arithmetic performance with number sense training: An investigation of underlying mechanism. *Cognition*, 133(1), pp. 188-200.

Rousselle, L., & Noël, M. P., 2007. Basic numerical skills in children with mathematics learning disabilities: A comparison of symbolic vs non-symbolic number magnitude processing. *Cognition*, 102(3), pp. 361-395.

Sasanguie, D. et al., 2012. Association between basic numerical abilities and mathematics achievement. *British Journal of Developmental Psychology*, 30(2), pp. 344-357.

Sasanguie, D. et al., 2014. The approximate number system is not predictive for symbolic number processing in kindergarteners. *The Quarterly Journal of Experimental Psychology*, 67(2), pp. 271-280.

Sasanguie, D. et al., 2013. Approximate number sense, symbolic number processing, or number–space mappings: What underlies mathematics achievement?. *Journal of Experimental Child Psychology*, 114(3), pp. 418-431.

Schwarz, G., 1978. Estimating the dimension of a model. *The Annals of Statistics*, 6, pp. 461-464.

Siegler, R. S., & Opfer, J. E., 2003. The development of numerical estimation: Evidence for multiple representations of numerical quantity. *Psychological Science*, 14(3), pp. 237-250.

Siegler, R.S., & Booth, J.L., 2004. Development of numerical estimation in young children. *Child Development*, 75, pp. 428– 444. doi:10.1111/j.1467-8624.2004.00684.x

Siegler, R.S., 2016. Magnitude knowledge: the common core of numerical development. *Developmental science*, 19(3), pp. 341-361.

Wilson, A.J. et al., 2006. An open trial assessment of 'The Number Race', an adaptive computer game for remediation of dyscalculia. *Behavioral and Brain Functions*, 2, available at: http:// www.behavioralandbrainfunctions.com/content/2/1/20.

EXPLORING THE IMPACT OF THE INFORMATIONAL VALUE OF FEEDBACK CHOICES ON PERFORMANCE OUTCOMES IN AN ONLINE ASSESSMENT GAME

Maria Cutumisu
Department of Educational Psychology, University of Alberta, Canada

ABSTRACT

This paper examines the impact of the informational value of feedback choices on students' performance, their choice to revise, and the time they spend designing posters and reading feedback in an assessment game. Choices to seek confirmatory or critical feedback and to revise posters in a poster design task were collected from a hundred and six Grade 8 students from a middle school in California via Posterlet, a computer-based assessment. Results show that critical uninformative feedback is associated with performance, critical informative feedback is associated with students' learning strategies (i.e., willingness to revise and feedback dwell time), while confirmatory informative feedback is negatively associated with performance and learning strategies. This research has implications for designing the informational content of feedback messages to support student performance on an open-ended design task.

KEYWORDS

Feedback, assessment, critical, informative, game, performance

1. INTRODUCTION

Feedback is an important aspect of learning performance, as it provides information about a learner's task performance (Hattie, 1999; Hattie & Timperley, 2007). However, despite a large body of feedback research, the mechanisms of feedback are still not well understood. For example, different feedback types (e.g., critical and confirmatory, immediate and delayed, etc.) have yielded mixed results for learning (Kulik & Kulik, 1988) and a meta-analysis found that feedback was even detrimental for performance in a third of the studies analyzed (Kluger & DeNisi, 1998). Feedback effectiveness is further influenced by individual differences, such as fixed versus growth mindset (Dweck & Leggett, 1988). Particularly, researchers differentiated between non-generic and generic feedback based on the informational value of feedback and they indicated that "non-generic feedback refers to a specific event and implies that performance is malleable, while generic feedback implies that task performance reflects an inherent ability" (Chiviacowsky & Drews, 2014).

The *information-processing* learning theory focuses on the individuals' cognitive ability to use the feedback information they encounter during a learning task not only to reinforce correct answers but also to correct errors (Hattie & Gan, 2011). In the *response certitude* model, instructional feedback messages include two components: verification and elaboration (Kulhavy & Stock, 1989). Verification feedback indicates whether the answer is right or wrong, while elaboration feedback aids the learner in error correction by including indications on how to correct errors or why an answer is correct (Hattie & Gan, 2011). There is a paucity of studies investigating the impact of non-generic elaboration feedback versus generic feedback on learning. Studies show that students perceive generic feedback as impersonal (Bray, 2016). Moreover, both praise and generic negative feedback were found to be detrimental to performance. In a study where 10-year old children (n = 40) kicked a soccer-ball at a target, the type of feedback (i.e., generic, such as "You are a great soccer player" versus non-generic, such as "The last kicks were great") was used to predict motor performance and learning. In their first experiment, researchers found that providing participants with generic feedback resulted in worse performance than providing non-generic feedback, after both groups received negative feedback (Chiviacowsky & Drews, 2014). In their second experiment that focused on the results of a retention task performed one day after practicing a throwing task, researchers showed that participants who received non-generic feedback during the performance significantly outperformed participants in the generic feedback group, after receiving negative feedback.

The current study focuses on the role of the informational value of feedback when students choose between confirmatory and critical feedback. Thus, the study examines the relation between the informational value and valence of feedback choices and students' task performance, choice to revise, and time spent reading feedback and designing posters. Here, we consider two types of feedback: informative elaboration feedback (i.e., non-generic, task-specific feedback) and uninformative feedback (i.e., generic, non-task specific feedback). Particularly, the study poses the following research questions:

1) Is informative feedback associated with in-game performance?
2) Is informative feedback associated with the choice to revise posters?
3) Is informative feedback associated with feedback dwell time or with time on task?

The remainder of this paper reviews the relevant literature, it describes the Posterlet assessment game that collects students' feedback and revision choices during a poster design task, and it presents empirical evidence that the informational feedback value impacts students' performance, choice to revise, and time spent reading feedback and designing posters.

2. LITERATURE REVIEW

Choice-Based Assessments. Posterlet is a choice-based assessment game (Schwartz & Arena, 2013) that draws on constructivist assessments (Bransford & Schwartz, 1999) and that focuses on the learning processes in which students engage when designing a poster. It collects students' choices to seek critical (i.e., negative) or confirmatory (i.e., positive) feedback and it enables the exploration of the impact of students' choices on performance. Here, the informational value of students' feedback choices is explored for the first time, with a focus on its impact on performance, choice to revise, and the time students spend reading their feedback.

Performance and Feedback Value. Informative feedback is a crucial factor in developing mastery (Ericsson, Krampe, & Tesch-Römer, 1993). Moreover, feedback research reveals that praise can be harmful for performance when it is directed to the student, rather than to the task (Hattie & Timperley, 2007). Previous research showed that choosing critical feedback was associated with better learning performance in and outside of the assessment environment (Cutumisu, Blair, Chin, & Schwartz, 2015; Cutumisu, Blair, Chin, & Schwartz, 2016). This research takes a step further and hypothesizes that students perform better when they encounter critical informative feedback.

Revision and Feedback Value. Although feedback from an expert is one of the most important factors in deliberate practice, feedback is most effective when learners apply it to revise and improve their performance (Ericsson et al., 1993; Kulik & Kulik, 1988). Despite research showing that feedback information is rarely used in revision of work (Carless, 2006), revision was strongly associated with willingness to choose critical feedback across many studies (Cutumisu et al., 2015; Cutumisu et al., 2016). In this paper, the relation between the informational value of feedback and students' choice to revise is explored for the first time.

Feedback Dwell Time, Value, and Time on Task. Previous research shows that the more the students choose to seek critical feedback, the more they dwell on feedback (Cutumisu et al., 2015). The current study aims to discern between the impact of informative and uninformative critical feedback on the time students take to read their feedback and design their posters.

The Posterlet Assessment Game. The Posterlet game tracks two learning choices students make while creating posters: the choice to seek confirmatory (positive) and critical (negative) feedback about their posters and the choice to revise their posters. On every game round, students choose either confirmatory or critical feedback from three virtual characters and choose whether to revise their poster. The feedback messages generated by the game were designed to alternate between informative (confirmatory: "Your poster helps people know where to go." or critical: "Where is the Fall Fair going to be?") and uninformative (confirmatory: "I like fairs" or critical "I don't like fairs."). This study investigates which type of feedback is associated with learning outcomes, depending on the learner's choices between confirmatory and critical feedback. For instance, if the student makes two same-valence choices on a poster, the first choice is always informative and the second is always uninformative. The game also produces a poster score as the number of tickets sold by each poster booth. An overall poster performance score is computed by adding the poster scores on each game round. More details about Posterlet are provided in prior work (Cutumisu et al., 2016).

3. METHODS

3.1 Participants and Procedures

Participants were n=106 Grade 8 students (60 female, 46 male), ranging in age from 13 to 14 years, from a public middle school in California. All students had the same science teacher and they played the Posterlet game in May 2015 designing three posters (M=14.76 minutes, SD=4.07) individually, as one of the assessments administered that day. Students who did not provide consent (n=9) or did not complete all posters (n=8) were excluded from analyses. Thus, the analyses included n=89 students (50 females).

3.2 Measures

Choices. *Critical Feedback* measures students' willingness to make "I don't like…" choices, ranging from 0 (no critical feedback chosen) to 9 (only critical feedback chosen). Feedback is divided into two orthogonal categories: valence (Confirmatory or Critical) by informational value (Informative or Uninformative). *Revision* measures students' willingness to revise their posters, ranging from 0 (no poster revised) to 3 (all posters revised). *Critical Informative Feedback* measures the number of informative critical feedback messages read by each participant (e.g., "You need to tell them what day the fair is."), while *Critical Uninformative Feedback* measures the number of uninformative critical feedback messages read by each participant (e.g., "I don't really like fairs"). Students chose the feedback valence (confirmatory or critical), not the feedback value (informative or uninformative). Critical Feedback is the sum of the Critical Informative and Critical Uninformative Feedback. *Confirmatory Feedback* is a complementary measure to Critical Feedback (i.e., 9 - Critical Feedback). Thus, *Confirmatory Informative Feedback* measures the number of informative confirmatory feedback messages (e.g., "It's good you told them what day the fair is."), while *Confirmatory Uninformative Feedback* measures the number of uninformative confirmatory feedback messages encountered (e.g., "I like fairs"). Confirmatory Feedback is the sum of Confirmatory Informative and Confirmatory Uninformative Feedback. Choices were measured by round and across the game.

In-game Poster Performance. Posterlet generates a *Poster Quality* score based on 21 design principles reflecting a student's poster performance across all rounds of the game. The quality of each poster is the sum of the scores for each of the 21 features: 1 if a feature is always used correctly on a poster, 0 if a feature is not included on the poster, and -1 if a feature is used incorrectly on a poster. Poster Quality measures the sum of the quality of students' posters by game round: *Poster Quality 1*, *Poster Quality 2*, and *Poster Quality 3*.

Feedback Dwell Time. *Feedback Dwell Time* measures the amount of time students spent reading feedback across the game. The amount of time students spent reading feedback on each game round was also computed as *Feedback Dwell Time 1, Feedback Dwell Time 2, and Feedback Dwell Time 3*, respectively.

Time on Task. *Design Duration* measures the time students take to design posters. It sums the time spent designing posters on each game round: *Design Duration 1*, *Design Duration 2*, and *Design Duration 3*.

4. RESULTS

4.1 Is Informative Feedback Associated with In-Game Performance?

Spearman correlation analyses were conducted to explore the association of the informative and uninformative feedback with poster performance by feedback valence (confirmatory or critical), as these variables were not normally distributed. Results showed that Poster Quality was positively associated with Critical Uninformative Feedback but not with Critical Informative Feedback, and negatively associated with both informative and uninformative confirmatory feedback, as shown in Table 1. Thus, the more the students engage with critical uninformative feedback, the better their posters are. More importantly, the more they engage with confirmatory feedback (informative or uninformative), the worse they perform on their posters.

Table 1. Correlations between performance and feedback information overall and by round ($^{***}p < .001$, $^{**}p < .01$)

Measure (n=89)	Critical Informative Feedback	Critical Uninformative Feedback	Confirmatory Informative Feedback	Confirmatory Uninformative Feedback
Poster Quality	.09	**.52*****	**-.36*****	**-.32****
Poster Quality Round 1	.20	.16	-.20	-.16
Poster Quality Round 2	.08	**.38*****	**-.29****	-.17
Poster Quality Round 3	-.09	**.50*****	**-.27****	**-.34****

Analyses by game round revealed that, on each of the second and third game rounds, poster performance (Poster Quality 2 and Poster Quality 3) correlated with Critical Uninformative Feedback and inversely with Confirmatory Informative Feedback, as shown in Table 1, consistent with the findings across the game. No correlations were found on the first round, perhaps because students were engaging in exploration and had not yet discovered a strategy. These results indicate that better poster performance is associated positively with both types of critical feedback (significantly only with critical uninformative feedback) and negatively with both types of confirmatory feedback (significantly only with confirmatory informative feedback).

A standard linear regression analysis was conducted to determine if informative and uninformative feedback messages were individual predictors of Poster Quality for each feedback valence. A model composed of critical informative and critical uninformative feedback predicted Poster Quality [$F(2,86) = 15.92$, $p < .001$, $R^2 = .27$, Adj. $R^2 = .25$], but only critical uninformative feedback ($\beta = .54$, $B = 4.82$, $p < .001$, $r = .52$, partial = .50, part = .50) was an individual predictor on Poster Quality, while critical informative feedback ($\beta = -.06$, $B = -.62$, $p = .52$, $r = .15$, partial = -.07, part = -.06) was not. In contrast, a model composed of confirmatory informative and uninformative feedback significantly predicted Poster Quality [$F(2,86) = 8.6$, $p < .001$, $R^2 = .17$, Adj. $R^2 = .15$], but confirmatory informative feedback ($\beta = -.24$, $B = -2.1$, $p = .07$, $r = -.38$, partial = -.19, part = -.18) and confirmatory uninformative feedback ($\beta = -.20$, $B = -2.55$, $p = .13$, $r = -.37$, partial = -.16, part = -.15) were not individual predictors. Thus, out of all types of feedback examined, critical uninformative feedback is the best predictor of Poster Quality.

4.2 Is Informative Feedback Associated with the Choice to Revise Posters?

Next, the study aimed to discern between the impact of the informative and uninformative value of critical and confirmatory feedback on students' choice to revise. Table 2 shows the average critical feedback, critical informative feedback, and critical uninformative feedback for the students who did not revise any of the three posters and for the students who revised at least one of the three posters, respectively.

Table 2. Average and standard deviation of critical feedback by informational value and revision

Choice (n=89)	Critical Feedback	Critical Informative Feedback	Critical Uninformative Feedback
No Revision (n=11)	4.27 (2.76)	2.55 (1.75)	1.73 (1.62)
Revision (n=78)	6.01 (1.86)	3.45 (1.04)	2.56 (1.21)

Results show that students who choose more critical feedback also revise their posters more. Students who encounter more critical informative feedback tend to revise more, as do students who encounter more critical uninformative feedback. Table 3 shows the equivalent information for confirmatory feedback. Conversely, students who encounter more confirmatory feedback tend to revise less. This low revising trend persisted for students who encountered more confirmatory informative and uninformative feedback. Table 4 shows the average critical and confirmatory feedback broken down by informational value. Results show that, on average, students chose more critical than confirmatory feedback across the game.

Table 3. Average and standard deviation of confirmatory feedback by informational value and revision

Choice (n=89)	Confirmatory Feedback	Confirmatory Informative Feedback	Confirmatory Uninformative Feedback
No Revision (n=11)	4.73 (2.76)	3.18 (1.83)	1.55 (1.13)
Revision (n=78)	2.99 (1.86)	2.18 (1.21)	.81 (.84)

Table 4. Average and standard deviation of critical and confirmatory feedback overall and by informational value

Choice (n=89)	All Feedback	Informative Feedback	Uninformative Feedback
Critical Feedback	5.80 (2.06)	3.34 (1.18)	2.46 (1.29)
Confirmatory Feedback	3.20 (2.06)	2.30 (1.33)	.90 (.90)

Spearman correlation analyses investigated which type of feedback (informative or uninformative) was associated with Revision for each feedback valence (confirmatory or critical). Across the game, Revision was positively associated with Critical Informative Feedback and with Critical Uninformative Feedback, but negatively associated with Confirmatory Informative Feedback and Confirmatory Uninformative Feedback, as shown in Table 5. Moreover, on each game round, Revision was positively associated with Critical Informative Feedback and negatively associated with Confirmatory Informative Feedback.

Table 5. Correlations between revision and feedback value overall and by round ($^{***}p<.001$, $^{**}p<.01$, $^{*}p<.05$)

Choice (n=89)	Critical Informative Feedback	Critical Uninformative Feedback	Confirmatory Informative Feedback	Confirmatory Uninformative Feedback
Revision	**.32****	**.39*****	**-.32****	**-.42*****
Revision 1	**.24***	**.29****	**-.24***	**-.29****
Revision 2	**.24***	-.03	-.18	-.04
Revision 3	**.32****	**.41*****	**-.34****	**-.51*****

A standard linear regression analysis was conducted to determine whether informative and uninformative feedback messages were individual predictors of revision, for each of the two feedback valences, critical and confirmatory. A model composed of critical informative and critical uninformative feedback significantly predicted Revision [$F(2,86) = 8.84$, $p < .001$, $R^2 = .17$, Adjusted $R^2 = .15$] and both critical informative ($\beta = .24$, $B = .21$, $p = .02$, $r = .34$, partial = .24, part = .23) and uninformative ($\beta = .25$, $B = .20$, $p = .02$, $r = .35$, partial = .24, part = .23) feedback were individual and medium predictors of Revision. In contrast, a model composed of confirmatory informative and confirmatory uninformative feedback significantly predicted Revision [$F(2,86) = 10.01$, $p < .001$, $R^2 = .19$, Adjusted $R^2 = .17$], but only confirmatory uninformative feedback ($\beta = -.35$, $B = -.40$, $p < .01$, $r = -.43$, partial = -.28, part = -.26) significantly and negatively predicted Revision, while confirmatory informative feedback was not a significant negative predictor ($\beta = -.11$, $B = -.08$, $p = .42$, $r = -.35$, partial = -.09, part = -.08).

4.3 Is Informative Feedback Associated with Dwell Time or Time on Task?

Finally, Spearman correlation analyses were conducted to investigate whether informative and uninformative feedback messages were differentially associated with the time students spent reading feedback, as well as with the time students spent designing their posters (i.e., time on task). We examined closely the last round of the game, when students presumably had found a stable learning strategy, judging by the significant differences from the first to the second round of the game in poster performance but a non-significant difference between the last two rounds of the game.

On round 3, the amount of time students took to read feedback was associated positively with Critical Informative Feedback and negatively with Confirmatory Uninformative Feedback, as shown in Table 6. This indicates that the more the students encounter critical informative feedback, the more time they spend reading feedback on the last round of the game. Conversely, the more time the students encounter confirmatory uninformative feedback, the less time they spend reading feedback on the last game round.

Table 6. Correlations between feedback dwell time and feedback value overall and by round ($^*p$<.05)

Choice (n=89)	Critical Informative Feedback	Critical Uninformative Feedback	Confirmatory Informative Feedback	Confirmatory Uninformative Feedback
Feedback Dwell Time	-.16	-.18	.14	**.24***
Feedback Dwell Time 1	-.11	**-.24***	.11	**.24***
Feedback Dwell Time 2	-.14	-.11	.14	.13
Feedback Dwell Time 3	**.22***	.11	-.13	**-.22***

The association between students' time on task (i.e., the amount of time students took to design each poster) and the informational value of critical and confirmatory feedback was also examined. Results shown in Table 7 revealed that, although significant only for the second round of the game, students' time on task was positively associated with critical feedback (both informative and uninformative) and negatively with confirmatory feedback (both informative and uninformative).

Table 7. Correlations between poster design duration and feedback value overall and by round ($^*p$<.05)

Choice (n=89)	Critical Informative Feedback	Critical Uninformative Feedback	Confirmatory Informative Feedback	Confirmatory Uninformative Feedback
Design Duration	.02	.05	-.10	.005
Design Duration 1	.15	-.002	-.15	.002
Design Duration 2	**.23***	**.21***	**-.27***	**-.22***
Design Duration 3	.08	.12	-.11	-.12

5. DISCUSSION, LIMITATIONS, AND FUTURE WORK

Performance and Feedback Value. The game did not provide a tutorial, thus, the first round of the game was an opportunity for students to explore the digital environment. Results revealed that the more the students encountered critical uninformative feedback, the better they performed on the poster design tasks. Although the association between poster performance and critical informative feedback was positive, it did not reach significance. When the individual contributions of the informative and uninformative feedback for each feedback valence in predicting poster performance were examined, critical uninformative feedback emerged as the only significant predictor. It is surprising that uninformative critical feedback proved to be more helpful for performance than informative critical feedback. One possible explanation is that students strive to identify the shortcomings of their poster when they encounter critical uninformative feedback, thus they work harder on subsequent posters. Results also showed that the less confirmatory informative feedback students encountered, the better they performed on the poster design tasks. This result supports previous findings that confirmatory feedback, and especially praise or confirmatory uninformative feedback, may be harmful for performance (Hattie & Timperley, 2007). This result also suggests that students already know the information provided by the confirmatory informative feedback, thus they may only improve their poster designs when they read critical informative feedback that fills a gap in their poster design knowledge. This hypothesis is supported by the findings related to revision and the informative value of feedback showing that the more the students encounter critical (informative and uninformative) feedback and the less they encounter confirmatory (informative and uninformative) feedback, the more they revise their posters. However, it could be that students who usually revise their work are more drawn to seeking critical rather than confirmatory feedback. Taken together, these results warrant further investigation, because when examining the associations over each of the last two rounds of the game between the different types of feedback and feedback dwell time, as well as time on task, we found that when students encountered more critical informative rather than uninformative feedback, they tended to spend more time reading the feedback and designing posters. This suggests that critical informative feedback may be more important than both critical uninformative feedback and confirmatory feedback, which was our initial hypothesis. A follow-up study will collect more data and will include a learning post-test, which was not possible for this study due to the limited time allotted for this assessment among a battery of assessments administered that day, to further clarify the relation between critical informative feedback and performance.

Revision and Feedback Value. Findings showed that the more the students encountered critical feedback (both informative and uninformative) and the less they encountered confirmatory feedback (both informative and uninformative), the more they chose to revise. Overall, students chose more than the average amount of critical feedback and less than the average amount of confirmatory feedback across the game. Due to the design of the informational value of feedback, students encountered a higher amount of informative than uninformative feedback for each feedback valence. The results broken down by students who revised at least once and students who never revised showed that students who more frequently chose critical than confirmatory feedback also revised more, supporting prior research (Cutumisu et al., 2015; Cutumisu et al., 2016). Conversely, students who more frequently chose confirmatory feedback also revised less. This result indicates that, for revision, the valence of feedback may be more important than the informational value of feedback, especially as critical and confirmatory informative feedback messages were designed to be equivalent in informational value and length in Posterlet. Moreover, this result was consistent on each game round as well. Thus, within the same feedback valence, the informative and uninformative feedback messages seem to be equally important. When examining the individual contributions of the informative and uninformative feedback for each feedback valence in predicting revision, informative and uninformative feedback messages were equivalent, significant, and unique predictors of revision for both critical and confirmatory feedback, respectively. These results show that the choice to revise is impacted by the valence of the feedback choice more than by its informational value. Critical feedback seems to determine students to try harder and revise their work (e.g., fix mistakes pointed out by the feedback), regardless of its specificity.

Feedback Dwell Time, Time on Task, and Feedback Value. On the last game round, findings indicate that the more the students encountered critical informative feedback and the less they encountered confirmatory uninformative feedback, the more time they spent reading feedback. Overall, this result is consistent with previous research showing that the more the students choose to seek critical feedback, the more they dwell on feedback (Cutumisu et al., 2015). This result suggests that, yet again, it is the critical informative feedback that is associated with better outcomes. The finding also suggests that the more the students encounter confirmatory uninformative feedback, the less attention they pay to this type of feedback. Results also showed that students' time on task was positively associated with critical feedback (both informative and uninformative) and negatively with confirmatory feedback (both informative and uninformative), although significantly only on the second round of the game. Taken together, these results support the findings regarding performance and revision and highlight the importance of critical over confirmatory feedback.

Limitations and Future Work. In Posterlet, students are given a choice regarding the valence of their feedback, but not regarding the informational value of feedback. The feedback system embedded in the Posterlet game is designed to alternate between informative and uninformative feedback of the same valence. For example, when choosing three pieces of critical feedback on a poster, the student may encounter two critical informative feedback messages and one critical uninformative. Moreover, if the student makes no design mistakes and chooses critical feedback, uninformative critical feedback is presented instead of critical informative feedback. Thus, a future experimental study will control both the valence and the informative value of the feedback students choose. In that case, would students choose more informative or more uninformative feedback and would their prefer critical over confirmatory feedback? Consequently, what would the students' performance be in each of these cases? Lastly, a follow-up study will explore the relation between feedback value and other factors, such as academic achievement and mindset.

6. CONCLUSIONS

The paper examined the impact of the informational value of feedback on students' performance, willingness to revise, and time spent reading feedback and designing posters. Findings showed that students' performance was positively associated with the critical uninformative feedback that they encountered and negatively associated with the confirmatory informative feedback that they encountered. Moreover, students' choice to revise was positively associated with the critical informative and uninformative feedback that they encountered and negatively associated with the confirmatory uninformative that they encountered. On the last round of the game, findings indicate that the more time the students spent reading feedback, the more critical informative feedback and the less confirmatory uninformative feedback they encountered on that round. The data provide evidence that critical uninformative feedback is helpful for performance, critical informative feedback is helpful for revision and time on task, and confirmatory informative feedback may be detrimental for performance, for students' willingness to revise their work, and for the time they spend reading feedback in a poster design task. These findings constitute a first step in gaining an insight into the value of feedback and its impact on performance and learning choices. This research has implications for the design of assessments and instructional materials that may help students engage more closely with feedback and revision, and, consequently, apply good learning choices to improve their performance.

ACKNOWLEDGMENTS

Many thanks to the students and teachers for their participation, to the Stanford AAA Lab members for their guidance, and to the University of Alberta Faculty of Education *Support for the Advancement of Scholarship* Grant #G018000473, the *Killam Research Fund Cornerstone* Grant #RES0032227, the *Killam Conference Travel* Grant #RES0031407, and the *SSHRC IDG* Grant RES0034954 for their generous support.

REFERENCES

Bransford, J. D., & Schwartz, D. L. (1999). Chapter 3: Rethinking transfer: A simple proposal with multiple implications. *Review of Research in Education, 24*(1), 61-100. doi:10.3102/0091732X024001061

Bray, J. P. (2016). Assessment feedback using comment banks: A useful approach? *Bournemouth University "Releasing Potential" Conference,* Bournemouth University.

Carless, D. (2006). Differing perceptions in the feedback process. *Studies in Higher Education, 31*(2), 219-233.

Chiviacowsky, S., & Drews, R. (2014). Effects of generic versus non-generic feedback on motor learning in children. *PloS One, 9*(2), e88989.

Cutumisu, M., Blair, K. P., Chin, D. B., & Schwartz, D. L. (2016). Assessing whether students seek constructive criticism: The design of an automated feedback system for a graphic design task. *International Journal of Artificial Intelligence in Education, online first*, 1-29. doi:10.1007/s40593-016-0137-5

Cutumisu, M., Blair, K. P., Chin, D. B., & Schwartz, D. L. (2015). Posterlet: A game-based assessment of children's choices to seek feedback and to revise. *Journal of Learning Analytics, 2*(1), 49-71.

Dweck, C. S., & Leggett, E. L. (1988). A social-cognitive approach to motivation and personality. *Psychological Review, 95*(2), 256-273.

Ericsson, K. A., Krampe, R. T., & Tesch-Römer, C. (1993). The role of deliberate practice in the acquisition of expert performance. *Psychological Review, 100*(3), 363.

Hattie, J. (1999). *Influences on student learning* (Inaugural Lecture: Professor of Education ed.). New Zealand: University of Auckland.

Hattie, J., & Gan, M. (2011). Instruction based on feedback. In R. Mayer, & P. Alexander (Eds.), *Handbook of research on learning and instruction* (1st ed., pp. 249-271). New York: Routledge.

Hattie, J., & Timperley, H. (2007). The power of feedback. *Review of Educational Research, 77*(1), 81-112. doi:10.3102/003465430298487

Kluger, A. N., & DeNisi, A. (1998). Feedback interventions: Toward the understanding of a double-edged sword. *Current Directions in Psychological Science, 7*(3), 67-72.

Kulhavy, R. W., & Stock, W. A. (1989). Feedback in written instruction: The place of response certitude. *Educational Psychology Review, 1*(4), 279-308.

Kulik, J. A., & Kulik, C. C. (1988). Timing of feedback and verbal learning. *Review of Educational Research, 58*(1), 79-97.

Schwartz, D. L., & Arena, D. (2013). *Measuring what matters most: Choice-based assessments for the digital age.* Cambridge, Massachusetts: MIT Press.

REFINING PRESENTATION DOCUMENTS WITH PRESENTATION SCHEMA

Yuki Obara and Akihiro Kashihara
Graduate School of Informatics and Engineering, The University of Electro-Communications
1-5-1, Chofugaoka, Chofu, Tokyo, 182-8585, Japan

ABSTRACT

Presentation is one of the important activities in research to publish research results. When we create presentation documents (P-documents for short), it is important to compose presentation structure (P-structure for short) that represents what to present and how to sequence the contents. To create proper P-documents, we need to learn how to create P-documents in the lab. In our previous work, we have helped unskilled researchers with presentation schema (P-schema for short), which is represented as an all-inclusive P-structure of P-documents accumulated in the lab. It allowed unskilled researchers to create proper P-documents. But, some learners could not properly segment research contents into slides. To solve this problem, this paper describes refinement of P-schema. This paper also reports a case study whose purpose was to assess whether the refined P-schema could promote segmentation by comparing P-documents and P-structure composed with the refined P-schema and composed with the original P-schema.

KEYWORDS

Presentation, Presentation Schema, Presentation Structure, Research Activity

1. INTRODUCTION

Among research activities, presentation is very important for publishing research results. In general, presentation is conducted under several restrictions such as time, place, audience, etc. It is necessary to consider such restrictions to create presentation documents (P-documents for short). There are accordingly many books about the ideas of presentation (Duarte 2008, Reynolds 2011). In order to create P-documents suitable for research contents, in addition, it is important to compose presentation structure (P-structure for short) that represents what to present and how to sequence the contents (Hasegawa and Kashihara 2013). The P-structure composition needs two tasks, which are segmentation and sequencing. Segmentation is to divide research contents into slides. Sequencing is to make a sequence of the slides. In order to properly carry out these tasks, it is necessary for researchers to have a lot of experience in creating P-documents.

On the other hand, unskilled researchers have fewer experiences in composing P-structure to create P-documents (Tanida 2008). They accordingly need to learn as learners how to create P-documents in lab, where they should have an apprentice role together with expert, and more skilled researchers (Collins 1988). From this apprenticeship point of view, we have addressed the issue how to improve their skills in composing P-structure by means of presentation schema (P-schema for short) as a scaffold that we have designed as an all-inclusive P-structure to be commonly used in lab. P-schema represents heuristics for creating P-documents in lab, which allows unskilled learners to properly compose P-structure and create P-documents. In addition, skills in composing P-structure could be improved due to P-schema (Shibata 2012, Shibata 2013).

We have conducted a number of case studies with P-schema in our lab to confirm so far that P-schema allows unskilled learners to create more proper P-documents. In addition, we also found some learners who could not properly segment research contents into slides with P-schema. Their P-documents included some slides with more than one topic, and missed some slides to be presented. There seem two reasons for this. First, P-schema could not represent P-structure as a suitable scaffold for segmenting research contents into slides. Second, unskilled researchers could not properly use P-schema as scaffold to segment.

Towards resolving these problems, this paper describes refinement of P-schema designed for our lab. The refined P-schema expects unskilled learners to improve segmenting their research contents into slides to create more proper P-documents. It is also expected to make clearer the heuristics for creating P-documents in lab.

This paper also reports a case study whose purpose was to assess whether the refined P-schema could promote proper P-structure composition and P-document creation. The results suggest that it allows unskilled learners to create more proper P-documents.

2. PRESENTATION DOCUMENTS

Research presentation requires the following three skills at least (Shibata 2013):

- Skill in composing P-structure for P-documents
- Skill in designing the contents of slides, and
- Skill in oral and gesture for presentation.

In this work, we focus on skill in composing P-structure. Let us here explain P-structure and P-schema in detail.

2.1 Presentation Structure

In creating P-documents suitable for research contents, it is very important to consider what to present and how to sequence the presented contents, which corresponds to P-structure. We represent P-structure with the following four metadata of P-documents (Tanida 2008):

- *Slide metadata*: Slide metadata shows the contents or role of each slide,
- *Segment metadata*: Segment metadata represents the role in which a sequence of several slides plays such as *Cover*, *Introduction*, *Research Goal and Approach*, *Theory and Model*, *System*, *Case Study*, and *Conclusion*,
- *Relation metadata*: Relation metadata represents the relationships between specific slides, such as *cause-problem*, *problem-solution*, *solution-implementation*, *implementation-functions*, and *solution-evaluation*, and
- *File metadata*: File metadata represents a context of presentation such as *presenter*, *conference type*, *place of presentation*, and *time limit*.

Figure 1 shows an example of P-structure embedded in a P-document created in our lab. As shown in Figure 1, P-structure is composed of four metadata, which forms a hierarchy. Slide metadata has its own hierarchy, and the leaf metadata corresponds to each slide. For example, the slide metadata from Background to Domain connects with each other by means of is-a relation. Segment metadata represents the role of a sequence of several slide metadata. Relation metadata connects between specific slide metadata. File metadata is located at the root of P-structure, which shows a context of presentation.

2.2 Presentation Schema

P-documents accumulated in the same lab tend to have a similar P-structure. This means that heuristics for creating P-documents are shared in the lab. In our previous work, we systematically extracted P-schema from a set of P-documents accumulated in our lab by means of machine learning technique, which represents a common P-structure among the documents like a result of logical multiplication (Hasegawa and Kashihara 2013). However, this schema could not represent contents unique to each P-document. In this work, we have accordingly defined an all-inclusive P-structure to be commonly used in our lab as P-schema, which expert researchers extracted. Such P-schema represents heuristics for creating P-documents in our lab. We think each lab has its own P-schema.

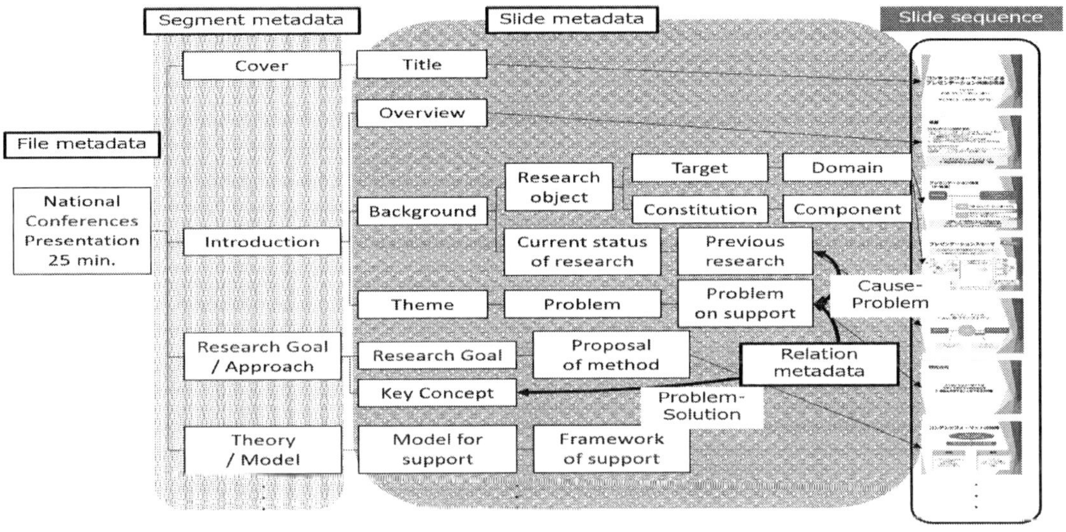

Figure 1. An example of presentation structure

3. SCAFFOLDING SYSTEM WITH PRESENTATION SCHEMA

We have developed a scaffolding system with P-schema as an add-in of Microsoft PowerPoint 2013. Figure 2 shows the user interface of this system. This system has two functions mainly, which are operable at the add-in tab in the upper part of the user interface shown in Figure 2.

The system first provides the function of displaying P-schema. P-schema is saved as an XML file, and it is inputted from the file and displayed at the left pane of the user interface when it is activated. P-schema is displayed as a hierarchy of metadata. When a mouse pointer is placed over slide metadata displayed in P-schema, a caption of the metadata will appear on the mouse pointer. The system second provides the function of composing P-structure, which allows learners to compose P-structure by referring to P-schema at the middle pane of the user interface. In generating and designing slides with PPT functionality, they could use P-schema as a scaffold for composing P-structure. In particular, they are expected to select and double-click metadata corresponding to the slides in the left pane (P-schema) to drop in the middle pane for composing P-structure.

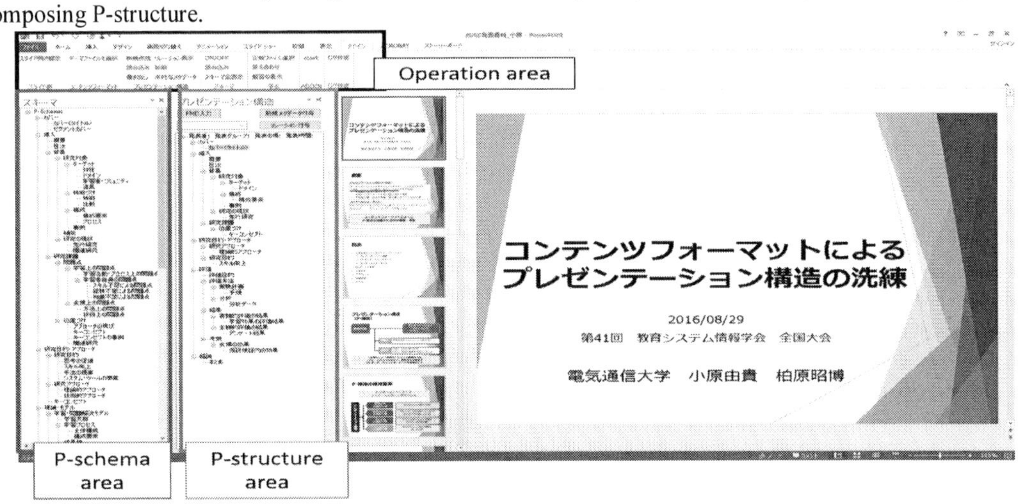

Figure 2. User interface of scaffolding system with P-schema

4. REFINEMENT OF PRESENTATION SCHEMA

4.1 Purpose

In our previous work, unskilled researchers were able to create proper P-documents using P-schema as a scaffold. On the other hand, P-documents created by unskilled researchers were not always improved. There are two reasons why these P-documents were insufficient. First, P-schema could not represent P-structure as a suitable scaffold. P-schema in the previous work was designed as an all-inclusive P-structure, but it was still inadequate. Second, unskilled researchers could not use P-schema properly as scaffold to segment. This shows that we should modify P-schema particularly words used for metadata. Towards these problems, we addressed refinement of P-schema.

4.2 Procedure

We first gathered P-documents that were accumulated in our lab, and selected 24 P-documents used in the final presentation for Master's thesis held in our university. The reason why we selected these P-documents for refining P-schema was that these were checked several times via presentation rehearsals and were sophisticated sufficiently. After the selection, we analyzed the P-structure embedded in these documents with the current P-schema and the scaffolding system, and then refined P-schema.

In analyzing the P-structure in the P-documents, we second followed the current P-schema to classify the slides for each segment metadata. Table 1 shows the results of the classification, which presents (a) the number and percentage of slide metadata per segment used in the P-structure, and (b) the number and percentage of slide metadata per segment in the P-schema. In (b), the percentages of slide metadata in "Introduction", "Theory / Model", and "Evaluation" segments are relatively high. It means that our lab emphasizes these contents as the presentation heuristics. Compared with (b), in addition, the usage percentage of slide metadata in "Research Goal / Approach" segment in (a) was high, and the usage percentages of slide metadata in "Theory / Model" segment was reversely low. These results suggest the possibility that the slide metadata in these segments are not used as expected. Particularly focusing on the segments "Research Goal / Approach" and "Theory / Model", we have reconsidered and subdivided slide metadata in P-schema in more detail to refine.

Table 1. Results of classifying slides and slide metadata in P-documents

Segment metadata	(a) Slide metadata in P-structure		(b) Slide metadata in P-schema	
	Number	Percentage	Number	Percentage
Cover	25	5.1	2	2.4
Introduction	118	23.9	21	25.3
Research Goal / Approach	50	10.1	5	6
Theory / Model	70	14.2	19	22.9
System	64	13	12	14.5
Evaluation	115	23.3	20	24.1
Conclusion	51	10.3	4	4.8
Total	493		83	

4.3 Refined Presentation Schema

Let us here compare P-schema and refined P-schema (called reP-Schema). There are two main differences between the P-schemata, which are slide metadata and hierarchy of slide metadata. Table 2 shows the number of slide metadata in the P-schema and reP-schema, and the rate of change and increase in slide metadata. In this table, let the total number of slide metadata in the P-schema be N_{old}, and the total number of slide metadata in the reP-schema be N_{new}. N_{new} includes newly added metadata (n_{new}), metadata partially-changed (n_{pc}), and metadata with no change (n_{nc}). The rate of change is calculated as $(n_{new} + n_{pc}) / N_{new}$. The rate of increase is also calculated as $(N_{new}-N_{old}) / N_{old}$.

As shown in Table 2, more than half of the metadata in the reP-schema have been changed in total. In particular, the rates of change in "Introduction", "Research Goal / Approach", and "Theory / Model" segments are high. The total rate of increase has been more than 30%. The rates in "Introduction" and "Research Goal / Approach" segments have been significantly increased.

As for the second difference between the P-schemata about hierarchy of slide metadata, Table 3 shows the number of slide metadata used in each depth of the hierarchy. In "Introduction" segment, the slide metadata are subdivided into deeper level in the refined P-schema. In "Research Goal / Approach" and "Evaluation" segments, the slide metadata increase at the deepest level in the reP-schema.

Table 2. Comparison between P-schema and reP-schema

Segment metadata	N_{old}	The number of slide metadata in the reP-schema					The rate of increase
		N_{new}	New (n_{new})	Partially-changed (n_{pc})	No change (n_{nc})	The rate of change ($n_{new}+n_{pc}$) / N_{new}	(N_{new}-N_{old})/ N_{old}
Cover	2	2	0	0	2	0	0
Introduction	21	36	22	6	8	0.78	0.71
Research Goal / Approach	5	9	4	2	3	0.67	0.8
Theory / Model	19	21	4	13	4	0.81	0.11
System	12	12	0	2	10	0.17	0
Evaluation	20	27	9	1	17	0.37	0.35
Conclusion	4	4	0	0	4	0	0
Total	83	111	39	24	48	0.57	0.34

Table 3. Hierarchies of slide metadata in P-schema and refined P-schema

Segment metadata	P-schema	The depth of the hierarchy				
		2	3	4	5	6
Introduction	P-schema	4	9	8	0	0
	reP-schema	4	5	12	12	3
Research Goal / Approach	P-schema	3	2	0	0	0
	reP-schema	3	6	0	0	0
Theory / Model	P-schema	4	8	7	0	0
	reP-schema	4	10	7	0	0
System	P-schema	3	4	5	0	0
	reP-schema	2	5	5	0	0
Evaluation	P-schema	5	6	9	0	0
	reP-schema	5	8	14	0	0

4.4 Expected Effects

We think there are two expected effects to be obtained from the P-schema refinement. In creating a P-document, unskilled researchers first tend to make a slide with a lot of information including different contents. Such slide causes the audience some difficulties in understanding the presentation. This is due to insufficient segmentation of contents. The reP-schema is expected to promote segmentation to improve making slides. Second, it is quite important for research lab to build up and share heuristics for continuing and developing research activities. It requires a lot of experience in carrying out the research activities, which also needs a lot of time. The reP-schema makes the heuristics for creating P-documents clearer. As a result, it could promote sharing the heuristics among the lab members, and improving P-documents creation.

5. CASE STUDY

We have conducted a case study whose purpose was to ascertain what kind of changes were seen in P-documents and P-structure composed with the reP-schema compared to the ones with the P-schema.

5.1 Preparation and Procedure

The participants were 9 graduate and undergraduate students (our lab students) in science and engineering. They were first asked to create P-documents and compose P-structure for their research contents with the P-schema. We then asked them to use the reP-schema, and to re-compose P-structure and modify their P-documents if necessary. We expected that the reP-schema allowed the participants to complement the contents missed and to subdivide the contents included in one slide into more slides and also to refine P-structure embedded in their P-documents. After the use of the reP-schema, we asked them to refer to their refined P-documents to answer a questionnaire including the question as follows:

Did you think whether your P-document was refined? (Yes or No)

5.2 Results

We evaluated P-structure and P-documents composed/modified by the participants. As for P-structure, we counted the number of changes in slide metadata before and after using the reP-schema, and analyzed how many new/partially-changed metadata defined in the reP-schema were used. As for P-documents, we counted the number of slides before and after using the reP-schema. Moreover, we evaluated the appropriateness of the slide metadata attached to each slide by the participants with three grades which were appropriate, partially appropriate, and inappropriate. "Appropriate" means the metadata represents the slide content. "Partially appropriate" means the metadata partially represents the slide contents. "Inappropriate" means the metadata does not represent the slide contents.

Table 4 shows the number of changes in metadata before and after using the reP-schema, the usage rate of the new/partially-changed metadata and its appropriateness, and the rate of "appropriate" and "partially appropriate". According to Table 4, the average rate of using new metadata exceeded 80%. Moreover, the total rate of "appropriate" and "partially appropriate" exceeds 80%, although the rates of participants E and G were lower. Table 5 shows the number of slides before and after using the reP-schema, its increase/decrease, and types/appropriateness of metadata attached to the increased slides. According to this table, 7 participants increased the number of slides, one did not change, and one decreased. 4 of the 7 participants also used new/partially-changed metadata, and most of them added the slides with appropriate metadata. As for the result of the questionnaire, all participants answered "Yes" to the question.

From the case study, the participants used new/partially-changed metadata positively and its usage was appropriate. This suggests that the reP-schema is appropriate for our lab, and properly represents our lab heuristics. In addition, most participants increased the number of slides and the slides were added with appropriate metadata. This suggests that segmentation is promoted by the reP-schema. In addition, we think it could contribute to refinement of the contents of P-documents.

Table 4. Number of changes in metadata before and after using the reP-schema, the usage rate of new/partially changed metadata, its appropriateness and rate of appropriate and partially appropriate

Participants	Number of changes	Types of metadata			Usage rate of new /partially-changed metadata	Appropriateness of new metadata used			Rate of appropriate and partially appropriate
		New	Partially-changed	Total		Appropriate	Partially appropriate	Inappropriate	
A	17	5	8	13	0.76	9	2	2	0.85
B	21	9	6	15	0.71	13	2	0	1
C	28	18	8	26	0.93	26	0	0	1
D	7	4	3	7	1	6	1	0	1
E	16	8	6	14	0.88	6	3	5	0.64
F	25	18	1	19	0.76	13	3	3	0.84
G	15	11	4	15	1	6	3	6	0.6
H	19	8	8	16	0.84	7	7	2	0.88
I	19	14	2	16	0.84	12	3	1	0.94
Average	18.6	10.6	5.1	15.7	0.84	10.9	2.7	2.1	0.87

Table 5. Number of slides before and after using the reP-schema, its increase/decrease, and types/appropriateness of metadata attached to the increased slide

Participants	Number of slides before using the reP-schema	Number of slides after using the reP-schema	Increase or decrease of slides	Types of metadata attached to the increased slides			Appropriateness of metadata attached to the increased slides		
				New	Partially-changed	No change	Appropriate	Partially appropriate	Inappropriate
A	27	28	1	0	0	1	1	0	0
B	38	40	2	0	0	2	2	0	0
C	36	40	4	4	0	0	3	1	0
D	15	16	1	0	1	0	1	0	0
E	26	25	-1	-	-	-	-	-	-
F	33	35	2	0	1	1	1	0	1
G	30	30	0	-	-	-	-	-	-
H	30	32	2	0	0	2	2	0	0
I	34	35	1	0	1	0	1	0	0

5.3 Additional Study

We had an additional study after the case study. 6 out of 9 participants (from D to I) participated. After the case study in 5.2, all of them had rehearsal with the expert researcher and then conducted their thesis presentation in our university. In order to investigate to what extent these 6 participants could create proper P-documents using the scaffolding system, we compared their P-documents refined with the reP-schema in the case study described in 5.2, and the P-documents used in their thesis presentation.

We counted the number of slides that did not change in the two documents. Table 6 shows the results. According to this table, participants D and F greatly changed the slides between the two P-documents, but the other participants changed almost half of the slides. This suggests that the reP-schema contributes to creating appropriate P-documents that are usable for actual thesis presentation. In addition, we analyzed the number of slides that did not change in each segment whose results are shown in Table 7. According to this table, almost half of the slides did not change in "Introduction", "Research Goal / Approach" and "Theory / Model" segments. In "System" and "Evaluation" segment, on the other hand, most of the slides changed. This suggests a positive effect on the refinement of P-schema, since we particularly refined and subdivided metadata in "Introduction", "Research Goal / Approach", and "Theory / Model" segments in this work.

Table 6. Number of slides that did not change in two documents

Participants	Number of slides		Number of slides without changes from *a* to *b* (*c*)	Rate of the number of slides without changes	
	Case study (*a*)	Thesis presentation (*b*)		R_1 (c/a)	R_2 (c/b)
D	16	20	1	0.06	0.05
E	25	25	14	0.56	0.56
F	35	36	6	0.17	0.17
G	30	27	14	0.47	0.52
H	32	33	16	0.5	0.48
I	35	33	20	0.57	0.6

Table 7. Number of slides that did not change in each segment

Participants	Number of slides created in the case study (*a*)	Number of slides without changes (*c*)	Cover		Introduction		Research Goal / Approach		Theory / Model		System		Evaluation		Conclusion	
			a	*c*	*a*	*c*	*a*	*c*	*a*	*c*	*a*	*c*	*a*	*c*	*a*	*c*
D	16	1	1	1	5	0	2	0	3	0	3	0	0	0	2	0
E	25	14	1	1	6	4	2	0	7	7	2	2	5	0	2	0
F	35	6	1	1	13	2	2	1	2	0	7	1	8	0	2	1
G	30	14	1	1	8	5	5	3	3	2	3	0	8	1	2	2
H	32	16	1	1	6	5	1	1	9	3	3	2	9	2	3	2
I	35	20	1	1	12	9	2	2	2	0	8	3	8	3	2	2
Total	173	71	6	6	50	25	14	7	26	12	26	8	38	6	13	7

6. CONCLUSION

In this work, we have refined the P-schema developed in our previous work and verified whether the participants in our lab could create P-document properly by using the refined P-schema. As a result of the case study, the participants used metadata in refined P-schema appropriately and segmented research contents.—Moreover, according to the additional study, the participants could create proper P-documents, which could be used for thesis presentation with the refined P-schema. In summary, the refined P-schema represents our heuristics more properly, promotes segmentation of research contents, and is effective to make P-documents that can be used for actual presentations.

In future, we need to explore whether the refined P-schema is valid not only in P-documents creation but also in other scene of presentation such as rehearsal. If the refined P-schema is properly displayed during the rehearsal of the presentation, the presenter could become aware of the inappropriate metadata that they would not notice when creating their P-documents.

ACKNOWLEDGEMENT

The work was supported in part by JSPS KAKENHI Grant Number 26282047 and 17H01992.

REFERENCES

Hasegawa, S. and Kashihara, A., 2013. A Mining Technique for Extraction of Presentation Schema from Presentation Documents Accumulated in Laboratory. *The Journal of Research and Practice in Technology Enhanced Learning (RPTEL),* Vol. 8, No.1, pp. 153-169.

Collins, A. et al, 1988. Cognitive Apprenticeship: Teaching the Craft of Reading, Writing and Mathematics. *Thinking: The Journal of Philosophy for Children*, Vol. 8, Issue 1, pp. 2-10.

Duarte, N., 2008. *Slide:ology: The Art and Science of Creating Great Presentations*, O'Reilly Media, USA.

Reynolds, G., 2011. *Presentation Zen: Simple Ideas on Presentation Design and Delivery*, New Riders Press, USA.

Tanida, A. et al, 2008. Proc. of The 16th International Conference on Computers in Education (ICCE2008), *Web 2.0 Services for Presentation Planning and Presentation Reflection*. Taipei, Taiwan, pp.565-572.

Shibata, Y. et al., 2012. Proc. of E-Learn2012, *Scaffolding with Schema for Creating Presentation Documents and Its Evaluation.* Montreal, Canada pp.2059-2066.

Shibata, Y. et al, 2013. Proc. of ITHET2013 (International Conference on Information Technology Based Higher Education and Training), *Skill Transfer from Learning to Creating Presentation Documents.* Antalya, Turkey.

THE KNOWLEDGE DEVELOPMENT MODEL: RESPONDING TO THE CHANGING LANDSCAPE OF LEARNING IN VIRTUAL ENVIRONMENTS

Nan B. Adams
Southeastern Louisiana University, United States

ABSTRACT

Society's relationship to knowledge and what is considered to be factual is changing. Effective teaching models focused on leveraging strategic control of the knowledge from teachers to learners in virtual learning environments are critical to insuring a positive path is charted. The Knowledge Development Model serves as the guide for determining how to move learners through stages of knowledge acquisition to knowledge application and ultimately to knowledge generation in virtual settings. Instructional strategies for fostering student engagement in a virtual learning environment are identified as critical, and a number of relevant theories focusing on student learning, affect, needs and adult concerns are presented to provide a basis for transfer of knowledge from teacher to learner. The validated (2009, Adams, DeVaney & Sawyer) Knowledge Development Model combines the dimensions of knowledge approach, knowledge authority and teaching approach to demonstrate the recursive and scaffolded design for creation of virtual learning environments.

KEYWORDS

Learning theory; social aspects of technological change

1. INTRODUCTION

The landscape of learning and knowledge is changing – rapidly, and in fits and starts. Knowledge and facts are being challenged in incredible ways. Adult learning is increasingly taking place virtually. Responsive design of virtual learning environments to address these changes offer challenges and opportunities for innovative teaching and enhancement of learning. In a previous discussion, Adams, DeVaney and Longstreet (2010) provided evidence for a change in the way people identify themselves in relation to groups, coining the term 'Digital Ethnicity'. Ethnicity has morphed in the age of digital technologies. Aspects of ethnicity that include Social Value Patterns, Orientation Mode, Intellectual Mode and Communication Mode (verbal, nonverbal and digital) have been identified that indicate a unique and Digital Ethnicity has emerged (Adams, DeVaney and Longstreet, 2013, 2010). This ongoing line of reasoning that seeks to describe changes in intelligence and intellectual style and the resultant needs for educational practices was started by Adams (2004) with her discussion of Digital Intelligence. The Knowledge Development Model for virtual learning environments presented here was designed to address these new ethnic, intellectual and communication styles. Validity for this model was established in 2009 (Adams, DeVaney, Sawyer). The theoretical design and practical use for this model is presented to demonstrate additional evidence and need for responsive virtual learning environments that utilize a valid framework for educational design and practice in virtual environments.

2. BODY OF PAPER

2.1 Learning Theory must drive Virtual Learning Environments

Strategies to foster transfer of knowledge generation dispositions from teacher to learner should be central to the design of virtual learning environments. Implicit in this process is the facility for transitioning newly acquired knowledge to become internalized knowledge for learners so they may address specific problems they encounter, which is often the ultimate goal of organized educational programs. In this facilitated-learning paradigm, gradual release of responsibility for the learning shifts, over time, from the teacher or facilitator to the learner. During this process, the learner ultimately develops strategic control of the knowledge as should be evidenced through social interaction within the virtual environment.

In traditional classrooms and educational activities, the teacher is central to the learning process. The teacher serves variously as guide, facilitator, motivator, and often as the authority for knowledge structure and student behavior when engaged in the learning process. This role changes in the virtual environment – where students often engage without observation or direct guidance from the teacher. The creator of a virtual learning environment must make certain assumptions. These assumptions are not small, but deal with the very nature of knowledge and knowing. These assumptions must be acknowledged and employed to guide the construction of virtual learning environments.

The theoretical conflict in construction of virtual learning environments often lies in the basic belief about what is considered knowledge, the structure of that knowledge, and what knowledge should be valued or championed. This may be illustrated by a brief discussion of the modern and postmodern views about reality and knowledge. Modernists believe that reality exists objectively and generally believe that knowledge has a definable structure. They believe it is the charge of the teacher to either lead or facilitate inquiry for students to discover this pre-existing structure and incorporate it into their own knowledge base to solve problems in a way that demonstrates their systematic understanding of a body of knowledge. Postmodernists believe that reality is a human creation that is socially constructed. The postmodern view that reality changes – and is constructed differently by each individual necessitates less structured, more individually-oriented learning environments that provide student choice and serve to rely on the strategy of gradually allowing the learner to explore existing knowledge structures as they create their own knowledge structures. The focus is on the learner ultimately generating his or her personal knowledge from existing knowledge and information they encounter. Context often provides the social element for construction.

Virtual environments exemplify postmodern belief. This highly changeable and infinitely responsive environment is wholly constructed by the mind of the author and then reconstructed by the mind of the visitor/learner. The notion that rigid structure should be applied in this environment is unrealistic. It is of great concern to the author that these virtual learning environments seek to develop whole, rather than partial constructions of reality, knowledge and knowing.

Modernist approaches to teaching and learning often utilize behavioral learning and instructional practices. Post-modern approaches to teaching and learning utilize constructivist teaching practices. These two major and somewhat opposing cognitive approaches to teaching currently guide educational practice, both in classrooms and in virtual learning environments. The proliferation of standardized testing has added to this problem – promoting the more behavioral approach to teaching and learning by requiring assessment in a totally objective 'only one answer' format. Arguably, we live in a post-modern world.

Programmed Instruction, the behavioral approach to teaching assumes teachable knowledge has a given structure and it is the task of the teacher to develop within the learner an understanding of this structure and an ability to utilize this knowledge to solve problems. The constructivist teaching approach assumes that knowledge is constructed and therefore the student must develop their own knowledge structure based on personal experience and through discovery and experimentation with the information that exists that surrounds this area of knowledge. Said plainly, behaviorism assumes a linear learning process that may be described as the learn/test cycle demonstrated by the prevalence of standardized tests with only one 'correct' answer and assumes 'mastery' when this one correct answer is given by the student.

Constructivism assumes a recursive learning process that allows the learner to develop and understanding of knowledge structures with the goal of gaining and strategic control of the knowledge to address contextual problems by applying acquired knowledge. Constructivism views knowledge as a product of reality. Constructivists consider learning to be an active process where knowledge is contextualized rather than acquired. Personal experiences guide the construction of knowledge. Learners continuously test their knowledge construction through social negotiation. The learner is not a blank slate (*tabula rasa*) but brings past experiences and cultural factors to a situation. The Knowledge Development Model for virtual learning environments melds the two approaches and suggests that the learning process requires BOTH to be comprise effective teaching design.

2.2 Foundational Theories for the Knowledge Development Model for Virtual Environments

Vygotsky (1978) proposed that social interaction profoundly influences cognitive development. His theory centers on the belief that biological and cultural development do not occur in isolation. He believed that the development process that begins at birth and continues until death is too complex to be defined by stages. His work describes a phenomena he termed the Zone of Proximal Development which is defined as the distance between the actual knowledge level as determined by independent problem solving and the level of potential development as determined through problem solving in collaboration with more capable peers. A central concept in Vygotsky's theory is the Zone of Proximal Development (ZPD), which may be explained as zone of potential for cognitive development that limited to a certain time span. He defines the ZPD as having four learning stages. These stages range between the lower limit of what the student knows and the upper limits of what the student has the potential of accomplishing. The 4 stages may be further divided as (p.35) Stage 1 – assistance provided by more capable others (experts or teachers); Stage 2 – assistance by self; Stage 3 – internalization; Stage 4 – recursiveness through prior stages. Vygotsky's theory promotes contexts in which students play an active role in learning. Roles of the teacher and student are therefore shifted, as a teacher should collaborate with students in order to help facilitate meaning construction. Learning becomes a reciprocal experience for the student and teacher. The transfer of knowledge from facilitator to learner in knowledge development occurs through the gradual release of responsibility from the inter-psychological plane of teacher and student to ultimately the intra-psychological plane of self. Students ultimately become 'owners' of their knowledge because they are highly participant in its construction.

Bruner (1996) proposed Discovery Learning Theory as a constructivist learning theory based in personal inquiry. Bruner describes learning as an active process in which learners construct new ideas or concepts based upon their current/past knowledge. Knowledge structures are used to provide meaning and organization to experiences and are intended to allow the learner to go beyond the information given. Bruner suggests the instructor should encourage students to construct hypotheses, makes decisions, and discover principles by themselves, in effect they should present information in such a way that students may build new knowledge on existing knowledge to facilitate a recursive learning process. It is assumed that students may be more likely to remember concepts and knowledge discovered on their own. This approach assumes that if learning activities foster student ownership of the knowledge, this knowledge will be meaningful to the learner. Bruner's constructivist theory may be applied to instructional practice, as Kearsley (1994) surmises, by applying the following principles: 1 - Instruction must be concerned with the experiences and contexts that make the student willing and able to learn (*readiness*), 2- Instruction must be structured such that it may be easily grasped by the student (*spiral organization*). 3 - Construction should be designed to facilitate extrapolation and or fill in the gaps (*going beyond the information given*).

Bloom's taxonomy is widely accepted and universally employed when developing instructional materials. Because this inquiry seeks to describe strategies for internalizing knowledge through ownership, Bloom's Affective Domain is considered for use within this model rather than the more commonly used Cognitive Domain Taxonomy. The Affective Domain Taxonomy is concerned with perception of value issues and ranges from mere awareness (receiving), through to being able to distinguish implicit values through analysis (1973). The model includes the following levels of affect, from least engaged to most engaged and include 1 - **Receiving Phenomena**: Learners are aware, willing to hear and receiving information; 2 - **Responding to Phenomena**: Learners are active participants with engaged responses that reflect personal motivation; 3 - **Valuing**: Learners begin to attach value or worth to a particular object, phenomenon, or behavior. This worth ranges from simple acceptance to the more complex state of commitment; 4 - **Organization**: The learner contrasts different values, resolving conflicts between them, and creating a unique and organized value system; 5 -**Internalizing values:** The learner possesses a value system that controls their behavior. The behavior is pervasive, consistent, predictable and characteristic of the learner.

Maslow (1954) sought to address the complexity of human behavior and presented the idea that human actions are directed toward goal attainment. He proposed that any given behavior could satisfy several functions at the same time; for instance, going to a bar could satisfy one's needs for self-esteem and for social interaction. Maslow's Hierarchy of Needs has often been represented in a hierarchical pyramid with five levels. The four levels (lower-order needs) are considered *physiological needs,* while the top level is considered *growth needs*. The lower level needs need to be satisfied before higher-order needs can influence behavior. The levels include **Self-actualization** - morality, creativity, problem solving, etc; **Esteem** - includes confidence, self-esteem, achievement, respect, etc.; **Belongingness** - includes love, friendship, intimacy, family, etc.; **Safety** - includes security of environment, employment, resources, health, property, etc.; **Physiological** - includes air, food, water, sex, sleep, other factors towards homeostasis, etc. A virtual environment focused on learning takes on the same characteristics as the physical environments we currently inhabit, one might consider that the complexities of human behavior continue to exist in virtual classrooms and should be addressed.

Kolb (1984) provides a descriptive model of the adult learning process. His model considers learning to be a recursive process that includes 4 progressive stages: *Concrete Experience* is followed by *Reflection* on that experience on a personal basis. This may then be followed by the derivation of general rules describing the experience, or the application of known theories to it (*Abstract Conceptualization*), and hence to the construction of ways of modifying the next occurrence of the experience (*Active Experimentation*), leading in turn to the next *Concrete Experience*. All this may happen instantaneously or over varied periods of time, depending on the topic. There may also be smaller recursion cycles of this process simultaneously.

Adopting change may be considered a learning process. Suggesting that a group should adopt or 'buy in' to a new way of thinking is surely an educational process. The Concerns Based Adoption Model (Hall, George & Rutherford, 1979) is included in this discussion because it focuses directly on the concerns of the individual who is in the process of adopting a new way of thinking or doing things. These concerns may pose barriers to accepting new information and therefore should be addressed when developing virtual learning environments for adults. This model includes identification of 4 general types of concerns that stretch across 7 stages of development that represent a cycle of student concerns about adopting new ideas or knowledge to include **Unrelated Concerns** are characterized by a lack of Awareness and need for Information. **Self Concerns** are characterized by need for personal context. **Task Concerns** are focused on learning to manage the new knowledge and **Impact Concerns** include consideration of the consequences of using this new knowledge, collaboration with others using this new knowledge and a refocusing to allow new uses for the newly incorporated knowledge.

The figure below (Figure 1.) has been developed to visually represent the contributing theories of learning. As the recursive nature of each theory demonstrates - learning theories, affective and need theories and adult learning theories are effectively attempting to accomplish the same task of fostering ownership for knowledge among learners. The graphical demonstration of shared purpose has been included to support those dimensions proposed in the Knowledge Development Model for virtual environments which include the learner's developing knowledge approach, the teacher-student relationship with regards to knowledge authority, and suggested teaching approaches for virtual learning environments.

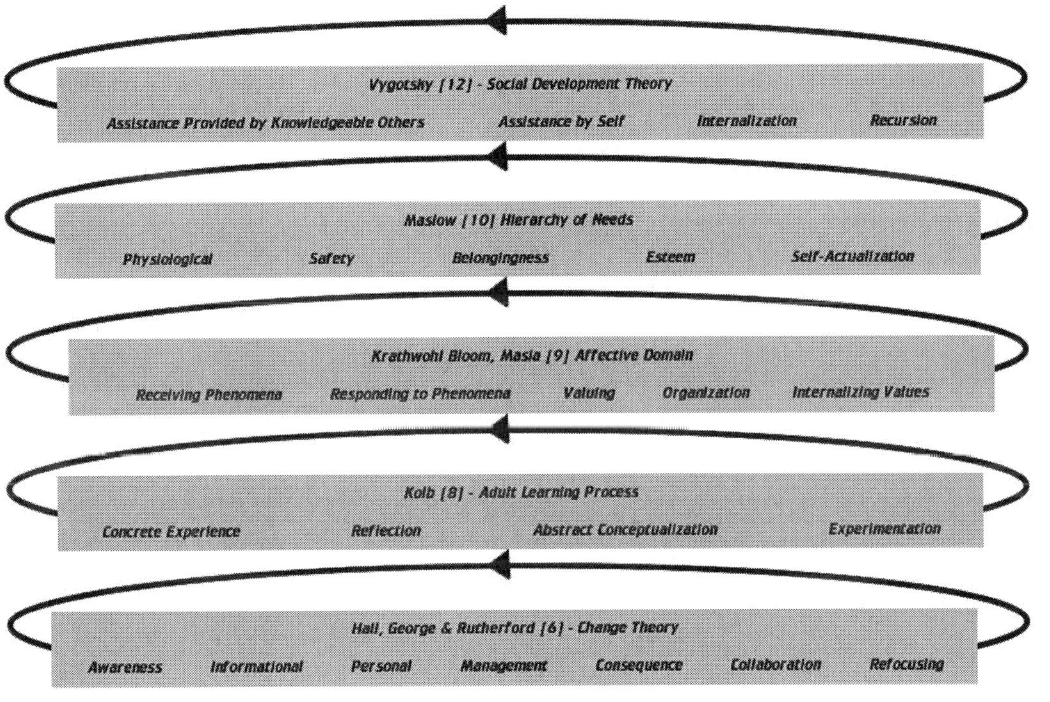

Figure 1. Contributing Recursive Developmental Learning Models

2.3 The Knowledge Development Model – a Recursive Model for Both Virtual and Physical Learning Environments

Most electronic learning environments seek to replicate existing traditional classroom teaching and learning practice. In this environment you will find word intensive pages that are intended for students to read and be expected to 'know' for a later demonstration. While these learning sites may be easy to construct, they are hardly virtual environments that create a variety of learning opportunities to foster knowledge development. Their focus is Knowledge Acquisition and they imply that knowledge authority is possessed by the teacher or site creator and are not particularly open to student manipulation.

As a virtual learning environment is developed the teacher or developer of the environment must consider the overall goals for student learning and within each of these goals determine the knowledge acquisition concerns, the knowledge application activities and determine how to foster knowledge generation through the discovery process. Using the Knowledge Development Model for Virtual Learning Environments, the following strategies are suggested for each of the proposed knowledge approaches.

After review of selected learning theories and their resultant models, the Knowledge Development Model was developed. The KDM is a derivative meta-model that seeks to address the domains of affect and need while employing discovery learning and scaffolding for recursive learning while recognizing the concerns of adult learners. This model deals with a description of three interrelated dimensions: the learner's developing knowledge approach, the teacher-student relationship with regards to knowledge authority, and suggested teaching approaches. It is assumed that each of these dimensions are cyclical and recursive and that this process may have several different instances occurring simultaneously.

2.3.1 Knowledge Authority – Leveraging the Teacher-Student Relationship

Vygotsky (1978) discusses the gradual release of knowledge from teacher or knowledgeable other to student or learner. Uniquely in the online environment, students are initially invested with the authority to move freely throughout the virtual environment. This may be controlled by timed offering of certain material and certain activities much as it is controlled by class meetings in the physical environment. It is suggested that much as students are provided the entire textbook in a face to face environment, virtual environments should be presented in their entirety (as a whole learning experience rather than disjointed parts) with the gradual release of knowledge authority from teacher to student demonstrated by the course organization. This provides a whole rather than partial view of the virtual reality construction of the knowledge to be explored. This also allows students to continually view the entire construction of the knowledge as they set about exploring the dimensions that make up this full construction.

2.3.2 Teaching Approach – Strategies for Learning

Teaching approaches range from the most behavioral strategy of drill and practice, through programmed instruction to constructivist statiges that include discovery learning and scaffolded learning activities. This model suggests that all of these techniques are useful in the virtual learning environment. A natural use of these stragegies might begin with more behavioral strategies to convey basic terminology and other supporting skills and progress to constructivist teaching approaches to foster the Knowledge Application and Knowledge Generation goals of this model. Scaffolding of learning activities to continually expand the student Zone of Proximal Development (Vygotsky, 1978) should be a central focus for continued knowledge transfer and generation. For when new knowledge is being generated, student ownership of knowledge is central to this new construction of knowledge to solve new problems.

2.3.3 Knowledge Approach – Outcomes for Learning

Knowledge Acquisition. If the goal for a certain learning activity is to foster knowledge acquisition, drill and practice and programmed instruction segments that provide supporting terminology and initial concepts to be used as building blocks for more sophisticated learning activities should be considered. Discovery learning may also be employed as the context and various PI modules may be supplied to inform this discovery process. Tutorials, informational web pages and databases to support student knowledge acquisition are useful tools for this phase of student learning.

Knowledge Application. Discovery learning may also serve as the context for knowledge application. Traditionally, knowledge application tasks include laboratory work, writing, preparing presentations and other activities that require the student to construct acquired knowledge to solve existing problems that have somewhat predictable outcomes. Collaboration among students often reinforces this process. The design of presentations or web pages that demonstrate a construction and application of the knowledge under investigation are appropriate virtual learning tools. These student products may be included for review as part of the virtual environment and serve to develop student ownership of course content, which is critical to fostering knowledge generation among students. The posted presentations demonstrate their knowledge and investment in the learning activities and ultimately their ownership of the knowledge. These constructions also allow the teacher to uncover common misconceptions about the knowledge base and facilitate discussion about these misconceptions to increase knowledge. Collaborative environments such as chat, threaded discussion boards, instant messaging and other collaborative tools are useful.

Knowledge Generation. A different level of discovery learning may be employed for fostering knowledge generation. Student ownership of this process is critical. Student brainstorming of problems to be solved creates the context for this ownership. Collaboration is critical among students and between students and faculty. Private discussion forums that foster risk taking may aid this process. As with knowledge application, collaborative environments such as chat, threaded discussion boards, instant messaging and other collaborative tools are useful. The design of presentations or web pages that demonstrate new construction and application of the knowledge under investigation are appropriate virtual learning tools. These student products should be provided space for private development either by singular students in collaboration with faculty or within student groups with faculty collaboration. The final projects should be included as part of the virtual environment and may be the capstone discussion activity of the learning cycle. These projects may easily reveal new areas of knowledge for exploration and may serve as the catalyst for another recursive learning cycle.

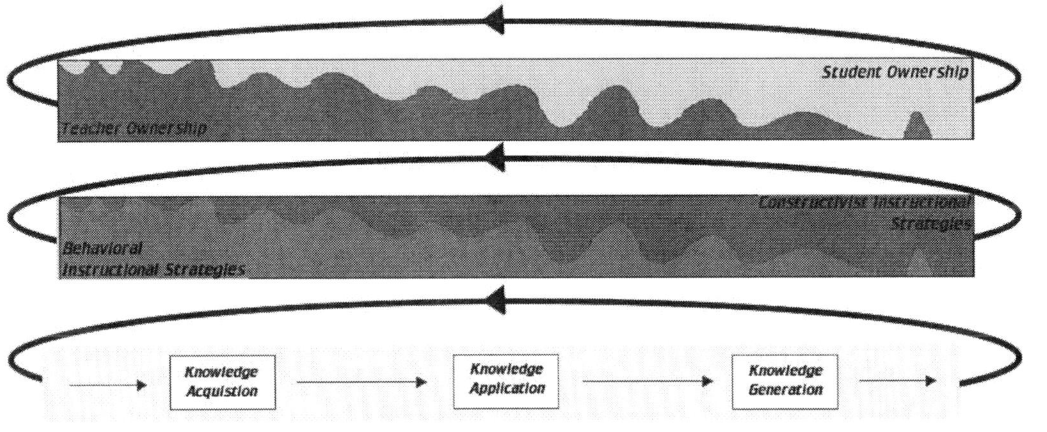

Figure 2. Knowledge Development Model in Virtual Environments

The model above (Figure 2.) combines the dimensions of Knowledge Approach, the teacher-student relationship with regards to Knowledge Authority and Teaching Approach to demonstrate the recursive and scaffolded design for creation of virtual learning environments. At this time, the author would like to offer a practical observation. In the context of course progression found in most learning institutions, these progressive knowledge approaches may occur repeatedly during one course or learning unit, or may stretch across two or more learning units or courses. The *focus* is to insure that all levels of knowledge engagement should be considered when creating *complete* knowledge transfer and foster ownership.

3. CONCLUSION

The social aspects of technological change greatly influence intellectual style and learning. Regardless of the modern or postmodern view held by the teacher and the learner and the assumptions about knowledge structure each reflects, student engagement is central to the learning process. The instructional strategies for fostering internalization and utilization of knowledge in a virtual environment are critical to the learner's strategic use of the knowledge. The instructional design to facilitate the transfer of knowledge so that it is strategically and gradually released to become internalized knowledge often occurs in the interactions between the facilitator of learning and the learner. The notion of scaffolded instructional strategies to support the transfer of knowledge is paramount to the goal of knowledge development and ultimately knowledge generation. Educational theory that has been accepted for traditional learning environments provides direct guidance as we seek to construct rich virtual learning environments that create whole learning experiences. Thus, instructional strategies and fertile learning environments that address the entire range of student learning likes, needs and concerns must be designed. The Knowledge Development Model for design of virtual learning environments was developed utilizing recursive learning theories that suggest targeted teaching strategies to yield learners with strategic control of knowledge.

REFERENCES

Adams, N. B. (2004) Digital intelligence fostered by technology. The *Journal of Technology Studies,* 30(2).

Adams, N.B., DeVaney, T.A., (2013) Aspects of an Emerging Digital Ethnicity. *Book Chapter.* Research Highlights in Technology and Teacher Education 2013. Society for Information Technology and Teacher Education.

Adams, N.B., DeVaney, T.A., (2011) Digital Ethnicity: Discussion of a Concept and Implications for Education. *Book Chapter.* e-Learning and e-Education.

Adams, N.B., DeVaney, T.A., Longstreet, W.S. (2010) Investigating aspects of an emerging digital ethnicity: Development of the Digital Ethnicity Scale, *Computers and Human Behavior*, 26 (2010) 1822–1830.

Adams, N.B., DeVaney, T.A. & Sawyer, S.G., (2009) Measuring Conditions Conducive to Knowledge Development in Virtual Learning Environments: Initial Development of a Model-Based Survey. *Journal of Technology, Learning and Assessment, 8*(1).

Bloom, B. S. (1956). *Taxonomy of educational objectives, Handbook 1: The Cognitive Domain.* New York: David McKay Co., Inc.

Bruner, J. (1966). *Toward a theory of instruction.* Cambridge, MA: Harvard University Press.

Hall, G. E.,George, A., & Rutherford, W. L. (1979) *Measuring stages of concern about the innovation: A manual for use of the SoC Questionnaire (Report No. 3032).* Austin: University of Texas at Austin, Research and Development Center for Teacher Education. (ERIC Document Reproduction Service No. ED 147 342)

Kearsley, G. (1994). *Constructivist theory (J. Bruner).* [Online]. Available: http://www.gwu.edu/~tip/bruner.html [May 30, 2007].

Kolb, D. A. (1984) *Experiential Learning: Experience as the source of learning and development* New Jersey: Prentice-Hall.

Krathwohl, D. R., Bloom, B. S., Masia, B. B. (1973). *Taxonomy of educational objectives, The classification of educational goals. Handbook II: The affective domain.* New York: David McKay Co.

Maslow, A. (1954). *Motivation and personality*. New York: Harper.

Vygotsky, L. S. (1978). *Mind and society: The development of higher mental processes*. Cambridge, MA: Harvard University Press.

MOBILE LEARNING ANALYTICS IN HIGHER EDUCATION: USABILITY TESTING AND EVALUATION OF AN APP PROTOTYPE

Matthias Kuhnel [1], Luisa Seiler [2], Andrea Honal [2] and Dirk Ifenthaler [1,3]
[1] University of Mannheim, [2] Cooperative State University Mannheim, Germany
[3] Curtin University, Australia

ABSTRACT

This study aims to test the usability of MyLA (My Learning Analytics), an application for students at two German universities: The Cooperative State University Mannheim and University of Mannheim. The participating universities focus on the support of personalized and self-regulated learning. MyLA collects data such as learning behavior and strategies as well as personality traits. This paper presents the findings of a usability test of the web app prototype. A total of 105 students from both universities participated in the study. In addition to a quantitative usability survey, the app navigation and design was evaluated through an eye tracking investigation with seven participants. The findings indicate that the MyLA prototype is easy to use but requires slight modifications concerning the app design.

KEYWORDS

Mobile Learning, Learning Analytics, App Prototype, Eye Tracking, Usability Testing

1. INTRODUCTION

The utilization of technologies in everyday life is constantly growing. For students, technologies are mostly indispensable. For example, 95 % of 14 to 29 years old Germans used a smartphone in 2016 (Statista / Bitkom, 2017). However, the potential of mobile devices has not been fully developed in many universities. There are numerous possibilities how digital technologies can improve learning at higher education institutions. In the NMC Horizon Report 2017, six key trends were identified to adopt technologies in the higher education sector: (a) *advancing cultures of learning* (higher involvement in innovation development processes), (b) *deeper learning approaches* (connection of learning with the real world), (c) *growing focus on measuring learning* (analytics of data out of learning environments), (d) *redesigning learning spaces* (improvement of the technical infrastructure), (e) *blended learning designs* (combination of online and face-to-face learning), and (f) *collaborative learning* (social interaction and intercultural experiences) (Adams Becker et al., 2017). The presented study covers two emerging fields of research in higher education: (1) learning analytics and (2) mobile learning.

Learning analytics (LA) use static and dynamic information to support students' learning process and optimize learning environments. Besides its flexibility, the main advantages of LA are personalization and the real-time availability of data (Ifenthaler et al., 2014). Lecturers can use rich data for pedagogical decision-making, understand individual performance development of students, identify potential lack of students' capabilities, or the need for curricular improvements (Mattingly et al., 2012). With LA, both students and lecturers can reflect on and improve their communication skills. By capturing, analyzing, and visualizing the available information about learning and teaching, lecturers are able to make more reliable predictions about their students' academic success (Macfadyen and Dawson, 2012). Furthermore, students at risk can be identified and given support through personalized pedagogical interventions (Lockyer et al., 2013). Successful applications of LA at universities are for example, *Course Signals* at Purdue University, which identifies students at risk using an approach similar to a traffic light system (green – no risk, yellow – potential risk, red – risky). Students and lecturers can identify needs for action to improve their learning situation. Furthermore, lecturers are able to intervene and help early (Ifenthaler and Schumacher, 2016). At the University of Wollongong, *SNAPP (Social Networks Adapting Pedagogical Practice)* is used. The main purpose of this system is to increase collaborative learning. For example, conversations in forums are analyzed for investigating the relationship between students and excluded students can be determined. The system is also used for reflection at the end of a lecture (Sclater et al., 2016).

Mobile Learning – m-learning – enables learning through personal portable electronic devices across multiple context. Through the usage of mobile devices students have access to learning materials more easily. The precondition is the availability of web-connected devices. In addition, students are independent from locations, time and they can communicate asynchronous (Lin et al., 2016). Mobile learning supports self-regulated learning on the one hand and it's an essential element of blended learning environments on the other hand (Al Saleh and Bhat, 2015). An example for a German mobile application is ARSnova of the THM University of Applied Sciences Gießen. ARS stands for Audience Response System. Via this app, students and lecturers can communicate interactively. For example, students can ask questions anonymously during a lecture and the lecturer is able to answer the questions in near real-time. Moreover, the communication can take place before or after a lecture. Another function is the evaluation of a lecture directly in the app (ARSnova, 2015).

The app MyLA (My Learning Analytics) of the Cooperative State University Mannheim and the University of Mannheim targets to improve learning processes at universities. MyLA provides ubiquitous communication in form of short messages from students to their lecturer and vice versa. This is especially useful for dual system courses where students are often away from the campus. Using this data, lecturers can adapt their lectures at university and implement personalized interventions, for example, adaption of learning materials or a detailed view at topics the students have problems with. Furthermore, the app supports a more personalized and individual way of learning. The students can document their learning motivation through their learning process. The app provides statistics, which enable students to observe their personal progress over time. In summary, MyLA combines learning analytics and mobile learning with the extension of personal learning.

This paper focuses on the components of the MyLA app prototype and the usability testing of the app.

2. MYLA APP

The web app prototype of MyLA (My Learning Analytics) consists of three different main units (see Figure 1): (I) My Profile, (II) My Learning, and (III) My Progress. The general page structure consists of the following:

- Header: with an icon for the side menu, the MyLA logo and an icon for the home button (except on the index page)
- Main: with contents (e.g. select lists in the profile data or pinboard elements like button and post)
- Footer: with the linked Cooperative State University Mannheim logo, imprint and privacy, icons linked to: contact, frequently asked questions (FAQ), settings and search function

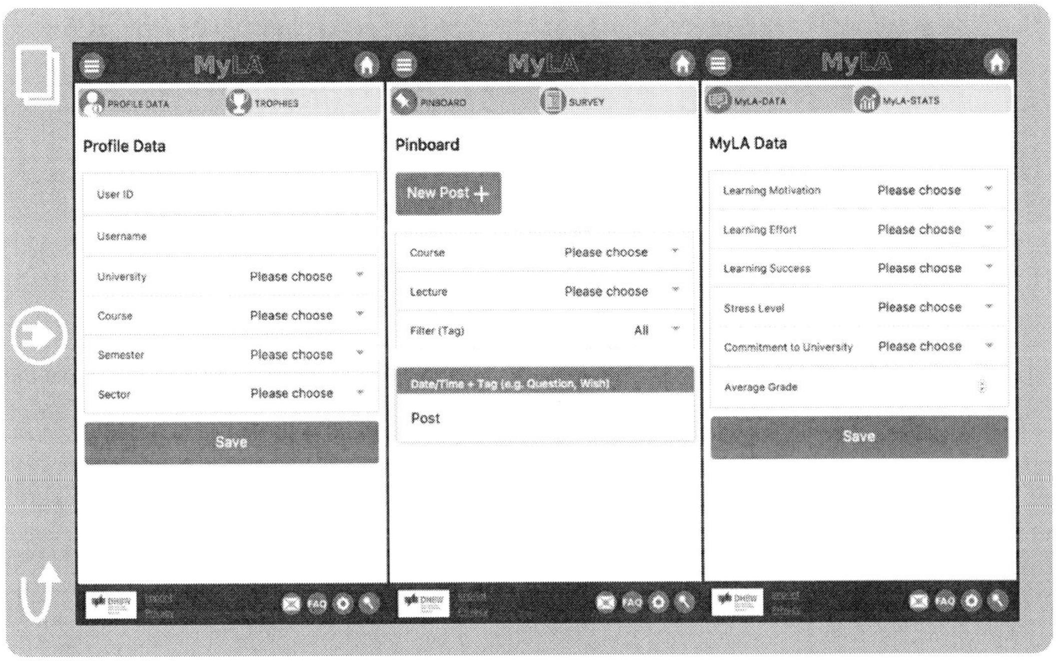

Figure 1. Web App Prototype MyLA (translated from German)

I. My Profile contains two subcategories: (1) *profile data* with input options like username or university and (2) the *trophy center* where app users have access to their rewards for i.e. when entering the profile data or participating on a certain questionnaire. This section includes administrative information of every app user.

II. My Learning contains two subcategories: (1) the *pinboard* where students can create posts for their lecturers and (2) the *survey center* where students can response to regular conducted questionnaires. Within this section of the app, the students can communicate with their lecturers and vice versa. Via pinboard, students can post messages by using tags (e.g. ask questions or point to a problem). This will be only visible for the responsible lecturer on their dashboard interface.

III. My Progress contains two subcategories: (1) *MyLA data* where students can enter personal data like learning motivation or learning effort and (2) *MyLA stats* where the MyLA data will be visualized in charts. This part displays the individual progress in additional (learning) factors.

The design of the app was realized to accommodate the corporate design of the Cooperative State University Mannheim and the University of Mannheim. Therefore, one significant color of each education institute had been extracted. As a next step, the colors were combined and supplemented by neutral colors.

According to the approach of learning analytics, the first prototype of MyLA app was designed to capture user data. Further steps will be collecting the data reports and deriving individual actions for students. Thereby, the main objective of developing personalized and adapted learning environments will be striven.

3. USABILITY TESTING

3.1 Research Questions

The usability testing focused on three major research questions:

1. How intuitive is the MyLA prototype (design, navigation) for students?
2. Is there room for improvement for the development of the MyLA prototype?
3. How can the empirical results (quantitative and qualitative) help to optimize the MyLA prototype for its initial implementation?

The questionnaire was conducted in order to evaluate design, navigation, text elements and used icons of MyLA. Beforehand, the students were shortly introduced to the topic of Learning Analytics. Afterwards, they were able to view the MyLA app either on web browser (Cooperative State University Mannheim) or on mobile browser (University of Mannheim) and afterwards responded to an online-questionnaire. For the purpose of comparability, none of the participants has used the MyLA web app before.

3.2 Methodology

3.2.1 Participants

The usability test was conducted with 105 students (56 Cooperative State University Mannheim, 49 University of Mannheim; 51 female, 54 male) in April 2017. The average age of the participants was 23.65 years (SD = 3.72, Min = 19, Max = 35). The majority of the respondents (N = 99) were studying in the field of business administration. More than half of the students were enrolled in a bachelor program (53.33 %) and 46.67 % were studying in a master program. In addition, seven students (4 female, 3 male) took part in an additional eye tracking study. In average, participants reported that they are spending 29 days (M = 28.90, SD = 4.56) per month with apps generally, but only four days (M = 3.65, SD = 6.06) days per month with apps for learning.

3.2.2 Design and Procedure

The usability test was divided into two parts using a standardized instrument (see 3.2.3): First, the participants made themselves familiar with MyLA app prototype via web browser or mobile browser. This included the navigation through the app and reviewing the design and the app's structure. Second, they responded to an online-questionnaire which was structured as follows: (1) Socio-demographic information, general usage of mobile devices and technologies, (2) MyLA-specific questions (open and closed questions). The MyLA-specific questions focused on navigation and navigation elements, design, and app structure. The main group (N = 98) followed this procedure. A smaller group (N = 7) participated in an eye tracking study (see 3.2.4). A significant difference between the participants was the device on which MyLA was tested: One group (Cooperative State University Mannheim) tested on a web browser via personal computer and another group (University of Mannheim) on a mobile browser via tablet. In order to ensure the anonymity various identification numbers had been given to the students.

3.2.3 Usability Instrument

The feedback of the students was committed via an online-questionnaire. The question pool within the MyLA-specific part was chosen following the usability testing instrument developed for HIMATT (or Highly integrated model assessment technology and tools). The instrument has been successfully tested for reliability and validity (see Pirnay-Dummer et al., 2010). For the MyLA Usability Testing, 13 items had been chosen. An example: "*I found it easy to navigate through the software*". All items were answered on a five-point Likert scale ranging from highly agree (5) to highly disagree (1). Figure 2 shows the thirteen items used in the usability testing.

3.2.4 Eye Tracking

According to Rayner (2009), eye movements are connected to a participant's attention and can therefore contribute to the usability testing of screen-based applications. Eye tracking is a standard methodology to record the eye movement of participants. The data evaluation is conducted with special eye tracking software. A very useful feature is the report function that visualizes the eye movements through heat maps or gaze plots (Kurzhals et al., 2017). Common observations in eye tracking studies include (Ehmke and Wilson, 2007):

- Fixation points: where participants have a long look,
- First look: where participants look first, or
- Non-looking: elements participants do not pay attention to.

After a short introduction, the students were instructed to solve three tasks by using the app prototype. The difficulty of each task was ascending. Therefore, seven AOI (Areas Of Interests) were defined for the analysis with Tobii Pro Studio software. All participants were recorded with regard to their "first look" and on which MyLA-contents they looked more often ("fixation points"). Furthermore, the student's solution approach was analyzed. The topics of the three tasks can be summarized as:

1. Calling the Cooperative State University Mannheim website as soon as possible.
2. Selecting and saving their respective university in the subcategory profile data.
3. Creating a post for a lecturer.

Students from the eye tracking study also participated in the survey-based usability test.

3.3 Results

The investigation of the results is divided into the survey-based and eye tracking usability test. Data analysis was conducted using IBM SPSS 23.0 and Tobii Pro Studio.

3.3.1 Survey-based Usability Test

The main part of the questionnaire was to investigate the app's navigation and design. Figure 2 shows the findings of the thirteen items from the survey-based usability test.

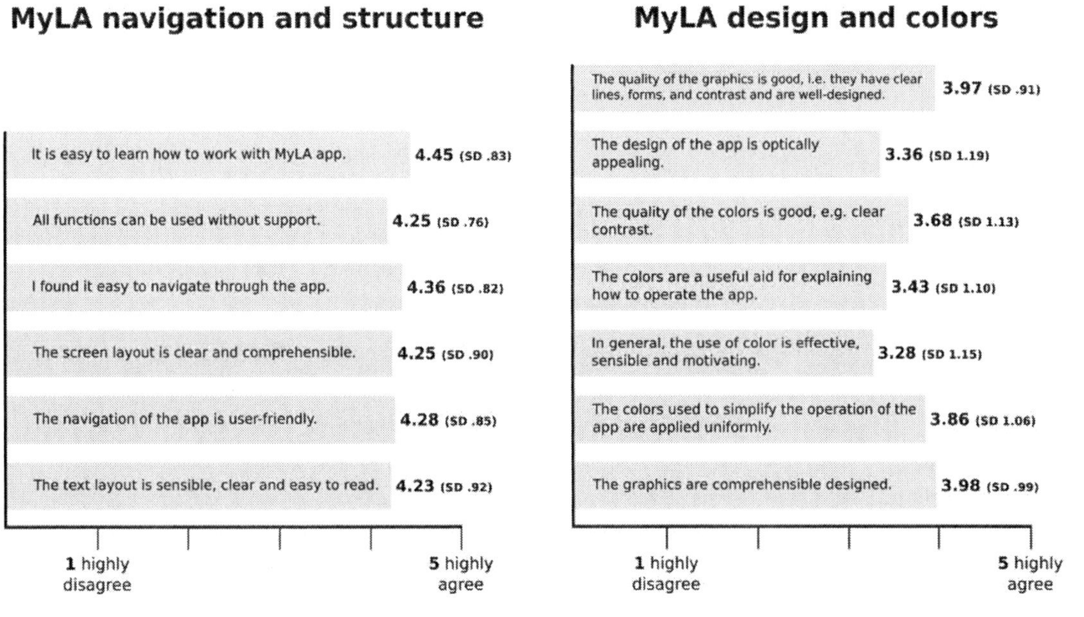

Figure 2. Bar Charts with the results of the MyLA-specific questions. Own Figure

The bar charts in Figure 2 are divided into two sections. The chart on left side shows the results concerning the navigation and structure of the MyLA prototype. The second chart on right side highlights the outcomes regarding the design and colors of MyLA. According to navigation and structure it is conspicuous that all six average values are constantly high. The highest value was reported for the simplicity of MyLA app prototype with an average of 4.45 (SD = .83). Followed by "*I found it easy to navigate through the app*" (M = 4.36, SD = .82) and "*The navigation of the app is user-friendly*" (M = 4.28, SD = .85). Based on the second chart it is obvious that there were some divergent opinions concerning the design and colors of MyLA. The lowest rated value was the use of color with an average of 3.28 (SD = 1.15). In addition, the participants ranked the design of MyLA as "*optically appealing*" with 3.36 (SD = 1.19).

3.3.2 Eye Tracking Usability Test

For the purpose of statistical analysis either the time of first fixation or the time to first mouse click were calculated. Table 1 shows the average times the pilot tester (conducted by a research team member) and the participants needed to complete the three tasks. The eye tracking study was implemented using the web browser version of MyLA (on a personal computer).

Table 1. Overview of the eye tracking usability test (all values in seconds)

Tasks	Pilot-Test (N = 1)	Participants (N = 7)
01 – Website challenge (click on a logo)	1.91	M = 4.86, SD = 2.46 (solved by 5 of 7)
02 – University selection (in the profile)	10.09	M = 14.55, SD = 9.43 (solved by 5 of 7)
03 – Pinboard post (create a new one)	4.81	M = 10.12, SD = 9.02 (solved by 7 of 7)

Table 1 shows that the majority of the participants (at least 5) were able to solve the simulated tasks. For task three, the students needed more time to find the solution in comparison to the first two tasks when compared to the benchmark of the pilot test. A possible explanation may be an unclear description of the task. Some students were not able to find the pinboard on a direct way (via chapter icon "My Learning"). However, all participants completed task three through an alternative solution (via side navigation menu).

As a next step, a heat map analysis was conducted which is a reflection of the screen where the participants viewed longer than other parts (Ehmke and Wilson, 2007) identifying gaze behavior precisely (Duchowski et al., 2012). Through the accumulation of all single viewpoints of a participant, the fixation points can be highlighted. Figure 3 shows the accumulation of the fixation points recorded by all participants. The viewpoints were predominantly recorded on the left side of MyLA prototype. For solving task one (pictured in the heat map of Figure 3), the participants had to look at the left side in order to find the Cooperative State University Mannheim logo. Additionally, it has to be considered that the participants saw the app via a desktop browser, hence, the screen width was obviously wider than on a mobile device.

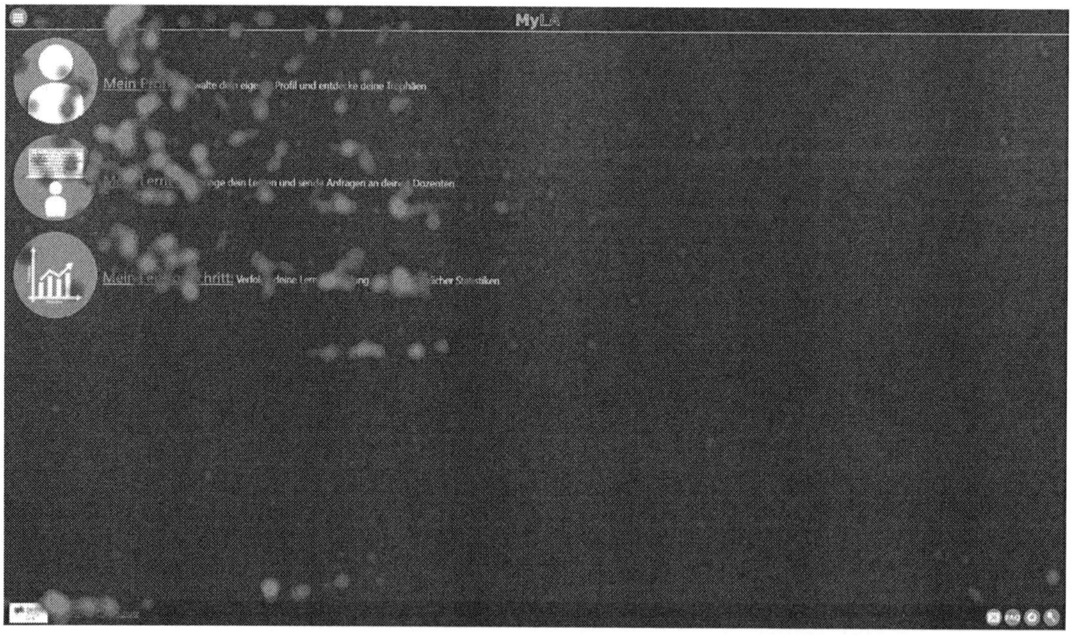

Figure 3. Heat map showing the cumulated fixation points of all Eye Tracking participants. Heat map exported using Tobii software

4. DISCUSSION AND CONCLUSION

Usability testing is a very useful and advantageous method for formative evaluation of the development process. The project MyLA can benefit from the valuable input of the potential app user.

With regard to research question 1 (*"How intuitive is the MyLA prototype (design, navigation) for students?"*), it can be suggested that the prototype is intuitive for the target group. Overall, the results were predominantly positive (all average values were higher than 3), however, some issues were identified for improvement, especially with regard to colors.

In addition, students provided feedback within the scope of open questions. The students evaluated the app's clarity, simplicity, navigation/structure and features as very positive. Regarding the assessment of the color scheme the responses were heterogeneous. Critical issues were partly used dark colors as well as color combinations. Moreover, some students mentioned that the app contained a broad color spectrum. Furthermore, they suggested additional features for future app versions, for example, a calendar function. With regard to research question 2 (*"Is there room for improvement for the development of MyLA prototype?"*), it can be summarized that the colors need to be adjusted.

To answer the research question 3 (*"How can the empirical results (quantitative and qualitative) help to optimize the MyLA prototype for the main survey?"*), the following aspects can be summarized: The involvement of the target group (students) was very important at this early project stage. The reason for that is very simple, because the students are prospective users of MyLA. Therefore, it is inevitable to get them highly involved. The success of a project depends on its acceptance. If the acceptance is high, the potential usage can be high, too. For reaching a large consumption of MyLA it is necessary to implement the students' feedback and recommendations. With help of these new insights future adaptions can be managed. Hence, the findings of the MyLA usability testing provided detailed insights to optimize the app prototype. Some lessons learned of the MyLA usability testing were the following proven statements:

- The handling of the MyLA web app prototype is intuitive.
- The app's structure is easy to learn.
- The navigation within the app is clear and user-friendly.
- The students mostly like the idea of MyLA.
- The design and colors can be improved, because the opinions deviate fairly high.

The next steps in the project will be the further development and implementation of the app prototype regarding the panel study in autumn 2017 Therefore, the technical infrastructure has to be developed. Furthermore, the feedback of the students concerning navigation and design has to be verified and adapted in the app. Additionally, the dashboard for lecturers, as associated software will be finalized. For generating a high acceptance within the project, the researchers want to involve the target group (students). By regularly viewing new features and other technical changes they make sure that the application will meet the students' needs.

Currently, the field implementation of the MyLA app is being prepared. Within this next project stage, more data will be available about the target group and the use of the application. According to the literature, the research area of learning analytics is still in its infancy in German-speaking countries (Ifenthaler and Schumacher, 2016). Moreover, with the advance of digital technologies, new skills and competencies are required from students at higher education institutions as well as their future workplace. In addition, the situation of non-traditional academics will be considered within the project. The combination of learning analytics and mobile learning seems to be beneficial in order to contribute to the individual demands of a diverse group of learners. For example, the project team wants to identify patterns of learning behavior and the management of learning tasks given a high demand of workload at the university and the workplace. In summary, the project can be seen as an important contribution to the topic of learning analytics for higher education in Germany.

ACKNOWLEDGEMENT

Funding for this project was provided by the Cooperative State University Mannheim and University of Mannheim as well as the Ministry of Science, Research and the Arts of the State of Baden-Württemberg, Germany. We thank all students who participated in the study.

REFERENCES

Adams Becker, S. et al. 2017. NMC Horizon Report: 2017 Higher Education Edition. The New Media Consortium, Austin, Texas, USA.

Al Saleh, S. & Bhat, S. A. 2015. Mobile Learning: A Systematic Review. *International Journal of Computer Applications*, 114(11), 1-5.

ARSnova. 2015. Feedback: Audience Response System für innovative Lehre. Technische Hochschule Mittelhessen (THM). Available at: https://arsnova.thm.de/blog/wp-content/uploads/2015/08/ARSnova-Produktprospekt-v5.pdf. [Accessed: 24 May 2017].

Duchwoski, A. T. et al. 2012. Aggregate Gaze Visualization with Real-time Heatmaps. *Proceedings of the Symposium on Eye Tracking Research and Applications*, Santa Barbara, California, USA, 13-20.

Ehmke, C. & Wilson, S. 2007. Identifying Web Usability Problems from Eye-Tracking Data. *Proceedings of the 12th International Conference on Human-Computer Interaction*, Beijing, P.R. China. Available at: http://www.bcs.org/upload/pdf/ewic_hc07_lppaper12.pdf. [Accessed: 4 May 2017].

Ifenthaler, D. et al. 2014. Challenges for Education in a Connected World: Digital Learning, Data Rich Environments, and Computer-Based Assessment – Introduction to the Inaugural Special Issue of Technology and Learning. *Technology, Knowledge and Learning, Springer Science+Business Media Dordrecht*, Tech Know Learn 2014, 19, 121-126.

Ifenthaler, D. & Schumacher, C. 2016. Learning Analytics im Hochschulkontext. *WiSt - Wirtschaftswissenschaftliches Studium,* 4, 172–177.

Kurzhals, K. et al. 2017. A Task-Based View on the Visual Analysis of Eye-Tracking Data. *Proceedings of the First Workshop on Eye Tracking and Visualization*, Chicago, Illinois, USA. Available at: http://www.springer.com/cda/content/document/cda_downloaddocument/9783319470238-c1.pdf?SGWID=0-0-45-1600732-p180288100. [Accessed: 18 May 2017].

Lin, H.-H. et al. 2016. Assessing Mobile Learning Systems Success. *International Journal of Information and Education Technology*, 6(7), 576-579.

Lockyer, L. et al. 2013. Informing Pedagogical Action: Aligning Learning Analytics With Learning Design. *American Behavioral Scientist*, 57(10), 1439–1459.

Mattingly, K. D. et al. 2012. Learning analytics as a tool for closing the assessment loop in higher education. *Knowledge Management & E-Learning: An International Journal*, 4(3), 236-247.

Macfadyen, L. & Dawson, S. 2012. Numbers are not enough: Why e-Learning analytics failed to inform an institutional strategic plan. *Educational Technology & Society*, 15(3), 149-163.

Pirnay-Dummer, P. et al. 2010. Highly integrated model assessment technology and tools. *Educational Technology Research and Development, Springer*, 58, 3-18.

Rayner, K. 2009. Eye movements and attention in reading, scene perception, and visual search. *The Quarterly Journal of Experimental Psychology*, 62(8), 1457-1506.

Sclater, N. et al. 2016. Learning Analytics in Higher Education: A review of UK and international practice: Full report. *Jisc*, p. 36.

Statista / Bitkom. 2017. Anteil der Smartphone-Nutzer in Deutschland nach Altersgruppe im Jahr 2016. Available at: https://de.statista.com/statistik/daten/studie/459963/umfrage/anteil-der-smartphone-nutzer-in-deutschland-nach-altersgruppe/. [Accessed: 28 April 2017].

DIGITAL COMPETENCE MODEL OF DISTANCE LEARNING STUDENTS

Ketia Kellen A. da Silva and Patricia A. Behar
Universidade Federal do Rio Grande do Sul - Brasil

ABSTRACT

This article presents the development of a digital competency model of Distance Learning (DL) students in Brazil called CompDigAl_EAD. The following topics were addressed in this study: Educational Competences, Digital Competences, and Distance Learning students. The model was developed between 2015 and 2016 and is being validated in 2017. It was created based on theoretical references and the mapping of competences in two classes, one a strictly distance learning undergraduate course and another a hybrid graduate course, to list the digital competences of students in this modality. As a result, a set of competences was obtained. It was analyzed by the DL students and specialists. Based on the results, the model was composed of seven general competences: 1. Computer use, 2. Internet and online communication, 3. Communication, 4. Information Management, 5. Creation and development of digital content, 6. Virtual profile management and, 7. Online Attendance. Currently, this model is in the final validation phase. The aim is that research results will support both the students and professors in the construction of digital competences in the DL modality.

KEYWORDS

Digital Competences, Distance Learning students, Distance Learning

1. INTRODUCTION

Distance Learning in Brazil has increased considerably in recent years, incorporating Information and Communication Technologies (ICT) through new instruments and criteria. However, the high levels of ICT use in distance learning requires students to continuously learn about different resources. In order to deal with these transformations, the concept of digital competences has been used as an alternative so that subjects have the chance to study more holistically through technology. However, studies specifically focused on digital competences for this profile are still incipient. Thus, this article aims to present the construction of a digital competence model for DL students. A model is seen as a way of establishing an analogous relationship with a simplified form of reality, a figurative system, according to Behar (2009). Thus, this proposal focuses on the construction of a digital competence model for DL students called CompDigAl_EAD.

Existing models of digital competences were analyzed through a bibliographical survey to inform this model, understand the profile of the distance learning student, and to map the competences that appear in the theoretical references. It became clear that many efforts have been made to define and create standards for digital competences. Being that the majority are from abroad, they translate a subject profile and educational level that does not align with this project. However, research in Brazil has been limited and there are no definitions or models focused on the DL student, which makes international studies the main theoretical basis for the present study. Thus, it was necessary to map the distance learning students, in order to have the resources to build a model focused on this subject profile.

Thus, this article presents the steps taken between from 2015 to 2017. It begins by mapping these competences, first based on the theoretical references and then with DL students. Subsequently, it examines the construction of the CompDigAL_EAD model and its validation, which is occurring presently . The work is therefore divided into sections that address digital competences, the profile of the student in the distance learning context, the construction of the digital competence model, CompDigAL_EAD, and lastly, the final considerations.

2. DIGITAL COMPETENCES

According to UNESCO reports (2006), digital competence is one of the eight core competences for lifelong development. However, there are few national and international studies available for understanding and developing this competence in education. Moreover, there is little research focused on DL. Most studies have come from international institutions, such as the European Commission (2003), Unesco (2006), and OECD (2005), and they generally define a list of digital competences for user profiles of these technologies that do not fit the needs of the DL student.

The definition of digital competences is interpreted in different ways in official and academic documents, which produces multiple meanings and a range of nomenclatures. A vast bibliography conceptualizing the term can be found, generating different definitions, some similar, some different, and many of them redundant. In fact, all descriptions seek to refer to how people should deal with ICT in different areas of life. Hence, the concept of digital competences has transformed as technologies have provoked transformations in society.

This study understands Digital Competences according to Ferrari (2012), as a "set of knowledge, skills, and attitudes, strategies and awareness that is needed when using ICT and digital media." Therefore, it is the mobilization of knowledge, skills, and attitudes (KSA) in a given context with the support of digital resources and technological tools. Yet, a DL student must also know about technology and its possibilities. Paloff and Pratt (2015) argue that there is not a single online learner profile, but a composition of subjects ranging from youth to adults. Thus it is necessary to go beyond the characteristics of the new generations and to focus on what it means to be a DL student. Rather than drawing generalizations based on generational differences, this entails taking into account that there are young people with less ICT skills than others, as well as different cultural, social, and economic contexts.

3. THE DISTANCE LEARNING STUDENT

Distance Learning using ICT resources redefines itself through virtual learning environments and new tools, creating an impact on the student profile of this new generation. In Brazil, Law 9.394 / 96 - Law of National Educational Guidelines and Foundations was introduced in 1996. It proposed Distance Learning as a new national educational modality. Years later guidelines for DL were created, which encouraged public institutions of higher education to create and develop courses. Moreover, the Open University System (UAB) and the Quality References for Distance Higher Education were also instituted in 2007, making the student the center of the educational process. In the DL quality references (BRASIL, 2007) the concept of DL proposes that all the subjects involved are responsible for their own development, considering their capacity for independent and autonomous learning, through interaction, organized and guided mediation, and with clearly defined evaluation criteria. Thus, the use of technologies in education must be supported by a philosophy of learning that provides students with opportunities for interaction and primarily the construction of knowledge (BRASIL, 2007).

According to the latest 2015 Brazilian DL Census (EAD.Br 2015), there were a total of 5,048,912 students enrolled in distance learning classes and the student profile was defined as subjects who primarily worked and studied and were between 21 and 30 years of age. In other words, they tend to be older than students in the traditional classroom. From this perspective, it is possible to note the development of DL in Brazil and its potential to democratize and elevate the quality standard of education. At the same time, student dropout rates have been shown to be one of the main obstacles faced by institutions with an average of 26% to 50% in 2015. According to the survey, the main factors that led students to dropout were lack of time to study and complete course activities, financial concerns, and the methodology applied by the institutions. Paloff and Pratt (2004, p. 112-113) argue that it is "the very elements that lead students to online education - the reality of restrictive working hours, the possibility of continuing to meet familial demands - interfere when it comes to staying in the course." Here the discussion of digital competences and their contribution to DL becomes quite apparent. Yet, according to Paloff and Pratt (2015), online learners range from younger students who have grown up with technology to older adults who are returning to college and looking for the convenience of online learning. Behar and Silva (2013) argue that students who seek distance learning need to develop a virtual student identity, which occurs through daily interactions with technology, where students will progressively appropriate the tools. Yet, there are three fundamental points that are be necessary to do so: 1. Student's strategic performance: time management, forms of communication, disposition, motivation related to the subject, etc.; 2. Understanding the characteristics of the group, the tasks, the objectives of the course, and the overall context; and, finally, 3. Technological abilities, which refer to the student's Internet connection, use of tools, and familiarity with technology. Students understanding regarding these points favors the development of their unique way of behaving in the DL context.

According to Gòmez (2015), the everyday life of the new generations is mediated by virtual social networks, which form new lifestyles, information processing, exchanges, expressions, and actions. Therefore, the characteristics of current students are very different from those of previous decades. According to Esteve, F.M., Duch, J. & Gisbert, M. (2014), the main terms used to define subjects and their relationship with technology are, Digital Natives (Prensky 2001), Generation Net (Tapscott, 1998), and Millennials (Howe and Strauss, 2000). However, according to Kennedy et. al. (2007), although these profiles possess certain ICT skills, they are technological skills that are often linked to social or leisure activities they cannot use to learn. Therefore, it is necessary that their technological confidence and experience is related to the development of digital competences aimed at their learning.

The methodological process carried out to construct the digital competence model of this research is presented in the next section.

4. DIGITAL COMPETENCES MODEL FOR DISTANCE LEARNING STUDENTS: COMPDIGAL_EAD

In order to construct the CompDigAl_EAD model, competences were mapped using the theoretical framework and with DL students. This article presents the four steps that have been taken so far. The model is being validated in 2017.

Step 1. Mapping of Digital Competencies from the bibliographic study - MAP 1;
Step 2. Mapping with DL students - MAP 2;
Step 3. Cross-referencing the results of MAP 1 with MAP 2, resulting in MAP 3;
Step 4. Validation of MAP 3 and construction of the CompDigAl_EAD model.
Each of these steps are explained in detail below.

4.1 Step 1

The first stage of the project was a bibliographic review related to the areas of knowledge involved. Thus, the themes of Competences in Education, Digital Competences, Distance Learning, and the Profile of the DL Student were further developed. A review of the existing models of digital competences at both the national and international level was also carried out. Fourteen models were selected and studied, as shown below in Table 1.

Table 1. Summary of Models studied

Year	Model Name	Location	Reference
1996	ECDL/ICDL	Spain	www.ecdl.org
2002	ICT – Literacy Framework	United States	Somerville et al. 2008 https://www.ets.org/
2003	DeSeCo – Competences	Europe	European Commission (2003)
2004	Digital Literacy	Israel	Eshet-Alkalai (2004 & 2009)
2005	DigEuLit	Europe	Martin (2005)
2006	E-Competences	Europe	http://www.ecompetences.eu/
2006	Key Competences for Lifelong Learning	Europe	http://eur-lex.europa.eu/
2007	NETs-S	United States	ISTE (2007)

2008	California ICT Digital Literacy Framework	United States	CEFT (2008 & 2010)
2009	ACTIC e COMPETIC	Catalonia	Department of Governmental Publications (2009)
2011	SIMCE-TIC	Chile	Enlaces (2011)
2012	Digital Competence	Spain	Larraz (2012)
2013	DIGICOMP	Europe	Ferrari (2013)
2013	Basic Competences for the digital environment	Catalonia	De. d'Ensenyame nt (2013)

Source: Created by the authors (2017)

These revealed a great diversity and lack of uniformity among the standards, which made the organization of an initial mapping quite difficult. Most only address knowledge related to digital literacy, limiting the results by not including skills and attitudes. In addition, the models tried to group the competences, but they have done so in many different ways with different names, such as domains, dimensions, categories, and areas. Another relevant point analyzed was proficiency, also called degrees or stages of development of digital competences. Therefore, all of the selected elements were arranged in a map and then in a single table, including their domains or categories, which resulted in 85 components. Subsequently, this was refined, combining those that were similar and distributing them in the identified competences, which were: Digital Literacy, Digital Fluency, Communication, and Teamwork. The following domains were found: Digital Security, Informational Literacy, Content Creation and Development. This first mapping is MAP 1. It clearly demonstrated the importance of mapping these elements focusing on DL students.

4.2 Step 2

In the second step, mapping of the digital competences with DL students was carried out, based on Leme (2012) and Torrezzan's (2014) methodologies. Two groups were used in 2015. One was a graduate course with 24 students between 25 and 50 years of age with different backgrounds, from experts to postdocs. The other was an undergraduate teaching course with a total of 10 students between 18 and 25 years old. A Learning Object (LO) developed about Digital Competences for DL students was used. In both classes the concept of digital competences and the DL student profile were initially discussed, referring to the first module of the LO as well as the challenges proposed in the LO. Then, in the second module, there was an orientation regarding the mapping of digital competences, where the students did the required readings and activities in groups. Both were given 20 hours to do the mapping, after having already discussed the concepts of DL, competences, and the profiles of DL subjects. The graduate group identified a list with 74 elements based on the activities, divided into knowledge, skills, and digital attitudes. These included basic issues such as turning the computer on and off, saving data, creating folders, knowing how to use e-mail, accessing the Virtual Learning Environment (VLE) on a regular basis, interacting with colleagues, meeting deadlines, responding to requests from the professor, as well as time management, as can be seen in Figure 1. The undergraduates identified 83 elements, highlighting the use of cellular phones and social networks to interact with groups, exchange ideas, and solve problems. They also emphasized creating websites, blogs, and games to broaden the ways of reading, thinking, and acting using technology, according to Figure 2.

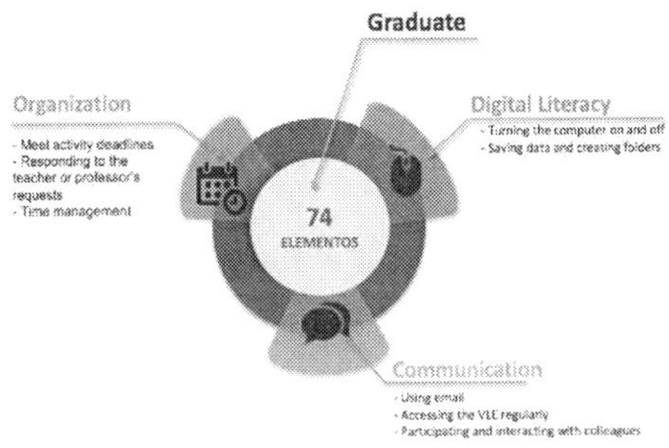

Figure 1. Main Competences for Graduate students

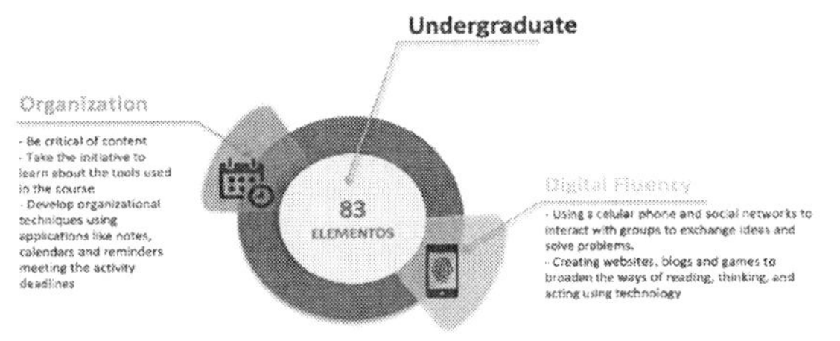

Figure 2. Main Competences for undergraduates

Source: Created by the authors (2017)

The elements listed in both groups were related to the competences: Digital Literacy, Digital Fluency, Organization, Communication, and Teamwork.

4.3 Step 3

The objective of the third step was to compare the competences identified in MAP 1 (theoretical references) with those of MAP 2 (mapping with the DL students). This was carried out through the four steps described below:

1. First, the results of the Digital Competence mapping activities from each class were organized in a table.
2. Then, the elements of the graduate and undergraduate mappings were combined separately by skills and attitudes in a new table. This was then refined by combining common points.
3. After combining the mappings in a single table with skills and attitudes, titled MAP 2, an analysis of similarities in MAP1 was performed, inserting knowledge and possible skills.
4. Finally, the elements were arranged by competencies and KSA, removing duplicate components and improving the writing. This final table was named MAP 3.

Although almost the same competences have been listed, the difference lies in the elements. While the theoretical framework presents an overview of these competences, the mapping with the DL students focuses on the student profile in the distance learning modality. Hence, when the elements were combined, the names of those that presented contributions to the subject profile were used, because it is the main objective of this research.

Step 4 corresponds to the validation of the mapping of digital competences with distance learning students.

4.4 Step 4

This step involves the validation of MAP 3, in order to transform it into a model containing the competences, KSA, and an evaluation of both focused on the DL student, or CompDigAL_EAD. This step took place in 2016/1 in the graduate class and 2016/2 with specialists. In the course, three classes were used for validation, this the group had already studied the concept of DL, Profiles, and Competences. The students were asked to reflect on MAP 3 through activities where the objective was to provoke ideas about what is needed in a digital competence model focused on distance learning and for the student profile. This was also done with experts, however in this case through an online questionnaire. From the results of this stage, the model could be organized as a list of competences that are directly linked to the student profile and their learning process in the distance learning modality. Therefore, the model had competences and KSA related to the technological domain which were: Functional Digital Literacy, Critical Digital Literacy, Digital Fluency, Communication, Information Management, Online Attendance, Creation and development of Digital content, and Virtual profile management.

According to Behar (2009), the technological domain consists of competences related to the use of technological resources in DL, such as virtual learning environments, learning objects, and tools in general. Thus, an analysis of the mappings carried out with the students was performed in conjunction with the bibliographic survey to adapt the elements to each competence. It became clear that for DL students to be digitally proficient, they need to develop a degree of Digital Fluency. Digital Fluency, therefore, becomes a central concept in this model. According to Machado et. al. (2016) there is a correlation between funcional and critical digital literacy and digital fluency. That is, in order for a student to reach the level of digital fluency, they must first have a level of literacy.

Therefore when analyzing the concepts of Functional and Critical Digital Literacy, and Digital Fluency, the complexity at each of these levels becomes clear, see Table 2.

Table 2. Conceptual Frameworks

Functional Digital Literacy	Equates the need to functionally master the technologies, reading, and writing to have access to digital and virtual knowledge (Coll, Illera, 2010). Functional Digital literacy is made up of competences related to the basic use of the computer and the Internet.
Critical Digital Literacy	Related to research, evaluation, reflection, and critical understanding of the information available on the Internet, as well as the use of digital tools for communication. Composed by a set of literacies, which are: informational, multimedia, communicational, and computational. (Ribeiro, 2013). Critical Digital Literacy is composed of competences such as Communication and Information Management in the network.
Digital Fluency	Linked to the use of technology in a way that the subject feels like a digitally active participant in technological advances. Fluency enables not only the use, but also the creation and production of content/materials. (Behar et al., 2009).

Source: Created by the authors (2017)

There is therefore a degree of complexity at each level which is composed of specific competences. Thus, during the organization of the mapped digital competences aimed at the technological domain, the organization that can be seen in Figure 4 emerged.

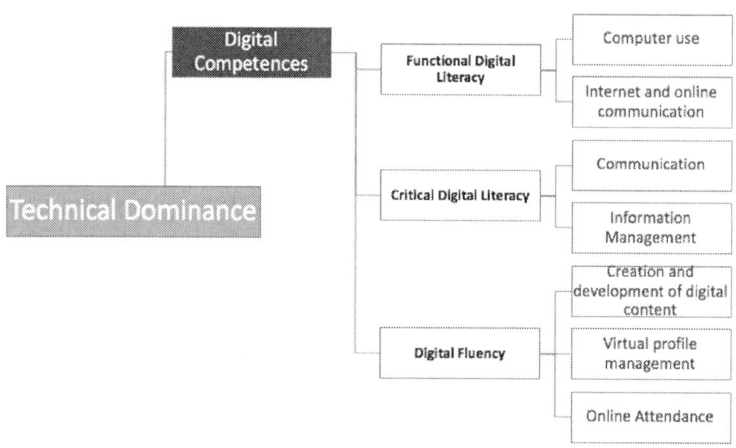

Figure 4. Technical Dominance and Digital Competences
Source: Created by the authors (2017)

Therefore, there is a non-hierarchical structure for the development of the digital competences, an organization of elements to be constructed by the DL students. Many times Critical Digital Literacy is not developed in all its elements, however the subject already has a degree of proficiency with respect to competences that belong to Digital Fluency.

The model, which is now in its final validation phase, consists of general and specific competences through the description of the elements: Knowledge, skills, and attitudes (KSA) and proficiency, basic, intermediate, and advanced levels with examples to illustrate each competence. Table 3 below shows the division of general and specific competences.

Table 3. General Organizational model of CompDigAl_EAD

Tecnological Domain		
Level	General Competences	Specific Competences
Functional Digital Literacy	Use of a computer	Basic notions of computers and devices;
		Tools for word processing, making charts, and presentations;
	Internet and online communication	Basic notions about Internet use;
		Basic use of E-mail
Criticatl Digital Literacy	Communication	Use of interaction and communication tools
		Sharing of information and content
		Internet etiquitte
	Information Management	Surfing, searching, and filtering information;
		Evaluating information;
		Saving and finding information;
Fluência Digital	Creation and development of digital content	Developing content
		Integrating and expanding content;
		Copyright and licenses;
		Programming;
	Virtual Profile Management	Protective devices;
		Protection of personal data
		Protection of physical and mental health
	Online Attendance	Virtual identity
		online attendance

Source: Created by the authors (2017)

It should be emphasized that digital competences must be constructed gradually over time, taking into account that technology is constantly evolving and provoking changes. Hence, this model is dynamic and must be constantly updated according to the needs of the target audience, in this case DL students.

5. FINAL CONSIDERATIONS

The main objective of this article was to present the steps taken to develop the digital competences model for DL students. Thus, a discussion of digital competences and the profile of the DL student was presented, in order to address the methodology used for the construction of the CompDigAL_EAD model, which is in its final validation phase.

A model of digital competences should be focused on the profile of the DL student, requiring specific knowledge of technology and its possibilities. One of the main questions therefore was focused on this subject. Research regarding these topics constitute a relatively unexplored territory and, therefore, it becomes a challenge for educational and technological to research.

Finally, the hope is that these results will enable the improvement of DL students' digital competences and can be an important resource for professors and students seeking knowledge about distance learning and digital competences.

REFERENCES

Behar, Patricia A.; Silva, Ketia Kellen. (2012) *Mapeamento de Competências: Um foco no aluno da Educação a Distância.* In: http://www.cinted.ufrgs.br/ciclo20/artigos/5a-ketia.pdf. Acess: 20 de mar. 2016

Behar, Patricia A. et al. (2009). *Modelos Pedagógicos em Educação à Distância.* Porto Alegre: Artmed.

Behar, Patricia, A. (Org.). (2013). *Competências em educação a distância.* Porto Alegre: Penso.

Brasil. Lei n. 9.394, de 20 de dezembro de 1996. *Estabelece as Diretrizes e Bases da Educação Nacional.* In: <http://www.planalto.gov.br/ccivil_03/Leis/L9394.htm>. Acess: 15 mai de 2017.

Brasil. (1999) Parecer CNE/CEB n ° 16/99. Trata das *Diretrizes Curriculares Nacionais para a Educação Profissional de Nível Técnico.* Brasília: Ministério da Educação, 1999a. In: <http://portal.mec.gov.br/setec/arquivos/pdf/PCNE_CEB16_99.pdf>. Acess: 14 mai. 2017.

Brasil. (2007) *Referenciais de Qualidade para Educação Superior a Distância.* Brasília: Ministério da Educação, Secretaria de Educação a Distância. In: <http://portal.mec.gov.br/seed/arquivos/pdf/referenciaisead.pdf>. Acess: 10 mar. 2017.

Brasil. (2015) *Censo Educação a Distância do Brasil 2014* (Censo EAD BR.2015). In Associação Brasileira de Educação a Distância. In: < http://abed.org.br/arquivos/Censo_EAD_2015_POR.pdf > Acess: 10 mai. 2017

Duncan-Howell, J.A. & Lee, K.T. (2007) *M-Learning: Innovations and Initiatives: Finding a place for mobile technologies within tertiary educational settings.* En Ascilite In: http://www.ascilite.org/conferences/singapore07/procs/duncan-howell.pdf Acess: 15 mai. 2017.

Esteve, F.M., Duch, J. & Gisbert, M. (2014). Los aprendices digitales en la literatura científica: diseño y aplicación de una revisión sistemática entre 2001 y 2010. *In. Revista de Medios y Educación.* Nº 45.

Ferrari, A. (2012) "Digital Competence in Practice: an analysis of Frameworks." Sevilla: JRC IPTS.

Gómez, A. I. Perez. (2015) *Educação na Era Digital: a escola educativa.*Tradução Marisa Guedes. Porto Alegre. Penso.

Helsper, Ellen and Eynon, Rebecca. (2009) *Digital natives: where is the evidence?* British educational research journal. pp. 1-18.

Howe, N., & Strauss, W. (2000). *Millennials rising: The next great generation.* New York: Vintage Original.

Illera, José Luiz Rodrigues; ROIG, Ana Escofet. (2010) Ensino e aprendizagem de competências comunicacionais em ambientes virtuais. In: COLL, Cesar; MONEREO, Carles (Org.), *Psicologia da Educação Virtual:* aprender e ensinar com as tecnologias da informação e da comunicação. Porto Alegre: Artmed. p. 329-345.

Kennedy, G. et al. (2007) The net generation are not big users of Web 2.0 technologies: Preliminary findings." En Ascilite 2007. *Universidad Tecnológica de Nanyang, Singapore.* in: http:// www.ascilite.or g.au/conferences/ singapore07/procs/kennedy.pdf Acess: 20 mai. 2017.

Leme, Rogério. (2012) *Aplicação prática de gestão de pessoas por competências – mapeamento, treinamento, seleção, avaliação e mensuração de resultados de treinamento.* Rio de Janeiro: Qualitymark, 244 p.

Machado, L; Grande, T. (2016). *Mapeamento de competências Digitais: a inclusão social dos idosos.* In: ETD – Revista de Educação e Temática Digital. Camp. SP, v.18, n.4, p.903-921.

Organisation for Economic Co-Operation and Development – OECD. *Are students ready for a technology-rich world?* What PISA studies tell us. Paris, 2005a. Disponível em: <http://www.oecd.org/dataoecd/28/4/35995145.pdf>. Acesso em: Mai. 2017.

Palloff, Rena M.; PRATT, Keith. (2004) *O aluno virtual: um guia para trabalhar com estudantes on-line.* Porto Alegre: Artmed.

Pallof, Rena M. (2015) *Lições da sala de aula virtual: As realidades on-line.* 2.ed. Porto Alegre: Penso.

Prensky, Mark. (2001) *Digital Natives, Digital Immigrants. In*: On the Horizon. NCB University Press, n. 5, v. 9.

Ribeiro, Ana Carolina Ribeiro. (2013). *Letramento digital: uma abordagem através das competências na formação docente.* 164 f. Tese (Mestrado em Educação) – Faculdade de Educação , Universidade Federal do Rio Grande do Sul, Porto Alegre,

Tapscott, D. (1998). *Growing up digital: The rise of the net generation.* New York: McGraw-Hill

Torrezzan, Cristina Alba Wildt. (2014) *ConstruMed: Metodologia para a construção de materiais educacionais digitais baseados no design pedagógico.* 240 f. Tese (Doutorado em Informática na Educação) – Centro de Estudos Interdisciplinares em Novas Tecnologias na Educação, Universidade Federal do Rio Grande do Sul, Porto Alegre, RS, 2014. Disponível em: < http://goo.gl/lq8B1g>. Acesso em: 05 mai. 2017.

UNESCO. (2006) *Padrões de competência em TIC para professores: módulos de padrão de competências.* Paris: Unesco, 2006. In:< http://unesdoc.unesco.org/images/0015/001562/156207por.pdf>. Acess: Abr. 2017.

HOW DISPOSITIONAL LEARNING ANALYTICS HELPS UNDERSTANDING THE WORKED-EXAMPLE PRINCIPLE

Dirk Tempelaar
Maastricht University School of Business and Economics
Tongersestraat 53, 6211 LM, Maastricht, Netherlands

ABSTRACT

This empirical study aims to demonstrate how Dispositional Learning Analytics can contribute in the investigation of the effectiveness of didactical scenarios in authentic settings, where previous research has mostly been laboratory based. Using a showcase based on learning processes of 1080 students in a blended introductory quantitative course, we analyse the use of worked examples by students. Our method is to combine demographic and trace data from technology enhanced systems with self-reports of several contemporary social-cognitive theories. We find that the same maladaptive learning orientations that play a role in worked examples learning theories as to explain the effectiveness of worked examples do predict the use of worked examples: this time in the role of individual learning dispositions.

KEYWORDS

Blended learning; dispositional learning analytics; e-tutorials; learning feedback; learning dispositions; worked examples.

1. INTRODUCTION

Although there exists little misunderstanding on what learning Analytics (LA) is supposed to study, LA practices seem to be at a large distance. '*Learning analytics uses dynamic information about learners and learning environments, assessing, eliciting and analysing it, for real-time modelling, prediction and optimisation of learning processes, learning environments and educational decision-making*' (Ifenthaler, 2015) is a broadly accepted description of all facets that are included in LA. In the same source, this definition is elaborated by enumerating all ten essential components of a holistic LA framework: information about the learners' individual characteristics, information from the social web, physical data, information from learners' activities in the online learning environment, curriculum information, the learning analytics engine, the reporting engine, and the personalisation and adaption engine (Ifenthaler, 2015). Yet, current LA practices typically incorporate only a few of these ten components, with a strong focus on building predictive models based on demographics, grades, and trace data.

To emphasize the importance of other data than trace or system data, Buckingham Shum and Crick (2012) proposed a Dispositional Learning Analytics (DLA) infrastructure that combines learning data (generated in learning activities through technology enhanced systems) with learner data (student dispositions, values, and attitudes measured through self-report surveys). Learning dispositions represent individual difference characteristics that impact all learning processes and include affective, behavioural and cognitive facets (Rienties, Cross, S., Zdrahal, 2017). Student's preferred learning approaches are examples of such dispositions of both cognitive and behavioural type; in research on their role in learning, they are often simply labelled as 'self-report data', and in the above description of the holistic LA framework, indicated as the learners' individual characteristics component (Ifenthaler, 2015). Different from LA research, stakeholders of DLA applications are typically restricted to students and teacher/tutors, as these applications can be positioned at both the meso- and micro-level (Ifenthaler, 2015), rather than the mega- or macro-level.

Our current study aims to provide a show case of the educational benefits of following this more holistic approach in the application of LA. We do so in the context of an instructional design issue: the worked examples principle (Renkl, 2014). The merits of using worked examples in the initial acquisition of cognitive skills are well documented. The evidence is without exception based on laboratory-based experimental studies, in which the effectiveness of different instructional designs is compared (Renkl, 2014). In this issue, the potential contribution of LA-based investigations in authentic contexts is that we can observe students' revealed preferences for learning with worked examples, rather than assigning them to a worked examples condition, and link the preferences to other observations: information about the learners' individual characteristics, information from the social web, and information from learners' activities in the online learning environment (the information components of Ifenthaler's holistic framework). By doing so, we aim to derive a characterization of students who actively apply worked examples, and those not doing so and link these characterizations to the outcomes of existing laboratory-based research. This study is a follow-up of previous DLA research by the authors on the use of worked examples (Tempelaar, Rienties, & Nguyen, 2017a). The focus of that previous research was on the timing of the use of worked examples: in the initial skills acquisition, or at a later stage in the learning process. The focus of the current research is on individual differences in the intensity of using worked examples.

2. WORKED EXAMPLES

The micro level pedagogical benefits that come with LA applications refer to the provision of 'personalized and adaptive scaffolds' supporting the learner in reaching the learning outcomes (Ifenthaler, 2015). Worked examples represent one of the scaffold formats in computer-enhanced environments (Duffy & Azevedo, 2015), formats that amongst others differ in the amount of guidance or assistance provided to students. Pedagogics has identified four main instructional approaches for assisting learners in problem-solving (McLaren, Van Gog, Ganoe, Karabinos, & Yaron, 2016), with varying degrees of learner support. First, the problem-solving approach is positioned in the low guidance end of the continuum, offering little or no feedback to learners. Second, tutored problem-solving provides learners with feedback and hints to solve the problem or construct the schema when a learner is stuck. This approach intervenes in the learning process only when help is needed; hence, it ensures learners will actively attempt to solve the problems. Third, erroneous examples present learners with flawed examples and instruct them to find, explain, and fix errors. Finally, at the high end of learner support McLaren et al. (2016) position the use of worked examples. The use of worked solutions in multi-media based learning environments stimulates gaining deep understanding (Renkl, 2014). When compared to the use of erroneous examples, tutored problem-solving, and problem-solving in computer-based environments, the use of worked examples may be more efficient as it reaches similar learning outcomes in less time and with less learning efforts (McLaren et al., 2016). The mechanism responsible for this outcome is disclosed in Renkl (2014, p. 400): '*examples relieve learners of problem solving that – in initial cognitive skill acquisition, when learners still lack understanding – is typically slow, error-prone, and driven by superficial strategies. When beginning learners solve problems, the corresponding demands may burden working memory capacities or even overload them, which strengthens learners' surface orientation. ... When learning from examples, learners have enough working memory capacity for self-explaining and comparing examples by which abstract principles can be considered, and those principles are then related to concrete exemplars. In this way, learners gain an understanding of how to apply principles in problem solving and how to relate problem cases to underlying principles*'.

Studies into the efficiency of worked examples are typically nested in laboratory settings, with students assigned to one of the several experimental conditions, each representing one unique pedagogical feedback scenario. In authentic settings, students mix and match diverse pedagogical feedback scenarios, and do so in different orders. For example, some students will avoid using worked examples; other students use just a single worked example at the very start of skills acquisition, whereas others apply worked examples exactly in the way the theory of example-based learning would indicate: self-explaining and comparing multiple examples as to '*represent principles in the form of abstract schema that are interrelated to multiple example cases so that learners know (1) how the abstract principles can be applied and (2) how concrete problem cases can be interpreted in terms of underlying principles*.' (Renkl, 2014, p. 400). Beyond detecting individual differences in preferences for pedagogical scenarios, a next step is to explain these based on differences in learning dispositions. For example, studies in gender differences in learning mathematics suggest that female students would profit more from having worked examples available at the very start of learning new mathematical concepts (Boltjens, 2004). Do such outcomes of experimental studies transfer to differences in revealed preferences in an authentic learning setting? And what other learning dispositions do make a difference in the use of worked examples beyond the potential role of gender?

3. METHODS

3.1 Context of the Empirical Study

This study takes place in a large-scale introductory mathematics and statistics course for first-year undergraduate students in a business and economics programme in the Netherlands. The educational system is best described as 'blended' or 'hybrid'. The main component is face-to-face: Problem-Based Learning (PBL), in small groups (14 students), coached by a content expert tutor (see Williams et al., 2016 for further information on PBL and the course design). Participation in tutorial groups is required. Optional is the online component of the blend: the use of the two e-tutorials SOWISO (https://sowiso.nl/) and MyStatLab (MSL) (Tempelaar, Rienties, & Nguyen, 2015, 2017b). This design is based on the philosophy of student-centred education, placing the responsibility for making educational choices primarily on the student. Since most of the learning takes place during self-study outside class through the e-tutorials or other learning materials, class time is used to discuss solving advanced problems. Thus, the instructional format is best characterized as a flipped-classroom design (Williams et al., 2016). Using and achieving good scores in the e-tutorial practice modes is incentivized by providing bonus points for good performance in quizzes that are taken every two weeks and consist of items that are drawn from the same item pools applied in the practicing mode. This approach was chosen in order to encourage students with limited prior knowledge to make intensive use of the e-tutorials.

The subject of this study is the full 2016/2017 cohort of students (1093 students). A large diversity in the student population was present: only 19% were educated in the Dutch high school system. In terms of nationality, the largest group, 44% of the students, was from Germany, followed by 23% Dutch and 19% Belgian students. In total, 50 nationalities were present. A large share of students was of European nationality, with only 3.9% of students from outside Europe. High school systems in Europe differ strongly, most particularly in the teaching of mathematics and statistics. For example, the Dutch high school system has a strong focus on the topic of statistics, but is mostly missing in high school programs of other countries. Therefore, it is crucial that this present introductory module is flexible and allows for individual learning paths (Williams et al., 2016). In this course, students spend on average 24 hours in SOWISO and 32 hours in MSL, which is 30% to 40% of the available time of 80 hours for learning on both topics.

3.2 Instruments and Procedure

The empirical analyses described in this contribution focus on the use of the MSL e-tutorial for learning statistics. Although Pearson MyLabs can be used as a learning environment in the broad sense of the word (it contains, among others, a digital version of the textbook), they represent primarily an environment for test-directed learning and practicing. Each step in the learning process is initiated by a question, and students are encouraged to (try to) answer each question. If a student does not master a question, she/he can either ask for help to solve the problem step-by-step (Help Me Solve This), or ask for a worked example (View an Example), as demonstrated in Figure 1 (left panel), in any lesson.

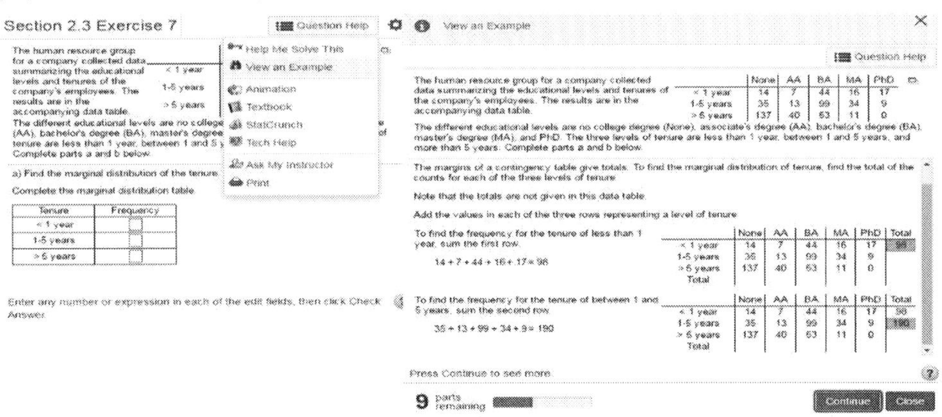

Figure 1. MSL exercise window, left panel, and worked example window, right panel

Students can call for multiple examples that differ in the context of the application of the same statistical principle, as indicated by the theory of example-based learning (Figure 1, right panel). When after studying these examples the student feels ready to make an own attempt, a new version of the problem loads (parameter based) to allow the student to demonstrate his/her newly acquired mastery.

Our study combines trace data of the MSL e-tutorial with self-report survey data measuring learning dispositions. Trace data is both of product and process type (Azevedo, Harley, Trevors, Duffy, Feyzi-Behnagh, & Bouchet, 2013). MSL reporting options of trace data are very broad, requiring making selections from the data. First, all dynamic trace data were aggregated over time, to arrive at static, full course period accounts of trace data. Second, from the large array of trace variables, a selection was made by focusing on process variables most strongly connected to alternative pedagogical behaviours of students. These include the alternative feedback modes preferred by students. In total, six trace variables were selected:

- *#Attempts*: total number of attempts of individual exercises;
- *#Examples*: total number of worked examples called;
- *#AttemptsCorrect*: total number of attempts with correct answers;
- *#AttemptsInCorr*: total number of attempts with incorrect answers; and
- *Mastery*: the proportion of the in total 160 exercises successfully answered.

In order to disentangle the effects of learning intensity from different learning approaches, we restricted the sample to those students who have been very active in the e-tutorial and achieved at least a 70% mastery level (that is, successfully solved at least 112 of the 160 exercises): 593 of the 1080 students. From this subset about 20% never used any worked example during the course. The other students were split into three equal-sized groups according to intensity of using worked examples. Table 1 provides descriptive statistics of these four sub-samples. *#Exerc* indicates the average number of exercises for which students called at least one example, and *#Example/Exerc* provides the average number of examples called in these exercises.

Table 1. Descriptive statistics of four sub-samples of students achieving at least 70% mastery level

Group	N	*Mastery*	*#Attempts*	*#Examples*	*#Exerc*	*#Example/Exerc*
NoExamples	114	90%	990	0	0	0
SomeExamples	159	91%	1211	34	12	2.9
AverageExampl	159	93%	1335	104	35	3.0
IntensiveExampl	161	93%	1719	242	57	4.3
Total	593	92%	1340	103	28	3.7

Mastery level is indeed invariant over groups. *#Attempts*, *#Examples*, *#Exercises* where examples are called, and *#Example/Exerc* do strongly increase over the four sub-samples. Since all observations are of count-type, they are all strongly right skewed. To diminish skewness and achieve better normality, we re-express all count data into square root transforms when applying correlation or regression analyses. As quantitative measures of how intensive students have used worked examples, we defined *#ExercExamplSqrt* as the square root of the number of exercises in which students called at least one example and *#ExercMultExamplSqrt* as the number of exercises in which the student called multiple examples, negatively exponentially weighted with the number of examples called.

In this study, we will make a selection with regard to the self-report surveys measuring student learning dispositions. More than a dozen were administered, ranging from affective learning emotions to cognitive learning processing strategies. We will focus here on a selection of six instruments measuring aspects of self-regulated learning (SRL), expectancy-value based learning attitudes, national culture dimensions and learning emotions, since these dispositions have been investigated in recent LA studies (see Azevedo et al., 2013; Duffy & Azevedo, 2015, Mittelmeier, Tempelaar, Rienties, & Nguyen, 2016 and references therein). All disposition surveys are measured using seven-point Likert scales; no transformations of variables were required except a logarithmic transform for the *Effort* variable.

In the characterisation of national cultural differences, research by Hofstede (Hofstede, Hofstede, & Minkov, 2010) takes a prominent position. Based on an analysis of attitude surveys obtained from employees in more than 50 countries, Hofstede identified six major dimensions on which cultures differ. Power distance (*PDI*) refers to the extent to which less powerful members of organisations and institutions accept and expect unequal distribution of power. Uncertainty avoidance (*UAI*) refers to society's tolerance for uncertainty and ambiguity. Individualism versus collectivism (*IND*) signals the degree to which individuals are integrated into groups: from loose ties between individuals and self-agency to integrated and strong, cohesive societies.

In masculine societies (*MAS*), emotional gender roles are rather distinct, whereas, in feminine societies, these roles overlap. Long-term orientation (*TOWVS*) distinguishes societies in being directed towards future rewards, or the fulfilment of present needs and desires. The final and most recently added cultural dimension is that of indulgence versus restraint (*IVR*) and signals the degree to which a culture allows or suppresses gratification of needs. In research applying national culture differences, students are assigned culture dimension scores based on their nationality (Mittelmeier, Tempelaar, Rienties, & Nguyen, 2016).

Preferred processing strategies of students, part of a broader array of self-regulated learning dispositions (Vermunt, 1996), allow for an ordinal classification from two deep learning orientations, *Critical processing*, and *Relating and structuring*, through *Concrete processing*, to two surface or step-wise learning orientations: *Analysing* and *Memorising*.

Expectancy-value based attitudes towards learning of statistics were assessed with the SATS instrument (Tempelaar, Gijselaers, Schim van der Loeff, & Nijhuis, 2007). The instrument contains six attitudes: *Affect*: students' feelings concerning mathematics; *CognComp*: students' self-perceptions of their intellectual knowledge and skills when applied to mathematics; *Value*: students attitudes about the usefulness, relevance, and worth of mathematics in personal and professional life; *NoDifficulty*: students' perceptions that mathematics as a subject is not difficult to learn; *Interest*: students' level of individual interest in mathematics; and *Effort*: the amount of work the student is willing to undertake to learn mathematics.

The Control-Value Theory of Achievement Emotions (CVTAE, Pekrun, 2006) postulates that emotions that arise in learning activities differ in valence, focus, and activation. Emotional valence can be positive (enjoyment) or negative (anxiety, hopelessness, boredom). CVTAE describes the emotions experienced in relation to an achievement activity (e.g. boredom experienced whilst preparing homework) or outcome (e.g. anxiety towards performing at an exam). The activation component describes emotions as activating (i.e. anxiety leading to action) versus deactivating (i.e. hopelessness leading to disengagement). From the Achievement Emotions Questionnaire (AEQ, Pekrun, Götz, Frenzel, Barchfeld, & Perry, 2011) measuring learning emotions we selected four scales: positive activating emotion *Enjoyment*, negative activating emotion *Anxiety*, neutral deactivating *Boredom* and negative deactivating *Hopelessness*. Next, *Academic Control* is included as the antecedent of all learning emotions. Learning emotions of epistemic type are related to cognitive aspects of the task itself (Pekrun, 2012). Prototypical epistemic emotions are curiosity and confusion. In this study, epistemic emotions were measured with the Epistemic Emotion Scales (EES, Pekrun & Meier, 2011), including *Surprise*, *Curiosity*, *Confusion*, *Anxiety*, *Frustration*, *Enjoyment*, and *Boredom*.

Course performance data is based on the final written exam, as well as the three intermediate quizzes. Quiz scores are averaged, and both exam and quiz are decomposed into two topic scores, resulting in *MathExam*, *StatsExam*, *MathQuiz* and *StatsQuiz*.

4. RESULTS

Grouping based on intensity of example use induces statistically significant but small group differences for gender (sign=.03, eta squared=1.5%), math prior education (sign=.009, eta squared=2.0%), and international students (sign<.001, eta squared=3.4%); see the left panel of Figure 2.

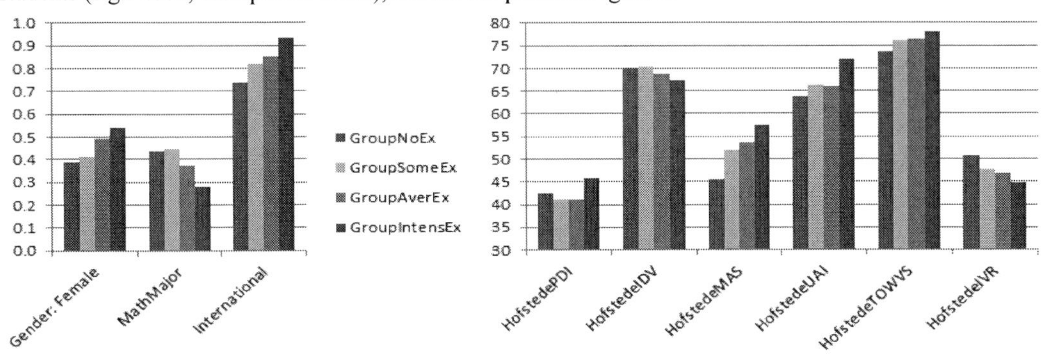

Figure 2. Group differences for demographics (left) and culture dimensions (right)

The same conclusion is reached for national culture dimensions: statistically significant but small group differences exist for *Power distance* (sign=.007, eta squared=2.0%), *Masculinity* (sign<.001, eta squared=4.0%), *Uncertainty avoidance* (sign<.001, eta squared=4.6%), *Long-term orientation* (sign=.014, eta squared=1.8%), and *Indulgence versus restraint* (sign=.001, eta squared=2.7%). Similar size differences are visible in the deep learning facets of the cognitive processing strategies: *Critical processing* (sign=.002, eta squared=2.6%), *Relating and structuring* (sign=.002, eta squared=2.6%), resulting in the aggregated group difference of the *Deep learning* scale being significant (sign<.001, eta squared=3.1%). Also, the *Concrete processing* scale demonstrates group differences (sign=.013, eta squared=1.8%), but not the two scales representing *Surface learning* approaches, *Analysing*, and *Memorizing* (Figure 3, left panel).

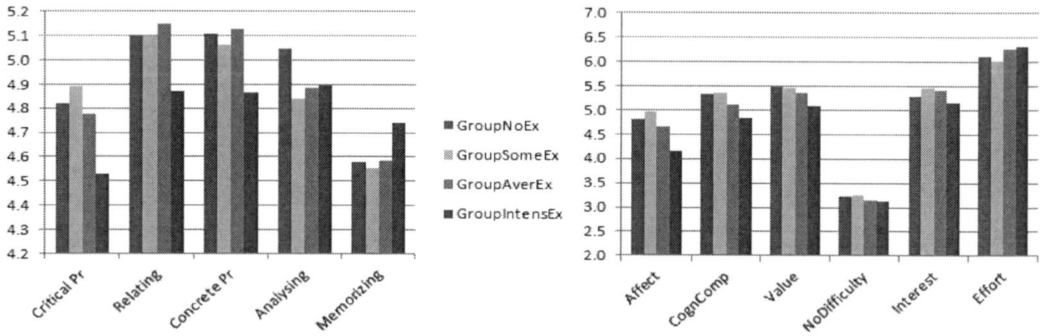

Figure 3. Group differences for cognitive processing strategies (left) and learning attitudes (right)

Learning attitudes exhibit group differences for *Affect* (sign<.001, eta squared=6.5%), *Cognitive competence* (sign<.001, eta squared=5.1%), *Value* (sign<.001, eta squared=3.8%), *Interest* (sign=.032, eta squared=1.5%) and *Effort* (sign<.024, eta squared=1.6%), but not for *NoDifficulty* (Figure 3, right panel). The effect of positive affect in the attitude scale is repeated in the two learning emotion scales. Epistemic emotions demonstrate group differences for the negative emotions *Confusion* (sign<.001, eta squared=3.3%), *Anxiety* (sign<.001, eta squared=4.8%), and *Frustration* (sign<.001, eta squared=3.6%), and the positive emotion *Enjoyment* (sign=.015, eta squared=1.8%): Figure 4, left panel. Emotions in the actual doing of learning activities, visible in the right panel of Figure 4, demonstrate even larger differences for *Academic control* (sign<.001, eta squared=5.0%), learning *Anxiety* (sign<.001, eta squared=5.9%), and learning *Hopelessness* (sign<.001, eta squared=5.2%), but not for learning *Boredom* and *Enjoyment*.

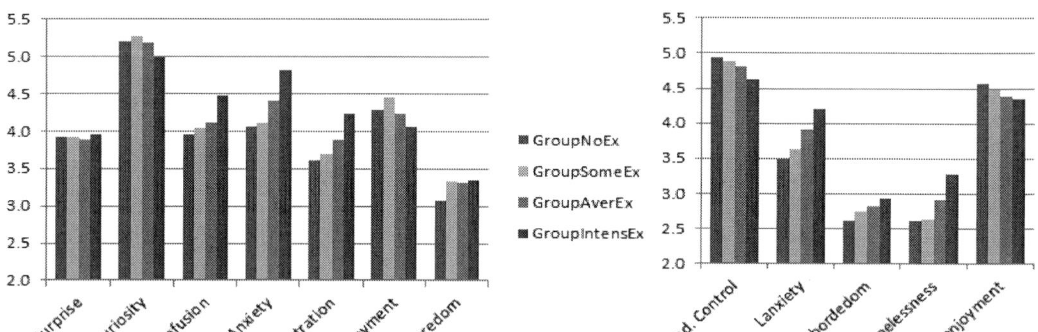

Figure 4. Group differences for epistemic emotions (left) and learning achievement emotions (right)

Last group differences refer to intensity of using the e-tutorial, and course performance: Figure 5. Significant differences exist in the square root transforms of *#Attempts* (sign<.001, eta squared=17.8%), *#AttemptsCorrect* (sign<.001, eta squared=3.0%), *#AttemptsInCorr* (sign<.001, eta squared=32.4%), as well as course performance measures *MathQuiz* (sign<.001, eta squared=7.3%), *StatsQuiz* (sign<.001, eta squared=14.0%), *MathExam* (sign<.001, eta squared=10.5%), and *StatsExam* (sign<.001, eta squared=13.0%). Outcomes of correlational analyses point in the same direction. The index for multiple use of examples, exponentially weighting for the number of repeated examples, correlates -.10 with *Critical* *processing*, -.07 with *Concrete processing*, .08 with *Relating*, .10 with *Memorizing*, .11 and .13 with epistemic *Anxiety* and *Frustration*, .13 with *Gender*, and -.15 for *StatsExam*, but not with *MathExam* (all significance levels below .01). In a multivariate context, the best prediction equation for multiple usage of examples, by step-wise regression, in standardized coefficients, is: *#ExercMultExamplSqrt* = .18*Masculinity* + .07*UncertaintyAv* + .09*Female* - .06*CriticalPr* -.10*Analysing* + .12*Memorizing* +.12*Effort* - .09*Value* with $R^2 = .32$.

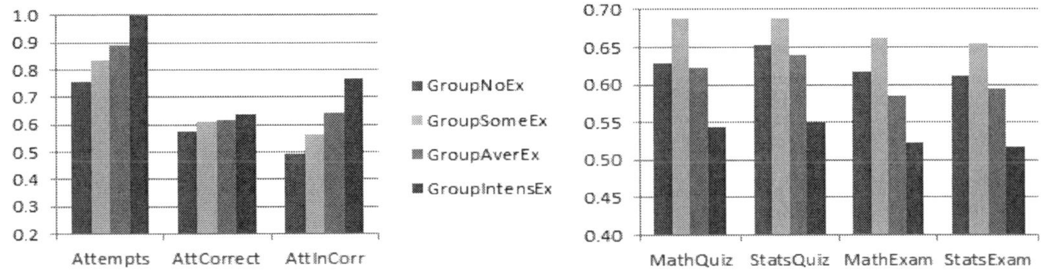

Figure 5. Group differences for e-tutorial activity (left) and course performance (right)

5. DISCUSSION AND CONCLUSION

The same mechanisms that explain why worked examples constitute an effective way of learning appear to explain individual differences in the preference for learning with worked examples when students can freely choose between alternative didactical scenarios. The danger of cognitive overload in the problem-solving scenario to strengthen a surface orientation of learning and to weaken the deep learning orientation of students (Renkl, 2014) is seen as a major merit of example-based learning. Exactly these same factors, the deep versus surface learning orientations, pop up as factors that explain individual differences in learning preferences. The *Critical processing* scale, most indicative for deep learning, is negatively related to the use of worked examples, whereas *Memorizing*, most indicative for surface learning, is positively related to the use of worked examples. But profiting from the availability of a large set of learning dispositions, we find that several other factors play a role, mostly of affective type. Adaptive antecedents as *Affect* and *Value* are negatively related to the use of examples, whereas maladaptive antecedents as epistemic *Confusion*, *Anxiety* and *Frustration*, and learning emotions *LAnxiety* and *Hopelessness*, are positively related to the use of worked examples. And in our international context, national culture impacts students learning preferences too, mainly through *Masculinity* and *UncertaintyAvoidance* being positively related to the use of examples. In total this suggests that where the use of (multiple) worked examples may help prevent students turning into maladaptive learning approaches because of cognitive overload, this help does not address all students in the same way. It is especially the group of students who score high on maladaptive dispositions, who are best helped by worked examples, whilst for a large category of students who opt out, using the examples only very infrequently or even not at all, worked examples seem to be of no added value. What suggests that a high level of adaptive learning dispositions protects these students from cognitive overload.

The story is richer than learning dispositions only. We do find gender and national culture effects: female students, and students from masculine and uncertainty avoiding cultures, do use worked examples more frequently than other students. The cultural facet in this may signal issues of adaptation of international students (Mittelheimer et al., 2016). The Dutch society, its educational systems, and PBL in specific, are strongly characterised by femininity and low levels of uncertainty avoidance and power distance. International students from cultures with opposite characteristics may choose to intensively use worked examples in their adaptation to the student-centred, PBL type of instruction they are so unfamiliar with.

The last conclusion relates the remarkable fact that intensity of usage of worked examples is as predictive for mathematics-related performance, as it is for statistics related performance. All worked examples in MSL focus on statistics topics; no one addresses any math topic. So from a cognitive perspective, there cannot be any effect from studying these worked examples on math performance. The only explanation that remains is that the frequent use of worked examples indeed signals higher levels of maladaptive dispositions.

This study is first and for all a showcase on the role of DLA in the provision of personalized, detailed learning feedback. No other program will apply the DLA with the same set of dispositions as described here. It is the general ability to identify students most in need of extra learning scaffolds that is the main lesson.

REFERENCES

Azevedo, R., Harley, J., Trevors, G., Duffy, M., Feyzi-Behnagh, R., Bouchet, F., et al. (2013). Using trace data to examine the complex roles of cognitive, metacognitive, and emotional self-regulatory processes during learning with multi-agents systems. In R. Azevedo & V. Aleven (Eds.), International handbook of metacognition and learning technologies, pp. 427–449. Amsterdam, The Netherlands: Springer.

Boltjens, E. (2004). Voorbeeld(ig) Onderwijs [Example-based education]. Maastricht, Netherlands: Maastricht University.

Buckingham Shum, S. & Deakin Crick, R. (2012). Learning Dispositions and Transferable Competencies: Pedagogy, Modelling and Learning Analytics. In S. Buckingham Shum, D. Gasevic, & R. Ferguson (Eds.). Proceedings of the 2nd International Conference on Learning Analytics and Knowledge, pp. 92-101. ACM, New York, NY, USA.

Duffy, M. C. & Azevedo, R. (2015). Motivation matters: Interactions between achievement goals and agent scaffolding for self-regulated learning within an intelligent tutoring system. Computers in Human Behavior, 52, 338-348.

Hofstede, G., Hofstede, G. J., & Minkov, M. (2010). *Cultures and Organizations: Software of the Mind* (3rd ed.): McGraw-Hill.

Ifenthaler, D. (2015). Learning analytics. In J. M. Spector (Ed.), Encyclopedia of educational technology (Vol. 2, pp. 447–451). Thousand Oaks, CA: Sage.

McLaren, B. M., Van Gog, T., Ganoe, C., Karabinos, M., & Yaron, D. (2016).The efficiency of worked examples compared to erroneous examples, tutored problem solving, and problem solving in computer-based learning environments. Computers in Human Behavior, 55, 87-99.

Mittelmeier, J., Tempelaar, D., Rienties, B., & Nguyen, Q. (2016). Learning analytics to understand cultural impacts on technology enhanced learning. In D. G. Sampson, J. M. Spector, D. Ifenthaler, & P. Isaias (Eds.), Proceedings 13th International Conference on Cognition and Exploratory Learning in Digital Age (CELDA 2016), pp. 236-243. International Association for Development of the Information Society, IADIS Press.

Pekrun, R. (2006). The control-value theory of achievement emotions: Assumptions, corollaries, and implications for educational research and practice. *Educational Psycholog Review, 18*(4), 315-341.

Pekrun, R. (2012). Emotions as drivers of learning and cognitive development, in: New perspectives on affect and learning technologies, pp. 23–39. New York: Springer.

Pekrun, R., Götz, T., Frenzel, A.C., Barchfeld, P., & Perry, R.P. (2011). Measuring emotions in students' learning and performance: The Achievement Emotions Questionnaire (AEQ), Contemporary Educational Psychology, 36, 36–48.

Pekrun R. & Meier E. (2011). Epistemic Emotion Scales (EES). Unpublished manuscript, Department of Psychology, University of Munich, Munich, Germany.

Renkl, A. (2014). The Worked Examples Principle in Multimedia Learning. In R. E. Mayer (Ed.), The Cambridge Handbook of Multimedia Learning, pp. 391-412. Cambridge, UK: Cambridge University Press.

Rienties, B., Cross, S., & Zdrahal, Z (2017). Implementing a Learning Analytics Intervention and Evaluation Framework: What Works? In B. Kei Daniel (Ed.), Big data and learning analytics: Current theory and practice in higher education (pp. 147–166). Cham: Springer International Publishing.

Tempelaar, D. T., Gijselaers, W. H., Schim van der Loeff, S. & Nijhuis, J. F. H. (2007). A structural equation model analyzing the relationship of student achievement motivations and personality factors in a range of academic subject-matter areas. Contemporary Educational Psychology, 32(1), 105-131.

Tempelaar, D. T., Rienties, B., & Giesbers, B. (2015). In search for the most informative data for feedback generation: Learning Analytics in a data-rich context. *Computers in Human Behavior, 47*(157-167).

Tempelaar, D.T., Rienties, B., & Nguyen, Q. (2017a). Adding dispositions to create pedagogy-based Learning Analytics. Zeitschrift für Hochschulentwicklung, ZFHE, 12(1).

Tempelaar, D.T., Rienties, B., & Nguyen, Q. (2017b). Achieving actionable learning analytics through dispositions. IEEE Transactions on Education, in press.

Vermunt, J. D. (1996). Metacognitive, cognitive and affective aspects of learning styles and strategies: A phenomenographic analysis. *Higher Education, 31*(1), 25-50.

Williams, A., Sun, Z., Xie, K., Garcia, E., Ashby, I., Exter, M., Largent, D., Lu, P., Szafron, D., Ahmed, S., Onuczko, T., Smith, J., Tempelaar, D. T., Bitting, K. S., Olcott Marshall, A., Christensen, E., Tseng, H., & Walsh, J. (2016). Flipping STEM. In L. Santos Green, J. Banas, R. Perkins (Eds.), The Flipped College Classroom, Conceptualized and Re-Conceptualized, Part II (pp. 149-186). Switzerland: Springer International Publishing.

PUSHING BUTTONS: A SOCIOMATERIAL EXPLORATION OF THE DISTRIBUTED LECTURE

Anna MacLeod, PhD, Paula Cameron, PhD, Olga Kits, MA and Cathy Fournier, MA
Faculty of Medicine, Dalhousie University, Canada

ABSTRACT

Current research on telepresence tends to engage a celebratory, taken-for-granted view of technology as a vehicle for improved communication and a mere backdrop against which communication unfolds. However, a growing body of literature interrogates the neutrality of technological environments in education. This paper considers the practice of lectures within distributed (multi-campus) medical education. Applying a sociomaterial theoretical lens, we analyze ethnographic data from a three-year study focused on the use of telepresence technology in the undergraduate medical program at Dalhousie University in Nova Scotia, Canada. Our research question was: How are material telepresence tools, processes and spaces enmeshed with student learning in the distributed lecture? We identified three sociomaterial complexities related to the practice of asking questions in this context: 1. Material presence and process of the button and screen in asking questions; 2. The ways in-class questions disrupt the flow of the distributed lecture; and 3. Tensions between ways in which questions are managed across sites. Attending to the seam between the social and material in the distributed lecture illuminates the challenges, barriers, and opportunities for student participation while unearthing innovative learning strategies.

KEYWORDS

Distributed learning, Higher education, telepresence, lecture, sociomaterial, ethnography

1. INTRODUCTION

This article considers the practice of lectures within distributed (multi-campus) undergraduate education. Applying a sociomaterial theoretical lens, we analyze ethnographic data from a three-year study focused on the use of telepresence in an undergraduate distributed medical education program at Dalhousie University in Nova Scotia, Canada. Our research question was: How are material telepresence tools, processes and spaces enmeshed with teaching and learning in the distributed medical education lecture?

Educational spaces have changed dramatically over the past century, from the static desks and slates of the late 1800s to the highly computerized learning spaces of present (Cleveland-Innes & Campbell, 2012). Undergraduate medical programs are no different in this regard, as medical schools increasingly engage in distributed medical education (DME) to increase access to education and address critical shortages of physicians in rural areas—the theory being that those who are educated in rural settings are more likely to stay and work in those settings (Strasser et al., 2009). In Canada, DME increasingly occurs using 'telepresence', where lectures are delivered to satellite campuses using state of the art digital telepresence technology (MacLeod et al., 2016; Snadden & Bates, 2009). Given the geographic vastness, pervasive issues with respect to attracting professionals to rural areas, and the ongoing developments in Information and Communication Technologies (ICTs), it is anticipated that Canadian distributed higher education will continue to grow (Kuehn, 2012).

Current research on telepresence tends to engage a celebratory, taken-for-granted view of technology as a vehicle for improved communication and a mere backdrop against which this communication unfolds (Logdlund, 2010). However, a growing body of literature interrogates the neutrality of technological environments in educational encounters, rather approaching telepresence and similar technologies as central to how and what teaching and learning happens. This research concludes that we cannot ignore the constitutive role of material and space within learning encounters, and must examine the ways in which technology enables, constrains, and essentially constitutes teaching and learning (Logdlund, 2010; Mannion, 2003; Roehl, 2012).

Existing literature in the broad area of distributed learning has focused largely on social, pedagogical and cognitive factors. While these factors are relevant, they do not exist independently from materiality, including telepresence technologies. Rather, social, pedagogical and cognitive factors are produced through and reinscribed by material factors. Given the growing numbers of DME programs, their reliance upon both ICTs and people, and the fact that they are delivered in geographically and materially diverse locations, it is imperative that our analyses of distributed medical education take both social and material considerations into account. Our study contributes to existing literature by critically examining sociomaterial effects of telepresence on lectures.

2. METHODS

2.1 Study Design

Our study builds on a rich 50-year tradition of ethnography in medical education research. Ethnography encompasses multiple methods of data collection and analysis, but consistently "involves lengthy participation or immersion in the everyday life of a chosen setting" by joining that everyday life and observing interactions and behavior (Pope, 2005, p.1180). In this case, the setting was the distributed medical program at a Canadian university, explored through observation, critical document analysis and open-ended interviews.

This ethnography was conceptually and theoretically framed in sociomaterialism, a heterogenous body of work. Our analysis is shaped by the following theoretical assumptions about sociomateriality: (1) that material entities are just as important as discourse and language; (2) the nature of reality is that the social and material are inextricable; (3) social and material entities do not have preexisting or inherent properties outside their interaction; (4) that the line drawn between social and material entities is abstract and artificial; and (5) that research must therefore focus on practices (Jones, 2014), where the social and the material hang together. We humans are constituted via materiality: our bodies, the tools we use, food, devices, which are also produced through human practices. This makes the distinction between humans and artifacts abstract (Orlikowski, 2007).

2.2 Setting

Data collection took place at two distributed campuses 400km apart. Campus A (in Halifax, Nova Scotia) is located in an established university in a small city and the second campus, Campus B (in St. John, New Brunswick) was established more recently in an area that has been challenged by physician recruitment and retention.

The Campus A classroom, where the bulk of the in-person teaching takes place, is a large 134-seat lecture theatre on the main floor of the medical building. This room features three large-scale screens at the front of the room, displaying the lecturer (left), PowerPoint slides (middle), and Campus B classroom (right screen). Three much smaller screens immediately below these giant screens project the same three views. Eight wall-mounted cameras are placed throughout the room, as are several white fabric wrapped acoustic panels. Seven rows of audience desks cascade down to the front of the room. A button activated microphone is shared between every two seats. The lecturer's podium features a computer monitor displaying PowerPoint slides and a small monitor that shows a map of the distant (Campus B) classroom, and features a silver button like the students', which flashes if a student button has been pushed at either campus. In front of the podium and under the first row of seating, three screens at lecturer eye level depict the PowerPoint slides (left screen), Campus B classroom (middle screen), and the lecturer herself (right screen, with a small screen in the right hand corner that depicts Campus A's view of the B classroom). An oblong light fixture contains a red light (indicating a local question) and green light (indicating a distant question). The audiovisual control room is located across the hall. More than 400 kilometres away, medical students at Campus B attend lectures in a small 30-seat room. Their classroom is built to mirror the Campus A site, though at a smaller scale, with three rows of seating that exactly allow for the smaller class. The Campus B audiovisual control room is located adjacent to the classroom, where audiovisual staff can directly observe the classroom through a tinted window.

2.3 Study Protocol

Our analysis focused on distributed learning activities on the two distributed campuses. Data methods included observations of distributed learning activities on two distributed campuses (n= 108 h) (Angrosino, 2007; Angrosino and de Perez, 2000), in-depth interviews with faculty, students, and audiovisual professionals (n= 33) (Kvale, 2007), and a critical textual analysis of a set of institutional documents and policies (n= 65) (Hodder, 2000; Rapley, 2007).

We gathered data over three years (2012-2015), learning about the Dalhousie medical program, and collecting formal and informal data. This longitudinal approach allowed us to gather a variety of data in order to build a progressive, in-depth analysis. Rather than focusing on specific curricular elements, the focus of our data collection was the educational technology itself (the telepresence videoconferencing system) and how people interacted with it, worked with or around it, and responded to it. We therefore focused on distributed events including large group lectures, but also experiential learning sessions, and meetings. For the purposes of this article, we will draw on observations of these lectures and 15 student interviews from participants at Campus A (n=7) and Campus B (n=8).

2.4 Data Analysis

Data analysis involved categorizing data to detect and interpret themes, attending to inconsistencies and contradictions. Data were analyzed according to Wolcott's (1994) three-step approach to ethnographic analysis: description; analysis; and interpretation. We examined data to develop a coding framework. This framework was then applied as the data were independently coded and analyzed. We organized this first by method (text, observation, interview) as an individual, site-specific data set, and then for the project as a whole. A core team took responsibility for analysis, while the wider group was involved in interpretation. We used qualitative analysis software (ATLAS.ti version 7.0) to assist with data sharing and management.

3. RESULTS

We identified three sociomaterial complexities related to the practice of asking questions in telepresence lectures: 1. Material presence and process of the button and screen in asking questions; 2. The ways in-class questions disrupted the flow of the distributed lecture; and 3. Tensions between ways in which questions are managed across the two sites.

3.1 The Button and Screen

Analysis of field note and interview data illustrates that rather than simply transferring in-person interactions to a virtual space, technological tools and processes in the distributed classroom radically mediate and shape the social interactions that are possible. Sociomaterial practices related to asking questions illustrate this point. Students we interviewed described the material processes involved in asking questions in a distributed lecture:

> You push a button and the light flashes. And then when it's your turn to go, the light stays on and the camera zooms in on you, and then you see your face up on the screen. And you ask your question [into the microphone], and [the opposite campus] can see you as well. That's sort of how it goes. So while the class is going on, there's the lecturer's slides on one screen and then there's also a picture of [other campus] on another.

There is a pause every time the camera pans to another student asking a question. Students who are seated within view of a question-asker are also frequently projected on the screen. Occasionally technical glitches occur, such as students lose their place in the queue or the camera zooms to the wrong student or into blank space.

3.2 Buttons Disrupt the Flow

Our analysis tended to frame question-asking as a disruptive force in the distributed lecture. The convergence of social processes and material technologies in the lecture appear to discourage students (and lecturers) from asking spontaneous questions, which in more traditional lectures are typically taken as a sign of engagement and investment in the topic at hand. Instead, through both normal processes and glitches, distance technologies can draw attention to the artifice of the "digitally extended classroom" and its deviation from a "seamless" extension of an in-person experience for human actors.

Our analysis of observation and interview data suggest that the materiality of the button and screen structures student engagement and questioning practices. Field notes indicate that it was unusual to see more than two questions per lecture. Early on in data collection, we noted, "No one is asking questions... Do people feel like they can ask a question as it comes up or are they worried [because] it is disruptive?" (Field notes). As the study progressed, it appeared that the large screens visually "expose" learners in their respective classroom. Students often appeared "very self-conscious and pained when they see themselves on the screen." This exposure extended to students sitting around the question asker, who were: "even more surprised and pained [to be caught on camera]. In some ways, they are 'collateral video damage' of the student... asking the question. ... Some look like they are 'caught' on the jumbotron at large sport events" (Field notes).

We asked students to describe their experiences with using the telepresence system to ask questions. We learned that the materiality of buttons, cameras, and screens involved in 'broadcasting' a question influences students' decisions to speak up. One interviewee, a first-year student at Campus B, attributed her hesitation to ask questions to "the uncomfortable nature of having your face zoomed in on when you're asking a question." In a traditional, in-person lecture, she noted, "students may turn around to look at you as you're speaking to the professor and to the class at large but you would never have such an in-your-face kind of sensation." Having your own image projected onto large screens "in-your-face" therefore can lead to a self-consciousness and sense of exposure that is heightened in the distributed classroom.

This student described technology as a distraction from learning, "particularly when you're trying to address the professor specifically and then you've got an image of yourself just adjacent, you know, watching yourself talk. It's just like an odd thing to experience." The self-consciousness sparked by being zoomed in on and projected onto large screens was one way that the material processes of telepresence are enmeshed with human actors in distributed lectures. The experience of being exposed whether one asked a question or not, underscores the inextricable nature of the social and technological processes in the distributed lecture. While students with questions can at least anticipate their projection on the screen, however uncomfortable, their neighbours may not be aware (or willing) that will be projected alongside them on the giant screen— "collateral video damage."

The distributed lecture is occasionally punctuated by glitches— visible and/or audible failures in material and virtual distributed learning spaces. During a lecture at Campus B, for example, one observer noted, "Student presses button - to turn off the mike[sic] or the camera? She presses it twice and looks unsure if it has worked but then her image shifts" (Field note). Full-on technical glitches can destabilize and disorient the human participants in distributed learning spaces. At one lecture, for example, a question is lost in the ether as the camera "pans out. [Campus A] student thinks it's her. Then the camera zooms out. It zooms around the room. Then it goes black." In the end, due to this material malfunction, "The student has no space to ask her question. It's lost. A [Campus B] student (next in the queue) asks his question" (Field note). On another day, the camera at the Campus A site fails to zoom in on the student asking a question, instead lurching around the room; "it is very disorienting as the camera zooms in it is like being on a rocky boat...then the screen focuses and then the screen turns black" (Field note). Technical glitches can also provide some levity. For example, after the "rocky boat" experience above, the class laughs and moves on to the next question.

Like students, lecturers also appeared to frame in-class questions as diversions. The material complexities of the button/screen system mean that often lecturers gloss over questions for either lip service invitations or avoidance altogether. As a researcher noted early on in the observation process: "No lecturer asks if there are any questions....which is a fairly common approach in most lectures. Is this related to the button? DISRUPTIVE?" (Field note). In one lecture at Campus A, we noted that "There has been no opportunity for interaction yet... it is unclear if the students understood the concepts – and unfortunately they did not have opportunity as they were going through to ask questions (nor encouraged to do so)" (Field note). This glossing over interaction was echoed by another lecturer administering "an online quiz [who] seems to be answering the questions himself...not a peep from [Campus B] (Field note), while yet another lecturer "asks if there are any questions very quickly to class but doesn't look to see if there are any questions from [Campus B]... she moves on very quickly (Field note).

3.3 Questions Across Sites

Data indicate that questions shape and are shaped by material forces in the distributed classroom, an effect experienced unevenly across campuses. Most lectures are delivered in person on the main (Campus A) campus, with the distributed (Campus B) class joining in via telepresence. Our field notes indicate that it was unusual for a question to originate from a distant site, which we linked to a sense of disconnection from the lecturer. Student interview data echoed this association. As one Campus B student noted:

> There really wasn't a lot of people asking a lot of questions on our end. And we would get teased for that. But it was like, "Well, come on, do you talk to your TV at home?" So there's sort of this feeling that we're kind of passive recipients.

We observed the frequent practice of students with questions waiting to approach the lecturer following the session, rather than using the telepresence technology. Another Campus B student was critical of Campus A students' tendency to approach the lecturer after class rather than asking questions during the lecture. This was substantiated by the lecturers we interviewed, with one saying: "always there would be 5 or 6 [students waiting to ask questions after the lecture] there was never anybody from [the distant site]." While asking questions after a lecture is not an occurrence unique to distributed medical education, we were surprised that the number of questions asked following the lecture outweighed the number asked during the lecture. Certainly, there are educational inequities associated with this practice, related to the physical location in which a learner is situated and the access to the physical presence of the lecturer as students navigate questions across sites.

When someone at a distant site did ask a question, there were sometimes elaborate workarounds put in place to make the question possible. As one second-year Campus A student noted: "They usually have a spokesperson that asks all the questions that's more confident talking in front of the class...they talk about which questions they want to ask and then he [confident person] would present them." Other strategies to avoid having to 'broadcast questions' were apparent and described by participants. One of the most interesting strategies involved self-directed or peer-supported teaching. One interviewee, a first-year Campus B student, noted: "We often just kind of try and figure out the answers to questions on our own or maybe we'll try and like email the professor afterwards rather than actually go ahead and ask the questions during class."

Students also noted that their smaller size and virtual participation in a lecture provided space for satellite students to override the technology (i.e. to keep microphones turned off) to create a student-centred space where they can collectively work through their questions. One first-year Campus A student described the class at Campus B as

> just very tight-knit and everyone knows each other a little better than here. ... there most of the time, the mic isn't on and they can kind of chat without the lecturer here knowing that they're chatting. So I find there's a lot more collaboration that goes on there.

The flip side to invisibility, in this case the satellite students' literal silence in the distributed classroom, is their ability to form a cohesive group and reclaim student centeredness for themselves. Learners thereby use their distance from the lecturer as an opportunity to engage with key concepts, problem-solve and work collaboratively, engaging in more self-directed learning.

Rather than technology extending the classroom space to the satellite site, and thereby enhancing communication and inclusion, telepresence appears to constructs two parallel but unequal worlds. These students also, however, in turn "push back" on the technology by enacting various material strategies to have their questions answered, including appointing informal "spokespeople" on either campus and creating alternative spaces (both virtual, via Facebook and texting, and in person, with the classroom microphones turned off) in which they collectively work through their own questions rather than disrupt the lecture with questions directed to the lecturer. In these cases, the classroom technologies both enable and make necessary creative workarounds for students to get their voices heard and learning needs met.

4. DISCUSSION

In distributed lectures, social practices regarding student questions are enmeshed with the materiality of distance technologies. These technologies constitute questions as disruptive within a distributed lecture. Asking a question leads to exposure for the asker and their neighbours, or "collateral video damage"—the price a student has to pay to formally ask a question during a lecture. Material telepresence tools and the students and lecturers come together in a way that constitutes spontaneous questions by students and lecturers as disruptive elements in the classroom. Unintended technical slips, however small, shape the quality and flow of learning in the distributed classroom, thereby complicating asking questions and drawing attention to the unfulfilled promise of the seamless extension of material into virtual space. Even with highly skilled audiovisual technicians helming the control room, there are moments of hesitation and uncertainty where learners and lecturers are unsure whether the button/microphone/screen process will work. This affirms sociomaterialists' challenge to the material as "neutral, passive and conformed by practice", reframing the ways in which telepresence technologies constrain, enable, and actually constitute, student learning in the distributed classroom— thus acting as "forcible mediators of communication" (Logdlund, 2010, p.183).

Our findings affirm a materialist emphasis on space within teaching and learning, conceptualized in two overlapping and equally important ways: first, a more traditional understanding of space as concrete (facilities, technical artifacts, and bodies), and second, space as social, that is, a set of relations between people within cognitive and virtual realms (Logdlund, 2010; Soja, 1985). Our findings underscore the ways in which concrete material space constrains and enables student learning through their manipulation (and/or avoidance) of the button and screen, and they ways in which telepresence technologies can resist and evade human manipulation through technical glitches. Tools and technologies implemented to facilitate communication in the distributed classroom can in fact encourage student passivity in distributed lectures by constructing student questions as disruptions. This finding echoes Logdlund's observation that student passivity in distributed learning largely takes root in students' hesitation to be visually exposed by the cameras and on the screen. Learners may not know exactly who is watching at any given time, and like lecturers, can seldom gauge the response of the audience at the other campus. Here material tools and technologies can be viewed as actors in the distributed lecture rather than passive and neutral backdrops to the educational encounters (Waltz, 2004).

This construction of questions as disruptions is experienced by students at both sites due to the presence of material technologies. Equally important as these concrete physical processes, however, are the social spaces in which learners inhabit and construct meaning. When we consider the findings in light of relations between individuals and groups within virtual and cognitive learning spaces, students at both campuses have equal access to these spaces. On the other hand, Campus B's physical participation, presence, and access to the lecturer in the physical learning space is usually mediated and at times silenced; their bodies are muted to the lecturer in a way that their colleagues on Campus A are not. In the physical space, their informal strategies to overcome or mitigate this unequal access includes participating in informal peer support and teaching, as well as relying on their colleagues on the Campus A to communicate their questions and concerns to lecturers. Peer-teaching by students at Campus B is therefore both facilitated and made necessary by the material realities of the distributed classroom. This affirms Logdlund's (2010) finding that activity in the distributed classroom appears to be divided between the main and distributed learning sites, the latter an alternative space where events can be seen (but not heard) as "a hidden 'secondary plot'" (p.189). This de-centering of both student and teacher by videoconferencing technology echoes Logdlund's finding that in distributed lectures, students participate as audience, while "the teacher is replaced by a television screen and authority that comes with the teacher's position in the classroom seems to be transferred to material design and technical artifacts" (p.190).

Our findings challenge the assumption that distance learning technologies simply extend the classroom into virtual space, thereby including a new group of learners as equal partners in the learning encounter. Instead, our findings resonate with Fenwick's (2014) assertion that "materials act together with other elements and forces (discourses, symbols, desires, etc.) to exclude, invite, and regulate particular forms of participation" (p.269). While distributed lectures can spark student engagement, it appears that due to significant tensions that emerge between students and technologies, this engagement often occurs in spite of, rather than because of, telepresence technologies and even most lecturers' attempts at student engagement. Due to these material technological constraints, however, student engagement, at least for distance students, spills outside the confines of traditional classroom participation with its reliance on asking questions in live time. Instead students improvise by engaging in peer supported learning. While distributed technologies clearly exclude certain kinds of participation, particularly for distance students, they also enable and invite others.

In Callon's (1986) words, the cameras, microphones and screens of the distributed medical lecture become an "obligatory point of passage," through which all players in the lecture: objects, bodies, and texts, must flow (Fenwick, 2014). Material practices in the distributed medical education classroom therefore shape and control the telepresence lecture in profound ways, from question-asking practices constrained and enabled by the button, microphone, and screen, to the social relations between local and distant site, including differently experienced classroom encounters for distance students inhabiting virtual space.

5. CONCLUSION

Everyday practices within distributed medical education are inextricably entangled with materiality of distance learning technologies. By resisting the tendency to render these educational technologies as neutral and passive background to the educational encounter, this research sheds light on the ways learners engage with and are engaged by these concrete tools and spaces. Theorizing materiality enables a more critical consideration of the ways educational technologies transform pedagogy by foreclosing certain teaching and learning practices and requiring, enabling, and shaping others. Before we can theorize about these practices we need to understand teaching and learning as an assemblage of human and non-human actors. Further qualitative research is required that takes a sociomaterial approach to teaching and learning in digital contexts in higher education, troubling the supposed inevitability, invisibility or neutrality of technological tools and spaces and critically considering what is gained, lost, and transformed in these contexts.

Sociomaterial perspectives and concerns can richly inform our efforts to move beyond taken-for-granted assumptions about "seamless" learning and teaching, to instead consider the often messy, contradictory, dynamic and multiple assemblages of tools, spaces, bodies and practices within distributed learning. Attending to the seam between the social and material in the distributed lecture illuminates the challenges, barriers, and opportunities for student participation while unearthing innovative strategies—as their learning shapes, and is shaped by, material technologies in the distributed classroom.

REFERENCES

Angrosino, M., 2007. *Doing Ethnographic and Observational Research*. Sage, London.

Angrosino, M. and de Perez, K., 2000. Rethinking Observation: From Method to Context. In: M. Denzin and Y. Lincoln, eds. *Handbook of Qualitative Research*. Sage, London, pp. 673-702.

Callon, M., 1986. Some Elements of a Sociology of Translation: Domestication of the Scallops and the Fishermen of St. Brieuc Bay. In: J. Law, ed. *Power, Action and Belief: A New Sociology of Knowledge? Sociological Review Monograph*, No. 32. Routledge, London, pp. 196-233.

Cleveland-Innes, M. & Campbell, P., 2012. Emotional Presence, Learning, and the Online Environment. In *International Review of Research in Open and Distance Learning*, Vol. 13, No. 4, pp. 269-292.

Fenwick, T., 2014. Knowledge Circulations in Inter-para/professional Practice: A Sociomaterial Enquiry. *Journal of Vocational Education and Training*, Vol. 66, No. 3, pp. 264-280.

Jones, M., 2014. A Matter of Life and Death: Exploring Conceptualizations of Sociomateriality in the Context of Critical Care. In *MIS Quarterly*, Vol. 38. No. 3, pp. 895-925.

Hodder, I., 2000. The Interpretation of Documents and Material Culture. In: M. Denzin and Y. Lincoln, eds. *Handbook of Qualitative Research*. Sage, London, pp. 703-715.

Kuehn, L., 2012. The "Voracious Appetite" of Online Learning. In *Policy Alternatives*, Vol. 21, No. 2, pp. 95-104.

Kvale, S., 2007. *Doing Interviews*. Sage, London.

Lögdlund, U., 2010. Constructing learning spaces? Videoconferencing at Local Learning Centres in Sweden. In *Studies in Continuing Education*, Vol. 32, No. 3, pp. 183-199.

MacLeod, A., Kits, O., Mann, K., Tummons, J., and Wilson, J., 2016. The Invisible Work of Distributed Medical Education: Exploring the Contributions of Audiovisual Professionals, Administrative Professionals, and Faculty Teachers. In *Advances in Health Sciences Education*. Advance online publication. doi:10.1007/s10459-016-9695-4.

Mannion, G., 2003. Learning, Participation and Identification through School Grounds Development. In: R. Edward and R. Usher, eds. *Space, Curriculum and Learning.* Information Age Publishing, Greenwich, pp. 61-78.

Orlikowski, W.J., 2007. Sociomaterial Practices: Exploring Technology at Work. In *Organization Studies*, Vol. 28, No. 9, pp. 1435–1448.

Paetcher, C. et al., eds, 2001. *Learning, Space and Identity.* Sage, London.

Pope C., 2005. Conducting Ethnography in Medical Settings. In *Medical Education*, Vol. 39, No. 12, pp.1180–1187.

Rapley, T., 2007. *Doing Conversation, Discourse and Document Analysis*. Sage, London.

Roehl, T., 2012. From Witnessing to Recording - Material Objects and the Epistemic Configuration of Science Classes, *Pedagogy, Culture & Society*, Vol. 20, No. 1, pp. 49-70.

Snadden, D. and Bates, J., 2005. Expanding Undergraduate Medical Education in British Columbia: A Distributed Campus Model. In *Canadian Medical Association Journal,* Vol. 173, No. 6, pp. 589-590.

Soja, E.W., 1985. The Spatiality of Social Life: Towards a Transformative Retheorisation. In D. Gregory and J. Urry, eds. *Social Relations and Spatial Structures.* Macmillan, London, pp. 90-□127.

Strasser, R.P. et al., 2009. Canada's New Medical School: The Northern Ontario School of Medicine: Social Accountability through Distributed Community Engaged Learning. In *Academic Medicine*, Vol. 84, No. 10, pp. 1459-1464.

Waltz, S.B. 2004. Giving Artifacts a Voice? Bringing into Account Technology in Educational Analysis. *Educational Theory,* Vol. 54, No. 2, pp. 157–72.

Wise, J.M., 2005. Assemblage. In: C.J. Stivale, ed. *Gilles Deleuze: Key Concepts*. McGill-Queen's University Press, Montreal, pp. 77-87.

Wolcott, H.F., 1994. *Transforming Qualitative Data: Description, Analysis, and Interpretation*. Sage, Thousand Oaks.

MULTIMODAL TEACHING AND LEARNING WITH THE USE OF TECHNOLOGY: MEANINGS, PRACTICES AND DISCOURSES

Vasiliki Papageorgiou and Petros Lameras
Coventry University, Priori Street, Coventry, United Kingdom, CV1 5FB

ABSTRACT

The aim of this paper is to report on teachers' experiences of, and approaches to, multimodality in teaching and learning. A small-scale online survey with closed and semi-structured questions has been deployed to school and university teachers (n=68) for eliciting their experiences in multimodal teaching and learning. Thematic analysis has been adopted as the overarching methodology for reporting patterns in the data from the survey. The results from the analysis showed that experiences of multimodality are discerned as: (1) imparting information, (2) enacting collaborative learning and (3) preparing students for exploring concepts. The process of meaning making is exemplified through a developmental progression from more teacher-directed modes through oral, written and visual representations to more student-centered through gestural representations as means of connecting and combining different modes triggered via visual communication, collaboration and exploration.

KEYWORDS

Multimodality, Technology-Enhanced Learning, Collaborative Learning

1. INTRODUCTION

There is an increasing body of evidence, which suggests that multimodality in learning is an active, student-centred approach in which students select the resources mostly relevant to them (Mayer, 2001). This means that students are responsible for organising learning content such as words and images into coherent verbal and visual models comprising their mental schemata and conceptual structures (ibid.). The essence of multimodality therefore is to provide different types of resources to the student for stimulating learning in meaningful ways within and across disciplines. To this end, multimodality is described as an interdisciplinary approach drawn with an emphasis on communication and representation (Jewitt, 2013). This is directly relevant to teachers in terms of using current theories of learning to engage students with student-centred pedagogies and resources of learning (Hassett & Curwood, 2009). Multimodality in today's classrooms refers to 'multiple' modes of representation, with combined elements of print, visual images and design (Jewitt, 2008). Multiple modes of representation include capabilities of combinations of oral and written language, visual, gestural, tactile and spatial representations (Cope & Kalantzis, 2009). This transitional shift from print-based education to multimodal education indicates the need to rethink how teaching and learning is conceived, approached and practiced.

A substantial body of research has reported on interventions, case studies, conceptual frameworks and design of teaching and learning activities using multimodal technologies and not on the actual multimodal teaching practices mediated by technologies currently used by teachers (Bell et al., 2010; Cope & Kalantzis, 2009). In this paper, it is argued that multimodality is based on the process of creating meaning through connecting and combining teaching strategies, approaches to teaching and learning with technologies that afford exploration, investigation and participatory learning. Against this background, meanings, practices and discourses were investigated in conceptualising and practicing multimodality in teaching and learning with the use of associated teaching approaches, technologies and resources. The research questions addressed in this study were the following:

1. What multimodality means for teaching and learning with the use of technology?
2. How multimodality is approached and practiced with the use of technology for enhancing teaching and learning?

The paper starts by contemplating on ways of understanding multimodality and elucidates on multimodality and digital technologies for teaching and learning. It then describes pedagogical approaches such as collaborative learning in tandem with more activity-led teaching advocating context-specific and personal construction of meaning. It continues with the methodology and research design adopted for the data collection and analysis. The results of the survey analysis are presented in the next section along with a discussion on connecting findings with research questions and implications for teaching practice and research. Finally, conclusions and future research are discussed based on the evidence from the survey.

2. WAYS OF UNDERSTANDING MULTIMODALITY

The way multimodality is perceived and enacted is in tandem with how technologies are deployed and used for designing and delivering learning content (Miller & McVee, 2013). Thus, it is less the technology itself and more about the individual and collaborative practices applied with technology including the mechanisms that teachers incorporate to create meaning to students. In essence, multimodality emphasises situated action, considering the social context as the key factor for meaning making, with special focus on how people use the resources available based on their cultural practices, personal beliefs and institutional contexts; rather than emphasising the attributes, behaviours and the system of the available resources (Kress, 2001). This introduces new possibilities for investigating, analysing and understanding the different ways which people use multimodality for creating, sustaining and transferring meaning to inter-related ecosystems and social contexts.

3. MULTIMODALITY, PEDAGOGICAL APPROACHES AND DIGITAL TECHNOLOGIES FOR TEACHING AND LEARNING

The advent of digital technologies for supporting teaching and learning has supplemented or amplified conventional non-digital activities (Beetham & Sharpe, 2013). Digitisation of administrative and routine tasks such as storing, transferring and retrieving information supplements traditional teaching and learning in the sense that the digital modalities used do not resemble or offer something novel to the way current teaching and learning processes and strategies are practiced. Indeed, learning technologies should help students to increase their capacities for innovation, leadership, multi-and inter-disciplinary collaboration, emotional intelligence, critical skills and collective problem solving in a participatory digital learning environment (Greenhow, et al., 2009). Multimedia resources and tools in these environments may include for example, interactive videos and images, recorded lecture presentations, online quizzes, discussion forums (synchronous and asynchronous), visual representations of student data to depict progress and on what the student is doing to learn (Sharples, et al., 2016). Currently many teachers tend to use digital technologies to support teacher-directed approaches with the aim of improving the quality of lecture presentations by using Interactive Whiteboards; PowerPoint for lecture notes and asynchronous discussion forums for the recreation of face-to-face tutorial discussions (Beetham & Sharpe, 2013). The affordances of the aforementioned technologies in these cases are mainly exploited to explain and visualise content knowledge or for engaging students in activities that require to visually absorb and manipulate information more actively than before. Mayer (2001) argues that student's learning becomes more meaningful when an array of interactive tools and resources are deployed rather using text alone. Moreover, the visual representation of content is vital for communicating subject matter and improving students' understanding (ibid.).

There is increasing research on collaborative multimedia learning in different subject domains (Bell, et al., 2010). Studies have shown that collaboration can enhance the quality of the learning process, hence the importance of achieving specific learning outcomes combining multimedia content with collaborative learning may lead to engaging, interactive and powerful multimedia learning environments (Dillenbourg, 1999). Students working collaboratively in groups have the opportunity to share their thoughts and prior knowledge. Collaborative dialogue supports learning by clarifying thinking and consolidating ideas (Hmelo-Silver, 2002). The "classroom learning communities" approach seeks to operationalize the benefits of learning through participation in communities of practice (Lave & Wenger, 1991). Multimodal collaborative learning promotes the idea of creating a learning community with a shared purpose of making sense of scientific ideas and practices (Harris & Rooks, 2010). Teachers, although still reluctant in using technology in pedagogically driven ways, have slowly started to integrate new educational teaching and learning practices (Miller & McVee, 2013) including but not limited to serious games, blogging, collaborative editing and online media manipulation. In this study, multimodality for teaching and learning is examined in terms of experiences on using different modalities (oral and written language, visual, gestural and tactile representations), technologies and teaching strategies (e.g. transmitting information, collaborative learning, informal learning) capturing more holistically the way multimodality is perceived and enacted by teachers.

4. METHODOLOGY AND RESEARCH DESIGN

A thematic analysis approach was adopted as the overarching methodology for this study. Thematic analysis is a method for identifying, analysing and reporting themes or patterns within data. Thematic analysis was selected because it offers a dynamic and flexible method to analysing qualitative data and it is ideal for thematic synthesis of primary research (Braun & Clarke, 2006; Boyatzis, 1998). Deciding to use thematic analysis was interlinked with our attempt in coding the different primary data on meanings, practices and discourses for multimodal teaching and learning. The data collection process started by designing an online survey for eliciting teachers' beliefs, intentions and actions in using multimodality for teaching and learning. The VARK[1] for 'Teachers and Trainers' questionnaire on multimodality has been adapted to encompass questions aligned towards identifying variation in ways of deploying teaching strategies, digital technology and modes of multimodal meaning as comprehended by teachers in three European countries. In particular, 30 teachers from Germany, 20 from Finland and 18 from Denmark (n=68) participated in this small-scale study. Purposive sampling aimed at selecting teachers from different disciplines for the facilitation of generalisability and validity.

The online survey has been translated in German, Finnish and Danish for ease of use for the participants of each country. The survey included 28 closed and semi-structured questions as to enable participants to instantly select the option mostly relevant to them (i.e. closed question) as well as to prompt for a more recursive process where participants had to go back and forth their descriptive answer for fine-tuning, refining and reflecting (i.e. semi-structured question). An informed consent form and information sheet were included in the survey for completion prior to main body of questions for seeking participants' agreement to take part in the study; and be ensured that all information provided would be treated in confidence.

The processes of analysis were adopted from a thematic analysis perspective for discovering the themes embodied in the evolving meanings of the data. In line to this, the following processes were carried out: (1) familiarization with the data, (2) generation of initial codes, (3) searching for themes, (4) review of themes, (5) definition of themes and (6) synthesis of themes. Repeating this process for all data-sets the data were categorised while considering connections and interconnections between codes and themes. Then, eight codings were generated (e.g. experiencing multimodality as imparting information) which were mainly emerged and resembled within the different sections of the survey.

5. RESULTS

This section reports on the results of the online survey for eliciting teachers' beliefs, intentions and actions in using multimodality for teaching and learning. The themes emerged from data analysis are presented below.

---

[1] http://vark-learn.com/the-vark-questionnaire/teaching-questionnaire/

5.1 Experiencing Multimodality as Imparting Information

The majority of the participants from Germany (53.3%) and Finland (50%) define multimodality as "a complex of modes including talk, visual communication, action, gesture, posture and movement", which shows a clear understanding of what is multimodality and in line with contemporary definitions revised in the literature (see Figure 1.). A considerable proportion of the teachers perceived that multimodality describes communication practices using modes to develop and deliver content, hence transferring information and content was the focus for multimodal teaching. Most of the teachers used technology for transferring information in static and linear way using voice and gestures via lectures and imparting knowledge via assignments and tests although there was a tendency to explain multimodality as a more interactive, constructive and interactive mode of teaching.

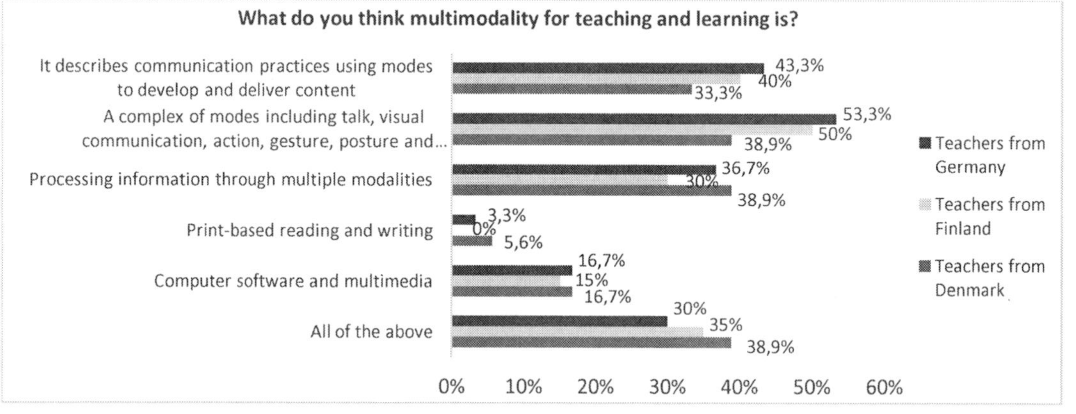

Figure 1. Teachers' definition of multimodality for teaching and learning

5.2 Experiencing Multimodality as Enacting Collaborative Learning

Teachers from Finland and Denmark (95% and 100% respectively) indicated that they use technology for collaborative learning practices. This may shows that the use of collaborative practices mediated by multimodal technologies is prevalent, as teachers increasingly seem to be confident in integrating collaborative activities that necessitate participatory tools and multiple modes. Participants were also asked to specify the modalities they use to enhance collaborative practices. Collectively the data show that the use of collaborative projects mediated by multimodal technologies was the most prominent choice between the others for the teachers from the three surveyed countries. Formative assessment seemed to be an important part of collaborative teaching strategies since the focus is to help the student understand comprehensively not only how to improve individually but also how the overall performance of the team could be enhanced to communally produce meaningful ideas. Interestingly, mostly the teachers from Finland and several teachers from Denmark appeared to use a variety of digital modalities (e.g. synchronous/asynchronous tools, social networking) to enhance collaboration and create a more dialogic and supportive learning culture. This result illustrates the importance of feedback and the ways that feedback is visualised to students for enhancing engagement (see Figure 2.).

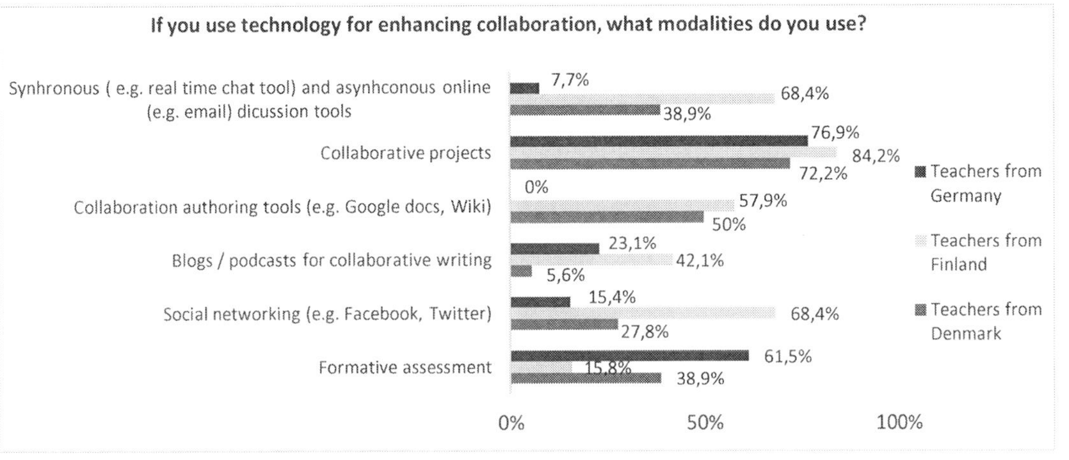

Figure 2. Modalities used by teachers for collaborative learning

5.3 Experiencing Multimodality as Preparing Students for Exploring Concepts

Participants were asked to make explicit their understanding concerning the strategies they would prefer to use in different teaching and learning situations. The teachers were enquired "How would you ideally prepare the first session of your course for your students?" Participants from Germany (46.7%) tend to introduce their session by an oral statement that stresses what students need to learn, absorb and memorise alluding to a behaviouristic approach to teaching. This result illustrates teachers' preference in more traditional-based practices via the use of the predominant oral communication modes. It also shows that less emphasis is given to the students' ideas and interests but mainly on teacher's organisation of content-based sessions and activities. Creating activities for students to collaboratively brainstorm on what they want to learn in this course via Google docs was the most popular option of the educators from Finland and Denmark (See Figure 3.). This approach highlights the teachers' learning design decisions informed by the students' personal interests, prior knowledge and interaction with peers; exemplifying a visual communication multimodality approach. Participants from Germany (30%), Finland (15%) and Denmark (38.9%) would ideally use a PowerPoint presentation showing examples and applications of how aspects of the course are beneficial for the society. Teachers attempted to use visual communication tools for explaining and clarifying concepts guided and directed by them and in line with the subject matter. This possibly reveals that teachers had difficulties in creating novel and complex multimodal artefacts for introducing concepts and ideas beyond the curriculum for initiating discussions that would help students to connect prior knowledge with novel concepts.

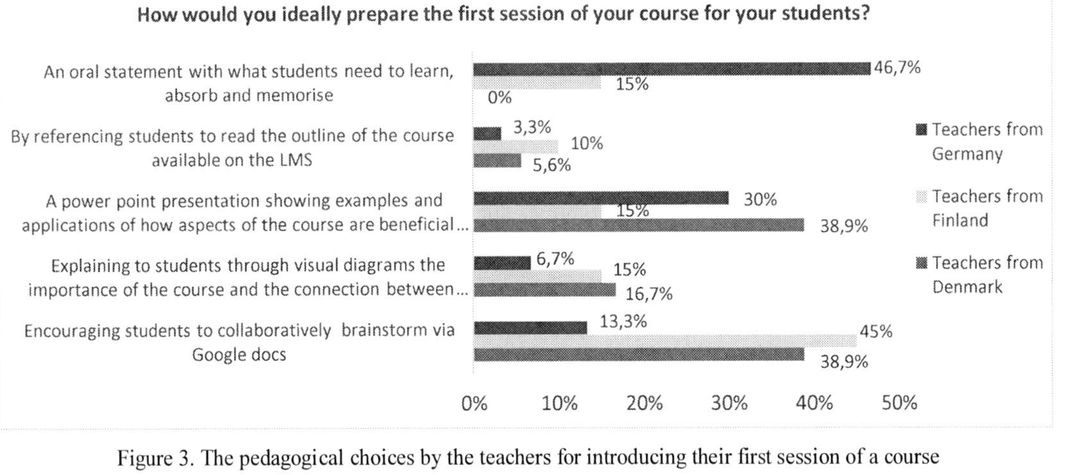

Figure 3. The pedagogical choices by the teachers for introducing their first session of a course

Responding to the question: "You have organised a field trip for your students to explore a topic in question. How would you prepare students?" Participants (see Figure 4.) perceived the usefulness of supporting students to design their own field trip preparation guidelines. Teacher's role is to provide the context for students to prepare and suggest resources and tools (mobile devices with gestural interfaces) to be used by students to plan their scientific investigations. The provision of different web links / web-quests for the preparation of the trip was also an option chosen by many teachers from Finland and Denmark, illustrating the vital role of multimodal technologies to empower students to enquire and conduct experiments in informal learning situations. However, oral means of communication still remain one of the central modes of content delivery as many teachers stated that they would orally suggest ways of preparing (as opposed to instructing students to follow a specific direction imparted by the teacher) that needs to be made by students in the classroom – because technology seemed to be obsolete when face-to-face teaching is the primary teaching mode. It was clear that the use of technology for multimodal teaching is experienced as a supplementary tool for face-to-face teaching for cementing a blended learning setting.

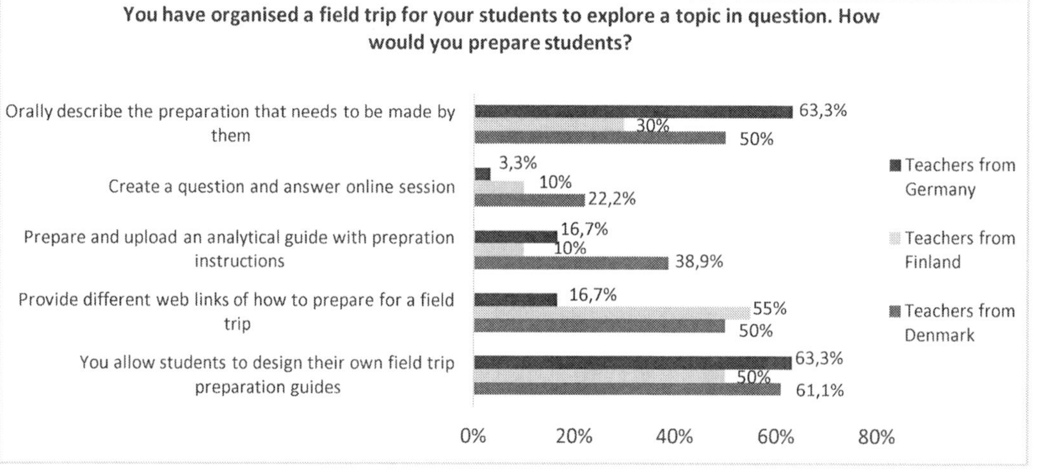

Figure 4. Strategies used by teachers for the exploration of a specific topic during a field trip

6. IMPLICATIONS FOR PRACTICE AND RESEARCH

Connecting the 3 emerging categories of experiencing multimodality as: imparting information, enacting collaborative learning and preparing students for exploring concepts to the two overarching research questions led to interesting experiences and practices for understanding how multimodality is approached with the use of technology. This section aims to provide a reflection on implications for multimodal practice and research in tandem to the research questions.

6.1 What Multimodality Means for Teaching and Learning with the use of Technology?

It is evident from the findings that multimodality is conceived as a cluster of modes increasingly being used as a communication mechanism for delivering information and content. This is in conjunction to using oral, written and visual representations for meaning making. The choice of modes, being used by participants include oral language (lecture), written language and visual communications (diagrams, PowerPoint). This creates an inventory of the meanings when technology is used in relation to storing content in a repository for rote learning. Essentially, building on the notion of using oral, written and visual descriptions, teachers' primary awareness is on constructing a system for imparting their knowledge and experiences through linear ways of representation. A demand of learning the foundations of the module based on subject matter or offering to students' information pre-selected, reviewed and evaluated by the teacher is the distinct aspect of meaning through the combination of oral/written and visual modes of meaning.

There were instances where multimodality via using technology was experienced as engaging students in activities for individual and collaborative construction of meaning and for preparing students to explore via field trips. An array of more 'developed' modes were evidenced such gestural for constructing meaning making processes that required students to take control of their learning by preparing to carry out investigations in field trips through smart devices. This demonstrated a more 'complete' understanding of multimodality in a more developmental sense, starting from a fragmented perception, that of using oral/written and visual descriptions for accessing and transferring information to a more cohesive- that of using gestural (via mobile devices for carrying out explorations during field trips) coupled with written/oral, audio and visual.

6.2 How Multimodality is Approached and Practiced with the use of Technology for Enhancing Teaching and Learning?

The findings revealed that there is a connection between 'espoused theories' and 'theories in use'. For example, participants that perceived multimodality as a linear contingent process emanated via oral/written language, the use of technologies that supported this view was more prevalent. Information transfer through lectures, presentations, learning repositories and written hand-outs were widely used. This was in tandem to influences derived from personal beliefs about teaching and learning, the role of the teacher in the classroom as well from institutional policies that might have pushed teaching to a certain pedagogical direction. It is however inconclusive to suggest that teachers' perceptions on 'fragmented' ways of using multimodal tools for teaching and learning are influenced only from their conceptions of teaching and learning.

More systematic research is needed for understanding, the connections between multimodal conceptions of learning and teaching with the way technology is used. Participants who felt that multimodality is enacted via more gestural, processes for meaning making, the use of technology was experienced as a process of engaging students in activities that could not be realised with conventional technology (PowerPoints). For example, teachers who experienced multimodality as an active process, the technologies deployed were more participatory, interactive and adaptive to student's interests and meaning making processes. Activities that involved collaborative projects and preparing for carrying out investigations through field trips encompassed a blending learning approach for synchronous and asynchronous communications, and the use of mobile devices for investigations, explorations and inquiry.

7. CONCLUSION

This paper investigated experiences of multimodality and their association to teaching and learning with the use of technology. Thematic analysis has been used to analyse the findings based on a survey with 68 teachers for eliciting experiences of multimodal teaching. The results showed a relation between multimodal meaning making descriptions, teaching approaches and technologies used for teaching and learning.

Limitations of this research were on the basis of discerning more detailed accounts of connections and influences that determined a specific way of conceiving the phenomenon in question. Sample restrictions were also a factor that prevented from getting more nuanced descriptions, particularly for identifying relations between ways of understanding multimodality, teaching strategies and technologies being used. More-over, due to the small-scale nature of this study, the findings are not generalizable to other contexts but rather may be used to provide insights on how teachers experience multimodal teaching and learning in specific contexts grounded to this study. Finally, it is acknowledged that multimodality is not a new concept for teaching and learning, however, this study might help to better understand how multimodality could work by using pedagogically driven approaches to teaching and learning mediated by technology that would help practitioners to design and support teaching and learning activities for enhancing students' learning experiences. Future research should closely investigate relations between multimodal meaning making and associated use of technology for discerning theories, practices and discourses. This will help the technology-enhanced learning research community to investigate and interpret multimodality in specific digital environments hence gauging larger-scale qualitative studies as means to surmount its impressionistic endeavour.

ACKNOWLEDGEMENT

The research leading to these results has received funding from the European Union Erasmus + programme, Key Action 2 Strategic Partnerships under grant agreement 2016-1-FR01-KA204-024178, STEAM project.

REFERENCES

Beetham, H. & Sharpe, R., 2013. *Rethinking Pedagogy for a digital age: Designing for 21st century learning.*. London: Routledge.

Bell, T., Urhahne, D., Schanze, S. & Ploetzner, R., 2010. Collaborative inquiry learning: Models, tools, and challenges. 32(3). *International journal of science education,* 32(3), pp. 349-377.

Boyatzis, R., 1998. *transforming Qualitative Information. Thematic Analysis and Code Development.* Cleveland: Sage.

Braun, V. & Clarke, V., 2006. Using thematic analysis in psychology. *Qualitative research in psychology,* 3(2), pp. 77-101.

Cope, B. & Kalantzis, M., 2009. "Multiliteracies": New literacies, new learning. *Pedagogies: An international journal,* 4(3), pp. 164-195.

Dillenbourg, P., 1999. What do you mean by collaborative learning? . In: *Collaborative-learning: Cognitive and computational approaches.* Oxford: Elsevier, pp. 1-15.

Greenhow, C., Robelia, B. & Hughes, J. E., 2009. Learning, teaching, and scholarship in a digital age Web 2.0 and classroom research: What path should we take now?. *Educational researcher,* 38(4), pp. 246-259.

Hennessy, S., 2011. The role of digital artefacts on the interactive whiteboard in supporting classroom dialogue. *Journal of Computer Assisted Learning,* 27: pp. 463–489.

Harris, C. J. & Rooks, D. L., 2010. Managing inquiry-based science: Challenges in enacting complex science instruction in elementary and middle school classrooms. *Journal of Science Teacher Education,* 21(2), pp. 227-240.

Hassett, D. D. & Curwood, J. S., 2009. Theories and practices of multimodal education: The instructional dynamics of picture books and primary classrooms.. *The Reading Teacher,* 63(4), pp. 270-282.

Hmelo-Silver, C. E., 2002. *Collaborative ways of knowing: Issues in facilitation.*. Boulder, Colorado, s.n.

Jewitt, C., 2008. Multimodality and literacy in school classrooms. *Review of research in education,* 32(1), pp. 241-267.

Jewitt, C., 2013. Multimodal methods for researching digital technologies. In: *The Sage handbook of digital technology research.* Los Angeles: SAGE, pp. 250-265.

Kress, G., 2001. *Multimodal teaching and learning: The rhetorics of the science classroom.*. London: Continuum .

Kress, G. & van Leeuwen, T., 2001. *Multimodal discourse: The modes and media of contemporary communication. London, UK: Edward Arnold.*. London, UK: Edward Arnold.

Lave, J. & Wenger, E., 1991. *Situated learning: Legitimate peripheral participation.*. Cambridge: Cambridge University press.

Mayer, R. E., 2001. *Multimedia learning.* New York: Cambridge University Press.

Miller, S. M. & McVee, M. B., 2013. *Multimodal composing in classrooms: Learning and teaching for the digital world.*. London: Routledge.

Redecker, C. et al., 2009. *Learning 2.0: The impact of Web 2.0 innovations on education and training in Europe (No. JRC55629).*, s.l.: Institute for Prospective and Technological Studies, Joint Research Centre..

Sharples, M. et al., 2016. *Innovating Pedagogy 2016: Open University Innovation Report 5,* Milton Keynes: Open University .

CONTRASTS IN OPENNESS TOWARD MOBILE LEARNING IN THE CLASSROOM: A STUDY OF ELEMENTARY, MIDDLE AND HIGH SCHOOL TEACHERS

Rhonda Christensen[1] and Gerald Knezek[2]
[1]*Institute for the Integration of Technology into Teaching and Learning, University of North Texas, Denton, Texas USA*
[2]*University of North Texas, Denton, Texas USA*

ABSTRACT

In a study involving 1414 elementary, middle school, and high school teachers from a large school district in the southwestern USA, the authors examine the similarities and differences among teachers at the three levels of K-12 education common in US school systems: elementary, middle school and high school. Major findings are that elementary school teachers are typically more open to mobile learning based on analysis of scores for three of the four factors (Possibilities, Benefits, and Preferences) assessed by the Mobile Learning Readiness Survey. For the fourth factor on the MLRS (External Influences), elementary teachers less strongly agree than either their middle school or high school counterparts that external influences determine whether it is practical to use mobile learning for teaching and learning in a classroom-centered context.

KEYWORDS

Mobile learning readiness, professional development, grade level teacher differences, technology integration

1. INTRODUCTION

Mobile learning in the classroom is become increasingly common in schools. The unique affordances of mobile learning are creating interest in different learning and teaching approaches. These devices offer the ability to collaborate (Corbeil & Valdes-Corbeil, 2007), to personalize instruction (Steel, 2012) and allow self-regulated learning (Sha, Looi et al, 2012). Other features useful for learning include audio and video recording, instant access to the Internet, texting, uploading and sharing files in addition to a growing number of learning apps. The portability of these mobile devices allows students to connect to content within and beyond the classroom walls.

A recent research report indicates that mobile devices are virtually ubiquitous for U.S. middle and high school students while one third of them are using mobile devices provided by their schools (Nagel, 2014). In order to address students who may not have a device, many districts are providing devices to students for learning initiatives. Parents also see the value of mobile learning in the classroom. In a 2010 survey conducted by Project Tomorrow, 62% of the responding parents would purchase a mobile device for their child if the school allowed the device to be used for educational purposes (Project Tomorrow, 2010). Yet teachers often remain reluctant to accept mobile devices as learning tools because they feel the need for additional support and training before they are comfortable using the devices with students (Messinger, 2011). Determining the best strategies for successful implementation of mobile devices to improve the learning environment is an important topic for research.

1.1 Impact of Mobile Learning

A meta-analysis of mobile learning in K-12 education reported overall positive gains in learning for students (Liu et al, 2014). A more recent meta-analysis of 110 studies related to mobile learning and student achievement (Sung, Chang, & Liu, 2016) reported an overall mean effect size of 0.523 (Cohen's *d*), indicating that learning with mobile devices can be more effective than traditional teaching methods that use pen and paper or desktop computers, to a moderate degree of magnitude (Cohen, 1988) that substantially exceeds the effect size = .3 standard beyond which an intervention is typically considered educationally meaningful (Bialo & Sivin-Kachala, 1996). Of the 110 articles in the meta-analysis, 38 were conducted at the elementary level, 10 at the middle school level and 10 at the high school level. The effect size differences for the elementary level were 0.654 while the effect sizes for the middle school level were 0.512 and high school 0.390. Additional reported findings indicated that implementation of handheld devices showed higher learning outcomes than the implementation of laptop computers. The authors conjectured that teaching with handheld devices uses more innovative teaching methods, including inquiry-based instruction (Sung, et al., 2016), while frequently laptops were replacements for desktop computers and used as such for note-taking and searching for information.

In a study of 224 teachers from 16 schools in Pennsylvania, Roche (2013) found that school level (elementary, middle or high school) and self-reported technology skill level are related to teachers' mobile learning attitudes. Teachers' perceptions regarding a change in their practices as well as their personal attitudes toward the change can significantly influence the successful implementation of mobile learning (Chao, 2005; Montrieux et al, 2014; Uzunboylu & Ozdamli, 2011). Roche (2013) also found significant differences by school level in how technology is used, specific technologies used and whether teachers created their own curriculum or used district curriculum.

1.2 Teacher Willingness to Accept Mobile Learning

Several factors are known to influence a teachers' willingness to use mobile technology in the classroom. These factors include student access, cost, class disruption, lack of teachers' technical and pedagogical skills, compelling evidence of effectiveness, and a lack of guidelines (Kim, 2013). In a study involving 1430 elementary, middle school, and high school teachers from a large school district in the southwestern USA, Christensen and Knezek (2017a) demonstrated that when aggregated across all school levels, teachers at different stages of technology integration proficiency also exhibit step-wise increments in their willingness to adopt mobile learning in their daily teaching and learning practices. In the current study, the authors examine the similarities and differences among teachers at the three levels of K-12 education common in US school systems: elementary (kindergarten – grade 5), middle school (grades 6-8) and high school (grades 9-12).

Little information was found in the literature regarding whether there are differences by school level in teachers' willingness to adopt mobile learning or regarding the underlying constructs that adequately describe teachers who are willing to accept and implement mobile learning. In addition, systematic study of the relationship of willingness to adopt mobile learning to classroom level of technology integration within a level of schooling is not fully developed. This led to the following research questions in the current study.

RQ1: To what extent do elementary school, middle school, and high school teachers differ in their willingness to adopt mobile learning in the classroom?

RQ2: To what extent are levels of technology integration proficiency related to willingness to adopt mobile learning among elementary, middle, and high school teachers?

2. THE STUDY

2.1 Methods

2.1.1 Participants

Educators from grades K-12 in a large school district in the southwestern US were invited to submit data related to mobile learning readiness in the fall of 2015. Of the 1,430 respondents, slightly fewer than half (n = 640, 44.8%) reported teaching at the elementary level with the remainder representing middle school (n = 370, 25.9%), high school (n = 404, 28.3%), or undesignated (n = 16, 1.1%). The undesignated participants were left out of the analysis for grade level taught due to the small number and undefined level.

2.1.2 Instrumentation

Participants were administered a battery of instruments including the Mobile Learning Readiness Survey (MLRS) and Stages of Adoption of Technology. The MLRS was designed to assess areas of needs for preparing teachers to teach with mobile devices in their classrooms (Christensen & Knezek, 2017b). The MLRS contains four constructs that measure different dimensions of teacher willingness to integrate mobile learning that can impact the preparation of classroom teachers. Twenty-eight (28) Likert-type items representing four factors were responded to by participants on a scale of 1 = Strongly Disagree to 5 = Strongly Agree. The reliabilities for four scales produced from this instrument, for this set of data are listed in Table 1.

Table 1. Internal Consistency Reliabilities for Four Scales of the MLRS

	Cronbach's Alpha	No. of Items
Factor 1 (Possibilities)	.92	8
Factor 2 (Benefits)	.91	10
Factor 3 (Preferences)	.79	5
Factor 4 (External Influences)	.61	4

Stages of Adoption of Technology (Christensen, 1997) is an instrument also administered to the teachers. Stages is a self-assessment of a teacher's level of adoption of technology, There are six possible stages in which educators rate themselves: Stage 1 - Awareness, Stage 2 - Learning the process, Stage 3 - Understanding and application of the process, Stage 4 - Familiarity and confidence, Stage 5 - Adaptation to other contexts, and Stage 6 - Creative application to new contexts. Demographic items such as years of teaching and grade level taught (elementary, middle and high school) were also completed by the teachers.

2.2 Results

2.2.1 Association of Mobile Learning Readiness and Grade Level Taught

As shown in Table 2, there were significant ($p < .05$) differences on all four of the MLRS factors by grade level taught. For Factor 1 *Possibilities*, Factor 2 *Benefits* and Factor 3 *Preferences*, elementary teachers were significantly higher ($p < .05$) than both middle school teachers and high school teachers in their dispositions. However, for Factor 4 (External Influences) the elementary teachers were significantly lower in their dispositions from both middle and high school teachers. As shown in Figure 1, the middle school and high school teachers were very similar in their dispositions for each of the four factors and overlay each other on the graph. In response to research Q1, a Tukey post hoc analysis revealed the significant differences for all four factors were elementary versus middle and high school teachers.

Table 2. Comparison of Four Mobile Learning Readiness Factors and Grade Level Taught

		N	Mean	SD	Sig.
Factor 1	Elementary School	640	4.38	.54	
Possibilities	Middle School	370	4.17	.62	
	High School	404	4.16	.62	
	Total	1414	4.26	.60	.0005
Factor 2	Elementary School	640	3.66	.62	
Benefits	Middle School	370	3.51	.65	
	High School	404	3.50	.66	
	Total	1414	3.58	.64	.0005
Factor 3	Elementary School	640	3.19	.80	
Preferences	Middle School	370	3.00	.79	
	High School	404	3.01	.82	
	Total	1414	3.09	.81	.0005
Factor 4	Elementary School	640	3.25	.68	
External Influences	Middle School	370	3.45	.70	
	High School	404	3.45	.67	
	Total	1414	3.36	.69	.0005

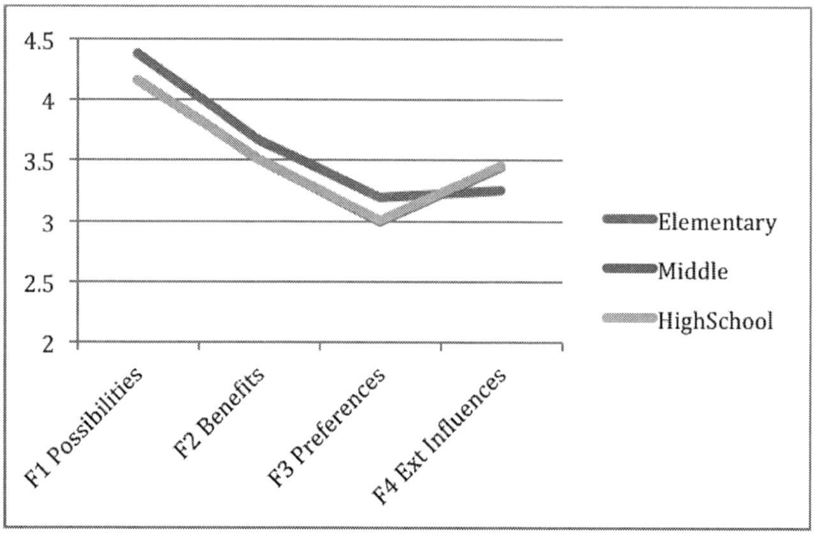

Figure 1. Four Factors of the MLRS by Grade Level Taught

2.2.2 Association of Technology Integration Measures and Grade Level Taught

An analysis of variance of Stages of Adoption of Technology by grade level taught showed significant ($p < .05$) differences among the three groups of teachers (Table 3). As revealed by a Tukey post hoc analysis, high school teachers were significantly ($p < .05$) higher in stages of technology integration than both elementary and middle school teachers.

Table 3. Analysis of Variance for Stages of Adoption of Technology by Grade Level Taught.

	N	Mean	SD	Sig.
Elementary School Teachers	640	4.45	1.062	
Middle School Teachers	370	4.41	1.121	
High School Teachers	404	4.68	1.134	
Total	1414	4.50	1.103	.001

2.2.3 Mobile Learning Measures by Stages of Adoption of Technology at Elementary, Middle and High School Levels

Analysis of variance for the four factors of the Mobile Learning Readiness Scale by Stages of Adoption of Technology were completed for each of the subpopulation samples of elementary, middle, and high school teachers listed in Table 3. The procedures followed were identical to those described in detail, for the combined group of 1400+ teachers in Christensen and Knezek (2017a). Results are illustrated in Figures 2-4. As shown in Figure 2, elementary teachers generally exhibit a smooth progression on all four factors of *Possibilities*, *Benefits*, *Preferences* and *External Influences* as proficiency in technology integration as indicated by Stages of Adoption of Technology, increases. For middle school teachers (Figure 3), the progression has a lesser slope (less rapid increase) but is still generally smoothly increasing as Stages of Adoption of Technology increase. For high school teachers (Figure 4), the transition changes appear to be more erratic possibly due to small numbers of teachers in Stage 1.

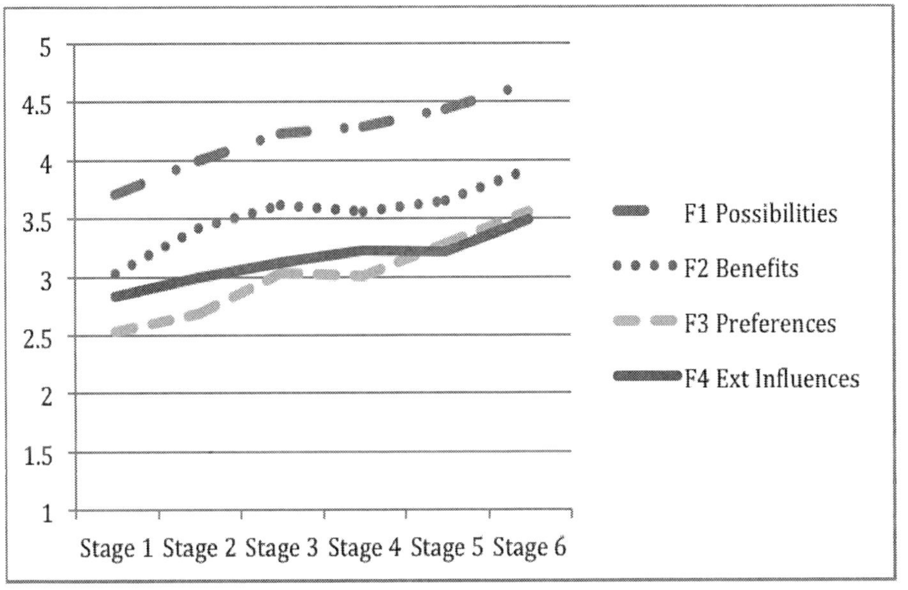

Figure 2. Elementary school teachers' MLRS factors by stage of adoption of technology

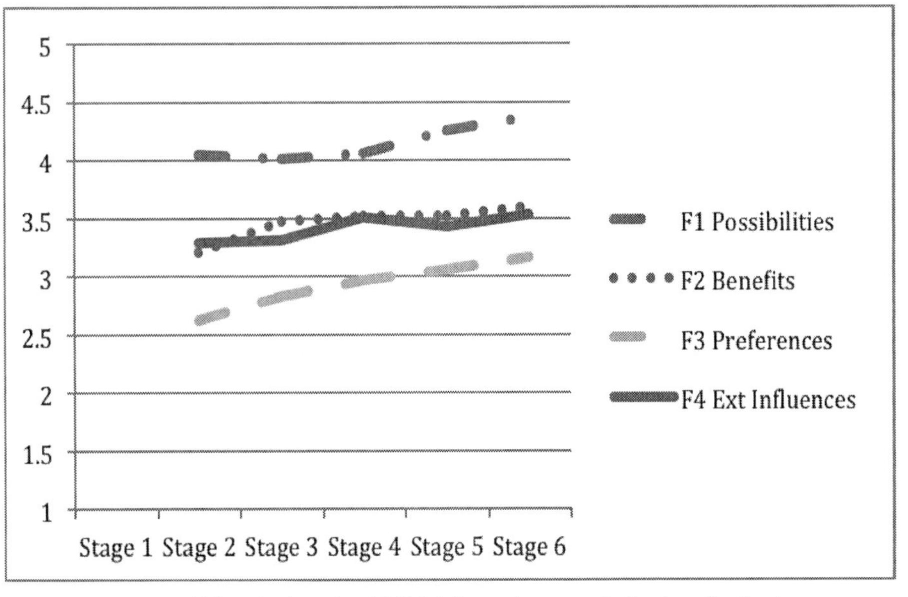

Figure 3. Middle school teachers' MLRS factors by stage of adoption of technology

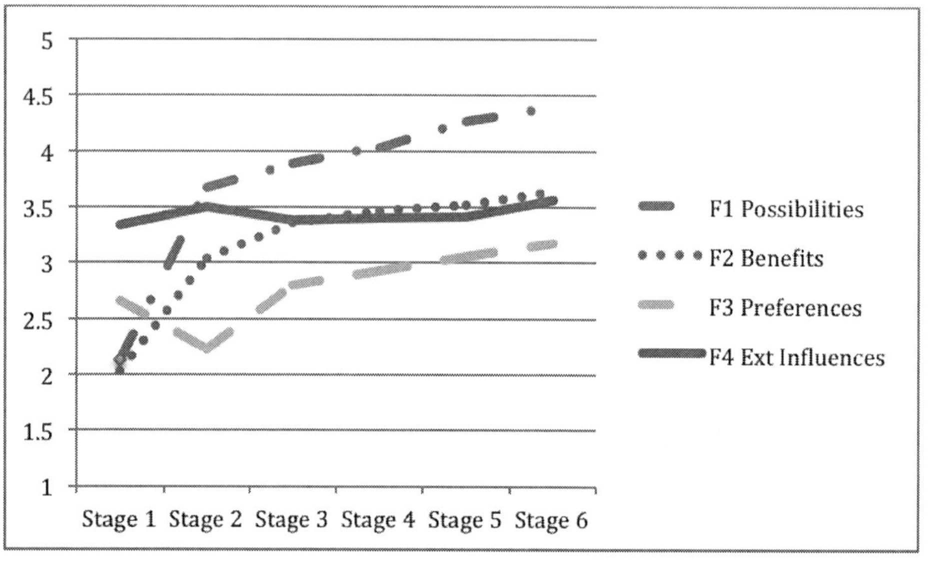

Figure 4. High school teachers' MLRS factors by stage of adoption of technology

With respect to research Q2, trends in the relationship of levels of technology integration to willingness to adopt mobile learning are similar for elementary, middle school and high school teachers. The positive linear association appears to be strongest for elementary school teachers.

2.2.4 Item Level Analysis

The 28 items were analyzed to compare teachers by grade level. Twenty-three (23) of the 28 items were significantly (p <.05) different by grade level taught. For 20 of the items with significant differences, elementary teachers reported higher means. Examples of these items are:

Item 2. Mobile learning will bring new opportunities for learning.
Item 17. The use of mobile technology in the classroom increases student engagement.
Item20. The use of mobile technology in the classroom allows students to develop creativity.

For 3 of the items elementary teachers reported lower means. These items were:

Item 24. Students are more knowledgeable than I am when it comes to using mobile technologies.
Item 27. My curriculum is conducive to students having their own technology.
Item 28. My administration is supportive of students having their own device.

Teachers at all grade levels seem to agree on five items related to mobile learning in the classroom in which there were no significant differences. Areas where teachers regardless of level of teaching tend to agree are:

Item 13. Teachers at all levels slightly prefer to use a traditional textbook rather than an electronic textbook.
Item 21. Teachers at all levels generally agree that mobile learning will improve communication between students and teachers.
Item 22. Teachers at all levels generally agree that mobile learning will improve communications among students.
Item 23. Teachers at all levels slightly agree that having a mobile device would improve student organization.
Item 25. Teachers at all levels generally agree that their school is doing a good job of using technology to enhance learning.

It appears that elementary teachers in this study are more open to embracing mobile learning in their classrooms but are not certain how it might fit into their current curriculum or whether the required support will be available. Teachers at all grade levels prefer the traditional teacher textbook to an electronic one, agree that mobile learning can support communication of different types and feel their schools are supportive of technology to enhance student learning.

3. DISCUSSION

The most surprising finding of this study is that elementary school teachers express the highest willingness to adopt mobile learning. This, combined with the conjectured and reconfirmed finding that the profiles of elementary, middle school, and high school teachers across the four scales of the Mobile Learning Readiness Survey differ greatly, implies that professional development activities for teachers, as well as learning activities for students, may differ greatly across these three levels. Perhaps the findings are related to the type of learning environment differences between primary (elementary) and secondary (middle and high) schools. Perhaps the differences are due to the ubiquitous access of mobile devices by middle and high school students (Nagel, 2014). These middle and high school teachers have experienced the difficulties involved in student devices brought to school, yet did not have the preparation to deal with the management and are reticent to embrace these devices for learning. Most elementary teachers may not have yet had to deal with these negative issues and are preparing to embrace mobile learning in a more systematic way as indicated in the more controlled studies found in the meta-analysis (Sung et al, 2016) that mobile learning device implementation had a more effective impact for elementary than middle and high school students.

4. CONCLUSIONS

In this study involving 1414 teachers from a large public school district in the southwestern USA, major findings are that elementary school teachers are more open to using smartphones, tablets and other hand-held information technology devices for mobile learning in their classrooms, when compared to middle school or high school teachers. For three of the four factors assessed by the Mobile Learning Readiness Survey (*Possibilities*, *Benefits*, and *Preferences*), elementary teachers as a group were found to be significantly ($p < .05$) more positive. For the fourth factor on the MLRS (*External Influences*), elementary teachers less strongly agree than either their middle school or high school counterparts that external influences determine whether it is practical to use mobile learning for teaching and learning in a classroom-centered context. These findings imply that there are likely different approaches and different types of professional development appropriate for elementary teachers versus middle and high school teachers. It appears that the elementary school level may be the most conducive for beginning a large-scale project such as a district-wide initiative if there is a need for a systematic implementation with the ability to measure impact. Middle school and high school teachers may need more focus on specific issues such as classroom management and implementation of an intervention that is based on having multiple classrooms of students for a limited period of time each day. Middle school and high school teachers may also need to be more versed in the integration of multiple types of personal devices brought to school by students. As shown in this study, teachers at different grade level bands have differing perceptions and needs when it comes to professional development for integrating mobile learning in the classroom. Additional research is needed to confirm whether the trends found in this study are applicable on a broad scale, across the US and in other portions of the world.

REFERENCES

Bialo, E. R. & Sivin-Kachala, J. 1996. The effectiveness of technology in schools: A summary of recent research. *School Library Media Quarterly, 25* (1), 51-57.

Chao, C. 2005. Evaluating teachers' attitudes toward the use of wireless-mobile technologies in supporting learning: An instrument development study. *Wireless and Mobile Technologies in Education, 2005. WMTE 2005. IEEE International Workshop on Advanced Learning Technologies,* 104-106.

Christensen, R., 1997. *Effect of technology integration education on the attitudes of teachers and their students*. Doctoral dissertation, University of North Texas.

Christensen, R. & Knezek, G. 2017a. Readiness for integrating mobile learning in the classroom: Challenges, preferences and possibilities. *Computers in Human Behavior, 76, 112-121.* doi.org/10.1016/j.chb.2017.07.014.

Christensen, R. & Knezek, G. 2017b. Validating a mobile learning readiness survey: Assessing teachers' dispositions toward adoption. *Journal of Digital Learning in Teacher Education, 33*(4). DOI:10.1080/21532974.2017.1347536.

Cohen, J., 1988. *Statistical power analysis for the behavioral sciences*. Hillsdale, NJ: Erlbaum.

Corbeil, J.R., & Valdes-Corbeil, M.E. 2007. Are you ready for mobile learning? *EDUCAUSE Quarterly, 30*(2), 51-48.

Kim, J. 2013. Measuring factors that influence teachers' willingness in using mobile phone in the classroom. In R. McBride & M. Searson (Eds.), *Proceedings of Society for Information Technology & Teacher Education International Conference 2013* (pp. 3730-3737). Chesapeake, VA: AACE. Retrieved March 16, 2014 from http://www.editlib.org/p/48689.

Liu, M., Scordino, R., Guertz, R., Navarrete, C., Ko, Y., & Lim, M. 2014. A look at research on mobile learning in K-12 education from 2007 to the present. *Journal of Research on Technology in Education, 46*(4), 325-372.

Messinger, J. 2011. M-learning: An exploration of the attitudes and perceptions of high school students versus teachers regarding the current and future use of mobile devices for learning. Doctoral Dissertation, Pepperdine University, ProQuest Dissertations Publishing, 2011. 3487951.

Montrieux, H., Courtois, C., DeGrove, F., Raes, A., Schellens, T., & DeMarez, L. 2014. Mobile learning in secondary education: Teachers' and students' perceptions and acceptance of tablet computers. *International Journal of Mobile and Blended Learning,* 6(2), 26-40.

Nagel, D. 2014. One-third of U.S. students use school-issued mobile devices. *THEJournal.* Available http://thejournal.com/Articles/2014/04/08/A-Third-of-Secondary-Students-Use-School-Issued-Mobile-Devices.aspx?m=2&p=1.

Project Tomorrow. 2010. Learning in the 21st century: Taking it mobile!. *Project Tomorrow and Blackboard K-12.* Www.tomorrow.org. Retrieved December 28, 2011 from http://www.tomorrow.org/speakup/MobileLearningReport_2010.html.

Roche, A.J. 2013. M-Learning: A Psychometric Study of the Mobile Learning Perception Scale. *Theses and Dissertations.* Paper 1607.

Sha, L., Looi, C., Chen, W., & Zhang, B.H. 2012. Understanding mobile learning from the perspective of self-regulated learning. *Journal of Computer Assisted Learning, 28*(4), 366-378.

Steel, C. 2012. Fitting learning into life: Language students' perspectives on benefits of using mobile apps. In M. Brown, M. Harnett, & T. Stewart (Eds.), *ascilite2012: Future challenges, sustainable futures* (pp. 875-880). Wellington, New Zealand.

Sung, Y-T., Chang, K-E., & Liu, T-C. 2016. The effects of integrating mobile devices with teaching and learning on students' learning performance: A meta-analysis and research synthesis. *Computers & Education, 94*, 252-275.

Uzunboylu, H., & Ozdamli, F. 2011. Teacher perception for m-learning: Scale development and teachers' perceptions. Journal of Computer Assisted Learning, 27, 544-556.

CLASSIFICATION OF LEARNING STYLES IN VIRTUAL LEARNING ENVIRONMENT USING J48 DECISION TREE

Renato R. Maaliw III[1] and Melvin A. Ballera[2]
[1]*Southern Luzon State University - Philippines*
[2]*AMA University - Philippines*

ABSTRACT

The usage of data mining has dramatically increased over the past few years and the education sector is leveraging this field in order to analyze and gain intuitive knowledge in terms of the vast accumulated data within its confines. The primary objective of this study is to compare the results of different classification techniques such as Naïve Bayes, Logistic Regression, Conjunctive Rule and J48 Decision Tree in detection and identification of student's learning styles in a Virtual Learning Environment to provide adaptation strategy according to identified learning styles of the students. The data sets were collected from 507 students of Computer Programming 1 course with a total of 52,815 rows of data extracted from their interaction logs and navigational patterns in a virtual learning environment. A mapping of student's learning style according to the selected learning style model had been accomplished. The performance of each classification techniques and its classification quality were measured in terms of correctly classified instances, kappa statistics, receiver operating characteristics, and area under the curve plots. Based from the analysis of the comparative results, the classification technique that has produced the highest collective average accuracy is the J48 Decision Tree with correctly predicted instances of 87.42%. The classification technique could be used to identify student's learning styles in a virtual learning environment.

KEYWORDS

Educational data mining, learning styles, learning style model, virtual learning environment, J48 decision tree

1. INTRODUCTION

The field of educational data mining (EDM) is an "emerging and evolving discipline that is particularly concern in creating and developing methods for exploring the different and unique types of data that comes from the educational settings". Higher Education Institutions (HEIs) have been investing thoroughly in providing educational infrastructure such as Virtual Learning Environment (VLE). This type of technology enables educators to represent knowledge by delivering different types of content and, monitor student participation that can enhance the learning process. VLE provides the creation of knowledge representation and contains set of tools for communications, assessments, and various features. Most universities employs traditional face-to-face interaction as the main approach in teaching in the sector of education but HEIs are investing on the infrastructure to supplement traditional methods of teaching with learning technologies in order to enhanced and improve the quality of learning (Dumcience et al., 2010). But despite the astronomical increase in practice of using VLEs in HEIs, the application of these technologies are still failing miserably in terms of inciting student motivation to learn, and "it fails to serve the ultimate goal of having on-line learning" (Ballera et al., 2013).

VLEs are rich sources of learner's data that the education sectors are completely overlooking and sometimes completely neglecting. It stores valuable source of information that should be considered in order to understand how student learns. The amount of data that can be extracted that are residing inside these VLEs can be exploited to better understand learner's behavior, improve the pedagogical process that leads to an efficient and streamlined teaching and learning progress. It can be used in the detection and identification of student's learning styles (LS) to provide adaptation strategies to the course design and contents of VLEs in order to match the student's preference in terms of their learning styles. There are substantial research studies that considered learning style as a vital factor that directly affects the student's learning process. It is one of the responsibilities of the teacher to understand how different learner learns in accordance to their learning styles. It cannot be denied that learners can encounter difficulties in an environment where their learning styles are not supported. This study focuses in the detection and identification of student's learning style in the context of a virtual learning environment using data mining techniques based from their extracted interaction logs and navigational patterns.

2. REVIEW OF RELATED LITERATURE

2.1 Learning Styles

Keefe (1979) defines learning styles as the "collective characteristics of affective, cognitive, and physiological factors serving as stable indicators of how a particular learner interacts with, perceives, and responds to a learning environment" while Stewart et al. (1992) defines learning styles as the "educational conditions under which a student is most likely to learn".

Learning style's primary concern is how an individual prefers to learns and not what the learner learns. When an individual tries to learn something new they vary regarding their preferences. Some learn by communicating to someone, some by reflecting about what they have learned, or prefers textual and graphical representation of the learning material. It can also be describe as a set of behaviors, and attitudes that enhance and streamline learning in any situation. Each individual has their own way of preferences when it comes to learning; it is an innate characteristic that are influenced by the environment, experiences, and developments. There are many learning style models that have existed in the literature but notable educational theorist are in agreement that each individual has their own preferred ways of learning that must be met by the learning environment. These learning styles are clear indicators of how learners perceive, react, interact with, and respond to the learning environments. There are "overwhelming evidences that learning styles are very diverse and educators should consider these differences in students to be taught in a method that are well-suited to their learning styles" (Pashler et al., 2008).

2.2 Dimensions of the Felder-Silverman Learning Style Model

The Felder-Silverman learning style model (FSLSM) is a learning style model based on the notion that students have preferences in terms of the way they receive and process information. The model presents different dimensions that are indicative of learning preferences. Four dimensions are described in the learning style model of FSLSM namely processing, perception, input, and understanding. Learner's learning styles are specifically defined for each of these dimensions. All dimensions are independent from one another and are based from major dimensions of learning styles. They describe learner's preferences to process information (active/reflective), perceive information (sensing/intuitive), receive information (visual/verbal), and organize (sequential/global) information.

Active learners are characterized as learners who prefer to process information by doing something with the learned material. The most obvious pattern of behavior of an active learner is that they have a strong tendency to discuss and interact with other learners. On the other hand, reflective learners prefer to think about the learning material and they work alone. In a VLE, active learners are expected to post more often in a forum while reflective learner's tendencies are to participate passively by visiting forum but rarely posting. Active learners also tends to attempt more self-assessment tests, a type of test where the result is not graded but it is important in order for the learner to assess their knowledge on a particular topic. The characteristic of reflective learner to think about the material leads to more visits in learning objects that are textual-based in context.

Sensing learners tends to repeatedly visit concrete learning materials that contains facts, data, and when a learning object is being linked to real life context whereas intuitive learners prefer to visit abstract learning materials that contains theories and their underlying meanings, histories, glossaries, syntax, and concepts. The number of visits on these kinds of learning objects serves as a pattern. On the other hand, intuitive learners supposed tendencies are to visit learning objects such as an example as a supplementary material. The number of visits on these kinds of learning objects tends to be higher for intuitive learners. Intuitive learners are also characterized as a careful worker. With regards to this, intuitive learners tend to be careful and tend to review their answers more when performing a test especially when it is being graded. The pattern can be conceived by the number of attempted answer reviews they made in an exercise before attempting to submit their answers.

Accordingly, verbal learner's preference on a learning object is composed chiefly of words or texts, they tend to like communication with others and discussions. Therefore, verbal learner's tendencies are to use the forum, thus a high number of forum postings can indicate a verbal learning style. On the opposite end, visual learners learn best from what they actually see. Therefore, they tend to view more learning objects that usually contains graphics such as diagrams, charts, and pictures. Video presentations also are highly preferred by visual learners while verbal learners are expected to visit a learning object of textual-based types.

Sequential learners are more comfortable with details, whereas global learners tend to be good in seeing the overall picture and connections to other fields. Because of this kind of behavior, global learners are interested in getting the "big picture" and an overview. Course outlines are especially important to them whereas sequential learners tend to skip these kinds of learning objects. A high number of visits spent on chapter outlines, course overview or chapter overview page indicate a global learning style. The navigational patterns of learners when using a VLE can be used also to differentiate sequential or global learning style as well. While sequential learners tend to go through the course step by step in a linear way, global learners tend to learn in large gaps by skipping learning objects and jumping to more complex and advanced learning objects. Therefore, the navigational patterns can be seen as an indicator to differentiate the two styles.

3. METHODOLOGY

3.1 Data Source and Methods of Collection

The data sets are based from the log files of Introduction to C++ Moodle Course (Computer Programming 1) in Southern Luzon State University (SLSU) in the Philippines. A blended learning environment has been implemented with this specific course by supplementing traditional face-to-face setup by a Moodle (Moodle Learning Management System) course that includes several and carefully designed learning objects such as chapter overviews, visual material, video presentation, textual material, audio material, examples, glossary, concrete, and abstract materials. Different types of assessment such as self-assessment and exercises are provided to allow students to practice their programming skills. Forum usage is also encouraged to increase interaction among students and to solve group related problems during the duration of the course. Although there are several courses in the virtual learning environment, this specific course was selected for it is found to have a large number of students enrolled thus it contains large amount of interaction and log data.

Five hundred seven (507) students have participated and answered the Index of Learning Style (ILS) questionnaires based from FSLSM. Students have been given ample amount of time and each question in the questionnaires is carefully explained to them to avoid contaminating the data. Table 1 shows the learning styles' distribution for all dimensions of the FSLSM without considering the degree of learning style preference.

Table 1. Distribution of learning styles based from ILS

Dimension	Processing	No. of Students	Percentage
Processing	Active	244	48.13%
	Reflective	263	51.87%
Perception	Sensing	348	68.64%
	Intuitive	159	31.365
Input	Visual	388	76.53%
	Verbal	119	23.47%
Understanding	Sequential	250	49.31%
	Global	257	50.69%

From the analysis of ILS questionnaires collected from 507 students, it reveals that at the processing dimension there are 263 (51.87%) students that have a reflective learning style while 244 (48.13%) students have an active learning style. This manifest that students learning styles in the processing dimension is fairly balanced. The perception dimension reveals that 348 (68.64%) students have a sensing learning style. This means that most students prefer learning objects that are based from real facts and data, and a learning object that is linked to real life situations. At the input dimension, the data collected reveals that 388 (76.53%) of students prefers learning objects that mostly contains graphics such as pictures, charts, diagrams, and video presentation materials. Finally, the data reveals that student's learning style in the understanding dimension is fairly balanced with 257 (50.69%) students with global learning styles and 250 (49.31%) students with sequential learning styles.

3.2 Mapping of Students Learning Styles in Virtual Learning Environment

Table 2 provides the lists of the learning style mapping of relevant student's behavior in a VLE. These sets of relevant behaviors were extracted from the VLE database to construct the data sets for data mining.

Table 2. Learning style mapping of relevant students' behavior in VLEs

Learning Style	Relevant Behavior	Attribute Name	Attribute Value
Active	Post more often in discussion forum	forum_posts	no. of posting in forum
	Perform more self-assessment tests	self_assesment	no. of viewed post in forum
Reflective	Reading post but rarely posting by themselves	forum_view	no. of viewed post in forum
	Prefers learning material in textual form	text_materials	no. of visits
Sensing	Prefers concrete learning materials (facts, data)	concrete_materials	no. of visits
	Prefers examples	examples	no. of visits
Intuitive	Prefers abstract learning material (definition, theories, syntax, flowcharts)	abstract_materials	no. of visits
	Prefers to review answers in graded exercise tests	exercises_rev	no. of attempted answer reviews
Visual	Prefers learning materials supplemented with pictures, diagrams, graphs	visual_materials	no. of visits
	Prefers learning materials presented in a video format	video_materials	no. of visits
Verbal	Prefers learning material presented in text or audio	text_materials	no. of visits
	Post more often in discussion forum	forum_post	no. of posting in discussion
Sequential	Prefers to go through the course step by step (linear way)	nav_pattern_dist	sequence of navigational pattern
Global	Prefers overviews, outlines	course_overviews	no. of visits
	Prefers to learn in large leaps by skipping learning material & jumping to more complex materials (non-linear way)	nav_pattern_dist	sequence of navigational pattern

3.3 Navigational Pattern Sequence Data Collection

Navigational patterns refers to how learners navigate through the course and in which order they visit certain types of learning objects. In a study by Imra et al. (2016) on personalized learning recommendation system, they have proposed identification of navigational sequence pattern using the formula for Euclidean distance to compute the similarity and difference between learners on their navigational characteristics. With this formula, navigational patterns of students in a Virtual Learning Environment can be inferred by analyzing and computing their navigational sequence distance values. In a similar research by Benlarmi (2003) on dynamic learning modeler, they have used approximately thirty (30) navigational sequences to cluster similarities between students navigational behavior in a hypermedia courseware. In accordance to previous studies, the navigational distance values in order to distinguish a user that are navigating sequentially or navigating globally can be tracked when accessing the online course.

3.4 Data Preprocessing, Transformation and Attribute Value Extraction

Every logs and activities of all students are recorded in the VLE database. Primarily, VLEs such as Moodle provides a module for extraction of user logs and activities for a specific course by exporting to varieties of file formats such as Microsoft Excel (*.xlsx) file. The table is comprised of data labels such as 'Time', 'User Full Name', 'Affected User', 'Event Context', 'Event Name', 'Description', 'Origin' and 'IP Address'. The initial data sets were subjected to data preprocessing by removing all unnecessary data. Interaction logs of each target students were extracted to produce a reduced log file that contains the data labels of 'User Full Name', 'Event Context', 'Event Name' and 'Type'.

The reduced log file extracted contains 52,815 rows of student logs and activities for the course that were used in classification of individual learning styles. With reference to Figure 1, a 'Learning Object Type' field has been created in order to identify as to what type of learning object each particular students interacts with. Identification of learning object type in the course was also mapped in order to identify as to what kind of learning object each truly represents based on the learning object literature types whether textual learning materials, visual learning materials, abstract learning materials, concrete learning materials and examples. These learning object type identification are evaluated by educational experts. It is necessary to distinguish these learning object types in order to effectively create data sets in inferring student's learning styles.

User full name	Event context	Event name	Learning Object Type
Beneluz Abustan	Page: Chapter 1 Overview	Course module viewed	course_overviews
Beneluz Abustan	Page: C++ Terminology	Course module viewed	abstract_materials
Beneluz Abustan	Page: Assignment Statements	Course module viewed	text_materials
Beneluz Abustan	Page: Assignment Statements	Course module viewed	text_materials
Beneluz Abustan	Page: Literals	Course module viewed	text_materials
Beneluz Abustan	Page: Literals	Course module viewed	text_materials

Figure 1. Excerpt of reduced log file of student's interaction and activities in a VLE

The next phase in the construction of the data sets is data transformation. The reduced log data in Microsoft Excel format is transformed and converted to a Microsoft Access file (*.accdb) format in order to easily aggregate the total number of interaction a particular learner to each learning objects. An aggregate SQL statement commands was used to extract the needed values for data mining and analysis. Derived variables was extracted by aggregating variables such as number of visits to a specific learning object, the number of submitted self-assessment tests, number of forum postings and views, and more.

The final phase in the construction of data sets is to arrange the derived values of number of interactions of the students to a specific learning object. It was arranged and categorized based from the learning behavior pattern mapping in Table 2. An excerpt of final data set construction is depicted in Figure 2. An additional data field was created to accommodate the reported learning styles of each student based from their answers from the ILS questionnaire. The results of the questionnaire served as the class labels of each student in terms of their learning styles for each learning style dimensions. The final data sets were used in data mining.

No.	Student	forum_post	forum_view	self_assesment	text_materials	PROCESSING
1	ABUSTAN, BENELUZ	1	2	8	27	ACTIVE
2	ABUAN, SIDNEY JANE	11	6	3	0	REFLECTIVE
3	ABULAR, MA. FREDA MAE	21	10	7	29	ACTIVE
4	ABULENCIA, APPLE GEM	9	2	8	1	ACTIVE
5	ABUSTAN, AUDREY CASSIE	4	3	8	17	ACTIVE
6	ACERO, CHANTREA FELICHE	15	11	0	14	ACTIVE

Figure 2. Excerpt of final data set construction (processing dimension)

3.5 Feature Selection

To determine the best features or attributes for determining the learning styles of the students in each dimension, attribute selection was used. Filtering method using Information Gain attribute evaluation was selected. The objective of feature selection technique testing is to empirically confirm and improve the classification performance of the predictors, providing faster and more cost-effective predictors, and providing a better understanding of the underlying process that generated the data. By applying attribute selection, significant predictors were extracted from each mapped attributes for each learning style dimensions. Summary of feature selection results can be seen in Table 3 and based from the results, eleven (11) attributes have been found to be significant in inferring learning styles in VLEs.

Table 3. Results of feature selection for each FSLSM Attributes

Information Gain Attribute Evaluation		
Processing Dimension Attributes	**Rank Value**	**Significant? (yes/no)**
forum_view	0.449	yes
self_assessment	0.338	yes
forum_posts	0.267	yes
textual_materials	0	no
Perception Dimension Attributes	**Rank Value**	**Significant? (yes/no)**
concrete_materials	0.353	yes
exercises_rev	0.241	yes
examples	0.107	yes
abstract_materials	0.093	yes
Input Dimension Attributes	**Rank Value**	**Significant? (yes/no)**
video_materials	0.382	yes
visual_materials	0.269	yes
forum_posts	0	no
textual_materials	0	no
Understanding Dimension Attributes	**Rank Value**	**Significant? (yes/no)**
course_overview	0.285	yes
nav_pattern_dist	0.039	yes

3.6 Pattern Discovery

In this phase, different classification data mining techniques was applied to the derived data sets. For the reason of its open-source implementation, Waikato Environment for Knowledge Analysis (WEKA) was used in order to analyze the performances of the selected classification methods to discover the most appropriate and best model that can be used for the future development of an adaptive VLE for different learning styles.

3.7 Evaluation

The model evaluation is an integral part of the model development process. The quality of classification was evaluated using the Receiver Operating Characteristics (ROC) and Area under the Curve (AUC) plots to measure the accuracy of the model. A random classifier has an area under the curve of 0.5, while AUC for a perfect classifier is equal to 1. In practice, most of the accurate classification models have an AUC between 0.5 and 1. A rough guide for classifying the quality of classification of the area under the curve is based on the traditional academic point system as shown in Table 4.

Table 4. Traditional Academic Point System

Range	Description
.90 – 1.00	Excellent
.80 - .90	Good
0.70 – 0.80	Fair
.60 - .70	Poor
.50 - .60	Fail

Another evaluation measure of classification quality in data mining is the Cohen's Kappa Equivalent. It is a coefficient which measures the inter-rater agreement for qualitative categorical items. The measurement was applied also to measure the classification accuracy when performing classification in data mining. Kappa statistics (Cohen, 1960) was used to assess the accuracy of any particular measuring cases. Cohen's kappa equivalent values are shown in Table 5.

Table 5. Cohen's Kappa equivalent values

Kappa Score	Equivalent
0.81 – 1.00	Perfect
0.61 – 0.80	Substantial
0.41 – 0.60	Moderate
0.21 – 0.40	Slight
<= 0	None

4. RESULTS AND DISCUSSIONS

A total of eight (8) classification techniques have been utilized to test the performance of the classifiers based on the final data sets but the top four performing algorithms such as Logistic Regression, Naïve Bayes, Conjunctive Rule and J48 Decision Tree were selected. Classification performances are tested on all four dimensions of the FSLSM. Comparative tests results can be seen in Table 6 and it is summarized based on classification accuracy and the kappa statistics values.

Table 6. Comparative performance results of classification using different techniques

Processing Dimension (Active/Reflective)				
	Simple Logistic	Naïve Bayes	Conjunctive Rule	J48
Correctly Classified Instances	85.99%	89.34%	75.14%	**92.50%**
Incorrectly Classified Instances	14.01%	10.65%	24.85%	7.49%
Kappa Statistics	0.719	0.786	0.497	0.849
Perception Dimension (Sensing/Intuitive)				
	Simple Logistic	Naïve Bayes	Conjunctive Rule	J48
Correctly Classified Instances	81.65%	82.24%	68.63%	**88.16%**
Incorrectly Classified Instances	18.34%	17.75%	31.36%	11.83%
Kappa Statistics	0.550	0.586	0	0.699
Input Dimension (Visual/Verbal)				
	Simple Logistic	Naïve Bayes	Conjunctive Rule	J48
Correctly Classified Instances	85.79%	85.99%	76.52%	**86.58%**
Incorrectly Classified Instances	14.20%	14.00%	23.47%	13.41%
Kappa Statistics	0.582	0.634	0	0.677
Understanding Dimension (Sequential/Global)				
	Simple Logistic	Naïve Bayes	Conjunctive Rule	J48
Correctly Classified Instances	80.27%	74.95%	81.26%	**82.44%**
Incorrectly Classified Instances	19.72%	25.04%	18.73%	17.55%
Kappa Statistics	0.605	0.500	0.624	0.647

Based on the comparative classification performance of different classification techniques, J48 decision tree classifier obtained the highest accuracy with an average of 87.42% collectively for all dimension. The Logistic Regression, Naïve Bayes and Conjunctive Rule yield a collective average accuracy across all learning dimension of 83.42%, 83.13% and 75.38% respectively. Kappa scores from the J48 method of 0.849, 0.699, 0.677, and 0.647 for the respective dimensions reflected that there is a 'Substantial' accuracy in classification.

To further test the classification quality of the J48 classification model, a total of four (4) ROC curve plots have been generated for each learning style dimension using KnowledgeFlow in WEKA.

The ROC curves for all learning style dimensions did not fall below the random guessing line threshold of 0.5 which suggests that the quality of qualification is well beyond random guessing and the classification did not happen by chance only. Furthermore, the values obtained from the AUC plots are 0.9176 (Excellent) for processing dimension, 0.8318 (Good) for perception dimension, 0.9016 (Excellent) for input dimension, and 0.8124 (Good) for the understanding dimension. Average AUC scores across all four dimensions are 0.86585 that signifies that the model provides a good classification quality. Having determined that the J48 classifier was the best fit for the classification purposes of learning styles, the rules generated from the J48 classification technique can be used in the development of a prototype of an adaptive VLE for different learning styles.

5. CONCLUSION

The interaction logs and navigational patterns of the participating students were extracted from the VLE's database. A total of 52,815 rows of data were extracted from the five hundred seven (507) participating students in the study. This study was limited only on the obtained Moodle log data for the specified course and did not consider the analysis of student's respective homework, recitation and discussion performances. The classification model was implemented on the data sets for the Introduction to C++ Moodle Course of SLSU in the Philippines. Based from the empirical results and comparative performance results of different classification algorithms, the technique by means of J48 decision tree classifier attained the highest accuracy with 87.52%.

Implementation of VLEs has been successful in most HEIs but in most cases this piece of technology fails to meet the unique needs of each students particularly their learning styles. Furthermore, there is no mechanism or a feature in most VLEs that automatically classifies student's based from their learning styles. The knowledge divulged from the empirical results can be a basis for HEIs, educators, and course developers that each student is unique in characteristics in terms of their learning styles thus they have different needs.

The next phase of the study is to develop a prototype software of an adaptive Virtual Learning Environment system in order to dynamically adjust its course design and contents to respond immediately to each student's needs based from the derived classification model from this study.

REFERENCES

Ballera, Melvin A., and Elssaedi, Mosbah Mohamed, 2013. New E-learning Strategy Paradigm: A Multi-Disciplinary Approach to Enhance Learning Delivery, *Proceedings of the 2nd E-learning Regional Conference*, State of Kuwait, pp. 25-27.

Benlarmi, S.K. 2003. A Dynamic Modeler for Navigational Sequence Patterns. *Journal of Research on Technology and Innovations*. vol 3., no. 2, pp. 121-127.

Carver, C.A., Howard, R.A., and Lane, W.D., Addressing Different Learning Styles through Course Hypermedia. IEEE Transactions on Education, vol. 42, no.1, pp. 33-38, 1999

Cohen J. A. 1960. Coefficient of Agreement for Nominal Scales. *Educational and Psychological Measurement*, 20, pp. 37-46.

Dumciene, A., Lapeniene, D., 2010. Possibilities of Developing Study Motivation in E-Learning Products. Electronics and Engineering. – Kaunas: Technolojia, No. (102) pp. 43-46.

Felder, R.M., and B.A. Soloman, 2016. Index of Learning Styles, http://www.ncsu.edu/felder-public/ILSpage.html, 2004, accessed May 2.

Felder, R.M., and Silverman, L.K., 1987. Learning Styles and Teaching Styles in Engineering Education. *Presented at the 1987 Annual Meeting of the American Institute of Chemical Engineers*, New York.

Garcia P., Amandi A., Schiaffin S., Campo M., 2007. Evaluating Bayesian Networks Precision for Detecting Student's Learning Styles. *Computers and Education*, 49, pp.794-808, Elsevier.

Imra J. and Zawili S., 2016. Personalized Learning Recommendation System for E-learning. *International Journal of Science and Technology*. vol.2, no. 1, pp. 85-90.

Keefe, J.W., 1979. Learning Style: An Overview. *In National Association of Secondary School Principlas (Ed.)*, Student Learning Styles: Diagnosing and Prescribing Programs, pp. 1-17

Moodle Learning Management System. [Online]. Available: http://www.moodle.org.

Pashler, H., McDaniel, M. Rohrer, D, Bjork, R., 2008. Learning Styles: Concepts and Evidence. *Psychological Science in the Public Interest*, vol. 9, pp. 105-119.

Stewart, K.L., Felicettie, L.A., 1992. Learning Styles of Marketing Majors. *Educational Research Quarterly*, 15(2), pp. 15-23.

WEKA at http://www.cs.waikato.ac.nz/~ml/weka. Retrieved April 29, 2016.

USING SHORT VIDEOS AS TESTING ELEMENTS IN SKILL MATCHING - TEST DESIGN IN THE SMART PROJECT

Marc Beutner and Frederike Anna Rüscher
University Paderborn, Chari Business and Human Resource Education II, Warburger Str. 100, 33098 Paderborn, Germany

ABSTRACT

This paper provides insights in the development of a skill matching test which addresses soft skills integrated videos as media to provide information about situations to be rated. The design of the skill testing and matching tool is situated in the educational ERASMUS+ project SMART which is presented as well. With a specific view on team work and the necessary skills, traits and interests this article provides insights into the representation of these aspects in the test and offers impression of the video and media design. These topics are combined with a presentation of the results of a qualitative study concerning this testing tool, which was conducted by expert interviews and analysed by using content analysis. These results highlight the advantages and challenges in the use of the testing tool.

KEYWORDS

Skill Matching, Competencies, Labour Market, Test Design, Qualitative Interviews, Youth

1. MEDIA TO FOSTER SKILL MATCHING ON THE LABOUR MARKET

Youth unemployment is an economic and social concern for almost every country affected by the economic crisis of the last decade. In Europe the unemployment rate rose from 14.7% in 2008 to 22.2% in 2014. While some countries, such as Germany, were able to maintain their unemployment rate (6.7% in March 2017), countries like Greece and Spain are suffering from youth unemployment of about 48% and 40.5% (ct. Statista 2017). In addition to that, nowadays many employers report difficulties in finding suitably skilled workers which often ends in a qualification mismatch (ct. GAC on Employment 2014). Qualification mismatch occurs when a candidate's qualification level is higher or lower than that required by the job position (ct. GAC on Employment 2014). Moreover, some job positions remain vacant whilst other jobs vanish. Due to digitisation, certain jobs are replaced by machines or parts of job tasks are taken over by machines, still those machines have to be operated (ct. Frey/ Osborne 2017: 257). Therefore, many job descriptions have changed over the years. New job types entered the labour market and new skills have to be developed to serve those needs (concerning labour market institutions, requirements and innovation see Bassanini / Ernst 2002). Another factor is the societies view on certain job positions which influence the decision of youth when applying for a job. Certain jobs have the tendency to be seen as 'unattractive' and are not included when deciding on a career. Concerning the development of job positions, companies often tend to set requirements which are too high and not necessarily needed to fulfil the tasks. These circumstances indicate the need of a regulated matching process for the applicants as well as for the companies by providing a framework for displaying the skills which are possessed by the applicant as well as which are really needed for a job position. Nowadays, many companies offer job positions via internet either through platforms or their own website (ct. Pommerien 2011: 53). Furthermore, they prefer applications for jobs in a digital form (ct. ibid). This allows companies to search for applicants worldwide. Applicants benefit from using the online application, because they are able to choose from a wider range of companies and job positions as well as cities or even countries. Hence, using digital media to find a job has become a daily routine. Regarding the youth unemployment rate, especially young people with low human capital and who are in the transitional system are at risk becoming unemployed (ct. Maxwell 2006: 9). Moreover, if living in rural areas it is even harder to find a suitable job position due to the fact that less job positions might be available. And some young people are unable to identify the skillset which they need to apply for a job. Skill tests are not uncommon (see e.g. Mind tools 2017 or Assessment Center HQ 2017) and are also available online, but a matching process is still missing. Providing a skill testing tool which also manages to match those skills to a vacant job position could be very helpful regarding youth, especially in rural areas. The importance of providing such a matching process via an online platform is undeniable, since a system can provide such algorithms more easily than people. Also a higher number of young learners can be reached via digital media and provided with the matching process. Addressing challenges is one of the objectives of the Europe 2020 strategy, the growth and employment strategy which is implemented by the European Commission during the last decade (ct. Erasmus+ Programme Guide: 14). The aim of the Europe 2020 strategy is to overcome the economic and social crisis and challenges of past years with intelligent, sustainable and inclusive growth. Erasmus+ is the European program to achieve these goals, especially in the context of education, training, youth and sport since the year 2014 up to 2020. Within the framework of this program special attention is paid to recognizing skills and qualifications as well as promoting justice and integration (ct. Erasmus+ Programme Guide: 5). These aspects incline that it is inevitable to help young people develop their human capital and become aware of their skills and qualification in order to find employment. The project SMART (see Beutner 2016) focuses on youth with school difficulties, economic obstacles or specific needs.

2. THE SMART PROJECT

SMART stands for 'Skill Matching Assistance and Reporting Tool' and is a ERASMUS+ funded project in the key action 'Cooperation for innovation and the exchange of good practices' which is embedded in the action 'Strategic Partnerships for youth' (see Beutner 2016). Therefore, the project is built with an educational background and focusses on the analysis of competences and skills. It is founded by the EU, started in April 2016 and will run until the end of March 2018. The project idea and structure of SMART was developed at the Department of Economic Education II of the University of Paderborn. Project coordinator is Asociatia Institutio Pro Educationem Transilvaniensis in Romania, who is characterised by its direct access to the target group of SMART, which is youth. Besides these two, three additional partners are assigned to the SMART project: University of Dundee in Scotland, Youth for Exchange and Understanding in Cyprus as well as Ingenious Knowledge who is responsible for the technical development of the tool. In the following the aims, structure and challenges of SMART as well as the SMART Matching Concept will be presented.

2.1 Aims, Challenges and Structure of Smart

The main aim of SMART is the development of a matching system which is able to keep pace with the changes in society and the labour market to support youth in comparing their competences with the requirements of the market (see Beutner 2017). The elements of the tool offer the possibility to create a very specific profile of the individuals. The idea is to recognize non-formally acquired skills and competences and therefore will be particularly useful for young, disadvantaged youth in the transnational systems who have to face different obstacles and who are looking for employment. Thus, SMART enables disadvantaged youth, who often lack formal qualifications, to show their real strengths and to present themselves in the most beneficial way. In addition to the identification of competences, traits, skills, interests as well as qualifications, the tool offers the possibility to match the individual profiles with open vacancies from companies, which can be contacted immediately by the user or vice versa (see Beutner 2016). The young people using the SMART tool can decide what information to share with potential employers. Due to the fact that SMART is developed on a European level the offer of job vacancies will be throughout Europe which provides a certain mobility for the youth. Furthermore, youth educators and youth workers can use the SMART tool to give young people the opportunity to gain a better understanding of themselves, their competences, traits, skills, interest and qualifications (see Beutner 2016 and Beutner 2017). Supporting high quality youth work is a necessity to offer occupational orientation. Developing such a tool with the aim to deliver a high quality product also entails certain challenges which need to be taken into consideration (Beutner 2016). One challenge is a reliable testing (see Golafshani 2003). Without that the tool would lack authenticity. The tool should provide fitting information not only to the young learners, but also to the companies. If the tool matches a non-fitting candidate to a job position or the other way around both parts will be disappointed and this needs to be avoided. Therefore, the available job position profiles have to be specific and reliable, too. Hence, the project partners conducted a sorrow research regarding the demanded skills of companies for low skilled job positions as well as identifying the most suitable method to conduct the skill testing. Further, regarding the development of the tool the challenge is to design a working matching concept. The tool demands a system which is able to produce a result by using the algorithms provided. Therefore, it is important how the skills are tested and what the results are and how the job positions are measured, because the system needs to connect these results to match the skills to a job profile and vice versa (concerning other ways of measuring person-job fit with profiles see Caldwell / O´Reilly 1990). Which means the system needs to be programmed in the demanded way as well as the design and output regarding the users has to be considered. In fact, the usability of this tool has to be taken into account. Therefore, whilst developing the tool, trial runs will give insight in possible improvements. Solving these challenges is crucial for providing a high quality tool for all target groups. The structure of the SMART tool entails two parts: (a) company related and (b) youth related. First, the system provides the companies with a framework for entering their company details. The next step is to provide information about open job positions which they want to occupy. Again, the system provides a framework for developing such a profile for open job positions in their companies. To ensure that the demands regarding those positions are set in proportion to the tasks the employee has to fulfil, the framework asks which skillsets are needed for the position and further asks for the priorities regarding those skills which is the first step towards the matching concept. The young applicants have to enter personal details guided by a framework at first. This is followed by the testing of their skills. Therefore, the young people have to rate certain reactions regarding a work situation presented to them per short videos. One video scenario tests different kinds of skills. Behind each rating will be a score. All scores regarding one skill will be added and represent the performance of the youth. This will be done for each and every skill. After this process the system has a profile regarding the skills of the young person. Those skills will be set in relation to each other and provided to the user in a positive way. This happens by not showing them their rates in numbers but the relation to each other. So, learners can recognise his or her strengths and weaknesses. Just numbers cannot provide any idea of improvements which are maybe needed, expected or which the user may wish to undertake. Due to this fact the young people get an overview of their skills, but without the judgement of numbers. So, a low skilled person won't be discouraged by only low numbers, because naturally one skill is more developed than another. Now, the youth will be matched with all available job positions and will be presented with the results. If the youth want to apply for one of those positions the information will be transferred to the companies. Each company will be presented with those candidates that match most with the offered position and can decide who they want to interview for the position.

2.2 The Smart Matching Concept

Besides providing an easy to understand user interface, the matching process is important. Matching the skills of the youth with the job profiles of the companies is, next to the testing, a main part of the SMART tool. The testing of the user skills is offered within different working situations through videos. After watching a video, the user gets different statements. The task is to rate on a scale how much he or she agrees with the single statements. Behind those statements lie skills. Each statement is designed to test a specific skill. By setting the scale the system gets the information how to measure this decision. This way it is harder to trick the system in answering in a way the user thinks he or she is supposed to. The user sees a rating scale next to the statement and has to rank the own opinions. Therefore, the scale is divided in different parts, which represent specific skills. Behind these skill parts lie numbers which the system adds up to a final score after all statements are rated. The same procedure is being applied for the job profile, only that the companies do not have to answer specific statements. The companies need to choose from a range of skills which are needed for this specific job position and as a final step have to rate those skills. Now, the system has a score for each skill of the user as well as for the job profile. At this moment a matching process is possible. At first, the system compares the score of the user skill with the company job profile score. For example, a user scored 86 in $skill_1$ and the company job profile scored 80 in $skill_1$ the system knows that this is a match, because as soon as a skill of a user reaches the same score or higher the system marks it as a match. If a $skill_n$ score of a user, in this example 63, is not reaching the companies job profile score, in this example 65, it is not a match. Depending on the number of matches a user generates when compared to a specific job profile it is a match. For each user the system compares the skill scores with each and every job profile that is available. After matching the skills with the job profiles available the system presents the user with all matches found. Now, the user can view the company's profiles and the specific job descriptions and apply for the most attractive job positions. The companies will be provided with a set of matching candidates available in the SMART tool. The most fitting candidate will be on top of the list followed by lesser fitting candidates, but still fitting ones. This way the company can check when receiving an application how fitting the candidate is and it can invite the most fitting candidates to an interview.

3. IDEO DESIGN FOR TESTING SOFT SKILLS

In SMART tests are crucial to provide enterprises and future employees with a basis for the matching of the qualifications of the applicant for a job and the requirements of the business. One important aspect is the analysis of soft skills, because they usually cannot be focused as easily as task related or subject oriented skills. But test designs which only refer to self-reflection and own estimates often lack a realistic background and objectivity. Therefore, the SMART research team decided to provide the job applicants with realistic situations and force them to make decisions which show their behavior and offer the chance to get ratings about their individual skills. Such rating can be used in two directions. First, they can be used to do the matching with a requirement profile provided by the enterprise and for the second, they can be used to provide feedback to the applicant about his or her own skill profile as a basis for future development strategies. The main challenge is to provide the applicant always with the same situations and to make the situations fit to different areas of soft skills. To handle the challenge of providing always the same situation to applicants, videos where created to assure comparability and a realistic setting. The use of videos offers the advantage to avoid long text descriptions which are not easy to interpret and often boring to the user.

3.1 Soft Skill Identification and Indication

One mayor aspect of soft skill which is often addressed by enterprises and in job descriptions is teamwork (see as well Robles 2012). But, usually this is not specified in job offers. This fact is challenging for both sides for the employer and the applicant. An employer has the problem that it is not easy to select persons which fit best, when it is not clear what criteria are really needed. And for the applicant the requirements are not transparent. Therefore, it was important in SMART to create a model to measure team competence. The team agreed on subskills, traits and interests which should specify this general competence (for a critical view on traits see Pervin 1994). Concerning skills, the project partners decided to focus on flexibility and communication skills. Herbst/ Guse 2017 defined three sub criteria to explain flexibility:

1. Willingness to work on short notice
2. Ability to change from one exercise to another
3. Willingness to try something new

And with regard to communication skills they decided to focus on

1. Ability to understand and express own and other intentions
2. Being able of suitable and adjusted expression
3. Willingness to give response/ feedback and to ask questions

Needed traits are emotional stability and conscientiousness. For emotional stability Herbst/ Guse offered:

1. Self confidence
2. Ability to control the own feelings
3. Ability to cope with stressful situations

Conscientiousness was addressed by

1. Sense of Responsibility
2. Neatness/ Thoroughness
3. Willingness to achieve effective performance

Concerning interests, the team differentiated between interest in traditional structured work and realistic interest. Traditional interest can be described by the following three criteria:

1. Favour material and financial possession
2. Favour clear instructions
3. Favour traditional roles

In contrast, realistic interests are:

1. Interest in physical work
2. Down-to-earth-mentality
3. Prefer concrete over abstract conditions

3.2 Example of a Video Scenario

An example how this video and scoring design can look like is the most appropriate way to provide an insight into the structure and testing approach at this point. Each video testing scenario is created on the basis of a short description which offers five core essentials about it and provides a short overview about the structure. They offer an insight in both, the video and the testing elements.

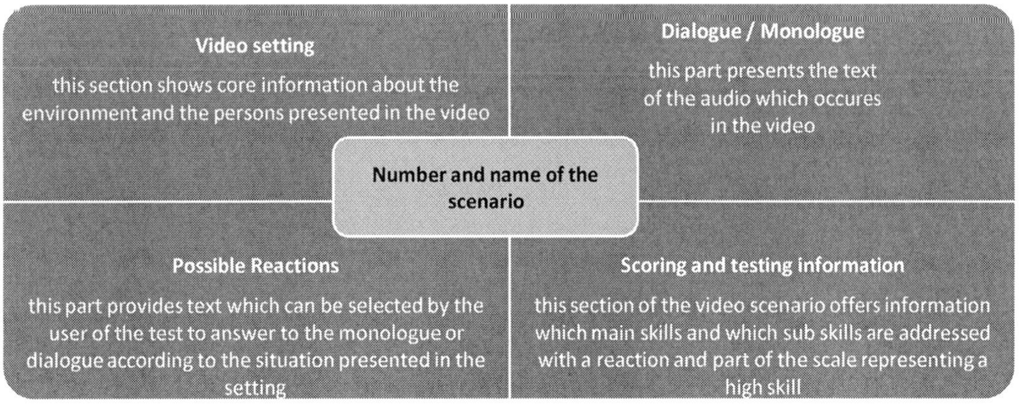

Figure 1. Essential elements of a video scenario description in SMART

These five essential elements are the basis for the design of each video and scoring part in the whole test. They show the connection between what the user hears and sees in the video, the user reactions on it and the scoring and skill identification.

To provide adequate feedback it is important to know which item presented in the possible reactions focusses on which main skill. Moreover, a main skill is becoming more concrete by being divided into sub skills. But, due to the fact that in a specific behaviour a sub skill cannot be seen directly, each item description, which represents a possible reaction, has to be connected to one sub skill. Like in reality it is possible to address several sub skills in a video. Therefore, the user has not to select between different reactions but has to score how much he or she agrees with this possible reaction. Here a slider will make scoring easier. The scale provided has always a high part, a middle part and a low part and it belongs to the way in which a possible reaction / the item is described where on the scale high skills are represented. This is important to know because in the aggregation process of the different answers to items related to a specific sub skill and a skill the rating of the users has to be transferred to single scale with one direction.

4. QUALITATIVE EXPERT STUDY CONCERNING THE VIDEO STRUCTURE

4.1 Methodology

After creating the description tables, it was important to provide the results to randomly selected experts to get an expert rating about the fit before the making of the video. To gather adequate feedback, the SMART project selected European educational experts. There were always two from UK, Germany, and Romania. The first set of six interviews were conducted in March 2017 within three weeks. The second set of interviews with another nine interviews was conducted at the end of May 2017 within one week. We did two sets because of some changes in the political situation due to elections and the focus on Education in Germany and to avoid that this will influence the results. But comparing the results of the first and the second set there was no structural or content related difference in the answers of the experts. So, it was possible to put both sets of interviews together. Therefore, we are able to derive our result from 15 expert interviews.

The average duration of each skype or telephone interview (see to the discussion on telephone interviews Novick 2008) was about 12 minutes. The interviewer conducted the research after first informative telephone contacts. These first information calls ensured that the experts are informed and available. The experts had a closer look at the description and the skill model and offered feedback in qualitative interviews. The interviews were conducted as telephone and skype interviews in a half-structured way (see Schnell / Hill / Esser 1999). Each interview opened with a narrative part, were the expert was able to express the most important aspects of the feedback. On the basis of an interview guideline it was assured that specific topics were always addressed in each interview: (a) adequacy of the video approach and the video length, (b) Connection between possible reactions, sub skills and skills, (c) scoring approach, (d) general feedback on the matching process and (e) adequacy of provided settings and dialogues.

The respondents had always the opportunity to provide additional information. Moreover, there were always several parts during the interviews where they could talk in a free not guided way about the topic (see Flick 1998; Strauss / Corbin 1998). All experts had the same material and the same introduction. They had at least one week before the interview to check the materials provided. In addition to that they got a short explanation why the SMART project is focusing on matching of qualifications and skills with the requirements of the labour market. They also got an overview about the SMART project. The skype and telephone interviews were immediately documented. This documentation process was done via text-recordings and structured via argumentation tables. It is important to compare and interpret the feedback and to categorise the answers to get deeper insight in a structured way. We used the method of content analysis (see Bos / Tarnai 1999) to achieve this aim and to analyse the data. In order to assure trustworthiness, the interviews were conducted by one interviewer, who could make sure that every expert had the same information and a similar interview structure. The interviews were designed to ensure credibility and validity. Validity is a core part of our study and could be realised by gathering all feedback and take everything into account. Therefore, all categories presented in the following results emerged from the data of the interviews. But, more important is that the categories and feedback components are also consistent with the understandings of the experts. For each expert a documentation file was created and named EX1 to EX15, which compiles direct quotes and the argumentation tables. These files are used in the content analysis.

4.2 Testing Results and Feedback

In total the experts stated that the video scenarios are an excellent way to gather the relevant information. Also, they agreed that the length of the video has to be very short to ensure that the whole test can be filled in with an appropriate time and does not get boring or too long. Concerning (a) adequacy of the video approach all 15 experts emphasised that a test on the basis of videos is a really adequate way to solve the task and to test the soft skills. One expert was really happy about the approach but added that not only soft skills should be addressed and mentioned that "expertise in the field is also needed" (EX3-P2-12). This could be addressed in different ways via video, via text based testing and tasks (see EX3-P2-16). The expert recognized that this is not the focus of SMART but stressed that this is important for employment as well.

The connection between possible reactions, sub skills and skills (b) was pretty clear for 13 of the experts. Three experts mentioned that it is not compulsory team work which is addressed with the skill set of SMART. One expert points out that for example communication is more general and not only related to team work (see EX2-P1-21). Nevertheless, it was clear to him that communication skills influence team work. Therefore, he was able to accept the skill model behind SMART. A second expert focused on the difference between interest in traditional structured work and realistic interest. This expert mentioned that also other interest could be taken into account like "interest in innovative modern and creative work" (EX3-P2-26).

With regard to the scoring approach (c) all experts agreed that the scoring system is an adequate way to collect and gather the data (see e.g. EX5-P1-16).

Concerning (d) the general feedback on the matching process the 12 of the experts agreed that the matching process is necessary and that rural areas need specific support in this field (see e.g. EX1-P1-13 or EX6-P2-2). Moreover, they stated that it is necessary to provide both, a feedback to the applicant as well as a feedback to the enterprise. One expert suggested: "It is not important that an enterprise gets all data of all applicants. Maybe you should take into account that only the information of the best fitting results should be provided. This could be the best fitting three applicants." (EX2-P3-5, translation from mother tongue into English by the authors of this article). The last expert added that the matching process is not only necessary for rural areas but also for the whole labour market with its sub markets (EX3-P2-19). Two experts didn't comment on that.

The adequacy of provided settings and dialogues (e) was discussed under different aspects. Some experts mentioned that the dialogues should me more realistic concerning wording (see e.g. EC2-P3-10). Other experts brought up that the description in the setting could be more concrete (see e.g. EX5-P2-12). All experts agreed that the settings and dialogues are a good basis for the filming and provide and excellent insight in the situations to decide on. All in all, the results can be shown in this category structure:

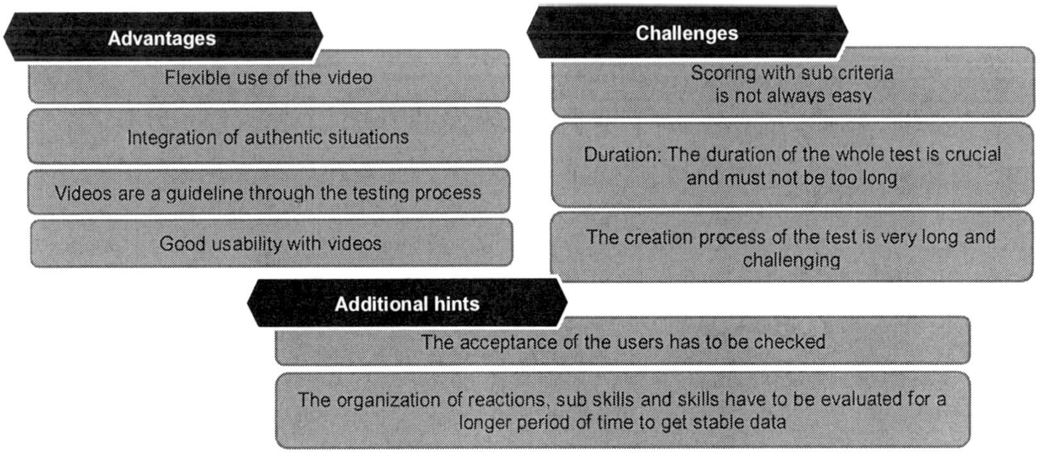

Figure 2. Insights in the categories found as results of the expert interviews

5. CONCLUSION

In SMART the results were taken into account and the wording is currently checked by the UK SMART team. Moreover, additional research perspectives especially in the field of usability (see Sardonick / Brau 2015) are set up. A usability study using the TAM model (see e.g. Beutner 2016b) will be conducted soon. In addition to that a quantitative field research with users will be a further step in SMART. Overall, the results are very positive. They encourage the project team to go further on this way of mapping and testing soft skills. The research results show that the use of media, especially videos, enriches and simplifies the diagnosis of soft skills and offers a possibility to enhance the process of matching on the labour market.

REFERENCES

Bassanini, A. / Ernst, E. (2002): Labour market institutions, product market regulation, and innovation: Cross-Country Evidence", OECD Economics Department Working Papers, No. 316, OECD Publishing, Paris. DOI: http://dx.doi.org/10.1787/002243151077.

Beutner, M. (2016). SMART – Skill Matching Assistance and Reporting Tool. Antrag. Paderborn 2016.

Beutner, M. (2016b): Sounds and Audios in E-learning scenarios. Köln 2016.

Beutner, M. (2017). SMART - Leichter auf den Arbeitsmarkt. Online Matching von Anforderungen und Qualifikationen in einem innovativen Tool. On the internet: https://www.portalderwirtschaft.de/ pressemitteilung/ 280854/smart-leichter-auf-den-arbeitsmarkt.html, date: 30.04.2017.

Bos, W. / Tarnai, C. (1999): Content analysis in empirical social research. In: International Journal of Educational Research. Vol., Issue 8, 1999, Pages 659–671.

Caldwell, David F.; O'Reilly III, Charles A. (1990): Measuring person-job fit with a profile-comparison process. In: Journal of Applied Psychology, Vol. 75(6), 1990, p.p. 648-657. On the internet: http://dx.doi.org/10.1037/0021-9010.75.6.648, date: 30.04.2017.

European Commission (2017): Erasmus+ Programme Guide. Version 2. 5, 14.

Flick, U. (1998): An introduction to qualitative research. London 1998.

Frey, C. B. / Osborne, M. A. (2017): The future of employment: How susceptible are jobs to computerisation?. Technological Forecasting and Social Change. 114. 245-280.

Global Agenda Council on Employment (GAC on Employment) (2014): Matching Skills and Labour Market Needs. Building Social Partnerships for Better Skills and Better Jobs. Davos-Klosters. Switzerland. January 2014.

Golafshani, N. (2003): Understanding Reliability and Validity in Qualitative Research. The Qualitative Report, 8(4), 597-606. On the internet: http://nsuworks.nova.edu/tqr/vol8/iss4/6, date: 30.04.2017.

Maxwell, N. L. (2006): The Working Life: The Labor Market for Workers in Low-skilled Jobs. Michigan 2006.

Novick, G. (2008): Is there a bias against telephone interviews in qualitative research? In: Research in Nursing and Health. Vol. 31, Issue 4, 2008, p.p. 391–398.

Pommerien, J. (2011): E-Recruiting aus Bewerbersicht: Der Einfluss von Persönlichkeit und Einstellung auf die Nutzung von Online-Bewerbungsverfahren. Journal of Business and Media Psychology. 2(1). 52-62.

Sardonick, F. / Brau, H. (2015): Methoden der Usability Evaluation. Wissenschaftliche Grundlagen und praktische Anwendung. 3. Aufl., Bern 2015.

Statista (2017): Europäische Union & Euro-Zone: Jugendarbeitslosenquote von 2006 bis 2016. On the internet: https://de.statista.com/statistik/daten/studie/249093/umfrage/jugendarbeitslosenquote-in-der-eu-und-der-euro-zone/. Date: 07.05.2017.

Statista (2017): Europäische Union: Jugendarbeitslosenquoten in den Mitgliedstatten im März 2017. On the internet: https://de.statista.com/statistik/daten/studie/74795/umfrage/jugendarbeitslosigkeit-in-europa/. Date: 07.05.2017.

Strauss, A. / Corbin, J. (1998): Basics of qualitative research: Techniques and procedures for developing grounded theory. 2nd ed. Thousand Oaks, CA 1998.

Schnell, R. / Hill, P. B. / Esser, E. (1999): Methoden der empirischen Sozialforschung. 10. Aufl., München 1999.

Mind Tools (2017): Get Started With Mind Tools. Test Your Skills! On the internet: https://www.mindtools.com/pages/article/get-started.htm, date: 30.04.2017.

Pervin, L.A. (1994): A critical analysis of current trait theory. In: Psychological Inquiry Vol. 5, Iss. 2, 1994.

Robles, M. M. (2012): Executive Perceptions of the Top 10 Soft Skills Needed in Today's Workplace. In: Business and Professional Communication Quarterly. Vol 75, Issue 4, 2012, pp. 453 – 465.

Assessment Centre HQ (2017): Numeracy Skills Test (QTS) – The Ultimate 2017 Success Guide. On the internet: https://www.assessmentcentrehq.com/numeracy-skills-test/, date: 30.04.2017.

I MIGHT NOT BE AS TECH AS YOU THINK: COLLEGIATE PRINT VERSUS DIGITAL PREFERENCES

Joan Ann Swanson[1], Susan L. Renes[2] and Anthony T. Strange[3]
[1]*Skidmore College, Saratoga Springs, NY, USA*
[2]*University of Alaska Fairbanks, Fairbanks, Alaska, USA*
[3]*Wayland Baptist University, Plainview, Texas, USA*

ABSTRACT

Participants in this study (N=1,986) were college students from four different regions of the United States: northeastern, southeastern, southwestern, and northwestern. Using survey methodology, participants indicated technology preferences and frequency of use as well as demographic information. Findings reveal a strong preference for print text; however frequency in digital use for contextualized purposes. Educational implications include professional development for educators to further understand these nuances and utilize tools and technology which most fit course and students' differentiated needs.

KEYWORDS

Print, Digital, e-Books, College Students, Preferences

1. INTRODUCTION

In an attempt to keep current with students, many professors are offering digital formats for their required readings. Society is increasingly moving toward digital reading formats. Mobile devices, such as tablets and e-readers have expanded reading in any location, at any time. Daily newspapers and news magazines such as Newsweek and U. S. News Report added a digital format to their print option and now send daily electronic communications. Some publications have stopped offering a print version altogether. Many book companies have moved to digital imprints and have become digital-only publishers (Thompson, 2013). Current trends in education have taken a similar course. Many grade schools have encouraged teachers to move toward digital books. School Library Journal reports 66% of schools across the United States offer e-books as of 2014 (Maughan, 2015). College students are now often required to read and submit work digitally. Entire collegiate courses and degrees are delivered digitally (Nelson, 2008). The acceleration toward digitalization in all areas of literacy is spiraling more rapidly than research about the implications of using digital devices including their impact upon learning (Niccoli, 2015).

The push for digital text affects courses delivery and the way students receive information. Renes (2015) suggests that because of e-learning options, higher education is becoming more accessible to students with disabilities, rural students, students with parental responsibilities and students serving in the military. The digital text can play a large role in such accessibility.

Many of these changes from print to digital are happening quickly, with limited and contradicting study on student preferences. Current research predominantly evaluates the technology used in educational situations and not actual student preference or what might be influencing these preferences. Many factors influence students' preferences and the question remains whether is it age alone, as those supporting digital native theories would suggest (Prensky, 2001), or potentially other demographic factors.

Educators, librarians, and researchers are questioning when and where texts should shift from print to digital (deNoyelles et al., 2015). The use of digital texts and more self-directed learning methodology is often fostered in online learning settings. The assumption of these learners being facile with such a setting is sometimes false since these constituents are often older, working adults who may have less experience with technology (Blondy, 2007). Sharpe et al. (2005) notes the need for more in-depth study on student perceptions of technology for learning purposes and how students are actually using that technology in their formal studies. After an initial study with undergraduates at one college, Patton (2014) also recommends analyzing perceptions of text and academic success using a larger population base. This paper provides a brief review concerning digital and print texts, and then examines survey results concerning technological preferences and practices of collegiate students of varied ages, diverse schools and geographic locations.

2. LITERATURE REVIEW

For the purpose of this paper, electronic reading (e-reading) will be called digital reading and print will be referred to as reading on actual paper. Each format may contain the same content but readers use different strategies to access that content, as well as interact and interface differently with those formats. The manner in which a digital text and print text can be utilized in courses also differs; both can be the main resource, supplementary reading, research resources, or just reference material. In situations where digital texts options are offered and students must choose, often students express uncertainly in which way to choose and for what reason (Patton, 2014). Instructors also wrestle with how and when to use digital texts understanding obvious pros and cons for each exist.

Niccoli, (2015), found 63 percent of colleges are using e-textbooks and others reporting they soon would be as well. The University of California and Springer Publishers surveyed college students about academic texts finding 49 percent of respondents' preferred print texts (Li, et al., 2011), and digital preferences increased with each academic degree level, with post-doctoral students most preferring digital. This finding differed from a University of Maryland survey where format preferences were more based on factors such as the text purpose (i.e. course text, conference proceedings, reference works) (Corlett-Rivera & Hackman, 2014). Similarly, Foasbergs (2014) tracked reading formats and practices using student journaling and found preferences for print related to academic purposes and digital for brief, non-academic pursuits. The shorter the passages, the more students tended to favor digital reading. With the continued technology experiences at younger ages, is it possible that the past preferences for print over digital for academics will reverse?

2.1 Text Choices

Digital books are changing how textbooks are used (McFall, 2005) so there are many considerations when instructors choose academic texts, such as whether the text meets the needs of the course and whether it is best accomplished through print or digital (Durwin & Sherman, 2008). Additionally, if an instructor's chosen text is not read by students, the objects and goals for using that text cannot be obtained, thus choosing text that will best engage students becomes paramount.

Textbooks and accompanying lectures are often the main delivery modes of information in courses, especially online courses. Landrum and colleagues (2012) remark that textbook remains a dominant part of collegiate courses. They assessed how these texts were used and subsequently impact academic performance. Whether students place value on using any digital or print text, according to Ainsa (2015), depends largely on how it is incorporated into the course (i.e. necessary for exams, papers, or assignments).

2.1.1 Print Benefits

Many describe comfort in printed text familiarity, noting a sensory experience of holding a printed book, with its marked pages and weighted essence. Print text, even for a range of media types, is regarded as personal and aesthetically pleasing (Krishen, et al., 2016; Mizrachi, 2015). Readers embrace the content structure familiarity of turning pages (Rose, 2011). Academic printed texts have been the standard in college courses until the recent proliferation of electronic media venues. Mizrachi (2015) acknowledges that contrary to popular stereotypes, college students continue to prefer academic text in print, but acknowledges the accessibility and affordability of digital influencing their practices.

2.1.2 Digital Benefits

Eden and Eshet-Alkalai (2013) purport students are gaining in proficiency of use with digital means simply because of societal increase in digital experience. They contend that it is no longer the case of just digital natives (Prensky, 2001) being comfortable with digital text, all ages now engage digitally.

Digital text offers an option that saves trees and the cost of making and shipping paper for printing. It is said to be convenient, cheaper and more portable (deNoyelles et al., 2005; Krishen, et al., 2016; Mizrachi, 2015). As compared to print, digital collections are less expensive, require less space and are easily accessed.

Digital texts also allows for rapid searching within the text (Mizrachi, 2015). These texts can be easily updated and sometimes provides additional multimedia features to enhance learning. Another benefit of digital course materials is that students in remote locations can receive their books much faster and do not have to order their print copies months in advance.

2.1.3 Digitization Issues

The rapid reproduction of texts in digital formats has resulted in some problems. When actual books designed for a printed page are scanned for digital reading, they often are more difficult to read; when text is digitized, the font and format changes, losing the original "feel" and look of the document (Rose, 2011). Differing page layouts (i.e. number of columns) or lack of page endings, make the digital reading experience different from the print experience (Niccoli, 2015). Rather than flipping page by page through a book, digital readers scroll, skip sections, brows for keywords, and other such habits that often cause "short-circuit comprehension" (Liu, 2005; Niccoli, 2015).

The physical experience of digital reading varies from print reading. Hillesund, (2010) observed reading patterns tend to differ between digital and print and noted digital readers tend to move from place to place in the text as they read rather than systematically across the page, thus impacting reading performance. While reading from a screen, many tend to become easily distracted and less emotionally engaged (Carusi, 2006). Additionally, when individuals focus on print on a screen, eye strain often occurs from the screen type or distance from the screen, resulting in quicker fatigue, and slower reading (Altonen et al. 2011; Eden & Eshet-Alkalai, 2013). Despite these noted digital text issues, Eden and Eshet-Alkalai (2013) found no significant difference in performance between digital and print college students' active reading abilities.

2.1.4 Digitization Preferences

As technological consumers become increasingly younger, there is more familiarity with digital media and modes of transforming information. Falc (2013) documented favorable attitudes towards academic digital text. There is seemingly a range of use and willingness to adapt to digital reading. Walton (2007) found more negative digital text use perceptions by faculty while there was more willingness toward digital utilization by students. Walton concluded this was in part faculty being unfamiliar and less comfortable with technology. Yet, even when the faculty member is familiar and comfortable with technology, digital text is often compartmentalized for specific use such as quick searches and news updates. Liu's (2006) found graduate students initially accessed academic readings digitally, then often printed them to read and study.

There continues to be mixed reports on how the type of text actually affects learning. Eshet-Alkalai and Geri (2007) found peoples' format preferences affects their performance with the information. Yet, Ainsa (2015) found the type of text students preferred did not affect their academic performance. Patton (2014) concluded that students' perceptions about print and digital text play a large role in the academic success while using that particular text. Since preferences seem to matter, Patton stresses the importance of letting the student choose the text format with which they most feel comfortable.

2.2 Learning Theory and Preferences

Preference theory (Hakim, 2003), recognizes there are lifestyle factors which become predictors of behavior. In essence, people have experiences, social expectations, and economic pressures that combine to influence preference decisions. Both faculty and students have preferences for text format. Both play a role in the success of the medium used as their preferences and opinions affect student learning. Preferences for different reading formats (digital or print) may be representative of how students learn differently. Many theorists such as Gardner (2003) and McCoog, (2007) understand that students have multiple ways of learning; however, when an educator can tap into preferred learning experiences, students will be more engaged, thus potentially maximizing potential learning. McCoog (2007) purports that multiple intelligence and technology should be utilized through differentiated instruction to effectively prepare students in today's global society and marketplace. Integration of technology into instruction offers different ways of presenting information, allowing for different ways of processing that information, resulting in potentially increased comprehension and understanding (Novak, 2003).

Both digital and print texts currently are playing a role in learning situations. Educators are beginning to see that the influx of technological tools, applications, and resources are indeed changing the way we teach, learn and assess learning. Research supports technologies are impacting the ways in which students learn (Conolea, et al., 2008; Oblinger & Oblinger, 2005, Prensky, 2001). As noted, classrooms from Kindergarten through graduate school have begun to utilize technological resources including digital texts. However, the use of such texts does not always come naturally to all learners. Wilson, et al., (2013) stress that it is necessary to prepare students for digital reading and the use of mobile devices in learning situations. In order to prepare, educators need deeper understanding of student preferences as means to further engage learning.

2.3 Research Questions

Since the interjection of technology and digital texts into the academic arena, there have been a few studies that examine print and digital preferences and their use in a comparative manner (Chen, et al., 2014; Eshet-Alkalai, & Geri, 2007; Falc, 2013; Foasberg, 2014; Liu, 2006; Maxwell, 2005; Rowlands, et al., 2007; Walton, 2007). Some of these studies emphasize specific areas such as cognitive load, reading patterns and library-related use. More information is needed in understanding the nuances of technology use in learning situations (Conole, et al., 2007). This paper takes the unique perspective of going one step further and delineating if any of these text versus print preferences are also affected by demographics such as age, gender, ethnicity, type of institution attended, major area of study and the purpose for reading.

1) Do college students prefer digital or print text?
2) What demographics or purposes for reading impact digital or print preferences?
3) What are the educational implications based upon digital and print preferences?

3. METHOD

This study was descriptive comparative and utilized survey methodology. This paper is part of a larger study that expanded upon previous work comparing college students' academic and non-academic technology use (author). Previous studies reviewing print versus digital use have stressed the need for increased demographic data (Sharpe et al., 2005). The study follows survey methodology suggestions of Busha and Harter (1980) seeking representative samples of collegiate experiences but also had the goal of increased demographic data enhancing comparative analysis.

3.1 Participants

Participants in this study (N=1,986) were college students from four different regions of the United States: northeastern, southeastern, southwestern, and northwestern. The institutions represented were coeducational, three public, one private, and had undergraduate through doctoral programs. Students, 31% male and 65% female, were enrolled in traditional, blended, or online programs (Table 1). Since there was a diversity in program types at these institutions, the age range of students covered a more wide span that just traditional undergraduates: students under 18 years (1%), 18-26 years (53%), over 27 years (44%), and 2% preferred not to answer. The largest area of academic study represented was social and behavioral sciences (47%) followed by applied science (22%) and natural sciences (10%).

Demographic self-reporting revealed cultural ethnicity representation including the following: African American (8%), Asian (5 %), European American (68%), Hispanic (11%), American/Alaskan Indian (8%), other (4%), and 6% preferred not to answer. Although 40 countries were represented, students' citizenship was reported as 89% from the United States, 3% international, 2% holding dual citizenship, and again 5% preferring not to answer. A total of 33 languages were identified as student's first language, in addition to English.

3.2 Survey

Data collection was completed using a self-report, anonymous Internet survey administered through Survey Monkey. Internal Review Board Approval was obtained at all four institutions. Students were invited by email to complete the survey and were offered the opportunity then to be entered into a random drawing for $25 gift certificates. The email invitation was sent to a potential of 23,319 students and gleaned a response of 1,986, resulting in a response rate of 9%.

The survey consisted of 21 questions including check-off boxes and ranking for Likert-type scaled responses, which indicated students' technology preferences and frequency of use as well as demographic information. Open-ended response boxes were also provided for comments.

Table 1. Comparison of survey respondents' enrollment by percent

Institution	Gender		International	Emer. Adult	Coursework			
	M	F			Traditional	Blended	Online	Other
A (Pri)	25.5	72.8	**	100	99	1	0	0
B (Pub)	21.1	75.7	2*	74	73.9	30.9	14.1	5.9
C (Pub)	40.7	58.7	2*	22	31.5	40.4	35.4	0.6
D (Pub)	32.2	65.7	5*	48	48.4	28.7	31.9	4.8
Total	31	65		53				

Note: *estimate as some preferred not to answer this. **citizenship was not asked for this institution. *Pri* represents private institutions and *Pub* represents public.

4. RESULTS

The results of the study are reported in response to the following research questions: 1) Do college students prefer digital or print text? 2) What demographics or purposes for reading impact digital or print preferences? 3) What are the educational implications based upon digital and print preferences?

4.1 Digital and Print Preferences

The preferences for digital versus print text varied by purpose (Figure 1). Most students preferred print text for academic reading (72%) and non-academic reading (64%). Preference for academic text type had a positive correlation for preference in leisure text r(1964) = .283, p< .01, R^2=.080. Virtual students were more likely to prefer digital reading for leisure, r(1913) = .123, p< .01, R^2=.015. However, there is a smaller relationship between classroom format and academic print preference, r(1913) = .068, p< .01, R^2=.005.

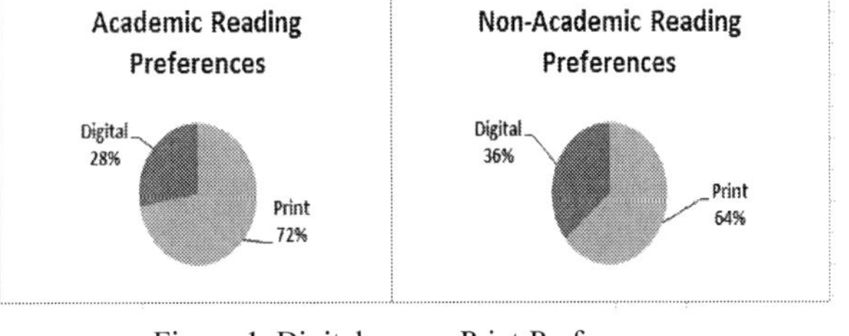

Figure 1. Digital versus Print Preferences

4.2 Demographics Impacting Preferences

4.2.1 Type of Institution

When preferences were examined in light of the type of institution, the pattern of preferring print for academics remained consistent. Each institutions mean response to preference for print over digital was low (print=1, digital=2). The private mostly undergrad institution had the strongest preference for print with a mean of 1.15 (SD = .362) for print and a mean of 1.26 (SD = .439) for leisure reading preference.

4.2.2 Gender and Age

Analysis of preferences for reading differed slightly by gender. Males reported preferring academic text in print (65%) over digital (35%) R^2=.016, and non-academic text also in print (56%) closely followed by digital (44%) R^2= .010. Females were slightly higher indicating preference for academic print (76%) to academic digital (24%) reading. Non-academic preferences for females were 68 % print and 32% digital.

Although most students reported preferences for print for academic text, age had some bearing on college student choices for reading preferences. With 1 indicating print preferences and 2 representing digital preferences, most respondents indicated a preference for print text particularly for academic use (academic M=1.28 SD=.449; digital M=1.36 SD=.481). Younger respondents were 2.1% more likely to prefer print over digital text in their leisure reading, r(1937) = .145, p< .01, R^2=.021, and 1.6% more likely to prefer print over digital text in their leisure reading, r(1933) = .129, p< .01, R^2=.016. Emerging Adults, ages 18-26 years who responded stated that they preferred print text for academic (77%) over print for leisure (66%). However, non-emerging adults over 27 years who responded stated they preferred print over digital for academic reading (71%) to print for non-academic text (47%). Non-emerging adults are increasingly utilizing digital for reading.

4.3 Educational Implications

Tools that students use to access academic material may play a large role in their frequency patterns for choosing their preferred reading mode for academic texts. Students in this survey reported daily use of their personal computer (87%) for academic purposes and non-academic purposes (82%). Computers are integral in today's educational process, whether to access text since they are already using that medium, or to complete assignments, etc.

Cell phones were also ranked high for both academic (65%) and non-academic (94%) uses. These mobile devices have become the most used technological tool by all students regardless of their age, institution, or type of program. This has significant implications for expanding pedagogical practices that utilize mobile technology.

Approximately half of the students surveyed stated they never use an iPad or tablet for academic (57%) or non-academic purposes (51%). Emerging adult students were 4.6% less likely than non-emerging adults to use an iPad or tablet for academic purposes $r(1899) = .214, p < .01, R^2=.046$ and were 6.1% more likely to use email for academic purposes $r(1899) = -.247, p < .01, R^2=.061$. Looking more deeply, the use of these devices becomes divided by age, leading to questions about what technology use represents developmentally and the impact of the context in which interactions with technology occurs.

Additionally, when examining time and tools, 50% of non-emerging adults reported spending 6-15 hours a week engaged in academic work outside of class and another 30% reported they spent 16 or more hours. Over half state 75 to 100% of that time was utilizing a technological tool. While 59% of emerging adults reported spending 6-15 hours a week on academics, a little less (27%) report spending more than 16 hours. Even though non-emerging adults report spending more devoted to academic, over half of both groups say 75-100% of that time involves technology. These findings confirm the importance of recognizing technology plays a significant role in collegiate education today.

5. CONCLUSION

Although the findings supports Conolea and colleagues (2008) earlier finding that students often by-pass institutional platforms in favor of their own personalized approach or preferred tools, there is evidence that institutional computers are accessed daily, evidence of a continued need for technological tools provided by institutions. Additionally, findings in this study reveal that individuals, who rely on institutional computers, did not prefer digital text. This population can take printed material with them without the need for a technological tool, which may not be suited for long readings (i.e. mobile phone). As a social justice issue, understanding resources among students vary, thus the authors highly recommended institutions provide access to computers. In the same manner, offering online course work also increases access to education for those who cannot be in a traditional class room for a multitude of reasons (Renes, 2015). The availability of digital texts are an asset in online education.

Demographics showed slight influence over preferences but still reflected the same dominant academic print preference. Males had a slightly higher preference for digital, especially in the area of non-academic print. Age followed a similar pattern with print having dominance, however, age had a positive correlation with digital academic text preference. One possible explanation for older college students using more digital would be that many of today's emerging adults have been introduced to technology as entertainment while non-emerging adults may likely have used technology for employment purposes. The purposes for which technology has been accessed may differ, thus, educational instructors need to clearly explain and demonstrate the use of digital texts in authentic and purposeful ways. "Choices are not made in a vacuum" (Hakim, 2003, p. 56) thus, instructors can help with guide choices.

The results in this study support other recent research that college students generally prefer print over digital reading for learning purposes (Mizrachi, 2014). College students from varied regions of the United States as well as students with international backgrounds continue to report print preference. However, most report that the time they spend on academics involves a technological tool. Regardless of this preference, they are immersed in the use of technology daily, often hourly. These findings support that college students are tightly connected to technological devices and utilize them for most academic purposes, truly "Technology is at the heart of all aspects of their lives" (Conolea et al., 2008, p. 519). It seems the point of access and communication has become through technology regardless of preferences. Students then adapt the technology to fit their needs and appreciate the accessibility and flexibility provided with technology.

Printed text and digital text both have value. The key is finding ways to help students benefit the most from technology within learning situations. Demographics slightly influence preferences for digital or print. Educators need to find the balance, as there is a time and place for technology use. Helping students adapt their technological skills for educational purposes will benefit college students. Providing further professional development related to technology use, and specifically in the use of digital texts, will assist instructors as they learn to model and facilitate appropriate ways to engage students with digital texts (deNoyelles et al., 2015). Educators need avoid technology related assumptions, and rather seek to recognize use patterns and preferences, and then adjust instruction to meet student needs, resulting in greater achievement, regardless of their preferences.

REFERENCES

Ainsa, P. 2015. Effects of college students' characteristics, culture, and language on using e-texts in distance learning. *Education*, Vol. 136, No.1, pp. 63-68.

Altonen, M., et al., 2011. Usability and compatibility of e-book readers in an academic environment: a collaborative study. *International Federation of Library Associations*, Vol. 37, No.1, pp.16–27.

Blondy, L. C., 2007. Evaluation and application of andragogical assuptions to the adult online learning environment. *Journal of Interactive Online Learning*, Vol. 6, No.2, pp. 116-130.

Busha, C. H., & Harter, S. P., 1980. *Research methods in librarianship: Techniques and interpretation*. Academic Press, Orlando, FL.

Carusi, A., 2006. Textual practitioners: A comparison of hypertext theory and phenomenology of reading. *Arts and Humanities in Higher Education*, Vol. 5, No. 2, pp.163–180.

Chen, G., et al., 2014. A comparison of reading comprehension across paper, computer screens, and tablets: Does tablet familiarity matter? *Journal of Computers in Education,* Vol.1, No. 2–3, pp. 213–225.

Conole, G., et al., (2008). 'Disruptive technologies', 'pedagogical innovation'" What's new? Findings from an in-depth study of students' use and perception of technology. *Computers & Education*, Vol. 50, pp. 511-524.

Corlett-Rivera, K. & Hackman, T., 2014. E-book use and attitudes in the humanities, social sciences, and education. *Libraries and the Academy*, Vol. 4, No.2, pp. 255-286.

deNoyelles, A., et al., 2015. Exploring students' e-textbook practices in higher education. *Educause Review*. Retrieved from http://er.educause.edu/articles/2015/7/exploring-students-etextbook-practices-in-higher-education

Durwin, C., & Sherman, W., 2008. Does choice of college textbook make a difference in students' comprehension? *College of Teaching*, Vol. 56, No.1, pp. 28-34.

Eden, S., & Eshet-Alkalai, Y., 2013. The effect of format on performance: Editing text in print versus digital formats. *British Journal of Educational Technology*, Vol. 44, No. 5, pp. 846-856. doi: 10.1111/j.1467-8535.2012.01332.x

Eshet-Alkalai, Y., & Geri, N., 2007. Does the medium affect the message? The influence of text representation format on critical thinking. *Human Systems Management*, Vol. 26, No.4, pp. 269–279.

Falc, E., 2013. An assessment of college students' attitudes towards using an online e-textbook. *Interdisciplinary Journal of E-Learning and Learning Objects*, Vol. 9, pp. 1-13.

Foasberg, N., 2014. Student reading practices in print and electronic media. *College and Research Libraries*, Vol. 75, No. 5, pp. 705–723.

Gardener, H., 2003. Multiple intelligences after twenty years. *Proceedings from the annual meeting of the American Educational Research Association*, Chicago.

Hakim, C., 2003. Competing family models, competing social policies. *Family Matters*, Vol. 6, No.4, pp. 52-61. Retrieved from http://www.catherinehakim.org/wp-content/uploads/2011/07/AIFSarticle.pdf

Hillesund, T., 2010. Digital reading spaces: How expert readers handle books, the Web and electronic paper. *First Monday*, Vol. 15, No. 4, pp. 503–520.

Retrieved from http://frodo.lib.uic.edu/ojsjournals/index.php/fm/article/view/2762

Krishen, A. S., et al., 2016. Do consumers dig it all? The interplay of digital and print formats in media. *Journal of Consumer Marketing*, Vol. 33, No.7, pp. 489-497.

Landrum, R., et al., 2012. Assessments of textbook usage and the relationship to student course performance. *College Teaching,* Vol. 60, pp. 17-24. doi: /10.1080/87567555.2011.609573

Li, C., et al., 2011. UC Libraries academic e-book usage survey.

Retrieved from http://www.cdlib.org/services/uxdesign/docs/2011/academic_ebook_usage_survey.pdf

Liu, Z., 2005. Reading behavior in the digital environment: Changes in reading behavior over the past ten years. *Journal of Documentation*, Vol. 61, No. 6, pp. 700–712.

Liu, Z., 2006. Print vs. electronic resources: A study of user perceptions, preferences, anduse. *Information Processing and Management*, Vol. 42, No.2, pp. 583–592.

Maughan, S., 2015. Going digital: How schools buy and use e-books. *Publishers Weekly*, Vol. 262, No. 35, pp. 18-33.

Maxwell, D. J., 2005. Digital versus print: The current state of reference affairs in school libraries. *Reference Librarian*, Vol. 44, No. 91, pp. 53-68. doi:10.1300/J120v44n9105

McCoog, I., 2007. Integrated instruction: Multiple intelligences and technology. *The Clearing House*, Vol. 81, No.1, pp. 25-28.

McFall, R., 2005. Electronic textbooks that transform how textbooks are used. *The ElectronicLibrary*, Vol. 23, No.1, pp. 72-81.

Mizrachi, D., 2015. Undergraduates' academic reading format preferences and behaviors. *Journal of Academic Librarianship*, Vol. 41, No.3, pp. 301-311. doi:10.1016/j.acalib.2015.03.009.

Nelson, M. R., 2008. E-books in higher education: nearing the end of the area of hype? *Educause Center for Applied Research Bulletin*, No.1, pp. 40–56. Retrieved from http://net.educause.edu/ir/library/pdf/ERM0822.pdf

Niccoli, A., 2015. Paper or tablet? Reading recall and comprehension. *EDUCAUSEreview*, Retrieved from: http://er.educause.edu/articles/2015/9/paper-or-tablet-reading-recall-and-comprehension.

Novak, J., 2003. The promise of new ideas and new technology for improving teaching and learning. *The American Society for Cell Biology*, Vol. 2, pp. 122-132.

Oblinger, D. G., & Oblinger, J. L., 2005. *Educating the net generation*, An Educause e-book publication, http://www.educause.edu/ir/library/pdf/pub7101.pdf.

Patton, K., 2014. *Digital vs. print textbooks: Relationships and trends for college students*. (Electronic Thesis) Bowling Green State University. Retrieved from https://etd.ohiolink.edu/

Prensky, M., 2001. Listen to the natives. *Educational Leadership*, Vol. 63, pp. 8–13.

Renes, S. L., 2015. Increasing access to higher education through e-learning, In *E-learning - Instructional design, organizational strategy and management*, Gradinarova, B. (Ed.), InTech, doi:10.5772/60906. Available from: https://www.intechopen.com/books/e-learning-instructional-design-organizational-strategy-and-management/increasing-access-to-higher-education-through-e-learning

Rose, E., 2011. The phenomenology of on-screen reading: University students' lived experience of digitized text. *British Journal of Educational Technology*, Vol. 42, No. 3, pp. 515-526. doi:10.1111/j.1467-8535.2009.01043.x

Thompson, M., 2013. Digital first. *EContent*, Vol. 36, No.3, pp.14-19.

Walton, E. W., 2007. Proceedings from the ACRL 13Th national conference: E-Book use versus users' perspective. *College and Undergraduate Libraries*, Vol. 14, No.4, pp.19-35.

Wilson, N., et al., 2013. Pedagogical frameworks of e-reader technologies in education. In J. Keengwe (Ed.), *Pedagogical Applications and Social Effects of Mobile Technology Integration*, IGI Global, Hershey, PA.

A VISUALIZATION SYSTEM FOR PREDICTING LEARNING ACTIVITIES USING STATE TRANSITION GRAPHS

Fumiya Okubo[1], Atsushi Shimada[2], Yuta Taniguchi[3] and Shin'ichi Konomi[1]
[1]*Faculty of arts and science, Kyushu University, 744 Motooka, Nishi-ku, Fukuoka 819-0395, Japan*
[2]*Graduate School of Information Science and Electrical Engineering, Kyushu University, 744 Motooka, Nishi-ku, Fukuoka 819-0395, Japan*
[3]*Research Institute for Information Technology, Kyushu University, 744 Motooka, Nishi-ku, Fukuoka 819-0395, Japan*

ABSTRACT

In this paper, we present a system for visualizing learning logs of a course in progress together with predictions of learning activities of the following week and the final grades of students by state transition graphs. Data are collected from 236 students attending the course in progress and from 209 students attending the past course for prediction. From these data, the system constructs a state transition graph, where the prediction is based on the Markov property. We verify the performance of predictions by experiments in which the accuracy of prediction using the data of the course in progress and the one by 5-fold cross validation.

KEYWORDS

Learning log, predication of learning activity, state transition graph

1. INTRODUCTION

In recent years, the use of the ICT based educational system, such as learning management systems and e-book systems, has been widely spread, especially in higher education. One of advantages to use such a system is that we can automatically collect several kinds of log data of students' learning activities on a system. Analyzing the collected learning logs by data mining technologies, teachers can observe students' typical learning behaviors (Baradwaj et al. (2011)).

At Kyushu University, a learning support system called the M2B system was introduced in October 2014. The M2B system consists of three subsystems, that is, the e-learning system Moodle, the e-portfolio system Mahara, and the e-book system BookLooper provided by Kyocera Maruzen, Inc. The feature of BookLooper is that detailed operation logs can be collected, such as moving back and forth between pages, the contents of memos, the kind of access device (PC or smartphone), etc., together with the user id and timestamp. This feature enabled us to analyze the learning behavior of students both inside and outside the university classroom. Our research group has conducted various investigations on learning analytics with the collected data. The details of the M2B system and our investigations are summarized in Ogata et al. (2015) and Ogata et al. (2017).

In the field of learning analytics, finding "at-risk" students who are likely to fail or drop out of class is important issue. A lot of methods for the early detection of at-risk students from data were intensively investigated, for example, in Baker et al. (2015), Romero & Ventura (2010) and Marbouti et al. (2016), where Logistic Regression, Support Vector Machine, Decision Tree, Multi-Layer Perceptron, Naïve Bayes Classifier, and K-Nearest Neighbor are guided. Moreover, Okubo et al. (2017) introduced the method by using Recurrent Neural Network that is known as a one of variants of Deep Neural Network. You (2016) showed meaningful learning logs based on the theory of self-regulation to predict students' final achievement by the statistical analysis method. Generally, the prediction of students' final achievement is based on data of previous courses, while in Hlosta et al. (2017) presented a method for finding "at-risk" students, which is depending only on the current course.

Not only analyzing data, giving appropriate feedback on the result of analysis to teachers and students is also important to improve their teaching activities and learning activities, respectively. For this purpose, in Okubo et al. (2015), a method for visualizing the four types of learning logs stored in the e-learning system and the e-book system namely, attendance, time spent for browsing slide, submission of a report, and quiz score, was presented. This method was realized by state transition graphs, where a state and an edge represent learning activities of a week and the number of students of such a transition, respectively, referring to the method proposed in Hlosta et al. (2014). Moreover, in Okubo et al. (2016), a method for identifying learning activities from the above four types of learning logs that are important for students to achieve a good final grade.

In this work, extending the method presented in Okubo et al. (2015), we propose a system for visualizing learning logs of an ongoing course together with predictions of student's learning activities of the following week and the final grade by state transition graphs. For predictions, learning logs of a course that has already finished are utilized. These methods are introduced in Section 2. Then, in Section 3, we verify the performance of prediction by experiments. Then, we compare the performance by using data of the past course for predicting with one by 5-fold cross validation. Moreover, we show results of questionnaire for students about this system. Finally, we give the conclusion and future research plans in Section 4.

2. METHOD

2.1 Data Collection

In order to employ the method of visualization, we need to collect learning logs from two courses, that is, one course that is in progress and another course that has already been finished. We expect that the two courses have a similar construction, for example, the past course is the same course as the course in progress by the same teacher opened one year ago.

In the two courses, the teacher and students use the LMS and the e-book system during lectures and preparation at all weeks of the courses. The lectures are presented by using several slides in the e-book system, each slide being associated with only one lecture. The slides are used by the students to complete their preparation sessions before each lecture. Furthermore, on some weeks, the students are required to submit a report and answer a quiz related to that week's lecture through the LMS.

Hence, in this study, we refer to the following four kinds of data stored in the LMS and the e-book system in this paper:

(i) attendance or absence,
(ii) the total time spent browsing the slides for preparation which reaches 600 seconds or above, or failure to do so,
(iii) the submission of a report or failure to do so,
(iv) the quiz score that reaches 70% or above, or failure to do so,

of each student participating in each week of the course. For each of the four items, we consider whether or not it is achieved. The achievement of an item is coded by "1" and the failure by "0". The courses are graded as A, B, C, D or F in the usual manner, with A being the best grade and F indicating failure of a course.

For an experiment, we collected learning logs from the following courses by the same teacher:

(1) The "Information Science" course, which is attended by 236 students and opened in the first term (8 weeks) in 2016, is treated as the course in progress,
(2) The "Information Science" course, which is attended by 209 students and opened in the first term (8 weeks) in 2015, is treated as the past course.

These courses are mainly for the first-year students of various departments. We note that in the second week of course (2), the submission of a report is required; however, in course (1), the submission of a report is not needed. This difference causes a difficulty in visualization in our method. Due to this reason, in order to adjust the logs of the two courses, we treat the data for item (iii) (the submission of a report) of the second week of course (1) as "0" for each student. Similarly, the data for item (iii) of the fifth week of course (2) is treated as "0" for all students.

2.2 Construction of a State Transition Graph

Using the logs of learning activities shown in Section 2.1, we construct a state transition graph to visualize the learning activities of the students in the course in progress and the prediction of learning activities. For this purpose, we assume that the target courses are opened through n weeks and the course in progress is finished until the m-th week.

A state in a state transition graph represents the learning activities of each week using four digits which refer to the achievements or failures in the four items (i), (ii), (iii), and (iv). For example, the state 1011 means that a student (i) attended the lecture, (ii) browsed the slides for preparation for less than 600 seconds, (iii) submitted a report, and (iv) obtained 70% or above in a quiz. The number of states is $2^4 = 16$ per week. Hence, the state transition graph consists of $16n$ states. The states are aligned such that the horizontal axis represents weeks from left to right, and the vertical axis represents states from bottom to top. In addition, the states representing the final grades are added to the right to the states of the n-th week.

An edge represents a transition of learning activities from the i-th week to the $i+1$-th week. An edge between state x of the i-th week and state y of the $i+1$-th lesson is constructed if there exists a student whose learning activities correspond to such a transition. The number of students having the same transition is expressed by the thickness of an edge. The edge is thin if the corresponding number is small. When the number of students who meet the condition increases, the edge thickness increases correspondingly. Similarly, edges from the states in the n-th week to the final grades are constructed. Figure 1 illustrates the example case where the number of transition from "1011" in the i-th week to "1011" in the i+1-th week is larger than the one from "1011" in the i-th week to "1010" in the i+1-th week. It is noted that if the i-th week is before the m-th week, we use the logs of the courses in progress; otherwise, we use the logs of the past courses.

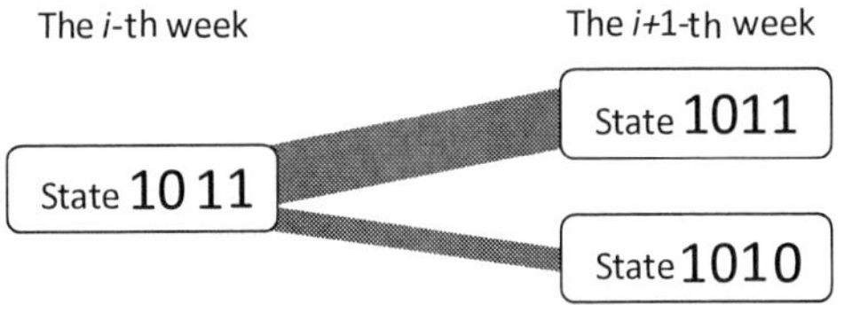

Figure 1. An example of a part of a state transition graph

2.3 Predication of Learning Activities and Final Grades

The logs of learning activities and the state transition graphs constructed by the above method can be utilized for predicting the learning activities and the final grades of students. Similar to Section 2.2, We assume that the target courses are opened through n weeks and the course in progress is finished until the m-th week.

From the state x in the m-th week of the course in progress, we can predict the next state y in the $m+1$-th week of this course by selecting the state y in the $m+1$-th week of the past course, where the number of students corresponding to this transition is the largest among all the transitions from the state x in the m-th week of the past course. This is represented by the thickest edge from the m-th week to the $m+1$-th week in the state transition graph.

The final grade is predicated by using the state x in the m-th week of the course in progress and the logs of the past course which indicates the final grade that is most likely to be obtained by a student who is in state x in the m-th week. This is represented by the thickest edge only from the last week to the final grades in the state transition graph.

3. IMPLEMENTATION AND EXPERIMENTS

3.1 Implementation

The system for constructing the state transition graphs that visualizing the learning activities of students was implemented as a plugin of Moodle (the e-Learning System in Kyushu University).

Teachers can add this system to their courses. After selecting the course that has already been finished in the setting screen of the system (Figure 2), the state transition graph at that time is displayed.

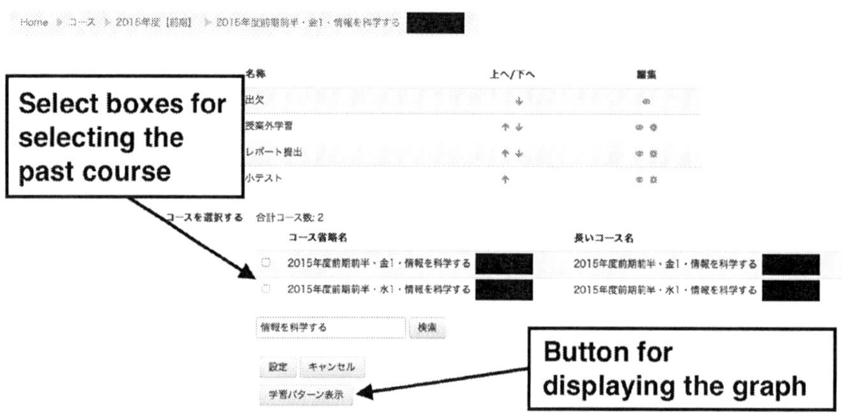

Figure 2. The setting screen of the system

We note that the states not reached by any student are omitted, for visibility. The system has two modes depending on the user: the teacher mode and the student mode. In the teacher mode, users can see all the user names displayed on the left end, while in the student mode, users can see only their own name.

Figure 3 displays the state transition graphs using the logs of course (1) as the course in progress, which finishes in the fourth week and course (2) as the past course (users' names are hidden by a black box).

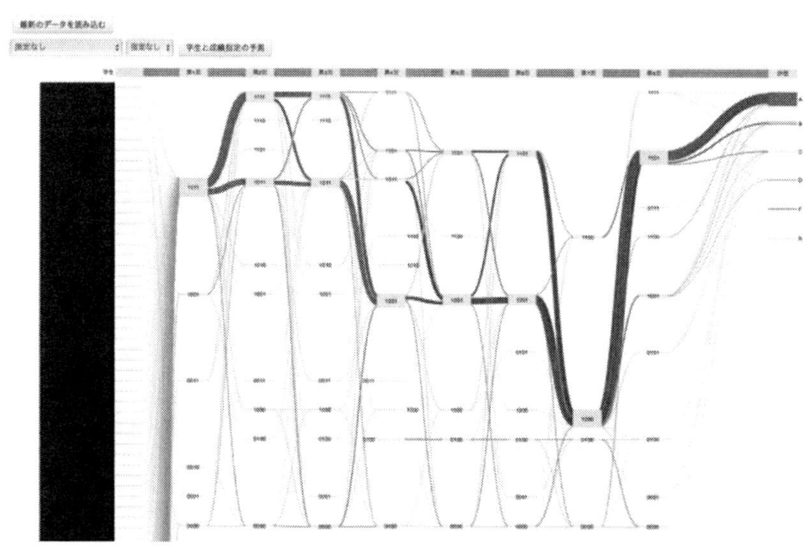

Figure 3. The state transition graph after finishing the fourth week

By clicking on a user's name, the following three changes occur (see Figure 4):

- the state transitions of the of the selected student until the fourth week are highlighted in red,
- the graph from the fourth week to the last week is reconstructed by using only the logs of the students who were at the same states of the fourth week in the past course as the selected student,

the percentage that the selected student is likely to obtain each final grade is calculated and displayed on the right of each grade.

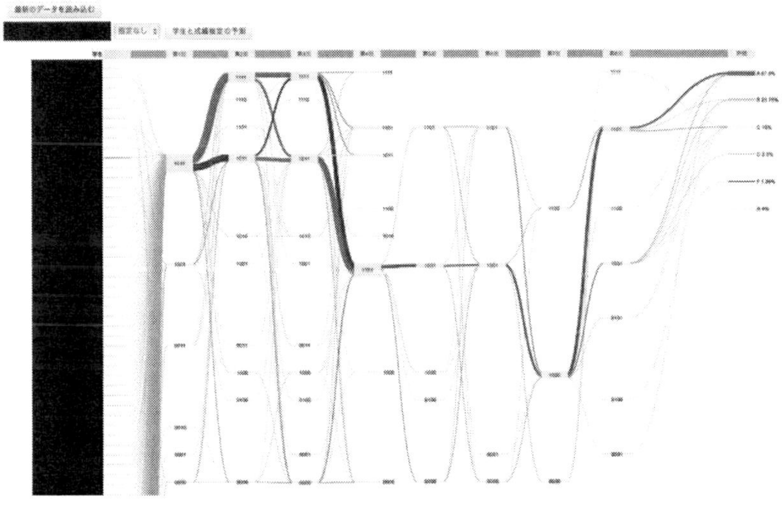

Figure 4. The state transition graph with the selected student

Students also can use this system, while users' names except oneself are anonymized.

3.2 Experiments

We conducted experiments to calculate the accuracy of the predictions of the learning activities of the following week and the final grade.

We applied our method to course (1) as the course in progress and course (2) as the past course. For each state in the i-th week with $1 < i < 7$, we predicted the state in the i+1-th week and calculated the accuracy of this prediction. Similarly, for each state in the j-th week with $1 < j < 8$, we predicted the final grade and calculated its accuracy.

Moreover, we also applied our method by means of 5-fold cross validation. Therefore, the data are separated into five parts, of which four parts are used as training data and the remaining part as test data. It is noted that in our method, training data are treated as the data of the past course and test data are treated as the data of the course in progress. In this case, there are five ways to choose the parts for training data and test data. Hence, the final result of this 5-fold cross validation is the average of the results of these five ways of choosing the training data and the test data.

The results regarding the accuracy of the prediction of the learning activities of the following week are summarized in Table 1. In the column titled by "i+1", the accuracy of the prediction for the state in the i+1-th week from the state in the i-th week is shown. The averages of the accuracies of the seven predictions are 37% in the case using the logs of the past course and 50% in the case of 5-fold cross validation.

Table 1. The accuracy of prediction for the following states

Method	2	3	4	5	6	7	8	Ave.
The past course	45%	45%	47%	22%	20%	58%	19%	37%
5-fold cross validation	45%	49%	47%	48%	41%	73%	46%	50%

The results regarding the accuracy of the prediction for the final grades are summarized in Table 2. In the column titled by "*i*", the accuracy of the prediction for the final grades from the state in the *i*-th week is shown. The averages of the accuracies of the eight predictions are 73% in the case using the logs of the past course and 84% in the case of 5-fold cross validation.

Table 2. The accuracy of prediction for the final grades

Method	1	2	3	4	5	6	7	8	Ave.
The past course	81%	71%	70%	85%	86%	25%	85%	78%	73%
5-fold cross validation	85%	84%	85%	85%	85%	83%	84%	84%	84%

3.3 Questionnaire for Students

We asked the students attending the "Information Science" course to use the system and then carried out the following questionnaire:

(a) How easy did you use this system?
(b) How useful was this system for reviewing your past learning?
(c) How much did you would like to change your learning in order to obtain better grades by looking at the results of prediction by this system?
(d) How much do you would like to use this system even in another class in the future?

201 students answered these questions. In Figure 5, the responses are summarized.

We can see that approximately 60% of the students felts that this system was useful for reviewing past learning, changing your learning in order to obtain better grades and they would like to use this system continuously. These results can be said to indicate that the system can solve the students' anxiety about learning strategies and final grades. On the other hand, the students who said this system is easy to use are less than 50%. Improvement of the user interface such as how to display the states of graph is an important future task.

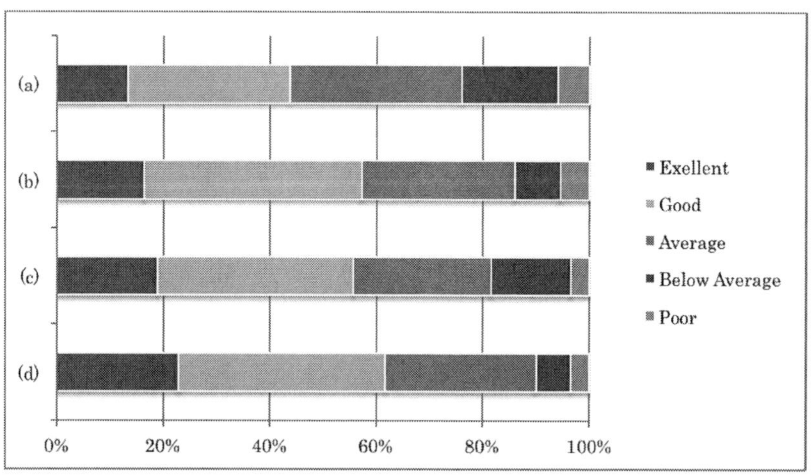

Figure 5. Summary of students' answer to questions regarding our system

4. DISCUSSION

From the results of the experiments described in Section 3.2, we can observe that in general, the accuracy of the prediction for the state in the following week is low. We consider that the main reason for the low prediction accuracy is that the prediction of the proposed method is based on the Markov property, that is, the possibility of reaching the state in the $i+1$-th week of the course in progress only depends on the state in the i-th week of the past course, or the test data in 5-fold cross validation (for more details of Markov property, refer to Norris (1998)). For improving the accuracy of prediction, we suggest that using the all the data from the first week to the i-th week for predicting the state in the $i+1$-th week may be effective. However, this plan has a limitation in that the predictions are difficult to visualize for teachers or students at least by using the state transition graphs proposed in this study.

In addition, we can observe that the accuracy of 5-fold cross validation is likely to be far higher than that of using the data of the past course in the predictions of both the following states and for the final grades. This observation implies that for the case using the data of the past course, the difference in construction (or instructions) of the course in progress and the past course sensitively affects the accuracy of the prediction, even when the two courses are the same and taught by the same teacher, although they are in different terms.

5. CONCLUSION

In this paper, we presented a system by which the learning activities of students in a course and the predictions of the learning activities of the following week and the final grades are visualized using state transition graphs. The learning activities of a week are represented by the four digits that means the achievements or non-achievements of attendance, the total time spent browsing the slides for preparation, the submission of a report, and the quiz score. A state transition graph is constructed from the logs of the two courses: the course in progress and the past course. If the course in progress is finished until the m-th week, the graph from the first week to the m-th week is constructed from the logs of the course in progress, and the rest part is from the one of the past course. A state in the graph represents the learning activities of each week using these four digits. An edge thickness between state x of the i-th week and state y of the $i+1$-th lesson is according to the number of students whose learning activities correspond to such a transition. This system enables teachers to overview the learning activities of students until the finished week and the learning activities that students are likely to do. Moreover, in the system, by clicking on a student's name, the state transitions of him/her until the finished week are highlighted in red, and the percentage that he/she is likely to obtain each final grade is calculated and displayed. This function may help the detection of student who likely to obtain the particular final grade.

We verified the performance of predictions of the following state and the final grades by experiments applying method using the data of the two same courses opened in the different term, namely, the first term in 2015 and the first term in 2016. The experiments by 5-fold cross validation was also conducted, where only the data of the course in 2016 were used, to comparing the results using the data of the past course. The accuracy of prediction for the final grades was fairly high, exceeding 70%, in both the cases of using the past data and 5-fold cross validation; however, the accuracy of prediction for the following states is low, because we use only the information of the previous one state for prediction. In addition, we can observe that the result of 5-fold cross validation is better than the one using the logs of the past course for prediction. This situation may be caused by the difference in construction or instructions of the course in progress and the past course. For enhancing the performance of prediction using the logs of the past course, we need to consider the model that is robust against such a difference.

The questionnaire for students about this system was also conducted. The results indicates that this system is useful for changing learning activities in order to obtain better grades, while improvement of the user interface is necessary.

There remain many subjects to be investigated along the research direction regarding visualization and prediction presented in this paper. Points of particular importance includes the followings:

- As stated in Section 3.3, for improving the accuracy of prediction, it may be effective to use the all the data from the first week to the i-th week for predicting the state in the $i+1$-th week or the final grade. The problem of this method is that the visualization of prediction is difficult by the similar way. For example, after finishing until the second week, for students "A" who is in state x_A in the first week and y in the second week and "B" who is in state x_B in the first week and y in the second week with $x_A \neq x_B$, the predictions for the third week of students A, B are different in general. But, this difference cannot be reflected in the state transition graph proposed in this paper.

- The thresholds which distinguish the achievement or the failure for the total time spent browsing the slides for preparation and the quiz score are manually decided in this paper. Finding the thresholds by which the accuracy of prediction is maximum is very important. It is also important to use another types of learning logs, such as the indicators based on the theory of self-regulated learning introduced in You (2016).

ACKNOWLEDGEMENT

The research results have been achieved by "Research and Development on Fundamental and Utilization Technologies for Social Big Data" (178A03), the Commissioned Research of National Institute of Information and Communications Technology (NICT), Japan.

REFERENCES

Baker, R. S., Lindrum, D., Lindrum, M. J. & Perkowski, D. 2015. Analyzing Early At-Risk Factors in Higher Education e-Learning Courses, *proc. EDM2015*, pp.150-155.

Baradwaj, B. & Pal, S. 2011. Mining Educational Data to Analyze Student's Performance, *International Journal of Advanced Computer Science and Applications*, vol. 6, 2, pp. 63-69.

Norris J. R. 1998, *Markov Chains*, Cambridge Series in Statistical and Probabilistic Mathematics, Cambridge University Press.

Hlosta, M., Herrmannová, D., Váchová, L., Kužílek, J., Zdrahal, Z. & Wolff, A. 2014. Modelling student online behaviour in a virtual learning environment, *Workshop Proc. LAK 2014*.

Hlosta, M., Zdrahal, Z., Zendulka, J. (2017). Ouroboros: Early identification of at-risk students without models based on legacy data, *proc. LAK2017*, pp.6-15.

Marbouti, F., H. A. Diefes-Dux & Madhavan, K. (2016) Models for early prediction of at-risk students in a course using standards-based grading, *Computer & Education*, pp. 1-15.

Ogata, H., Taniguchi, Y., Suehiro, T., Shimada, A., Oi, M., Okubo, F., Yamada, M., Kojima, K. (2017). M2B System: A Digital Learning Platform for Traditional Classrooms in University, *Practitioner Track Proc. of LAK2017*, pp.154-161.

Ogata, H., Yin, C., Oi, M., Okubo, F., Shimada, A., Kojima, K. & Yamada, M. 2015. E-Book-based Learning Analytics in University Education, *proc. ICCE2015*, pp.401-406.

Okubo, F., Hirokawa, S., Oi, M., Shimada, A., Kojima, K. & Yamada, M. & Ogata, H. 2016. Learning Activity Features of High Performance Students, *Proc. the 1st International Workshop on Learning Analytics Across Physical and Digital Spaces (Cross-LAK 2016)*, pp.28-33.

Okubo, F., Shimada, A., Yin, C. & Ogata, H. 2015. Visualization and Prediction of Learning Activities by Using Discrete Graphs, *proc. ICCE2015*, pp.739-744.

Okubo, F., Yamashita, T., Shimada, A. & Ogata, H. (2017). A Neural Network Approach for Students' Performance Prediction, *proc. LAK2017*, pp.598-599.

Romero, C. & Ventura, S. (2010) Educational Data Mining: A Review of the State of the Art, *IEEE Transactions on Systems, Man, and Cybernetics, Part C (Applications and Reviews)*, 40(6), pp.601-618.

Wolff, A., Zdrahal, Z., Herrmannová, D., Kužílek, J. & Hlosta, M. 2014. Developing predictive models for early detection of at-risk students on distance learning modules, *Workshop Proc. LAK 2014*.

You, J. W. 2016. Identifying significant indicators using LMS data to predict course achievement in online learning, *Internet and Higher Education*, vol.29, pp.23-30.

OCRA, A MOBILE LEARNING PROTOTYPE FOR UNDERSTANDING CHEMISTRY CONCEPTS

Tenku Putri Norishah Tenku Shariman[1] and Othman Talib[2]
[1]*Multimedia University, Cyberjaya 63000, Selangor, Malaysia*
[2]*University Putra Malaysia, Serdang 43400, Selangor, Malaysia*

ABSTRACT

This research studies the effects of an interactive multimedia mobile learning application on students' understanding of chemistry concepts. The Organic Chemistry Reaction Application (OCRA), a mobile learning prototype with touch screen commands, was applied in this research. Through interactive multimedia techniques, students can create and visualize the mechanistic steps of an organic chemistry reaction. Ninety-two students who were either assigned to a control or an experimental group participated in the research. Data collection included achievement in the pre- and posttest, and students' responses in a questionnaire that examined their perception towards the OCRA. The findings demonstrated that students' attitudes towards the OCRA were positive while their test scores have improved. It is concluded that the teaching and learning approach applied in the OCRA has engaged students in learning organic chemistry and develop their conceptual thinking, leading to deeper understanding of chemistry concepts.

KEYWORDS

Interactive multimedia, Mobile Learning, Engaging, and Chemistry Concepts

1. INTRODUCTION

In the last decade, there has been intense research in studying the impact and advancement of multimedia and mobile technology on learning environments that involved students in diverse learning activities. These technologies have influenced the design of curriculum in many universities for they offer flexibility and mobility in everyday learning. Mobile learning, (M-learning) for example, provides four universal qualities that add value for learners: any time, any place, widen participation and personalized learning (Park, 2011). Additionally, multimedia has revolutionized traditional educational methods. Integrating multimedia elements increase student retention, and create interesting and interactive learning environments (Mayer and Moreno, 2010).

When combined with multimedia, learning then becomes a more dynamic process. Mayer (2009) championed multimedia as the means to "engage learners in the cognitive processes required for meaningful learning within the visual and verbal information processing systems" (p. 4). Meaningful learning in a multimedia environment occurs when students are given the choice of selecting words and images from a learning material, and independently organize and integrate these verbal and visual representations into a coherent mental representation (Mayer and Moreno, 2010). This study demonstrates that the use of an interactive multimedia content with a mobile device provide students with opportunities to reflect and build their understanding of chemistry concepts through a meaningful, and cognitively engaging task.

2. PROBLEM STATEMENT

One of the current aims of chemistry education in Malaysia is to provide students with the knowledge and skills that would enable them to solve problems that range from specific types of calculations to open-ended situations. However, the latest findings of the *Secondary School Performance Report 2015* (Ministry of Education, 2016) by the Ministry's Examination Division regarding the chemistry performance of students are incongruent with this aim. It was found that the "majority of candidates did not understand and have not mastered the concepts of chemistry" (MOE, 2016, p.14). In particular, the report found weaknesses in the responses towards organic chemistry questions and concluded that the majority of candidates have failed to acquire basic conceptual understandings (MOE, 2016). Students were able to provide answers for questions that required simple recall of scientific facts, but had problems with analyzing abstract processes and failed to classify, synthesize and evaluate information. Farhan and Zainun (2013) revealed that the traditional direct transmission approach is a practice widely used by chemistry teachers in Malaysia to explain and draw chemical reactions, while students passively listen and take notes. They stated that chemistry teachers preferred to use only the whiteboard or static images to illustrate the organic synthesis process although constructivist teaching strategies are encouraged by the MOE. Consequently, students who function largely as passive recipients of knowledge have a negative attitude towards chemistry; they often perceive the subject as being boring and difficult to comprehend. These views are consistent with those of Hutchinson (2000, p.3), when he claimed that in general, chemistry in the United States of America is taught to students mostly based on "expository and explanatory statements of concepts and applications......clearly verifies the pervasiveness of traditional approach." The guided-inquiry approach promoted by the MOE is mainly implemented in science laboratory activities. However, most teachers are only interested to conduct selected guided-inquiry experiments for the purpose of answering examination questions rather than developing students' process skills or conceptualizing scientific phenomena (MOE, 2016). It can be argued then that the direct transmission approach and the minimal implementation of the guided-inquiry approach has not led to positive changes in students' conceptual understanding of science that go beyond rote memorization.

3. LITERATURE REVIEW

Learning is an active process of knowledge construction that humans perform naturally, but not everyone is an effective and efficient independent learner. Indeed, most learners benefit from some level of support. First, successful teaching and learning involve a variety of strategies for engaging, and motivating learners over and above merely presenting them with well-designed learning materials (Lukerson, 2014). There are a number of pedagogical techniques that focus on providing activities for learners to perform either in groups or as individuals that help to create deeper, swifter and more effective learning like discussion, simulations, or problem based learning. Secondly, successful teaching and learning is not just the creation of thoughtful and engaging activities for students to undertake, but also giving thought to the sequential order and timing of the various activities and the presentation of the resources needed to support them (Lukerson, 2014). Over the last two decades the mode of learning has gradually shifted away from education that is teacher-centered to student-centered, from rote learning to learning as reflection and from face to face learning to mobile learning (Jarvis, Holford and Griffin, 2003). According to Conole and Oliver (2007), the emergence of new approaches to learning has led to new perspectives on learning presented through different theoretical lenses.

The teaching and learning of science is always perceived as the teaching and learning of concepts that are often organized from the simple to the most complex. In the context of teaching and learning organic chemistry, the "arrow pushing" technique is widely used to present the mechanic aspects of the organic reaction mechanism under investigation. However, this talk and chalk technique is incapable of visualizing the actual processes during the organic reaction mechanism; consequently, students have failed to grasp the organic reaction mechanism in the same way as their teachers (Berg and Ghosh, 2013). Interactive multimedia offers great potential for bridging the gap between what students already know and the targeted concept that needs to be understood. For example, through a multimedia content, students can visualize the abstract and dynamic chemical processes that occur in an organic reaction mechanism. As stressed by the MOE (2016, p. 14), "multimedia are effective tools for the teaching and learning of abstract or difficult science concepts." A teacher can also convey a meaning or concept clearly which might be often difficult to explain verbally to students. According to Lafarge, Morge, and Meheut (2014), conceptual questions in chemistry often involve the solution of a problem through a step by step approach. Since chemistry concepts have diverse characteristics with different types of abstractions, it is necessary to consider how these concepts can be visualised to students. This is in line with Montes, Prieto and Garcia (2002) view that a multimedia content could enhance students' understanding of the chemistry reaction processes that are dynamic and abstract in order to solve a problem.

One of the rapidly advancing areas of education in the world today is the development of mobile learning content, which adopts multimedia and mobile technology for education purposes. Multimedia has been shown to elicit the highest rate of information retention and results in shorter learning time (Alessi & Trollip, 2001), whereas Kulkuska-Hulme (2005) has asserted that mobile learning facilitates learner engagement without the constraints of a fixed, pre-determined physical environment. However, Ng and Nicholas (2013) have cautioned that mobile learning is not just learning using mobile devices, but learning through context. Mobile devices have the capability of catering to various learning theories and methods, either behaviourist, cognitivist, or constructivist theories, or whether through games, social networking, video or multimedia applications (Keskin and Metcalf, 2011) to enhance and extend the incentives and mechanisms of teaching and learning to support and motivate students individually or collaboratively. The emergence of mobile technology fosters teachers to experiment with digital materials in and outside the classroom. When preparing mobile learning experiences, it is advisable to avoid replicating the direct instruction model applied in classrooms; instead teachers should strive to apply more effective models to convey instruction (Ng and Nicholas, 2013). Understanding the use of M-learning tools for mediation will be crucial to discourage educators and designers from simply swapping printed worksheets for mobile devices with the expectation that students or learners will perform better (Liaw, Hatala, and Huang, 2010).

4. AN INTERACTVE MULTIMEDIA MOBILE PROTOTYPE

This paper presents an interactive multimedia mobile learning prototype, namely the Organic Chemistry Reaction Application (OCRA) which is used for learning fundamental concepts of organic reaction mechanism. This application), as shown in Figure 1 below, can be used effectively with mobile devices, such as smartphones and tablets. OCRA is not intended to be used as a prime teaching tool in a classroom but only as a supplementary tool to learn and understand organic reaction mechanism.

Figure 1. An Interactive multimedia M-learning prototype

For the Net-generation students, those who have grown up with Internet access and are accustomed to using mobile devices in their daily lives, OCRA is considered a M-learning solution that facilitates understanding through multimedia, including digital imagery, sound, and animation, as well as through coordination of students' interactivity with the animation to generate immersive learning experiences. According to Anderson (2008), "this new generation of learners is smart and creative, but impatient, expecting results immediately, and like to customize the objects they choose (p. 203).

OCRA offers convenience and flexibility, and uses a touch screen feature to demonstrate and conceptually visualize the mechanistic steps in an organic reaction mechanism. By transferring the control of learning to students with its touch-screen feature, students are able to form and break apart a chemical bond by sliding their fingers on the screen to move electrons or atoms, and predict logically the mechanistic steps of the three fundamental organic reactions - addition, substitution, and elimination. This technique enables the users to understand the particulate nature of organic reaction mechanism. Mediated through interactive practice activities, the interactive multimedia content enhances students' confidence in learning organic reaction mechanism. Developed based on the revised Bloom's taxonomy model – Remember, Understand, Apply, Analyses, Evaluate, and Create (Krathwohl 2002), the basic premise of OCRA is to immerse students in hands-on experiences that apply the principles of nucleophile, electrophile, and free radicals in the organic reaction mechanism. An example is illustrated in Figure 2 below.

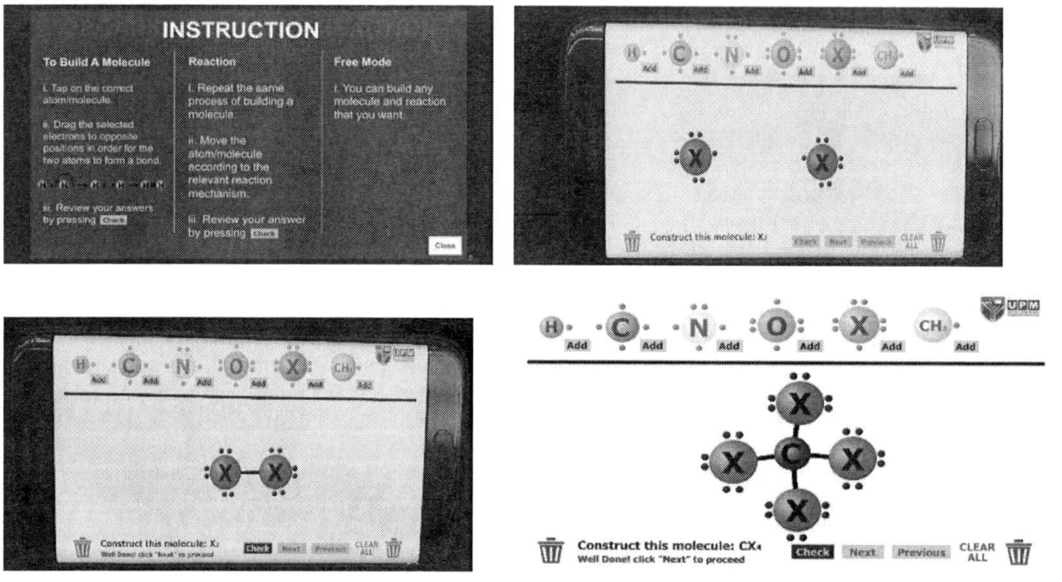

Figure 2. An example of an interactive practice activity using multimedia content

These immersive experiences enable students to analyse every movement of the electrons, including the breaking apart and the formation of covalent bonds. Moreover, critical thinking is encouraged since they are expected to observe, evaluate and come to a decision regarding the arrangement of the molecules to create a possible final product. Finally, the students can check if they have completed the process accurately. Thus, OCRA has the capability to activate users' learning by aiding students to create their own molecules and organic reaction mechanism.

4.1 Interface

The interface of OCRA consists of the five basic atoms in organic chemistry that are shown in different colours with their valence electrons, in terms of the Lewis dot structure, at the top of the screen as shown in Figure 3 below.

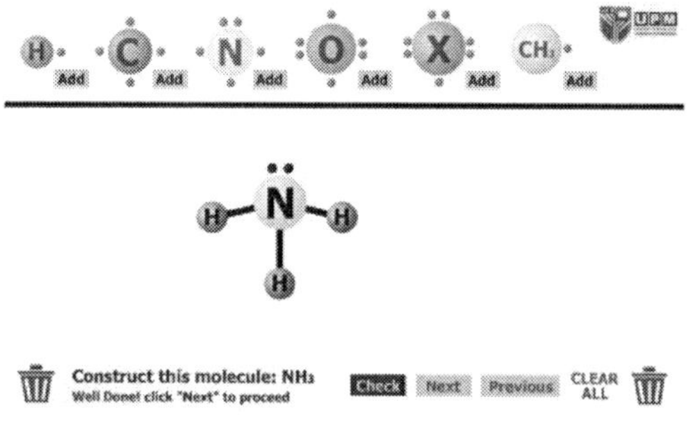

Figure 3. The Interface of an Interactive multimedia M-learning prototype

Most organic molecules are made up from these atoms. Students need to click or tap on the atoms to build a molecule with single, double or triple bonds. Then, students can refer to the simple instruction at the bottom of the screen to construct the different molecules listed before they proceed to interactively try out any basic organic reaction mechanism, leading to the creation of a molecule. The users can try the next exercise by tapping on the "CLEAR ALL" button, and then, the 'NEXT' button. After an activity has been completed, the students can tap on the "CHECK" button to check their answers.

5. METHOD AND PROCEDURE

For this research, the researcher had used the quasi-experimental method. To test the effectiveness of an interactive multimedia approach through the use of a mobile device, two sample groups participated in the research which were a control group and an experimental group. The two groups consisted of 92 students from the Science Foundation Program of a university in Malaysia who were taking the Introduction to Chemistry course with 46 individuals in each group. The control group had learned the organic chemistry concepts fully using traditional teaching and learning methods while the experimental group had learned the organic chemistry concepts with the assistance of the interactive multimedia m-learning prototype, Organic Chemistry Reaction Application (OCRA).

To recognise the perception of students towards the interactive multimedia m-learning prototype, questionnaires were distributed among 100 students, fifty four (54) students from an earlier cohort who had taken the Introduction to Chemistry course during the previous semester as well as the forty six (46) students who were taking the Introduction to Chemistry course at the time of the study. The questionnaire was divided into 4 sections and used the Likert scale that has a ratio of 1 to 4. The key question of this study was, "If students are using interactive multimedia content for learning organic chemistry concepts with a m-learning prototype, what are the outcomes in relation to learning, motivation and engagement'? A complementary question is "What are the benefits of using an interactive multimedia m-learning prototype as perceived by students?" These two questions seek to measure the effectiveness of using the interactive multimedia content, provided in the m-learning prototype and accessed through a mobile device, by examining students' perception about their learning preferences as well as their experiences in understanding organic chemistry reaction concepts.

6. RESULTS AND DISCUSSION OF DATA

A comparison was made between two groups, the control group and the experimental group, with an assumption that these two groups had similar levels of academic achievement. The analysis was carried out using the t-test approach. Through the t-test analysis, a comparison between the minimum achievement value of the tests conducted on the control group and experimental group was performed.

Analysis of the t-test between the Pre-Test and Post-Test achievement for the Control Group is presented in Table 1:

Table 1. t-test for control group

Test	Number of Sample, N	Min	Standard deviation	t value
Pre	46	22.62	7.79	-9.77
Post	46	40.86	10.90	

Table 1 demonstrates there is a significant difference ($p<.05$) between the scores of the pre-test and post-test for the control group which is a total increase of 18.24 marks. This means that the traditional approach of teaching and learning was able to improve students' understanding of organic chemistry concepts. However, the achievement of students is not outstanding.

Analysis of the t-test between the Pre-Test and Post-Test achievement for the Experimental Group is presented in Table 2:

Table 2. t-test for experimental group

Test	Number of Sample, N	Min	Standard deveiation	t value
Pre	46	27.86	7.00	15.83
Post	46	62.24	12.22	

Table 2 demonstrates there is a significant difference ($p < .05$) between the scores of the pre-test and post-test for the experimental group which is a total increase of 34.38 marks. This shows that the teaching and learning approach of using the interactive multimedia m-learning prototype among the experimental group is more effective to improve students' performance in the organic chemistry reaction topic compared to the traditional approach.

Analysis of t-test for the Pre-test Achievement between the two groups of students is presented in Table 3:

Table 3. t-test for pre-test achievement between the control group and experimental group

Group	Numberof sample, N	Min	Standard deviation	t value
Control	46	22.62	7.79	-3.43
Experimental	46	27.86	7.00	

Table 3 shows that the two groups have the same level of achievement ($p > .05$) even though the minimum score for the experimental group is higher than the minimum score for the control group although there is only a difference of five marks. This imply both groups have the same level of pre-knowledge understanding of the organic chemistry concepts.

Analysis of t-test for the Post-test Achievement between the two groups of students is presented in Table 4:

Table 4. t-test for post-test achievement between the control group and experimental group

Group	Number of sample, N	Min	Standard deviation	t-value
Control	46	40.86	10.90	-8.12
Experimental	46	62.24	12.22	

Table 4 shows the minimum score for the experimental group is significantly higher ($p < .05$) compared to the control group. This suggest that students were able to improve their understanding of organic chemistry concepts, especially for the fundamental organic reaction mechanism concept, with the assistance of the interactive multimedia m-learning prototype.

Generally, the t-tests conducted on every minimum score achievement showed that both the traditional teaching and learning approach and the interactive multimedia m-learning approach increased students' understanding. However it is discovered that the use of the interactive multimedia content, delivered through the m-learning prototype, has more effectively improved the performance scores of students; in fact students in the experimental group obtained a higher percentage of improvement in performance their scores compared to the control group. Table 5 clearly shows that the post test for the experimental group has a higher percentage which is 62.24% compared to the control group which is 40.86%.

Table 5. Pre- and Post-Test Achievement for the Control and Experimental Group

Group	Number of sample	Pre-test	Post-test
Control	46	22.62	40.86
Experimental	46	27.86	62.24

Finally, a survey was conducted among the students to investigate the perception of students about the OCRA, the interactive multimedia m-learning prototype. Two main factors were studied in this survey namely the suitability of the OCRA for teaching and learning and the quality of the Interface. Data for the average score of students' perception towards the suitability of OCRA for teaching and learning is given in Table 6 below:

Table 6. Average mean of students' perception of the M-learning prototype for teaching and learning

No.	Statement	Average Score
1	The interactive multimedia content helped in my learning process to understand the topic in organic chemistry reactions.	4.41
2	The interactive activity of multimedia content enabled me to learn the steps of organic reaction mechanism through practice.	4.21
3	The sequence of content delivered with interactive multimedia content is easy to follow.	4.50
4	The sequence of content delivered with interactive multimedia content engages my attention.	4.26
5	The interactive multimedia content is relevant with the organic chemistry reaction mechanism topic.	4.45
6	The interactive multimedia content motivated me to further foster my knowledge of these topics.	4.56
7	The presentation for the topic improved my memory retention of the topic.	4.44
8	The interface of the M-learning prototype is easy to use so I am able to continue following the content until the conclusion.	4.51
9	Learning the organic chemistry concepts with the M-learning prototype is enjoyable because it is convenient.	4.49
10	The M-learning prototype provided a supportive learning environment to enhance understanding of concepts and topics covered in the chemistry course.	4.58
	Average Mean	**4.44**

Table 6 shows the mean score of students' perception towards the suitability of the interactive multimedia M-learning prototype for teaching and learning chemistry concepts; the results demonstrated that there is no apparent difference between all items. The total average mean for this part is 4.44; the results of the survey confirm that majority of students have a positive perception on the suitability of OCRA to positively impact their experiences, motivation and engagement in learning organic chemistry concepts. The use of multimedia based presentations in science education may not necessarily be effective in assisting students to understand a concept. The mere movement of words or objects, and changes to the colours or size of objects may not be able to fully explain a science concept that is often abstract and dynamic, and needs detailed explanation at the macroscopic and microscopic level (Lowe, 2004). Conversely when multimedia based content is used in an interactive task that expected students to be actively involved in applying the Bloom's 'Remember, Understand, Apply, Analyses, Evaluate, and Create' Model, it is found that eventually the students were able to produce a solution to a difficult organic chemistry problem.

7. CONCLUSION

The findings of the study has demonstrated that the interactive multimedia content in the m-learning prototype has served as a learning aid for students and has significantly improved students understanding of organic chemistry concepts, particularly for the organic reaction mechanism topic. In testing the effectiveness of the interactive multimedia m-learning prototype, it is found that the experimental group experienced an increase in percentage in their test score compared to the control group. Moreover, the survey conducted has identified that students have a positive perception of the interactive multimedia m-learning prototype with an overall mean average of 4.44 from the Likert scale that ranges between the degree of 1 to 5. Even though this research has shown promising results, to date the research has not yet included other instruments to obtain data such as interviews. A more detailed statistical analysis is needed to identify and confirm students' perception and acceptance of the interactive multimedia m-learning prototype. Therefore, field trials with different groups of students and the shifting of focus from only organic chemistry reactions to other difficult concepts will be conducted and further explored.

Mobile applications that highlight student-centred content generation, like OCRA, provide ample opportunities for students to optimize their understanding of concepts through multimedia content; the content offer interactivity and information related to the fundamental concepts of organic reaction mechanism. As an alternative learning tool, students are able to experiment with examples of the substitution, elimination and addition reaction for any basic form of molecule in organic chemistry. As mentioned before, continual use of the traditional talk and chalk approach has limited students' ability to visualize the electrons involved in making or breaking a bond nor are they able to conceptualize a synthesis reaction where two or more substances combine to form a new compound. However, the comprehension of electrophile, nucleophile as well as the octet rule concepts can be assessed through OCRA. In Malaysia, the most common initiative in educational technology has been focused on developing and delivering digital content to students as online study notes or guidelines which students tend to download and study off line. From this study, we have observed that true education must go beyond mere access to information, but should involve students in constructing and applying knowledge (Miyazoe, 2010). It is highly recommended that mobile learning applications that take into consideration the current pedagogical approaches in education, especially for the Net Generation, should continue to be developed. OCRA, an interactive multimedia m-learning prototype, is a promising example of an alternative teaching and learning tool that improvises on the traditional teaching and learning approach. This educational approach is a step towards upgrading the effectiveness of teaching and learning in Malaysia, especially in this era of innovative technological advancement.

ACKNOWLEDGEMENT

The authors would like to acknowledge the Research Grant provided by University Putra Malaysia to develop the m-learning application, in collaboration with Multimedia University, Malaysia.

REFERENCES

Alessi, S. M. and Trollip, R. S, 2001. *Computer Based Instruction; Methods and Development.* (3rd. ed.), Allyn and Bacon, Boston. M.A.

Berg, S. and Ghosh, A. 2013. Six Impossible Mechanisms Before Breakfast: Arrow Pushing as an Instructional Device in Inorganic Chemistry. *Journal of Chemical Education,* Vol 90, No. 11, pp 1446–1451.

Conole, G. and Oliver, M. eds., 2007. *Contemporary perspectives in e-learning research: themes, methods and impact on practice.* The Open and Flexible Learning Series. London, UK: Routledge.

Farhana, Y., and Zainun, M.A., 2013. Attitude towards Learning Chemistry among Secondary School Students in Malaysia. *Journal of Asian Behavioural Studies*, Vol. 3, No. 11, pp. 1-11.

Hutchinson, J.S. , 2000. Teaching Introductory Chemistry using Concept Development Case Studies: Interactive and Inductive Learning. *University Chemistry Education*, Vol.4, pp. 3-7.

Keskin, O. N., & Metcalf, D., 2011. The current perspectives, theories and practices of mobile learning. *The Turkish Online Journal of Educational Technology* (TOJET), Vol. 10, No. 2, pp. 202-208.

Kulkuska-Hulme, 2007. Mobile usability in Educational Contexts: What have we learn? *International review of Research in Open and Distance Learning.* Vol. 8, No. 2, pp 1-6.

Jarvis, P., Holford, J. and Griffin, C., 2003. *The Theory and Practice of Learning*, Rougledge Falmer, London, U.K.

Lafarge, D.L., Morge, L.M., and Meheut, M.M., 2014. A New Higher Education Curriculum in Organic Chemistry: What Questions Should Be Asked? *Journal of Chemical Education.* Vol. 91, No. 2, pp 173–178.

Liaw, S. S., Hatala, M., and Huang, H. M., 2010. Investigating acceptance toward mobile learning to assist individual knowledge management: based on activity theory approach. *Computers & Education*, Vol. 54, No.2, 446-454. Luckerson, V, 2014. Too cool for school. *Time,* Vol. 184, No. 11, p. 16.

Mayer, R. E., 2009. *Multimedia learning,* (2nd ed.). Cambridge University Press, Cambridge, M.A.Mayer, R. E., and Moreno, R., 2010. Techniques that reduce extraneous cognitive load and manage intrinsic cognitive load during multimedia learning. In J. L. Plass, R. Moreno, & R. Brunken (Eds.), *Cognitive load theory* (pp. 131–152). Cambridge University Press, New York, N.Y.

Ministry of Education, 2016. *Laporan Prestasi SPM 2015* [Report on SPM Performance 2015]. MOE Examination Division, Kuala Lumpur, Malaysia

Miyazoe, T., and Anderson, T., 2010. The interaction equivalency theorem. *Journal of Interactive Online Learning*, Vol. 9, No. 2, pp. 94–104.

Montes, I., Prieto, J. A., and García, M., 2002. Using Molecular Modeling in the in the Organic Chemistry Course for Majors. *The Chemical Educator,* Vol. 7, pp. 293-296

Ng, W., and Nicholas, H., 2013. A framework for sustainable mobile learning in schools. *British Journal of Educational Technology*, Vol. 44, No. 5, pp. 695-715

Park, Y., 2011. A pedagogical framework for mobile learning: Categorizing educational applications of mobile technologies into four types. *International Review of Research in Open and Distance Learning*, Vol. 12, No.2, pp. 78-102. Retrieved from http://www.irrodl.org/index.php/irrodl/article/view/791/169

TEACHING STRATEGIES AND METHODS IN MODERN ENVIRONMENTS FOR LEARNING OF PROGRAMMING

Slobodanka Djenic and Jelena Mitic
The School of Electrical and Computer Engineering of Applied Studies, Vojvode Stepe 283, 11000 Belgrade, Serbia

ABSTRACT

This paper presents teaching strategies and methods, applicable in modern blended environments for learning of programming. Given the fact that the manner of applying teaching strategies always depends on the specific requirements of a certain area of learning, the paper outlines the basic principles of teaching in programming courses, as well as the possibilities for applying modern teaching strategies in this area. Blended learning of programming is gaining dominance in higher education, through combining traditional and modern technologies and teaching methodologies in classroom and via the internet: in traditional courses – with lessons in the classroom and regular additional forms of teaching via the Internet and in distance courses - with regular lessons and additional forms of teaching in the classroom / via the internet. This paper describes teaching strategies which are implemented within the blended programming traditional and distance courses in the School of Electrical and Computer Engineering of Applied Studies in Belgrade: Programming fundamentals, Programming languages and Object oriented design. The methods recommended for carrying out teaching strategies in this area have been described: modernized teaching strategies and the increasingly popular strategies of collaborative, situated and self-directed learning. Considering all the above, this paper can in fact motivate teachers in the given area to improve their teaching and adjust it to modern generations of students.

KEYWORDS

Teaching strategies, learning of programming, collaborative learning

1. INTRODUCTION

Development and use of internet have made significant changes in education. The very beginning of this century is considered as a breakthrough in higher education, as there have been significant transformations in teaching approach as well as teaching strategies and methods. Now there are final solutions of modern blended learning environments, which include teaching and learning via the internet in many different forms (without terminating traditional learning in classroom), as well as new teaching methodologies and technologies (without dismissing those previously developed and rather modernizing them). Because that, methodology of teaching does not represent a package of "ready-to-wear" recipes, as was the case with traditional learning environments, but has a rather flexible basis for the development of the existing and finding new methods of modern teaching strategies.

In the area of programming as well, teaching methodology is being constantly improved and combines different methods of applied strategies. The reasons for this can easily be found in the basics of learning in this area: learning of programming includes learning the theory in the form of basic elements and programme algorithms, as well as a practical part in the form of mastering the skill of using modern environment for the sake of program development and the logic programming through as many different problems as possible in the chosen programming method and language. In the very beginning of your programming learning, you can benefit greatly from standard surrounding libraries of program development and already solved problems in various textbooks and other similar teaching materials, as well as discussions with teachers considering the way of solving problems. As far as further development is concerned, individual and team program solving with the help of developing surroundings and tools is the best way to go.

In this paper, there is an overview of applied a modern teaching strategies and methods in learning of programming in blended courses: Programming fundamentals, Programming languages and Object oriented design, in the School of Electrical and Computer Engineering of Applied Studies in Belgrade, which constantly follows and applies advances in education. Mentioned courses are developing in this School, in classical and distance studies since 2012/13 academic year.

Simultaneously, this paper touches current questions in higher education, such as: How do you keep traditional methods and strategies that are proven to be efficient, but at the same time introduce new ones, supported by modern technologies and which are of great importance to new generations of students? How do you enable students to be active in certain segments of lessons and not just passive observers? How do you obtain and maintain the collaborative teacher-student relationship?

2. TEACHING STRATEGIES - FROM TRADITIONAL TO MODERN

If we consider teaching strategies in modern learning environments, we cannot generalize when it comes to advantages of ones over the others, nor when it comes to strategies and their methods which are unchangeable. For developing highly efficient learning environments in any area, depending on the specific requirements and available experience of the already developed environments, it is necessary to choose teaching strategies, and after this gradually implement all the acquired experience with the applied strategies into their further development.

Teaching strategies in modern blended learning environments [Petrina, 2007] are student-oriented: The structure of learning environment is totally adjusted to students; The process of teaching is fully directed to students; During the teaching, the students are encouraged not only to take in information, but do more research, critically contemplate on the teaching material, perform individual or team work on solving specific problems they encounter during teaching; Both teachers and students are simultaneously encouraged to continuously, during the process of teaching and learning, act as a team which cooperates in this process [Hart, 2014].

To make a suitable choice of strategies in a certain area, it is first of all necessary to study general characteristics of specific actual teaching strategies [Bullen, Janes, 2007]:

- Direct Instruction Strategy – implies learning from the previously defined content of the teaching material, prepared by the teacher. The traditional direct instruction strategy mostly involved a passive absorption of the content by the students, while with modern forms of the same strategy, a constant student activity in the process of teaching and learning is implied, due to the existence of internet platforms which stimulate active learning, and interactive content of the teaching material [Ruth, 2008].
- Collaborative Learning Strategy – means learning through communication on the teaching material between teacher and students and among students themselves, as well as an active student teamwork on problems and projects, or simply put - a cooperation between teachers and students in the process of learning, a live one, but also with the help of different modern web tools for communication and online teamwork. With modern forms of this strategy, the process of teaching is rather adjusted to individual students.
- Situated Learning Strategy – means learning through practical problem solving, practical exercises, experiments, seminar papers and projects, all accompanied by the instructions and help of the teachers, and supported by a wide spectrum of web and multimedia technologies, animations and simulations in virtual labs. Modern forms of this strategy enable a rather active participation of students in the process of teaching.
- Self-directed Learning Strategy – means learning from the teaching material, as little as possible recommended by the teacher, and as much as possible researched by the students themselves. Earlier forms of this strategy involved researching of the printed material, and its modern forms also require browsing the material on internet platforms for learning, web pages, wikis, blogs and social networks. This strategy is characterised by active student involvement, and the process of teaching adjusted to their individual needs.

Each modern teaching strategy requires a special approach to teaching, and specific forms of teaching organisation, as shown in Table 1.

Table 1. Basic characteristics of modern teaching strategies

Teaching strategy	Approach to teaching	Forms of organising teaching
Direct Instruction	Learning Transmission	Working on presenting the content
Collaborative Learning	Learning in Society	Working on preparing cooperation in learning
Situated Learning	Learning Environment	Working on preparing practical work in learning
Self-directed Learning	Learning through Research	Working on preparing for research in learning

There is no universal recipe for choosing a teaching strategy and method in blended learning environment. Experience shows [Bonk, Graham, 2006.] that choosing the right blended model presents a very important step there. If a model is well chosen there are conditions for its implementation - with the use of appropriate strategies and methods - to give the expected results. Experiences also show that the choice of strategy and method, which is made according to the instructional design for every particular blended model, is just a guideline for the further development of teaching activities. Encouraging active student participation in teaching, continuous communications and cooperation between teacher and students, provide outlines and within them teachers' and students' activities are further formed.

This paper further presents experiences in the choice and use of teaching strategies and methods in developed and implemented blended learning environment for teaching of programming in the School of Electrical and Computer Engineering of Applied Studies in Belgrade:

- in classical studies – with the initially applied basic blended learning environment model, along with the advanced blended learning model, from school year 2006/7;
- in distance studies – with the advanced blended learning environment model from school year 2012/13.

3. MODERN ENVIRONMENTS FOR PROGRAMMING COURSES

When selecting the teaching strategies which will be used in a specific area through their methods, it is, at very start, necessary to take into account the specificity of the area in question and basic principles of teaching in this area. The coming section of this paper gives a brief overview of the basic principles of teaching in programming courses.

3.1 Basic Principles of Teaching and Contents Specifics in Programming Courses

Modern learning environments for programming [Djenic, Krneta and Mitic, 2011], [Hadjerrouit, 2007], [Hadjerrouit, 2008] are constantly improved so they would be more efficient, but at the same time, they use basic principles of teaching programming, which are given below:

- Teaching theory is a guideline for praxis - although it goes without saying that every programming language can be learned best through praxis, the best "guide" for it, just like in all the other areas, is theory. Teaching theory here implies learning the syntax, definitions of certain groups of programme elements, the manner of connecting these elements, algorithms and methods of their application in programmes;
- Practical teaching is crucial – a programming is mainly learned through practical work on the programmes. Practical teaching in this area involves giving instructions and help in solving problems in a specific programming language, initially based on the examples of solved programmes in the same language, and later in finding original solutions for diverse problems of programme tasks, within exercises and projects;
- The principle of connection between theory and praxis – the theory of programming is a precondition for practical work in this area, since it is essential that students adopt it before beginning with the analysis of the completed programme solutions. On the other hand, practical work on programme tasks may serve to students to better grasp the theory and check the importance of theoretical knowledge;
- The principle of availability - to prevent certain concepts in the area of programming from being abstract, their descriptions should be clear and available - adjusted to students and based on the pre-knowledge expected from them. When teaching any programming language, it is necessary to explain them. In modern conditions, this is considerably supported by multimedia;
- The principle of active student role – in learning of programming, the priority has always been in the active role of students. Students are expected to show initiative, work individually or in teams on problem solving, ask questions in order to clarify certain situations they encounter in problem solving, and participate in discussions on the teaching material with teachers. In all this, web tools are used quite efficiently;
- Principle of interaction - student-teacher, student-student and student-content type of interactions are quite important in the theoretical and practical part of teaching in this area. In today's conditions interactivity is rather present, given the development of multimedia content, animations and simulations, which require constant student activity, together with different forms of online communication on the teaching material;

The forms in which certain segments of the content in this area are prepared are: theory in lessons, examples of solved programmes, programming tasks and questions:

- Theory in lessons can be prepared in the form of: text with programme elements definitions; illustrations with algorithms of basic programming structures. Electronic materials can have an addition: interactive lesson content, animations which complement or substitute the text, the purpose of which is to explain abstract concepts to students, through their visualization;
- Examples of solved programmes usually contain: text with the source code and additional explanation of the source code programme and illustrations with memory overview and programme execution output. Electronic editions of solved programme collections can also contain: interactive textual content for programme examples; animations for explaining the itinerary of programme execution and;
- Programme tasks should be systematized into those for research, team and individual homework, seminar paper or project, and prepare as a text of concrete tasks which should be solved in the required programming language, possibly with illustrations. In the electronic form the text of the task can be a content within the interactive applications, uploaded via the forum or other web tools;
- Questions in this area, with: connecting programme elements and their descriptions, alternative choice, multiple choice, filling in the programme elements or open-type. Just like tasks, the questions in the electronic form can be prepared within interactive applications of all kinds.

3.2 Development of Modern Blended Programming Courses

Modern blended learning environment [Bonk, Graham, 2006] is a environment the purpose of which adjustment to new the generation of students, which is achieved through combining of different: media and technologies in learning and teaching [Picciano, Dziuban, 2007]; teaching approaches, strategies and teaching methods; classroom and learning via internet.

In the first blended learning environments, classroom learning and teaching were dominant. The constant development of interactive multimedia, web systems and technologies, created a possibility for the development of new learning environments, and that was a significant step in the development of these environments. In modern blended learning environments, the following principles are insisted upon: adaptable classroom, flexible learning time, individual learning dynamics, regular communication throughout teaching and learning. Unlike the traditional learning environments, in which it was possible to implement only the original forms of the mentioned strategies of teaching of programming, modern blended environments introduce the internet, and partly become virtual, as shown in Table 2.

Table 2. Current strategies in the learning of programming and the environmental change for their realization

Teaching strategy	Forms of learning	Traditional environment	Modern environment
Direct Instruction	Listening, reading and analysing	Classroom, computer lab	Web platform for learning
Collaborative Learning	Team work; Exchange of ideas	Computer lab	Web tools for teamwork
Situated Learning	Practical work	Computer lab	Virtual lab
Self-directed Learning	Researching, revealing solutions	Computer lab	Web resources; Virtual lab

Blended courses implies using knowledge and experience of traditional environments, but it is necessary to work extra on broadening this knowledge and experience in modern conditions:

- Basic blended model of teaching (enhanced f2f learning) - realised within traditional studies, with 100% classroom lessons and extra forms of teaching via the internet;
- Advanced blended model of teaching (f2f & online, more online learning) - realised within distance studies: by substituting about 90% of all the lessons by online lessons, and realising via the internet all additional forms of teaching. Here too, the internet platform is using for online lessons and additional forms of teaching, but with much more complete teaching material: recordings of classroom lessons / audio-video presentations / multimedia textbooks with interactive simulations / applications for knowledge check.

Perennial research in the area of modern teaching methodology for programming by the authors of this paper, resulted in the development and realization of blended courses in this area, according to basic blended model of teaching in classical studies and according to advanced blended model of teaching in distance studies since, 2012/13 academic year. The teaching plans for these courses, Programming fundamentals, Programming languages and Object oriented design, are shown in Table 3.

Table 3. Teaching plan for described programming courses

"Programming fundamentals" topics
Structural programming, Algorithms of the program structures, language C
Data types, Operators and standard functions, Commands for flow control, language C
Arrays, Sorting of arrays, Use of pointers in arrays, Functions, language C
"Programming languages" topics
Dynamic memory assignment, Data structures, Dynamic linked lists, languages C/C++
Data input from command line, Working with text- and binary files, languages C/C++
Modular programming, language C, I/O streams, Classes and objects, language C++
"Object oriented design" topics
Classes features, Encapsulation, Inheritance, Polymorphism, language Java
Data and expressions, Working with data bases, Exceptions, language Java
Class diagrams, Activity Diagrams, Basic concepts of program design, language Java

4. EXPERIENCES IN APPLYING MODERN TEACHING STRATEGY METHODS IN PROGRAMMING COURSES

Every teaching strategy defines its own methods for interaction in the process of teaching and learning: teacher-content, student-content, teacher-student and student-student. Different strategies use different methods with various levels of teaching control and student activity in the teaching process, for the fulfilment of all these types of interaction. The same goes for the area of programming.

4.1 Modern Teaching Strategy Methods Implemented in Programming Courses

Short descriptions of modern teaching strategy methods which are implemented in blended courses of programming in the School of Electrical and Computer Engineering of Applied Studies in Belgrade, are shown in Table 4.

Table 4. Modern strategy methods implemented in the programming courses

Teaching strategy	The most common activities in the classroom / via the internet
Direct Instruction	**Teachers' activities:** Lecturing, presenting and reviewing programme elements and algorithms; Instructions on learning programme syntax; Demonstration on completed solved programmes; **Students' activities:** Interactive lectures following; Asking questions regarding elements and algorithms and completed solved programmes;
Collaborative Learning	**Teachers' activities:** Creating working teams or suggestions on the same; Instructions for team problem solving; Leading the discussion on the material; **Students' activities:** Team projects and problem solving; Active in the discussion on the material and problems; Indication of discussion on the lectures and problems;
Situated Learning	**Teachers' activities:** Instructions for using developed tools and surroundings; Instructions on programme solving and exercises; Instructions on writing programme seminars; **Students' activities:** Mastering using developed tools and surroundings; Programme solving; Writing programme seminars; Solving potential practical problems; Working on simulations of previously solved programmes; Researching previously solved programmes;
Self-directed Learning	**Teachers' activities:** Directions and recommendations for research on certain subject; **Students' activities:** Researching all of the subjects; Partial or complete reviews; Professional practice;

In modern environments for learning of programming, relation between present types of teacher and student activity is significantly changed compared to traditional systems [Watkins, 2005]. There were many more forms of teachers' activities in the lecturing strategy which dominated in the traditional learning environment whereas now it is insisted upon the change of this relation because certain forms of students' are present in the same level or more in some learning strategies which can be seen in Figure 1.

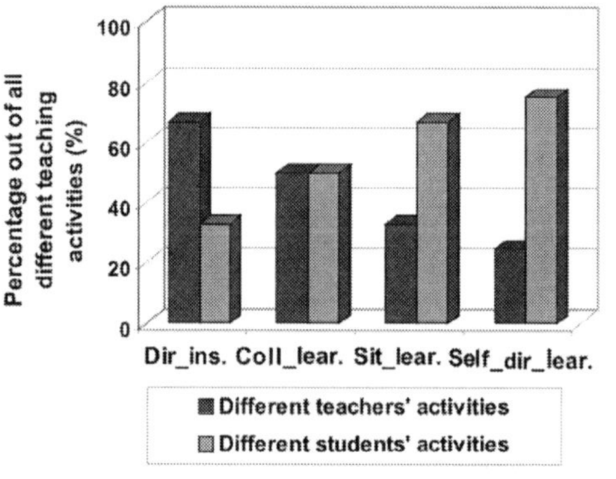

Figure 1. The relation between present forms of teachers' and students' activities in some modern teaching strategies for programming: direct instruction, collaborative, situated and self-directed learning

Experiences in applying above mentioned teaching strategies and methods in implemented blended learning environment in programming courses are briefly described further in this paper.

Experiences in applying modern teaching strategy methods - new forms for presenting teaching material with interactive smart board and internet access are very important for lessons in programming. Teaching materials can be available on the web, audio/video recordings of lessons in classrooms can be followed online or downloaded and used locally, watching audio/video material can be delayed and possible an arbitrary number of times, lessons and consulting can be implemented through audio/video conferences and other communication tools - this requires more teachers' than students' teaching activities.

Experiences in applying the collaborative learning method - cooperation is very important in modern learning environments. Discussions have become a necessary method in the collaborative learning strategy but also, the commonly used method in other modern strategies in learning of programming. It is no longer a question whether discussions should be included in programming courses because the experiences in their implementation show that they can offer great help to all participants - this requires the around same amount of teachers' and students' teaching activities.

Experiences in applying the situated learning strategy - this strategy demands that students practice solving problems that appear in real situations by simulating real conditions in programming. Students that learn in a blended environment get the chance to learn in a more situated manner because their participation in teaching and learning outside of the traditional classroom requires exactly that. Practical work commonly provides better understanding of abstract terms and success in studying after reading and listening to theory of programming - this requires more students' than teachers' teaching activities.

Experiences in applying the self-directed learning method - in this strategy, students are given recommendations and are free to research and get familiar with the theory that way and solve practical problems in programming. This strategy is used in different ways: checking material, essays and reports on covered teaching content on wiki pages and on blogs, practice in an online lab, working on tasks with the help of web tools. Practicing the use of this strategy in programming shows that it is very useful if students have mutually different pre-knowledge - this requires much more students' than teachers' teaching activities.

4.2 Recommendations: Modern Teaching – Enterprise of Teachers and Students

Experience from blended environments on the large number of programming courses ensues recommendations for the preparation of such teaching:

- use good experience with traditional teaching strategies and methods;
- set out all the conditions for realisation of the new teaching activities, long before the planned course;
- involve consultants in the specific area and pedagogy in the preparation of the new teaching activities;
- prepare online platform for learning, as well as all other planned web tools for the new teaching activities;
- make a detailed plan of teaching activities;
- try, if possible, to realise the planned teaching activities with other teachers;
- formulate the rules for the individual and team work for students;
- prepare the plan for communication with students about the teaching material;

Technology changes strategies and methods of teaching and consequently the roles of teachers and students. Experience suggests that the basic condition for modernizing teaching is that teachers accept innovations in order for students to do the same.

Teachers get new, highly demanding roles and assignments, but also an opportunity to have insight into learning methods of their students and to familiarize themselves better with them.

Students assume a very active role, while teachers are always available to answer all their questions, comments and objections related to the teaching material.

4.3 Development Trends and Future Research of Teaching Methods

There are high expectations for the results of future research in teaching strategies and methods, considering the constant development of new technologies and new roles of teachers and students. It is the same expectations in the area of programming:

- development of the learning environment for mobile devices constitute "mobile classroom" - teaching methods for programming are expected to be improved with:
  - uploading and views of audio / video content of lessons and exercises, instructions for tasks and practical work in programming – in mobile devices;
  - regular knowledge self - checks and discussions on teaching material and tasks - via mobile device;
  - teachers' and students' use of mobile devices in programming courses, both outside the classroom and in it, which represents trend of "bring your own device" in working context.
- development of the learning environment with distance online tools, in the form of virtual classroom constitute so called "classroom in the cloud":
  - preparing, development and views of lessons, exercises, knowledge self - checks and discussions on teaching material - on the cloud, without installing any kind of tools in local teachers' and students' computer devices;
  - working on solutions in programming, design, implementation and testing of code - on the cloud;
  - teachers' and students' activities more reliable and adaptive, free of charge or very affordable due to the reduced need for the local maintenance of programming environment and tools.
- development of the learning environment, web platforms, teaching materials and activities in the blended classroom, so called "flipped classroom":
  - outside the classroom: preparing, downloading, uploading and views of lessons, work instructions, programme examples and tasks;
  - outside the classroom: working on programme solutions, design, implementation and testing of code;
  - in the classroom: views of teaching material, questions and answers, discussions on teaching material and knowledge checks.

Blended learning environments for programming have already entered the practice of highly renowned education institutions all around the globe [Djenic, Krneta and Mitic, 2011]. In this area, like in all others, current teaching methods are constantly being modernized and the new ones are being developed, and the concept of teaching has shifted towards flexible cooperation between teachers and students.

5. CONCLUSION

Continuous work on the modernization of traditional, and the development of new teaching strategies and methods, as well as their application to modern blended learning environments, is currently an important strategic move in the development of higher education.

Learning of programming is closely related to the development of modern information and communication technologies, and it is therefore vital to continuously apply the latest achievements of modern teaching methodology in this area.

Perennial research in the area of modern teaching methodology for programming by the authors of this paper, indicated that the methods of all current teaching strategies are preferred in this study area. Modern teaching strategy methods incorporate interactive multimedia and interaction in teaching, which are important for this study area; Collaborative learning methods develop greatly needed creativity in solving programme tasks and stimulate the vital exchange of programming experience; Situated learning methods increase motivation and students' interest in solving programme problems, which are dominant in this study area; Self - directed learning methods capacitate student for lifelong development in this area, which is important for the further development of technologies.

In the application and further development of teaching methods in all the above mentioned strategies of this area, teachers have the task to explore / prepare / recommend students: web environment and tools for learning, as much interactive multimedia content as possible, animations and simulations, verified techniques for communication about teaching material and tasks, as well as mechanisms necessary for the evaluation of applied teaching methods.

The conducted research indicates that, with regard to combining various strategies and methods, blended learning environments require early and more thorough preparation than the traditional learning environments. Improvement of current strategies and methods, involves greater focus on the role of the teacher, as a tutor and mentor for students in the work on programming tasks and discussions on teaching material, as well as concentrating on the active role of students in employing these teaching methods.

Long-term experience in development of blended learning courses for programming indicates that in this area, establishing and encouraging cooperation between teachers and students in the process of learning, their joint work on solving practical problems that students have in mastering the teaching content and getting practice, as well as joint research in the learning area, can all lead to successful application and improvement of teaching strategies and methods in this area.

REFERENCES

Bonk C, Graham C, 2006, *The Handbook of Blended Learning Global Perspectives, Local Designs*, Pfeiffer An Imprint of Wiley, San Francisco.

Bullen M, Janes D, 2007, *Making the Transition to E-Learning: Strategies and Issues*, Information Science Publishing.

Djenic S, Krneta R, Mitic J, 2011, Blended Learning of Programming in the Internet Age, *IEEE Transactions on Education, vol. 54, no. 2, 247-254.*

Hadjerrouit S, 2007, A Blended Learning Model in Java Programming: A design-Based Research Approach, *Computer Science and IT Education*, pp. 283-308.

Hadjerrouit S, 2008, , Towards a Blended Learning Model for Teaching and Learning Computer Programming: *A Case Study*, Informatics in Education, vol. 7, no. 2, pp. 181-210.

Hart J, 2014, *Social Learning Handbook*, C4LPT.

Petrina S, 2007, *Advanced Teaching Methods for the Technology Classroom*, *Information Science Publishing*, London.

Picciano A, Dziuban C, 2007, *Blended Learning, Research Perspectives*, the Sloan Consortium, USA.

Ruth C, 2008, *Cognitive Methods for Training and Performance Improvement*, Society for Performance Improvement.

Watkins A, 2005, *e-learning Activities*, John Wiley & Sons, USA.

A LECTURE SUPPORTING SYSTEM BASED ON REAL-TIME LEARNING ANALYTICS

Atsushi Shimada and Shin'ichi Konomi
Kyushu University, Japan

ABSTRACT

A new lecture supporting system based on real-time learning analytics is proposed. Our target is on-site classrooms where teachers give their lectures, and a lot of students listen to teachers' explanation, conduct exercises etc. We utilize not only an e-Learning system, but also an e-Book system to collect real-time learning activities during the lectures. The proposed system is useful for a teacher just before lecture starts and during the lecture. The system provides summary reports of the previews of given materials and quiz results. The teacher can check which pages were well previewed and which pages were not previewed by students using the preview achievement graph. Additionally, the teacher can check which quizzes were difficult for students, and the suggested pages that should be explained in the lecture to aid students. During the lecture, real-time analytics graphs are shown on the teacher's PC. The teacher can easily grasp students status whether or not students are following the teacher's explanation. Through a case study, we confirmed the effectiveness of the proposed system, in terms of high synchronization between a teacher and students, i.e., the teacher adjusted the speed of his lecture based on the real-time feedback, and many students followed the teacher's explanation.

KEYWORDS

Learning analytics, real-time feedback, on-site classrooms, lecture supporting system

1. INTRODUCTION

Learning analytics (Khalil 2016) has attracted many researchers recent years. One of the important issues in learning analytics is not only to perform analysis of data about learners, but also to realize feedbacks for optimizing the learning environment and learners themselves. There are roughly three types of feedback loops in terms of their frequency: yearly, weekly and real-time feedbacks. A typical example of a yearly (or term-by-term) feedback loop is the assessment and improvement of education. Students' grades, examination results, class questionnaires, and so on are typically analyzed and evaluated (Mouri 2016, Okubo 2016). The yearly feedback loop is designed so that the feedback results will be delivered in the next year (or term). In other words, students and teachers will not directly receive the feedback results acquired by analyzing their own learning logs. A weekly feedback loop can recommend related material based on student status determined using a prediction of academic performance through the analysis of learning logs such as attendance reports and quiz results (Shimada 2015, Shimada 2016). In contrast to a yearly feedback loop, the analysis results are directly fed back to the students and teachers who provide the learning logs. The main difference between weekly and real-time feedback loops is that the analysis results can be fed back to the on-site students and teachers even during a lecture. A teacher can check what students are doing, e.g., whether students are following the explanation, or whether they are doing something not related to the lecture. A teacher can flexibly control the speed of the lecture, and/or take more time for exercises rather than a nonstop talk, and so on.

There are several related work, which tackles real-time learning analytics. Minovic et al. proposed a visualization tool for teachers to track students learning progress in real-time, while in gameplay session (Minovic, 2013). Piech et al. collected tens of thousands of program codes, and applied a machine learning approach to identify "sink" states of students. A feedback is achieved for students just before they are about to enter such problematic "sink" states (Piech 2012). Fu et al. also proposed a real-time analysis of program codes (Fu 2017). They provides a learning dashboard to capture the behavior of students in the classroom and identify different difficulties faced by students. Although these studies realize real-time feedbacks, the target of the analytics and its feedback are activities in virtual learning environments.

Our study has focused on feedback, specifically, how to feedback efficient information to on-site classrooms even during lectures. The aim of this research is to realize real-time feedback, which has not often been discussed with respect to on-site educational environments. Our target is on-site classrooms where teachers give their lectures, and a lot of students listen to teachers' explanation, conduct exercises etc. In such a large classroom, it is not easy for teachers to grasp students' situations and activities. We utilize not only an e-Learning system, but also an e-Book system to collect real-time learning activities during the lectures. We have developed two main feedback systems. One is useful for a teacher just before lecture starts. The system provides summary reports of the previews of given materials and quiz results. The teacher can check which pages were well previewed and which pages were not previewed by students using the preview achievement graph. Additionally, the teacher can check which quizzes were difficult for students, and the suggested pages that should be explained in the lecture to aid students. The other is real-time analytics graphs which are helpful for the teacher to control his/her lecture speed during the lecture. The system collects e-Book logs operated by students sequentially, and performs analytics in real time how many students are following the teacher's explanation. In the rest of this paper, we introduce the details of our real-time feedback system and report experimental results.

2. IMPLEMENTATION

2.1 Learning Logs

The e-Book logs were collected via an e-Book system called "BookRoll". Figure 1 shows samples of e-Book logs. There are many types of operations recorded in the logs, for example, OPEN means that the student opened the e-book file and NEXT means that the student clicked the next button to move to the subsequent page. The browsing duration for each page can be calculated by subtracting the subsequent timestamps. Learning logs on the e-Leaning system such as attendances and quiz scores are collected from tables in the Moodle database. The system analyzes the quiz scores and class attendances by integrating related tables.

User	Material	Operation	PageNo	Date	Time
X	00000000NLAT	OPEN	0	2014/10/15	9:01:09
X	00000000NLAT	CLOSE	1	2014/10/15	9:01:13
Y	00000000P82P	PREV	25	2014/10/29	10:05:35
Y	00000000P855	NEXT	2	2014/11/19	8:52:47
Z	00000000P84Z	NEXT	9	2014/11/12	9:31:30
...	...	...	...	...	...

Figure 1. Samples e-Book logs

2.2 On-site Lecture Supporting System

We present the example case study shown in Figure 2, which was actually applied to a lecture in our university. The time line is divided into two parts: before starting a class and during a class. During the previous lecture, a teacher gave students some preview materials, that were automatically generated by summarization technique (Shimada 2017). Students previewed the given materials before the class, and the operation logs recorded during the previews were collected by the system. Before the class started, students answered the quizzes and the results were collected on the server.

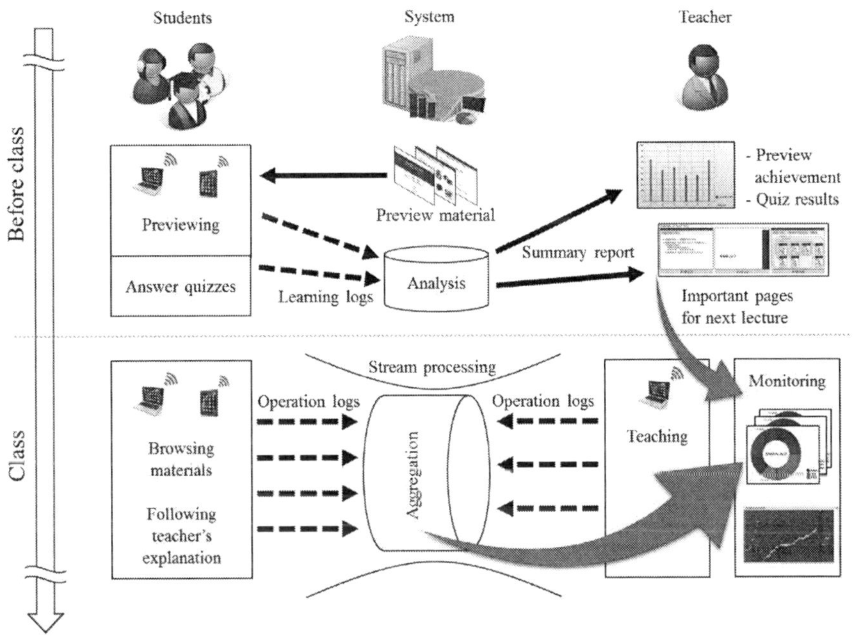

Figure 2. A case study. Students previewed materials before their class and answered the quizzes. Learning logs (e-book operation logs and quiz results) were collected in the system and summary reports were sent to the teacher. The teacher checked the preview achievements (which page was browsed the most, which page was not read, etc.) and quiz results before starting their lecture. Additionally, they were told some important pages that should be explained well in the next lecture. During the lecture, the operation logs of the teacher and students were collected and analyzed. The results were immediately visualized on the teacher's PC. The teacher could check the students' activities (e.g., how many students were following the lecture) and adjust the their speed accordingly

Just before the lecture started, our system analyzed the learning logs to make a summary report containing previews of the achievement and quiz results (details are given in the section 2.6. Additionally, the system provided information regarding important pages that should be explained well in the lecture. For example, the teacher should focus on pages that are related to the quizzes, especially those that have led to lower quiz scores. Our system analyzed the relationship between quiz statements and their related pages in the lecture material in advance. Section 2.3 explains how we automatically discover important pages.

During the lecture, a teacher explained the contents of the materials and students browsed the materials in their lap-top PCs. In our university, students are asked to open and browse the same page as the teacher, and to put highlights or notes on the important points. During the lecture, learning logs were sequentially collected and stored. The analysis results were immediately visualized on the web interface, and updated each minute. Therefore, the teacher could check the latest student activities. The visualization included real-time information regarding how many students were following the lecture, how many students were browsing previous pages, etc. The web interface is described in section 2.6. The teacher adaptively controlled the speed of the lecture according to the students. For example, if many students were not following the lecture and were still on previous page, the teacher slowed down the lecture.

2.3 Important Page Mining

There are strong relationships between lecture materials and quizzes, because quizzes are often generated using the contents of the lecture materials. Related pages are important to understanding the contents of the materials. However, lecture materials and quizzes are stored separately, or are very weakly connected in the system using, for example, subject names. We can manually assess the relationship between a quiz item and its related pages, but this is not easy nor realistic when the number of quiz items and/or the number of pages increase. Furthermore, if the lecture material is updated, i.e., the page numbering changes, the teacher must update the correspondence. Therefore, we developed a method that automatically determines the correspondences.

Our strategy assumes that a related page contains the same keyword as the quiz statement. Each quiz statement, QS, is divided into morphemes. Then, we extract the nouns n $(1, \cdots, n, \cdots, N)$. For each noun n, a normalized histogram h_n is created. Each bin $b_{u,n}$ of the histogram h_n represents how many times page u contains noun n. Note that the bins are normalized after counting the number of times noun n appears in all the pages. To acquire the final result, we sum the frequencies of all nouns. We define the normalized value r_u as the related score of page u.

Although the mining method finds pages that are highly related to a given quiz statement, it does not consider the relationships among pages. Therefore, we also apply a ranking method that assigns a ranking score to each page. The idea was inspired by VisualRank (Jing 2008). A ranking vector R is iteratively updated using

$$R = \alpha(S \times R) + (1 - \alpha)B$$

where S is the column normalized similarity matrix, and $S_{u,v}$ measures the page similarity between pages u and v. In this study, we simply evaluate the similarity using the L2 norm between two feature vectors represented by bag of words (Zhang 2010). B is a bias vector. We use the relate score r_u as an element of B. R is repeatedly updated until it converges. α, $(0 \leq \alpha \leq 1)$ controls the balance between the similarity matrix and the bias vector. According to the literature (Jing 2008), $\alpha > 0.8$ is often used in practice. After the ranking vector R converges, pages that are related to important pages have larger ranking scores. We select the top N ranked pages as important.

2.4 Preview Achievement

By analyzing e-book operation logs, we can know how long students spend previewing each page of a given material. The previewing time period for each page can be easily acquired by subtracting two successive time stamps from the operation logs. Note that we ignored durations less than 3 seconds and more than 600 seconds to discard skipped and abandoned pages. Figure 4 shows an example of a visualized result of preview achievement. A teacher can check the preview status of given materials in advance before beginning his/her lecture.

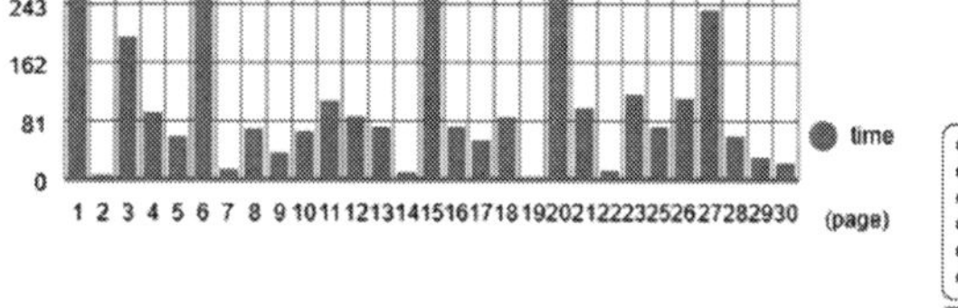

Figure 3. Example preview achievement. The horizontal axis is the page number and the vertical axis is the time spent previewing by students

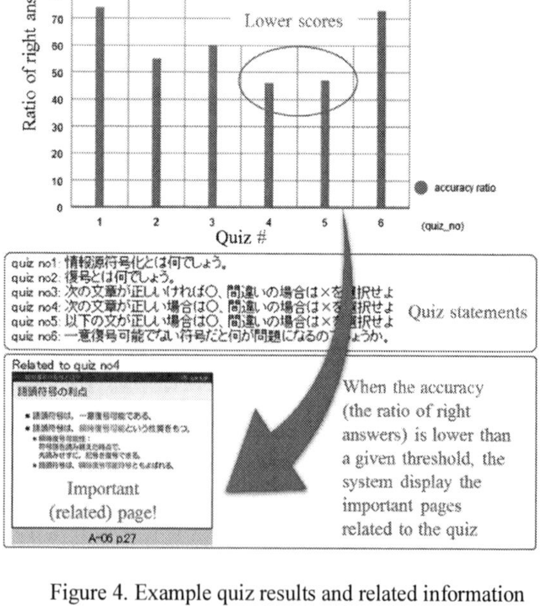

Figure 4. Example quiz results and related information

2.5 Quiz Results

The quiz results and questions are collected from the e-Learning system, and the scores are aggregated in the class. We set a threshold for the ratio of correct answers (in our implementation, we set the threshold to 50), and if the accuracy is lower than the threshold, important pages, which are automatically mined in advance, are displayed below the summary graph. See Figure 3 for an example of the web page. A summary graph of the quiz results is followed by the quiz statements, and related page information if necessary.

2.6 Visualizer on Web Pages

The proposed visualizer of the analysis results was implemented as a web system. A teacher can easily access the web page from a PC. Before the lecture starts, a teacher can access the web pages that provide summary reports of the previews of given materials and quiz results, as shown in Figure 4 and Figure 3. The teacher can check which pages were well previewed and which pages were not previewed by students using the preview achievement graph. Additionally, the teacher can check which quizzes were difficult for students, and the suggested pages that should be explained in the lecture to aid students.

During the lecture, the teacher can access to two kinds of real-time analytics graphs. One is the real-time heat map shown in Figure 5. The horizontal and vertical axes represent the time of day and the page number, respectively. In other words, a vertical line corresponds to the distribution of the number of students who are browsing each page. The vertical lines are updated each minute, i.e., a new line is added per minute. Each cell represents the number of students. The page being explained by the teacher is highlighted by red colored rectangles. If a brighter color (red, orange, yellow, or green) is used on the page being explained by the teacher, most of students are following the teacher's explanation. Students are asked to try to be on the same page as the teacher, and to add highlights or notes if necessary. Therefore, when the distribution of the students is skewed to the below direction, some students are still browsing previous pages. In such a case, the teacher should slow down the lecture so that students can catch up.

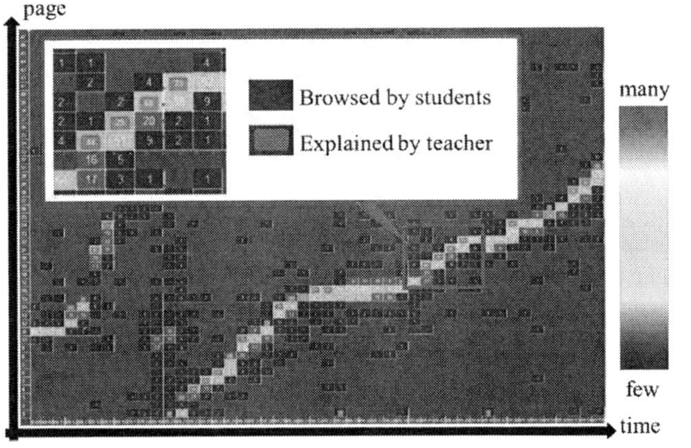

Figure 5. Real-time heat map of browsed pages. The horizontal axis is the time of day, and the vertical axis is the page number. A column corresponds to the distribution of the number of students browsing each page. The page explained by the teacher is highlighted by a red colored rectangle. The heat map is automatically updated minute-by-minute

The other real-time analytics graph is the circular chart (left part of Figure 6), which is a summarized version of above heat map. A teacher could take some time to check and understand the situation from the heat map. To just visualize a summary of the heat map, the second visual focuses on the ratio of three types of students: browsing previous pages (blue), browsing the same page as the teacher (green); and browsing the next pages (red). This chart is also updated each minute to display the latest status of students. The visualizer also provides a breakdown of the three types based on whether students previewed the page in advance (light color) or not (dark color). For example, if many students are still browsing previous pages, most of them had previewed the pages in advance, and the pages are suggested as important ones that are related to a difficult quiz, the teacher should wait for students and explain the material slowly and carefully. Another example is that a teacher should proceed with the lecture when many students are browsing the next pages, and most of them have previewed the materials in advance. In such a situation, students may have got bored during a teacher's long explanation, or some students may have finished a given exercise.

The right part of Figure 6 is a time-series of the circular chart. The teacher can see the recent trends of each status. As described above, the real-time analytics graphs provide an opportunity to flexibly adjust the lecture progress based on the statuses of students.

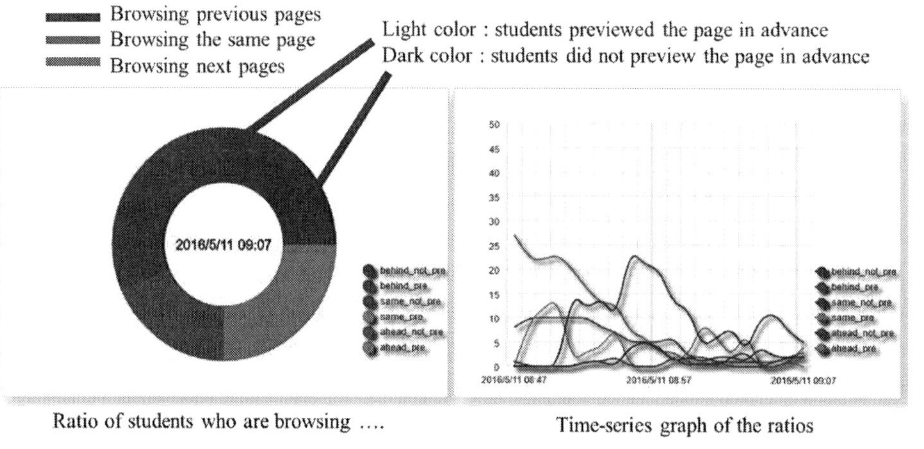

Figure 6. Real-time circular chart of student status. There are three kinds of status: browsing previous pages (blue), browsing the same page as the teacher (green), and browsing next pages (red). In each status, the system uses different brightness of colors to distinguish whether students previewed the page in advance (i.e., previewed the page before the lecture started)

3. EXPERIMENTAL RESULTS

3.1 Settings

We investigated the effectiveness of the proposed system in two classes at Kyushu University, Japan. One was a control group (N = 58) without the system, and the other was an experimental group (N = 157) with the system. The contents of two lectures are completely the same. Students chose one of them according to their schedules accordingly. Therefore, the number of students are not balanced between two classes. The class was designed to provide an introduction to information and communication technology in a number of disciplines. First-year students, including both arts and science students, attended the class, which commenced in October 2016. All of the students brought their own laptops to the class.

The lecture was given by the same teacher using the same materials. The teacher used two materials: material 1 consists of 37 pages, and material 2 consists of 47 pages. The teacher firstly began with the material 1 followed by material 2, and asked students to follow the page of materials with putting bookmarks, highlights and notes. Operation logs were sequentially collected to the server, and real-time analysis was performed. The results were fed back to the teacher minute-by-minute in the class of experimental group only. More details are summarized in Table 1. We conducted a pre-test to check the basic knowledge about information science. There was not significant difference between two groups.

Table 1. Detailed information of each group. n.s.: not significant

	control	experimental	p-value
# of students	58	157	
pre-test average	6.85±2.28	6.99±2.38	n.s.
e-Book logs	16335	39722	
logs / students	281.6±123.3	253.0±129.1	n.s.

3.2 Synchronization

When the teacher gave his lecture to students in the experimental group, he monitored the display on which real-time analysis results were drawn. He controlled the speed of lecture to make students catch up the lecture as much as possible. We evaluated the synchronization of classroom; how many students opened the pages which were explained by the teacher. We counted up the number minute-by-minute with setting allowable delay, which is a short period to accept the delay of e-Book operations.

Table 2 shows the ratio of synchronization of each group. For example, if we set the allowable delay to be 3 minutes (i.e., if students opened the same page with the teacher within 3-minute delay), the synchronization ratio of the experimental group was 0.7661. The score was significantly different from the score of the control group. In other allowable delay settings, the synchronization ratios of the experimental groups were higher than those of the control group. We consider that such high synchronization was realized by the lecture speed control through the real-time feedback of classroom activities.

Table 2. Synchronization ratio of each group in three length of allowable delay. *: p<0.05, **: p<0.01

	control	experimental	p-value
1 min.	0.4275	0.5174	0.0403 *
3 min.	0.6598	0.7661	0.0033 **
5 min.	0.7508	0.8599	0.0014 **

3.3 Effectiveness of Important Page Suggestion

The analyses of preview status and quiz scores were performed just before the lecture started. The system reported that most students wrongly answered two of eleven questions. The pages related to the quizzes (actually, the page #10 of material 1 and the page #27 of material 2) were shown on the display, and the teacher confirmed them. The teacher spent a little bit longer time for the explanation of these pages. In fact, the page #10 was opened by the teacher for 3 minutes in the experimental group, meanwhile one minute for the control group.

We analyzed the number of bookmarks, highlights and notes on the above two pages, where the teacher emphasized the explanation. About 61% of students used the functions in the experiment group. On the other hand, about 53% of the students in the control group used the functions.

In addition, we analyzed utilization ratios of three functions through the materials, and compared the ratios between two groups. Table 3 shows that more students in the experimental group used the functions compared with the students in the control group. We guess that students in the experimental group had enough time to put bookmark, highlight and/or note because the teacher emphasized the explanation about important pages with adjusting the speed of his lecture based on the real-time situation of the classroom.

Table 3. Utilization ratios of three functions during the lecture

function	control	experimental
bookmarks	0.828	0.904
highlight	0.759	0.834
note	0.293	0.471

4. CONCLUSION

We proposed a lecture supporting system based on real-time learning analytics, which is available in on-site classrooms. Our system provided summary reports of previewing and quiz scores just before a lecture had started. The report was helpful for a teacher to check which pages were well previewed and which pages were not previewed by students using the preview achievement graph. Additionally, the teacher can check which quizzes were difficult for students. Our system automatically suggested related pages that should be explained in the lecture to aid students. Furthermore, real-time analytics graphs were helpful for the teacher to control his/her lecture speed during the lecture. We conducted a case study of real-time learning analytics in our university. Through the experiments, we found out the following things. The proposed real-time learning analytics system supported the on-site lecture in terms of following aspects.

- The teacher could adjust the speed of his lecture based on the real-time feedback system.
- The teacher emphasized the important points which were mistakenly understood by the students.

As the results, the following effects were confirmed.

- The students could catch up the lecture with following pages explained by the teacher.
- Many students put bookmarks, highlights and memos on important pages.

In our future work, we will continue to use the proposed real-time learning analytics system for further evaluation. Besides, we are going to develop other report graphs which support teachers' decision in classrooms.

ACKNOWLEDGEMENT

This work was supported by JST PRESTO Grant Number JPMJPR1505, Japan.

REFERENCES

M. Khalil and M. Ebner. 2016. What is learning analytics about? A survey of different methods used in 2013-2015. *In Proceedings of Smart Learning Conference*, pp. 294-304

K. Mouri. et al, 2016. Bayesian network for predicting students' final grade using e-book logs in university education. *In IEEE International Conference on Advanced Learning Technologies(ICALT2016)*, pp. 85-89.

F. Okubo. et al, 2016. Learning activity features of high performance students. *In Cross-LAK2016.*

A. Shimada. et al, 2015. Automatic summarization of lecture slides for enhanced student preview. *In The 23rd International Conference on Computers in Education.*

A. Shimada. et al, 2016. Automatic generation of personalized review materials based on across-learning-system analysis. *In Cross-LAK2016.*

M. Minovic and M. Milovanovic, 2013. Real-time learning analytics in educational games. *the First International Conference on Technological Ecosystem for Enhancing Multiculturality*, pp.245-251.

C. Piech. et al, 2012. Modeling how students learn to program. *In Proceedings of the 43rd ACM Technical Symposium on Computer Science Education, SIGCSE'12*, pp.153-160.

X. Fu. et al, 2017. Real-time Learning Analytics for C Programming Language Courses. *The 7th International Conference on Learning Analytics & Knowledge Understanding*

A. Shimada. et al, 2017. Automatic Summarization of Lecture Slides for Enhanced Student Preview -Technical Report and User Study-. *IEEE Transactions on Learning Technologies*, Vol.PP, No.99

Y. Jing and S. Baluja, 2008. Visualrank: Applying pagerank to large-scale image search. *IEEE Transactions on Pattern Analysis and Machine Intelligence*, Vol. 30, pp.1877-1890.

Y. Zhang. et al, 2010. Understanding bag-of-words model: a statistical framework. *Int. J. Machine Learning and Cybernetics*, pp.43-52.

CHARACTERISTICS OF EFFECTIVE PEDAGOGICAL STRATEGIES FOR SELF-REGULATED LEARNING IN TECHNOLOGY-ENHANCED ENVIRONMENTS: TOWARDS IMPROVING LEARNING OUTCOME

Ian S. McGowan
University of Technology, Jamaica

ABSTRACT

The purpose of this study is to investigate the primary features of self-regulated learning (SRL) treatments and strategies employed in technology-enhanced learning environments (TELEs) that could enhance learning outcome. A total of twenty related academic articles were identified and examined for key independent SRL variable features, SRL support strategies and SRL outcomes. The findings of the study are important in terms of advising TELE educators of the existing leading SRL treatment frameworks for consideration. The results showed some of the characteristics of learning outcomes influenced by self-regulation. The results show that SRL are sometimes taught during online courses, while in other courses, the SRL are embedded inside the TELE, giving students important and timely feedback as they evaluate themselves, and learn.

KEYWORDS

e-learning, Pedagogical Strategies, Self-regulation, Metacognitive

1. INTRODUCTION

In technology enhanced learning environments (TELEs), the absence of the instructor, and the increased responsibility demanded of learners to effectively engage in learning tasks, may present difficulties for learners, particularly those with low self-regulatory (SR) skills (Shen, et al 2007).

Interest in academic SR has increased considerably in recent years as investigators and practitioners attempt to understand how students become master of their own learning processes (Artino, et al 2013). Artino also concluded that effective self-regulated learning (SRL) may be critical in distance learning situations due to the high degree of student autonomy resulting from the instructor's physical absence.

A SRL perspective on students' learning and achievement is not only distinctive, but it has profound implications for the way teachers should interact with students while teaching, and the manner in which schools should be organized in relation to course deliveries (Zimmerman, 1990).

Demand for and the technological advancements in e-learning, more-so over the past decade, have seen more universities and colleges across the globe delivering more of their courses through these modes. It is even predicted that the global demand for higher education will expand from less than 100 million students in 2000 to over 250 million students in 2025 (Unesco, 2011). A growing momentum towards open educational approaches and resources, and advances in technology-enabled learning, have resulted in the emergence of a plethora of digital platforms and portals which offer easy access to educational resources and course materials from institutions across the globe, and have allowed individuals to undertake a vast range of courses online (European Commission, 2014). Both traditional higher education institutions and new types of providers have developed or are now developing a range of online offerings spanning full degree programs, continuing professional development and shorter type courses.

As universities and colleges move more and more towards flexible mode of course deliveries, as educators come to terms with the challenges of developing courses to be taught remotely and asynchronously, and as students battle with these new modes of delivery, a study was needed in the best practices by educators that foster effective SRL (McMahon, 2012). A body of literature investigating relationships between effective SRL and positive learning outcome has reported a mix of results. Zarei, et all (2012). Pintrich et all (1990)

In this proposed contribution, we'll attempt to answer the following research questions:

What are the key features in some of the pedagogical strategies or tools that effectively support learner SRL practices in TELEs?

Is there empirical evidence that those pedagogical strategies and tools do improve student learning outcome?

2. IMPORTANCE OF PEDAGOGICAL STRATEGIES IN SRL PRACTICE

Influencing learning and academic success, the research on the concept of self-regulation emerged in the mid-1980s to answer the question, "How can students manage their own learning processes?" (Bozpolat, 2016).

Interest in academic SR has increased considerably in recent years as investigators and practitioners attempt to understand how students become masters of their learning process (Artino, et al 2013).

In Azevedo et al (2015), it was shown that understanding the acquisition, retention, use and transfer of SRL skills, is key to enhancing comprehension in science learning online. Nejabati (2015) established a significant positive relationship between EFL (English as foreign language) learners' improved reading comprehension and a prior SRL treatment.

The findings in Artino et al (2013) suggest that faculty of online courses, should design their instruction and learning requirements in a manner that helps learners not only appreciate the value or importance of content or skills, but also supports and scaffolds their attempt to master them.

Cho (2004) explained that exposing students to practice or the use of SRL skills, is not enough to promote their self-regulated learning. They need continuous interactions with peers or with instructors about their progress. Interview results from the Cho study showed that many students were not able to fully understand the purpose of SRL, and why they were doing the activities. Cho showed that interactions with others will remind them to think continuously about their activities and progresses.

Marini (2014), studying the relationship among variables associated with SRL showed that intrinsic motivation had a statistically significant association with the use of cognitive and metacognitive learning strategies. These are some of the key variables that educators must appreciate in depth in order to better support student SRL practices.

3. WHAT IS SRL?

A wide body of literature supports the notion that high achievers reported more use of SRL strategies than lower achievers. Nejobi (2015) argues that SRL has deep implications for teacher-learner interaction during course delivery.

SRL was defined by Zimmerman (1990) as the degree to which learners are meta-cognitively, motivationally and behaviorally active participants in their own learning processes.

In terms of metacognitive processes, learners plan their steps, organize themselves to follow these steps, routinely monitor and compare actual steps to planned, and self-evaluating themselves at various points. Zimmerman described motivational process as learners reporting high self-efficacy, self-attributions and intrinsic task interest.

SR students have been described as confident, autonomous, inquisitive learners who employ meta-cognitive strategies to facilitate their learning (Alraggad, 2014). Since SR is not a personality trait, students can control their behavior in order to improve their academic learning and performance.

4. METHOD

Data collection

A total of 20 academic articles relating to SRL TELEs and SRL variables were identified and considered, from which 10 were selected.

Identification procedure

The primary procedure used was a search of appropriate electronic databases to identify relevant literature (Pickering et al, 2014)

Some of the key search terms included:

"e-learning self-regulated learning"
"design in self-regulated learning e-learning"
"e-learning self-regulated learning treatment"
"e-learning self-regulated learning strategies"

Some of the electronic database searched

ACM Digital Library
Google Scholar

The secondary identification procedure used was the reference list of some of the articles found (Pickering et al 2014).

Article Inclusion Selection Procedure

The following selection criteria was applied, in keeping with the recommendation in Pickering et al (2014):

- Peer reviewed
- Applied SRL strategy related with a quantitative analysis
- Reproducible post-SRL statistical analysis

Items selected from included articles

Five (5) items were selected as data from each article. These seem best to describe and report on their chosen SRL treatment:

1. The research questions
2. The independent SRL variables being studied
3. SRL support strategies/tools
4. Details of the experiment and study group
5. SRL outcome statistical results

Table 1 shows the papers studied

Table 1. Papers studied

Paper	RQs
1. Chen, Wang, Chen (2014)	Whether the proposed Digital Reading Annotation e-Learning System (DRAS) with SRL mechanisms, can promote reading comprehension annotation abilities in individual learners?
2. Hu, Driscoll (2013)	Whether a web-based SRL strategy training will positively influence (1) achievement measured with individual assignment scores and final grade for the course (2) learner motivation in terms of task-value, self-efficacy, goal-orientation and self-satisfaction, and (3) learners' self-reported use of strategies
3. Shen et al (2007)	What are the effects of web-based problem-based learning and SRL on the development of computing skills?
4. Lawanto et al (2013)	To what degree students' grade performance change after using EGN (enhanced guided notes)? To what degree students' SRL profiles change after using the EGN?
5. Al Khatib (2010)	What is the extent to which the following variables (intrinsic goal orientation, extrinsic goal orientation, task value, control beliefs, self-efficacy, and test anxiety), account for college students' course scores?
6. Lawanto et all (2014)	What was the students' task value? and to what degree did they exercise SRL while engaged in a web-intensive engineering course? While students were engaged in a web-intensive engineering course, were there significant correlations between: -task value and learning performance -SRL and learning performance -task value and SRL What was the relative importance of task value and SRL with regard to their impact on students' learning performance?
7. Chen C. (2002)	What SRL strategies are related to achievement in a lecture learning environment in an information systems course? Does prior computer experience and software used affect achievement? What SRL strategies are related to achievement in a computer hands-on learning environment of an IS course? Does prior computer experience and software used affect achievement?
8. Zara-ee, A (2007)	What is the relationship of test takers use of cognitive and metacognitive strategies with EFL (English as a foreign language) reading test performance?
9. Cigdem, H (2015)	Is there any significant correlation between student's success and learner self-regulation, perceived usefulness, perceived satisfaction, perceived self-efficacy, perceived anxiety, and interactivity in the online learning environment?
10. Chyung et al (2010)	What levels of intrinsic motivation and self-efficacy do students have in an introductory engineering class? What role do students' intrinsic goal orientation, self-efficacy and e-learning practice play in their learning?

5. FINDINGS

Research Question 1: **What are the key features in some of the pedagogical strategies or tools that effectively support learner SRL practices in TELEs?**

Table 2 summarizes the data collected. No significant pattern emerged in terms of approaches to SRL treatment strategies applied. Motivated Strategies for Learning Questionnaire (MSLQ) was the preferred questionnaire model in 5 of the 10 studies (#2, #5, #6, #7 and #10). MSLQ (Pintrich et al, 1991) is a self-report instrument designed to assess college students' motivational orientations and their use of different learning strategies for a college course. The MSLQ has been widely adopted in studying the impacts of students' motivational orientations and use of different learning strategies on their performances (Fang, 2014).

Five of these achieved the recommended Cronbach alpha reliability score range of 0.70 – 0.90 (Santos 1999). Two of the studies (2 & 6) were above the 0.90 mark which could suggest too many or redundant (Tavakol et all 2011) SRL items. The MSLQs used in studies #2 and #6 therefore appear to be both unreliable and ineffective pedagogical tools.

Only three of the studies (#5, #7 and #9), used a sample size of 100 or higher as suggested by Santos for the SRL questionnaires to be useful.

From table 3 which highlights the focus SRL variables of the studies, we can see that among the most included are self-efficacy (#5, #9 and #10), intrinsic goal orientation (#2, #5 and #10), learning time (#1, #6 and #7), and metacognitive SR (#5, #7 and #8), each appearing in three of the ten studies. This suggests any pedagogical strategy to support SRL practices by the learner, should include all four SRL components at the minimum.

Learning time was used in study #6 as part of the study's performance control strategy. It measured how students' allocate study time for online courses, how they schedule and observe study times, and how they distribute study times across days (MSLQ e.g. "I try to schedule the same time every day or week to study for my online courses, and I observe my schedule").

In study #1, learning time was used a SRL competence measure index, and a factor in a SRL status indicator to help remind and motivate the learner during the course. Used as a part of resource management strategies in study #7, learning time measured use of study time, sticking to a study schedule, keeping up regularly, tardiness in attending class, and time to review course material (MSLQ e.g. "I find it hard to stick to a study schedule", "I rarely find time to review my notes or readings before an exam").

Self-efficacy (SE) is defined as people's beliefs about their capabilities to produce designated levels of performance that exercise influence over events that affect their lives (Bandura, A. 1997). SE beliefs determine how people feel, think, motivate themselves and behave.

Self-efficacy (SE) in study #5 measured the extent to which students believed that were competent in terms in terms of task-related abilities and skills, and had a high likelihood of a successful academic performance (e.g. "I believe I will receive an excellent grade in this class").

Study #9 concluded that learners who were more satisfied with the online mode of blended learning, and found it is more interactive and useful, reported a higher level of self-regulation in online mode of the blended Computer Programming course. SE in study #9 measured students' confidence levels using a course portal, perceived satisfaction, perceived usefulness, and interactivity in the online learning environment.

In study #10, SE measured students' confidence levels in learning and performance at the end of an introductory engineering class (e.g. "I'm certain I can understand the most difficult material presented in the readings for this course.", " I'm confident I can understand the basic concepts taught in this course").

Intrinsic goal orientation (IGO) refers to the drive inherent in an activity itself, as when the student engages in an activity for its own sake, the enjoyment it provides, the learning it permits, or the feelings of accomplishment it evokes (Khatib, 2010).

IGO in study #5 was used to assess the degree to which learners perceived themselves to be engaged in academic tasks in order to meet a personal challenge, satisfy personal curiosity, and/or attain personal mastery over the elements of the task (e.g. "In a class like this, I prefer course material that arouses my curiosity, even if it is difficult to learn").

In study #10, IGO was used to measure how students perceive themselves to be participating in a task for reasons such as challenge, curiosity, and mastery (e.g. "In a class like this, I prefer course material that really challenges me so I can learn new things. ", "The most satisfying thing for me in this course is trying to understand the content as thoroughly as possible", "When I have the opportunity in this class, I choose course assignments that I can learn from even if they don't guarantee a good grade").

Table 2. Features of the SRL treatments applied

Paper	1	2	3	4	5	6	7	8	9	10
SRL embedded into the TELE	√									
n										
1 – 20		√								
21 – 39	√							√		
40 – 79			√			√				√
80 – 129				√						
130 – 149										
150 – 199							√			
≥ 200					√				√	
SRL q'nnaire										
MSLQ										
Pintrich, 1991		√			√	√ √	√			√
Butler, 2004				√						
Barnard, 2008						√				
Purpura, 1999								√		
Alpha coefficient										
0.50 – 0.59										
0.60 – 0.69										
0.70 – 0.79										
0.80 – 0.89		√		√	√	√				√
0.90									√	
0.91 – 0.99		√ √				√				
Likert scale										
1 – 4				√						
1 – 5		√				√		√		
1 – 6										
1 – 7						√	√		√	√
Item count										
1 – 20						√ √				√
21 – 39						√		√	√	
40 – 59					√		√			
60 – 100		√								
BEFORE COURSE										
Admin SQL q'nnaire				√	√			√	√	
DURING COURSE										
Admin SRL q'nnaire		√					√			
Taught SRL	√	√	√							
Allowed SRL practice	√	√	√							
AT END OF COURSE										
Admin SRL q'nnaire		√		√		√				√

Table 3. SRL variables used

	Paper									
SRL Variables	1	2	3	4	5	6	7	8	9	10
Cognitive strategies								√		
Concentrated learning	√									
Control beliefs					√					
Effort for learning courseware	√						√			
e-learning practice										√
Environment structuring						√	√			
Extrinsic goal orientation		√			√					
Goal seeking						√				
Help seeking						√	√			
Importance						√				
Interactively in the on-line									√	
learning environment										
Interest						√				
Intrinsic goal orientation		√			√					√
Learning time	√					√	√			
Metacognitive SR					√		√	√		
Monitoring Strategies				√						
Peer learning							√			
Perceived anxiety					√				√	
Perceived satisfaction									√	
Perceived usefulness									√	
Planning Strategies				√						
Prior computer experience							√			
Problem-based learning			√							
Reading rate	√									
Regulatory Strategies				√						
Reported Use of Strategies		√								
Self-efficacy					√				√	√
Self-evaluation						√				
Self-Satisfaction		√								
Software used							√			
SRL			√						√	
Task strategies						√				
Task Value		√			√					
Utility						√				

The findings by Pintrich et all (1990), that *meta-cognitive self-regulation* (mCSR) was the best predictor of academic performance on all the outcome measures, suggests that the use of self-regulating strategies, such as comprehension monitoring, goal setting, planning, and effort management and persistence, is essential for academic performance on different types of actual classroom tasks.

mCSR in study #5 was one of the predictors of college students' academic performance, and was used to assess the degree to which the students monitor and regulate their use of cognitive state (e.g. "when I become confused about something I'm reading for this class, I go back and try to figure it out").

mCSR is study #7 was used to measure how students handle challenging new topics while being delivered in class and studied, how students handle distractions or being confused, and how they use goals in studying.

Research Question 2: **Is there empirical evidence that those pedagogical strategies and tools do improve student learning outcome?**

Table 4. Summarised Statistical Overall Learning Outcome Results

			Mean Test Scores					
			Control	Exprmnt				
Study	*n*	Assessment	Group	Group	*t*	*p*	sig	r^2
1	32/32	Reading	45.31	60.63	-2.5840		0.0120	
			45.00	56.72	-2.4730		0.0160	
			47.34	62.19	-2.7020		0.0090	
		Annotation	14.34	34.53	-4.4020		0.0000	
			14.16	27.28	-3.0380		0.0040	
			16.41	27.94	-2.6400		0.1000	
2	13/8	Test	85.92	91.13		< 0.05		0.5100
		Paper	58.38	87.63		< 0.05		0.4800
		Final Exam	83.77	89.13		< 0.05		0.4800
3	52/54	MS-Word	58.21	63.11	2.0180	0.0460		
4	97	Exams 1/2			-7.9700	0.0000		
		Exams 2/3			-4.1300	0.0000		
		Exams 3/Final			5.0300	0.0000		
5	404	Final Exam				< 0.001		0.4050
6	57	Final Exam				0.0040		0.3710
7	197	Test				< 0.000		0.2290
8	30	Test					0.0340	0.3880
							0.5000	0.1280
9	267					< 0.005		
10	50	Test				0.0070		0.2400

Table 4 shows overall learning outcome performance statistically for each of the studies.

Study #1 shows significant better leaner performance in the mean test scores by the experiment group over the control group (Reading Test #1 – 45.31/60.63, #2 – 45.00/56.72 and Test #3 – 47.34/62.19 . Annotation scores at p = 0.0000 appears very significant. *n* is small at 32, but both groups were randomly assigned (Cohen et al 2005). These results suggest the results could be repeated using the same pedagogical strategies for another English-Language reading group. In this study, the SRL components were embedded in the TELe. The participants received regular SRL performance feedback during the course.

With $n = 97$ engineering students (selected by survey results, not at random), study #4 showed statistical very significant ($p = 0.000$) improved performances exam to exam (t = -7.79 and -4.13). The final exam (at t = 5.03) performance fell however.

In Study #5 40% of the test scores were predicted with a 95% confidence level and strong *p* below 0.001. *n* at 404 represented 100% coverage over five general education courses. Perhaps providing written procedural instructions and the purpose of the study to the participants contributed to the strong level of performances. In keeping with Cohen et at (2005) we could expect a repeat of these results over another large population using the same pedagogical strategies for the same courses.

Study #8 resulted with only 39% of the final exam scores explained by the cognitive strategies with low significance of 0.03, and 12% of the final exam scores explained by the meta-cognitive strategies with non-significance of 0.50. Study #8 used only the two SRL variables. Perhaps the inclusion of at least one more key variable would have strengthened the learner performance outcomes.

6. DISCUSSION

The findings of this study are important in terms of advising TELE educators on some of the existing leading SRL treatment frameworks for consideration. Previous studies on individual SRL treatment strategies to improve learning outcome, show how SRL treatments are applicable across many academic subject areas focusing on particular SRL variables and features.

Research also has shown that SRL skills need to be adopted in formal e-learning coursework as cognitive toolsets (Leacock et al 2006). This study provides educators with some of the key elements of established cognitive toolsets and stages in an e-learning course that could be applied.

Our analysis of ten studies showed some of the SRL treatment and strategy frameworks adapted by researchers in teaching cognitive skills in experiment. The features of the frameworks included the use and structure of SRL knowledge acquisition questionnaires, administering the questionnaires before, during and at the end of the courses, teaching SRL early in a course and allowing students to practice SRL during a course.

The data analysis in this study showed the sets of SRL variables considered crucial by researchers. From the statistical results provided, we later identified the four strongest variables.

Zumbrum et al (2011) found that learners who were taught SRL skills through monitoring and imitation, were more likely to elicit higher levels of academic self-efficacy (i.e. confidence). Code et al (2006) argued that intrinsic goal orientation provides students with a sense of control and resilience in the face of external challenges.

Based on the results of this study, and considering some of the strengths and weaknesses of the ten studies, we could recommend a pedagogical strategy to promote SRL practice among students in a TELe to include:

- Preparing a 21-39 item MSLQ questionnaire adapted from Pintrich (1991) to include subscales self-efficacy, intrinsic goal orientation, meta-cognitive self-regulation and time management at the minimum
- Administering the MSLQ at the beginning of course
- Preparing and delivering SRL workshops during the course based on the responses from the MSLQ
- Allowing the students to practice SRL during the course
- Administering the same questionnaire at the end of the course to assess the SRL behavioral changes

7. CONCLUSION

The main contribution of the present study was to investigate the primary features of the self-regulated learning treatments and strategies employed in TELEs that could enhance learning outcome. The results showed the characteristics in summary, of the SRL treatments and strategies that were investigated. The characteristics of and use of SRL knowledge questionnaires, how and when they are administered, where provided. The results showed that SRL are sometimes taught during a course, while another course embedded the SRL inside the TELE giving the students important feedback as they learn and evaluate themselves. The results also showed the focus SRL variables used in the studies, and how wide and indifferent there were. Some of the variables however where shown to be similar among the studies and formed the basis of consensus that the four variable identified are among the strongest that could best lead to improved learning outcome, if taught well to the students. The statistical results in provided in the studies confirmed the consensus, about which needs further analysis for future work.

ACKNOWLEDGMENT

This research was undertaken as part of the PhD in E-research and Technology Enhanced Learning in the Department of Educational Research at Lancaster University. I am pleased to acknowledge the contribution of tutors and peers in supporting the development of this study and its report as an assignment paper.

REFERENCES

Al Khatib, S. A. (2010). Meta-cognitive self-regulated learning and motivational beliefs as predictors of college students' performance. *International Journal for Research in Education*

Alraggad, F. E. A, Abou-Ameerh, O. A., Al-Sabeelah, A. M. S. (2014). Investigation the Relationshibetween Goal Orientation and Self-Regulated Learning among Sample Jordanian University Students. *Journal of Education and Practice*

Artino Jr, A. R. & Stephens, J. M. (2013). Learning Online: Motivated to Self-Regulate? *www.sp.uconn.edu*

Azevedo, R., Johnson, A., Burkett, C. (2015). Does Training of Cognitive and Metacognitive Regulatory Processes Enhance Learning and Deployment of Processes with Hypermedia? *mindmodeling.org/cogsci2015/papers*

Bandura, A. (1997). Self-efficacy: The exercise of control. New York: *W.H. Freeman.*

Bozpolat, E. (2016). Investigation of the self-regulated learning strategies of students from the faculty of education using ordinal logistic regression analysis. *Educational Sciences: Theory & Practice*

Chen, C. S. (2002). Self-regulated learning strategies and achievement in an introduction to Information Technology. *Learning, and Performance Journal*

Chen, C. M., Wang, J. Y., Chen, Y. C. (2014). Facilitating English-Language Reading Performance by a Digital Reading Annotation System with Self-Regulated Learning Mechanisms. *Educational Technology & Society*

Cho, M. (2004). The Effects of Design Strategies for Promoting Students' Self-regulated Learning Skills on Students' Self-Regulation and Achievements in Online Learning Environments. *eric.ed.gov*

Chyung, S. Y., Moll, A. J., Berg, S. A. (2010). The Role of Intrinsic Goal Orientation, Self-Efficacy, and E-Learning Practice in Engineering Education. *The Journal of Effective Teaching*

Cigdem, H. (2015). How Does Self-Regulation Affect Computer-Programming Achievement in a Blended Context? *Contemporary Educational Technology*

Code, J. R., MacAllister, K., Gress, C. L. Z., Nesbit, J. C. (2006). Self-Regulated Learning, Motivation and Goal Theory: Implications for Instructional Design and E-Learning. *Sixth International Conference on Advanced Learning Technologies (ICALT'06)*

Cohen, L., Manion, L., Morrison, K. (2005). Research methods in education (5th ed.). *Taylor & Francis e-Library*

da Silva Marini, J. A., Boruchovitch, E. (2014). Self-Regulated Learning in Students of Pedagogy *Paidéia*

European Commission, 2014. Report to the European Commission on new modes of learning and teaching in higher education.

Fang, N (2014). Correlation between students' motivated strategies for learning and academic achievement in an engineering dynamics course. *Global Journal of Engineering Education*

Hu, H. & Driscoll, M. P. (2013). Self-Regulation in e-Learning Environments: A Remedy for Community College. *Educational Technology & Society*

Lawanto, D. & Santoso, H. (2013). Self-Regulated Learning Strategies of Engineering College Students While Learning Electric Circuit Concepts with Enhanced Guided Notes. *International Education Studies*

Lawanto, O., Santoso, H. B., Goodridge, W., Lawanto, K. N. (2014). Task Value, Self-Regulated Learning, and Performance in a Web-Intensive Undergraduate Engineering Course: How Are They Related? *MERLOT Journal of Online Learning and Teaching*

Leacock, T. L. & Nesbit, J. C. (2006). Cognitive tools for self-regulated e-learning. Making the Transition to E-learning: Strategies and Issues. *Hershey, PA: Information Science Publishing.*

McMahon, M. & Oliver, R. (2012). Promoting Self-Regulated Learning in an On-Line Environment

Nejabati, N. (2015). The Effects of Teaching Self-regulated Learning Strategies on EFL Students' Reading Comprehension. *Journal of Language Teaching and Research*

Pickering, C. & Bryne J. (2013). The Benefits of publishing systematic quantitative literature reviews for PhD candidates and other early-career researchers. *Higher Education Research & Development*

Pintrich, P. R., Smith, D. A. F., Garcia, T., McKeachie, W. J. (1991). A manual for the use of Motivated Strategies for Learning Questionnaire (MSLQ). *University of Michigan, National Center for Research to Improve Postsecondary Teaching and Learning*

Pintrich, P. R. & Elisabeth V. De Groot, E. V. (1990). Motivational and Self-Regulated Learning Components of Classroom Academic Performance. *Journal of Educational Psychology.*

Shen, P., Lee, T., Tsai, C. (2007). Applying Web-Enabled Problem-Based Learning and Self-Regulated Learning to Enhance Computing Skills of Taiwan's Vocational Students: a Quasi-Experimental Study of a Short-Term Module. *Electronic Journal of e-Learning*

Tavakol, M. & Dennick, R. (2011). Making sense of Cronbach's alpha. *International Journal of Medical Education*

UNESCO. Rankings and Accountability in Higher Education: Uses and Misuses. *UNESCO Global Forum, Ma 2011.* http://unesdoc.unesco.org/images/0019/001924/192417m.pdf

Zarei, A. A. & Hatami, G (2012). On the Relationship between Self-regulated Learning Components and L2 Vocabulary. *Knowledge and Reading Comprehension.*

Zare-ee, A. (2007). The Relationship between Cognitive and Meta-cognitive Strategy use and EFL Reading Achievement. *Journal of Applied Psychology*

Zimmerman, B. J. (1990). Self-Regulated Learning and Academic Achievement: An Overview. *Educational Psychologist*

Zumbrunn, S., Tadlock, J., Roberts, E. D. (2011). Encouraging Self-Regulated Learning in the Classroom: A Review of the Literature. *Metropolitan Educational Research Consortium (MERC)*

PSEUDO-HAPTIC FEEDBACK FOR PROMOTING NARRATIVE COMPREHENSION

Kazuaki Umetsu and Akihiro Kashihara
Graduate School of Informatics and Engineering, The University of Electro-Communications
1-5-1, Chofugaoka, Chofu, Tokyo, 182-8585, Japan

ABSTRACT

Skill in reading comprehension requires reading sentences to understand an intention embedded between the lines. In the case of narrative, it is particularly necessary to read a narrative and find essential concepts such as emotions of the characters embedded between the lines for comprehending an intention of the narrative. In this work, we focus on reading between the lines and to require learners to compose a narrative map including a concept (called interlinear concept) between the lines, which is related to the narrative intention. We also demonstrate a tablet tool, which allows learners to compose a narrative map including interlinear concept from narrative. This tool presents pseudo-haptic feedback when learners operate the nodes and links representing the interlinear concept and narrative intention on the map. The results of a case study suggest that the pseudo-haptic feedback could enhance awareness of the interlinear concept and narrative intention.

KEYWORDS

Narrative, Narrative map, Pseudo-haptic feedback, Tablet media

1. INTRODUCTION

OECD (Organization for Economic Co-operation and Development)'s PISA survey pointed out the decline of Japanese reading comprehension (Ministry of education 2005). In particular, it showed that Japanese children were weak in reading sentences to understand an intention embedded between the lines. In particular, they seem to have difficulties in finding essentials embedded in sentences, which allow them to understand it. In the case of explanatory text, such essentials are clearly described in the text. But, these are embedded in the case of narrative. It is accordingly necessary to read narrative and find essential concepts such as background and emotions of the characters embedded between the lines for comprehending an intention of the narrative.

The main issue addressed here is how to help learners find essential concepts embedded in narrative to understand an intention of the narrative. Our approach to this issue is to focus on reading between the lines and to require learners to compose a concept map including the essential concepts. In concept map composition, learners are expected to make links among nodes indicating the concepts represented in the narrative. It accordingly allows them to make clear the relationships between the concepts and to promote understanding the narrative.

We have developed a tablet tool that scaffolds composing a concept map from a narrative. In this tool, learners are expected to read the narrative sentences to link the nodes prepared in advance according to the contents of the narrative. If the composed map is not correct, they are also expected to re-read the sentences to re-compose the map until the correct map is obtained.

Although such concept map composition is useful for understanding the contents of narrative, an essential concept embedded between the lines is often missing on the map. Our approach to this is to propose a narrative map including a concept (called interlinear concept) between the lines, which is related to the narrative intention. In addition, the intention of narrative varies with viewpoints of the readers. In this work, the tablet tool provides learners with a viewpoint before composing a narrative map so that the intention of the narrative can be uniquely decided. The tablet tool also presents an interlinear concept for the narrative map composition, which serves as a clue for comprehending the intention of the narrative.

In composing such a narrative map, in addition, it is not so easy particularly for learners with lower reading comprehension skill to become aware of the interlinear concept and the intention of narrative. We accordingly propose a method for presenting pseudo-haptic feedback when learners operate nodes/links representing the interlinear concept and the narrative intention. In this paper, we demonstrate the tablet tool with pseudo-haptic feedback. We also report a case study whose results suggest it could enhance awareness of the interlinear concept and narrative intention.

2. NARRATIVE UNDERSTANDING

In understanding a narrative, it is important to draw out the narrative intention as learning of linguistic culture (Ministry of education 2009). It is also necessary to infer the emotions of the characters and the atmosphere embedded between the lines. However, it requires a deeper understanding of the narrative including the intention of the author and the interlinear concept. Even though learners could grasp the contents of the story, it is not easy to obtain such deeper understanding. In this work, we focus on how to help learners read between the lines in narrative, which is essential in narrative comprehension.

3. NARRATIVE MAP

In order to promote understanding narrative, we introduce a concept map representing concepts appearing in the narrative and their relationships. The concept map visually represents the structure of the sentences with nodes as concepts and links as the relationships between the concepts. Composing such a map makes it possible to clarify the relationships and to promote understanding of the sentences. In the narrative comprehension, however, it is important to comprehend the intention of narrative embedded in the sentences. In general, information such as emotion and background embedded between the lines is not represented in the map.

We accordingly propose a narrative map, which includes the interlinear concept in addition to the concepts clearly described in the narrative. The interlinear concept affords a clue to grasp the narrative intention. In composing such narrative map in concurrent with reading the narrative, learners are expected to become aware of the interlinear concept and the narrative intention. Since the intention of narrative could be interpreted differently depending on viewpoints of the readers, in addition, we give learners one viewpoint so that an intention can be given.

Let us demonstrate narrative map composition with Figure 1. Figure 1 (A) shows a part of narrative sentences, which corresponds to a paragraph on *"Ozbel and the Elephant"* (Kenji Miyazawa,1989). Figure1 (B) shows a narrative map to be composed from Figure 1 (A) with 9 nodes and 11 links. Links are expressed with labels such as "action", "casual", "object" and "state".

In this narrative, *white elephants laughed with lonesome*. However, the reason why *white elephant laughed with lonesome* isn't described, which is an important interlinear concept in this narrative. We accordingly give learners a viewpoint of the narrative such as "consider why *white elephant laughed with lonesome*?" before starting map composition. This viewpoint could allow learners to become aware that a feeling of guilty that is caused by "*crushing the master Ozbel*". The feeling of guilty is viewed as an interlinear concept.

In Figure 1 (B), this is represented with the relationships among the nodes "*white elephant*", "*feel guilty*", and " *laugh with lonesome*", and the causal relationship between the nodes "*crush*" and "*feel guilty*". The node "*feel guilty*" represents the interlinear concept. An intention of the narrative can be interpreted as "killing the master produces feel guilty", which is expressed as a partial of the narrative map shown in Figure 1 (B).

In this work, we prepare and present some concepts according to the sentences and an interlinear concept as nodes in advance, then require learners to compose a narrative map in concurrent with reading the sentences. However, all nodes have no visual differences.

Although learners with high reading comprehension skill are expected to correctly understand the intention of narrative while linking the interlinear concept and other concepts, it is not so easy particularly for learners with low skill to become aware of the interlinear concept node and the partial structure representing the narrative intention. In order to address this issue, we introduce pseudo-haptic feedback into the narrative map composition process. Pseudo-haptic feedback could promote such cognitive awareness to bring about understanding of the narrative intention (Kashihara and Shiota 2014).

> .
> .
> .
>
> Ozbel was already crushed while holding the case of the gun.
> As soon as the gate opens, the elephant pours. "Where is the prison?" Everyone rushes into the cabin. The logs were folded like a match, that white elephant ran out of the hut badly. "Well, I'm glad, did not you?" Everyone quietly removed the chain and copper. "Oh, thank you, I was saved." White elephant laughed with lonesome.

(A) A Paragraph on *"Ozbel and the Elephant"* (Kenji Miyazawa,1989)"

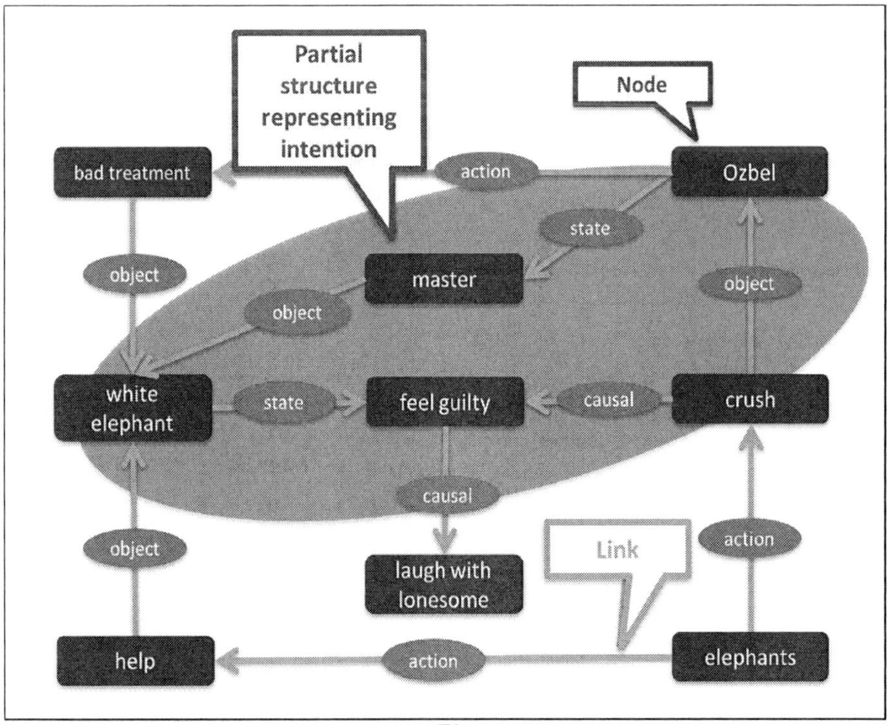

(B)

Figure 1. A narrative map of *"Ozbel and the Elephant" (Kenji Miyazawa,1989)*

4. PSEUDO-HAPTIC

Pseudo-haptic is illusion about tactile sense caused by uncomfortable feeling between physical manipulation of an object and its visual movement. While moving an object on a tablet with finger, for example, learners can get a feeling that the object is heavy as the movement of the object slows down (Lecuyer 2009). We have already ascertained that pseudo-haptic feedback for manipulating a concept map representing knowledge learned from an instructional text could promote an awareness of important concepts or important relationships embedded in the text (Kashihara and Shiota 2015).

In this paper, we introduce pseudo-haptics into the narrative map composition. Learners are provided with pseudo-haptic feedback as shown in Table 1. Let us consider the first feedback shown in Table 1 with Figure 2. When a learner touch-operates a node representing interlinear concept such as *feel guilty*, it moves with a delay in comparison with the touch operation. The visual movement represents heaviness of the node as the pseudo-haptic feedback. It expects learners to explore into the text the reason why the pseudo-haptic feedback occurs. Such exploration brings about cognitive awareness that the node represents an interlinear concept.

In addition, let us also consider the second feedback shown in Table 1 with Figure 3. When a learner moves a node linking another node, the link usually lengthens or shortens according to the positions of the nodes. When the learner moves a node belonging to the partial structure representing the narrative intention, all the nodes and links included in the partial structure move accordingly without shortening/lengthening the links. In other words, all the nodes representing the intention move together. This visual movement represents hardness of the links as the pseudo-haptic feedback. It also expects learners to explore the reason in the text to become aware that the partial structure represents the narrative intention.

Table 1. Pseudo-haptic feedback from operation

Operation on narrative map	**Pseudo-haptic feedback**	**Cognitive awareness**
Interlinear node operation	Node heaviness	Interlinear concept
Operating nodes belonging to the partial structure representing the narrative intention	Link hardness	Intention of narrative

Figure 2. Example of pseudo-haptics for "node heaviness"

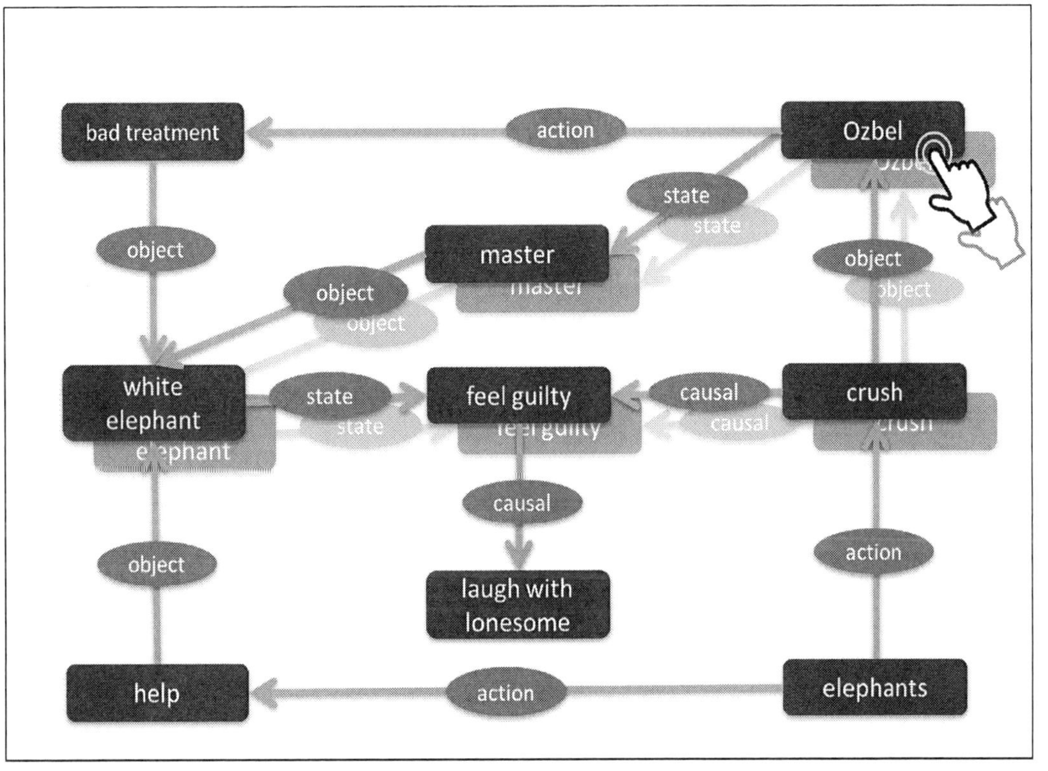

Figure 3. Example of pseudo-haptics for "link hardness"

5. TABLET TOOL

We have developed a tablet tool on iPad, which provides learners with pseudo-haptic feedback according to Table 1. Figure 4 shows the user interface of the tool. Let us here describe the framework of the tool, the narrative map composition on the tool, and the learning process expected.

5.1 Framework

This tool prepares a narrative text and the corresponding correct narrative map including an interlinear concept and the intention embedded in the text. On the left pane of the interface, the tool displays the text. On the right pane, the tool provides a space for narrative map composition. As the initial setting, the tool put the nodes on this pane, which represent the interlinear concept and the concepts used in the narrative text.

Before the narrative map composition, the tool presents a viewpoint of the narrative at the top pane of the interface. The learners are then required to follow the viewpoint to read the text and compose a narrative map corresponding to the correct map. The correct relationships among the nodes are defined in the tool. When the learners move the nodes that embed the pseudo-haptic feedback, they are provided with the corresponding feedback according to Table 1. They are then expected to explore into the text the reason why the visual movement defined by the pseudo-haptic feedback occurs. Such exploration brings about cognitive awareness expected by the feedback. When learners complete the map, they can check the correctness by pushing the "Answer" button.

5.2 Map Operations

This tool provides learners with the touch operations: node movement, link generation/deletion, and attachment/change of link labels. The learners can touch and drag the node with fingers they want to move. Link generation is operated by tap and draw. The learners can tap a node to become the starting point of the link. They can then draw the link to another node. Change of link label is operated by tap. The learners can tap a label to change and select one of 4 types of labels "action", "casual", "object" and "state". Link deletion is operated by long tap. The learners can do long press on the links they want to delete.

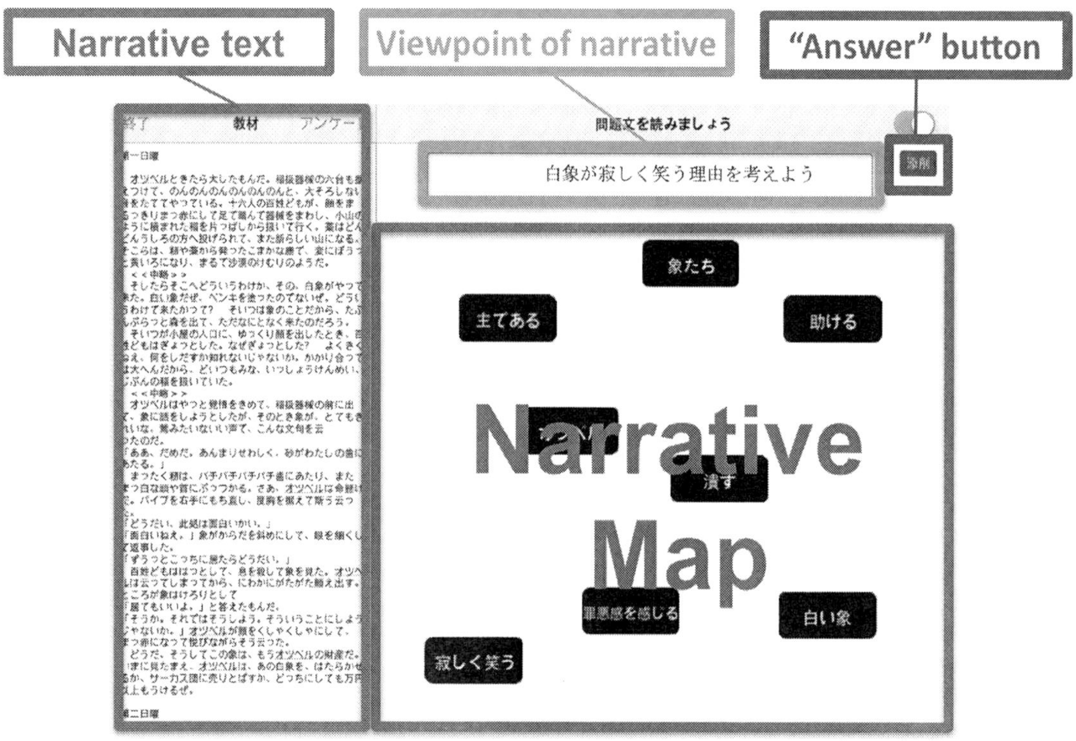

Figure 4. User interface

6. CASE STUDY

6.1 Purpose and Procedure

We have had a case study whose purpose was to ascertain whether the tablet tool could provide pseudo-haptic sense and cognitive awareness as shown in Table 1 compared to narrative map composition only with touch operation (without pseudo-haptic feedback). In order to allow the participants to compose a narrative map without pseudo-haptics, we prepared the control tool that removed the function of demonstrating the visual movements for the pseudo-haptics from the tablet tool. The participants were 6 graduate and undergraduate students in science and engineering. We set two conditions, which were (a) narrative map composition with the tablet tool (PseudoHaptic-group), and (b) narrative map composition with the control tool (Visual-group). We assigned 3 participants per condition.

In this case study, all participants were required to read a narrative text *"Ozbel and the Elephant"* (Kenji Miyazawa,1926), and to compose a narrative map with the tool. After map composition, they were required to refer to their composed map and to answer the questionnaire about pseudo-haptic sense and cognitive awareness brought about by pseudo-haptic feedback.

In order to evaluate the effects of the table tool, we compared the results of the questionnaire. The questionnaire included the following four questions:

(1) Select the nodes that felt important from the composed map
(2) Select the nodes included the part that felt an intention of the narrative from the composed map
(3) Select the node that felt heavy from the composed map
(4) Select the links in which you felt hard from the composed map

We used the answers to these questions to analyze.

6.2 Results and Consideration

Table 2 shows the results of the questionnaire. Node importance shows whether the node corresponding to the interlinear concept "*feel guilty*" felt important. Partial structure representing the intention shows how many nodes included in it felt representative of the narrative intention. Node heaviness shows whether the node corresponding to the interlinear concept felt heavy. Link hardness also shows how many links in the partial structure felt hard.

The results suggest that both group obtained almost the same cognitive awareness about the interlinear concept and narrative intention. As for PseudoHaptic-group, on the other hand, the participants obtained less pseudo-haptic sense about node heaviness, although the participant B obtained cognitive awareness of the interlinear concept.

Table 2. Cognitive awareness brought by presentation of pseudo-haptic and Awareness of presentation of pseudo-haptic

		(1)Node importance	(2)Partial structure representing the intention	(3)Node heaviness	(4)Link hardness
PseudoHaptic-group	A	incorrect	3 correct nodes	incorrect	2 correct links
	B	correct	4 correct nodes	incorrect	3 correct links
	C	correct	4 correct nodes	correct	5 correct links
Visual-group	D	correct	5 correct nodes	n.a	n.a
	E	correct	4 correct nodes	n.a	n.a
	F	correct	4 correct nodes	n.a	n.a

7. CONCLUSION

This paper has described the narrative map composition with pseudo-haptic feedback, which promotes the understanding the narrative intention. We have also demonstrated a narrative map generation tool on iPad, which could produce pseudo-haptic feedback such as heaviness and hardness on touch operations. The results of the preliminary case study suggest the possibility that the tablet tool could provide cognitive awareness of interlinear concept and narrative intention. However, the results also suggest we need to modify the pseudo-haptic feedback so that learners can obtain the pseudo-haptic sense in addition to cognitive awareness.

In future, we need to reconsider the method of pseudo-haptic feedback, and must have case studies with more subjects to evaluate the possibility of pseudo-haptic feedback. In addition, we will check whether the tablet tool can promote narrative intention understanding.

ACKNOWLEDGEMENT

This work was in part supported by JSPS KAKENHI Grand Number 15K12408 and 17H01992.

REFERENCES

Ministry of education(2005), "Reading Comprehension Program", available at: www.mext.go.jp/a_menu/shotou/gakuryoku/siryo/05122201/014/005.htm (accessed 3 Jane 2017).

Ministry of education(2009), "Course of guidance 'Living power'", available at: http://www.mext.go.jp/a_menu/shotou/new-cs/youryou/chu/koku.htm (accessed 3 Jane 2017).

Kashihara, A., Shiota, G.: Knowledge Construction with Pseudo-Haptics, Proc of ITS2014, LNCS 8474, Springer, pp.61-68, Hawaii, U.S.A. (2014).

Kashihara, A., Shiota, G.: Knowledge Construction with Visual and Pseudo-Haptic Senses, IEICE transaction, Vol.J98-D, No1, pp.104-116, 2015.01, in Japanese.

Kenji, M. (1989), Ozbel and elephant.

Lecuyer, A.: Simulating Haptic Feedback Using Vision: a Survey of Research and Applica- tions of Pseudo-Haptic Feedback, Teleoperators and Virtual Environments, Vol.18, No.1, pp.39-53, MIT Press, 2009

Short Papers

DEVELOPMENT OF A SUPPORT APPLICATION AND A TEXTBOOK FOR PRACTICING FACIAL EXPRESSION DETECTION FOR STUDENTS WITH VISUAL IMPAIRMENT

Hirotaka Saito*, Akinobu Ando*, Shota Itagaki**, Taku Kawada**,
Darold Davis*** and Nobuyuki Nagai*
**Miyagi University of Education, 149 Aramaki,aza-Aoba, Aoba-ku,Sendai, Miyagi, Japan*
***Tohoku University, 6-3-9 Aramaki,aza-Aoba,Aoba-ku, Sendai, Miyagi, Japan*
****Replicant AD, LLC, 535 Liberty Street, Apt. 302, El Cerrito, CA 94530, USA*

ABSTRACT

Until now, when practicing facial expression recognition skills in nonverbal communication areas of SST, judgment of facial expression was not quantitative because the subjects of SST were judged by teachers. Therefore, we thought whether SST could be performed using facial expression detection devices that can quantitatively measure facial expressions. In this research, we developed an application software using a facial expression recognition device connected to a smartphone and a practice book. With opening the book, one situation is described. A student makes a facial expression as he/she thinks is best. Our application judge's the expression and gives feedback of whether it is proper or not. A total of 28 students practiced it at two visual support schools and a class guidance classroom. As a result, all of the students were able to repeatedly make their intended face expression each time they tried. And from the observations and interviews with the students, we found the students were pleased and proud with the result.

KEYWORDS

Special support education, SST, Facial expression recognition, Facial expression practice

1. INTRODUCTION

Today it is known that utilizing ICT equipment in special support education can be expected to have educational benefits such as improving learning or living difficulties of students with disabilities and leading to active social participation. According to a survey conducted by Miyagi University of Education on the status of ICT equipment usage in classrooms targeting students with developmental disabilities, there are 55% of classes utilizing PCs, with more than half found to be teaching using PCs. However according to the survey on usage, it turned out that it was used in 88% of "support of study subjects", 31% by "school life support" and 26% by "information sharing". For this reason, PC usage in special support services in resource rooms are mostly occupied by utilization in the support of subjects of learning, and there are present circumstances that utilization in support of school life is not yet popular. According to the survey results on the actual state of educational information at schools conducted by the Ministry of Education, Culture, Sports, Science and Technology, the average WLAN maintenance rate in ordinary classrooms is 26.1% nationwide. It was also revealed that the WLAN is not maintained in the ordinary classroom at the rate of 3 out of 4 schools, and the application that requires communication with tablet terminals etc. cannot be utilized.

Additionally, in the field of special support education, SST (social skill training) is being implemented as support for this school life. According to Onuki et al. (2004), the area of SST can be divided into 5 areas, 17 skills. Until now, when practicing facial expression recognition skills in nonverbal communication areas of SST, judgment of facial expression was not quantitative because the subjects in SST were judged by teachers. Therefore, we thought whether SST could be performed using facial expression detection devices that can quantitatively measure facial expressions.

In recent years, Kinect of Microsoft Corp. and Human Vision Components-Consumer (HVC-C) of OMRON Co., Ltd. released technology having facial expression detection functionality. Both of them have the feature that makes it is possible to quantitatively identify facial expressions, and in addition to the expression detection function, it is also possible to acquire information such as body information, sex, age, etc. with motion capture and gaze tracking. In addition, since these development environments are also open source, it is now possible to develop applications using equipment having facial expression detection functions, and various applications are being developed. However, practice using devices equipped with this facial expression detection function in educational environments is mostly for sensing movement of the body, and practice using facial expression detection function is not yet widespread.

From the above, it can be considered that a device with facial expression detection function can be used in the field of facial expression recognition technology in SST nonverbal communication area. By using SST equipped with facial expression detection function, it is thought that utilization of ICT equipment and popularization of facial expression detection equipment in lifestyle habit situations will be achieved. Also, it is considered necessary to operate a system that operates even in environments where information communication with outside schools and classrooms in Japan is restricted, and can use facial expression training without restrictions in other places.

Therefore, in this research, we aim to develop a simple feedback method using facial expression recognition device for SST and SST teaching material, and to develop applications to support facial expression exercise practice.

2. OUTLINE OF THE SYSTEM

2.1 About Facial Expression Recognition Device

In the past, research has been conducted to make artificial intelligence deeply learn every expression in order to improve accuracy as a method of detecting facial expressions. However, in such research, it can be said that it is generally difficult to utilize it in educational environments because it requires a huge expression sample set to let artificial intelligence learn, and takes time to make deep learning. Therefore, in this research, we emphasized easy detection of facial expression and decided to adopt OMRON HVC-C, a facial expression recognition device that is on the market. With this facial expression recognition device, not only facial expression estimation but also impression parameters such as "positive degree" and "negative degree" can be acquired. However, in the device standard specification, since the prediction result of the expression is greatly different from the actual expression, the original adjustment is performed in consideration of the impression parameter.

2.2 About the Expression Practice Application

We developed an expression practice application using the facial expression detection device as mentioned above. This facial expression training application adopts the basic training model of SST and evaluates to which expression the personal expression is close to and the degree of expressiveness. The flow of this system is shown in Figure 1. At first, thinking about the facial expression that matches the question. Next, making facial expression and detect it with HVC - C. Then, the application feedbacks the results detected by HVC-C by means of both of voice and text information. One set of the practice consists of 10 questions. All of the questions are as shown in Table 1.

This application will be practiced with the cooperation of the school and for five students in Sendai City GoJo Junior High School Commuting Classroom, six students in Miyagi Prefectural Vision Support School and 17 students in Yamagata School for the Blind School of Yamagata Prefecture.

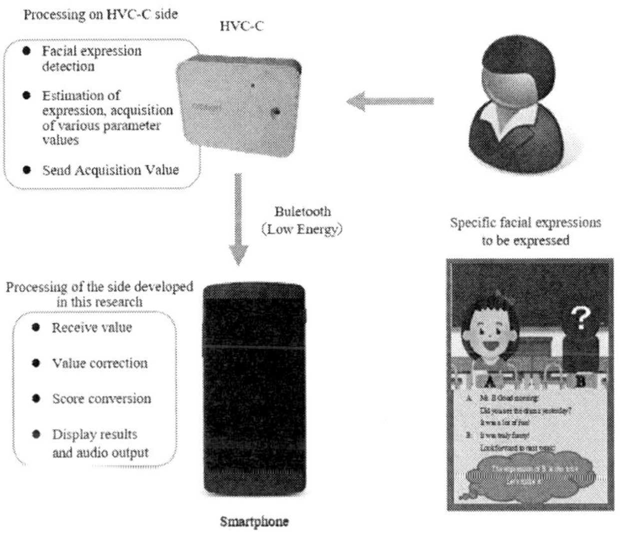

Figure 1. Outline of a face detection system and procedure

Table 1. Contents of a question

Situation	Contents	
Conversation with my mother	Mom:	How long are you going to sleep! Get up early!
Teacher's remarks	Teacher:	How long are you talking! Get on your seat!
Usual conversation with a friend	D:	How was the result of the math test?
(Results of examination)	B:	It was 100 points! Perfect!
Usual conversation with a friend	D:	How was the result of the math test?
(Results of examination)	B:	I couldn't do it at all ... It was a shock ...
Usual conversation with a friend	A:	Good morning! Did you see the drama yesterday?
(TV drama program)		It was a lot of fun!
	B:	It was really interesting! Look forward to next week!
Usual conversation with a friend	A:	That was funny. But, the hero was to be taken ill...
(TV drama program)	B:	That's right. It was a shock ...
Usual conversation with a friend	C:	Good morning! This is a note when you were absent yesterday.
(I was absent)	B:	Borrow C note. Thank you very much.
Usual conversation with a friend	E:	Physical education is swimming. Change clothes in swimwear.
(Physical education class)	B:	Physical education is swimming ...I can't swim, I do not want.
Usual conversation with a friend	C:	Good morning! Did you do your homework in Japanese?
(Homework)	B:	Huh, did you have homework? I heard it for the first time ...
Usual conversation with a friend	A:	The actor X got married! Did you know?
(Famous actor's marriage)	B:	Really? Surprised!

3. RESULT

Firstly, from observations made of the practice sessions and through interview survey results with the teacher and students at the time of application at Commuting Classroom, we found that the cooperating students were able to repeatedly make the intended expression every time they practiced. Secondly, from further observations and interview surveys conducted during the practice sessions at Vision Support School, we found that the cooperating students were pleased with their expressions and that this promoted understanding of what kind of impression the usual expression gives to others, gaining confidence that they were able to express intended facial expressions. The surveys also found that practicing expressions with a machine partner has less resistance to practice than doing practice in face to face with an instructor. However, as this practice was temporary, we wondered what kind of transformation could be seen in expressing facial expressions through a medium to long term use of continuous practicing, and whether such long term use would cause a reduction of the sense of resistance, and the need to create a problem tailored to the tendency of the targeted student's good or weak facial expression. Therefore, based on the premise that it can be practiced in the medium to long term with no sense of resistance, it is considered necessary to have a system for automatically generating problems based on the basic training model, and a system for managing the results of exercises.

4. FUTURE WORKS

Recently, learning from the instructors does not occur face to face, but there are also forms of teaching that utilize ICT-based e-learning and MOOCs (Massive Open Online Courses). However, these learning approaches are mainly aimed at acquiring knowledge. Meanwhile, Itagaki et al. (2017) also developed an e-learning material for the skills of kana. As next steps, we also need to develop e-learning teaching materials and LMS (Learning Management System) equipped with a system that records and manages the results of expression facial expression practice for grasping how facial expression skills have improved.

5. CONCLUSION

In this study, we developed a facial expression detection software and a situation exercise book. A total of 28 students used the software and we observed the situations and interviewed them. The results we could find followings.

- Each time students practiced, they were able to make the facial expression they intended on their own.
- Students were found to be pleased about their facial expression.
- Students were found to be able to gain confidence by expressing their intended facial expression.
- Students were able to practice with less sense of resistance than they practiced with an instructor/teacher in person.

On the other hand, the followings was observed:

- Assessment from long term practice.
- How to keep students' motivation in continuous practice.
- Developing making situations functions adaptably with each student.

ACKNOWLEDGEMENT

This work was supported by KAKENHI (15K01013).

REFERENCES

Ministry of education,2010. *Guide on informatization of education.* Ministry of education,Japan.

Ministry of education,2016, *Survey results on actual situation of information conversion of education in school in FY2015.*Tokyo,Japan,pp1-15.

Miyagi University of Education,2014. *ICT Utilization Handbook for Children with Developmental Disabilities Classroom.* Miyagi University of Education,japan.

Satoru,K. et al, 2004 *LD · ADHD social skills training.* Japanese culture science company,Tokyo,Japan.

Syota,I. et al,2017 Development and evaluation of lesson system to support learning of Kanna, *The Journal of the Japan Society of Educational Technology Engineering*,Vol.41,No.1,pp65-75

TEACHING MEDIA DESIGN BY USING SCRUM. A QUALITATIVE STUDY WITHIN A MEDIA INFORMATICS' ELECTIVE COURSE

Ines Herrmann[1], Sander Münster[2], Vincent Tietz [3] and Rainer Uhlemann[4]
[1] *Department of Literatures, Cultures and Languages Oak Hall, University of Connecticut*
[2] *TU Dresden, Media Center*
[3] *Otto Group Solution Provider (OSP) Dresden GmbH*
[4] *lightframe visual effects*

ABSTRACT

Cross-disciplinary skills are today's key skills for media informatics students to gain employment after graduation. However, such problem-based learning projects almost never take place due to organizational struggles. The authors suggest Scrum, a framework that is increasingly used in software engineering, as a solution for the challenges. Scrum has been implemented in a 3D media design project seminar at Dresden University of Technology during the cross-disciplinary project "SUFUvet" which took place in cooperation with University of Leipzig in 2016. The authors evaluated the use of Scrum qualitatively during the project and after. This paper explains methodology and results of the studies. Results shall be presented in four hypotheses within this paper.

KEYWORDS

Visual media design, Scrum, 3D visualizations, Higher Education, Media Informatics.

1. INTRODUCTION

As investigated in former courses (Kröber and Münster, 2016), complex learning settings like team problem- or project-based learning (PBL) require a high degree of supervision and much time to be carried out (cf. Blumenfeld et al., 1991, Barron et al., 1998). One of the reasons is the complexity and massive cognitive load for participants caused by the multitude of tasks especially in the initial stages of these seminars. With regard to these challenges, the employment of an organizational framework like Scrum, which was primarily used for Agile Programming approaches for software development (Davies and Sedley, 2009) has been proposed as a promising solution (cf. Münster et al., 2015). To assess this assumption empirically, the educational project "SUFUvet" took place in spring and summer of 2016 as a joint cooperation involving the Technische Universität Dresden and the University of Leipzig. The project assignment was to create 3D visualized multimedia material for an e-learning course about ante-mortem and post-mortem meat inspection of domestic pigs (cf. Maurer et al., 2016). 10 students from a media informatics master level course and 3 veterinary students from the University of Leipzig carried out the task. Both media informatics students and veterinary students formed teams, each of whom was responsible for one of three 3D visualizations. Due to the unique setting of the course, our interest was to qualitatively investigate, how Scrum works in an educational setting. Related questions are:

- How would the application of Scrum work in general?
- How would Scrum influence the overall workflow as well as the transparency and documentation of the project and students' performance?

2. METHODOLOGY

Complex learning settings as PBL for multimedia creation "require[s] deeper integration of ideas" and an intense coordination of team members (Mintzberg and Westley, 2010). Scrum seems promising for mastering some of the issues of relevance for complex learning scenarios as for instance the lack of "strategies for planning and guiding" for problem solving as well as the lack of knowledge of cooperative social interaction and discourse practices (Reiser, 2004) and to iteratively estimate, plan and perform tasks together using self-organization and collaboration.

Application of Scrum

The main focus of Scrum is to deliver significant value in short iterative production cycles as so called "Sprints" (cf. Figure 1). The cycle begins with a Project Vision which is created by the so called *Product Owner* with all stakeholders. Each Sprint starts with a Sprint Planning Meeting. The Scrum Team discusses which Backlog Items of high priority should be considered for inclusion in the Sprint. During the Sprint the Scrum Team realizes a potentially shippable Deliverable or product increment. During short Daily Standup Meetings team members discuss the daily progress, identify impediments or coordinate their current tasks. At the end of the Sprint, a Review Meeting is held during which the Team gives a demonstration of all Deliverables to the *Product Owner* and relevant stakeholders. The Sprint cycle ends with a Sprint Retrospective Meeting where the team discusses ways to improve processes and performance. While Scrum is basically used in software and web engineering, some teachers adopted Scrum for a production of e-learning courses and materials (eg. Tselentis, 2014, Davey and Parker, 2010, Boyle et al., 2006, Winckler de Bettio et al., 2013). Especially for those non-engineering scenarios and educational purposes the Scrum method needs to be adopted (Popovic, 2012, Winckler de Bettio et al., 2013).

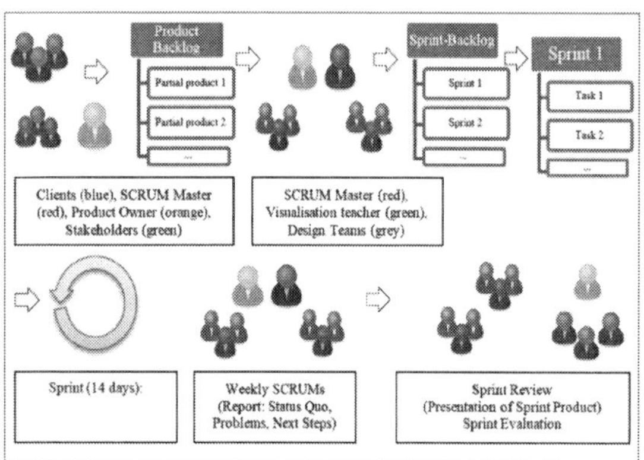

Figure 1. SCRUM procedure within the SUFUvet project (cf. Schwaber and Sutherland, 2011)

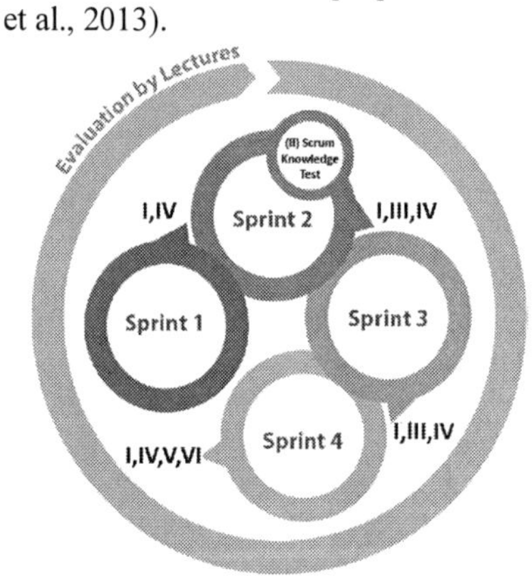

Figure 2. Assessment instruments within the SUFUvet project

Since visual media design class at university is a very particular setting for the implementation of Scrum, we applied various changes of the methodology as marked in Figure 1, in particular to Scrum meeting intervals plus several roles within the framework. At the beginning of the project, we expected it to be a main challenge "to split overall visualization goal(s) into independent subtasks that can be prioritized freely by each person in a design team" (Maurer et al., 2016), but we also hoped that this splitting would help students to structure and plan the work right from the start. Our project had four Sprints with durations between 1 and 3 weeks. Once a week students met in class for a three hour work session with a 20 minute break halfway through. They were tutored by a 3D modelling expert.

Assessment strategy

While a primary goal of formative assessment is "to provide feedback to teachers and students over the course of instruction" (Boston, 2002, p.1), a summative approach evaluates competencies or outcomes at a specific time and "sums up the performance or learning level of achievement" (Dumit, 2012, slide 10). According to several studies (eg. Igaki et al., 2014, Santos and Pinto, 2013, Scharf and Koch, 2013, Vasilevskaya et al., 2014), Scrum is a very handy method to evaluate workflow progress and assess team performance both formative and summative in a PBL scenario due to its periodic and intensive process documentation. Furthermore, there are reflections on usability studies within Scrum (eg. Jia et al., 2012, Lizano et al., 2014) but none on how to check the surplus value of Scrum itself especially in university education. That is why the evaluation of Scrum in a non-software or web engineering surrounding is a pilot project. We installed the following formative and summative assessment instruments within the proposed PBL course (Figure 2):

I. After each of the four sprints we arranged a review by guideline-based questionnaires to assess a quality of outcomes.
II. During the second sprint, students did a Scrum Knowledge Test in which they a) proved knowledge on the Scrum method as well as b) reflected on advantages and disadvantages. The latter was a qualitative evaluation by students in an open text question.
III. Following the second and third sprint, a teacher-provided assessment based on individual process information in Scrum desk was provided.
IV. After the sprints one, two and three, each Design Team held a Sprint Retrospective reflecting: “What was good?”, “What was bad?” as well as set the Action Points for the next sprint.
V. The end of sprint four marked the end of the project. Students were asked to do final presentations on their own progress, work and the Scrum implementations before the final review took place.
VI. After the last sprint, a Project Retrospective with all stakeholders and students assessed the Scrum implementation as well as further discussed results of stage III.

We find the **process quality** assessed through II, III and IV. The **performance** has been evaluated with the teacher-provided assessment mentioned in III. It shows that the possibility for III could be a first proof of Scrums handiness concerning a simple assessment. **Output assessment** was realized through I, V and VI and the installation of I also guarantees the **client satisfaction**.

3. RESULTS

3.1 Scrum Knowledge Test & Evaluation by Lecturers

At the end of the second sprint, students took part in a Scrum Knowledge Test that consisted of 15 compulsory questions, one additional question and an elective one: “What advantages or disadvantages do you see in the implementation of Scrum into media design processes?” Five out of nine students answered this question. Students appreciated the structure that was given by the Scrum framework and acknowledged clearly defined rules, efficiency increase by retrospectives and the team experience in Scrum as well as the well-organized overall project. Two students stated that the Scrum framework is a better approach for organization and coordination than the approaches previously known to them. Scrum was also seen as a possible bridge between traditional software engineering and traditional design processes by one student. On the other hand, one student declared that there are no advantages about the Scrum implementation and that it is a useless theory. Also, it was declared a disadvantage that the Scrum theory and application needs to be trained first. Considering this in addition to the repeated complaint about the Scrum organization being very time consuming and parts of it not always being useful or doable for media design processes (e.g. documentation and splitting the product into pieces that can be done by different persons), one student's statement summarizes the overall evaluation: *“It is a way of organization, and that is always depending on preferences. Though, it is nice to get to know it”* (translated from German by Authors).

Lecturers have been asked to evaluate the implementation separately at the end of the class. From a Scrum master's point of view, Scrum helps to define the media product with the highest business value for the client because there is a steady communication about it. This is also supported by short iterations which imply fast intermediate results which the client can comment on so that it can be improved easily and to the client's needs. In this case, design teams do not spend too much time on unnecessary work. During Scrum, teams estimate workload and time effort and if so, the client gets planning certainty. Transparency eliminates the risk of immoderate expectations of what the teams may accomplish. Creativity and problem solving are provided by the whole interdisciplinary team. On the other hand, media design products often have to be aesthetic in a way, and it is difficult to find hard criteria of what is aesthetic. This affects the Scrum organization partly (so-called acceptance criteria). Media design products often cannot be split and combined in the end (unlike programmed software elements). Moreover, tasks are rather dependent of one another, and for Scrum to be effective, the question is how this can be altered. For a media design expert, the advantages of team communication which is necessarily part of the Scrum process as well as its quality protection throughout the iterations by transparency and feedback are obvious. On the other hand, the team organization workload and the dependence on others as well as the splitting problem gives cause for consideration.

3.2 Sprint Reviews & Retrospectives

Veterinary project students & stakeholders have evaluated the design work during the Sprint Reviews in Scrum. Therefore, they filled in their data in a questionnaire that was solely created for the documentation of these reviews. To give an idea, we have the documentation of all three design work pieces for the first and the second sprint. Due to some project related events[1], only one of the work pieces reviews is available for all sprints: the gastrointestinal system (design piece 1). These documentations show that a) the students' priorization did increasingly meet the clients' priorization from sprint to sprint, b) the students produced little during the first sprint and then started to design schematic models of almost all parts during the second sprint which c) met the clients' acceptance criteria in sprint three already and d) the visualization has been finalized in sprint four. This documentation leads to the following interpretation:

- Reviews helped the students to gather the information they needed and to overcome problems which popped up at the very beginning of the design process because they could request e.g. image sources that met their needs for 3D modelling.
- The regular feedback during the reviews led to an improvement of the media design product.
- Especially it eased the design teams' work to meet the clients' needs.

Let us look at the Retrospective of the teams to gain even more insights. The design team of design piece (2) consisted of two persons. The work was done by mainly one person who was experienced in 3D modelling but did not communicate or exchange data as well as it was expected but absent during the first review. Both design team members complained about Scrum and refused to document their work in Scrum desk from the very beginning. Design team of the work piece (3) got the unexperienced team member during sprint three. Because he, but also another team member, were missing every now and then but did not communicate about it, the team got into time troubles. Meanwhile, they were able to solve a data exchange problem via Dropbox which is documented as an action point and reflection in the retrospectives of sprint two and three. While this team was able to split the work very well, it was an issue for the design team (1) of the gastrointestinal system from sprint three on in their retrospectives. The latter design team, though, got the experienced team member of team (2) and therewith had a pretty helping hand. We assume that,

- the speedy result of design team 2 is rather due to the experienced team member in 3D modelling than to Scrum organization, but also
- the workflow of design team 1 may be due to the Scrum organization but also because of their experienced help from sprint three on.
- Scrum is only working with reliable and team-minded persons and
- Retrospectives have the potential to identify problems of the teams and to solve them.

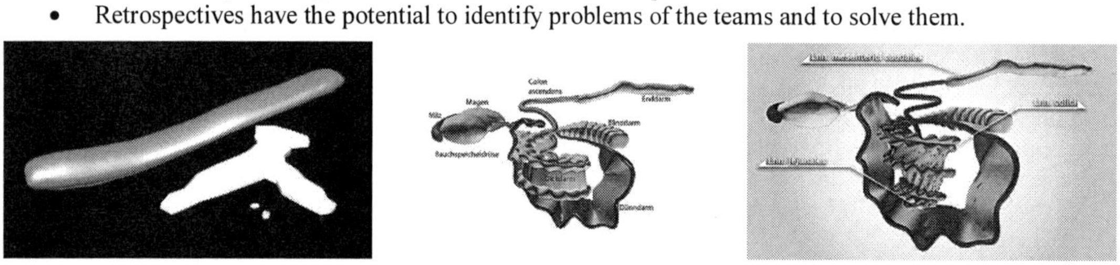

Figure 3. Results of the first, third and fourth sprint of the design team "gastrointestinal system"

3.3 Students Presentation & Project Retrospective

Students had to give short presentations on their progress and results and to reflect the learning and working process for themselves and their design team critically. These presentations included various reflections on

[1] For example, one of the pieces was finished after the second sprint and only the visualization was then slightly changed to fit afterwards. There is only one other documentation for the fourth sprint.

the class & project. It has been stated that the use of Scrum led to effective time management as well as to good teamwork. Other reflections cannot be linked to Scrum. Still, we compared the students' reflections with those from a previously mentioned former project to indicate changes. Whereas the students of the former project reflected on the fact that they felt lost and needed a lot of input to get structured and to understand what the work was about, students in the recently done project focused on time and software problems. Although, the students involved in our current project argued, that the Scrum organization consumed much time yet. Additionally, we had a final group discussion with all participants involved in our last session. The so called Project Retrospective, referring to the sprint retrospective, had a time-line design and concluded all reflections on the class and project itself (see Figure 3). All parties wrote positive, neutral and negative feedback on colored paper and talked about it. Also, every student could mark the statements that he or she most agreed with. Two students voted positively for the Sprint Retrospectives to improve the project's work flow as well as the combination of Scrum and 3D modelling, and the visits by the veterinary students during the reviews in Scrum. One student voted neutral for Scrum desk as it is not always useful for media design, for example to keep record of who does what. A non-digital solution was not preferred. Three students voted negatively for the Scrum overhead. Still, already in sprint two, there are two positive votes for a structured work and routine and ten positive votes for a relaxed atmosphere.

4. CONCLUSION

Summarizing, it can be said that Scrum helped to structure the work and improve the work process of this project class. But it needs to be even more simplified to meet the requirements of a 3D modelling even better. We conclude that

- Scrum supported the complex PBL scenario in the SUFUvet project. Both the lecturers and students voted positively on the structure and the review culture that is given by Scrum. In comparison to the last project, there have also been fewer complaints about challenges to organize the work. Instead, students stated that Scrum helped them a lot on that matter but they faced struggles with a Scrum-work-overload.
- Scrum simplifies a formative and summative assessment. The documentation of all steps of Scrum allows an all-time overview of what is happening and how it is evaluated by the persons involved. Our additional tools, like the questionnaire for the students from Leipzig, helped to gain more information on how usable the media products were and how these could be improved during the short iterations.
- Our assumption that the use of non-digital documentation instead of Scrum desk would minimize the overload of Scrum has been declined by the students in the Project Retrospective. When looking for ways to solve this overload problem after all, we come to see that:
- Generally speaking, Scrum is transferrable to other fields like media design and can be useful for them. But we plead to reduce Scrum to its helpful elements such as reviews and retrospectives instead of clinging to the original concept and to support a documentation structure that only covers meaningful items for the assessment.

To us, the parallel work of design teams and design team members is particularly useful for 3D contexts since for a 3D scene one often has to create and texture multiple 3D models. To artificially separate parts of 3D models, though, is not recommended. In Scrum, it can be seen as a challenge to create work tasks that take about the same amount of work for everyone involved as well as to train the necessary communication level within and between the design teams. Since the described research was intended as initial exploration, we currently plan for a more detailed study to validate findings.

ACKNOWLEDGEMENTS

The educational project "SUFUvet - Multimedia, 3D visualized teaching-learning class about ante-mortem and post-mortem meat inspection of domestic swine" was funded by the Saxon Center for Higher Education in 2016 within the Learning in Transfer scheme. We are very thankful to Patric Maurer as lead project conceptor and coordinator as well as to Antonia Christine Raida who supervised the research work at the University of Leipzig. Moreover, we'd like to acknowledge the valuable contribution of all seminar students.

REFERENCES

Barron, B. J. S., Schwartz, D. L., Vye, N. J., Moore, A., Petrosino, A., Zech, L., Bransford, J. D. & Vanderbilt, T. C. A. T. G. A. 1998. Doing with understanding: Lessons from research on problem- and project-based learning. *The Journal of the Learning Sciences,* 7, 271-311.

Blumenfeld, P. C., Soloway, E., Marx, R. W., Joseph S. Krajcik, Guzdial, M. & Palincsar, A. 1991. Motivating Project-Based Learning: Sustaining the Doing, Supporting the Learning. *Educational Psychologist,* 26.

Boston, C. 2002. *The Concept of Formative Assessment. ERIC Digest.,* Boston, ERIC Clearinghouse on Assessment and Evaluation College.

Boyle, T., Cook, J., Windle, R., Wharrad, H., Leeder, D. & Alton, R. 2006. An agile method for developing learning objects. *Proceedings of the 23rd Annual Ascilite Conference. Autralia.*

Davey, B. & Parker, K., R. 2010. Technology in education: an agile systems approach. *Proceedings of Informing Science & IT Education Conference (InSITE), Italy.*

Davies, R. & Sedley, L. 2009. *Agile Coaching,* Raleigh, The Pragmatic Bookshelf.

Dumit, N. Y. 2012. *Diagnostic/Formative/Summative Assessment,* n.n.

Igaki, H., Fukuyasu, N., Saiki, S., Matsumoto, S. & Kusumoto, S. 2014. Quantitative assessment with using ticket driven development for teaching scrum framework. *ICSE Companion'14, May 31 – June 7, 2014.* Hyderabad, India.

Jia, Y., Larusdottir, M. K. & Cajander, Å. 2012. The Usage of Usability Techniques in Scrum Projects. *In:* WINCKLER, M., Forbrig, P. & Bernhaupt, R. (eds.) *HCSE 2012.* Cham: Springer.

Kröber, C. & Münster, S. 2016. Educational App Creation for the Cathedral in Freiberg. *In:* Spector, J. M., Ifenthaler, D., Sampson, D. G. & Isaias, P. (eds.) *Competencies, Challenges, and Changes in Teaching, Learning and Educational Leadership in the Digital Age.* Cham: Springer.

Lizano, F., Sandoval, M. M. & Stage, J. 2014. Integrating Usability Evaluations into Scrum: A Case Study Based on Remote Synchronous User Testing. *In:* Kurosu, M. (ed.) *Human-Computer Interaction, Part I, HCII 2014.* Cham: Springer.

Maurer, P., Raida, A., Münster, S. & Lücker, E. 2016. Visual media as tool to acquire soft skills – interdisciplinary teaching-learning project SUFUvet. *In:* SPENDER, J., SCHIUMA, G. & NÖNNIG, J. R. (eds.) *Proceedings of the 11th International Forum on Knowledge Asset Dynamics (IFKAD 2016) Dresden, Germany. June 15-17th 2016.* Dresden: University of Basilicata.

Mintzberg, H. & Westley, F. 2010. Decision Making: It's Not What You Think. *In:* Nutt, P. C. & Wilson, D. (eds.) *Handbook Of Decision Making.* Oxford: Wiley-Blackwell.

Münster, S., Kröber, C., Schlenker, L. & Bergert, A. 2015. Employing SCRUM methods for a cooperative virtual reconstruction of architectural heritage. *In:* Schiuma, G. (ed.) *IFKAD 2015.* Bari: International Forum on Knowledge Asset Dynamics.

Popovic, T. 2012. Is anyone using Scrum in research projects at universities?

Reiser, B. F. 2004. Scaffolding Complex Learning: The Mechanisms of Structuring and Problematizing Student Work. *The Journal of the Learning Sciences, 13(3), 273–304 Copyright © 2004, Lawrence Erlbaum Associates, Inc.*

Santos, S. C. D. & Pinto, A. 2013. Authentic Assessment in Software Engineering Education Based on PBL Principles. A Case Study in the Telecom Market. *ICSE 2013.* San Francisco, CA, USA.

Scharf, A. & Koch, A. 2013. Scrum in a Software Engineering Course: An In-Depth Praxis Report. *CSEE&T 2013.* San Francisco, CA, USA.

Schwaber, K. & Sutherland, J. 2011. *The Scrum Guide. The Definitive Guide to Scrum. The Rules of the Game,* Scrum.org.

Tselentis, J. 2014. *How to Use Scrum for Your Team and for Print Projects.*

Vasilevskaya, M., Broman, D. & Sandahl, K. 2014. An assessment model for large project courses. *SIGCSE'14, March 5–8, 2014.* Atlanta, GA, USA.

Winckler De Bettio, R., Pereira, D. A., Martins, R. X. & Heinfarth, T. 2013. The Experience of Using the Scrum Process in the Production of Learning Objects for Blended Learning. *Informatics in Education,* 12, 29–41.

AN ARCHITECTURE TO SUPPORT WEARABLES IN EDUCATION AND WELLBEING

Fernando Luis-Ferreira[1], Andreia Artifice[1], Gary McManus[2] and João Sarraipa[1]
[1]*Departamento de Engenharia Electrotecnica, DEE, CTS, FCT-UNL, Campus da FCT-UNL, 2829-516 Caparica, Portugal*
[2]*Telecommunications Software & Systems Group Waterford Institute of Technology, WIT, West Campus, Carriganore, Waterford, Ireland*

ABSTRACT

Technological devices help extending a person's sensory experience of the environment. From sensors to cameras, devices currently use embedded systems that can be used for the main goal they were designed but they can also be used for other objectives without additional costs of material or service subscription. Emotional assessment is a useful tool for students' assessment of motivation and engagement on learning activities while it is also a valuable tool to evaluate elder mental status. On the other hand, the same devices are useful to monitor health risks in young and older individuals. The present work aims at tackling students' dropout, by emotional reasons, and emotional problems of elderly people, both considered serious cases as the dropout in South America and ageing worldwide. Considering the identified needs, it is proposed an architecture that aims at supporting people in the learning process while providing advice and ensuring support in case of permanent or temporary cognitive disabilities. The present research work is in merged fields of education within the scope of ACACIA project and elderly support within the scope of CARELINK project. It is proposed a technological solution, based on a wearable, that covers a wide range of ages and different cognitive stages.

KEYWORDS

Emotions, ECG, Wearables, Healthcare, Safety, Ageing

1. INTRODUCTION

The emerging field of internet of things is growing at a fast pace as it is expected that by 25 billion Internet-connected things by 2020 (Gartner 2015). Wearables are user centric devices that follow that line with an increasing adoption, with a rise in shipped devices from about 13 million in 2013 to 130 million in 2018 (Wei 2014). Those devices can be used for diverse purposes as in the case of fitness bracelets that can track a person's movement, sleep and infer burned calories and stress level. There are different configurations for wearable devices, like bracelets, clothing and even the smartwatches can provide wearable functionalities since the accelerometers measure physical activity and some use cameras to measure a person's heartbeat with a high degree of accuracy (Pelegris et al. 2010). Heartrate and skin conductance are both used to assess a person's emotional state (Luis-Ferreira 2015) (Lee et al. 2005). But there is also strong evidence that heartrate (HR) and heartrate variability (HRV) are related with a person's emotional states and may, per se, constitute a source of information about the person's emotion psychophysiology (Anttonen & Surakka 2005).

Emotions play a relevant role in humans' lives. Its importance relates with success and failure and augment or reduce cognitive capacities. Damasio states that 'We feel therefore we learn' to highlight the importance of affective and social neurosciences in education (Immordino-Yang & Damasio 2007). Diverse technics can be used to identify emotional status in a classroom and by informing the teacher or trainer about the class affective state while learning thus providing tools to actively promote the quality of the teaching environment (Sarraipa et al. 2016). With this in mind, it is possible to envisage that emotional evaluation can have a strong impact in preparing classes and managing the ongoing of a class, promoting the quality of the learning environment and preventing students dropout, a serious problem in many developing countries (Gutiérrez y Restrepo et al. 2016). On the other hand, it is possible, and desirable, to stimulate fitness practices and health monitoring. That is precisely the aim of most of fitness device and it became an area with multiple solutions but most of the times restricted to physical exercise. The balance can arrive while using the same devices explore other regions like the above mentioned, students' emotional status and collective affective reactions towards teaching environment. Beyond that, considering lifelong learning and elderly engagement in classes that aspect becomes also sensitive since demotivation plays an important role in elder disengagement from learning and other stimulating cognitive activities. It is possible to reason about physiological measurements in order to infer about a person's emotional state (Mauss & Robinson 2009). Those measurements, provided by the above-mentioned wearables and, in the same process, ensure the person's safety, in cases related with Alzheimer or other dementia cases as a surplus of the wearables in use. That is a path towards a rational use of all the data collected, by applying that to different purposes while using the same device and thus maximizing its utility and reducing expenses. In overall, the assessment behind the current work is that data generated by wearable devices is used for a main purpose, established by manufacturers, but it can be used for many other purposes. Among those purposes the present work elects emotional engagement to the learning process, in young and lifelong learners while providing health safety in case of impairments like those related to aging. The paper is divided in three main sections, this introduction presented the case to be addressed and the motivation, the second section presents an architecture that addresses those objectives and finally section 3 debates the results and prospects for future work.

2. AN ARCHICTECTURE FOR TEACHING AND HEALTH

The architecture presented in this section has multiple finalities from coaching students and assisting the learning environment to assisting elder people while learning, in a lifelong learning strategy but also ensuring health safety and security. Those objectives are achievable without adding hardware and result from the exploitation of the flexibility of the architecture presented next in **Figure 1**.

The research question that motivated such architecture can be instantiated as; If we can use smartphones for emotional evaluation, helping students to outperform, supporting older people to perform daily routines while being cognitively stimulated, why not developing a system that does it all?

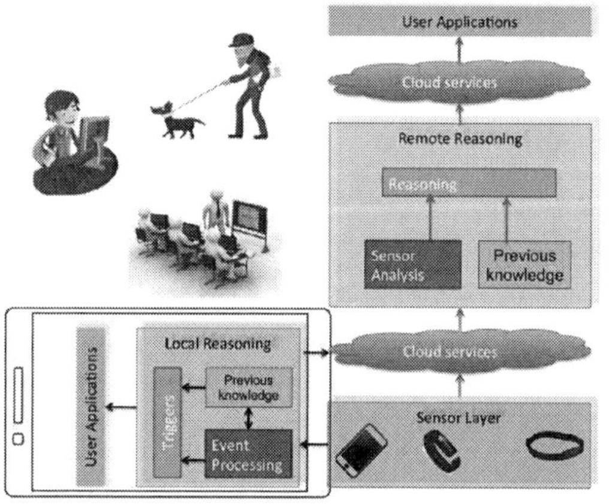

Figure 1. Architecture based on a smartphone for education, teaching and safety

In the proposed architecture, two approaches are considered; one that is a local system, contained in a smartphone, that is permanently monitoring the person and as a main function is ready to respond to health threats. The other is a system that uploads data to the cloud and can use data analysis and reasoning to feed more complex applications.

The Local System (LS) captures data from sensors being those of the smartphone supporting also others wirelessly connected (e.g. by Bluetooth, Wi-Fi). It relies on real-time measurements of heartrate for local assessment of vital signals so that emergency situations can be tackled immediately. It also uses known algorithms over heartrate measurements in order to provide clues about a persons' emotional state. The goal is not to characterize to detail a person's emotional state but rather tell if the person is unresponsive or with low response to external stimuli. As in what regards to students it can report their state of alertness or boredom thus providing clues to the teacher's system about the behavior of the class. These local applications are also able to provide feedback to web-services in a cloud where a more complete analysis is made and that will not condition the need for network access as data can be uploaded asynchronously. That is of particular importance as the system remains autonomous but while possible it uploads anonymized data. Services in the cloud will be used to improve algorithms and perform analysis of the classroom students' performance, or reason about a person's health status providing valuable feedback.

The Remote Reasoning System (RRS) is accessed by web services supported by the cloud and thus providing powerful tools that cannot be supported on a smartphone. The RRS also depends on connectivity that may not be accessible all the time due to location or strategy to preserve smartphone energy. The services on the cloud will perform analysis over the available sensors, with strategies of data mining, data extraction and sensory fusion. While the smartphone easily obtains HR measurements and performs HR, HRV analysis, other measurements can be executed (e.g. Galvanic Skin Response, Blood Pressure). Reasoning will be performed using previous knowledge that may include teachers' instructions or clinical guidance but also background knowledge on cognitive issues or clinical aspects. The analysis to be executed over the cloud can become available for diverse types of applications from health to education.

The sensors within a flexible sensor layer can be of diverse type; while in the local system they should be restricted those of the smartphone, in the remote system they can be of any type according to the objective to be achieved.

In overall, the system aims at using the available sensory capacity already embedded in smartphones, to diverse goals supported by the proposed architecture. The architecture is based on results already achieved in the scope of the ACACIA project (https://acacia.digital/en/) and the starting CARELINK project. While ACACIA supports education and prevents dropout in south America, CARELINK helps elder to perform their tasks safely by monitoring health and avoiding losing track due to dementia associated projects. The proposed architecture aims at providing a holistic solution both for young and old population, learning or just doing daily routines and preventing hazardous behaviors while monitoring health in older or young at risk.

3. CONCLUSION

The usage of wearable devices is becoming a reality that can be adopted in diverse societal domains including health, wellbeing and learning. The work hereby presented aims to address those mentioned areas, empowering the student's performance and the citizens health track while centered on the individual. The proposed architecture was partially implemented with results that encourage the continuation. It is also to mention that the pilot experiments made with students in the scope of this research work, correlate physiological measurements with emotions and are suitable to be integrated in the proposed framework (Kadar et al. 2016). As for the real impact of the work hereby described, it has been tested in pilot studies in universities of South American countries, in the scope of ACACIA project, with results that encourage its adoption tackling heavy numbers of students' dropout from university. Aiming at a broader utility, the present work is to prove that solutions can be of large spectrum on the opposite of the traditional reductionist approach focused on limited solutions. The present technological solution can be deployed for the student and grandparents supporting teaching or daily activities. It can be useful for young and old with physical or cognitive impairments while using devices as common as smartphones or not that common as fitness bands or smartwatches.

The results achieved so far are encourage the usage of emotional assessment to prevent dropout and stimulate students' learning activities. Future research will aim at designing nonobtrusive devices that can be used daily without minimum impact along with new methods, including data mining and machine learning, for determining emotional and behavioral changes and its impact on people's lives. Those objectives will be pursued in the scope of the CARELINK project and ACACIA project using cloud services and local deployments in the case that online services are not available.

ACKNOWLEDGEMENT

The research leading to these results has received funding from the European union Erasmus+ program under grant agreement EAC/A04/2014 ACACIA. The work has also been promoted under the project CARELINK, AAL-CAL-2016-049 funded by AAL JP, and co-funded by the European commission and national funding authorities of Ireland, Belgium, Portugal and Switzerland.

REFERENCES

Anttonen, J. & Surakka, V., 2005. Emotions and heart rate while sitting on a chair. In *Proceedings of the SIGCHI conference on Human factors in computing systems - CHI '05*. New York, New York, USA: ACM Press, p. 491. Available at: http://dl.acm.org/citation.cfm?id=1054972.1055040 [Accessed March 11, 2015].

Gartner, 2015. The Internet of Things and the Enterprise - Smarter With Gartner. Available at: http://www.gartner.com/smarterwithgartner/the-internet-of-things-and-the-enterprise/?cm_mmc=social-_-rm-_-gart-_-swg [Accessed July 12, 2017].

Gutiérrez y Restrepo, E. et al., 2016. Enhanced Affective Factors Management for HEI Students Dropout Prevention. In P. Zaphiris & A. Ioannou, eds. *Learning and Collaboration Technologies: Third International Conference, LCT 2016, Held as Part of HCI International 2016, Toronto, ON, Canada, July 17-22, 2016, Proceedings*. Cham: Springer International Publishing, pp. 675–684.

Immordino-Yang, M.H. & Damasio, A., 2007. We Feel, Therefore We Learn: The Relevance of Affective and Social Neuroscience to Education. *Mind, Brain, and Education*, 1(1), pp.3–10. Available at: http://doi.wiley.com/10.1111/j.1751-228X.2007.00004.x [Accessed March 18, 2012].

Kadar, M. et al., 2016. Affective Computing to Enhance Emotional Sustainability of Students in Dropout Prevention. In *Proceedings of the 7th International Conference on Software Development and Technologies for Enhancing Accessibility and Fighting Info-exclusion - DSAI 2016*. New York, New York, USA: ACM Press, pp. 85–91. Available at: http://dl.acm.org/citation.cfm?doid=3019943.3019956 [Accessed July 14, 2017].

Lee, C.K. et al., 2005. Using Neural Network to Recognize Human Emotions from Heart Rate Variability and Skin Resistance. In *2005 IEEE Engineering in Medicine and Biology 27th Annual Conference*. IEEE, pp. 5523–5525. Available at: http://ieeexplore.ieee.org/document/1615734/ [Accessed July 13, 2017].

Luis-Ferreira, F., 2015. *Knowledge management framework based on brain models and human physiology*. Available at: http://run.unl.pt//handle/10362/15445 [Accessed November 4, 2015].

Mauss, I.B. & Robinson, M.D., 2009. Measures of emotion: A review. *Cognition & emotion*, 23(2), pp.209–237. Available at: http://www.pubmedcentral.nih.gov/articlerender.fcgi?artid=2756702&tool=pmcentrez&rendertype=abstract [Accessed July 14, 2014].

Pelegris, P. et al., 2010. A novel method to detect Heart Beat Rate using a mobile phone. In *2010 Annual International Conference of the IEEE Engineering in Medicine and Biology*. IEEE, pp. 5488–5491. Available at: http://ieeexplore.ieee.org/document/5626580/ [Accessed July 13, 2017].

Sarraipa, J. et al., 2016. Smart Techniques for Emotional Status Detectionof Students During ClassroomAttendance. In *Smart Applications & Technologies for Electronic Engineering, SATEE 2016*. Alba Lulia, Romania.

Wei, J., 2014. How Wearables Intersect with the Cloud and the Internet of Things : Considerations for the developers of wearables. *IEEE Consumer Electronics Magazine*, 3(3), pp.53–56. Available at: http://ieeexplore.ieee.org/document/6844949/ [Accessed July 12, 2017].

DIFFERENTIATED LEARNING ENVIRONMENT – A CLASSROOM FOR QUADRATIC EQUATION, FUNCTION AND GRAPHS

Emre Dinç
M.Ed. in Educational Technology, University of Delaware, Newark, Delaware, USA

ABSTRACT

This paper will cover the design of a learning environment as a classroom regarding the Quadratic Equations, Functions and Graphs. The goal of the learning environment offered in the paper is to design a classroom where students will enjoy the process, use their skills they already have during the learning process, control and plan their learning process, and have the right of free choice of which way they can learn easily. Besides, it is alleged that in the paper, students will be more engaged, motivated and self-confident in this learning environment in terms of theories and approaches. Besides, students will have computers and graph calculators in the classroom, and some applications and programs will be provided such as Cabri, Maple, Derive, etc.

KEYWORDS

Differentiated-learning, technology-based, student-centered, quadratic

1. INTRODUCTION

Learning happens in its natural habitat throughout history. People discover, explore, and learn in their daily life because, just like Dewey said, *"I believe that education, therefore, is a process of living and not a preparation for future living.*[1]*"* If we would like to design an effective learning environment, this learning environment should represent the real life and contain the abilities of human being. Otherwise, as we all observe, students don't want to go to school. Fostering students to go to school voluntarily may be the hardest thing to be achieved. However, if learning environment – classroom – gives students the opportunities to use their own abilities that they already have, it will foster the students to learn willingly. Students are already learning what they need to learn in their daily experiences, so they can learn in the classroom as well.

According the Gardner, it is a huge mistake to treat all children like they are different samples of the same individual, and this mistake leads to the formation of another mistake which is to try teaching the same things to all children in the same way. One of the main aims of this learning environment is to allow the students to enjoy the process, making them become willing to learn and assume the responsibility of their learning experiences.

The need for learning differs because of the existence and unique nature of man. When we look at the basis of education in education systems, the goals identified for the behavioral change to be gained by everyone are determined by assuming that the students have common characteristics in terms of their motoric, mental and affective developmental characteristics. Although individuals show similarities in terms of some mental and kinetic developmental characteristics, there are different forms of learning that emerge due to individual differences.

This study will cover the design of a learning environment for a classroom regarding the Quadratic Equations, Functions and Graphs that high school students find more difficult to learn. If we provide them an effective learning environment, the learning process of this topic would be beneficial. There are many studies

[1] This quote is from John Dewey's *My Pedagogic Creed* (1987), Article Two: What the School is.

made to show the difficulties that students faced through learning equations, functions and graphs in the literature (Bayazit, 2011; Golderberg & Kliman, 1988; Sezgin-Memnun et al., 2015).

Specifically, quadratic equations, functions and graphs are included in one of the categories of mathematics education which is algebra. Algebra contains abstract thinking in it, and with abstract structures, students can improve their critical thinking abilities and ability of noticing relationships of elements related to mathematics. Because of that, students' inability to learn algebra may lead them not to be capable of understand higher level mathematical matters, and withhold them to be successful in their educational lives (Williams, 1997). Functions and equations as abstract subjects in algebra are hard to comprehend, but they could be easier through graphs. Since, graphs are the visible way to understand what functions and equations represent. Graphical demonstrations of functions or expressions of equations both enhance students' reasoning skills and boost their mathematical skills including interpreting mathematical elements (Sezgin-Memnun et al., 2015).

2. THE LEARNING ENVIRONMENT

The class will be divided into three divisions. At the front of the class there will be a section where the students who want to listen to the teacher will be figured. In the middle of the class there will be round tables where group work can be performed, and the third part will be located at the back side of the classroom where the graph calculator can be used. This divisions will appeal to students' differences. If a student doesn't want to join a group work, that students will work independently in the setting, or if a student is motivated by recent technologies that s/he has never seen, that students will go towards to graph calculators.

In this learning environment, students need to control their learning throughout process. To foster voluntarily learning, students should set short-term and/or long-term objectives for themselves. People are committed to a goal in everything they do in their lives, therefore in education, setting a goal is not a different thing, it is the reflection of life. Secondly, planning can help students to engage in learning tasks easily. From the aspect of self-regulation, setting goals is the beginning of planning the learning process. With the help of goals, students can direct their attention and effort to the tasks they need to complete. While planning, students can use their prior knowledge or experience – they can use the knowledge of graph and relations from the subject of pattern. They can choose activities freely based on their own goals.

Functions can be visualized by graphs, so to engage students with the tasks, technological tools such as computer and graph calculator will be used to motivate students. Admittedly, in 21st-century students are already inundated with technology, therefore they are already accustomed to using technology. If we use technology as a tool or a platform (to create *macros*), it will automatically motivate students to engage with the subject. Hollar & Norwood (1999) reported that the graphing calculator facilitates to move among the representations fast. It should be noted that it does not have to be graphing calculator to use in the classroom, any graphing program would be useful for meaningful learning (such as Cabri, Maple, Derive, etc.). In this point, I need to indicate that students have different learning styles, and they are motivated by different technologies. Moreover, some of them may not be motivated by technology. In this learning environment, in front of every students will be computer, and in a corner of the classroom there will be graph calculator section, but the teacher never forces students to use them. If students would like to choose the traditional way to understand function, equation and graph, they will use pen and paper. Since, when any method, specifically technology is forced in the classroom, it might create motivational complications. Students will be free to choose their learning way. Therefore, students control their learning with setting goals, planning and motivating themselves with the learning style they choose according to their prior experiences, we can say that this learning environment will be learner-centered learning environment. Students can only learn deeper conceptual understanding by actively participating in their own learning (Sawyer, 2014).

In addition to the setting goals, planning and motivating, self-monitoring will be encouraged by the teacher. Self-monitoring is a self-regulation process, and it affects academic performance since it includes self-assessment and self-recording (Shapiro et al., 2002, Graham et al., 1992). While drawing a graph or writing the function from graph, students will keep a record of the number of times they work on a specific task, the time that spends on working on the task and the steps faced with failure or success (the task could be drawing a graph, writing the function or implementing the graph). This self-monitoring helps students to observe and evaluate their development and make changes while needed. Just as working on a specific learning task, students will seek help from other students or the teacher. Consequently, social support will turn into feedback, naturally. With this feature, the learning environment turns into assessment-centered learning setting. The key principles of assessment in this kind of learning environment are that they provide opportunities for revision and feedback (Bransford, Brown & Cocking, 1999).

As Sezgin-Memnun et al. (2015) indicated that memorizing is the problem in learning with understanding. In this environment, learning and interpreting the equations, functions and graphs is easier to achieve than memorizing them. This environment is evaluating the understanding rather than memorization, it provides a depth of study. Planning will be a strong element through process, since it helps the knowledge to be well-organized. Also, with the help of records, understanding will be considered carefully and students will improve metacognitively by expecting additional information to make sense and asking for clarification when they face with complication during keeping record. Considering these features that the learning environment provide, we can name it as knowledge-centered learning setting. Since, knowledge-centered environments emphasis on sense-making, makes students more knowledgeable and consider students' preconceptions brought to the environment (Brandsford, Brown & Cocking, 1999).

2.1 Affecting Theories

In education, Piaget, the Swiss developmental psychologist, described constructivism as the process that students constructed their own knowledge. Constructivism based on Piaget's research results is not an instructional approach, but an information learning approach (Pehlivan, 2010). As a result, teachers focus on individual process of knowledge construction rather than imposing upon their own knowledge. Papert, a student of Piaget, expanded his teacher's strategy to constructionism by helping students construct their own knowledge that others can see and criticize (Papert & Harel, 1991; Kafai, 2006). Besides, constructivism is affected by Vygotsky's theory (Vygotsky, 1978), there are three major points alleged: (i) social interaction plays a significant role through cognitive development, (ii) having at least one person who has better understanding in the environment – this person could be a teacher or a peer, and (iii) the Zone of Proximal Development which is the distance between a student's ability to perform a task with guidance or a peer and ability to study independently. Vygotsky said that learning takes place in this zone.

In addition to these, constructivism is linked to instructional approaches and strategies such as metacognition and self-regulation. Both have important roles in students' learning process and refer to; process of monitoring, self-management, and evaluating a students' understanding (Hattie et al., 1996; Dignath et al., 2008). Metacognition means that one is aware of his own processes of thinking and can control these processes (Jaleel, 2016). Metacognitive approach is crucial because it encourages the students to think creatively and solve problems, and helps them to use their prior knowledge and experiences (Salmon, 2008). This theory claims that individuals must be the one who builds the knowledge, therefore, during process students regulate their own cognitive structure. When looking at the cognitive constructive view, self-regulation must be considered.

When it comes to learning process of equations, function and graphs, in this learning setting students will be encouraged to construct their own knowledge, and teacher has a role which is just a counselor, facilitator and scaffolder. When a student faced with problems to understand, another student can assist him/her or the teacher will scaffold the learner. So, this verifies Vygotsky's second point. As students creating and interpreting the function, equation and graph with the help of apps, calculators or just using pen and paper, teacher will give directions instead of imposing his/her own understanding to the students. Additionally, during the process that students exert effort to find out the conception that the facts bear out related to subject, they will need help and they will be in search of assistance. At this juncture, social interaction with peers or the teacher will be formed as feedback. Just as the constructionist approach advocates, other learners will see and critique the construction built by a learner. This confirms Vygotsky's first and third points. The records kept throughout process will provide monitoring students' understanding, and help the teacher to specify the misunderstandings and/or misconception. This will make easier the evaluation for the teacher. The process of monitoring derives the most effective assessment, and permanent and strong learning. An important goal of this environment is that fostering voluntarily study including setting goals, monitoring the process and evaluating the learning. Students will take active roles and the setting will provide them great opportunities to reflect on what they learn and how they learn with their peers and the teacher.

3. CONCLUSION

Given the structure, the number of students should be limited because there are some reports that indicates the class size is a significant element for the benefit of learning (Farrie et al, 2016; Bosworth, 2014). Students can get more attention from teacher, and teachers know well their students. Every student will be involved to the process, and none of them will be neglected.

Because all the information is transferred from teacher to themselves in current educational system – teacher-centered, students will have difficulties in controlling their learning and studying on their own. However, problems and difficulties would be eliminated with a well-trained teacher about counseling, scaffolding, self-regulated learning and educational psychology. At this point, we need to assume that the teacher has the abilities mentioned above.

Students will learn the understanding of function, equation and graphs in a unique way rather than traditional learning. Also, with the help of interaction and having the freedom to choose the learning way, the ability of working with other people would be improved, their self-esteem and confidence would be settled, and their construction of knowledge will be cumulated by means of others feedback. Students will understand and see the true meaning of and differences between function, equation and graphs, and can easily interpret and recognize them.

REFERENCES

Bayazıt, İ., 2011. Öğretmen adaylarının grafikler konusundaki bilgi düzeyleri. *Gaziantep Üniversitesi Sosyal Bilimler Dergisi,* Vol. 10, No. 4, pp. 1325-1346.

Bosworth, R. 2014. Class size, class composition, and the distribution of student achievement. *Education Economics*, Vol. 22, No. 2, pp. 141-165.

Bransford, J.D. et al, 1999. *How people learn.* National Academy Press, Washington, DC:

Dignath, C. et al, 2008. How can primary school students learn self-regulated learning strategies most effectively? A meta-analysis on self-regulation training programmes. *Educational Research Review,* Vol. 3, pp. 101-129.

Farrie, D. et al, 2016. Reducing Class Size in New York City: Promise vs. Practice. *Education Law Center.*

Goldberg, E.P. and Kliman, M., 1988. *Metaphors for understanding graphs: What you see is what you see.* Educational Technology Center, pp. 1-27, Cambridge, MA.

Graham, S. et al, 1992. Developing self-regulated learners. *Focus on Exceptional Children,* Vol. 24, No. 6, pp. 1–16.

Hattie, J.A. et al, 1996. Effects of learning skills interventions on student learning: A meta-analysis. *Review of Educational Research,* Vol. 66, No. 2, pp. 99-136

Hollar, J.C. and Norwood, K., 1999. The effects of a graphing-approach intermediate algebra curriculum on students' understanding of function. *Journal for Research in Mathematics Education,* Vol. 30, No. 2, pp. 220-226.

Jaleel, S., 2016. A study on the metacognitive awareness of secondary school students. *Universal Journal of Educational Research*, Vol. 4, No. 1, pp. 165-172.

Kafai, Y., 2006. Constructionism. In R.K. Sawyer (Ed.), *The Cambridge Handbook of the Learning Sciences*, pp. 35-46. Cambridge University Press, Cambridge, MA.

Papert, S. and Harel, I., 1991. *Constructionism.* Ablex Publishing Corporation, Westport, CT, US.

Pehlivan, H., 2010. Egitimde Yapilandirmaci Yaklasim. *1st Ulusal Egitim Programlari ve Ogretim Kongresi*. 13-15 May. Balikesir Universitesi, Balikesir, Ayvalik.

Salmon, A., 2008. Promoting a culture of thinking in the young child. *Early Childhood Education Journal*, Vol. 35, pp. 457-461.

Sawyer, K., 2014. Introduction: The new science of learning. In R.K. Sawyer (Ed.). *The Cambridge Handbook of the Learning Sciences*, pp. 1-18. Cambridge University Press, Cambridge, MA.

Sezgin-Memnun, D. et al., 2015. Failures and inabilities of high school students about quadratic equations and functions. *Journal of Education and Training Studies,* Vol. 3, No. 6, pp. 50-60.

Shapiro, E. S. et al, 2002. Self-monitoring interventions for children and adolescents. In M. R. Shinn, H. M. Walker, & G. Stoner (Eds.), *Interventions for Academic and Behavior Problems II: Preventive and Remedial Approaches*, pp. 913–938. NASP, Bethesda, MD.

Vygotsky, L.S., 1978. *Mind and society, The development of Higher Mental Processes*. Harvard University Press, Cambridge, MA.

Williams, S., 1997. Algebra: What students can learn. The nature and algebra in the K-14 curriculum. *Proceedings of a National Symposium,* Washington, DC, May 27-28.

LEVERAGING THE AFFORDANCES OF MOBILE LEARNING FOR VOCABULARY GAINS

Michael Bowles
Zayed University , Academic City, Dubai, PO Box 19282, United Arab Emirates

ABSTRACT

According to research findings, learners who are about to commence an undergraduate degree course with English as the medium of instruction (EMI), require a minimum English vocabulary size in order to decode and comprehend the academic texts that they have to read (Hazenberg and Hulstijn, 1996; Staehr, 2008; Laufer and Ravenhorst-Kalovski, 2010; Schmitt, 2010; Nation, 2013, Milton and Treffers-Daller, 2013). In the United Arab Emirates, several thousand Emirati students attend English foundation programmes prior to starting their EMI degrees in order to improve their academic skills, such as reading and vocabulary knowledge. However, despite the increased use of Technology-Enhanced Learning (TEL) and the introduction of mobile learning in 2012, the results of this study show that the vast majority of female Emirati still have an insufficient receptive vocabulary size for beginning an EMI undergraduate degree course. In addition, the use of a generic vocabulary learning app over a four-month period has not led to a significant increase in most students' vocabulary size. The reasons for this could include the fact that the generic app does not fully utilise the affordances of mobile learning, it is not underpinned by pedagogically-sound vocabulary learning principles and that it does not focus on the particular learning needs and lexical weakness of Emirati students. Therefore, the author has worked as part of a team to develop and build a new, customised, mobile app that has attempted to address these weaknesses and help Zayed University students reach the required vocabulary learning goal.

KEYWORDS

Foreign languages; vocabulary; apps; affordances; mobile learning; adaptive learning

1. INTRODUCTION

The ability to read academic texts is important for all students in higher education, but it is a particular issue for students for whom English is not their first language and who are about to embark on an EMI (English as the medium of instruction) undergraduate degree course. In order to read and understand these academic texts, it is important that students possess a sufficient knowledge of the appropriate English vocabulary or lexical items so that they can recognise and decode the words on the page. Several studies show that learners require a receptive knowledge of at least the first 3,000 most frequent word families in order to understand these texts with the help of an instructor (Nation, 2013: 208).

In order to achieve this learning goal of 3,000 word families, students need to actively learn and practice the most frequent words families in English (Nation, 2013). An ideal tool to do this a vocabulary learning app on a mobile device, such as a tablets or smartphone. This takes advantages of many of the affordances of mobile technology, such as ubiquitous learning, multimodal meaning, recursive feedback and differentiated learning (Cope & Kalantzis, 2017) and navigationism (Moran, 2008).

At Zayed University in the UAE, these affordances have been harnessed to develop a context-specific, vocabulary learning app that supports learners in acquiring 600 of the most useful and frequent general and general academic word families in English. This paper first identifies the issues as described in the literature, as well as the learning context. It then describes how the features of the new app leverage the affordances of e-learning and mobile learning, and finally how these features are based on key pedagogical principles and process of learning vocabulary.

2. LITERATURE REVIEW

2.1 Conceptualising Vocabulary

Vocabulary knowledge in any language can be conceptualised in terms of breadth or depth. Vocabulary breadth, or vocabulary size, refers to the number of words or word families a person knows, while vocabulary depth refers to how much a person knows about each word (Milton, 2013, p. 60). Another important distinction is between the written or orthographic form of a word that is used in reading and writing and its aural or phonological form used in listening and speaking (Nation, 2013).

2.2 Vocabulary Size

There is already a clear relationship between reading comprehension and breadth of receptive vocabulary knowledge in a language. Nation (2013: 208) states that knowledge of the 3-4,000 most frequent word families in English will enable readers to recognise and comprehend 95% of the words in most written texts with instructional support from the teacher. However, in order to read and understand most texts independently of a teacher, and be able to guess the meaning of the remaining unknown words, learners need to know 98% of the words in a text. This is equivalent to knowledge of 8-9,000 word families (Ibid). This is supported by Laufer & Ravenhorst-Kalovski (2010:15), who also identified 8,000 word families as an optimal size for reading comprehension.

2.3 Learning Context

Zayed University is one of three federal higher education institutions in the United Arab Emirates in which English is the medium of instruction (EMI) on all degree courses. Prior to starting their 4-year degree course, students with a lower level of English ability have to join a foundation program for a maximum of eight months over one academic year of two semesters. On this program they undertake intensive English for General Academic Purposes (EGAP) courses of up to twenty hours per week in order to gain the necessary English language and academic skills. Technology is widely used throughout the program, both in terms of the hardware and software. Since August 2012, the use of iPads was mandated in all classes and they became the primary tool for the students to consume and produce learning content. Students also make use of their smartphones for certain learning tasks and activities. For each of the three levels in the Foundation program, there are clear vocabulary learning objectives that focus on receptive vocabulary knowledge. The learning outcome is for students to learn 600 word families over a period of 16 weeks.

2.4 Current Vocabulary Knowledge

At the end of the 2016 Fall semester, 252 students in the final level of the foundation program completed an online vocabulary size test. The results showed that nearly 50% of the students had a receptive vocabulary size of only 2,000 word families, while approximately 24% of students had a vocabulary size of less than 2,000 word families. Only 14% of students at the end of the ABP demonstrated a vocabulary size of 3,000 word families, which has been identified as an absolute minimum for starting a degree course in English.

2.5 Mobile Apps for Learning Vocabulary

Since the introduction of mobile devices, such as tablets and smartphones, a plethora of commercial mobile apps have been developed that support the learning of different aspects of vocabulary in various languages. These include those that focus on general language development (Duolingo), storing vocabulary (MyWordBook) and retrieving vocabulary (Quizlet).

In addition, there have been several attempts by teachers and academics to develop English vocabulary learning mobile apps for their particular learning context and their research findings show how mobile learning apps can enhance English vocabulary learning. For example, Wu (2015) reports on the development of a Basic4Android smartphone app to help college students in China improve their English vocabulary. She shows that the students who used the app "significantly outperformed those in the control group in acquiring new vocabulary" (2015: 170). Similarly, Wang (2017) designed an Android app that presented 720 lexical items from the New General Service List (NGSL) of the most frequent words in English to her class of university students in Taiwan. Feedback from her students suggested that for the vast majority, the app gave them more opportunities for learning English and allowed them to learn every day.

2.6 Generic Vocabulary App

In terms of the Foundation program Zayed University, a generic, off-the-shelf app and website – 'Vocabulary and Spelling City', was introduced at the beginning of the 2015 academic year as a way for students to try and learn the 600 word families specified in the curriculum.

In order to measure the effectiveness of the app, students were asked to complete an online vocabulary size test at the beginning of the Fall semester in September 2016 and again at the end of the semester in early December 2016. The test scores are presented as knowledge of vocabulary in bands of 500 word families. Table 1 shows the changes in the overall vocabulary band scores for the 212 students who completed both tests. 103 or nearly half of all the students showed no change in the size of their vocabulary, as measured by the test. 56 students or about a quarter of the total increased their vocabulary by one band and 22 students or 10% of the total increased it by two bands. At the other end of the scale, 23 students or 10% of the total experienced a decline in their receptive vocabulary by on band.

Table 1. Changes in Vocabulary Sizes for EGAP4 students between Sept. and Dec. 2016

Change in Band Scores	Number of students	Percentage of total number of students
Decreased 3 Bands	1	0.47%
Decreased 2 Bands	6	2.83%
Decreased 1 Band	23	10.85%
No Change in Band	103	48.58%
Increased 1 Band	56	26.42%
Increased 2 Bands	22	10.38%
Increased 5 Bands	1	0.47%
TOTALS	**212**	**100%**

Overall, the learning gains from using the generic vocabulary app have been far from impressive. There could be several reasons for this. Firstly, the generic app does not fully utilise the affordances of mobile learning. Secondly, it is not underpinned by sound vocabulary learning principles. Finally, it does not focus on the particular learning needs and lexical weakness of Emirati students. Therefore, the author has worked as part of a team to develop and build a new, customised, mobile app that has attempted to address these weaknesses and help Zayed University students reach the required vocabulary learning goal.

3. AFFORDANCES OF A CUSTOM-BUILT APP

The Academic Vocabulary App (AVA) was designed by instructors in the foundation program in conjunction with instructional designers from the university's Centre for Educational Innovation (CEI). All the content was localized for the context and it has been designed to take advantage of many of the affordances advocated by leading educationalists in e-learning, such as Cope & Kalantzis (2017).

3.1 Ubiquitous Learning

The app is primarily designed to be used by the learners as a self-access tool outside the classroom, using their smart phones or tablets. Learners can take advantage of the anytime, anywhere, anyhow aspect of mobile learning and are actively encouraged to use the app whenever they have even five minutes of free time. Instructors can also make use of it in class to play team games to review word families.

3.2 Multimodal Meaning

As well as static text and images, the app also uses sound files to allow users to hear each word being pronounced by a speaker of either British or American English. This allows users to make a much stronger connection between the orthographic (written) representation and the phonological (aural) representation of the meaning.

3.3 Differentiated Learning

In order to take advantage of the ability of the technology to differentiate learning for each individual, AVA features elements of individualized and adaptive learning. Firstly, items within each stage are completely randomized, so no two learners will get the same sequence of items. In addition, if a user gets an item wrong, it is re-presented later within the same stage. Finally, the app records which words and items a user has had problems with and saves these as Weak Words. Users can then complete Weak Word Quizzes that only contain items for these words.

3.4 Recursive Feedback

At all stages, feedback is constant and immediate. For individual items, users get instant feedback on whether their answers are correct or not. If they are incorrect, they get the opportunity later to answer the same question again. At the end of each Stage, block and Unit, users get feedback on which words were weak and are directed to complete extra activities to strengthen these.

3.5 Navigationism

Finally, the structure of the app has been designed so that learners can follow the built in learning sequence to maximize learning gains or, if they prefer, go to the Stages in the app that they feel they need more practice with, such as learning collocations. This encourages learners to develop their skills in navigationism (Moran, 2008) so that they can steer their own path through the learning materials without a teacher being there to dictate their learning pathway.

4. VOCABULARY LEARNING PRINCIPALS

AVA is also based on four important vocabulary learning principles or processes that make it unique amongst mobile vocabulary learning apps.

4.1 Noticing

This process simply refers to learners giving attention to a particular word or lexical item. In the app the meaning and form of each new word is presented very clearly in the initial stage so that users can connect the two in several different activities.

4.2 Encoding

Encoding is the process by which a new trace of information is laid down in memory. According to Kihlstrom (2013) a stronger memory is created "when we process an item deeply, connecting it to our rich fund of pre-existing knowledge." (Kihlstrom, 2013, p. 3). AVA incorporates this principle by presenting new words in sentences that are localized and relevant to Emirati learners. This makes them more meaningful and therefore more likely to be remembered.

4.3 Generating

Previously met words need to be subsequently used in ways that are different from the previous meeting with the word (Nation, 2013, p. 68-72). These new meetings force learners to reconceptualise and strengthen their knowledge of that word within their long-term memories. In AVA, there are six different stages that users can pass through and each one focuses on a different aspect of vocabulary, including spelling, collocations and word families. Each stage enables users to see the same words in different contexts, which are more likely to help preserve and enhance the long term memory trace of that word.

4.4 Retrieving

This final process involves actively remembering and recalling the form and meaning of a word at different points (Nation, 2001, p. 66-68). To maximize the effectiveness of retrieval, learners require at least seven opportunities to retrieve the word from their memory (Nation, 2001:67). Within each block of 10 words in AVA, users encounter each word at least 10 times over a 30-minute period.

5. CONCLUSION

As has been described in this paper, the development of a custom-built, vocabulary learning app has been based on substantial research into both the affordances of e-learning and mobile technology, as well as key vocabulary learning principles. For the Fall 2017 semester, all learners in the final level of the program will use the app for the first time and a measurement of their vocabulary sizes will be taken at the beginning and end of the semester. It is hoped that the consistent use of the app by learners on the foundation program will lead to a greater number reaching the learning objective of 3,000 of the most frequent word families in English and, therefore, being better able to cope with the academic texts they are required to read on their EMI undergraduate courses.

REFERENCES

Cope, B. & Kalantzis, M., 2017. *e-Learning Ecologies: Principles for new learning and assessment.* Routledge, New York, USA.

Hazenberg, S. & Hulstijn, J. H., 1996. Defining a minimal receptive second-language vocabualry for non-native university students: An empirical investigation. *Applied Linguistics*, Volume 17, pp. 145-163.

Kihlstrom, J. F. 2011. How students learn and how we can help them. Retrieved from
http://socrates.berkeley.edu/~kihlstrm/GSI_2011.htm

Laufer, B. & Ravenhorst-Kalovski, G. C., 2010. Lexical Threshold revisited: Lexical text coverage, learners' vocabulary size and reading comprehension. *Reading in a foreign language*, April, 22(1), pp. 15-30.

Lin, C.-C. & Yu, Y.-C., 2016. Effects of presentation modes on mobile-assisted vocabulary learning and cognitive load. *Interactive Learning Environments*, DOI: 10.1080/1049820.2016.1155160

Milton, J., 2013. Measuring the contribution of vocabualry knowledge to proficiency in the four skills. L2 vocabulary acquisition, knowledge and use. *Eurosla Monographs Series 1,* pp. 57-78.

Milton, J. & Treffers- Daller, J., 2013. Vocabulary size revisited: the link between vocabulary size and academic achievement. Applied Linguistics Review, Volume 4, pp. 151-172.

Moran, S., 2008. After behaviourism, navigationism? *Irish Educational Studies*, September, Volume 27, No. 3, pp.209-221.

Nation & I. S. P., 2008. *Teaching Vocabulary: Strategies and Techniques*. Heinle, Boston, USA.

Nation, I. S. P., 2013. *Learning Vocabulary in Another Language (2nd Edition)*. Cambridge University Press,
Cambridge, UK.

Schmitt, N., 2010. Key issues in teaching and learning vocabulary. Insights into Non-native Vocabulary Teaching and Learning. *Multilingual Matters*.

Wang, B.-T., 2017. Designing mobile apps for English Vocabulary Learning. *International Journal of Information and Education Technology*, April, 7(4), pp. 279-283.

Wu, Q., 2015. Designing a smartphone app to teach English (L2) vocabulary. *Computers & Education*, Volume 85, pp. 170-179.

TOWARDS A FRAMEWORK OF USING KNOWLEDGE TOOLS FOR TEACHING BY SOLVING PROBLEMS IN TECHNOLOGY-ENHANCED LEARNING ENVIRONMENT*

Sergei Kostousov[1] and Dmitry Kudryavtsev[2]
[1]*Saint-Petersburg Peter the Great Polytechnic University, Polytechnicheskaya ulitsa, 29, Russia*
[2]*Graduate School of Management, St. Petersburg University, Volkhovskiy Pereulok, 3, Russia*

ABSTRACT

Problem solving is a critical competency for modern world and also an effective way of learning. Education should not only transfer domain-specific knowledge to students, but also prepare them to solve real-life problems – to apply knowledge from one or several domains within specific situation. Problem solving as teaching tool is known for a long time, but our aim is to enhance it by suggesting knowledge tools for different stages of problem solving process. Knowledge tools involve students in the process of knowledge construction that contributes to understanding of subject and help students to organize and present their own knowledge. An overview of software, which help to apply the suggested knowledge tools, is presented as well. Finally we illustrate our approach with two examples of teaching school and university students.

KEYWORDS

Education, problem solving, knowledge tools, knowledge construction, technology-enhanced learning

1. INTRODUCTION

Contemporary world requires the use of new technologies in learning process as the traditional educational methods cannot manage increasing amount of information. Education should not only give information to students, but also provide the methods of knowledge production and information technologies can make this process more effective and efficient. The use of IT in education should not be limited by the change of the communication channel for information transfer: "from teacher to learner" to "from the multimedia system to learner." Computer technology should provide conditions for students to design, present and express their knowledge by themselves rather than on a pre-programmed pattern (Jonassen et al, 1998; Jonassen, 2005). The learning environment is necessary to provide an opportunity for students to produce, present and express knowledge. The use of computers in this case means not only the use of various forms of presentation and communication of information (Kalantarov, 2014).

The use of problem-solving method in the learning process helps students in construction of their own knowledge and allow instructors to individualize the learning process, as students will generate their own decisions with the teacher's support and not use the already existing ones (Jonassen, 2004). This helps to understand the studied subjects better and improve problem-solving skills, regardless of the field of study.

Existing research (De Corte et al, 2004) shows the effectiveness of applying problem solving for educational results and improvement of learning and adaptation skills, but the suggested environment does not specify the role of IT. Computer system in this case should serve as a catalyst for the acquisition of knowledge and skills. Other research (Kim, Hannafin, 2011) illustrates the possibilities of scaffolding problem solving in technology enhanced environment, but without use of knowledge tools.

Knowledge tools help in the transfer of knowledge from teacher to student, making the process more clear and understandable, and enable students to construct their own knowledge and mental models. Knowledge tools involve students in the process of knowledge construction that contributes to understanding of subject, and not only the playback from the memory of what has been received from a teacher or other source of knowledge. These tools help students to organize and present their own knowledge. That is why we decided

* Research has been conducted with financial support from Russian Science Foundation grant (project No. 15-18-30048).

to make an environment where students would be given the opportunity to use knowledge tools to construct their own mental models and apply them to solve problems.

The aim of this paper is to propose a framework of using knowledge tools for teaching by solving problems and to suggest a corresponding IT support.

2. PROBLEM SOLVING AS A TEACHING TOOL

Problem solving is usually one of the most important cognitive skills in education, profession and everyday life (Jonassen, 2000). Problem is the task that requires study and subsequent decision, that contains the following (Jonassen, 1997): domain, type, solving process and solution. Domain defines concepts and elements of issues, concepts and principles adopted by it. Solving process is a set of operations to reduce the impact of the problem and to approach targets (Wood, 1983). Problem type prescribes the rules and procedures necessary for its solution. Well-structured and ill-structured problems can be allocated (Jonassen, 1997). Dividing problems in two categories is important for our framework because different types of problems can appear and different kinds of tools can be used for them. We summarized characteristics of problems in Table 1 (Jonassen, 1997; Wood, 1983; Kitchner, 1983).

Table 1. Characteristics of well- and ill-structured problems

	Well-Structured	**Ill-Structured**
Context dependence	Weak	Strong
The initial state	Well defined	Undefined
The final (target) state	Well known	Unknown
Number of solutions	One solution	Many solutions
Similar problems	Similar solution	Solutions can differ because of context dependence
Required skills	Knowledge Base	Personal experience in the field of problem Extensive knowledge of the issues and related fields The ability to argue and defend their point of view
Solving process	Spent circuit solutions Iterative search	Design and synthesis solutions Collection of evidence in favor solutions Discussions for the selection decision Monitoring of selected solutions
Evaluation	The effectiveness of the chosen schema	Only empirically
Relation with real life	Weak	Most real-world problems

According to (Jonassen, 2004; Kim, Hannafin, 2011) we can highlight the following stages of solving process for different types of problems: 1. Identify problem; 2. Create problem space (including context); 3. Search potential solutions; 4. Evaluate and choose solutions; 5. Implement solution; 6. Check and verify; 7. Reflection.

3. KNOWLEDGE TOOLS FOR TEACHING BY SOLVING PROBLEMS

The use of knowledge tools helps in the construction of knowledge by a student and becomes a key ingredient of active and continuous learning (Gavrilova, 2010; Gavrilova et al, 2011; Jonassen et al, 1998; Jonassen, 2005; Koznov, Pliskin, 2008). The article (Wang et al., 2013) illustrates the possibilities of using cognitive tools to scaffold the whole problem solving process and shows its effectiveness. Argument and concepts maps are used there together.

The current work is in line with the design science research methodology. The following requirements are specified for the framework: support of different stages of problem solving process; application of tools, which supports knowledge structuring and production; specifics of problems must be taken in to account; guidelines for implementation of IT support must be provided.

We analyzed and selected knowledge tools that can be applied effectively at different stages of problem-solving in teaching. The main sources of information were (Jonassen, 2005; Gavrilova et al, 2012; Young, 2010; Kudravtsev, Gavrilova, 2017). Our framework does not mean the use of all the proposed knowledge tools, but shows possible ones. Although some tools may be used at several stages, we tried to define the most important "stage-tool" links. The selection criterion for tools was a type of knowledge that is needed at the stage of problem solving. Also those tools were selected that are easy to learn and do not require a lot of time to study because they are ancillary.

3.1 Framework of Using Knowledge Tools on Stages of Problem Solving

The main part of our framework is based on visual knowledge structuring tools. First of all, elements of problem should be presented by student. Problem presentation is the key to problem solving (Jonassen, 2005). Knowledge visualization facilitates intuitive understanding (Mayer, 1989). Main parts of a problem situation and actions in problem-solving process as well as their relationships should be visualized. Mind maps can be used to show them. Then we should create problem space: understand relations between problem elements. Concept maps can visualize all relations. For ill-structured problems we should take into account context dependencies as well and simple overview of similar problems cannot give enough information in current situation. So causal models can be used to describe root causes and different consequences of a problem, they can also illustrate by (+) factors, that have positive impact, and by (-) factors, that have negative impact. The goal tree can be used for ill-structured problem because it can have multiple target states, which are associated to different goals, and we don't know the best one. Both well- and ill-structured problems can have several methods of solution: in this case, decision tree helps to visualize them. Argument mapping can help during choosing the best solution of that have been found by visualizing benefits and limitations of them. Such an evidence in favor or against solutions is especially relevant for ill-structured problems. When solution is chosen, diagrams may help to visualize its implementation plan in terms of projects and processes (for example, Gantt charts). After the implementation stage we should verify the solution. With argument map we can check solution by illustrating what have been and have not been done. On the last step mind map can be used again to summarize experience and make knowledge more structured. The framework is presented on table 2.

Table 2. Knowledge visualization tools supporting different stages of problem solving

<table>
<tr><th>Stage</th><th>Well-Structured problem</th><th>Ill-Structured problem</th></tr>
<tr><td>1. Identify problem</td><td colspan="2">Mind map</td></tr>
<tr><td rowspan="2">2. Create problem space (incl. context)</td><td colspan="2">Concept map</td></tr>
<tr><td>–</td><td>Causal model</td></tr>
<tr><td rowspan="2">3. Search potential solutions</td><td>–</td><td>Goal tree</td></tr>
<tr><td colspan="2">Decision tree</td></tr>
<tr><td>4. Evaluate and choose solutions</td><td>–</td><td>Argument map</td></tr>
<tr><td>5. Implement solution</td><td colspan="2">Project diagram, Process diagram</td></tr>
<tr><td>6. Check and verify</td><td colspan="2">Argument mapping</td></tr>
<tr><td>7. Reflection</td><td colspan="2">Mind map</td></tr>
</table>

However, not only knowledge visualization tools can be useful. Brainstorming can be used to identify problem in the group. Libraries with example solutions and case studies should help to understand meaningful objects of problem space and can show possible ways of the solution. Means-end analysis can be used for well-structured problems as we know initial and final state. For ill-structured problems brainstorm can help generate different solutions. Also decision tables can help to generate and organize possible solutions and then this tool can help to select the way to reach the best one. After action review and formulation of lessons learned can be used to evaluate chosen solution, get a feedback from students and accumulate their knowledge.

3.2 Software for Supporting Proposed Framework of Using Knowledge Tools

To scaffold our framework we reviewed some software tools to create heterogeneous technology-enhanced learning environment. Listed software (table 3) was chosen based on author's experience, literature review and product's descriptions.

Table 3. Software supporting knowledge visualization

Knowledge visualization tool	Possible software
Mind map	MindManager, MindMapper, ThinkGraph, FreeMind, MyMind, Xmind
Concept map	CmapTool, Inspiration
Argument map	Reason!Able, Athena, Debatabase, Agora, Rationale
Decision tree	PrecisionTree, Flying Logic
Project diagram	Microsoft Project
Process diagram	Microsoft Visio

Another option is software integrated in a learning management system. Benefit of this approach is that software tools are standardized and visual models can be produced, saved and checked directly in learning environment. Moreover, integration gives an opportunity to use one tool for knowledge transfer from teacher, knowledge construction by student and assessment of education results. We analysed Moodle system (https://moodle.org/) as an integration platform. Moodle is a learning platform designed to provide educators, administrators and learners with a single robust, secure and integrated system to create learning environments. Standard activities like forums, chats and wiki can be used for brainstorming, after action review and lessons learned and also to describe and accumulate cases and worked examples.

Visual knowledge tools can be installed as well. We have found activity plugins for mind mapping (Mind Map, Advanced MindMap, Mappa) and question type plugin for concept mapping (Concept Map). Hierarchical structure of mind maps allows using this tool for goal and decision trees, using colors on mind map can make it suitable for argument map creation and a complement of this tool by chat gives a visual tool for brainstorming. A substitution of relations in concept map by + and – allows to make causal models.

4. DEMONSTRATION

Our approach now is on the stage of approbation. For case and field studies we decided to implement our framework and added problem solving as an instrument of education in two courses: for programming learners at school and for university learners of business engineering (enterprise architecture).

First group includes school learners 14-15 years old that study programming and have a task of making course project. They should choose well-structured problem. To enhance this process it is required to build mind map of their problem to make it more obviously. After the information model of program was build students should apply means-ends analysis to make effective and optimized algorithm. If pupils do not implement it, they can choose any working solution without comparing so they will not get metacognitive skills. After making of programs all students will have to discuss not only their own works but try to evaluate other solutions through common after action review.

University students study business engineering (enterprise architecture) through semester-long problem-oriented project. They should choose an enterprise, find «bottle necks» and suggest solution. This task is ill-structured. Students create standard enterprise architecture models during analysis and synthesis phases of problem solving. Students should make a mind-map in order to organize knowledge about an enterprise and understand context. Goal tree is created and causal map for root-cause analysis is developed. Brainstorm can be applied for searching possible solutions by group. Overview of existing solutions for similar problems and work with case library will help to avoid wheel reinvention. Many solutions are possible because this problem is ill-structured – we cannot know the ideal goal state for enterprise. Argument mapping can help to choose the best solution and develop skills of reasoning and defending point of view. After the solution was created students have to consolidate gathered knowledge by formulating lessons learned.

It should be noted that the use of knowledge tools is an additional cognitive load. However, the expected effect of improving learning skills and deeper understanding of the subject, in our view, justifies this approach. Further research will be dedicated to more detailed analysis of relationship between knowledge tools and different stages of problem solving, besides more sound evaluation of the proposed framework is required.

5. CONCLUSION

Contemporary world requires the use of new technologies in learning process. Education should not only give domain-knowledge but has to provide the methods of knowledge production and information technologies can make this process more efficient. Principles of education through problem solving were discussed. Problems as educational instrument can let students get metacognitive skills and not only domain specific knowledges. To make the process of transferring of knowledge from teacher to student clearer and to help student construct own knowledge we proposed the framework of using knowledge tools and methods on different stages of problem solving. Knowledge tools involve students in the process of knowledge production that contributes to their profound understanding of subject. IT environment can help to make this process more effective. The results of the research can be used for creating courses and applying specific IT-tools and plugins on various stages of training.

REFERENCES

De Corte E., Verschaffel L., Masui C. (2004). The CLIA-model: A framework for designing powerful learning environments for thinking and problem solving. European Journal of Psychology of Education, 19(4), 365-384.

Gavrilova T., Leshcheva I., Strakhovich E. (2011). On the use of visual conceptual models in teaching // Bulletin of St. Petersburg State University, a series of management, № 4, 125-151. (in Russian)

Gavrilova, T. (2010). Knowledge engineering for non-engineers. Intelligent Information Processing, IFIP Advances in Information and Communication Technology, Springer, 340, 225-233.

Jonassen D. H. (1997). Instructional design models for well-structured and III-structured problem-solving learning outcomes. Educational Technology Research and Development, 45(1), 65-94.

Jonassen, D. H., Carr, C., & Yueh, H. P. (1998). Computers as mindtools for engaging learners in critical thinking. TechTrends, 43(2), 24-32.

Jonassen D. H. (2000). Toward a design theory of problem solving. Educational technology research and development, 48(4), 63-85.

Jonassen D. H. (2004). Learning to solve problems: An instructional design guide (Vol. 6). John Wiley & Sons.

Jonassen, D. H. (2005). Tools for representing problems and the knowledge required to solve them. In Knowledge and information visualization, Springer Berlin Heidelberg, 82-94.

Kalontarov J., Kandy P.A. (2014). Basic directions and tendencies in the process of using of informational technology in education. STUDIA, (5), 75 (in Russian).

Kim M. C., & Hannafin, M. J. (2011). Scaffolding problem solving in technology-enhanced learning environments (TELEs): Bridging research and theory with practice. Computers & Education, 56(2), 403-417.

Kitchner K.S. (1983). Cognition, metacognition, and epistemic cognition: A three-level model of cognitive processing. Human Development, 26, 222-232.

Koznov, D., & Pliskin, M. (2008). Computer-supported collaborative learning with mind-maps. Communications in Computer and Information Science, 17, 478-489.

Kudryavtsev D., Gavrilova T. (2017). From Anarchy to System: A Novel Classification of Visual Knowledge Codification Techniques. Knowledge and Process Management, 24(1), 3-13.

Mayer R. E. (1989). Models for understanding. Review of Educational Research, 59(1), 43-64.

Wang M., Wu B., Chen N.S., Spector J.M. (2013). Connecting problem-solving and knowledge-construction processes in a visualization-based learning environment. Computers & Education, 68, 293-306.

Wood P.K. (1983). Inquiring systems and problem structures: Implications for cognitive development. Human Development, 26, 249-265.

Young R. (2010). Knowledge management tools and techniques manual. Asian Productivity Organization.

EXPLORING STUDENTS' LEARNING JOURNALS WITH WEB-BASED INTERACTIVE REPORT TOOL

Yuta Taniguchi[1], Fumiya Okubo[2], Atsushi Shimada[3] and Shin'ichi Konomi[2]
[1]*Research Institute for Information Technology, Kyushu University, Japan, 744 Motooka,, Nishi-ku, Fukuoka 819-0395, Japan*
[2]*Faculty of Arts and Science, Kyushu University, Japan, 744 Motooka,, Nishi-ku, Fukuoka 819-0395, Japan*
[3]*Information Science and Electrical Engineering, Kyushu University, Japan, 744 Motooka,, Nishi-ku, Fukuoka 819-0395, Japan*

ABSTRACT

Students' journal writings could be useful resources for teachers to grasp their understandings and to see their own teaching objectively. However, reading a large number of journals thoroughly is not always realistic for teachers. Although various automatic analysis methods have been proposed to understand learning journals, they does not necessarily fit needs of teachers and tend to overlook minor opinions. In this paper, we propose an interactive report tool for exploring journal writings. Focusing on the efficiency of reading learning journals, it employs weekly keywords extracted from journals as entry points for journal sentences. It enables us to read journal sentences selectively. The tool also provides lists of most used adjectives from week to week, which is helpful for teachers to grasp the temporal variation of opinions through a semester. We conducted a preliminary questionnaire about the usefulness of the report tool targeting teachers of the course "Information Science" in our university. Most of them evaluated our tool positively although the number of answers were small.

KEYWORDS

Learning journals, teaching support, understanding journal writings, interactive user interface

1. INTRODUCTION

Journal writing in an educational context is an important approach for fostering writing skills, for deepening understandings of concepts (Scouller, 1998), for reflection (Boud, 2001), and so on. Students' learning journals contain their thoughts, feelings, and ideas, which come up to their mind during a class. These are useful for teachers to see their teaching activity objectively from student's perspective. By reading journals, teachers can find which topics interested students, what confused them, and how they understood concepts. Such observation gives teachers many insights that lead to improvements of course materials and their own teaching.

Reading journals thoroughly, however, takes a long time when a class is large, and it is not always possible for teachers to read journals of all students. It is also difficult to summarize a number of opinions without overlooking minor but important opinions. In recent years, text mining techniques has been employed to automatically analyze learning journals; for example, a topic modeling technique was employed for grading reflections (Chen et al., 2016), and subjective and affective features were captured from reflective texts (Gibson and Kitto, 2015).

Although such analysis methods help us to understand journals to some extent, they only provide a fixed view of journals and does not always fit teacher's need. Therefore, it remains important to read individual entries of journals in an efficient manner. Our research question is how we could improve teachers' reading experience especially for learning journals without losing flexibility and efficiency.

In this study, we propose an interactive report tool based on web technologies, which makes it possible for teachers to explore students' journal writings without losing details of the writings. We employed weekly keywords (Taniguchi et al., 2017) as entry points to actual journal texts, which enables teachers to read journal entries selectively. We implemented our interactive reports on our Mahara e-portfolio system as a web-based tool, and conducted a preliminary questionnaire about its usefulness. In the rest of the paper, we detail the design and implementation of our proposed interactive report tool, and then discuss the result of the questionnaire.

2. METHOD

2.1 Design of Interactive Report

We propose a web-based interactive report tool for journal entries, which provides word-based navigation mechanism and shows patterns of word usages. We consider a kind of keyword that helps us to understand a wide variety of topics of journal entries. The graphical user interface displays such keywords as entry points of journal exploration. The keywords are shown in ranking tables for each week, and we can see how the usage of words varies from week to week. We also show most frequent adjectives for every week, which presents the temporal change in sentiment.

We employ the importance measure proposed in (Taniguchi et al., 2017), which identifies weekly keywords. Minor opinions or topics are relatively difficult to notice when we read students' journals in a limited time. Most of the journal entries usually share the common topics, and thus we can skip some redundant entries. The importance measure balances between minor and major topics by taking into account both the frequency and the week-specificity of a word, where week-specificity is computed from the week frequency of the word in a dataset. Since minor opinions highly related to particular course topics tend to include week-specific words, we can efficiently ignore redundant entries by choosing entries that includes weekly keywords.

2.2 Implementation Detail

The users of our Mahara system can use the interactive report tool as a part of the system. The tool shows an interactive report for selected classes. A report consists of three sections. The first section presents a simple statistical information about journal texts. Figure 1 shows an example of the section. It includes the total of entries, the total of words, the average number of words per sentence, and so on. These numbers shows how much students wrote in journals.

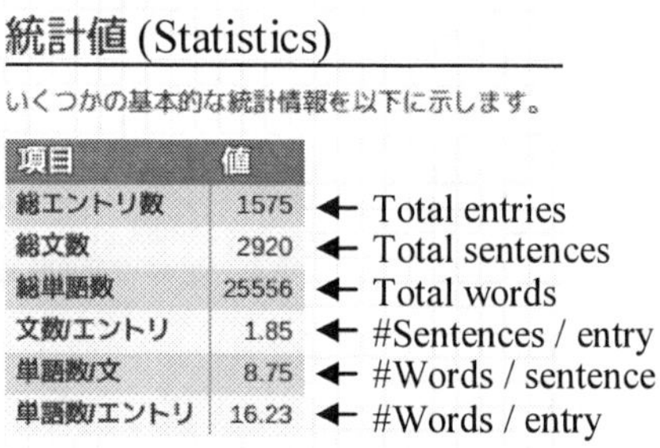

Figure 1. The first section showing statistics such as total numbers and average numbers of entries, sentences, and words

The second section gives us the main interactive interface for journal exploration. There are four subsections corresponding to part of speeches of nouns, adjectives, verbs, and adverbs. Each subsection shows a ranking table of words of the corresponding part of speech for every week. Figure 2 shows an example table for nouns on the left hand side, and additional three dynamic features on the right hand side.

The first dynamic feature is a pop-up sentence view. When we hold a mouse cursor on a word in tables, a popup appears and it shows the sentences containing the selected word and emphasizes its occurrences. It is helpful for us to understand in what context and how the word is used in real sentences.

The second one is word highlighting feature which emphasize all occurrences of a pointed word across ranking tables. Since the ranking table presents a relative importance in a particular week, this feature makes it possible to see how the usage pattern of the word changes through a semester.

The last feature is grouping feature of adjective and verbal words by their polarity based on a dictionary. We can toggle the feature, and get *positive* and *negative* words in ranking tables colored with green and red colors, respectively. It is helpful to quickly understand journal contents from the sentimental point of view.

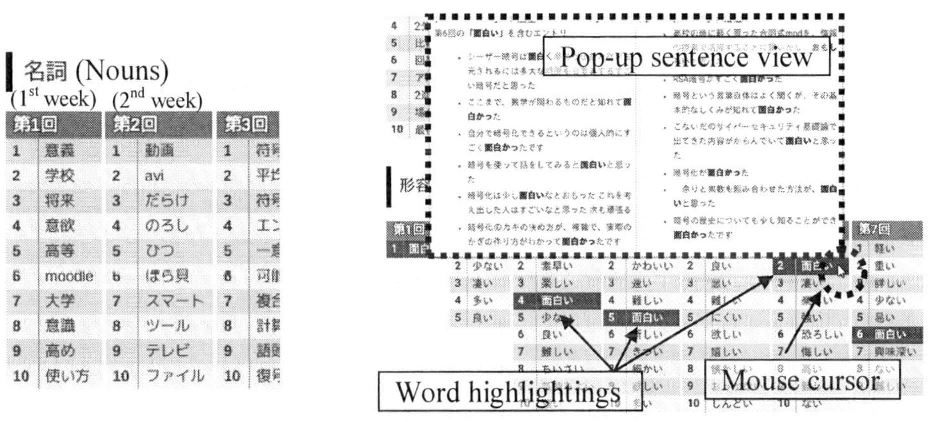

Figure 2. The second section showing weekly keyword rankings. On the left hand side, rankings of noun keywords for the first three weeks are shown. Additional dynamic features are shown on the right hand side

The last section focuses on adjectives and includes two types of stacked bar charts as shown in Figure 3. On the left hand side of the figure, the numbers of occurrences are shown for each major adjective word. In contrast, on the right hand side, adjective words are grouped into positive ones, negative ones, and the others;

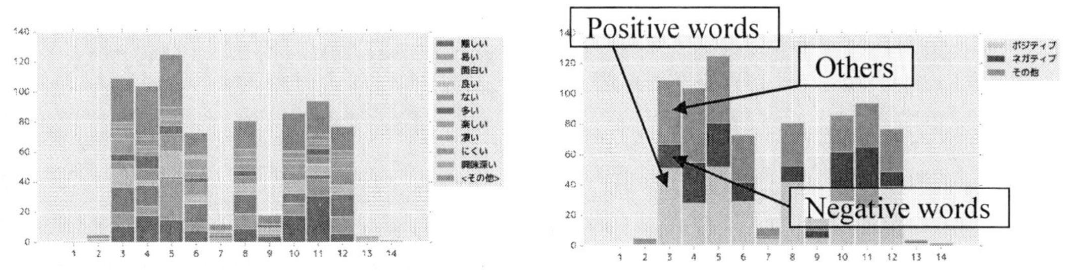

Figure 3. The third section that shows temporal changes in adjective word usage. The frequencies of individual words is shown as a stacked bar chart on the left hand side. The same for three word groups of *positive*, *negative*, and *other* is shown on the right hand side

and it roughly shows how opinions changes. These charts make it possible for teachers to track the temporal change in adjective word usage, which in turn helps them identify topics interesting or difficult for students.

3. RESULT & DISCUSSION

We did a questionnaire about the use of students' journal for improving teaching and about the usefulness of our report tool. We asked ten teachers to use our interactive report tool and to answer the questionnaire, who conducted classes of Information Science course held for the first grade students during the first semester 2016 in our university. In the classes, students were instructed to write a journal entry per week after a class with the content including their impression after class, what they learned, what aspects they found interesting, and so on. All the learning journals are collected in our Mahara e-portfolio system.

Since we obtained answers from only several teachers, we abandoned to quantitatively evaluate our report tool. We only shows some of the answers in this paper. Only two out of five teachers answered they had browsed students' learning journals before, and had read journals of all students. A teacher commented that he could find what students feel difficult. Another teacher pointed that he was able to understand which weeks have many negative opinions at a glance. In comparison to the user interface of Mahara system, three persons answered it is easier to read and analyze.

4. CONCLUSION

We designed and implemented an user interface for exploring students' learning journals interactively. Based on weekly keyword rankings, our tool provides a way to access important entries efficiently without overlooking minor opinions. From the questionnaire for a preliminary evaluation, we obtained some positive feedback. However, the number of answers is very small, and thus the evaluation is very limited. In future study, we will conduct expanded survey for quantitatively evaluate our tool. Our interactive report tool can be used to promote the use of students' journals for improving teaching, and it would be useful for comparatively analyze different teaching styles.

ACKNOWLEDGEMENT

This work was supported by Grant-in-Aid for Scientific Research (B) No. JP16H03080.

REFERENCES

Boud, D., 2001. Using journal writing to enhance reflective practice. *New directions for adult and continuing education*, 2001(90), pp. 9-18.

Chen, Y. et al., 2016. Topic Modeling for Evaluating Students' Reflective Writing: a Case Study of Pre-service Teachers' Journals. *Proceedings of Learning Analytics & Knowledge Conference.* Edinburgh, United Kingdom, pp. 1-5.

Gibson, A. and Kitto, K., 2015. Analysing Reflective Text for Learning Analytics: An Approach Using Anomaly Recontextualisation. *Proceedings of Learning Analytics & Knowledge Conference.* New York, United States of America, pp. 275-279.

Scouller, K., 1998. The influence of assessment method on students' learning approaches: Multiple choice question examination versus assignment essay. *Higher Education*, 35(4), pp. 453-472.

Taniguchi, Y. et al, 2017. Revealing Hidden Impression Topics in Students' Journals Based on Nonnegative Matrix Factorization. *Proceedings of IEEE International Conference on Advanced Learning Technologies.* Timisoara, Romania, pp. 298-300.

THE FRAMEWORK OF INTERVENTION ENGINE BASED ON LEARNING ANALYTICS

Muhittin Şahin and Halil Yurdugül
Hacettepe University , Faculty of Education, Department of Computer Education and Instructional Technology, Ankara, Turkey

ABSTRACT

Learning analytics primarily deals with the optimization of learning environments and the ultimate goal of learning analytics is to improve learning and teaching efficiency. Studies on learning analytics seem to have been made in the form of adaptation engine and intervention engine. Adaptation engine studies are quite widespread, but intervention engine work has been seen to studies very few. For the intervention engine studies, it was generally determined that interventions were made with feedback and dashboards. The aim of this study is to reveal an intervention engine framework which is based on learning analytics. Within this framework, a system design has been put forward which can provide instructional, supportive and motivational interventions to learners. These interventions are based on both the learning outputs of the learners and their learning experiences. Instructional interventions are planned to be based on learning outputs, supportive and motivational interventions are based on learning experiences.

KEYWORDS

Learning analytics, intervention engine, learner output, learner experience

1. INTRODUCTION

Learning analytics primarily deals with the optimization of learning environments. So far, this optimization has been based on two basic components. These are adaptation engines and intervention engines. Numerous designs and researchers are being conducted for the adaptation engine. Whereas studies on intervention engines have, unfortunately, been limited to dashboards and feedback. The weakness of the intervention engine designs based on learning analytics is that the theoretical construct is not adequately addressed. However, the intervention is a concept that includes specific methods and models in psychology. Intervention defined; interact with people to help them in an ongoing system (Argyris, 1970). The dimensions of the intervention concept and types of intervention in the related field are stated as instructional, supportive and motivational interventions (Geller, 2005). But, the theory of intervention is structured in the field of behavioral psychology. Therefore, intervention theory based on behavioral psychology principles is not suitable for learning environments based on the constructivist learning approach. The aim of this study is to create an intervention engine framework which is based on learning analytics. Instructional, supportive and motivational interventions will be included in this intervention engine.

1.1 Learning Analytics and Intervention

E-learning provides a lot of benefits to learner and instructor designers. Besides this, there are some barriers in e-learning processes. One of the most important of these barriers is that online learning processes are biased. Here, the biggest bias is mentioned; online learning processes provide more benefits for self-directed learners. In other words, in online learning environments; a process that works against the learners who need intervention in favor of autonomous learners. In the solution of this negativity learning analytics is an intensively studied subject. For solving these problems, learning analytics offers opportunities for instructional designers, instructors, and researchers. Moreover, the main aim of learning analytics is to improve learning and optimize learning environments. Siemens and Gasevic (2012) proposed the concept of learning analytics in this direction: "Analyzing, measuring and reporting on learners and learning environments data in order to understand and improve learning environments and processes". In this context, it appears that learning analytics will play an important role in facilitating learning and increasing performance. Because; the ultimate goal of learning analytics is to improve learning and teaching efficiency (Elias, 2011). Learning analytics provide a great deal of power to improve learners' learning performance and increase learning efficiency (Dyckhoff vd., 2012). Besides, that learning analytics can ensure better feedback on the learning process (Kloos vd., 2013). Based on the feedback obtained, environment designs are reviewed and improved to create more appropriate environments.

Learning analytics often rises on the educational data mining background. Educational data mining is the subject of analysis based on log data of learners in learning management systems. The relationship and / or difference between the two concepts can be sought in terms of analyze-analytic concepts. The concept of analysis refers to pattern discovery based on data, whereas analytic refers to the use of these patterns in a specific area. In this direction; while the educational data mining aims to discover the patterns of learning data in instructional environments, learning analytics requires the use of these patterns with instructional purposes.

With the use of learning analytics, it became possible for learners in e-learning environments to intervene and improve the learning environment during their learning experiences. The ultimate goal of the interventions; improve learner achievement or improve learners' learning experiences (Pardo & Dawson, 2016). But the delay of feedback and the inability to use real-time information is a concerning topic for adaptive diagnosis and intervention in e-learning environments (Wu, Huang & Zou, 2015). With the intervention engines, it is possible to give immediate feedback to learners and to use the interaction data in e-learning environments. In addition, if the successes and interactions of learners are ignored learners' successes and their environment engagement can be negatively affected. Effective interventions have been shown to have a significant impact on encouraging learners' performance of learning (Chen, 2011). A structured intervention model which is developed with learning analytics to support learning and teaching can improve the learning performance of learners(Wu, Huang & Zou, 2015). Studies on learning analytics have just begun. So, research on improving the learning environment seems to be lacking. The main reason of this lacking is that there is not enough study on the intervention engines.

1.2 Design of Intervetion Engine

In this research, an intervention engine framework which is based on learning analytics is presented. In the next stage, an intervention engine design and development will be done using the developmental research method. Before designing the intervention engine it is necessary to define the intervention which is a psycho-educational structure. Intervention is defined that interact with people to help them in an ongoing system (Argyris, 1970). Intervention theory and intervention models in the field of psychology have been put forward. In this research, "*ABC (activator-behavior-consequence)*" which is intervention model developed by Geller (2005) will be used. In this model; there are three types of intervention which are instructional, supportive, and motivational.

Table 1. Intervention types and definitions (Geller 2005)

Intervention Type	Definition
Instructional	Use an activator or antecedent to start a new behavior.
Supportive	If an individual learns what is right behavior and exhibits behavior, it can be used to turn it into a routine in daily life or to automate the behavior.
Motivational	Person know the right behavior but if it does not show it; he/she needs an encouragement from the outside or the interventions.

As we can see in the definitions interventions use for the changing the behavior. Interventions and intervention types are used to create about behavioral changes because of the concept of intervention is a psycho-educational structure. In the context of this research, this structure has been included in the intervention engine design in accordance with the e-learning environments. The aim of the intervention is improving the learning. These interventions both can be directly made based on learning outputs, and they can be indirect interventions to based on learning experiences. In the studies of the related field, it was seen that the interventions to learners were usually based on learning outputs. In this research, interventions are based on both learners' learning outputs and learning experiences. Instructional interventions based on learners' learning outcomes and supportive and motivational interventions based on learning experiences are structured.

2. METHOD

Research is planned as developmental research. Developmental research is defined as; "*Design, development, and evaluation of a specific product*" (Richey, Klein & Nelson, 2004). The research process is conducted in accordance with the developmental research approach suggested by Reeves (2000).

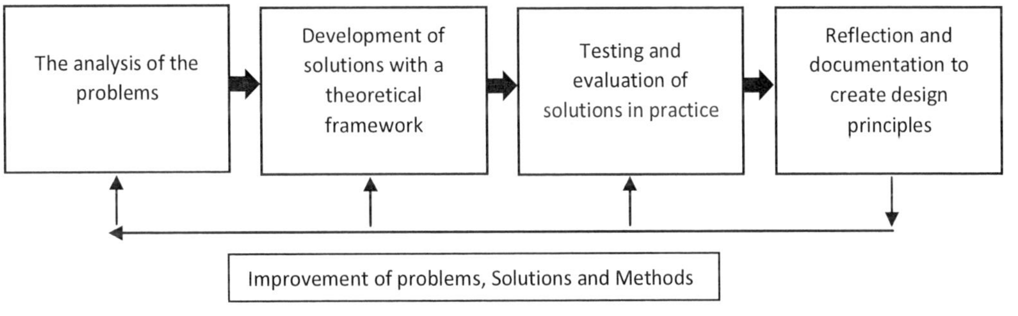

Figure 1. The process of developmental research

As you can see in Figure 1, developmental research is an iterative process that starts with needs analysis and ends with designing and documentation. In the context of needs analysis, focus group interviews were made with the learners by the semi-structured interview form. Then, we were decided from the obtained findings the interventions which are used in the intervention engine design. After the interventions have been determined, the prototype will be developed. After the final prototype is determined, the e-learning environment will be developed.

2.1 Framework of Intervention Engine

The intervention engine framework includes instructional, supportive and motivational interventions. Instructional interventions based on outputs of learning tasks; supportive and motivational interventions based on learning processes/experiences. The intervention engine framework which is planned to be developed is presented in Figure 2.

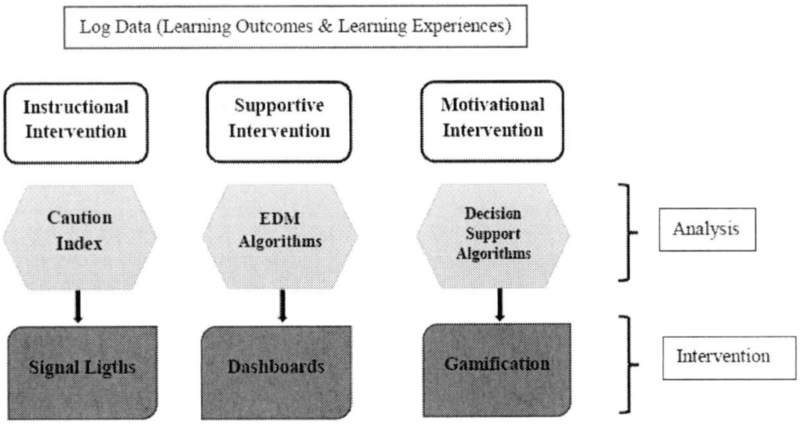

Figure 2. The intervention engine framework

As can be seen in Figure 2, instructional interventions will be done using the caution index based on the notes that learners have taken from learning tasks. According to the results obtained, direct feedback is given to the learners and information about weak or strong topics will be given by signal lights.

Supportive interventions which based on learners' experiences' data will be calculated by using educational data mining algorithms. The results will be presented to the learners via dashboards. In this type of intervention, predictions which the success status of learners will also be made.

Motivational interventions which based on learners' experiences' data will be calculated by using decision support algorithms. According to the results, the motivation items will be presented to the learners via gamification components.

3. CONCLUSION

In this research, an intervention engine framework based on learning analytics has been revealed. There are educational, supportive and motivational interventions in the scope of the intervention engine. Instructional interventions will be calculated according to the results of learning outputs of learners via the caution index. Learners will be presented information which is about their performance via direct feedback and signal lights. Educational data mining algorithms will use for supportive interventions and dashboards will be used to display the results. The gamification items will be used in the e-learning environment for motivational interventions. As a result of the research, an intervention engine for e-learning environments has been put forward. At the next stage, the intervention engine will be developed.

REFERENCES

Argyris, C. (1970). İntervention Theory and Methods. Addison-Wesley Publishing Co, Massachusetts, USA. 15-20 p. http://web.mit.edu/curhan/www/docs/Articles/15341_Readings/Organizational_Learning_and_Change/Argyris_Intervention_Theory_&_Methods_Classic_Readings_pp587-591.pdf

Chen, L.H. (2011). Enhancement of student learning performance using personalized diagnosis and remedial learning system. *Computers & Education,* 56(1). 289-299p.

Dyckhoff, A.L., Zielke, D., Bültmann, M., Chatti, M.A. ve Schroeder, U. (2012). Design and implementation of a learning analytics toolkit for teachers. *Educational Technology & Society, 15 (3).* 58–76p.

Elias, T. (2011). Learning analytics: definitions, process and potential. http://learninganalytics.net/LearningAnalyticsDefinitionsProcessesPotential.pdf

Geller, E.S. (2005). Behavior-based safety and occupational risk management. *Behavior Modification*, 29(3). 539-561p. DOI: 10.1177/0145445504273287

Kloos, C.D., Pardo, A., Muñoz-Merino, P.J., Gutiérrez, I. ve Leony, D. (2013). Learning Analytics @ UC3M. 2013 IEEE Global Engineering Education Conference (EDUCON), 13-15 March, Berlin, Germany.

Pardo, A. & Dawson, S. (2016). Measuring and Visualizing Learning in the Information-Rich Classroom. Peter Reimann (Ed.), Learning analytics (41-55p.). Routledge, UK.

Richey, R.C., Klein, J.D. & Nelson, W.A. (2004). Developmental Research: Studies Of Instructional Design And Development. http://aect.org/edtech/41.pdf.

Siemens, G., & Gasevic, D. (2012). Guest Editorial - Learning and Knowledge Analytics. *Educational Technology & Society, 15*(3), 1–2.

Wu, F., Huang, L. & Zou, R. (2015). The design of intervention model and strategy based on the behavior data of learners: A learning analytics perspective. *Hybrid Learning: Innovation in Educational Practices*, 9167. 294-301p.

ON THE USE OF E-TPCK FOR SITUATED TEACHER PROFESSIONAL DEVELOPMENT

Maria Mama Timotheou[1], Andri Christodoulou and Charoula Angeli
Department of Education, University of Cyprus, P.O. Box 20537, 1678 Nicosia, Cyprus

ABSTRACT

The authors herein justify the need for e-TPCK, an adaptive e-learning system for teaching in-service teachers how to teach with technology. Outlining the instructional design process involved and the adaptivity feature of e-TPCK, it is explained how the system promotes and measures the development of teachers' Technological Pedagogical Content Knowledge (TPCK). Considering the novel alternative of the system to more traditional professional development approaches, the authors conclude with the argument for employing e-TPCK in real classroom settings in a situated way.

KEYWORDS

e-TPCK, instructional design, adaptive learning, technology-enhanced practice, situated professional development

1. INTRODUCTION

Despite the massive investments to integrate technology in education, teachers still appear unprepared to engagingly link technology to their pedagogy and competently use it in their daily practice. These limitations have been attributed to several barriers, including teachers' inadequate technical skills and limited understanding of the pedagogical affordances of technology (Fu, 2013). To secure sustained technology-enhanced classroom practice, it has been consistently suggested that substantial efforts focus on teachers' professional development. However, the literature reveals that training programs often prove ineffective due to insufficient emphasis placed on the pedagogy behind technology use (Kirschner & Davis, 2003).

Scholarly work over the last decade has focused on developing theoretical frameworks to ground research in the area of teaching with technology; extending Shulman's (1987) Pedagogical Content Knowledge, researchers have proposed Technological Pedagogical Content Knowledge (TPCK), a new body of knowledge that teachers need to possess to effectively teach with technology. There are two theoretical conceptualizations of TPCK, the integrative view (Mishra & Koehler, 2006), and the transformative view (Angeli & Valanides, 2005). Research has indicated that measuring empirical evidence of TPCK development appears more reliable following the latter (Graham, 2011), which is the view we adopt here and which addresses TPCK as a unique body of knowledge conceptualized in terms of: technology knowledge, pedagogical knowledge, content knowledge, knowledge of learners and knowledge of context. In brief, TPCK is described as the ways knowledge about technology, pedagogy, content, learners and context form an understanding of how subject-matter topics can be taught with technology, for specific learners in specific contexts, to maximize learning outcomes (Angeli, Valanides, Mavroudi, Christodoulou, & Georgiou, 2015).

Acknowledging the struggle of traditional training programs to engage teachers in purposeful integration of technology, TPCK has been proposed as an appropriate framework for the design of professional development (Niess, 2011). This is a crucial step toward successful integration of technology into teaching; yet, in view of research evidence suggesting the importance of contextualized and personalized training programs according to the teachers' needs (Kopcha, 2012), we further emphasize the need for e-TPCK, an adaptive and interactive e-learning system for promoting teachers' TPCK (Angeli et al., 2015). Based on an instructional design approach, e-TPCK could prove highly effective in situated professional development.

---

[1] mamatimo@cantab.net

2. E-TPCK AND ADAPTIVE INSTRUCTIONAL DESIGN

Designed following a Design-Based Research approach, the e-TPCK aspires to promote teachers' ongoing TPCK development by personalizing the content of technology-infused design scenarios; each of these scenarios is structured to guide teachers through a series of instructional design decisions about how to teach a particular topic using specific digital tools (Angeli et al., 2015). The system is inspired by socio-cultural theories of learning and capitalizes on the concepts of scaffolding and self-regulated learning. Aiming to reduce cognitive load, adaptive scaffolding of various forms is implemented according to the users' knowledge, understanding and choices; as the users attain competence fading of scaffolding becomes available upon request, enabling them to regulate their experience and engage in task definition, goal setting and planning, monitoring and control of their learning, and reaction/reflection (ibid). Below, the instructional design principles and the need for the adaptivity feature of e-TPCK are explained.

2.1 Instructional Design and Development of TPCK

Being student-centered and goals-oriented, the instructional design (ID) process is characterized by procedures for systematically developing education and training materials (Reiser & Dempsey, 2012). In this respect, instruction is viewed as a system emphasizing the key role of all components in the process and their interaction. The literature is saturated with different ID models, with Gagne's taxonomy (Gagne & Briggs, 1974) being perhaps the most popular in the field because of its clear distinction between abstract and concrete definitions of learning. Despite their variety, traditional ID models include the phases of 'ADDIE', an acronym for: Analysis (identification of a problem and goal setting), Design (articulate measurable objectives), Development (preparation of instructional materials), Implementation (delivery of instruction) and Evaluation (formative/summative evaluation and revision of instruction) (Reiser & Dempsey, 2012). Scholars in the field have also considered the content, objectives and learners in selecting the media in the ID process, yet many addressed these in a rather generic and de-contextualized way (Angeli & Valanides, 2005).

Identifying major differences between typical ID and teachers' actual instructional decision-making, recent ID models emphasize the need to identify specific content but also analyze learners' characteristics and contextual elements (Angeli & Valanides, 2005; Dick, Carey, & Carey, 2005). Capitalizing on the fact that teachers' design decisions are influenced by their personal beliefs and classroom experiences and that their content knowledge interacts with their knowledge of curriculum, learners, pedagogy and context, Angeli & Valanides have associated instructional design with the development of TPCK and proposed Technology Mapping as the core of an ID model which is situated in teachers' actual practice (Angeli & Valanides, 2005, 2013). This approach to instructional design is depicted on the structure of the technology-infused learning design scenarios of the e-TPCK system. Specifically, each scenario includes the following phases: 1) Rationale of topic selection; 2) Brief subject-matter content description; 3) Learning objectives (lower-order objectives, higher-order objectives, ICT-related objectives); 4) Learning methodology/model; 5) Sequence of classroom activities: a) Attract student interest, b) Identify students' initial understandings or misconceptions, c) Destabilization of initial perceptions – cognitive conflict, d) Student engagement in knowledge construction, e) Application of new knowledge, f) Revision and comparison with initial perceptions.

As reflected on the structure of the design scenarios in e-TPCK, teachers' development of TPCK is measured in terms of distinct instructional design competencies (Angeli & Valanides, 2013). The first competency is related to the identification of topics to teach with technology in ways that signify the added value of ICT tools. As a next step, teachers are required to consider the tool affordances to identify representations for transforming the content to be taught into forms that are comprehensible to students and difficult to support by traditional means. Still considering the tool affordances, teachers must then identify teaching strategies that are difficult or impossible to implement by other means. Next, they need to select tools with inherent affordances to support the previous two steps. Finally, teachers need to design and infuse technology-enhanced learning activities in the classroom.

2.2 Adaptivity and Adaptive Learning Design

The importance of engaging teachers in systematic design of the learning scenarios in their classroom, especially in the new media era, cannot be stressed enough. The adaptivity of the e-TPCK system seeks to further empower teachers' design thinking providing personalized e-learning. The operational principle of any adaptive system is that an effective instruction process should consider individual learners' characteristics and profiles (Towle & Halm, 2005).

Adaptation may be system-controlled, with the system adapting to perceived learner profiles, or user-controlled, with the system being adaptable by the learners. In the case of e-TPCK, adaptation and instructional control is shared between the teacher user and the system (Angeli et al., 2015). More specifically, there are three different categories of design scenarios: completed scenarios, semi-completed scenarios and new scenarios that teachers need to complete from scratch. There are four different types – levels of semi-completed scenarios, according to the amount of scaffolding provided to the users to complete the design. The higher the scenario level the more phases (of those outlined in Section 2.1) are missing and intended for teachers to complete. It is made clear that when logged-in to the system, the teacher is asked to choose the ICT tool involved in the learning activity and the difficulty level of a design scenario. Scaffolding is provided based on the teacher's Likert-scale rating of the cognitive effort they experience, after specific phases of a scenario are completed. According to their rating, the system asks if a less or more demanding design scenario is preferred or if the user wants to continue with the same scenario. Therefore, the adaptive learning strategy employed here consists of the adaption rules, i.e. the rules that assign shared control between the system and the user, the adaptation parameters, i.e. the user's perceived cognitive load, choice of ICT tools and the difficulty level of the scenario, and the adaptation methods, i.e. tailoring content, learning flow and sequencing of activities (ibid).

Adaptive scaffolding to foster self-regulated learning is also implemented through prompts to teachers for progress monitoring and reflection on their competency, the task or the context. Activity monitoring and reflection are also facilitated through the learning analytics incorporated in the e-TPCK system. In addition, adaptive feedback is assigned to encourage metacognitive reaction and assist with the completion of the semi-completed design scenarios and the development of new design scenarios.

The above remarks emphasize the fact that the e-TPCK system capitalizes on adaptivity to develop teachers' TPCK, facilitating their instructional design thinking. Moreover, it is further argued that the adaptive process and the reflection it engages teachers in could improve their own understanding of adaptive instruction. Teachers being designers of adaptive technology-enhanced learning would be an important step in addressing students' divergent needs more effectively and optimizing their learning experiences. The design principles of adaptive learning and the Technology Mapping to develop TPCK incorporated in the foundations of e-TPCK, could prove valuable in training teachers in the design of adaptive instruction.

3. SITUATED USE IN REAL CLASSROOM SETTINGS

The previous discussion on adaptive instructional design highlights the novelty of the e-TPCK system compared to more traditional approaches to professional development which, as noted earlier, often fail to engage teachers in ICT-enhanced pedagogical reasoning and practice. The system adaptivity, a feature not usually available in typical training programs, is central in accommodating teachers' diverse needs, knowledge, abilities and experiences toward the development of their TPCK. Moreover, even though the e-TPCK objectives and structure apply to both pre-service and in-service teacher education, in this paper we see great value in the situated use of the system in real classroom settings. Besides, research evidence strongly indicates the potential of situated professional development to promote sustainable classroom practice with technology (Kopcha, 2012).

What is key to stress is that the structure of the e-TPCK design scenarios guides teachers to identify and purposefully employ technology affordances within the context of an authentic design task directly related to a specific subject-matter topic and the curriculum. This way, lack of connection to actual classroom practice, which has been repeatedly acknowledged as a major drawback of traditional professional development, is not a concern. Then, the design process is context-sensitive with teachers being invited to consider their real contextual conditions (related to their classroom, school, system) and their students' profiles when defining the learning objectives and planning the activities in any scenario, corroborating the situated use of the system. Additionally, contrary to stand-alone workshop training for technology integration or even mentor-based professional development, the e-learning platform provides ubiquitous access to teachers allowing them to resort to e-TPCK at any preferred point in their daily professional routine. Beyond the convenience aspect, this flexibility is argued to encourage reflection and intended involvement in the instructional design.

In proposing e-TPCK as a novel professional development system, the 'default' socio-cultural aspect in any situated learning setting is another point to acknowledge. Drawing upon research on professional development on technology integration (Mouza, 2006), but also the literature on professional learning communities (Vescio, Ross, & Adams, 2008), we acknowledge the importance of collective participation and interaction toward the establishment of a collaborative work culture. To this end, a 'social networking tools' area is integrated in the e-TPCK system where teachers can discuss and exchange ideas with others synchronously or asynchronously. Moreover, any semi-completed or new design scenario fully completed by a user and approved by the instructional designer/tutor, is added in the design scenarios database for sharing. In a more systematic approach, enabling sharing of teachers' different knowledge, competencies and experiences, the e-TPCK system could facilitate the development of communities of practice. In such communities, especially when fostered within the same school unit, teachers' development of TPCK would be further promoted, eventually leading to a sustainable integration culture.

4. CONCLUSION

The purpose of this work-in-progress paper was to discuss the instructional design process of the e-TPCK e-learning system toward the development of teachers' TPCK in the context of professional development, considering the adaptivity feature of the system. Thus, the novelty of the system compared to more traditional professional development programs is underlined, while the contribution of the paper lies in the argument for the appropriate and effective use of e-TPCK in real classroom settings in a situated way, especially in relation to the buildup of communities of practice.

REFERENCES

Angeli, C., & Valanides, N. (2005). Preservice teachers as ICT designers: An instructional design model based on an expanded view of pedagogical content knowledge. *Journal of Computer-Assisted Learning, 21*(4), 292-302.

Angeli, C., & Valanides, N. (2013). Technology mapping: An approach for developing technological pedagogical content knowledge. *Journal of educational computing research, 48*(2), 199-221.

Angeli, C., Valanides, N., Mavroudi, A., Christodoulou, A., & Georgiou, K. (2015). Introducing e-TPCK: An Adaptive E-Learning Technology for the Development of Teachers' Technological Pedagogical Content Knowledge. In C. Angeli & N. Valanides (Eds.), *Technological Pedagogical Content Knowledge: Exploring, Developing, and Assessing TPCK* (pp. 305-317). Boston, MA: Springer US.

Dick, W., Carey, L., & Carey, J. O. (2005). *The systematic design of instruction* (6th ed.). New York: HarperCollins Publishers. .

Fu, J. S. (2013). ICT in education: A critical literature review and its implications. *International Journal of Education and Development using Information and Communication Technology, 9*(1), 112.

Gagne, R. M., & Briggs, L. J. (1974). *Principles of instructional design*: Holt, Rinehart & Winston.

Graham, C. R. (2011). Theoretical considerations for understanding technological pedagogical content knowledge (TPACK). *Computers & education, 57*(3), 1953-1960.

Kirschner, P., & Davis, N. (2003). Pedagogic benchmarks for information and communications technology in teacher education. *Technology, Pedagogy and Education, 12*(1), 125-147.

Kopcha, T. J. (2012). Teachers' perceptions of the barriers to technology integration and practices with technology under situated professional development. *Computers & education, 59*(4), 1109-1121.

Mishra, P., & Koehler, M. J. (2006). Technological pedagogical content knowledge: A framework for teacher knowledge. *Teachers college record, 108*(6), 1017.

Mouza, C. (2006). Linking professional development to teacher learning and practice: A multi-case study analysis of urban teachers. *Journal of educational computing research, 34*(4), 405-440.

Niess, M. (2011). Investigating TPACK: Knowledge growth in teaching with technology. *Journal of educational computing research, 44*(3), 299-317.

Reiser, R. A., & Dempsey, J. V. (2012). *Trends and issues in instructional design and technology*: Pearson Boston, MA.

Shulman, L. (1987). Knowledge and teaching: Foundations of the new reform. *Harvard educational review, 57*(1), 1-23.

Towle, B., & Halm, M. (2005). Designing adaptive learning environments with learning design. *Learning design*, 215-226.

Vescio, V., Ross, D., & Adams, A. (2008). A review of research on the impact of professional learning communities on teaching practice and student learning. *Teaching and teacher education, 24*(1), 80-91.

NARB-BASED ANALYSIS OF TWEETS RELATED TO UNITED AIRLINES CONTROVERSY: LEARNING BEYOND THE MEDIA

Ananda Mitra
Wake Forest University, USA

ABSTRACT

The use of narrative bits – narbs – has been discussed as an alternative means of looking at opinions of those who are producing narbs, for instance, in the form of tweets. The American carrier, United Airlines, came under media attention in April 2016 when a passenger was forcibly removed from a flight. This resulted in a spike in tweets around the #unitedairlines and the narrative that emerged from a selection of the tweets demonstrate that there were negative opinions not only about the airlines, but also about the aviation industry and passengers. This analysis demonstrates that it is increasingly important to supplement traditional learning of contemporary affairs with a systematic analysis of narbs that offer alternative perspectives of what the traditional learning offers.

KEYWORDS

Narb; discourse; narrative; analysis, politics, United Airlines, opinion

1. NARRATIVE ANALYSIS

The construct of looking at culture, communication and human behavior and beliefs through the lens of a narrative was suggested by the work of Walter Fisher (1984) who in turn based his work on earlier scholars who identified the importance of story-telling and narratives in the process of making meaning of everyday life as people operate within the cultural and social spaces that they occupy (see, e.g., Andrews, 1982; Gadamer, 1982; MacIntyre, 1981; Ricouer, 1977; White, 1984).

It is possible to understand what people learn by systematically analyzing the stories that are being told. In the case of social media systems these stories appear as collection of narbs, or *nar*rative *b*its, that are made up of the different ways people express themselves – from simple status updates to the elaborate process of offering visual information that makes up the elements of the narrative. One of the most popular form of narbs that is currently available are tweets which are considered micro-blogs as different people express themselves through the short narbs that often become immensely popular and become the focus of analysis by many institutions ranging from the institutional media to political institutions.

2. THE UNITED INCIDENT

On April 9, 2017 a passenger was removed from a flight operated by United Airlines. The removal was involuntary, and there was the need to use law enforcers to physically dislodge the person from the aircraft. The event was unusual for two inter-related reasons. First, there has not been any notable similar event related to a legitimate passenger, use of force and the airlines, and secondly, because the matter was copiously video recorded by other passengers and immediately made available to the larger digitally networked space. The matter was rapidly absorbed by institutional media and major television networks began to "cover" the story by talking to specialists and "pundits" who claimed either knowledge about the specific incident or were knowledgeable about policies regarding issues such as "overbooking" and other intricacies of the aviation industry in the USA. The issue continued to remain in view of the popular cultural space and on the following days newspapers carried headlines such as "United case expose lack of right

(USA Today, April 11, 2017) and "United Airlines passenger Dragged From an Overbooked Flight" (New York Times, April 10, 2017), and similar stories appeared in the institutional media around the World. The World learnt of the details of the incident and its implication through these traditional media outlets. However, a simultaneous narrative was also being created and propagated in the realm of the virtual where non-specialists were crafting the narrative from the information that was available in the mainstream media, and other information including personal experience and anecdotes that was available to the "general public" with access to Twitter. I argue that these tweets offer another way of learning about the incident a slightly different learning outcome can be obtained when learning is based on the tweets. To understand what is learnt from the tweets, it is useful to consider each tweet as a narb.

As established in the existing literature, a narb is a *nar*rative *b*it of information that an individual produces every time the advance information in a digital space (see, e.g., Mitra, 2010). Narbs are comprised of updates on social media systems, entries on micro-blogs, and contributions to blogs and additional online platforms that shape the discourse that is occurring in the virtual space. In this case study, the focus is on tweets which serve as the units of analysis.

Corporate use of tweets has been examined to understand how different kinds of companies use Twitter as a communication channel to address internal and external issues, with some researchers looking specifically at the way in which airline companies use tweets (see, e.g., Budd, 2012; Tarhan, et. al., 2013; Wigley and Lewis, 2012; Zhang, et. al. 2016). Most of the studies look at the way in which the corporations actually use the tweet platform for different kinds of communication. However, in the case study presented here the focus shifts away from the airline industry or the passengers on the specific flight where the incident happened. A different kind of information is learnt from tweets produced by people who are presenting their opinion, based on the information gathered primarily from institutional media, and thus crafting a specific narrative. This story emerges from the analysis of the tweets, and offers a different learning about the specific event.

3. DATA AND ANALYSIS

In this case, the narbs were composed of nearly 12,000 tweets that were collected when the hashtag "unitedairlines" was "trending" as a popular topic amongst the people using the micro-blogging system. The specific tweets were collected and the content of the tweets were then analyzed to extract a narrative map which is a visual representation of specific narrative categories, which are represented as the nodes of the map, and the strength of connection between the nodes represented by the relative thickness of the lines connecting the nodes.

As has been pointed out in years of research on text analysis, it is known that texts are often connected with other texts – thus the notions of inter-textuality. Similarly, texts have multiple meanings – thus the notion of polysemy. Texts are also sensitive to the culture within which it is produced. Yet, much of the automated analysis miss these nuances of texts that are fundamental to the way in which texts are able to tell stories and illuminate specific attributes of the author as suggested in the narrative paradigm. In the analysis offered here, the automation is coupled with contextualizing of the dictionary and offering an intermediary step that mimics the traditional coding process of earlier textual analysis allowing for the recognition and incorporation of the context under which the unstructured big data has been produced. This is the process that was used on the narbs extracted for this case study.

4. FINDINGS

The analysis results in the production of narrative maps that offer visualization of the narratives by showing the connection between the key categories in the narrative. In these maps, the size of the circle, or node, representing the narrative category indicates the frequency with which that category appears in the narbs, and the thickness of the line between the nodes indicates the strength of the relationship.

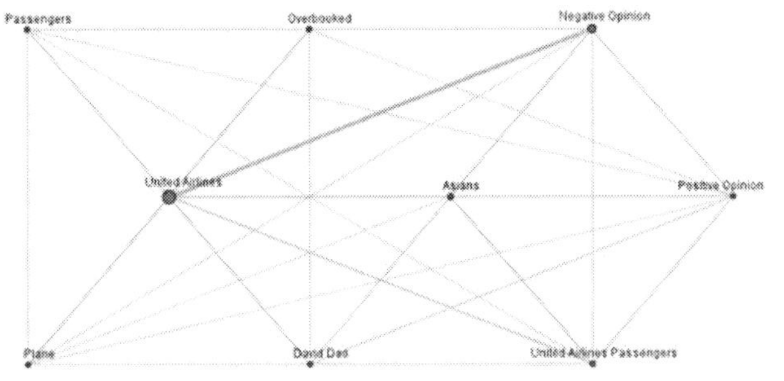

Figure 1. Narrative map of analysis of "unitedairlines"

It is important to note that the narrative is fundamentally ambiguous. The narbs do not attempt to offer a starkly "negative" or "positive" opinion, which is often the tendency in stories offered by institutions. The connection between the narrative categories of "negative" and "positive" opinion represent that the narbs would simultaneously state something bad and good about a specific narrative category. Thus, the narbs show that those who were creating the narbs, in summation of their narbs, were creating a story that attributed positive qualities to the airlines unlike what was demonstrated in a majority of the stories that were available in the media which tends to polarize the narratives.

It is also important to observe how the story is composed of many different narrative categories, which are all inter-connected. The narbs offer a narrative where many different issues are being talked about simultaneously. Thus, most of the narrative categories are connected with each other suggesting that those who are creating the narbs see the inherent connection between all the different elements and the consequent complexity of the narrative. This is another demonstration that the narb-based analysis offer a story where all the elements are important and connected with each other. Although the size of the nodes show that some of the narrative categories are discussed more frequently, it is still the case that different narrative categories emerge from the narbs. In this case, connections exist where expected – narbs are talking about overbooking and passengers, or about being Asian and the specific passenger. However, the lack of connection between being Asian and overbooking suggests that the narrative does not make that connection.

Additionally, the findings represented in the narrative map offers an "open-ended" narrative that is open for interpretation in many different ways. The narrative map offers a visualization of the narrative for the reader of the map. However, unlike other story-telling tools, such as a book or television, the story is not pre-constructed. For instance, in the case of television news, a location shot of an event is invariably accompanied with a reported interpreting and describing what the viewer is seeing. In the case of narrative maps, the viewer can extract multiple stories, with different nuances, from a map that distills the Big Data into a manageable summary. This offers a mode of learning about an event, such as the United Airlines event, which requires a cognitive engagement with the narrative in an active way unlike the passivity of being an audience of a story. With the narrative map, the reader is required to examine the map and learn from the map on a manner which is usually unavailable in other forms of storytelling.

5. DISCUSSION

The narrative map demonstrates that there is a strong negative opinion about United Airlines in the story that emerges from the narbs used in this analysis. Indeed, nearly 97% of the tweets that had something negative to say mentioned United Airlines. From another perspective, out of the 10,257 tweets that included the narrative category of "United Airlines," 4,229 also included the narrative category of "negative opinion." The story certainly demonstrates a strong negative opinion about the company. At the same time, the story does not attach a large amount of importance to the issue of overbooking. Those who were tweeting about the event appeared less concerned about the issue of overbooking. Even though overbooking of flights could be an inconvenience, it is not something that appears to be a matter of great concern, similar to all the other narrative categories all of which are less important in the narrative.

This finding is important for United Airlines, because the negativity about the company is connected with other narrative categories. The story suggests that there are negative feelings about the company and all the other narrative categories. The company could benefit from this learning and note that the story emerging from these tweets are speaking negatively about the manner in which United deals with its passengers, where customer service is a strong component of the narrative. However, it is useful for the company to note that the story based on the tweets also places some blame on the specific passenger involved in the narrative. There were 337 tweets that included the narrative category "David Dao" and 87 (26%) had a negative opinion about the passenger. This is a finding that was not available through the traditional channels of learning about the event, but this narrative analysis offer that perspective. Notable in the narrative is also the negative connection that emerges about Asians, especially in the fact that a line in the map connects negative opinion with the particular passenger and the narrative category of "Asians" offering a racial overtone to the narrative as well.

6. CONCLUSION

The key to narb-based narrative analysis is that it offers an alternative way of learning about issues. In an era where the availability of Big Data is only expected to increase there are different options to learning. As I have argued earlier, there needs to be systematic ways of extracting the information from narbs to offer the student or learner ways in which they can interpret the information. There is an inherent open-ended potential to what *can* be learnt from narbs as opposed to the more closed-ended situation that tells what *must* be learned.

REFERENCES

Andrews, J. D. (1982). The structuralist study of narrative: its history, use and limits. In. P. Hernadi (Ed.). The horizon of literature (pp. 99-124). Lincoln, NE: The University of Nebraska Press.

Budd, L. (2012). @doesyourairlinetweet? An empirical examination of the use of twitter by 50 international airlines. Journal of Airline and Airport Management, [S.l.], v. 2, n. 2, p. 124-135. Available at: <http://www.jairm.org/index.php/jairm/article/view/10>.

Fisher, W. R. (1984). Narration as Human Communication Paradigm: The Case of Public Moral Argument, Communication Monographs, 51, 1–22.

Gadamer, H. G. (1982). Truth and method. New York, NY: Crossword Publishing.

MacIntyre, A. (1981). After virtue: A study in moral theory (2nd ed). Notre Dame, IN: The University of Notre Dame Press.

Mitra, A. (2010). Creating a Presence on Social Networks via Narbs. Global Media Journal, 9(16).

Murthy, D., & Petto, L. R. (2014). Comparing print coverage and tweets in elections: A case study of the 2011–2012 U.S. Republican primaries. Social Science Computer Review. Advance online publication. doi:10.1177/0894439314541925

Propp, V. (1968). Morphology of the Folktale: Second Edition. Austin, TX: University of Texas Press.

Ricouer, P. (1977). The model of the text: Meaningful action considered as text. In F. R. Dallmayr & T. A. McCarthy (Eds.), Understanding and social inquiry (pp. 316-334). Notre Dame, IN: The University of Notre Dame Press.

Tarhan, A., Canoz, K., and Bakan, O. (2013). Airline Companies' use of Social Media: A Content Analysis of Airlines' Companies Tweeter Messages. Proceedings of The Asian Conference on Social Sciences.

Todorov, T. (1977). The Poetics of Prose. Ithaca, NY: Cornell University Press.

Wigley, S. and Lewis, B. K. (2012). Rules of engagement: Practice what you tweet. Public Relations Review, 38(1), 165-167.

Zhang B., Kotkov D., Veijalainen J., Semenov A. (2016) Online Stakeholder Interaction of Some Airlines in the Light of Situational Crisis Communication Theory. In: Dwivedi Y. et al. (eds) Social Media: The Good, the Bad, and the Ugly. I3E 2016. Lecture Notes in Computer Science, vol 9844. Springer, Cham.

LEARNERS' AND TEACHERS' PERCEPTIONS OF LEARNING ANALYTICS (LA): A CASE STUDY OF SOUTHAMPTON SOLENT UNIVERSITY (SSU)

Osama Khan
Southampton Solent University, East Park Terrace, Southampton, Hampshire SO14 0YN, UK

ABSTRACT

This paper depicts a perceptual picture of learning analytics based on the understanding of learners and teachers at the SSU as a case study. The existing literature covers technical challenges of learning analytics (LA) and how it creates better social construct for enhanced learning support, however, there has not been adequate research on whether learners and teachers understand the significance of LA and how they can utilise it for enhancement of learning and teaching. This qualitative study helps to shape understanding of an LA initiative based on one university, but with implications for other universities. Shared stakeholders' understanding of LA with an institutional strategic priority supported by a collaborative delivery would ensure a successful implementation of LA.

KEYWORDS

Learning Analytics, Case Study, Perception

1. INTRODUCTION

The purpose of this study is to find out how LA is perceived by the learners, teachers and other staff members of the Southampton Solent University (SSU) as a case study. Daniel (2015) mentions there are institutional challenges of collecting big data in a warehouse and subsequently analysing and visualising such data for the betterment of learning and teaching. In this paper the stakeholders are the learners, teachers and support staff members for LA as identified by Reyes (2015). The research paper presents a case study of SSU, a relatively new university gaining university charter in July 2005 (Southampton Solent University 2016). The university has a history of education dating back to 1856 and transformed itself into a higher education institution in 1989. It has always been a teaching intense university transforming local and national workforce. There is large body of highly technical literatures in LA and big data as well as non-technical literatures exploring the challenges and ethical dilemmas (Picciano 2014, Slavakis, Giannakis & Mateos 2014, Anonymous2015, Daniel 2015, Kash, Thappa & Kavitha 2015, Reyes 2015, Madhavan, Richey 2016) This research contributes into the social aspects of using LA. The research findings are highly relevant for any teaching intense university with social inclusivity as a major agenda and learning and teaching being a core academic activity.

2. THE FIELD OF LEARNING ANALYTICS

Enter the text here. Although LA is a relatively new concept, the literature is significantly large, varying from highly technical research papers to studies concentrating on the educational value of such technological intervention. Based on the research context, this paper identifies the proximate topics: definition, issues, and outcomes of learning analytics (Daniel 2015).

As Daniel (2015) highlights, LA is "an interdisciplinary area focusing on methodologies for identifying and extracting useful and meaningful patterns from large data sets" (p 906). The methodology "draws upon research in statistics, databases, pattern recognition, machine learning, data visualisation, optimisation and high performance computing" (p 906). LA is defined as a technological intervention based on large amounts of data on learners and teachers to enhance learning experiences and aid progression (Slade, Prinsloo 2013) Oblinger (2012) indicates that LA is set of data about individual learners that helps the institution and the teachers to support the student in learning. Oblinger (2012) and Sclater, Peasgood and Mullan (2016) differentiate between academic analytics and learning analytics, where academic analytics refers to macro data that helps the management of a higher education institution. On the other hand, there has to be an appreciation of how this supports educational decision making to ensure effective resource allocation, educational guidance, and enhanced retention through student success (Conde, Hernández-García 2015). The empirical literatures in development of LA as presented in Ali *et al.* (2012) , Ali *et al.* (2013) and Fidalgo-Blanco *et al.* (2015) also broadly agree with the above definitions. Siemens (2013) showcases how LA and related research has given rise to an emerging area of study in educational research.

The ultimate power of LA lies with its predictability (Dietz-Uhler, Hurn 2013, Agudo-Peregrina et al. 2014, Strang 2016b, Strang 2016a). A substantial data warehouse containing big data on learners can be analysed using statistical modeling to produce predictive analytics (Strang 2016b). However there should be proper reflection on the ethical issues surrounding learning and predictive analytics (Slade, Prinsloo 2013) The predictability should not be used in isolation and without the social context for a learner or group of learners (Hernández-García et al. 2015). On the other hand, Gašević *et al.* (2016) argue that learning conditions are an important factor to consider while using LA. There is a need for an appreciation of the value LA adds to the process of learning and teaching. For example, Persico (2015) explains how LA can inform the learning design. van Leeuwen *et al.* (2015) showed how teachers can benefit in their educational rationale by using LA. Whereas, Strang (2016a) and Strang (2016b) present how student learning outcomes and achievements can be predicted by LA.

3. RESEARCH DESIGN

This is a post-positivist research that applies a subjectivist paradigm (Cohen 2011, Lincoln, Guba 2003). This exploratory research applies case study methodology through a series of key stakeholder semi-structured interviews (Vanwynsberghe, Khan 2007, Yin 2003, Creswell 2014). SSU is the case in this study that constructs a holistic single-case design (Yin 2003), where the researcher builds an institutional perception as readiness for using LA within the SSU. Because the author is part of the LA initiative at the SSU, the axiological aspect demands the research to apply constructivist approaches to learning. The research tries to identify the perceptions of the stakeholders around LA in the SSU, where the context, existing belief systems, and institutional values stipulated by the mission statement create a local understanding of the topic. Cronje (2006) and Chen (2007) argue that objectivist and constructivist paradigms of learning can co-exist while designing learning environments. Therefore, in this research, there are multiple paradigms being applied i.e. post-positivist, subjectivist, and constructivist. The research addresses the following three questions:

RQ1: What is the perception of LA among the major stakeholders?
RQ2: Who are the wider stakeholders of LA?
RQ3: What are the challenges around LA as perceived by the stakeholders?

4. PERCEPTUAL FINDINGS

4.1 Student Perceptions

The students had no idea about LA and the author had to define LA. They thought presenting non-attendance with potential impact on academic performance would be useful for those who tend to miss learning opportunities. In a nutshell, they wanted to find out the correlation between missing learning opportunities and someone's grades, indicating the predictive analysis of learning opportunities. This demonstrates that students perceived LA as a support for learning (Oblinger 2012, Slade, Prinsloo 2013) while appreciating the predictive capability of such tool (Dietz-Uhler, Hurn 2013, Agudo-Peregrina et al. 2014, Tempelaar, Rienties & Giesbers 2015, Strang 2016a, Strang 2016b). They highlighted other engagement data to be correlated with academic performance e.g. library attendance and VLE attendance. These SSU students perceived comprehensive data collection on learners' activities useful (Sclater, Peasgood & Mullan 2016). When asked who else could have access to this sort of data, they replied negatively, as there could be personal reasons for non-attendance bringing the social dimension of LA (Hernández-García et al. 2015). However, they thought this sorts of data could be anonymous and be used in academic analytics as management information (Oblinger 2012, Sclater, Peasgood & Mullan 2016). The author asked about teachers as being potential stakeholders for such data and they replied that might be useful as long as students could opt out of such data disclosure (Slade, Prinsloo 2013). The students also felt comparative analytics could be useful as long as it was compared with a relevant cohort. This indicates that the university may want to include carefully chosen peer comparison within the analytical engine (Sclater, Peasgood & Mullan 2016).

4.2 Academic Staff Perceptions

The academic staff, unlike the students, knew about LA and defined it as a process of measuring some data about learners (Oblinger 2012, Slade, Prinsloo 2013, Sclater, Peasgood & Mullan 2016). They said the measurement involves collecting, analysing, reporting and making decisions about learners in order to achieve some strategic aims as defined by Daniel (2015) and Sclater, Peasgood & Mullan (2016) They emphasised the need for the accuracy of data collection and thorough data cleansing (Strang 2016b, Daniel 2015) before analysing the data to support institutional performance (Oblinger 2012, Sclater, Peasgood & Mullan 2016). They highlighted that it was more important to collect big data and analysed them for performance enhancement (Ali et al. 2013, Ali et al. 2012, Conde, Hernández-García 2015, Fidalgo-Blanco et al. 2015) irrespective of its usage at micro level or macro level. When asked what LA would be useful to enhance their teaching, the academics replied any data about the learners could be useful to custom tailor their teaching materials (van Leeuwen et al. 2014) for the learners for better engagement (Oblinger 2012, Slade, Prinsloo 2013). The academics wanted all sorts of factual data about their learners to be included in LA, e.g. demographic data, past educational attainments (Strang 2016a, Strang 2016b), professional experiences, engagement with learning activities (Slade, Prinsloo 2013, van Leeuwen et al. 2014), accessibility requirements, specific health requirements (Hernández-García et al. 2015).

The academics mentioned that having access to all data about learners was not useful for an academic rather it would be useful to have some insights about learners drawn from LA (actionable data mentioned by Slade and Prinsloo (2013), which can be readily utilised for enhanced pedagogy (Ali et al. 2012, Ali et al. 2013, van Leeuwen et al. 2014, Conde, Hernández-García 2015, Fidalgo-Blanco et al. 2015). The academics also thought all student support systems should have access to LA and their actions must be driven by data (Slade, Prinsloo 2013). Academics believed that the biggest technological challenge (Daniel 2015, Strang 2016b) of LA is the data collections that were not from application forms but through human interactions. This statement confirms with (Hernández-García et al. 2015) who spoke about the social context of LA. The academics mentioned about challenges around spotting patterns across big data and trying to predict situations in timely fashion to support systems that could make a difference (Dietz-Uhler, Hurn 2013, Agudo-Peregrina et al. 2014, Tempelaar, Rienties & Giesbers 2015, Strang 2016a, Strang 2016b).

4.3 Student Support Staff Perceptions

One of the student support manager, currently working on the SSU LA project, defined LA as big data appropriately presented to learners, teachers, support staff and management (Oblinger 2012, Slade, Prinsloo 2013) to facilitate their decision-making from their contexts (Gašević et al. 2016). She thought the purpose of LA for all of these stakeholders was to improve respective performances (Ali et al. 2012, Ali et al. 2013, Conde, Hernández-García 2015, Fidalgo-Blanco et al. 2015, Strang 2016a, Strang 2016b). She said it would also help the SSU to formulate relevant strategies, e.g. around retention and progression and would allow the organisation to measure progress against such strategies (Slade, Prinsloo 2013, Sclater, Peasgood & Mullan 2016) . She also described how LA could support course management and organisation (Persico, Pozzi 2015) and could support learners to achieve their personal goals (Strang 2016a, Strang 2016b). She clearly articulated a phased roll-out of LA but ultimately reaching every stakeholder, to make decisions based on data. While addressing potential benefits of LA for her student support team, she clearly mentioned predictive analytics (Hernández-García et al. 2015), which would predict current and future students at risk based on past patterns and trends in data (Daniel 2015, Sclater, Peasgood & Mullan 2016). This would particularly support her team to address retention issues with the SSU (Ali et al. 2012, Ali et al. 2013, Conde, Hernández-García 2015, Fidalgo-Blanco et al. 2015). She highlighted there needed to be a significant cultural shift at the SSU for successful LA to drive decision-making with accountability (Slade, Prinsloo 2013). The interviewee did not perceive any ethical dilemma and felt ethical issues can be managed with appropriate policy and procedures in place around usage of big data.

4.4 System Support Staff Perceptions

The system support staff member, currently working on the LA project, thought the learner in this digital age would understand what data could do to enhance their learning experiences but might just be struggling with the specific term LA. She initially thought learners' engagements understood by different touch points (VLE login, library attendance, classroom attendance etc.) would mean LA, but after the Jisc engagement, she realised that LA broadly dealt with macro and micro level data on learners (Sclater, Peasgood & Mullan 2016). She thought there might be academic staff that kept themselves informed about contemporary development in pedagogy (Persico, Pozzi 2015) and in the process learnt about LA. In response to the stakeholder question, she answered that the academic staff members, support staff members, and the management would be the key stakeholders of LA for daily operations (Oblinger 2012, Slade, Prinsloo 2013), whereas the information technology support staff would be fundamental in delivering the project around LA. Interestingly she did not think that the learners were stakeholders for LA. She thought of involving the student union or a recent SSU graduate employee to join the implementation project. She identified that there are very little offerings in the market place to amalgamate big data on learners encapsulating all the touch points. She understands that LA have predictive capability for which statistical analysis are needed. When asked about ethical dilemmas, she highlighted the implication of the Data Protection Act (1998) on LA (Slade, Prinsloo 2013).

5. CONCLUSION

The students at SSU do not understand the concept of LA. In contrast, there is a broad understanding among the academic and support staff members that aligns with existing literatures. The system staff member, though aware of the technological complexity, does not possess a fully evolved understanding of LA. The SSU staff members are more open in sharing relevant LA as long as the ethical issues are dealt with proper adherence of the Data Protection Act (1998). The SSU students questioned wider sharing of their data and comparative analysis that may disengage learners with poorer achievement records. In general they do not understand the technological complexity of LA. The support staff and academic staff members advocate a strong cultural shift for any LA related project to be successful, invoked by an institutional strategy based on a shared understanding of LA. The SSU staff members also appreciate the outcome driven and purposeful usage of LA for enhanced pedagogy, learners' achievement, and efficient resource allocation highlighted by existing literature. Interestingly no one at the SSU thought that LA should be a multidisciplinary and multi-stakeholder initiative (Reyes 2015, Daniel 2015). Neither anyone at the SSU understands that data could be learners generated as learning is a temporal dynamic construct, which can largely mitigate ethical issues (Slade, Prinsloo 2013). The research also discovered that there is little understanding around statistical modelling within an analytical engine to deliver LA (Daniel 2015, Tempelaar, Rienties & Giesbers 2015, Strang 2016a, Sclater, Peasgood & Mullan 2016). Completing similar case studies across several other universities would further strengthen these research outcomes to be more meaningful for teaching-intense universities.

ACKNOWLEDGEMENT

This research has been completed as part of the doctoral study at the Department of Educational Research, Lancaster University, Bailrigg, Lancaster LA1 4YW, UK. The author is grateful for support and guidance from Dr Kyungmee Lee and Prof Don Passey.

REFERENCES

"Special issue on learning analytics", 2015, *Learning Technologies, IEEE Transactions on,* vol. 8, no. 3, pp. 322-323.

Agudo-Peregrina, ÁF., Iglesias-Pradas, S., Conde-González, M.Á & Hernández-García, Á 2014, "Can we predict success from log data in VLEs? Classification of interactions for learning analytics and their relation with performance in VLE-supported F2F and online learning", *Computers in Human Behavior,* vol. 31, pp. 542-550.

Ali, L., Asadi, M., Gašević, D., Jovanović, J. & Hatala, M. 2013, "Factors influencing beliefs for adoption of a learning analytics tool: An empirical study", *Computers & Education,* vol. 62, pp. 130-148.

Ali, L., Hatala, M., Gasevic, D. & Jovanovic, J. 2012, "A Qualitative Evaluation of Evolution of a Learning Analytics Tool", *Computers & Education,* vol. 58, no. 1, pp. 470-489.

Chen, S. 2007, "Instructional design strategies for intensive online courses: An objectivist-constructivist blended approach", *Journal of interactive online learning,* vol. 6, no. 1, pp. 72-86.

Cohen, L. 2011, *Research methods in education,* 7th ed. edn, London : Routledge.

Conde, M.Á & Hernández-García, Á 2015, *Learning analytics for educational decision making.*

Creswell, J.W. 2014, *Educational research electronic resource] : planning, conducting, and evaluating quantitative and qualitative research,* Fourth edition.; Pearson new international edition. edn, .

Cronje, J. 2006, "Paradigms Regained: Toward Integrating Objectivism and Constructivism in Instructional Design and the Learning Sciences", *Educational Technology Research and Development,* vol. 54, no. 4, pp. 387-416.

Daniel, B. 2015, "Big Data and Analytics in Higher Education: Opportunities and Challenges", *British Journal of Educational Technology,* vol. 46, no. 5, pp. 904-920.

Dietz-Uhler, B. & Hurn, J.E. 2013, "Using learning analytics to predict (and improve) student success: A faculty perspective", *Journal of Interactive Online Learning,* vol. 12, no. 1, pp. 17-26.

Fidalgo-Blanco, Á, Sein-Echaluce, M., García-Peñalvo, F.J. & Conde, M.Á 2015, "Using Learning Analytics to improve teamwork assessment", *Computers in Human Behavior,* vol. 47, pp. 149-156.

Gašević, D., Dawson, S., Rogers, T. & Gasevic, D. 2016, "Learning analytics should not promote one size fits all: The effects of instructional conditions in predicting academic success", *Internet and Higher Education,* vol. 28, pp. 68-84.

Hernández-García, Á, González-González, I., Jiménez-Zarco, A.I. & Chaparro-Peláez, J. 2015, "Applying social learning analytics to message boards in online distance learning: A case study", *Computers in Human Behavior,* vol. 47, pp. 68-80.

Kash, B.R.P., Thappa, D.M.H. & Kavitha, V. 2015, "Big Data in Educational Data Mining and Learning Analytics", *International Journal of Innovative Research in Computer and Communication Engineering,* vol. 02, no. 12, pp. 7515-7520.

Lincoln, Y.S. & Guba, E.G. 2003, "Paradigmatic controversies, contradictions, and emerging confluences (Chapter 8)" in *Handbook of qualitative research*, eds. N.K. Denizen & Y.S.(.). Lincoln, 3rd edn, Sage, Thousand Oaks, CA, pp. 191-215.

Madhavan, K. & Richey, M.C. 2016, "Problems in Big Data Analytics in Learning", *Journal of Engineering Education,* vol. 105, no. 1, pp. 6-14.

Oblinger, D.G. 2012, "Let's Talk... Analytics", *EDUCAUSE Review,* vol. 47, no. 4, pp. 10-13.

Persico, D. & Pozzi, F. 2015, *Informing learning design with learning analytics to improve teacher inquiry.*

Picciano, A.G. 2014, "Big Data and Learning Analytics in Blended Learning Environments: Benefits and Concerns", *International Journal of Interactive Multimedia and Artificial Intelligence,* vol. 2, no. 7, pp. 35-43.

Reyes, J. 2015, "The skinny on big data in education: Learning analytics simplified", *TechTrends; Linking Research and Practice to Improve Learning A publication of the Association for Educational Communications & Technology,* vol. 59, no. 2, pp. 75-80.

Sclater, N., Peasgood, A. & Mullan, J. 2016, *Learning analytics in higher education A review of UK and international practice.*, JISC, Bristol.

Siemens, G. 2013, "Learning Analytics: The Emergence of a Discipline", *The American Behavioral Scientist,* vol. 57, no. 10, pp. 1380.

Slade, S. & Prinsloo, P. 2013, "Learning Analytics: Ethical Issues and Dilemmas", *The American Behavioral Scientist,* vol. 57, no. 10, pp. 1510.

Slavakis, K., Giannakis, G.B. & Mateos, G. 2014, "Modeling and Optimization for Big Data Analytics: (Statistical) learning tools for our era of data deluge", *Signal Processing Magazine, IEEE,* vol. 31, no. 5, pp. 18-31.

Southampton Solent University 2016, , *Our History.* Available: http://www.solent.ac.uk/about/history/history.aspx [2016, 05/07].

Strang, K.D. 2016a, "Beyond engagement analytics: which online mixed-data factors predict student learning outcomes?", *Education and Information Technologies,* , pp. 1-21.

Strang, K.D. 2016b, "Do the Critical Success Factors From Learning Analytics Predict Student Outcomes?", *Journal of Educational Technology Systems,* vol. 44, no. 3, pp. 273-299.

Tempelaar, D.T., Rienties, B. & Giesbers, B. 2015, "In search for the most informative data for feedback generation: Learning analytics in a data-rich context", *Computers in Human Behavior,* vol. 47, pp. 157-167.

van Leeuwen, A., Janssen, J., Erkens, G. & Brekelmans, M. 2015, "Teacher regulation of cognitive activities during student collaboration: Effects of learning analytics", *Computers & Education; Comput.Educ.,* vol. 90, pp. 80-94.

van Leeuwen, A., Janssen, J., Erkens, G. & Brekelmans, M. 2014, "Supporting teachers in guiding collaborating students: Effects of learning analytics in CSCL", *Computers & Education,* vol. 79, pp. 28-39.

Vanwynsberghe, R. & Khan, S. 2007, "Redefining case study", *International journal of qualitative methods,* vol. 6, no. 2, pp. 80-94.

Yin, R.K. 2003, "Designing case studies" in *Case study research: design and methods*, ed. R.K. Yin, 3rd edn, Sage, London, pp. 19-56.

ISSUES OF IT-PROFESSIONALS TRAINING IN TRADITIONAL EDUCATIONAL PROCESS

Farid Eminov[1] and Irina Golitsyna[2]
[1]*Automated Information Processing Systems and Control department, Kazan National Research Technical University named after A.N. Tupolev, 420111 Kazan, 10 Karl Marx street, Russia*
[2]*Department of Software Engineering, High School of Information Technologies and Information Systems, Kazan (Volga) Federal University, 420008 Kazan, 35 Kremlevskaya street, Russia*

ABSTRACT

The paper presents issues of modern IT-specialists training. Formation of information- educational environment of IT-professionals is discussed. Studying of enterprise infocommunication infrastructure and its management features within a framework of the traditional educational process is considered.

KEYWORDS

Educational process, IT-professionals, electronic information-educational environment, flexible learning, enterprise network infrastructure

1. INTRODUCTION

Organization of educational process of modern IT-specialists requires modern methods and forms of teaching and learning that correspond to a rapid pace of information technologies development. Training of such specialists has following features (Eminov, 2009):

- Enterprises require qualified graduates who have to be prepared to start on their jobs right after graduation.
- Field of information technologies is changing rapidly, new technologies are developing continually.
- Forms and methods of training adjust to a rapidly changing informational educational environment.

Training of labor market-viable specialists requires arranging educational process taking into account features stated above.

To ensure proper quality of modern professional training, teachers have to be constantly updated on educational content. In order to do this, they use various approaches, such as re-processing and periodic re-issue of study books and manuals, development of electronic educational resources based on specialized systems and web-resources, use of a professional software products, including those available on the Internet, development of their own software-environments for teaching, including these based on mobile technologies.

Our experience of e-learning courses implementation shows, that they allow to create a virtual learning environment, to expand and change the content of disciplines in terms of educational standards, to organize individual, group and collective forms of learning activities, to organize self-directed learning for students to reach educational goals (Golitsyna, 2013). At the same time, forms and methods of teaching have to correspond to educational content of disciplines.

This paper presents approaches to formation of information- educational environment of modern IT-specialists, as well as to organization of traditional educational process through the studying of enterprise infocommunication infrastructure and its management features.

In organization of educational process we were directed by demands of Federal State Educational Standards of higher education in the field of training 09.03.01 Informatics and computer technology, 09.03.02 Information systems and technologies, 09.03.03 Applied Informatics.

2. EDUCATIONAL PROCESS IN INFORMATION-EDUCATIONAL ENVIRONMENT

Electronic information-educational environment of an educational institution provides interaction between participants of educational process, including synchronous and (or) asynchronous communication via Internet . Formation of information-educational environment of organization brings changes to teachers' activity in a way that elements of distance learning are increasingly used in traditional educational process (Solovov , Men'shikova, 2015). These processes lead to the fact that traditional learning process acquires features of "flexible learning". Flexibility is considered as an attribute of both learners and teachers; it can also be understood as a characteristic of institutional educational strategies (Wanner, Palmer, 2015). Researchers emphasize that under "flexible training" conditions teacher has to take a role of a guide and encourage students to be independent and flexible within an educational framework (Agudelo, Salinas, 2015). Flexible learning technologies can be used productively also in a traditional educational process of IT-professionals (Golitsyna, 2017b).

On practical classes of our course "Infocommunication systems and networks" for bachelor program 09.03.02 Information systems and technologies and at the course "Operations research and optimization methods" for bachelor program 09.03.03 Applied Informatics were used following forms of educational activity (Golitsyna, 2017a):

1. Using educational resources of the Internet have been prepared guidelines, giving brief theoretical information on topic and hands-on assignments and tasks for solving problems for each practice session.
2. Students were free to choose software environment or online resources for problem solving. Students had to choose tools for problem solving themselves, including mobile tools.
3. Control in a classroom was in a form of personal discussion with students about practical lessons topics.

This form of training and teaching of classes allowed:

1. To choose and use the most qualitative and methodically prepared educational resources for studying each topic of a taught discipline.
2. To arrange an individual conversation with every student, before which students have to be prepared and answer all the questions on a topic of a lesson. Under preparation for a verbal response, student should actualize task formulation, method of its solution, justify a choice of means of problem solving or task accomplishment method. This form of control, in our opinion, is especially relevant under the modern educational process conditions, when verbal forms are often replaced by computer interaction such as tests, reports, learning activity with LMS etc.
3. Let students choose freely methods and means of problem solving and managing of practical tasks. As a result students' independent practical work was personified. Students could independently chose tools for assigned problem solving, including use of mobile devices. Students worked on their tasks at an individual pace, including their time outside a classroom as part of independent work.

Organization of flexible learning of IT-specialties students is especially efficient due to the fact that students actively begin to use professional environment to work on assigned problems. Within a framework of the traditional educational process, students get an opportunity to master methods of self-education and continuous education in electronic educational environment which necessary for successful professional activity of IT-professionals.

Virtual learning environment creates the platform to provide permanent access to educational recourses from mobile devices. This option helps students to use opportunities of mobile learning in the educational process.

Web-services are the main tools for self-education for students of IT-specialties. Application of web-resources in a process of self-education leads to formation of informational personal-oriented educational environment for every student. Students widely use web-resources for self-education and academic problems solving (Golitsyna, 2015): they learn distantly using open educational resources. Students use specialized forums for studying of programming languages, as well as for programming from mobile devices, programming online in integrated programming environments IDE. Often they start to program in a framework of self-education.

Thus, flexible learning technology promotes of educational process personalization, which is one of the global trends in development of modern higher education (Burnashov, 2017).

3. EDUCATIONAL PROCESS THROUGH ENTERPRISE INFOCOMMUNICATION INFRASTRUCTURE

Information technologies at enterprises required to provide users with information system services, whose work is supported by enterprise infocommunication infrastructure.

Under teaching of IT-professionals, management of an information network infrastructure has to be taken into account. Information technologies systems are getting more complicated and require creation of information technology service management systems.

Problems of IT- resources management and IT-services effectiveness improvement (ITSM - Information Technology Service Management) were formulated in the 1980s. This methodology has been highly demanded since the beginning of this century, with the transition from the traditional model - support of enterprises' informational and communicational infrastructure, to the model oriented on servicing core business of an enterprise. On enterprises were formed departments (IT-departments), providing functional departments with various services related to information technologies. Additionally to operational services provided to functional departments of an enterprise to ensure proper functioning of its IT-systems, IT-departments have work to improve their own efficiency level.

Nowadays, enterprises require use of information technologies in such areas as: maintaining of electronic correspondence flow, use of the Internet, automating of inner business-processes, supporting interactions with partners etc. Modern IT-departments have service-oriented structure, which is built as a system of processes managing services (Eminov, 2015). IT-departments support and develop infrastructure according to requested services and specified quality. Functional department sets its requirements for a specified type of required services and their quality. In this connection, IT-department of an enterprise becomes an important resource for enterprise management system.

Every type of enterprise infrastructure defines an educational content of IT-students. For example, when students study disciplines corresponding to network infrastructure of information systems, first they need to study basic knowledge, which, in our opinion, can contain following topics:

1. Definition of distributed processing. Possible structures of distributed information processing systems.
2. Basic concepts and definitions of information (computing) networks, such as: network architecture, network protocols and interfaces, concept of "open systems", international standards for network interactions implementation, OSI / ISO model, "client-server" technology etc.
3. Basic modern network technologies of local and corporate networks for office use, based on cable and wireless connections, namely: standards for these technologies, possible data communication environments, access methods to data communication environments, methods of signals and data coding, interface with data communication environments.
4. Basic information about network interactions and network services, particularly: networks interaction organization, network interfaces and protocols, network services, addressing in networks etc.

Hierarchical structure of corporate management system of manufacturing enterprise has to be taken into account while building a training system (Eminov, 2015), which has production character of activity.

Every level designed to perform specific management functions. Each hierarchical management level has its own computing environment, which is a network generally. Information networks with their functioning characteristics are formed on every management level. We will review studying features of office networks, corresponding to upper and middle levels of corporate management system hierarchy.

Possible form of educational activity is a training based on specially organized training ground. Particularly, such training ground was organized for students of bachelor program 09.03.02 Information systems and technologies and bachelor program 09.03.01 Informatics and computer technology in following disciplines: "Infocommunication systems and networks", "Network technologies" and "Corporate information systems ".

Students perform necessary operations to create local network infrastructure, using provided to them computers. Modern infocommunication infrastructure of an enterprise is integrated and formed by a combination of cable and wireless components (Eminov, 2017). Students consistently create separate fragments of local network, installing cable systems, computers and communication equipment, making necessary adjustments and tests of single elements of infocommunication system and networks.

After mastering basics of installation, adjustment and testing of infocommunication infrastructure, students move on to learning of administration basics. For solution of this problem they use virtual environments. Each student creates on PC a virtual environment which usually includes a server that has a special role in learning environment and one (or more if necessary) network workstation. Student learns in created virtual environment and getting necessary skills in setting up various network services required for a normal functioning of enterprise information systems.

After mastering deployment skills of basic network services of enterprise, students begin to administrate more complex services in terms of their formation and configuration parameters. During operations implementation of network and information systems administration, students master skills of creating terminal access, organizing secure data transmission tunnels, creating directory services and solving other tasks of managing enterprise infrastructure.

4. CONCLUSION

Information-educational environment of modern IT-professionals is developing according of development of education and the professional environment. These changes require organization of special learning approaches. These approaches are dictated, on one hand, by industry and business requirements to IT-professionals, on the other hand, by rapid development of professional environment of IT-specialists.

Application of web-resources and mobile devices facilitates infiltration of flexible learning technologies into traditional learning process, which creates additional opportunities for organizing independent work of students and provides personalization of training.

As shows our experience, teachers need:

- to participate in continuous development of the information-educational environment of educational institutions according modern educational standards;
- to work on constant update of educational disciplines content according to condition of professional environment of IT-specialists.

REFERENCES

Agudelo O. L., Salinas J., 2015, Flexible Learning Itineraries Based on Conceptual Maps// *New approaches in educational research,* July 2015, Vol. 4, No. 2, pp. 70-76.

Burnashov B.A., 2017. [Personalization as a global trend of e-learning in higher education institutions] // *Sovremennyye problemy nauki i obrazovaniya (Modern problems of science and education),* No.1. (In Russ.) - https://www.science-education.ru/ru/article/view?id=26078

Eminov F., 2009. [Formation of competitive specialists for IT-services of enterprises] // *Mezhdunarodnyy elektronnyy zhurnal "Obrazovatel'nyye tekhnologii i obshchestvo* (*Educational Technology & Society*) ".Vol. 12, No.1, pp. 436-442. (In Russ., abstract in Eng.) - http://ifets.ieee.org/russian/depository/v12_i1/html/10.htm

Eminov F., 2015. [*Information technologies of enterprises management]*. The Master Line, Kazan, Russia, 144 pp. (In Russ.)

Eminov F., 2016. [*Office and industrial information networks].* The Master Line, Kazan, Russia, 346 pp. (In Russ.)

Golitsyna, I. N., 2013. Creation of e-learning resources for Web-oriented disciplines //*International Conference on Interactive Collaborative Learning (ICL)*, Kazan, Russia, pp. 266 – 275.

Golitsyna I., 2015. Application of web services in teaching of IT-discipline// *Procedia - Social and Behavioral Sciences,* Vol. 214, 5 Dec. 2015, pp. 578-585. - http://www.sciencedirect.com/science/article/pii/S1877042815061182

Golitsyna I., 2017a. Educational process in electronic information-educational environment// *Procedia - Social and Behavioral Sciences,* Vol. 37, 21 February 2017, pp. 939-944. - http://www.sciencedirect.com/science/article/pii/S1877042817301325

Golitsyna, I.N., 2017b. [Flexible learning in a traditional educational process]. *Vysshee obrazovanie v Rossii [Higher Education in Russia]*, No. 5, pp. 113-117. (In Russ., abstract in Eng.) - http://vovr.ru/upload/5-17.pdf

Solovov A. V., Men'shikova A. A., 2015. [E-learning: development vector] // *Vysshee obrazovanie v Rossii [Higher Education in Russia]*. No. 11, C. 66-75. (In Russ., abstract in Eng.) - http://vovr.ru/upload/11-15.pdf

Wanner T., Palmer E., 2015, Personalising learning: Exploring student and teacher perceptions about flexible learning and assessment in a flipped university course // *Computers & Education*, Vol. 88, October 2015, pp. 354–369.

THE ISOLATION EMOTION: AN EMOTIONAL POINT OF VIEW ON TEAMING AND GROUP TOOLS IN E-LEARNING ENVIRONMENTS

Tarek Boutefara (*)(**) and Latifa Mahdaoui (***)
(*) Computer Science Dept, Faculty of Exact Sciences and Computer Sciences, University of Mohammed Seddik Benyahia, Jijel, Algeria.
(**) Doctoral School STIC, National High School of Computer Sciences, Algiers, Algeria.
(***) RIIMA Laboratory, Computer Science Dept, USTHB, Algiers, Algeria

ABSTRACT

The Socio-constructive approach applied by the largely used e-Learning platforms tries to give the learners the ability to build their own knowledge by searching, analyzing and discussing information in a collaborative environment. This approach has known a large success. In this paper, we will look to this approach from an emotional point of view. The idea is to understand the emotional dimension of the collaborative tools that allow the realization of Socio-constructive learning activities. To do so, we have chosen to use a 3D learning environment in a, attempt to understand the link to the isolation emotion which is generally expressed in text-based environments. The main idea is to prove the presence of an emotional dimension in every component of e-Learning platform. If proven, this affirmation could help us to define new design approaches that exploit this emotional dimension and don't need additional emotion-dedicated components.

KEYWORDS

Emotions; Isolation emotion; 3D Environments; E-Learning

1. INTRODUCTION

Emotions are strongly related to learning activity (Picard, 1995)(O'Regan, 2003). Today, studying and analyzing learning emotions are a key factor in providing a better learning experience (Lin, & al., 2010). This importance becomes more urgent in an e-Learning context (Lin, & al., 2010). With the absence of the human contact, the teacher is no longer able to detect the emotional state of the learner; an ability that can be seen as trivial in a classic classroom course (Lin, & al., 2010). Consequently, providing course adaptation and motivational support becomes more difficult (Picard, 1995)(Lin, & al., 2010).

One of the first and most used framework to represent learning emotions is the FEASP named after the five emotions: Fear, Envy, Anger, Sympathy and Pleasure (Astleitner, 2001). In larger emotional theories, these emotions are seen as basic emotions (Geslin, 2012)(Ekman, 1999). In this paper, we will try to put in focus another less studied emotion that is the emotion of isolation.

Isolation can be defined as "having a well-functioning social network but still feels emotionally separated from others" (Helgason & al., 2001); we can adapt this notion to a learning group by saying that intentional isolation during a learning session is the sensation of separation from the other members of the learning group. It can be seen as the contrary of belongingness where the learner sees himself as a part of the team (Baumeister & Leary, 1995). In a learning context, teaming is a powerful tool in organizations; including classrooms (Quinn, 2016). Its importance allowed the proposition of a whole new pedagogical approach known as "Socio-constructivism" (Raynal & Rieunier, 1997). This approach came to complete the constuctivism approach which sees the learner as an active agent during the learning process (Quinn, 2016)(Raynal & Rieunier, 1997). In the socio-constructivism approach, the learners are seen as a set of teams that build actively their knowledge by searching and analyzing information and performing experiments (Raynal & Rieunier, 1997).

In e-Learning context, a large part of these notions are lost with the absence of the human to human (direct) communication (Lin, & al., 2010). The teaming in text-based environment such as chat rooms and forum groups seems to be very limited compared to teaming and grouping in real-life classic classroom environments (Cruz-Lara, 2010). Consequently, the emotion of isolation appears more frequently in e-Learning context (Cruz-Lara, 2010).

To resolve this problem, we can proceed with the generic approach of emotion integration in e-Learning systems (Lin, & al., 2010). This approach defines three steps: emotional indicators' collection, emotion recognition and system reaction (Lin, & al., 2010)(Geslin, 2012). This approach can be applied in different situations and integrated in different e-Learning platforms; however, it represents a very high coast in implementation, integration and evaluation. It can, also, require the use of particular equipments (Boutefara & Mahdaoui, 2015).

In this paper, we explore another option to prevent the isolation emotion: the use of 3D environments. The idea finds its roots in two main points. First, the success of virtual agents and emojis as an enhancement of the on line communication in there absence of the face-to-face (human-to-human communication) (Cruz-Lara, 2010)(Kim, 2015). Second, the success of the Socio-constructivism approach in teaching (Raynal & Rieunier, 1997). In an emotional point of view, we think that the success does not reside in the value of interactions only but by the emotional state of the group members which can be seen as the opposite of the isolation emotional state (Baumeister & Leary, 1995).

In this paper, we present a local experiment which aims to provide emotional feedback, mainly about the isolation emotion, during a learning activity in a 3D environment. The paper is devised to three main sections. First, the related work section presents briefly a set of important notions for the realized work. Second, the experiment section presents the used tool, the experiment plan and the experiment result. Finally, the discussion section presents a critical analyze of the obtained results.

2. RELATED WORKS

In a learning context, such as e-Learning, the obtained results in the cognitive field represent a sufficient justification to study the possibilities and opportunities to take in count the learner emotional state on e-Learning platforms (Picard, 1995).

The largely used e-Learning platforms, such as Moodle (http://www.moodle.org/), try to give support for the socio-constructivism learning approach. They offer a set of tools such as forums, chat and blogging to allow communication between the teacher and his learners and the communication between learners during learning activities (Angeli & al., 2003)(Naidu, 2006). We think that these tools have an emotional dimension that can be exploited in taking in count the learner emotional state during learning activities.

A platform that takes in count the learner emotional state should be able to accomplish more that the detection; it should be able to influence the emotional state to obtain the more adequate emotional state for the current learning activity or to prevent emotional states with negative effect on learning activity such as frustration (Lin, & al., 2010)(Geslin, 2012). To achieve this goal, many works have been realized. Some of these works use virtual agents (Faiver & al., 2002). Virtual agents try to simulate the presence of a human being that accompanies the learner during the learning activity (Faiver & al., 2002). The main reason that justifies its utilization is the limited possibilities given by the textual tools as support of communication. Virtual agents are also used in 3D and VR environments (Cruz-Lara, 2010).

Taking these points and the precision that we are trying to adopt an emotional point of view, we define the following hypothesis: it is possible to realize an e-Learning environment that can have a well known and manipulated emotional effect on learners without the need for additional dedicated tools.

3. EXPERIMENTATION

The defined hypothesis is a generalization of perceived facts; we will not be able to validate it with one experiment. Therefore, the realized experiment had as main goal the obtaining of explicit feedback from learners about the isolation emotional state after using a 3D e-Learning environment.

3.1 Open Wonderland

Open Wonderland (http://www.openwonderland.org/) is an open-source toolkit for creating collaborative 3D virtual worlds. The learners are present by their avatars and can move from a location to another by walking and they can express body gestures. This environment offers a set of collaborative tools such as chat, the collaborative white board, live conferencing and screen sharing. These tools allow the design and deployment of different forms of learning resources and the performance of live demonstrations and experiments.

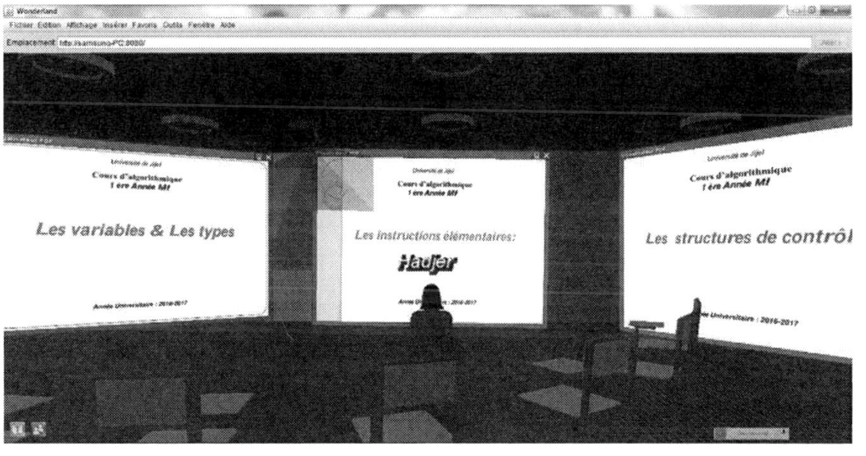

Figure 1. File display component, one among many collaborative tools in Open Wonderland

3.2 Experiment Plan

Given that the aimed emotion in this study is the isolation emotional state, we have to conceive an experimentation that tries to eliminate other learning emotions that can affect our experimentation. Thus, we have not included grading activities and prerequisite knowledge to avoid Fear, Anger and Envy.

The experiment has been performed by 20 students; each one has assisted to Algorithmic learning session of 30 to 40 minutes with the ability to use different collaborative tools. The feedback is gathered using a form that every participant will fill just after the end of the experiment and through a set of observation notes.

3.3 Results and Discussion

The experiment has been held recently; we are still analyzing and mining all the significant paths in the collected data. This is a first impression of the obtained result while:

- Attention and implication: the learners have all presented a very good level of implication, attention and activity during the learning session.
- Similarity to classic classrooms: 60% have said that the 3D environment is very similar, on communication aspect, to the classic classrooms compared to 40% for fairy similar.
- In comparison to text-based e-Learning environment, the simulated presence of the teacher has been seen as the most valuable aspect. Having the sensation of a direct human-to-human communication have been felt by 90% of the students.

The first feedbacks from the experimentation are very encouraging. The feeling of having a human-to-human communication means that the emotional state of isolation has been avoided in the 3D learning environment. The experiment does not imply all the factors related to isolation emotional state or all the possibilities of text-based and 3D based e-Learning environments. However, being able to exploit the nature and the emotional characteristics of the learning support, in this case the 3D environment, to induct or to avoid a particular emotional state without the need to implement or to integrate a full stack emotional systems (detecting and reacting system) is an encouraging validation (even partial) for the fixed hypothesis.

4. CONCLUSION

In this paper, we have tried to study the effect of a 3D learning and collaborative environment on the isolation emotional states to the learner. The main motivation for this work is to understand the emotional dimension in the Socio-constructivism tools. Understanding this dimension can help us to design and build on line courses that take in count the learner emotional state without the need to implement an emotion detection and reaction system. In this work, we have limited our field of action to one emotional state which is the isolation emotion. A 3D environment has been chosen to simulate a classic classroom.

The realized experiment on 20 students that tries to limit the influence of other learning emotion to allow a better observation of the isolation emotional state helped us to obtain a significant feedback from the students. The obtained results are very encouraging; the virtual presence was seen by most learners as very similar to the physical presence and their implication in the activity was very strong. The emotional state of isolation was not observed, therefore, we can say that the nature of the 3D environments gives the opportunity to design and build an on line learning experience with no isolation emotional state.

This reasoning can be generalized in farther studies to define explicitly the emotional state of every available tool on today e-Learning platform; the obtained data can be included in the course design to take in count the emotional dimension of the learner without the need for additional or dedicated components.

REFERENCES

Angeli, C. & al, (2003). Communication in a web-based conferencing system: the quality of computer-mediated interactions. *British Journal of Educational Technology* , Vol 34, No. 1, pp 31-43.

Astleitner, H. (2001). Designing Emotionally Sound Instruction--An Empirical Validation of the FEASP-Approach. *Journal of Instructional Psychology*, Vol 28, No. 3, pp 209-219.

Baumeister, R. F., & Leary, M. R. (1995), The need to belong: Desire for interpersonal attachments as a fundamental human motivation. *Psychological Bulletin*, Vol 117, No. 3, pp 497-529.

Boutefara, T. & Mahdaoui, L. (2015). Emoticon-based Feedback Tool for e-Learning Platforms. *The 16th International Arab Conference on Information Technology*. Zarqaa University, Amman, Jordan.

Cruz-Lara, S. (2010). Standards for communication and e-learning in Virtual Worlds : The multilingual-assisted chat interface. *12th International Conference on Enterprise Information Systems,* Funchal, Madeira, Portugal.

Ekman, P. (1999). Basic Emotions. *In Handbook of Cognition and Emotion.* John Wiley & Sons Ltd, New York City, USA, pp 46-60.

Faivre, J. & al. (2002). Gestion Emotionnelle dans les Systèmes Tuteurs Intelligents. Frasson C., Pécuchet J.-P. *Technologies de l'Information et de la Communication dans les Enseignements d'ingénieurs et dans l'industrie*, Villeurbanne, France. Institut National des Sciences Appliquées de Lyon, France, pp.73-80.

Geslin, E. (2012). Method of induction of basic and complex emotions in video games and virtual environments. *SIGGRAPH ASIA2012.* Singapore.

Helgason, A. R. & al, (2001). Emotional Isolation: Prevalence and the Effect on Well-being among 50–80-Year-Old Prostate Cancer Patients. *Scand J Urol Nephrol*, Vol 35, pp 97-101.

Kim C. M. (2015). Boosting learning-by-teaching in virtual tutoring. *Computers & Education.* Vol 82, pp 129-140.

Lin H. & al, (2010). Affective Computing in e-Learning, *in e-Learning*, InTech Publisher, ISBN 978-953-7619-95-4, pp 117-128.

Naidu, S. (2006). *E-Learning A Guidebook of Principles, Procedures and Practices*. Commonwealth Educational Media Center for Asia, New Delhi, India.

O'Regan, O. (2003). Emotion and e-Learning. *JALN,* Vol. 7, Issue 3, pp 78-92.

Picard, R. W. (1995), Affective Computing. *M.I.T Media Laboratory Perceptual Computing Section Technical Report,* No. 321.

Quinn, C. (2016). The New Organizational Learning: A Review of Teaming. *Elearn Magazine,* Vol 5.

Raynal, F. & Rieunier, A. (1997). *Pédagogie: dictionnaire des concepts clés, apprentissage, formation et psychologie cognitive.* ESF éditeur, Paris, France.

DEVELOPMENT OF CRITICAL THINKING WITH METACOGNITIVE REGULATION AND TOULMIN MODEL

Yasushi Gotoh
Niigata University, 8050,Ikarashi-2nocho, Nishi ward, Niigata City, Niigata, Japan

ABSTRACT

Developing critical thinking is an important factor in education. In this study, the author defines critical thinking as the set of skills and dispositions which enable one to solve problems logically and to attempt to reflect autonomously by means of metacognitive regulation of one's own problem-solving processes. To identify the validity and reliability of students' self -assessment, the critical thinking rubric and Toulmin model combination was introduced. At the end of the lesson all Toulmin model work sheets written by students were revised correctly. It was discovered that students solve problems logically. This shows that a high level of critical thinking among students is reliable and valid.

KEYWORDS

Critical Thinking, Metacognitive regulation, Toulmin model, Knowledge-constructive jigsaw method

1. INTRODUCTION

The ATCS21 (Assessing and Teaching 21st Century Skills) Project proposes ways of thinking; tools for working; ways of working; and ways of living in the world as the skills needed for the 21st century. According to ATCS21, critical thinking is one aspect of ways of thinking. Developing critical thinking is an important factor in education. A number of researchers such as Dewey (1910), Glaser (1941), and Ennis (1985) define critical thinking as reflective and logical thinking.

In this study, the author defines critical thinking as the set of skills and dispositions which enable one to solve problems logically and to attempt to reflect autonomously by means of metacognitive regulation of one's own problem-solving processes. AACU also provides a rubric known as a value rubric as a critical thinking assessment tool. In order to develop their critical thinking skills, it is important for students to be able to use this rubric and assess themselves.

In Gotoh (2016) it was suggested that metacognitive regulation with this critical thinking rubric as the criterion could enhance students' critical thinking ability (Gotoh2016). On the other hand, the following two problems remain. The first problem concerns the validity and reliability of students' self-assessment. Basically, the achievement level of critical thinking using the critical thinking rubric is dependent on students' judgment. To identify the validity and reliability of students' own self-assessment, some kind of tool is needed. At this point, the author introduces the Toulmin model as a tool to evaluate students' level of logical organization. The Toulmin model consists of six parts: ground, claim, warrant, backing, rebuttal and qualifier. If students' logical organization is deficient, even high self-assessments are not reliable and valid.

Incidentally, introducing the Toulmin model will assist students in their problem- solving. Will students feel that the combination of the critical thinking rubric and the Toulmin model is useful? In this study, the author considers this point.

The second problem concerns differences among individuals. In particular, nobody yet knows the difference in critical thinking achievement levels between those who have an aptitude for critical thinking and those who do not. Comparative study is needed.A template is a set of styles and page layout settings that determine the appearance of a document.

2. METHOD

2.1 Knowledge-constructive Jigsaw Method

27 university students took part in the study. Cooperative problem-solving methods such as the knowledge-constructive jigsaw method were selected as materials. The research project consisted of the knowledge-constructive jigsaw method and metacognitive regulation. Students held a discussion on the subject of introducing non-Japanese workers into Japan. Four types of different information were provided separately: depopulation in Japanese society; disadvantages and difficulties of employing non-Japanese workers; an overseas case study; and trends among non-Japanese workers in selecting an employment destination. After reading these different types of information individually, the students discussed the following topic: "Should Japan bring in more foreign workers?"

The entire discussion was audio-recorded and a lesson protocol was developed to be used in subsequent metacognitive regulation and reflection. Students were asked to carry out self-assessment using the critical thinking rubric（Gotoh2016）.

- I pay attention to the information source (who wrote it).
- I pay attention to the information destination (who reads it).
- I pay attention to the information purpose (agenda).
- I assume information from an opposing point of view.
- I pay attention to information period (when it was produced).
- I pay attention to inconsistencies and missing information.
- I pay attention to gaps in the argument.
- I make an impartial valuation of information that goes against my own opinion.
- If necessary, I reserve judgment.
- If necessary, I make a conditional judgment.

Self-assessment was carried out while listening to the audio recording of the discussion and reading the lesson protocol. Students were asked to self-assess their critical thinking ability on three levels: achieved, partly achieved, failed. Students were asked to explain their logic using the Toulmin model work sheet. The Toulmin model consists of six parts: ground, claim, warrant, backing, rebuttal and qualifier. The validity or non-validity of students' logic was evaluated according to whether they could correctly describe the relationship among claim, ground and warrant. Figures should de numbered consecutively as they appear in the text.

2.2 Metacognitive Regulation and Reflection

Students were asked to reflect on their learning using the critical thinking rubric and a rating scale, and by writing comments. These activities are themselves metacognitive regulation. Items on the rating scale are as follows:

- Using the critical thinking rubric and Toulmin model, it is easy to make a correct judgment.
- Using the critical thinking rubric and Toulmin model, it is easy to organize a discussion.
- Using the critical thinking rubric and Toulmin model, it is possible to clarify the problem.
- The critical thinking rubric and Toulmin model are useful in daily life.

The critical thinking rubric and Toulmin model are difficult to use. In order to focus on critical thinking dispositions, the Critical Thinking Disposition Scale (Hirayama & Kusumi, 2004) was used. This scale consists of four factors: awareness of logical thinking, spirit of inquiry, objectivity and emphasis on evidence. The scores of 33 items on this 4-point scale were totaled and the top two students and lowest two students were extracted.

Comparison and analysis of the top 50% and lowest 50% and the top 25 % and lowest 25% were also carried out.

3. RESULTS

3.1 Achievement Levels in the Critical Thinking Rubric

Figure 1 shows achievement levels in the critical thinking rubric. Over 90% of students had a high level of achievement in the following items: "I make an impartial evaluation of information that goes against my own opinion," "If necessary, I reserve judgment," I pay attention to the information source (who wrote it)" "I pay attention to inconsistencies and missing information," and "I assume information from an opposing point of view." Over 70% of students had a high level of achievement in the following items: "I pay attention to the information period (when it was produced)" and "I pay attention to the information destination (who reads it)." In comparison with the above, there was a lower level of achievement in the following items: "I pay attention to the information source (who wrote it)" and "I pay attention to gaps in the argument."

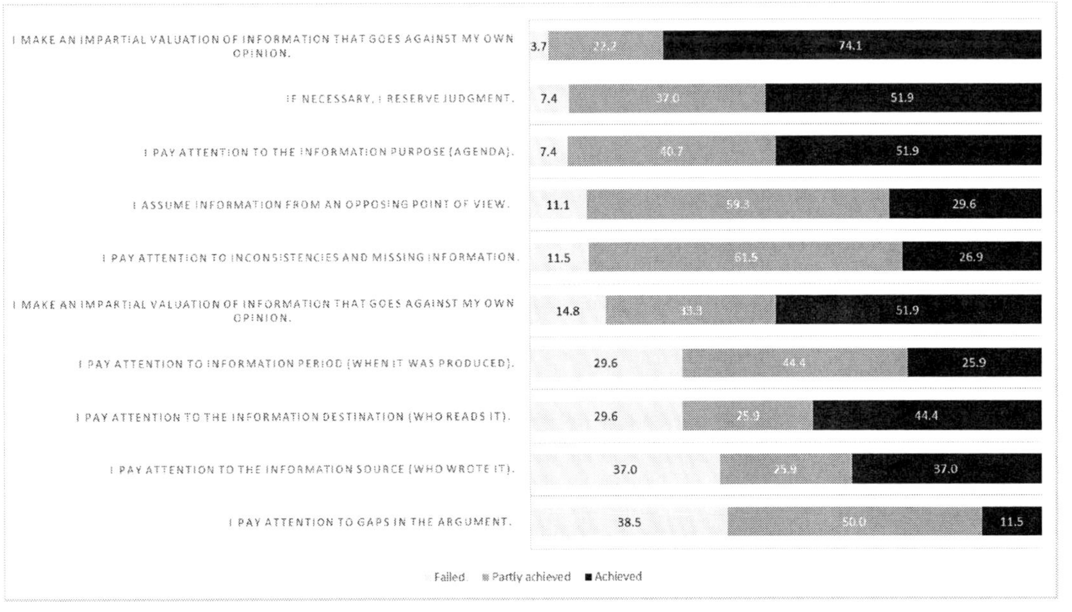

Figure 1. Achievement levels in the critical thinking rubric

3.2 Evaluation of Logical Organization

The relationship among ground, claim and warrant was evaluated using the Toulmin model work sheet. At first, some students described the relationship among these three components incorrectly. However, at the end of the lesson, as a result of discussions with each other, all the Toulmin model work sheets were revised correctly. Evaluation of the critical thinking rubric and Toulmin model

Figure 2 shows the evaluation of the critical thinking rubric and Toulmin model. Using the critical thinking rubric and Toulmin model, about 90% of students feel "It is easy to make a correct judgment," "It is easy to organize a discussion," and "It is easy to clarify the problem." On the other hand, students also feel that the critical thinking rubric and Toulmin model is hard to use (about 50%) and difficult to use in daily life (about 40%).

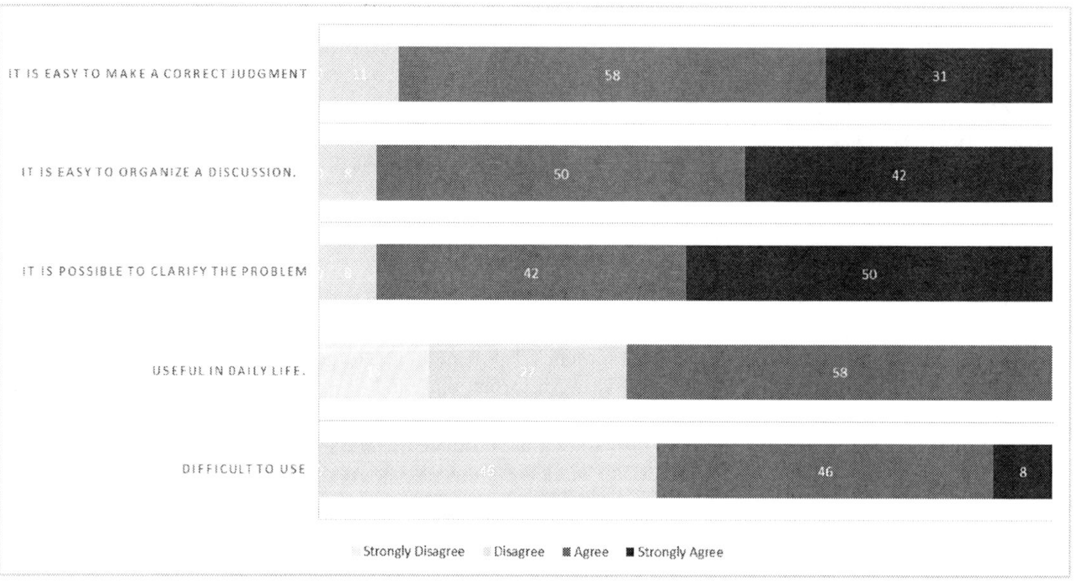

Figure 2. Evaluation of the critical thinking rubric and Toulmin model

3.3 Contents Analysis of Evaluation of Critical Thinking Rubric and Toulmin Model

In comparison with Gotoh(2016), which did not use the Toulmin model, many students referred to logical organization and rebuttal. I realized that in daily life, I never consider evidence for information rebuttal and I always swallow information uncritically. Considering rebuttal evidence is useful in judging the reliability of information. Using the Toulmin model, I can clearly focus on the crux of the problem. In comparison with writing about claim and ground, it takes me much longer to write a rebuttal so I realize I am not very good at thinking about something from different points of view.

3.4 Comparison of Critical Thinking Dispositions

Critical thinking disposition score was calculated (average score 111.18, max score 153, minimum score 84). The top 2 students and lowest 2 students, the top 50% and lowest 50% and the top 25 % and lowest 25% were extracted. Three types of comparison studies (a comparison of the top 2 students and lowest 2 students, the top 50% and lowest 50% and the top 25 % and lowest 25%) were carried out. As a result of cross tabulation of achievement levels in the critical thinking rubric, no significant difference was found in any comparisons (Cramer V ns.). In the evaluation of the critical thinking rubric and Toulmin model, a significant difference was found between the top 2 students and the lowest 2 students. In the case of high critical thinking dispositions, the critical thinking rubric and Toulmin model tended to be useful for the item about clarifying the crux of the problem (Cramer V.046). No significant difference was found among any groups (Cramer V ns.) .

4. CONCLUSION

To identify the validity and reliability of students' self -assessment, the critical thinking rubric and Toulmin model combination was introduced. At the end of the lesson all Toulmin model work sheets written by students were revised correctly. It was discovered that students solve problems logically. This shows that a high level of critical thinking among students is reliable and valid.

It was also discovered that students are aware of the importance and usefulness of considering rebuttal evidence using the critical thinking rubric and Toulmin model combination.

On the other hand, there was no clear difference between high and low dispositions for critical thinking.

In this research the sample size was extremely limited. In the near future, the author hopes to collect a large data sample. Differences among individuals, such as differences in personality and knowledge will also be taken into consideration.

ACKNOWLEDGEMENT

This work was supported by JSPS KAKENHI Grant Number 15K01020.

REFERENCES

Assessment & teaching of 21st century skills 2015 21st skills. http://www.atc21s.org/

Dewey,J.1933.How we think (Revised and expanded edition). MA: Houghton Mifflin Company.

Ennis,R.H. 1985 A logical basis for measuring critical thinking skills. Educational Leadership, 43, 44-48

Gotoh,Y. 2016 Development of Critical Thinking with Metacognitive Regulation. Proceedings of 13th international Conference on Cognition and Exploratory Learning in Digital Age(CELDA2016), 353- 356

Gotoh,Y. 2015 Development of Critical Thinking Self-Assessment System using Wearable Device. Proceedings of 12th international Conference on Cognition and Exploratory Learning in Digital Age(CELDA2015), 387- 389

Gotoh,Y. 2013 Visualization of Understanding of Media Characteristics Using Analytic Hierarchy Process. Computer Technology and Application, Vol.4, pp.563-567

Graser, E.M. 1941 An experiment in the development of critical thinking. New York: Teachers College of Columbia University, Bureau of Publications.

Hirayama,R. & Kusumi,T.2004 Effect of Critical Thinking Disposition on Interpretation of Controversial Issues : Evaluating Evidences and Drawing Conclusions. Japan Journal of Educational Psychology, Vol.52(2),186-198 in JAPANESE

Ministry of education, culture, sports science and technology Japan 2015 Result of National Assessment of Information Utilization Ability in Japan. http://www.mext.go.jp/a_menu/shotou/zyouhou/1356188.htm

The Association of American Colleges and Universities 2015 Critical thinking value rubric https://www.aacu.org/value/rubrics/critical-thinking

A PRELIMINARY INVESTIGATION INTO PARENTS' CONCERNS ABOUT PROGRAMMING EDUCATION IN JAPANESE PRIMARY SCHOOLS

Yukiko Maruyama[1], Hiroko Kanoh[2] and Kinya Adachi[3]
[1]*Tokai University, Hiratsuka Kanagawa, Japan*
[2]*Yamagata University, Yamagata, Japan*
[3]*Sagami Primary School, Yamagata, Japan*

ABSTRACT

To investigate parents' concerns about programming education in primary school, a preliminary online survey was carried out as a first step of the study. The result of the survey shows that parents seem to think that aim of programming education in primary school is not only learning coding.

KEYWORDS

Programming education, primary school, parents' concerns, computing thinking, logical thinking, problem-solving

1. INTRODUCTION

Attempts to bring computational thinking to primary/secondary or K-12 education have been widespread (Barr 2011, Grover 2013). The term "computational thinking" was first used by Papert (1993) and popularized by Wing (2006). According to Wing, "'Computational thinking' involves solving problems, designing systems, and understanding human behavior, by drawing on concepts fundamental to computer science" (p. 33). Moreover, she stated that computational thinking is a fundamental skill for everyone and that we should add computational thinking to every child's analytical ability. The article received attention from many education researchers and educators, and many researches related to computational thinking in K-12 have since been carried out. In the United Kingdom, a new subject "computing" was introduced into primary/secondary schools. In a guide to the subject "computing" for primary teachers, the importance of computational thinking is repeatedly stated.

As computational thinking gains increasing attention, programming education is also receiving attention as one of the ways of teaching computational thinking. Lye and Koh (2014) state that "[p]rogramming is more than just coding, for, it exposes students to computational thinking which involves problem-solving using computer science concepts and useful in their daily lives" (p.51). In Japan, the central council for education in the Ministry of Education, Culture, Sports, Science and Technology submitted a report that mentioned the introduction of programming education into primary school. In another council report, it is said that programming education in primary school should not aim to teach students coding itself, but rather to foster students' programming thinking. Programming thinking is considered a similar concept to computational thinking and included in computational thinking. Though, having said that , it also appears that a misconception has started to spread among parents that the aim of programming education is to learn coding.. The parents' role in primary education is a very important one, and their attitude toward education has considerable influence on children's attitudes. Indeed, some researchers have investigated parent-child collaboration in learning programming (Lin and Liu 2012, Hart 2010). Parents' misconceptions and anxiety related to programming education could become obstacles for their involvement into children's learning. To introduce computer education into primary school smoothly and appropriately, it is important to know parents' concerns about programming education. Moreover, it is necessary to support parents to become involved in programming education. This study aims to make a clear case for establishing a support system for parents to become involved in programming education in primary education.

This paper provides the result of a preliminary investigation into parents' concerns about programming education in Japanese primary school, and constitutes the first step in clarifying this issues in detail.

2. INVESTIGATION

The survey for this study was conducted in April and May 2017. Participants were invited to the survey with e-mail which were sent by authors or authors' acquaintance. There were 20 participants in the survey were: 14 were mothers and the rest were fathers of primary school children. Two of them participated in a programming seminar for children, which was held by the authors. The survey was carried out as online questionnaire, which included the following sections: 1) attitudes towards programming education in primary school, 2) expectations for introducing programming education into primary school, 3) views on programming education out of school, and 4) their experiences of computer usage. There were some other questions related to English education and education in general in primary school; however, the results of these questions have not been included in this paper.

Table 1. Ages of participants

Age	Frequency
-39	4
40 - 44	7
45 - 49	7
50 -	1
non-response	1

Table 2. School years of participants' children

School year	Frequency
1	1
2	7
3	2
4	1
5	5
6	3
non-response	1

3. RESULTS AND DISCUSSION

3.1 Attitudes toward Programming Education in Primary School

Eighteen participants responded that they were strongly or relatively interested in programming education in primary school. All of the respondents but one agreed strongly or relatively with introducing programming education into primary school. Figure 1 shows parents' responses to questions concerned with attitudes toward programming education. It shows that participants generally have relatively positive attitudes toward introducing programming education into primary school, but they do not want programming to be a subject. Moreover, eight responded that they did not know that how programming education would be taught in the next course of study at all and ten answered that they were unsure. And five responded that they did not know what their children learnt about programming.

Table 3. Questions concerned with parents' attitudes

(1) Everyone needs to know how to program.
(2) Programming should be learned starting in elementary school.
(3) Programming will be required in the society of the future, so it should be learned in elementary school.
(4) Elementary school is too early to learn programming.
(5) Programming should be part of the elementary school curriculum.
(6) Programming will affect students' other studies, so it should not be taught in elementary school.

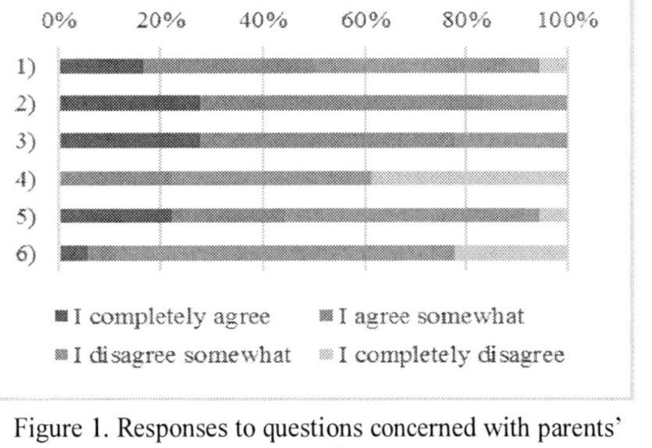

Figure 1. Responses to questions concerned with parents' attitudes

These results show that parents are open to introducing programming education and are interested in it; however, they are not provided with enough information about it.

3.2 Expectations for Introducing Programming Education into Primary School

Figure 2 shows the responses to the following question: "Do you expect the following outcomes as a result of introducing programming education?" and Table 2 shows items. Respondents placed high expectations on the usefulness of programming education for work in the future, They also expected their children to become accustomed to the knowledge and skills used in ICT. The outcomes "Children will like using a computer" and "Children will learn to think logically" were also relatively highly expected. On the other hand, the outcomes "Children will learn how to express themselves" and "Children will be better able to communicate" were expected to a lesser extent. By contrast, there was a relatively high expectation that children would become accustomed to creativity, problem-solving and problem-finding skills. Finally, the outcomes of "It will foster personnel with advanced ICT skills" and "It will make Japan a global powerhouse in ICT" were expected to a lesser extent.

It seems that parents' expectations of programming education are generally high; however, they do not expect that learning programming results in fostering ICT specialists. Moreover, they expected children to become accustomed to logical thinking, creativity, problem-solving and problem-identifying. They understand to a certain extent that programming is more than just coding.

Table 4. Questions concerned with parents' expectation for introducing programming education

1)Children will become skilled at using a computer
2)Children will like using a computer
3)Children will learn to think logically
4)It will help with work in the future
5)Children will like arithmetic and science
6)Children will learn about using ICT
7)Children will learn ICT skills
8)It will foster personnel with advanced ICT skills
9)It will make Japan a global powerhouse in ICT
10)Children will learn problem-solving skills
11)Children will learn to be creative
12)Children will learn how to express themselves
13)Children will learn how to problem-identifying skill
14)Children will be better able to communicate

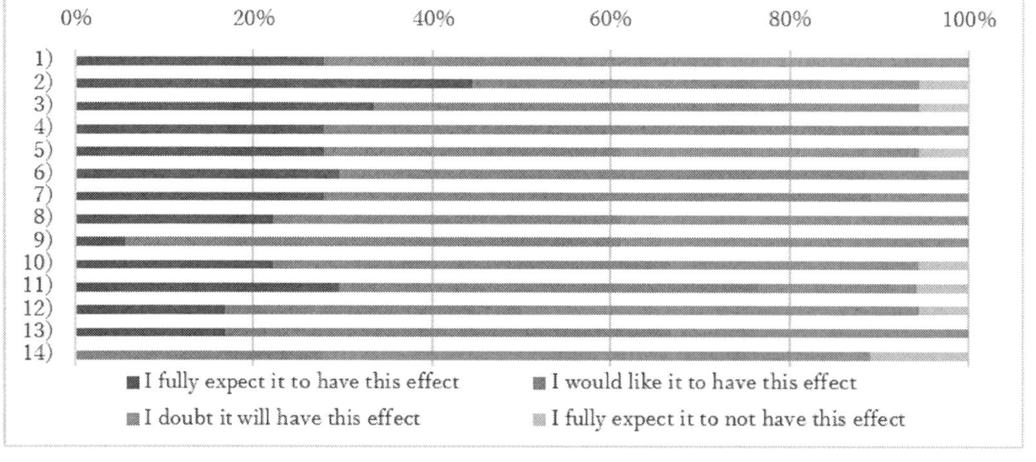

Figure 2. Responses to the question "Do you expect the following outcomes by introducing programming education?

Figure 3 shows the participants' responses to the following question: "To what extent do you expect that students will be able to achieve the following as a result of programming education?" and Table 3 shows items. The expectation that their child "Children will understand how a computer works" was highest. It was also expected that children would be "Children will be able to use a computer to write compositions," "Children will be adept at using a computer," and "Children will learn how to use the Internet" were expected. Following these expectations, it was also hoped that children would be "Children will be able to write computer programs," "Children will learn to think logically," and "Children will think about the steps one must follow when performing a task."

It seems that parents expect their children to be able to use computer to a certain extent as a result of programming education. Additionally, becoming accustomed to coding and developing logical thinking are regarded as secondary aims. This shows that parents think that the aim of programming education in primary school is not only learning coding.

Table 5. Questions concerned with parents' expectation for their children's achievement as a result of programming education

1)Children will like using a computer.
2)Children will be inclined to use a computer.
3)Children will be able to use a computer to write compositions.
4)Children will be able to use a computer to draw pictures.
5)Children will understand how a computer works.
6)Children will be able to write computer programs.
7)Children will be adept at using a computer.
8)Children will learn how to use the Internet.
9)Children will be able to understand arithmetic and science.
10)Children will learn to think logically.
11)Children will think about the steps one must follow when performing a task.
12)Children will be better able to study other subjects.
13)Children will be better able to communicate their thoughts.
14)Children will be better able to work with others.

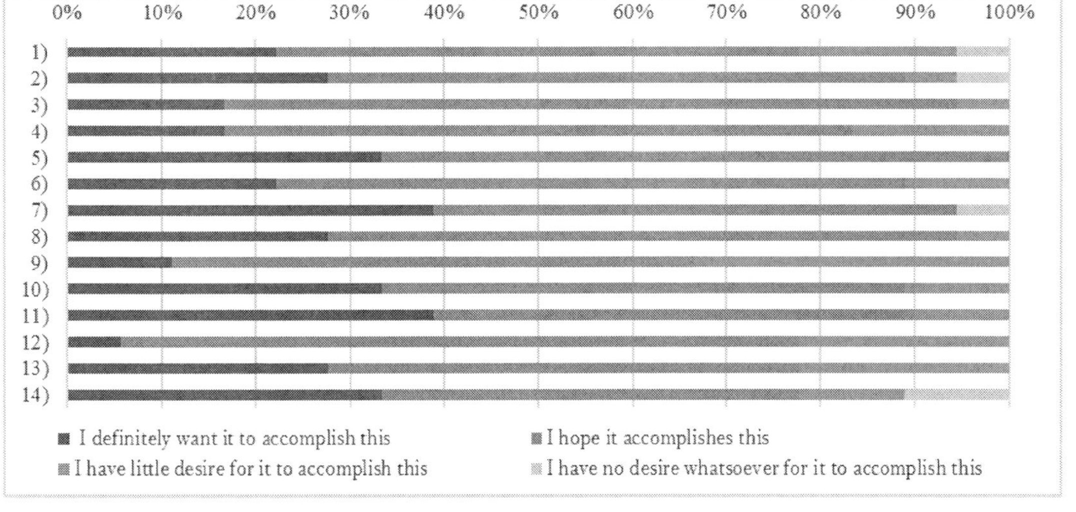

Figure 3. Responses for a question "To what extent do you expect that students will be able to achieve the following as a result of programming education?"

3.3 Programming Education Out of School and Parents' Own Experiences of Computer Usage

Six respondents answered that their children had participated in programming lessons or short courses out of school. Thirteen responded that they did not receive information about programming lessons or short courses out of school enough or at all. This suggests that it is necessary to provide parents information about programming education out of school.

Tables 4, 5, and 6 show responses to questions related to parents' own experiences. Almost half responded that they were good at using computers. More than half responded that they use computers at work and in daily life. It thus seems that respondents in this study were relatively familiar with computers. Future work is needed to expand subjects.

Table 6. Self-evaluation for using computers

Quite skilled	3
Capable	6
Basic operations only	5
No skill at all	3

Table 7. Experience of using computers at work

I have a computer-related job	1
I use a computer for work	8
I seldom use a computer for work	4
I never use a computer for work	2

Table 8. Experience of using computers in daily life

I use one often	8
I use one sometimes	5
I seldom use one	3
I never use one	1

4. CONCLUSION AND FUTURE WORK

To investigate parents' concerns about programming education in primary school, a preliminary online survey was carried out as a first step of the study. The results of the survey are outlined below.

1) Parents are open to introducing programming education and are interested in it; however, not enough information about programming education is provided.
2) Parents' expectation of programming education are generally high; however, they do not expect that learning programming leads to fostering experts. Moreover, they expected children to become accustomed to logical thinking, creativity, problem-solving and problem-identifying.
3) Parents expect children to be able to use computers to a certain extent as a result of programming education. Additionally, becoming accustomed to coding and developing logical thinking are regarded as secondary aims.

Parents seem to think that aim of programming education in primary school is not only learning coding.

This survey is just a preliminary survey, thus the number of participants was limited. It is necessary to carry out the survey with more participants. The questions were also limited; as a next step, we would like to add questions related to anxiety surrounding the introduction of programming education in primary school.

REFERENCES

Barr, V., and Stephenson, C. 2011. Bringing computational thinking to K-12: What is involved and what is the role of the computer science education community? *Acm Inroads*, Vol. 2, No. 1, pp. 48-54.

Grover, S., and Pea, R. 2013. Computational thinking in K–12: A review of the state of the field. *Educational Researcher*, Vol. 42, No. 1, pp. 38-43.

Hart, M. L., Making contact with the forgotten K-12 influence: Are you smarter than YOUR 5th grader? *Proceedings of the 41st ACM technical symposium on Computer science education*, Wisconsin, USA, pp. 254-258.

Lin, J. M.-C., and Liu, S.-F. 2012. An investigation into parent-child collaboration in learning computer programming. *Educational Technology & Society*, Vol.15, No.1, pp162–173.

Lye, S. Y., and Koh, J. H. L., 2014, Review on teaching and learning of computational thinking through programming: What is next for K-12? *Computers in Human Behavior*, Vol. 41, pp. 51-61.

Papert, S. 1993. *Mindstorms: Children, Computers, and Powerful Ideas, 2nd ed*, Basic Books, New York.

Wing, J.M. 2006. Computational Thinking, *Communications of the ACM*, Vol. 49, No. 3, pp. 33-35.

DESIGNING PHILADELPHIA LAND SCIENCE AS A GAME TO PROMOTE IDENTITY EXPLORATION

Amanda Barany[1], Mamta Shah[1], Jessica Cellitti[1], Migela Duka[1], Zachari Swiecki[2], Amanda Evenstone[2], Hannah Kinley[2], Peter Quigley[2], David Williamson Shaffer[2] and Aroutis Foster[1]
[1]*Drexel University, USA*
[2]*University of Wisconsin-Madison, USA*

ABSTRACT

Few digital tools are designed to support identity exploration around careers in science, technology, engineering, and mathematics (STEM) that may help close existing representation gaps in STEM fields. The aim of this project is to inform the design of games that facilitate learning as identity change as defined by the Projective Reflection theoretical framework. Projective Reflection is the process by which a person who is engaging in digital gameplay or a virtual environment constructs and/or enacts an identity that has the potential to modify the person's possible/future self and lead to a new sense of identity in a domain (Foster, 2014). This paper reports on *Philadelphia Land Science*, an educational web-based game that allows players to explore roles related to urban planning and environmental science careers as they connect to a Philadelphia context. We describe game design and iterative changes as backed by theory and existing research. The game iteration is detailed in terms of the embedded content, the pedagogical approaches used, and the technological features that support the learning goals.

KEYWORDS

Projective Reflection, STEM, Game-Based Learning, Game Design, Identity Exploration, Identity Change

1. INTRODUCTION

Identity exploration, or "the deliberate internal or external action of seeking and processing information in relation to the self," (Flum & Kaplan, 2006, pp 100), has been identified as an essential tool for learners adapting to the needs of a 21st century workforce (Kaplan et al., 2014). Supporting students in this intentional process of identity self-construction could prove particularly useful for increasing representation in science, technology, engineering, and mathematics (STEM) careers, given workforce statistics that illustrate limited gender and racial diversity in these fields (US Congress Joint Economic Committee, 2012). Student identity exploration can lead to targeted identity change when a curriculum supports intentional reflection on their starting/current selves (who they are), through exploration of possible selves (who they might want or expect to be), and on their new selves that emerge at the end of a learning experience (Foster et al., 2017). Tracking student identity exploration over a period of time (long or short) can also illustrate when and how students synthesize developing experiences with a given STEM domain into understandings of self.

Games can also influence players' identity exploration and change processes by illuminating the personal relevance and utility of STEM content beyond school settings (Foster, 2008). For example, an examination of engineering virtual internships Nephrotex and Rescushell by Chesler and colleagues (2015) demonstrates how games can offer authentic virtual environments that emulate professional settings, support situated understandings of content, and allow players to explore domain-related identities. Such affordances might encourage students to consider career domains with limited acquisition rates, or those lacking positive social status among youth (i.e. careers in STEM domains).

We argue that game design and implementation supported by identity exploration theory could encourage student identity change toward STEM careers, particularly among students who may not be prompted to explore STEM identities in other ways (i.e. minority students with few existing professional examples to identify with) (Foster & Shah, 2016). However, research on facilitating identity exploration through game-based learning is still an emerging area.

This work details the design of *Philadelphia Land* Science (*PLS)*, which was informed by what was learned from existing exemplary games to optimally support students' identity exploration as they take on roles as urban planning interns at a virtual city design firm. The Projective Reflection theoretical framework, used to operationalize identity exploration in game-based learning contexts, was used to structure design changes made to the original game to enhance its capacity for supporting identity exploration and change around urban planning and environmental science careers.

2. PROJECTIVE REFLECTION

The Projective Reflection (PR) framework frames identity change in an individual as a process of identity exploration over time. Adapted from Kaplan and Garner's (2016) Dynamic Systems Model of Role Identity (DSMRI), Projective Reflection frames identity exploration in a game-based learning context as changes in: a) content knowledge and game or technical literacy (Kereluik et al., 2013), b) regulated actions (i.e. self-organization and control) (Hadwin & Oshige, 2011), c) interests and valuing of domain (Foster, 2008), and d) self-perceptions and self-definitions (Kaplan et al., 2014). The framework comprehensively informs the process of identity exploration as it is measured at repeated points over the course of students' learning experiences, thereby tracking learning as identity change over time in a targeted academic domain (Foster et al., 2017; Foster & Shah, 2016). Projective Reflection can be used to inform both assessment and design of games and supportive curricula for identity exploration.

3. METHODS

The design, development, and implementation of a digital tool to support learning as intentional student identity exploration is part of a 5-year NSF CAREER project (Foster, 2014). Early phases of the project involved the examination of existing games with exemplary design characteristics for promoting science learning and identity exploration: *EcoMUVE*, *Land Science (LS),* and *River City* (Foster et al., 2017). From 2014-, we analyzed the design features of each game using the four PR constructs to understand how these environments excelled at encouraging some aspects of identity exploration, and to identify opportunities to design for closer alignment with PR in future design. The playing research method (Aarseth, 2003) guided this process through analysis of both firsthand gameplay experiences and secondary game information (e.g. research papers).

From 2016-2017, authors partnered with Epistemic Games Group in the development of a new design iteration of *Land Science* that implemented what was learned from game analysis using the Virtual Internship Authoring (VIA) tool. This paper introduces the design characteristics of this iteration, named *Philadelphia Land Science (PLS)*, illustrating how it capitalizes on the game's existing characteristics to support comprehensive identity exploration through PR.

3.1 *Land Science* and Existing Context

Land Science was designed to serve as a virtual internship for students studying urban planning, or other related environmental, economic, and engineering concepts. Students play as interns at Regional Design Associates, a fictitious urban planning firm that models how real-world professional settings are structured. Groups of students are synchronously guided through the process of creating zoning plans for the city of Lowell, Massachusetts by online mentors.

First, students read about the city's unique history and structure, researching the needs of key stakeholder groups introduced through community brochures. Then, student groups engage in a virtual professional meeting, in which knowledge is exchanged between players. Players then individually use an interactive digital map of the city to rezone areas as commercial, industrial, open space, wetlands, or single-family, two-family (duplexes), or multi-family housing. As players experiment with different zoning combinations, they develop contextualized understandings of how different city designs influence environmental and economic issues such as housing density, job growth, pollution control, wildlife protection, and waste disposal. Finally, groups receive feedback on their collection of city designs from virtual non-player characters representing key community members, and the iterative process of meeting, redesign, and feedback begins again, until individual final proposals are developed and submitted electronically.

3.2 *Philadelphia Land Science*

To pilot the *Philadelphia Land Science* implementation, researchers collaborated with a science museum in downtown Philadelphia that partners with a local public magnet high school to offer STEM-focused, entrepreneurial, and practice-centered learning experiences. Forty ninth-grade students met at the museum for one of two eight-week 'Virtual City Planning' courses in fall 2016 and winter 2017. This describes key design differences between *Land Science* and *Philadelphia Land Science* with consideration for this classroom context. Table 1 offers an overview of *Philadelphia Land Science* modifications to enhance *Land Science*'s alignment with PR constructs.

Table 1. Summary of design changes made in *Philadelphia Land Science*

Change	*Land Science* characteristics	*PLS* design changes	Enhanced PR constructs
1. Context	• *LS* is set in Lowell, MA • Interactive map design matched Lowell context (i.e. two-family "duplexes") • Stakeholder groups set in Lowell • NPC's representative by gender; limited racial/ethnic diversity in NPC biographies	• *PLS* is set in Philadelphia, PA, where students live • Interactive map aligned with Philadelphia context (i.e. medium-density "row houses") • Stakeholder groups set in Philadelphia • New NPC's representative based on gender, race, and ethnic background	• Interests and valuing • Content knowledge
2. Writing deliverables	• Players summarize what they learned from meetings, map design, and NPC feedback as professional "notebooks"	• 7 new deliverables prompt students to reflect on developing interests, valuing, self-perceptions and self-definitions	• Interests and valuing • Self-perceptions/ definitions
3. Intake + exit surveys	• Intake/exit interviews assess changes in knowledge, self-organization and self-control	• Intake/exit questions added to assess changes in self-perceptions and definitions, interests and valuing	• Interests and valuing • Self- perceptions/ definitions
4. Role-plays	• Virtual meetings" facilitated by online urban planning mentors; co-regulated learning	• In-person instructor roleplaying as an urban planner, facilitating socially-shared and self-regulated learning	• Self-organization and self-control
5. Game scaffolding	• Chat log plays key role in peer/mentor interaction • Example final proposals and other texts provided; plagiarism noted in existing play data	• Chat log takes on secondary role to in-person interactions • Examples replaced with 1-2 line prompts specifically describing what players should write about	• Game literacy • Self-organization and self-control

3.2.1 Change 1: Content and Context

Much of the existing game content was either retained in *Philadelphia Land Science*, or mirrored to reflect a Philadelphia context. Redesigning the game for the city of Philadelphia was intended to develop student engagement and understanding of the relevance of urban planning in their lives. For example, *Philadelphia Land Science* maintained the general design of the interactive map, but shifted the setting from Lowell to Philadelphia. Some of the zoning codes on the map also shifted; single-family, two-family, and multi-family residential were renamed low, medium, and high-density housing. For students residing in an urban center, researchers recognized that two-family housing in particular might be an unfamiliar concept. Redefining housing density codes allowed for descriptions that aligned more closely with students' urban lived experiences, and illustrated the nuances of housing density in downtown Philadelphia more accurately.

Environmental and economic issues addressed in the game were largely analogous to Philadelphia, though environmental variables related to animal populations in Massachusetts shifted to represent Philadelphia-native species: Eastern Bluebirds and Eastern Mud Turtles. Philadelphia-specific brochures and biographies describing fictitious community stakeholders were also developed for *Philadelphia Land Science*, organized into stakeholder groups with varying combinations of economic and environmental values.

Philadelphia Land Science capitalized on opportunities to demonstrate diverse employees and leaders in urban planning. Portraying urban planners with whom players can identify is key to the development of possible selves in the domain, as it encourages players to see themselves in a given role and develop domain-specific knowledge (Foster, 2008). Male and female non-player characters with Latina-American, African-American, and Indian-American heritages were added.

3.2.2 Change 2: Writing Deliverables

Land Science was designed with a cyclical pedagogical structure that progresses students through one "room" of activities to the next, to guide players through the process of developing urban planning proposals. Activities such as researching stakeholders, participating in professional peer meetings, making zoning changes to the interactive maps, and reviewing NPC feedback on map designs, are each encapsulated in a room. Rooms start with an email from the supervisor that introduces the activity, and outlines how students will summarize their experiences in a concluding "notebook entry."

Analysis of *Land Science* illustrated how writing deliverables encouraged students to recount in detail what they had learned, but could be further leveraged to support reflections on students' changing interests and valuing of urban planning, and of changing perceptions and definitions of self in relation to the experience. *Philadelphia Land Science* maintained room structures and existing writing prompts, but included seven new deliverables prompting consideration of developing interests and values (e.g. submit "a formal summary of the changes you would make to meet your own needs as a citizen of Philadelphia"), as well as their self-perceptions and self-definitions as related to urban planning (e.g. "reflect on your role in this internship and your expectations about this role going forward").

3.2.3 Change 3: Intake and Exit Surveys

Questions on the intake and exit surveys in *Philadelphia Land Science* were also designed to assess aspects of student identity, including player knowledge, interest and valuing, patterns of regulation, and self-perceptions and definitions. Items consisted of short answer, multiple choice, and Likert-style survey questions that take an estimated total of 20 minutes to complete. Intake and exit surveys bookend identity exploration in the game, allowing researchers to track student changes from starting selves, through identity exploration during gameplay, to new selves upon completion.

3.2.4 Change 4: Role-plays

The most significant pedagogical changes in *Philadelphia Land Science* related to the enactment of professional peer-to-peer meetings. In *Land Science*, remote mentors communicated with players via chat, answering questions and leading meetings using scripted discussion questions. Analysis of *Land Science* play data revealed that these meetings excelled at providing opportunities for co-regulated learning supported by mentors, and offered some opportunities for socially-shared learning between peers. To better align with Projective Reflection constructs, the redesign of meetings in *Philadelphia Land Science* offered more opportunities for socially-shared and self-regulated learning.

In the Philadelphia museum classroom, players led in-person meetings at round tables, supported by instructors roleplaying as urban planning professionals. The "urban planners" introduced meeting topics and highlighted important points where needed, but also allowed student discussion to develop naturally and for student leaders to emerge in group discussions. During gameplay, urban planners would move around the room, providing individualized support where needed, then stepping back to allow students to self-regulate or receive assistance from peers. Supplemental opportunities for curricular activities, reflection, and discussion were designed and implemented in the classroom environment as supported by the Play, Curricular activity, Reflection, and Discussion model for game-based learning (Foster & Shah, 2015).

3.2.5 Change 5: Game Scaffolding

Most technological features of *Land Science* were retained in *Philadelphia Land Science*, as they were found to support student game literacy development over time. Though the majority of peer-to-peer and peer-to-mentor interactions migrated to real-world role-play in *PLS,* the chat feature was kept so that players could communicate with the online moderator as needed; for example, if students submitted a notebook entry before it was completed, the moderator could coach them through the retrieval process before advancing game activities.

Land Science also included sample notebook entries that students could reference as they developed skill in professional writing and speaking; review of the *LS* gameplay data showed some copied sections of sample text to construct their notebook responses. Given the emphasis on personal reflection and regulated learning practices in *PLS*, designers shifted support texts from *how* a notebook was written towards *what* players should write in their entries. For example, a prompt in the Entrance Interview room asked students to "please include a short summary of your experience completing the Entrance Interview." This change further supported student development of game literacy by simplifying the game interface; instead of clicking between an external example and the notebook text box, *PLS* writing prompts were directly embedded in the text boxes for ease of access.

4. CONCLUSION

In this paper, Projective Reflection (PR) was introduced as a framework for facilitating learning as identity change through an intentional process of identity exploration in a given domain or career. Projective Reflection informed game redesign to support identity change towards STEM careers. *Philadelphia Land Science* builds upon the strengths of the original virtual internship to facilitate an intentional process of learning as identity change that emphasizes knowledge construction, interest and valuing, regulated action as self-organization and self-control, and self-perceptions and self-definitions. Future design iterations will involve (a) the incorporation of a procedurally generated map of Philadelphia that updates to reflect real-time zoning changes and open-source data, (b) map and game development around different city sections or of the city as a whole, and (c) the inclusion of more land use codes and variables to support value-driven, personalized learning as identity change.

ACKNOWLEDGEMENT

The project is supported by a National Science Foundation CAREER Award, titled CAREER: Projective Reflection: Learning as Identity Exploration within Games for Science. The primary investigator is Aroutis Foster, recipient of the NSF Faculty Early Career Development (CAREER) Program: DRL-1350707. This work was funded in part by the National Science Foundation (DRL-0918409, DRL-0946372, DRL-1247262, DRL-1418288, DUE-0919347, DUE-1225885, EEC-1232656, EEC-1340402, REC-0347000), the MacArthur Foundation, the Spencer Foundation, the Wisconsin Alumni Research Foundation, and the Office of the Vice Chancellor for Research and Graduate Education at the University of Wisconsin-Madison. All opinions and results are by the researchers and do not reflect the views of funding agencies.

REFERENCES

Aarseth, E., 2003. Playing Research: Methodological Approaches to Game Analysis. In *Proceedings of the Digital Arts and Culture Conference*, pp 28-29.

Chesler, N. et al., 2015. A Novel Paradigm for Engineering Education: Virtual Internships with Individualized Mentoring and Assessment of Engineering Thinking. *Journal of Biomedical Engineering*, Vol. 137, No. 2, pp 024701.

Foster, A., 2008. Games and Motivation to Learn Science: Personal Identity, Applicability, Relevance, and Meaningfulness. *Journal of Interactive Learning Research*, Vol. 19, No. 4, pp 597.

Foster, A., 2014. CAREER: Projective Reflection: Learning as Identity Exploration within Games for science. *Drexel University: National Science Foundation*.

Foster, A. and Shah, M., 2015. The Play Curricular activity Reflection Discussion model for Game-Based Learning. *Journal of Research on Technology in Education*, Vol. 47, No. 2, pp 71-88.

Foster, A. and Shah, M., 2016. Knew Me and New Me: Facilitating Student Identity Exploration and Learning through Game Integration. *International Journal of Gaming Computer-Mediated Simulation*, Vol. 8, No. 3.

Foster, A. et al., 2017. Facilitating Learning as Identity Change through Game-Based Learning. In Y. Baek (Ed). *Game-Based Learning: Theory, Strategies and Performance Outcomes.* Nova Publishers. New York, NY.

Hadwin, A. and Oshige, M., 2011. Self-Regulation, Co-Regulation, and Socially Shared Regulation: Exploring Perspectives of Social in Self-Regulated Learning Theory. *Teachers College Record,* Vol. 113, pp 240-264.

Kaplan, A. and Garner, J. K., 2016. Handbook and Analytical Manual for the Dynamic Systems Model of Role Identity. *Temple University and Old Dominion University.*

Kaplan, A. et al., 2014. Design-Based Interventions for Promoting Students' Identity Exploration within the School Curriculum. *Advances in Motivation and Achievement*, Vol. 18, pp 247-295.

Kereluik, P. et al., 2013. What Knowledge is of Most Worth: Teacher Knowledge for 21st Century Learning. *Journal of Digital Learning in Teacher Education*, Vol. 29, No. 4, pp 127-140.

US Congress Joint Economic Committee, 2012. STEM Education: Preparing for the Jobs of the Future. *Washington DC.*

JUXTAPOSE: AN EXPLORATION OF MOBILE AUGMENTED REALITY COLLABORATIONS AND PROFESSIONAL PRACTICES IN A CREATIVE LEARNING ENVIRONMENT

Darren Menorath[1] and Laurent Antonczak[2]
[1]*COLABxMINA (AUT), Auckland, New Zealand*
[2]*Auckland University of Technology (AUT), Auckland, New Zealand*

ABSTRACT

This paper examines the state of the art of mobile Augmented Reality (AR) and mobile Virtual Reality (VR) in relation to collaboration and professional practices in a creative digital environment and higher education. To support their discussion, the authors use a recent design-based research project named *Juxtapose,* which explores tensions between the digital and the analogue. Also *Juxtapose* explores the possibilities of interaction resulting from the use of multiple markers to create a playful semi-tangible object, whilst proposing a networked model of content creation in *augmented space*. In this paper, following a narrative and empirical base, the authors argue that their approach is very similar to Wenger's concept of legitimate peripheral participation leading to active participation within communities of practice and can be beneficial to redesign and improve some of the creative curriculum in higher education.

KEYWORDS

AR, VR, mobile, higher education, community of practice, prosumer

1. INTRODUCTION

Augmented Reality (AR) can be considered "the overlapping of virtual information in real space (…) mixing virtual objects generated by computers with a real environment, generating a mixed environment that can be viewed through any technological device in real time." (Redondo, Puig, Fonseca, Villagrasa & Navarro. 2014. p. 16). The project *Juxtapose* (Menorath, 2016) focuses on print-based AR which serves as one of the main components of Mixed Reality (MR), an umbrella term for "technologies that involve merging of real and virtual worlds" (Milgram, 1994. p.3). Because an *augmented space* (Manovich 2002) relies on the Internet to display and connect to others in an AR environment, this paper investigates Internet and creative collaboration, more specifically how communities provide one key aspect: a participatory model of creating art and design. This exploration opens up discussion around AR content and how it could potentially be made and whom it could be made by, and what AR practices may look like according to current creative and collaborative movements in relation to universities curriculum design. This paper is organised into four sections: the context; the methodology; the design practice, development and critical analysis; and the conclusion.

2. CONTEXT

This first section discusses Danvers (2003) idea that designing transformative learning environments involves cultivating a sense of supporting and encouraging student creativity. The topic of an augmented space and its relation to the theoretical context of everyone being able to create their own AR will be discussed in the second part.

Due to the lack of public knowledge and very limited course development around the creation of marker-based AR, many people think that integrating AR into everyday objects is complicated. By identifying these issues alongside the development of smart devices, AR companies such as *Layar Creator* (2009), *Qualcomm Vuforia* (2011), and *Augment Desktop* (2016) have created platforms and apps that allow anyone to quickly produce AR content. Free user-friendly AR tools that are available to the public, open up the opportunity for designers, students and Internet creative groups to take advantage of the technology and make it their own. *Juxtapose* [1], a design project which aims at concealing print-based and digital content, contributes to the movement of democratised AR by presenting an artefact that exemplifies simple AR techniques that anyone can do themselves.

Also, being a hybrid publication that merges print tangibility and virtual augmentation, *Juxtapose's* artefact raises some question about the way higher education curriculum are designed and, currently, lacking of opportunity to allow for cross-disciplinary delivery. Though this project looks specifically at print based AR publication, its technical function can be applied to any other content, including topic such as engineering or mathematics. This draw on Danvers' (2003) notion who argues that designing transformative learning environments involves cultivating a sense of supporting and encouraging student creativity:

> "Creativity thrives in an atmosphere that is supportive, dynamic, and receptive to new ideas and activities. The learning environment has to encourage interactions between learners in which: action and reflection are carefully counter-balanced… stimulating inputs and staff interventions interwoven with periods in which learners develop ideas and constructs at their own pace." (p. 52)

The concept of an *augmented space* could soon be a reality with the development of AR-based technologies such as Google's *AR smart lenses* (2014) and Microsoft *HoloLens* (2016). Cara Kahl (2009) identifies prosumers[2] (producer + consumers) needing to be addressed in the wider context of education, implying that, "Social groups play an integral part in establishing creativity. Their perception and evaluation processes may be hard to decipher in an increasingly networked world, but ignoring this complexity does not necessarily facilitate scientific comprehension of creativity". Developing a creative learning culture can be achieved by using an ecological approach to curriculum design that identifies the key components required to support the graduate outcomes of a course. According to Danvers concept of radical pedagogy (2003), an example of an ecological model of education is Cormier's (2008) rhizomatic learning for enabling self-determined learning communities (cMOOCs) based upon the analogy of the decentralised root structure of rhizomes.

Internet communities provide some models and context in order to create AR content in the situation of an augmented space. Cyber communities such as *Vaporwave* (Menorath, 2016) provides a model of how Internet communities function and create AR content in the context of an augmented space. This participatory model of content creation presented in the *Virtual Plaza* identifies how individuals will gravitate to Internet forums as a form of collective guidance and inspiration with AR opens up a public participatory design space that disrupts traditional boundaries between creator and consumer, academia and industry. In fact, *Juxtapose's* design model incorporates some aspects of *Vaporwave*'s model, such as using social media platforms to enhance members' connectivity and exchange, whilst highlighting the growing use of a *prosumer* model in today's sub-cultures. Hence, the scholarship of technology-enabled learning (SoTEL)[3] which improve teaching, its effectiveness evaluation, excellence aspiration, and to make sure that all learners can get pertinent and relevant results, as explained Frielick in *Education Review* (October 2016).

Furthermore, Cormier (2008) has proposed an ecological model for enabling self-determined learning communities. Pachler, Bachair and Cook (2010) have also linked the concept of an ecology of resources model for enabling learner-generated contexts via mobile learning. Within our framework for creative curriculum design, *Juxtapose* uses an ecology of resources based upon mobile social media to facilitate triggering events for cultivating participants creativity.

---

[1] Menorath, D. (2015). Juxtapose: An exploration of the technical and aesthetic potential of print-based augmented reality design. Auckland: Auckland University of Technology.

[2] A term coined by Futurist, Alvin Toffer meaning "one who is both producer and consumer" (Ritzer, Dean & Jurgenson 2012. p.2).

[3] Retrieved from http://www.educationreview.co.nz/magazine/october-2016/researching-teaching-the-importance-of-sotl/

3. METHODOLOGY

Due to the complex nature of the technology development, the authors employed an empirical and heuristic form of research which allows a systematic approach to the practice-led research, and that utilises a rinse-and-repeat method supported by a phenomenological framework. The broad framework for all design-led research is analysis and synthesis, based on the authors interpretation of the tacit, explicit and new knowledge gained through case studies and practice. However, the collaborative element of such projects needs to be clearly defined, then students experience of being active members within an authentic professional global community of practice can provide new learning experience for most of participants, including professionals or amateurs.

The authors also highlight the need for establishing a significant level of trust among the participants of global collaborations that takes time to establish. This trust can be nurtured through the use of mobile social media both asynchronously:

> "Design projects must ultimately pass through three spaces: Inspiration, Ideation, and Implementation (…) Projects will loop back through these spaces—particularly the first two— more than once as ideas are refined and new directions taken" (Brown, 2008. p. 4).

This refers to Puentedura (2014) who developed a simple framework that identifies four levels of educational technology adoption: SAMR framework (Substitution, Augmentation, Modification, Redefinition). Cochrane et al. argue that the SAMR framework aligns with a conception of three levels of creativity: replication, incrementation, and redirection. Within an educational context using new technologies, for example modifying activities and assessments to involve student-generated projects and the learning experience by using new technologies to redefine practice, the SAMR model is one that can usefully be applied to the design of mobile AR/VR learning activities. In contrast mobile AR projects can involve the "incorporation of student-negotiated projects that harness the geolocation services of smartphones to create an AR environment for mobile content production and sharing, thus representing a redefinition of previous teacher-delivered content and teacher-directed assessment and course activities" (Cochrane et al., 2016).

4. DESIGN PRACTICE, DEVELOPMENT AND CRITICAL ANALYSIS

4.1 The Software Used

The current issue with most AR software is the unfamiliarity of the user interface (UI), and the availability of resources such as software tutorials. *Juxtapose* is created with Qualcomm's software development kit (SDK) *Vuforia* (2011) because it provides a plethora of information and guides on how to use their product, whilst having a Unity[4] SDK option, allowing users the flexibility to create both simple or code-aided AR. *Juxtapose* is sitting on the cusp of coding, programming (hard science) on one side, and designing user experience, creative interfaces (soft science) on the other side. As of this moment, AR is predominately taught in creative technology labs such as MIT's Media Lab[5], AUT's CoLab[6] and Georgia Tech GVU[7]. While the artefact lacks in coding and interactive components, *Juxtapose's* hybrid publications serve as a precursor that encourages other *prosumers* to take print-based AR beyond the conventional and to encourage higher education to allow more permissibility in-between faculties, schools and departments.

[4] Unity is a 2D/3D game developing platform that is highly flexible in terms of platform compatibility.
[5] http://fluid.media.mit.edu/projects/smarter-objects
[6] https://colab.aut.ac.nz/
[7] http://www.gvu.gatech.edu/research/labs

4.2 Process of Design

Correspondingly, the challenge for higher education is to adopt a different learning and teaching model and to open up conventional and predominant Learning Management System (top-down, teacher/lecturer-centred) for more flexible and interaction for the participant/contributors. This can be done with more emphasis on fostering a global localisation community of practice and reassessing current practices.

This form of cyber participation will be a key aspect in the future creation of AR/VR in an augmented space. Nevertheless, it is important to note biases present in the different social platforms and how themes specific to the platforms affect the popularity of the design. From observation and experience, the authors identify a serious lack of degrees structured in ways to incorporate this kind of approach also.

During the production of the zines and AR content, there was a re-occurring issue regarding the tensions between publication and smart device, due to different ways each medium display information. *Juxtapose* embraces and explores this tension between screen and book by using glitches as part of the experience. This kind of mindset, called heuristics approach in academia, is not often supported, nor taught in curriculum, especially outside of creative ones. Because of their constantly changing nature AR and VR are challenging higher education paradigm, alike pointed by Sir Ken Robinson in his TED Talk (2010) *Changing education paradigms.*

Juxtapose as a project could have benefited more from programming commands in its AR content on *Unity*, and was restricted due to the limited knowledge of C# from both authors. As a graphic designer, coding languages such as C# was not taught during their different time of studies in Applied Arts (France) or Art and Design (New Zealand). Although Cochrane et al. argue that the creation of mobile AR environments is relatively simple, this investigation suggests that future graphic designers incorporate disciplines outside of their conventions, such as programming and AR. Michael Rock adds to this notion in Albinson's, Giampietro & Leslie's (2011) book, *Graphic Design: Now in Production* stating: "The true investment is the investment in design itself, as a discipline that conducts research and generates knowledge—knowledge that makes it possible to seriously participate in discussions that are not about design" (p.18).

This point is not in contradiction with earlier statement praising AR/VR simplicity. It openly and precisely addresses the dichotomy of achieving quickly some basic results and struggling while dealing with more complex content, or formal aspects. At this point of the discussion, it is important to acknowledge the potentials of AR/VR and the crucial that could play education is enhancing SoTEL and fostering multiple fields perspective.

5. CONCLUSION

In this paper, the authors presented and contextualised the possibility of indie-based hybrid products development and more specifically through *Juxtapose* which exemplifies the possibility of AR/VR and content being created and dictated not only by designers, but also by various empowered creative groups, by *prosumers*. Research conducted for *Juxtapose* looked into three key aspects that could potentially play a part in customised AR for a broad public in the near future: AR mode of creation (*Vaporwave*), the democratisation of AR software and design tools that encourages a possible participatory design space, and the tension between physical and virtual (smart device and image marker/AR, the smartphone, and print).

This investigation led the authors to three conclusions relating to the technological and educative aspects of AR/VR: the use of AR in conjunction with *Vaporwave*'s model of creation opens up notions around a participatory design space that disrupts traditional boundaries between professional and amateur/creator and consumer/professional and students; this investigation also suggests that AR as creative medium plays an integral role in graphic design development, enriching those who incorporate it into their practice and it as a profession as well as in any curriculum development in higher education; lastly, AR is one of many mediated reality technologies that will shape the way information will be communicated in the future. Designers/students must be ready to explore this medium, collaborate with others and create immersive works that redefine current AR norms. This investigation concludes by suggesting that teaching AR in graphic design schools can help enrich the profession and could potentially be further explored and developed in the future. The authors agree with Maeda (2016) who argue that "we must consciously invest in education to develop a more hybrid perspective on creativity in the 21st century: Technology x Business x

Design." and that designing creative learning environments involves not only facilitating student creativity, but also modelling creative pedagogical practice. It is also important that higher education foster more collaboration between academia and industry by correlating students' daily experiences and transfiguring them into a new learning environment, a mixed reality space full of opportunities.

REFERENCES

Augment. (2016). Augment Desktop [Software]. http://www.augment.com/augment- desktop/

Albinson, I., Giampietro, R., & Leslie, J. (2011) book, *Graphic design: now in production* Minneapolis, MN: Walker Art Centre.

Brown, T. (2008). Design Thinking. In *Harvard Business review,* June 2008 (pp.1-10). Retrieved from https://botfl.nd.edu/pdf/HBR%20Design%20Thinking.pdf

Cochrane, T., Antonczak, L. (2015). Connecting the theory and practice of mobile learning: a framework for creative pedagogies using mobile social media. *Media Education*, Vol. 6, n. 2, 2015, pp. 248-269.

Cochrane, T., Narayan, V. & Antonczak, L. (2015). Designing Collaborative Learning Environments Using Mobile AR. In S. Carliner, C. Fulford & N. Ostashewski (Eds.), Proceedings of EdMedia: World Conference on Educational Media and Technology 2015 (pp. 1394-1402). Association for the Advancement of Computing in Education (AACE).

Cormier, D. (2008). Rhizomatic education: Community as curriculum. *Innovate*, 4(5), np. Retrieved from http://davecormier.com/edblog/2008/2006/2003/rhizomatic-educationcommunity-as-curriculum/

Danvers J. (2003), Towards a radical pedagogy: Provisional notes on learning and teaching in art & design, «*International Journal of Art & Design Education*», vol. 22, n. 1, pp. 47-57.

Google (2014). *Smart Contact lens.* Retrieved from https://googleblog.blogspot.co.nz/2014/01/introducing-our-smart-contact-lens.html

Frielick, S (2016). *Researching teaching: the importance of SoTL.* Retrieved from http://www.educationreview.co.nz/magazine/october-2016/researching-teaching-the-importance-of-sotl/

Jenkins, H., Ford, S., & Green, J. (2013). *Spreadable media: Creating value and meaning in a networked culture postmillennial pop.* New York, NY: NYU Press.

Kahl, C. H., da Fonseca, L. H., and Witte, E. H. (2009). *Revisiting creativity research: An investigation of contemporary approaches.* Creativity Research Journal, 21 (1), pp. 1-5.

LAYAR. (2009). *Layar Creator* [Content Management System]. Retrieved from https://www.layar.com/creator/

Maeda, J. (2016). *#DesignInTech Report 2016.* Kleiner Perkins Caufield & Byers, (2016). Retrieved from http://www.slideshare.net/kleinerperkins/design-in-tech-report-2016

Manovich, L. (2002). *The Poetics of Augmented Space.* Retrieved from http://manovich.net/index.php/projects/the-poetics-of-augmented-space

Menorath D. (2016). *Juxtapose: An exploration of the technical and aesthetic potential.* Master's thesis Auckland University of Technology, Auckland, New Zealand.

Microsoft. (2016). *Microsoft HoloLens*. Retrieved from https://www.microsoft.com/microsoft-hololens/en-us

Milgram, P. (1994). A taxonomy of Mixed Reality visual displays. Paper presented in *IEICE Transactions on Information Systems*, Vol E77-D, No.12 December 1994.

Pachler, N., Bachmair, B., & Cook, J. (2010). Mobile learning: Structures, agency, practices. London: Springer.

Qualcomm. (2011). *Vuforia Augmented Reality* [Software]. Retrieved from https://www.vuforia.com/

Puentedura, R.R (2014). SAMR and TPCK: A Hands-On Approach to Classroom Practice. Retrieved from http://www.hippasus.com/rrpweblog/archives/2014/06/29/LearningTechnologySAMRModel.pdf

Redondo, E., Puig, J., Fonseca, D., Villagrasa, Navarro, I. (2014). Augmented and geo-located information in an architectural education framework. In proceedings of the *Virtual, augmented and mixed reality. applications of virtual and augmented reality*: 6th International Conference, VAMR 2014, Held as Part of HCI International 2014, Heraklion, Crete, Greece, June 22-27, 2014, Proceedings, Part II.

Ritzer, G., Dean, P., & Jurgenson, N. (2012). The coming of age. In *American Behavioural Scientist* 56(4) 379–398. doi: 10.1177/0002764211429368

Wenger, E. (1998). Communities of Practice: Learning, Meaning, and Identity. Cambridge: Cambridge University Press.

GENDER, GAMES AND SPACE

Suzanne de Castell[1], Hector Larios[1] and Jennifer Jenson[2]
[1]*University of Ontario Institute of Technology, 2000 Simcoe St N, Oshawa, ON L1H 7K4, Canada*
[2]*York University, 4700 Keel St., Toronto, Ontario, M3J1P3, Canada*

ABSTRACT

We report here a study of spatial learning and action videogame play based on Feng et al.'s (2007) finding that 10 hours spent playing an action videogame significantly improved selective attention and mental rotation. Students with above-average scores on measures of spatial abilities, such as mental rotation, prove more successful in Science, Technology, Engineering, and Mathematics (STEM) fields (Lubinski & Benbow 2006), however females demonstrate significantly less ability in mental rotation and spatial navigation than males (Astur et al. 1998) and are, as well, significantly under-represented in STEM subjects and fields (Beede et al. 2011; Hango, 2013). This study aims to better understand the factors that affect abilities to navigate virtual spaces, to identify underlying processes different users bring to bear when navigating virtual environments, and to identify design modifications guiding the development of game-based virtual environments that support improvement in spatial cognition. A Virtual Morris Water Maze is used to assess whether and how playing either FPS (First Person Shooter) or puzzle games appears to impact the navigational performance of male and female participants. Concluding suggestions are (tentatively) offered about specific features of games that appear to support increased success in highly valued STEM subjects and fields and that might assist in re-mediating this persistently gendered disadvantage.

KEYWORDS

Game-based learning, spatial abilities, gender, STEM

1. INTRODUCTION

Playing videogames has become an increasingly popular pastime among both children and adults, and with it has come a growing interest in questions about what and how players learn from videogame play. This study is part of a larger project to identify evidence-based, replicable studies of game-based learning, since much research on that question reports on small-scale, anecdotal and largely qualitative work. Relatively recent research has shown that videogame play could have a positive impact on spatial abilities such as mental rotation and selective attention (De Lisi & Wolford 2002; Green & Bavelier 2003; Feng et al. 2007; Boot et al 2011), but there are still many issues that remain unresolved. This research is of particular interest because we know that students with above-average scores on measures of cognitive ability such as mental rotation tend to be successful in Science, Technology, Engineering, and Mathematical (STEM) fields (Lubinski & Benbow 2006). We also know that females and males use different strategies to solve spatial tasks. We need to know more about how males' and females' spatial perception and cognition are affected by videogame play. This research could lead to identifying ways to maximize skills and abilities that are useful in STEM subjects and fields.

This study of spatial learning and action videogame play builds on the work of Feng et al. (2007), which found that 10 hours spent playing an action videogame significantly improved selective attention and mental rotation. Successful replication will considerably strengthen the evidential basis of investigations into whether and how training with an action video game affects performance in measures of attention, mental rotation, spatial learning and memory. Although not an exact replication, in our study, as in the Feng et al study, participants will be trained in either an action video game or a puzzle game for 10 hours to see how their experience impacts performance on measures of spatial cognition. Both prior to and following 10 hours of action game or puzzle game play, participants complete a test of mental rotation, and a navigation task in a 3D virtual environment.

Spatial cognition encompasses an array of skills and abilities at multiple levels of processing. As Feng et al. (2007) indicate, for instance, "attentional processes are intimately involved in higher-level tasks in spatial cognition." Thus, the ability to deploy attention across space is a "building block" for higher-level cognitive processes such as mental rotation. They found that action video games do improve lower-level attentional processes, and this may be one of the factors that lead to improvement on more complex abilities like mental rotation. As far as we are aware there has been no systematic research into whether video games also lead to improvements in cognitive processes measured at a higher level, and that may depend on mental rotation as a building block. Past research has found a correlation between mental rotation and navigation strategies as measured with maps (Dabbs et al. 1998) and real-world environments (Malinowski 2001). These findings suggest that mental rotation supports more complex tasks such as navigation, which is a form of spatial learning and memory. Discovery of a causal relationship between video game playing and spatial learning and memory, as mediated by mental rotation, would prove important not only at a theoretical but also practical level.

In this study we are using a 3D virtual version of the Morris Water Maze, which has been extensively used to measure spatial learning and memory in non-human subjects (Morris 1984), and more recently, in its virtual versions, to assess spatial cognition in human participants (Astur et al. 1998; Hamilton et al. 2002; and Mueller et al. 2008) as an experimental tool to investigate the extent to which video games lead to improvement not only in mental rotation but also in higher-order spatial learning and memory.

2. PRIOR RESEARCH

In a previous study of gender and (virtual) spatial navigation, we tested 82 undergraduate students, 50 females and 32 males, at a technology-focused School for Interactive Arts and Technology. Using a Virtual Morris Water Maze (https://youtu.be/v1EPF3YGaHo), we assessed navigational competence by comparing participants' search times to locate a hidden target, and their dwell times in the target area. Results showed videogame experience and spatial ability to be significantly correlated (de Castell et al. 2015). Those results indicated that past 3D video game experience was generally associated with better navigation performance in most, but not all, instances.

We found in that prior study a gender-differentiated uptake of distal and proximal cues, with navigators of high spatial ability being less reliant on salient proximal cues than navigators of low spatial ability --but we were also able to demonstrate how, with the provision of proximal cues, in the form of landmarks on the circumference of a virtual pool, these gender-based differences in navigational performance were significantly diminished. Given that spatial abilities have been correlated with positive educational outcomes in STEM subjects, and that female students have been and remain under-represented in these subject areas despite their centrality to 21st century educational and occupational demands, understanding the underlying processes that different users bring to bear when navigating 3D virtual environments, and knowing what design modifications, support improvements in performance, is of utmost importance in advancing educational access and opportunity.

2.1 Correlation to causation: Strengthening Connections between Claims and Evidence for Game-Based Learning

Participants in this study are 32 undergraduate students, 16 male and 16 female. The data collection procedure has four phases: pre-training, training, post-training, and follow-up. In the pre-training phase, participants complete a mental rotation test (Ganis & Kievit 2015) which involves viewing digital images of abstract three-dimensional objects (Figure 1) and determining if they are the same or different. This task has been used extensively to assess ability to visualize and mentally manipulate 3D figures.

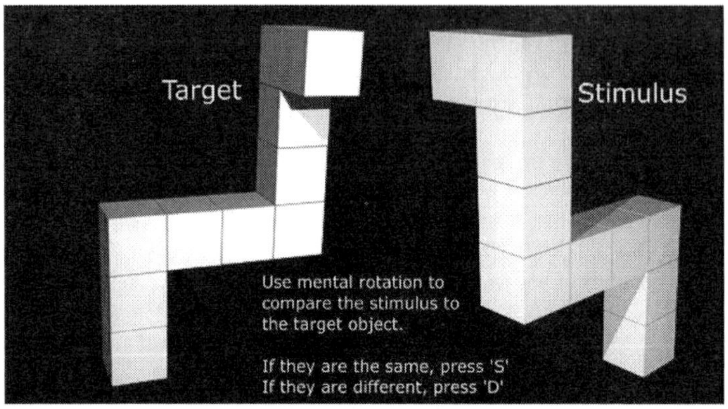

Figure 1. Sample figures used in the mental rotation test (adapted from Ganis & Kievit 2015)

After completing the mental rotation test, the participant's navigation abilities will be assessed with the Virtual Morris Water Maze (VMWM) task. Our VMWM (Figure 2) consists of a virtual environment that contains a pool full of water within a rectangular room. Hidden beneath the water is a platform that is activated whenever a participant swims over it. This task is believed be an accurate measure of spatial learning and memory (D'Hooge & De Deyn 2001). In the present study, all proximal cues have been removed from the pool wall so that successful completion depends upon ability to make use of distal cues to create and manipulate a mental representation of the environment.

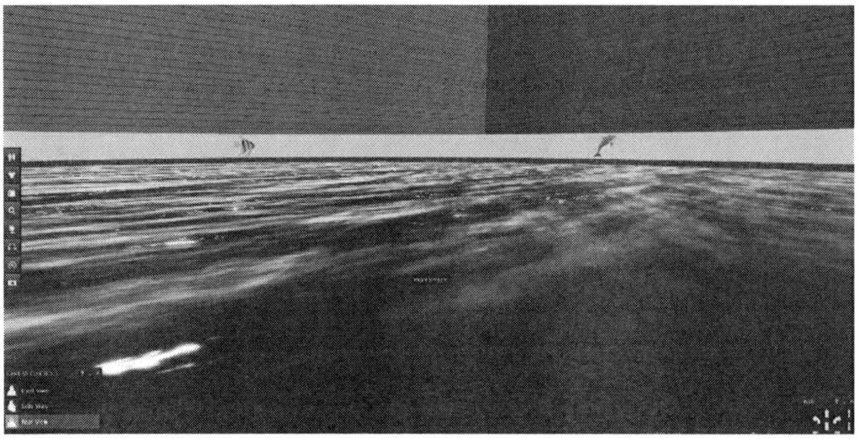

Figure 2. The Virtual Morris Water Maze. The figure shows the room walls and the pool, with proximal cues along the pool wall

Participants use the keyboard to move an avatar, in the form of a lab rat, to learn the location of the hidden platform. There are 15 trials in total, all of which are video-recorded. After participants complete these tasks, they are asked to fill out a video game and demographics questionnaire. The video game training phase randomly assigns participants to play either an action game (Call of Duty 2) or a puzzle game (Puzzle Ball) for a total of 10 hours. In the post-training phase, the participants will again complete both a mental rotation test and 15 trials in the virtual maze. In a follow-up phase designed to evaluate retention of learning, participants will again to complete the mental rotation test and the VMWM task, as well as a short questionnaire to assess their video game habits over the six months since the completion of training.

This study's results will help us understand the factors that affect abilities to navigate virtual spaces, identify the underlying processes different users bring to bear when navigating 3D virtual environments, and identify design modifications to guide the development of game-based virtual environments that support improvements in performance.

3. CONCLUSION

The advantages of this approach are both theoretical and practical: virtual environments, paradoxically enough, can enable more naturalistic assessments of the complex and diverse abilities involved in spatial navigation, than could previous assessments reliant on narrow psychometric tests, paradigmatically pen and paper mental rotation tests. As they become increasingly ubiquitous, virtual environments afford wide availability of computationally powerful technologies for experimentation. Unlike 'real world' experimental conditions, they enable greater control, and support complex and realistic scenarios that can be easily modified to test specific variables, for instance proximal cues can be inserted or removed, trial times can be lengthened or reduced, performance can be easily tracked in a variety of different ways (e.g. latency, path length, movement patterns, goal completion, etc.), and data capture storage and retrieval, as well as some forms of analysis can be automated. The 'portability' of virtual environments such as the VMWM mean experimentation is no longer restricted to the lab, the range of potential ethical concerns is greatly reduced and accessibility for differently-abled participants made possible. Such on-line experimental environments also allow for dissemination and knowledge-sharing and comparative analysis across locations on an unprecedented scale. Moreover, most of the research on sex differences in spatial abilities, and specifically research using the Morris Water Maze, has been conducted with animals, but the VMWM allows us to test a wide range of questions using human participants, thus enabling cross-species comparisons.

Limitations of our experimental approach are that directional cues are not fully 3-D---however this limitation will in time be circumvented by new developments in virtual reality technologies. Other limitations include possible gender differences in the ways males and females interact with virtual stimuli, (Viaud-Delmon et al.,1998; Wooley et al., 2010), specifically gender-differentiated responses to expanding both field of view and shape of the visual display, the fact that the VMWM has not yet been extensively studied and there are several design and protocol differences in the research which has been reported---and that it remains possible that differences in virtual maze performance may have less to do with spatial abilities than with the typical and often-reported 'hesitation' phenomena displayed by female subjects, both animal and human, interestingly enough (Shore et al, 2001,Wooley et al, 2010).

Implications for future work relate to the potential uses of the VMWM to easily, affordably and accurately assess spatial abilities, and to inform the design of game-based training instruments to remediate those abilities. As Feng et al. point out, given the evidence that quite specific cognitive abilities are associated with success in specific educational and vocational fields, and the evidence that these abilities can, indeed, be ameliorated through specific kinds of digital gameplay, "training with appropriately designed action video games could play a significant role as part of a larger strategy designed to interest women in science and engineering careers". (Feng et al, 2007, p.854).

ACKNOWLEDGEMENTS

The authors are indebted to Walter R. Boot, David Harris Smith, and John Murray. This research was supported by the Social Sciences and Humanities Research Council of Canada

REFERENCES

Astur, R.S. et al, 1998. A characterization of performance by men and women in a virtual Morris water task: A large and reliable sex difference. *Behavioural Brain Research* 93, 185–190.

Beede, D.N. et al, 2011. Women in STEM: A Gender Gap to Innovation (SSRN Scholarly Paper No. ID 1964782). *Social Science Research Network*, Rochester, NY.

Boot, W.R. and Blakely, D.P., 2011. Do action video games improve perception and cognition? Front. *Psychology* 2, 226.

Dabbs, J.M. et al, 1998. Spatial ability, navigation strategy, and geographic knowledge among men and women. *Evolution and Human Behavior* 19, 89–98.

de Castell, S. et al. 2015. The role of video game experience in spatial learning and memory. *Journal of Gaming & Virtual Worlds*, 7(1), 21–40.

De Lisi, R. and Wolford, J.L., 2002. Improving children's mental rotation accuracy with computer game playing. *The Journal of Genetic Psychology: Research and Theory on Human Development* 163, 272–282.

Feng, J. et al, 2007. Playing an action video game reduces gender differences in spatial cognition. *Psychological Science* 18, 850–855.

Ganis G. and Kievit, R. 2015. A New Set of Three-Dimensional Shapes for Investigating Mental Rotation Processes: Validation Data and Stimulus Set. *Journal of Open Psychology Data* URL https://openpsychologydata.metajnl.com/articles/10.5334/jopd.ai/ (accessed 10.1.15)

Green, C.S. and Bavelier, D., 2003. Action video game modifies visual selective attention. *Nature* 423, 534–537.

Hango, D. 2013. Gender differences in science, technology, engineering, mathematics and computer science (STEM) programs at university. Retrieved September 28, 2016, from http://www.statcan.gc.ca/pub/75-006-x/2013001/article/11874-eng.htm

Lubinski, D. and Benbow, C.P., 2006. Study of Mathematically Precocious Youth After 35 Years: Uncovering Antecedents for the Development of Math-Science Expertise. *Perspectives on Psychological Science* 1, 316–345.

Malinowski, J.C., 2001. Mental rotation and real-world wayfinding. *Percept Mot Skills* 92, 19–30.

Morris, R., 1984. Developments of a water-maze procedure for studying spatial learning in the rat. *Journal of Neuroscience Methods* 11, 47–60.

Mueller, S.C. et al, 2008. Sex differences in a virtual water maze: An eye tracking and pupillometry study. *Behavioural Brain Research* 193, 209–215.

Murray, J. et al. 2016. Something in the way we move: Quantifying patterns of exploration in virtual spaces - *Semantic Scholar*. Retrieved August 23, 2016, from https://www.semanticscholar.org/paper/Something-In-The-Way-We-Move-Quantifying-patterns-Murray-Chow/8411622a906971fe2230e5b978a536baa741b762

Shore, D.I. et al, 2001. Of mice and men: virtual Hebb-Williams mazes permit comparison of spatial learning across species. *Cognitive, Affective, & Behavioral Neuroscience* 1, 83–89.

Viaud-Delmon, I. et al, 1998. Sex, Lies and Virtual Reality. *Nat Neurosci* 1, 15–16.

Woolley, D.G. et al, Wagemans, J., Gantois, I., D'Hooge, R., Swinnen, S.P., Wenderoth, N., 2010. Sex differences in human virtual water maze performance: Novel measures reveal the relative contribution of directional responding and spatial knowledge. *Behavioural Brain Research* 208, 408–414.

THE CONTRIBUTION OF COLLECTIVE INTELLIGENCE FOR THE ANALYSIS OF THE PHENOMENON OF STUDENTS OVERCROWDING

Dikagma Bassagou and Luigi Lancieri
University of Lille, Citée Scientifique, Villeneuve d'Ascq, France

ABSTRACT

This paper presents a method aiming at analyzing a problem of overpopulation at the university of Lomé (Togo). In this perspective, we associate the teachers' perceptions with that of students through two kind of questionnaires, static and interactive. We describe this methodology to survey large groups of students. The results allows to better understand the teaching context of students, their difficulties but also the hidden potential of their situation. In background the feasibility of distant learning is also analyzed through this method of investigation.

KEYWORDS

Interactive questionnaires, context analysis

1. INTRODUCTION

The understanding of complex problems escapes to traditional rational methods of investigation. In organizational contexts for example, when political, economics or technological factors interplay, the behavior of individuals may appear out of control. In such cases, collective approaches of analyze such as brainstorming have been introduced in the last century but methodologies are still discussed. One of the problem is to decide who should participate to these collective investigations. A second question is to identify an easygoing method that facilitate the contribution of participants including online. In this paper, we developed this reflexion in an educational context.

For several years, the university of Lomé (Togo) faced various problems related to a large and growing population. For example, the number of students enrolled in mathematical analysis was 3778 in 2015 against 3612 in 2014 (+ 4.6%). Given that no amphitheater of the university can accommodate this enrollment, the first solution was to create two groups and to do the course twice a week. Unfortunately, the organizational problem has not been resolved because the largest amphitheater can only contain 1500 students and because students do not comply with rules and often switch groups. Moreover, for logistical and cost considerations, it is not possible to create more than 2 groups at the moment. Various other solutions are being studied (distance training, construction of a new amphitheater, ..) but, due to strong economic constraints, it is vital to carefully analyze the effectiveness of envisaged options. Not only the administration and the educative staff should agree with the final choice but also students. Without this overall consensus, the risk of being ineffective and losing money remains high. But how can we take all perspectives into account in a practical and productive way?

In order to investigate the depth of this consensus and better understand the reality on the ground, we developed a method exploiting, in a complementary way, two forms of online questionnaires. The first one, fairly classical, consists of 38 multiple-choice questions designed by the teaching staff who has made a first analysis of the problem of overcrowding. Students, therefore, only answer the problem (i.e. the questions) as analyzed by teachers. The objective of this first survey is to better understand the conditions of students' training, their feelings and their rates of equipments, in particular, to measure the feasibility of distance learning. The second questionnaire is based on the idea that the problem should be analyzed by students. It should be up to them to find the questions that express their situation and to propose answers. The interest of this second questionnaire, therefore, lies not only in answers but equally in the formulation of questions (words used, ..) (Lancieri et al, 2015). The rate of participation also gives a good indication on how the situation impacts students.

The device used for this second survey was conceived as an interactive adaptation of online multi choices forms where each student can interactively add questions, suggest answers and vote. In order to simplify as possible these operations, a special effort was done to keep the user interface basic and user friendly. Initially, teachers identify one or two generic questions in order to initiate the process of interaction between students. At the end of each day, the system automatically ask, by e-mail, all participants to reply to new questions or to add other questions (or answers) if they deem it necessary. Students may also change their initial answers if new choices of responses, provided by others, seem more appropriate. The analysis of these changes of opinion is key to understand the problem complexity as well as the process of consensus building. This e-brainstorming system has previously been used in several online experiments with small groups (20 individuals) (Veilleroy et al, 20013). This study is the first attempt to target large groups (225 individuals).

2. ANALYSIS OF FIRST RESULTS

The first questionnaire, formulated by teachers, was submitted to 501 students enrolled in a class of first year of university (400 of them answered). The population of students was in majority composed with male (69,7 %) and have from 18 to 26 years old (21 on average).

The responses show that, because of the plethora of students, 81.9% of respondents came early to university to find a seat (39.2% at 4 am, 35.6% at 5 am). When the amphitheater is full, 61.4% of students declare they must regularly stand and 95% feel they can not follow the course. The given reasons were: noise (according to 77 %), heat (82.7%), distraction (49.1%), lack of interaction with the teacher (70.4%). At the same time, the survey shows that a significant proportion of students could take part in distance learning. Indeed, some of them connect to the Internet from their home (38.8%, against 72.7% in cybers) and are rather equipped with nomadic tools (laptop 41%, smartphones 45%). In addition, 77% of students have a positive opinion on distance education.

To complement this “static”vision, the interactive questionnaire was submitted to two groups of students (a total of 225 individuals) with two startup questions on the topic: "How to facilitate the follow-up of courses when students are numerous? ". After two weeks of interactions, students proposed 31 (group 1) and 35 (group 2) new questions. The average number of responses per question is of 4 for the first group and 3 for the second. The response rate is lower than for the static questionnaire. Of the 225 students, 95 were connected but only 66 responded to at least one question. However, the participation rate of 29.3% is higher than what is usually the case when individuals are invited by e-mail to respond to an on-line questionnaire (24,8%).

We observed a clear difference from users’ viewpoint between the static questionnaire produced by teachers and the interactive one produced by students. While the former “describes the situation” as it is perceived, in the second, students tend to express the perceived “causes of the situation”. We observed that new questions and answers are often politically oriented. For example: "Why the state does not multiply universities? For 58.33% of students, the state lacks of teachers. Furthermore, 100% of participants blamed the lack of follow-up in the management of students. In reality, university administrations are unable to manage the overwhelming number of students due to a lack of resources and because information and communication technologies are not there. This lack of resources is also reflected in the fact that courses are more theoretical than practical (lack of equipments). Students indicate spontaneously their preference for activities in autonomy, 78% prefer practical work and projects rather than lectures.

We also noted that 29 participants (near to a half of respondents) modified at least one of their responses during the survey period. This is a sign that the causes of the overpopulation problem are not clear for all students. The contributions (new questions and answers) from the group make students to have a wider view of the situation and then call in question their first opinion. Let us remark that the capacity to monitor the change of opinions within the group over the time is one of the most important feature of this tool. It allows to better understand how works the collective intelligence.

This study allows us to have a first vision of a complex training context. While distance learning seems to be the most practical solution to the overpopulation problem, it can not be deployed yet in a massive way. Regardless of the lack of equipment, the limited monitoring capacities may penalize the less autonomous students. In an other hand a sub group with the most motivated and autonomous students could certainly take benefit from distance learning. But how to identify these students ? In further works we will tackle this difficult question.

3. DISCUSSION

Several studies focus on the consequences of universities overpopulation in Africa. In other more developed countries, this question is little mentioned probably because consequences are, at the moment, more limited.

In most of the cases, these situations are analyzed by a core team of education specialists who proposes consensual solutions. However, studies show that this approach is not always the best. In his book, "The wisdom of crowds", J. Surowiecki gives many examples showing that merging different skills, even with basic qualifications, is often more creative and productive than a team of specialists (Surowiecki, 2005). In this domain, questionnaires and polls are a way to exploit the collective intelligence in computer mediated environments (Lancieri, 2016). But traditional questionnaires are very regulated and constrained (check boxes, radio buttons, etc.), impossible to go back (later) to modify answers. At the other end, open questionnaires allow interactivity and creativity but the final result is very hard to exploit due to the heterogeneity of the responses textual structure. A difficult and time-consuming human analysis is necessary in most of the cases.

Interactive multi-choices questionnaires are a solution between these 2 extremes modes (open and closed surveys). In this perspective, the Delphi method, introduced in the 1940s and later the RT Delphi is a structured communication technique, which tries to get opinions, judgments and justifications from the participants. It seeks a consensus, with a carefully predefined set of questions, but here the creativity is controlled and contained. There are multiple rounds where questionnaires allow experts to provide their judgment, then to revise their answers (Powell, 2003). But Delphi may be found long, expensive, tedious and requires a lot of efforts (Ekionea et al, 2011). Furthermore, this method is not adapted for a survey of a large population. Inquiry based learning that put ahead the role of questioning is also a new trend in modern education (Baron et al, 2008).

The method we proposed in this paper is a way to adapt a brainstorming process to a large population while monitoring users interactions during the survey. This allows to better follow and explain the dynamic of collective behaviors such as opinion leaderships, change of mind or consensus building. In further works we will increase the surveyed population. We will also study the effect of a larger implication of teachers in the e-brainstorming process. At present, they only provide startup questions. What would be the effects if they add more oriented questions during the survey process ?

Finally, our method consists in trying to turn a problem into a solution. Indeed, the large number of students is a problem in the sens that it hampers the education system. In the other hand it turns into a solution in the sens that collective intelligence provides insights for solving the problem. Of course, this is a preliminary work and we don't yet answer all of our questions. But, trough our 2 combined modes of survey, we obtain a kind of "stereoscopic" picture and a more precise view of our eduction context. For example, we imagined that some students have to come early in the morning in order to find a seat but not at 4 am. We also imagined that some students have a computer but probably not 41%. In addition, combining the outcomes of both questionnaires, we see that the overcrowding situation is perceived as critical by students. We also see that in our context, the distance learning is perceived by all actors (teaching team and students) as a real potential option. Of course, this feeling is one thing but implementing a large scale distance learning system is another thing. Outside economic questions, a key problem is to identify autonomous and motivated students who have the most chances to succeed through distance learning.

REFERENCES

Barron, B., and Darling-Hammond, L. (2008). Teaching for Meaningful Learning: A Review of Research on Inquiry-Based and Cooperative Learning. Book Excerpt. George Lucas Educational Foundation.

Ekionea J.P. , Bernard P., and Plaisent M., (2011). Consensus par la méthode Delphi sur les concepts clés des capacités organisationnelles spécifiques de la gestion des connaissances. Recherches qualitatives, 2011, pp. 168

Lancieri, L.(2014) Collective intelligence in a computer mediated environment (Chapter 8); in Handbook of Research on Democratic Strategies and Citizen-Centered E-Government Services; collective book coordinated by Ejub Kajan; 2014; DOI: 10.4018/978-1-4666-7266-6, ISBN13: 9781466672666; IGI Global Editor.

Lancieri, L. and Leprêtre, E. (2015) A new linguistic approach to assess the opinion of users in social network environments; Application of Social Media and Social Network Analysis" that is going to be published by Springer in the series: Lecture Notes in Social Networks (LNSN) Editors Przemyslaw Kazienko, Nitesh Chawla.

Powell, C. (2003). The Delphi technique: myths and realities. Journal of advanced nursing,41(4), 376-382.

Surowiecki James (2005), The Wisdom of Crowds. Paperback – August 16, 2005

Veilleroy Yann, Eurin Gabriel, Hoogstoel Frédéric and Lancieri Luigi (2013) Exploring Collective Intelligence in Online Brainstorming, The Third International Conference on Advanced Collaborative Networks, Systems and Applications (Colla2013)

INTEGRATED COLLABORATIVE E-LEARNING FOR THE GLOBAL MANAGEMENT EDUCATION IN THE 21ST CENTURY

Barbara W. K. Son
California State University at Los Angeles, 5151 State University Drive, Los Angeles, CA 90032, USA

ABSTRACT

Rapidly growing information and communications technology and more interconnected global world offer benefits and challenges to global business organizations. While exploring benefits from global workforce and global production, they must successfully adapt to their local market conditions and manage their multicultural resources. How can we teach these rising complex global management challenges effectively in the 21st century global management classrooms? We need to pursue a new learning paradigm to foster active learners with innovative and critical global management thinking. Global management curricula should be designed to constantly draw forth active learning feedback to facilitate innovative learner-centered interactive classrooms. We closely examined the interactive learning models at the previous AACE Conferences (Son & Goldstone, 2012; Son & Simonian, 2014; Son, 2016). At the current Conference, we will discuss how integrated collaborative e-learning should be designed to improve these models using the example of a global online MBA course at Anaheim University. Using innovation and entrepreneurship as the subject matter, we closely examine the three pillars for global management education: leadership education, responsible education, and experiential education.

KEYWORDS

Global Management Education, Integrated Interactive E-Learning, Active Learning, Experiential Education, Leadership Education, Responsible Education

1. INTRODUCTION

As information and communications technology has made its progress, the global market is more interconnected and the digital world is experiencing spectacular growth. Emerging market and developing economies will continue to represent the major portion of global growth. These rising trends pose challenges to multinational and multicultural organizations. They have to explore flexible and adaptable strategies to deal with complexity costs and global risks (Dewhurst, Harris, & Heywood, 2012). How can we teach these rising complex global management challenges effectively in the global management classrooms? We need to pursue a new learning paradigm to foster active learners with innovative and critical global management thinking. Fast growing mobile world and advances in multimedia instructional technology are facilitating a significant paradigm shift from traditional learning to learner centered collaborative and engaged learning (Son & Simonian, 2016).

Global management curricula should be designed to constantly draw forth active learning feedback to facilitate innovative learner-centered interactive classrooms. As students demand more up-to-date learning materials in the fast moving business world, global management classrooms have to deliver learner-friendly complex content promptly and effectively. In addition, global education programs and instructors ought to tailor interactive materials for different learning styles. We closely examined these challenges at the previous AACE Conferences (Son & Goldstone, 2012; Son & Simonian, 2014; Son, 2016).

At the current Conference, we apply flipped learning to the three pillars for global management education: leadership education, responsible education, and experiential education. We illustrate how active learning, collaborative learning, and experiential learning are vital components in the 21st century global management learning paradigm.

2. NEW PARADIGM IN THE 21ST CENTURY GLOBAL MANAGEMENT EDUCATION

Learner-centered nurturing pedagogy in global management education must address the complex and dynamic challenges of global business environment. Active learners in global management education need to be adaptive and explore creative and flexible solutions. To facilitate these learning outcomes, innovative pedagogical techniques must be incorporated into global management curricula in the 21st century. As Figure 1 portrays, there are three pillars for global management education in the 21st century: leadership education, responsible education, and experiential education. In the globalized world, leaders and entrepreneurs in multinational and multi-cultural organizations ought to be equipped with global mindset and cultural intelligence and possess social responsibility (Anderson, Mason, Hibbert, & Rivers, 2017).

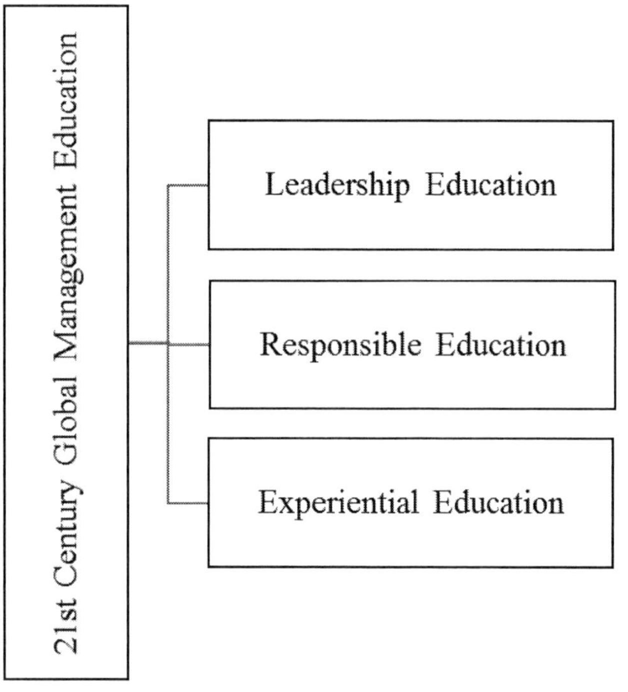

Figure 1. Three pillars in the 21st century global management education

2.1 Flipped Learning in Leadership Education

Multinational and multi-cultural organizations demand effective and flexible leadership approaches to meet complex challenges (Amagoh, 2009). It is hence critical for leaders and entrepreneurs to think globally and lead locally through cultural intelligence and a global mindset (Gutierrez, Spencer & Zhu, 2012; Lovvorn & Chen, 2011; Aggarwa, 2011). Furthermore, as organizational complexity grows, global management education has to prepare students to be effective leaders who drive organizational performance and competitiveness. Our students who are global business professionals have contributed to these learning objectives. In our innovation and entrepreneurship class, we apply flipped learning pedagogical techniques through learner-centered collaborative learning and multi-disciplinary case studies and projects. Flipped learning combines constructivist learning theory and behaviorist learning theory (Roach, 2014). We emphasize flipped learning practices through which our active learners gain perspectives toward complex business markets, have understanding for multi-dimensional management challenges, and develop leadership and entrepreneurship skills.

2.2 Flipped Learning in Responsible Education

Globally responsible leaders are called upon to create and foster their desired work culture based on ethics and accountability and to develop diverse and inclusive workplace. Accordingly, management curriculums must address practice-based learning and development, so that students learn and build these responsible leadership skills. As the United Nations' Principles for Responsible Management Education advocates, today's global management education is expected to promote corporate social responsibility and sustainability (Alcaraz & Thiruvattal, 2010). Consequently, global and interdisciplinary pedagogies are required to cultivate these responsible education values (Lund Dean & Forray, 2017) and to facilitate positive social changes (Anderson, et al., 2017). Our innovation and entrepreneurship class examines the implementation of these values in multinational organizations. We apply flipped learning pedagogical techniques through collaborative and active learning. We integrate corporate social responsibility and sustainability issues in the case studies, reflective exercises, and group practices, while focusing on the creative and innovative side of entrepreneurship. In addition, we explore the complex problems and challenges faced by leaders and entrepreneurs in this process.

2.3 Flipped Learning in Experiential Education

The 2015 Global Management Education Survey of 3,329 graduating business school students in 29 countries reported that they prefer case studies and experiential learning, but these learning methods represent just one third of the instruction time (Plompen, 2015). To adapt management education to the new global market realities, management education paradigm must shift to support experiential learning. To embed experiential learning in management classes, management educators must possess the following four areas of experience and expertise: "industry experience, consultancy experience, research experience and teaching experience (Balaji, 2013, p.1262). In our innovation and entrepreneurship class, we draw on our experiences in these areas to apply experiential learning methods such as management case studies, consulting exercises, and multinational group collaborations. These methods along with cross-cultural experiences are vital for students to learn and build their effective management competencies (Caligiuri & Tarique, 2012). We play as active learning facilitators to help students practice experiential applied learning (Ash & Clayton, 2009).

3. CONCLUSION

Active learners in global management education need to be adaptive and explore creative and flexible solutions to the rising complex global management challenges. To facilitate these learning outcomes, innovative pedagogical techniques must be incorporated into global management curricula in the 21st century. Global management curricula should be designed to constantly draw forth active learning feedback to facilitate innovative learner-centered interactive classrooms. Accordingly, we closely examined the three pillars for global management education: leadership education, responsible education, and experiential education. As we have earlier examined, active learning, collaborative learning, and experiential learning are vital components in the 21st century global management learning paradigm. Therefore, management learning system should be tailored to stir innovative and effective managerial thinking, knowledge and skills vital to success in the global business environment.

ACKNOWLEDGEMENT

We'd like to thank the anonymous reviewers for helpful comments.

REFERENCES

Aggarwa, R., 2011. Developing a global mindset: Integrating demographics, sustainability, technology, and globalization. *Journal of Teaching in International Business*, Vol. 22, No. 1, pp. 51-69.

Alcaraz, J.M. and Thiruvattal, E., 2010. An Interview with Manuel Escudero The United Nations' Principles for Responsible Management Education: A Global Call for Sustainability. *Academy of Management Learning & Education*, Vol. 9, No. 3, pp. 542–550.

Amagoh, F., 2009. Leadership development and leadership effectiveness. *Management Decision*, Vol. 47, No. 6, pp. 989-999.

Anaheim University, 2015. Student Resources. Retrieved from https://www.anaheim.edu/student-resources/online-discussion-forum

Anderson, L., Mason, K., Hibbert, P., Rivers, C., 2017. Management Education in Turbulent Times. *Journal of Management Education*, Vol. 41, No. 2, pp. 303-306.

Ash, S. and Clayton, P., 2009. Generating, Deepening, and Documenting Learning: the Power of Critical Reflection in Applied Learning. *Journal of Applied Learning in Higher Education*, Vol. 1, pp. 25-48.

Balaji, R., 2013. Trends, Issues and Challenges in Management Education. *International Journal of Innovative Research in Science, Engineering and Technology,* Vol. 2, No. 4, pp. 1257-1262.

Caligiuri, P. and Tarique, I., 2012. Dynamic cross-cultural competencies and global leadership effectiveness. *Journal of World Business*, Vol. 47, No. 4, pp. 612-622.

Gutierrez, B., Spencer, S.M., and Zhu, G., 2012. Thinking globally, leading locally: Chinese, Indian, and Western leadership. *Cross Cultural Management: An International Journal*, Vol. 19, No. 1, pp. 67-89.

Dewhurst, M., Harris, J., and Heywood, S., 2012. The global company's challenge. *McKinsey Quarterly* June. Retrieved from http://www.mckinsey.com/business-functions/organization/our-insights/the-global-companys-challenge

Lund Dean, K. and Forray, J.M., 2017. You're Just WEIRD: Considering the Nature of Today's Management Students. *Journal of Management Education,* Vol. 41, No. 2, pp. 175–180.

Lovvorn, A.S. and Chen, J., 2011. Developing a Global Mindset: The Relationship between an International Assignment and Cultural Intelligence. *International Journal of Business and Social Science*, Vol. 2, No. 9, pp. 275-283.

Plompen, M., 2015. Global Management Education: Return on Investment and Employment Outlook. Retrieved from https://www.efmd.org/efmd-deans-across-frontiers/view/869-global-management-education-return-on-investment-and-employment-outlook

Reuters, 2008. Anaheim University Ranks #1 in Japan's Nikkei BP MBA Rankings. Retrieved from http://www.reuters.com/article/pressRelease/idUS110001+12-May-2008+MW20080512

Roach, T., 2014. Student perceptions toward flipped learning: New methods to increase interaction and active learning in economics. *The International Review of Economics Education,* Vol. 17, pp. 74-84.

Son, B. and Goldstone, B., 2012. Innovative Live Lecture Strategies for Integrated Interactive e-Learning at DeVry Online. *AACE Proceedings of Global TIME 2012 — Online Conference on Technology, Innovation, Media & Education*, Chesapeake, VA, pp. 184-190.

Son, B. and Simonian, M., 2014. Using Mobile Learning to Enhance Innovative Interactive Learning at DeVry Online. *EdMedia-- World Conference on Educational Multimedia, Hypermedia and Telecommunications*, Chesapeake, VA, pp. 546–552.

Son, B. and Simonian, M., 2016. An Integrated Multimedia Learning Model vs. The Traditional Face-to-Face Learning Model: An Examination of College Economics Classes. *Journal of Educational Multimedia and Hypermedia*, Vol. 25, No. 4, pp. 305-321.

Son, B., 2016. Innovative Collaborative Learning Strategies for Integrated Interactive E-Learning in the 21st Century. *International Conference on Cognition and Exploratory Learning*, Mannheim, Germany, pp. 315-318.

RELATIONS BETWEEN COGNITIVE RESOURCES AND TWO TYPES OF GERMANE LOAD FOR LEARNING

Kazuhisa Miwa[1], Hitoshi Terai[2] and Yosuke Mizuno[3]
[1]*Graduate School of Informatics, Nagoya University, Nagoya, 4648601 Japan*
[2]*Faculty of Humanity-Oriented Science and Engineering, Kindai University, Fukuoka, 820–8555 Japan*
[3]*School of Information Science, Nagoya University, Nagoya, 4648601 Japan*

ABSTRACT

Cognitive load theory (CLT) distinguishes three types of cognitive loads: intrinsic, extraneous, and germane, of which the latter is generally imposed in learning activities. To examine the nature of germane cognitive load, the participants engaged in 8-by-8 Reversi games against computerized opponents. The experimental results indicated that germane load decreases as extraneous load increases because the cognitive resources for assigning the germane load are exhausted by the extraneous load, and that there are two types of germane load: one that increases with an increase in intrinsic load and the other increases as intrinsic load decreases.

KEYWORDS

Cognitive load theory, extraneous load, intrinsic load, germane load

1. INTRODUCTION

Cognitive load theory (CLT) plays a central role in designing learning environments (Sweller, 1988; Sweller, Van Merrienboer, & Paas, 1998). The theory distinguishes three types of cognitive loads: intrinsic, extraneous, and germane. Previous CLT studies have focused on the distinction between intrinsic and extraneous load. In this regard, intrinsic load is the basic cognitive load required to perform a particular task. Conversely, extraneous load is defined as the wasted cognitive load that is unrelated to primary cognitive activities. Overall, extraneous load can have a negative impact on learning activities. On the other hand, positive cognitive load that increases learning effects was found in the mid-1990s. Some studies reported that, when a large cognitive load was imposed on the participants in an experimental group, there were significant learning gains. Such a cognitive load is defined as germane load, which is the load used for learning (Paas & Van Merrienboer, 1994; Paas & van Gog, 2006; Ayres & van Gog, 2009).

Although the negative impact of extraneous load on learning has been widely accepted, the effects of germane load have been subject to debate. Essentially, there are two views regarding the relationship between intrinsic and germane cognitive loads:

Part-of-intrinsic view: Germane cognitive load is a part of intrinsic cognitive load; that is, germane load emerges in cooperation with intrinsic load.

Independent-from-intrinsic view: The nature of germane and intrinsic cognitive loads differs; that is, germane cognitive load independently emerges from intrinsic cognitive load.

The present study measures germane load as learning effects. More specifically, it manipulates the amounts of extraneous and intrinsic loads as independent variables, and measures germane load as a dependent variable. The following hypotheses are posited:

Hypothesis 1: This hypothesis is clearly drawn from numerous CLT studies that have indicated the negative impacts of extraneous load on learning activities. When extraneous load increases, germane load decreases, since the cognitive resources for assigning the germane load are exhausted by the extraneous load.

Hypotheses 2a and 2b refer to a relationship of intrinsic and germane cognitive loads.

Hypothesis 2a: This hypothesis is drawn from the part-of-intrinsic view. Germane load increases with an increase in intrinsic load, since the amounts of both cognitive loads are correlated.

Hypothesis 2b: This hypothesis is drawn from the independent-from-intrinsic view. Germane load increases with a decrease in intrinsic load, since this decrease causes an increase in the cognitive resources for assigning germane load in working memory capacity.

2. EXPERIMENT

2.1 Procedure

The task used in this study was an 8-by-8, computer-based Reversi game. The participants play the game against a computerized opponent (i.e., opponent agent). Meanwhile, the computerized partner-agent assists the participant in selecting the winning moves. Both agents (i.e., the opponent and partner) are controlled by the Reversi engine (Edax 4.0), which suggests the best moves by assessing the situation in the game.

2.2 Procedure

In order to determine the baseline for measuring learning gains, the participants performed a pre-test consisting of 12 problems. Then, the participants moved on to the learning (training) phase in which they played 16 games. Each game started in the middle stage in which approximately half of the discs were already placed on the board. The learning phase consisted of four blocks in which the participants played four games in each block. A set of winning strategies in Reverse games was known. The trainings in each block were intended to allow the participants to learn one of the strategies. The first three games in each block began with an identical disc arrangement, while the fourth (final) game began with a different arrangement from the arrangement in the preceding three games. After the learning phase, the participants performed a post-test consisting of the same 12 problems as those in the pre-test.

2.3 Independent Variable

Two factors, i.e., the disc representation factor and the hint information factor, were applied for manipulation. The former factor was expected to manipulate the extraneous load, whereas the latter factor was expected to manipulate the intrinsic load.

Disc representation factor: Figure 1 presents a sample disc arrangement of the Black and White and L and rL (reversal L) conditions.

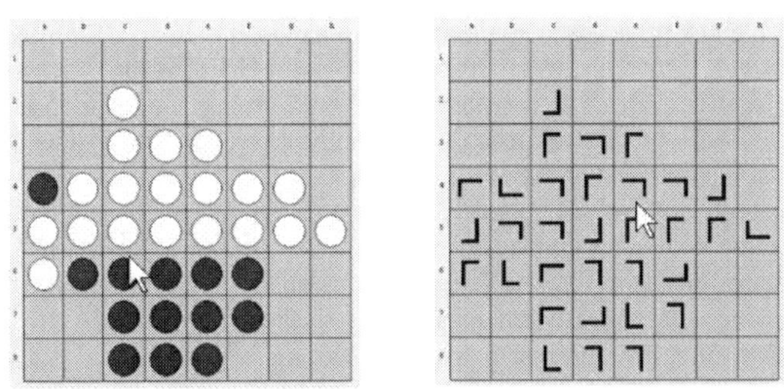

(a) Black and White condition (b) L and reversal L condition

Figure 1. A screenshot of the game board in the Black and White and L and rL (reversal L) conditions

When the Black and White condition was considered, the Black and White discs were arranged, whereas when the L and rL condition was considered, the Ls or rotated Ls (black discs) and the mirror reversal Ls or rotated reversal Ls (white discs) were arranged. In the L and rL condition, in order to perceive the status of the disc arrangement and decide the best move, the participants had to mentally rotate the L or reversal L images in each trial, thus causing significant extraneous load. As a result, the L and rL condition increased the extraneous load more than the Black and White condition.

Hint information factor: In each trial of the game, the main task was to choose the best move for winning the game. In order to do so, the participants had to understand the status of the disc arrangement, search the problem space, and estimate the best move, thus increasing intrinsic load. Under the hint presentation condition, the computerized partner-agent suggested the best moves to the participants, whereas under the no hint condition, no such information was presented. This suggests that the intrinsic load of the participants was lower in the hint presentation condition than in the no hint condition.

2.4 Experimental Conditions

Based on the aforementioned understandings, three experimental conditions were established:

No hint and Black and White condition: A small extraneous load is imposed, and a large intrinsic load would emerge.

Hint presentation and Black and White condition: A small extraneous load is imposed, and an intrinsic load would be minimized.

Hint presentation and L and rL condition: A significant extraneous load is imposed; therefore, only little cognitive resource to which the intrinsic and germane loads are assigned.

2.5 Dependent Variable

Pre- and post-tests were performed in order to evaluate the learning gains. Each test consisted of 12 problems, and the problems used in the post-test were identical to those in the pre-test. In each problem, the participants were presented with a disc arrangement, after which they were required to determine the best possible move. The 12 problems were grouped into the following three categories, each of which consisted of four problems:

Identical problems: The disc arrangements, identical to those used in the training phase, were presented.

Near transfer problems: The presented disc arrangements were modified from the original arrangements used in the learning phase. More specifically, they were rotated 90, 180 or 270 degrees from the original arrangements or mirror-reversed from the rotated arrangements.

Far transfer problems: The presented disc arrangements were new. However, the participants were able to determine the best possible move if they had learned the strategies that were intended to be found during the learning phase.

Since the number of problems in each category was four, the full score was also four. This study used the increase in the scores from the pre- to the post-test as a dependent variable (i.e., learning gains). The germane load assigned in the learning phase was evaluated based on the increase of the test scores.

2.6 Participants

A total of 61 undergraduates from Nagoya University participated in this study. All of the participants were not experts in playing Reversi, even though they had some experience with the game. The participants were divided into three groups: 21 for the no hint and Black and White condition; 19 for the hint presentation and Black and White condition; and 21 for the hint presentation and L and rL condition.

3. RESULTS

3.1 Prediction

Since the germane load is evaluated based on the increase of the test scores, the following predictions are made: Hypothesis 1 predicts: (1) no increase in the test scores under the hint presentation and L and rL condition, and (2) substantial increases in the hint presentation and Black and White condition as well as in the no hint and Black and White condition, compared to the hint presentation and L and rL condition. More specifically, Hypothesis 2a predicts an increase in the test scores under the no hint and Black and White condition, whereas Hypothesis 2b predicts an increase in the hint presentation and Black and White condition.

3.2 Increase of Test Scores from Pre to Post Test

Table 1 shows the increase in the test scores from the pre- to the post-test in the identical problem category. In order to confirm whether significant increases in the test scores occurred, one-sample t-tests were conducted, which indicated that there were substantial increases in the no hint and Black and White condition as well as in the hint presentation and Black and White condition ($t(20) = 3.09$, $p < 0.01$; $t(18) = 4.72$, $p < 0.001$). Conversely, there was no increase in the hint presentation and L and rL condition ($t(20) < 1$, n.s.).

Table 1. Increases in the test scores from the pre- to the post-test in three experimental conditions. * shows a substantial increase, while the numerals in parentheses show the standard errors

	No Hint Black/White	Hint Black/White	Hint L/rL
Identical	0.90* (0.28)	1.16* (0.24)	-0.05 (0.16)
Near Transfer	0.76* (0.24)	1.21* (0.24)	0.29 (0.22)
Far Transfer	0.33 (0.35)	0.58 (0.27)	0.24 (0.29)

Similarly, the table presents the results of the near transfer problem category. The same one-sample t-tests were conducted to confirm whether there were significant increases in the test scores. Similar results were obtained, thus indicating substantial increases in the no hint and Black and White condition as well as in the hint presentation and Black and White condition ($t(20) = 3.07$, $p < 0.01$; $t(18) = 4.86$, $p < 0.001$), whereas no increase was found in the hint presentation and L and rL condition ($t(20) = 1.24$, n.s.). In the far transfer problem category, no increases were found in all three conditions ($t(20) < 1$, n.s.; $t(18) = 2.07$, n.s.; $t(20) < 1$, n.s.).

4. CONCLUSION

First, the results of this study confirmed Hypothesis 1. In the L and rL condition, a significant extraneous cognitive load was expected to emerge through the irrelevant cognitive activities such as performing mental rotations of L and reversal L.

Second, both Hypothesis 2a and 2b were also confirmed, implying that there are two types of germane load relating to the part-of and independent-from intrinsic views. However, the generality of the two hypotheses is still limited. Although substantial increases were found in the test scores from the pre- to the post-test in Black and White conditions, the increases were only found in the identical and near transfer problem categories. Meanwhile, no increases were found in the far transfer problems.

REFERENCES

Ayres, P. & van Gog, T. (2009). State of the art research into cognitive load theory. *Computers in Human Behavior*, 25, 253-257.

Paas, F.G. & Van Merrienboer, J.J. (1994). Variability of worked examples and transfer of geometrical problem-solving skills: A cognitive-load approach. *Journal of Educational Psychology*, 86(1), 122-133.

Paas, F. & van Gog, T. (2006). Optimising worked example instruction: Different ways to increase germane cognitive load. *Learning and Instruction*, 16(2), 87-91.

Sweller, J. (1988). Cognitve load during problem solving: Effects on learning. *Cognitive Science*, 12(2), 257-285.

Sweller, J., Van Merrienboer, J. J., & Paas, F.G. (1998). Cognitive architecture and instructional design. *Educational psychology review*, 10(3), 251-296.

A FRAMEWORK FOR PEOPLE RE-IDENTIFICATION IN MULTI-CAMERA SURVEILLANCE SYSTEMS

Sirine Ammar, Nizar Zaghden and Mahmoud Neji
MIRACL: Multimedia InfoRmation systems and Advanced Computing Laboratory, Tunisia

ABSTRACT

People re-identification has been a very active research topic recently in computer vision. It is an important application in surveillance system with disjoint cameras. This paper is focused on the implementation of a human re-identification system. First the face of detected people is divided into three parts and some soft-biometric traits are extracted from each part. In second step, we can recognize people even if their faces are hidden or they are with back appearance. The features extraction will be carried out according to the overall characteristics of the complete images of different persons. An algorithm that identifies people from their body shape will be developed. A powerful representation of the person based on the characteristics of color, texture and shape as well as different soft-biometric features is suggested. The experiments are carried out on SAIVT-SoftBio database which consists of videos from disjoint surveillance cameras as well as some static image based datasets (MUCT, VIPeR, CVSRP).

KEYWORDS

People Re-Identification, Soft-Biometric, Surveillance System

1. INTRODUCTION

Today, video surveillance systems are widely used in our daily life. These surveillance systems are applied in many areas including home security, surveillance of public places, control some private access, resolution of criminal investigations and so on. In many surveillance purposes, it is desirable to determine whether a person has already been detected by a multi-camera system, known as people re-identification. Biometric information can be very effective in identifying people, but there are limits to use them, namely the need for high-resolution images and are captured in the closest distance. In fact, the principal problem in tracking or people re-identifying is to create a model that can represent people in a unique and accurate way. In this paper, a framework is suggested to construct human appearance model for people re-identification in disjointed camera surveillance system. This approach allows to resolve some problems (theft in public or private places, criminal investigations, etc) and their possible unfavorable results.

The rest of the paper is organized as follows: Section 2 gives a general view on re-identification approaches, followed by the choice of our method compared to the state of the art in section 3. Finally, conclusion is addressed in section 4.

2. GENERAL VIEW ON RE-IDENTIFICATION APPROACHES

2.1 Global Approaches vs. Local Approaches

2.1.1 Global Approaches

The global approaches allow the recognition of images based on visual similarities measured on the whole images. A globally described image is represented by a single attribute vector. Many global approaches exist to make re-identification of people. Among the best known are the works of (D. Gray / 2008) which consist of extracting texture features such as Schmid and Gabor, as well as eight color channels from the RGB, YCbCr, and HSV color spaces. In (A Derbel et al. / 2014), two new representations of the motion distribution named gait frequency representation (RFD) and gait envelope representation (RED) are presesnted. These two representations are computed from the binary images of the silhouettes. In the work of (Nakayima et al. 2003) Two-dimensional normalized color histograms are computed; r = R/(R+G+B), g = G/(R+G+B). The characteristics of shapes were calculated by counting the pixels along the rows and columns of the extracted body images.

2.1.2 Local Approaches

This type of approaches consists of segmenting the image to divide it into local areas and then calculating the characteristics for each of the extracted regions. Most of these methods use points of interest (Nizar Zaghden et al/2013) that are based on characteristic structures (blobs or ridges) in the image. Many local approaches exist to make re-identification of person. Among the best known, we can cite the work (W. Schwartz et al/2010), in which characteristics of texture (Local Binary Pattern) and shape (Histogram of Oriented Gradient) and color (captured by averaging the intensities of pixels) are combined to represent each block of the cropped face. (O. Hamdoun / 2008) uses interest points descriptors to obtain the signature for a person. In (Vaquero, 2009) First, human body is segmented in face, torso and legs. Then, Normalized color histogram is extracted for each body part in HSL space. The region of the face is partitioned into three parts as presented in Figure 1 and some soft biometric features are extracted from each head area.

Figure 1. Body Parts and Attributes Considered in the Implementation

In (Lyes Hamoudi / 2011) the elements of the foreground are obtained. After, the entire blob is divided into three areas using height ratios equal to [1/5, 3/10, 1/2] of the total blob size as presented in Figure 2. The color characteristics used are the mean values of the colors. The extracted texture characteristics are based on the co-occurrence matrix.

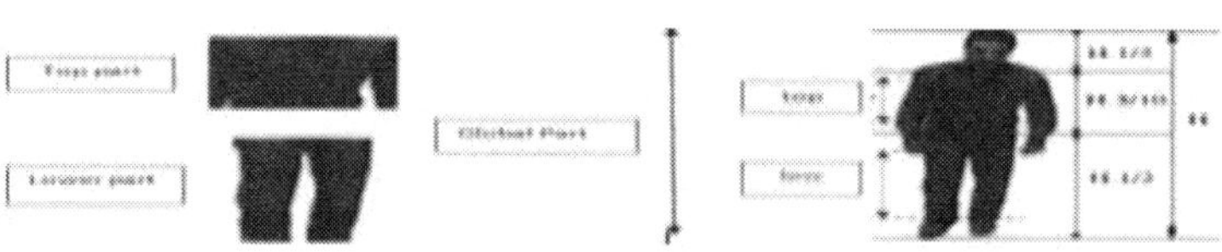

Figure 2. Body Detection and Split Procedure

In (Farenzena / 2010), a System Drive Accumulation of Local Features (SDALF) approach is presented. In order to individualize the human parts, the author used the bilateral chromatic operator and the spatial coverage operator. As for the representation, weighted color histogram, Maximally Stable Color Regions (MSCR) and Recurrent High-Structured Patches (RHSP) are described.

2.2 Intrusive Approaches vs. Non-Intrusive Approaches

Approaches can be categorized into two broad groups: intrusive or non-intrusive. Intrusive techniques require that the individual be in direct contact with the acquisition equipment or located at a small distance compared to the camera. The non-intrusive approaches consist of identifying persons without having touch with the acquisition equipment. Among these methods we can cite the works of (Vaquero/2009) and (Lyes Hamoudi/2011).

In the table below (table1), we present a classification of the different approaches of people re-identification by focusing on the human model.

Table 1. Summary Table of People Re-Identification Approaches

References	Features	Categories		representation			Categories	
		local	global	color	texture	shape	intrusive	Non-intrusive
(D. Gray/2008)	Schmid, Gabor, eight color channels		✓	✓	✓			✓
(Ahmed Derbel / 2014)	RFD, RED		✓			✓		✓
(C. Nakajima et al. 2003)	Color histogram, shape histogram		✓	✓		✓		✓
(W. Schwartz et al/2010)	LBP, HOG, average color values	✓		✓	✓	✓		✓
(O.Hamdoun /2008) (Nizar Zaghden /2013)	interest points descriptors	✓				✓		✓
(Vaquero/2009)	A normalized color histogram.	✓		✓				✓
(Lyes Hamoudi/2011)	Average color values, The co-occurrence matrix	✓		✓	✓			✓
(Farenzena/2010)	weighted color histogram, MSCR, RHSP	✓		✓	✓			✓

2.3 Supervised Approaches vs. Unsupervised Approaches

2.3.1 Supervised Approaches

In this classification approach, knowledge of the meaning of each class is required. The number of classes is fixed (in prior) and the available images are already allocated to the different classes of the database. The aim is thus to assign new images to the appropriate classes following two types of methods.

Discriminative methods - Discriminative models like SVM and boosting are widely used for feature learning in order to find the discriminant representations of the Region Of Interest. The matching phase, in (Truong Cong et al. 2010a) is based on the SVM method. In (Gray et al. / 2008). The proposed similarity function is a weighted ensemble of likelihood ratio tests, constructed with the AdaBoost algorithm.

Metric learning - Another direction is to learn task-specific distance functions with metric learning algorithms. (Weinberger and Saul/2009) briefly introduce the metric learning framework for large margin nearest neighbor (LMNN) classifier. The goal is to learn a linear transformation which minimizes the distance between each point of the small learning set and its K nearest neighbors similarly labeled, while maximizing the distance between all points labeled differently according to a constant margin.

2.3.2 Unsupervised Approaches

The unsupervised approach consists in determining the different classes without any previous knowledge. In (Farenzena *et al.* /2010) [6] As for matching, similarity between two images is defined as the weighted sum of the Bhattacharyya and the euclidean distances.

In the table2, we present a classification of different similarity calculation and machine learning methods.

Table 2. Summary Table of Similarity Measures and Matching Methods of People Re-Identification Approaches

references	method	classification	
		Supervised	Unsupervised
(Gray *et al.* / 2008)	Boosting	✓	
(Farenzena/2010)	Bhattacharyya distance, Euclidean distance		✓
(Truong Cong *et al.*/2010a)	Support Vector Machine	✓	
(Weinberger andSaul/2009)	LMNN	✓	

3. CHOICE OF OUR METHOD COMPARED TO THE STATE OF THE ART

The characteristics presented in global approaches are calculated in an overall aspect on the image. Although the overall representations of the images are easy to construct and invariant to the position of the objects, they only provide a rough and not detailed aspect of the image, therefore, some localized information are lost. In order to overcome these problems the image can be represented as set of local image parts. On the other hand, dealing only with local characteristics risks losing the overall sense of the image, by submerging it in a stream of unnecessary little details. Furthermore, this type of approaches require good image resolution. In our image search system, we combine global and local approaches in the measurement of the similarity between two images. To identify people by face, it requires videos or images with high resolution and being captured in nearest distance. Also, face identification is mainly focusing in the frontal face. That's why the intervention of people is required. We can recognize people even if their faces are hidden or they are with back appearance. An algorithm that identifies people from their body features will be developed. First of all, it is imperative to carry out a robust and adequate segmentation of human body, which is to isolate and identify each of the person's limbs. Then, several measurements may be taken. In matching phase, If an entire appearance of the person's body is available, it will be better to use this information in order to limit the number of searches in the database. This means that it is not necessary to browse the entire database, because many people will be eliminated only at the sight of the body.Thus, sufficient precision must be achieved for this be truly discriminatory and for candidates not to be falsely identified and / or excluded.

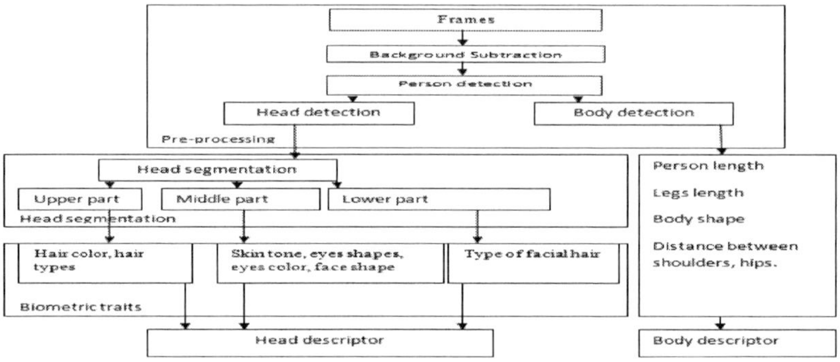

Figure 3. Overview of the Proposed Framework

4. CONCLUSION

In this paper, we present a person re-identification framework for multi-camera surveillance system based on both soft-biometric features and the overall appearance of person body. People detection, body segmentation and features extraction are included in this framework. In correspondence phase, first the comparison will be carried out according to the captures of faces of the different people. In second stage the comparison will be carried out according to the overall characteristics of the complete images of the different persons.

REFERENCES

Ahmed Derbel et al, Jun 2014 Human identification in frontal view using the silhouette motion distribution. *Shape Recognition and Artificial Intelligence (RFIA)* 2014, France.

C. Nakayima et al, September 2003. Full-body person recognition system. *Pattern Recognition*, 36(9) :1997–2006.

D. A. Vaquero et al, 2009. Attribute-based people search in surveillance environments, in: *Workshop on Applications of Computer Vision (WACV),* pp. 1–8.

D. Gray, H. Tao, 2008 Viewpoint invariant pedestrian recognition with an ensemble of localized features, in: *Proc. European Conference on Computer Vision (ECCV)*, pp. 262–275.

Lyes Hamoudi, 2011 Learning techniques application to person detection and recognition, à Lille 1

M. Farenzena et al,2010 Person re-identification by symmetry-driven accumulation of local features, in: *IEEE Conference on Computer Vision and Pattern Recognition (CVPR)*, pp. 2360–2367. pp. 381–390.

Nizar Zaghden, Remy Mullot, and Adel M.Alimi, « Categorizing ancient documents », IJCSI 2013, Vol. 10, Issue 2, No 2, March 2013.

O. Hamdoun et al, 2008 Person re-identification in multi-camera system by signature based on interest point descriptors collected on short video sequences, in: *Second ACM/IEEE International Conference on Distributed Smart Cameras (ICDSC),* pp. 1–6.

Truong Cong et al, (2010a). People re-identification by spectral classification of silhouettes. *Signal Processing,* 90(8): 2362–2374.

Weinberger, K., Saul, L(2009). Distance metric learning for large margin nearest neighbor classification. *The Journal of Machine Learning Research* 10, 207–244.

William Schwartz et al. 2010 A robust and scalable approach to face identification. *European Conference on Computer Vision (ECCV),* pages 476–489.

CONNECTING THE DOTS: LINKING CREATIVITY, SYNTHESIS SKILLS, AND THE STUDENTS' ANXIETY ABOUT THE FUTURE

Ioan Susnea, Emilia Pecheanu, Luminita Dumitriu and Adina Cocu
University "Dunarea de Jos" of Galati, Department of Computer and Information Technology
Galati, Romania

ABSTRACT

In the past few years we have participated in several EU funded projects, aimed to create the educational content and auxiliary ICT tools to support the development of some essential soft skills of the students: the creativity, and the ability to write syntheses of the ideas extracted from various sources. In this context, we produced an easy to use web application for the assessment of creativity based on a new scale, and we also proposed a methodology to evaluate the quality of text summaries written by our students starting from a given source. Through a serendipitous coincidence, this research occurred while we were in search of a means to assess the risk in education, and noticed that the students' anxiety about the future (AAF) might be a good measure of this risk. This paper is an attempt to make sense of the data collected using the newly created tools, by exploring the possible correlations between creativity, summarization skills, and AAF from the perspective of the students' ability to cope with the uncertainties of the future

KEYWORDS

Creativity, Synthesis skills, Anxiety about the future, Risk in education

1. INTRODUCTION

School is, certainly, a future oriented business. As educators, we claim that we "provide the students with the knowledge and skills they need to enjoy fruitful and meaningful lives" (Perna, 2013) in 10 - 20 years or more from now. But, since the future remains shrouded in uncertainty even for much shorter time horizons, this claim looks more like an example of "epistemic arrogance" (Taleb, 2007) than like a serious strategic objective. Thus, if we agree that risk is the result of the "uncertainty regarding the outcome of certain actions or events" (see Aven & Renn, 2009), it appears "that any activity expected to last, or to produce effects over a long period of time, is highly affected by risk." (Susnea et al., 2016b).

Education is a typical example of this kind of activity.

We discussed these topics from an ethical perspective in (Susnea et al., 2014), and from the perspective of the risk in education in (Susnea et al., 2016b). In both cases, we suggested that a systematic effort to develop the students' creativity could provide the students with the ability to better cope with the uncertainties of the future, and thus to mitigate the overall risk of schooling.

But we did more than just discussing these issues. In the project "Tecrino – Teaching Creativity in Engineering" (http://www.tecrino-project.eu), we developed educational content for an e-learning platform dedicated to teaching creativity (Susnea et al. 2015a, 2015b), and also a software application (Susnea & Vasiliu, 2016) for fast and easy assessment of the individual creativity (available online at http://dev.ugal.ro/creativity/). In the project iLab2 – Innovation Laboratories for the Quality of Vocational Education (www.ilab2.eu – see also Cocu et al, 2015) we focused on creating an "extraordinary environment" aimed to stimulate the group creativity, and – finally - in the project "Explain – How to Tell What You Know Well" (www.explainwell.org) we created educational content for other useful soft skills: the ability to synthesize the ideas from various sources in a text summary, the ability to create and handle mind maps and concept maps, and to improve the oral performances for public presentations. In the same project, we also proposed a methodology to measure the value of a text summary in the educational context (Susnea & Pecheanu, 2017).

In the course of the development of the above mentioned tools, we collected a wealth of experimental data. Though we don't have yet a thorough statistical analysis of this information, in the following sections we outline some preliminary results of this work

2. A WORD ABOUT THE METHODOLOGY

Basically, what we tried to do was to measure the individual creativity, the AAF scores and the summarization skills of a group of students, and look for possible correlations between these variables.

We measured the individual creativity quotient CQ using our own scale and a dedicated software application described in (Susnea & Vasiliu, 2016). For the AAF, we initially used the Bolanowski AAF scale (Bolanowski, 2005), and later we added one item to the questionnaire: "I worry that I will not be able to complete my studies". In what concerns the synthesis skill, we used the methods described in (Garner, 1982) and (Susnea & Pecheanu, 2017) to compute a "summary efficiency quotient SEQ", as follows:

$$SEQ = \frac{AR}{CF} * K \qquad (1)$$

Where:

AR - is the *"accuracy rate"*, defined as the ratio between the number of ideas correctly identified N_i, and the total number of ideas in the source text N_t.

$$AR = \frac{N_i}{N_t} \qquad (2)$$

CF is a *"compression factor"*, defined as the ratio between the number of words in the output summary text, NW_o, and the number of words in the initial text NW_i.

$$CF = \frac{NW_o}{NW_i} \qquad (3)$$

Finally, K is a scaling factor used to normalize the results in the interval [0-100].

In the early stage of the experiments, we simply applied the creativity test (Susnea & Vasiliu, 2016) and the unmodified Bolanowski test for AAF (Bolanowski, 2005) on a group of 30 students in the 5'th semester at the Department of Computer Science of our University, and we noticed a pretty clear negative correlation between the creativity quotient (CQ) and the AAF score. In parallel, we measured the CQ and SEQ quotients for a group of N=27 students, and again we noticed a correlation between the two variables (Susnea & Pecheanu, 2017).

However, the students who participated in these preliminary experiments were volunteers having overall exam results above the average, thus the sample was not really representative for the population considered. Therefore, we decided to repeat the experiment with a larger (N=62), and more diverse group of students. This time we added an item to the Bolanowski scale, and we eliminated the "manual" adjustment of the SEQ scores (aiming to a greater objectivity of the evaluation, but losing information about the ability of the students to formulate the ideas with their own words). The results are presented in the following section.

3. EXPERIMENTAL RESULTS

The charts indicating the values of the variables Cq, AAF, and SEQ for the group with size N=62 are shown in figure 1. We found that the Pearson correlation factor for the pair CQ-AAF was r=-0.27, indicating a weak negative linear correlation. This results supports the findings of our initial experiment, but the correlation is weaker.

For the second pair of variables CQ-SEQ, the Pearson correlation factor for this pair was r=-0.14 – indicating that there is no linear correlation between the students' creativity and their synthesis ability. This contradicts the results of our initial experiment with a smaller group of students, but it is unclear whether this is due to the change in the methodology of evaluating the SEQ, or to some other factor related to the structure and the size of the sample group.

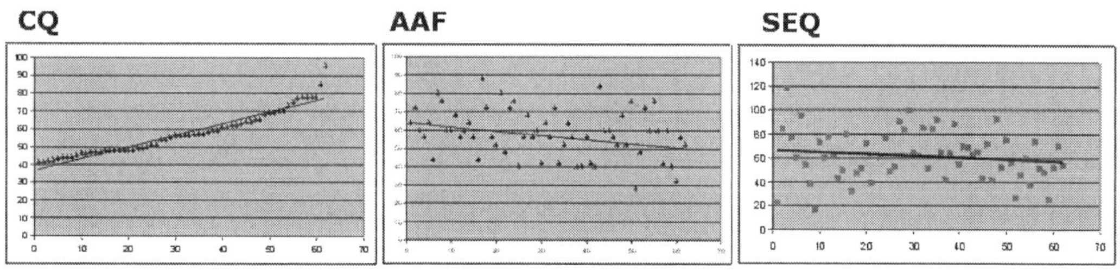

Figure 1. CQ vs AAF and SEQ comparison chearts

4. DISCUSSION AND CONCLUSIONS

It appears that there is indeed a weak negative linear correlation between the students' creativity and their level of anxiety about the future.

The reason for this may be that more creative students feel better prepared to face the future, or maybe they simply care less about the future. According to Zimbardo and Boyd (2008), people having a "present hedonistic" type of personality, as determined by means of the Zimbardo Time Perspective Inventory (ZTPI see Zimbardo & Boyd, 2015) are more creative, probably because they perceive the future as distant i.e. having a higher "psychological distance" from the present (see also Chiu, 2012 and Trope, Y., & Liberman, 2010).

Further research by applying the ZTPI test to the same group of students might clarify this aspect.

It should be noted that the Bolanowki scale – designed and tested on medical students only - may not be the best instrument to measure the AAF of other young adults.

Our experimental data show that there is no correlation between the creativity quotient and the summary writing skills. However, it is possible that the correlation between CQ and SEQ is in fact nonlinear (we tried a polynomial regression and it seems to fit better on the CQ-SEQ data sets).

This may be explained by the fact that we have evaluated the SEQ based only of the verbal processing of the information, which is a typical left brain (non-creative) activity. It is likely that a methodology of evaluating the synthesis abilities starting from visual representations of the information (e.g. mind maps) may lead to different results.

Since the general topic of the risk in education seems to be only marginally studied, further research is also needed to investigate the interdependence between the AAF and the overall risk in education.

ACKNOWLEDGEMENT

This research is partly supported from the project ERASMUS+ KA2 Strategic Partnerships Italy 2014 -1-IT01- KA200 – 002650 "EXPLAIN – How to tell what you know well" (http://explainwell.org/)

This project has been funded with support from the European Commission.

This publication reflects the views only of the authors, and the Commission cannot be held responsible for any use which may be made of the information contained therein.

REFERENCES

Aven, T., & Renn, O. 2009 On risk defined as an event where the outcome is uncertain. *Journal of risk research, 121*, 1-11,.

Bolanowski, W. 2005. Anxiety about professional future among young doctors. *International journal of occupational medicine and environmental health, 184*, 367-374.

Chiu, F. C. 2012. Fit between future thinking and future orientation on creative imagination. *Thinking Skills and Creativity, 73*, 234-244

Cocu, A., Pecheanu, E., & Susnea, I. 2015. Stimulating Creativity through Collaboration in an Innovation Laboratory. *Procedia-Social and Behavioral Sciences, 182*, 173-178.

Garner, R. 1982. Efficient text summarization: Cost and benefit. Journal of Educational Research, Vol 75, pp:275–279.

Perna, L. W. 2013. Preparing today's students for tomorrow's jobs in metropolitan America. University of Pennsylvania Press.

Susnea, I., Pecheanu, E., Tudorie, C., & Cocu, A. 2014. The education for creativity–the only student's tool for coping with the uncertainties of the future. In *MAC ETEL 2014–International Conference on Education, Teaching and e-Learning, Prague.*

Susnea, I. Pecheanu E.,Tudorie, C. 2015a. Initiatives towards an education for creativity. *Procedia-Social and Behavioral Sciences, 180*, 1520-1526..

Susnea, I., Pecheanu, E., & Costache, S. 2015b. Challenges of an e-Learning Platform for Teaching Creativity. In *The International Scientific Conference eLearning and Software for Education* Vol. 1, p. 376. " Carol I" National Defence University, Bucharest, Romania.

Susnea, I. Pecheanu, E. Dumitriu, L. 2016a. The Education for Creativity May Lower the Students' Anxiety About the Future, Proceedings of the 7'th Edu-World International Conference

Susnea, I. Pecheanu, E. Dumitriu, L. 2016b. The School in Extremistan – How the Research on Creativity May Lower the Risk in Education , Proceedings of the 2'nd MIC Conference, The Marconi Institute for Creativity, Bologna, Italy

Susnea, I., & Vasiliu, G. 2016. A Fuzzy Logic Software Instrument and a New Scale for the Assessment of Creativity. *International Journal of Computers Communications & Control, 113*, 441-449

Susnea, I. Pecheanu, E. 2017. Exploring the Connection Between the Students' Creativity and Summary Writing Skills, Proceedings of EDUCON 2017, Athens, Greece

Taleb, N. N. 2007. *The black swan: The impact of the highly improbable* Random House

Trope, Y., & Liberman, N. 2010. Construal-level theory of psychological distance. *Psychological review, 1172*, 440

Zimbardo, P., & Boyd, J. 2008. *The time paradox: The new psychology of time that will change your life*. Simon and Schuster.

Zimbardo, P. G., & Boyd, J. N. 2015. Putting time in perspective: A valid, reliable individual-differences metric. In *Time Perspective Theory; Review, Research and Application* pp. 17-55. Springer International Publishing

Reflection Papers

LOCALISING CONTENT FOR AN XMOOC IN THE UAE

Jenny Eppard and Preeya Reddy
Zayed University, UAE

ABSTRACT

Universities in the UAE are entering the age of virtual and open access education. This paper describes the evolution of a MOOC at a state-funded university in Dubai. We will describe the challenges as well as a reflection of our experiences as creating virtual learning spaces in this culture differs somewhat from Western models.

KEYWORDS

MOOCs, xMOOCs, UAE, higher education, virtual learning, online learning.

1. INTRODUCTION

During the Fall semester 2016, a team of teachers at Zayed University were asked to create two virtual learning modules. The first provided units of instruction of basic English skills (24 grammar units) and the second facilitated professional development for educators (37 units on teaching practice) in the United Arab Emirates. The following reflection paper will aim to provide an academic justification for the creation process finally reflecting on the evolution of the project.

2. BACKGROUND

MOOCs (Massive Open Online Courses) are created to support university curricula, community outreach professional development, and corporate training applications. They can be either cMOOCs, xMOOCS or a combination of both.

Bates (2014) argued that xMOOCs are characterized by the following: software design for large numbers of students, video lectures (under 15 minutes), computer marked assignments, peer assessment, supporting materials, shared comment discussion space, no or very light discussion moderation, badges or certificates learning analytics. Bates describes the other forms of cMOOCs as autonomy of the learner, diversity of tools used, cooperative learning, open access, use of social media, participant driven, distributed communication and lack of formal assessments. The only true characteristic of a cMOOC that we incorporated was that our materials were open access.

Wright (2003) provided several levels of criteria when designing MOOCs. Due to cultural constraints, we could not include all his recommendations. An important specification we did consider was the learners' backgrounds, ability levels and expectations. The UAE educational context historically had, and continues to have, a strong connection with Islamic education (Dailo, 2014). This was a key consideration for us.Also, we wanted to ensure that learners were given feedback about their progression which made learning analytics and assessment results available (Yousef, Chatti, Schroeder and Wosnitza 2014).

3. REFLECTION

The projects provided challenges for numerous reasons. At this point, we can only reflect on the instructional design phase as students have not started using the materials in a systematic way.Creating a resource for virtual online learning in this region was still relatively new. The materials created were trailed in the classroom by teachers with a knowledge of the local cultureto ensure their usability reliability and validity.

Even though experiences we had with developing the modules were overwhelming positive, there were a few issues. For one, there was little release time from a teaching workload to develop the project. Also, finding images that were copyright free and culturally appropriate was time-consuming and expensive. The final obstacle was designing materials to work in an online environment.

There is a need for ongoing research on how culturally acceptable student collaboration would be on a shared discussion platform. Furthermore, one must consider how much teacher interaction is needed for students who use English as a second languageto benefit from the courses.Noting these changes may provide some general recommendations for creating similar courses in future.

REFERENCES

Anders, A. (2015). Theories and Applications of Massive Online Open Courses (MOOCs) : The

Case for Hybrid Design. *The International Review Of Research In Open And Distributed Learning, 16*(6). doi:http://dx.doi.org/10.19173/irrodl.v16i6.2185

Bates, T. (2014). Comparing xMOOCs and cMOOCs: philosophy and practice. *Online*

learning and distance education resources.

Conole, G. G. (2015). MOOCs as disruptive technologies: strategies for enhancing the learner experience

and quality of MOOCs. *Revista de Educación a Distancia*, (39).

Diallo, I. (2014). Emirati students encounter Western teachers: tensions and identity resistance. Learning and Teaching in Higher Education: Gulf Perspectives, 11(2).

Wright, C. R. (2003). Criteria for evaluating the quality of online courses. *Alberta Distance*

Education and Training Association, *16*, 2.

Yousef, A. M. F., Chatti, M. A., Schroeder, U., &Wosnitza, M. (2014, July). What drives a

successful MOOC? An empirical examination of criteria to assure design quality of MOOCs. In *Advanced Learning Technologies (ICALT), 2014 IEEE 14th International Conference on* (pp. 44-48). IEEE.

ACADEMIC READING ON A COLLABORATIVE, ONLINE PLATFORM

Jenny Eppard and Preeya Reddy
Zayed University, UAE

ABSTRACT

Academic reading circles can be adapted from in class to an online platform where students can work collaboratively. This paper outlines how reading circles are used online with Second Language Learners. A description of the stages and necessary roles is provided.

KEYWORDS

Academic reading circles, collaborative learning, online collaboration, constructivism

1. BACKGROUND INFORMATION

Government run universities in the UAE are moving away from teaching English for General Purposes and moving toward supporting students with academic English at both the pre-sessional and in-sessional levels. Faculty who teach content-based courses often give students academic tasks that are beyond their language abilities. As a result, students arrive in class without completing the required reading or the coursework. In-sessional faculty have reported that instead of facilitating students' learning, they are spending a large amount of time covering the materials students should have studied outside of class. The following paper will describe an approach used to encourage students to read outside of class collaboratively through online tools and reading circles.

Collaborative learning is an educational approach to teaching and learning that involves groups of two or more students working together to solve a problem, complete a task, or create a product. While Dillenbourg (1999) emphasizes that this definition does not encompass all aspects of collaborative learning; this is the most flexible definition for our purpose. Daniels (1994) coined the term "literature circles" as small temporary discussion groups who have chosen to read the same poem, story, article or book. The aims of these circles are to make reading more manageable and less overwhelming, to expose students to different reading strategies and to encourage learner autonomy. Seburn (2016) argues that there are three components to the academic reading circles: the text, the group with each member given a responsibility and the group discussion. According to this model, the group consists of the following: (1) the leader (facilitator), (2) the contextualiser (explains the who, what, when, where and why - can be recorded), (3) the visualiser (uses and develops graphical interpretations), (4) the connector (connects concepts with real-world situations), (5) the highlighter (facilitates vocabulary comprehension (Seburn, 2016).

One way to collaborate in reading circles is through online collaborative tools such as wikis and online writing tools These are seen by many educators as a way to enhance collaborative learning (Binbin 2015). This aligns with the reflective and collaborative nature of constructivism. Through online collaborative tools, learners reflect and build knowledge collectively (Parker & Chao, 2007). Kessler and Bikowski (2010) found that second language learners were able to increase learner autonomy and practice their writing through online collaborative tools. Collaborative learning online can be assessed using two different methods. For one, students can be assessed by their peers. De Wever, Van Keer, Schellens and Valcke (2011) had success with peer assessment using rubrics that targeted contribution, sources, discussion and social behavior. Teacher rubrics are another method used to evaluate collaborative work (Lai & Ng, 2011).

2. CONSIDERATIONS FOR IMPLEMENTATION

When implementing reading circles online, there are a number of factors that need to be addressed. The overall implementation should be mapped using principles of instructional design such as the ADDIE model. (ref) Starting with a clear analysis of the program needs: Why is this needed? Where are the current gaps that this program would address? For our program, the students are second language learners and therefore the reading texts (which come from textbooks that are in English) are difficult for students and reading circles helps with students better analyze texts. Also, our students have a limited time on campus. Therefore, an online venue is an appropriate choice for our specific population. After the analysis phase, the program needs to be designed to outline exactly what will be included based on the program and student needs. For this phase, specific texts will be targeted and chosen and a timeline created. Also, a firm outline of what will be included in the online learning reading circles and how it will be assessed is needed. We bypassed this important step when developing our program, which is unfortunate because it would have been useful and clarified roles and tasks. The next step is developing the materials. We did this but not in a systematic way with a clear design. After this step, is the implementation phase, which is self-explanatory. The program would be closely monitored to determine and note any issues that arise. When we implemented our program, it was not systematic and addressed only ad hoc needs that came up. The final step is evaluation, this could be evaluating the program as a whole and/or evaluation of students understanding of the materials. For our program, we sent out a survey to the teachers but we did not include the students and also we did not check students' understanding of the materials to determine if the online reading circles were effective.

REFERENCES

Binbin Zheng, Melissa Niiya & Mark Warschauer (2015) Wikis and collaborative learning in higher education, Technology, Pedagogy and Education, 24:3, 357-374, DOI: 10.1080/1475939X.2014.948041

Dillenbourg, P. (1999). *Collaborative learning: Cognitive and computational approaches. advances in learning and instruction series*. Elsevier Science, Inc., PO Box 945, Madison Square Station, New York, NY 10160-0757.

Daniels, H. (2002). Literature circles: Voice and choice in book clubs and reading groups. (2nd ed.). Portland, ME: Stenhouse.

Kessler, G., & Bikowski, D. (2010). Developing collaborative autonomous learning abilities in computer mediated language learning: Attention to meaning among students in wiki space. Computer Assisted Language Learning, 23, 41–58.

Lai, Y. C., & Ng, E. M. W. (2011). Using wikis to develop student teachers' learning, teaching, and assessment capabilities. The Internet and Higher Education, 14, 15–26.

Parker, K. R., & Chao, J. T. (2007). Wiki as a teaching tool. Interdisciplinary Journal of Knowledge and Learning Objects, 3, 57–72.

Schifter, D and Simon, M. (1992). Assessing teachers' development of a constructivist view of mathematics learning. *Teaching and Teacher Education*, 8(2): 187–197.

AUTHOR INDEX

International Association for Development of the Information Society (IADIS)
Rua Sao Sebastiao Da Pedreira
No. 100, 30, 1050-209
Lisbon, Portugal

ISBN 978-1-5108-5320-1

9 781510 853201